ECONOMY AND ECONOMIC ANALYSIS

ECONOMY AND ECONOMIC ANALYSIS

Robert Black

2004

Economy and Economic Analysis
Robert A. Black

Direct correspondence and permission requests to one of the following:

E-mail: info@trianglepublishing.com
Web site: www.trianglepublishing.com
Mail: Triangle Publishing
4301 South Washington Street
Marion, Indiana 46953
USA

Black, Robert
Economy and Economic Analysis

ISBN: 1-931283-10-9

Cover Design: Susan Spiegel
Layout Design: Jennifer Mattison
Graphic Design: Lyn Rayn

Printed in the United States of America
Evangel Press, Nappanee, Indiana

Contents in Brief

TABLE OF CONTENTS

SECTION III: Introduction to Macroeconomics

PREFACE

This text is a brief introduction to economy and economic analysis. With a mathematical focus confined mainly to demand and supply, the circular flow, and aggregate demand and aggregate supply, the text avoids the apparatus of intermediate economics that has slipped into principles texts. This text introduces students to the basic principles of micro and macroeconomics and their applications. It is suitable for a one-semester course in economics or, with a few supplements, as a first course in a two-semester sequence.

Overview of the Chapters

The Introduction explores the intersection of Christian faith and economics. Chapter 1 reviews the economic problem of scarcity in detail, highlighting how people have battled scarcity through history. Chapter 2 introduces the economic analysis of scarcity, including price as a measure of scarcity, demand and supply as the model of price determination, and various measures of economic efficiency and opportunity cost as the economists' preferred measure of cost. The chapter weaves together these ideas to make clear early on why economics is defined as the science of the efficient use of resources. Having defined efficiency at the start, students can use the important concepts of productive, allocative, macroeconomic, and institutional efficiency throughout the course.

Chapter 3 summarizes the history of economic thought for those who want to survey the various schools and major writers. Chapter 4 reviews principles of economic behavior, including rationality, voluntary association, opportunism, and strategic games. Chapter 5 then reviews principles of economic method in general and the difference between microeconomics and macroeconomics, with emphasis on explaining economic causality, the marginal method, consumer surplus, willingness to pay as a measure of economic value, *ceteris paribus*, and aggregate economics.

Chapters 6 through 10 give a broad overview of the nature of economy, its complexity and its problems. Reading these after the introductory chapters will give the course a wider ranging and more integrative focus. Chapter 6 introduces economy as a complex system of institutions and organizations by which people use endowments of scarce resources to pursue the fundamental economic activities: production, distribution, and consumption. This chapter highlights the complexity and variety of economic systems, as well as the tendency of economists to ignore pluralistic culture and focus only on the debate over free markets and government control. Chapter 7 explores in more detail an economy's endowments of resources, organizations, and institutions, with emphasis on human capital and moral capital. Chapter 8 explores the nature and causes of individual wealth and poverty, distinguishing between absolute and relative poverty and between distributing and creating wealth. Chapter 9 examines the causes of wealth and poverty in many nations through a historical summary of key theories of economic growth, from Adam Smith to institutional explanations. Chapter 10 explores the powers of, limits on, and economic functions of government, emphasizing the rule of law, U.S.

Constitutional history, and various perspectives on the role of government.

The introduction to microeconomics begins with chapter 11, but it can be read any time after reading chapter 2 or chapter 5, especially to give the course a stronger microeconomics focus at the beginning. Chapters 11 and 12 examine the major economic activities of consumption and production, with emphasis on the important principles of diminishing marginal utility and diminishing marginal product. Chapter 13 reviews price theory, including shifts in demand and supply (and various determinants), elasticity of demand and supply, market structure, and transfer pricing.

The introduction to macroeconomics follows, beginning with chapter 14. To lend a macroeconomic focus early on, this material could be read after chapter 5. Chapter 14 introduces the problems, statistics, theory, and brief history of macroeconomics. The theory and history discussion introduces aggregate demand and supply and the equation of exchange. Chapter 15 develops a more detailed circular flow of income and expenditure, emphasizing the money flows and indicators of household and business activity. The full circular flow includes financial, governmental, and international sectors; the final section of this chapter shows how to illustrate historical macroeconomic shocks with the circular flow. Chapter 16 explains in more detail the role of financial markets and their effect on the macroeconomy. It includes a brief introduction to the central bank and to the effects of central banking and financial flows on interest rates.

Distinctives of the Text

This text develops mainstream economic ideas while offering a running commentary from other perspectives, including the ethical, institutional, psychological, radical, and sociological points of view. The text highlights the relatively recent contributions of new institutional economists, especially in chapters 3 and 4, and—in more detail—in chapters 9 and 12. The ideas developed in these chapters are referenced throughout the remainder of the text.

Chapter sections and a series of Expansion Points develop the connections between economic analysis and other fields. For example, chapter 11 on consumption briefly reviews psychological and sociological perspectives, and also discusses economic analysis in the context of household budgeting. Chapter 12 on production incorporates an accounting income statement and balance sheet to show students more detail about calculating economic versus accounting rates of return. Throughout the text, examples incorporate ideas from literature, ethics, religion, law, and history.

Many Thanks!

This project would not have been possible without the help of a number of able advisors, editors, and encouragers. Willing colleagues, students, friends, and family members have contributed significantly by reacting to earlier versions of each of these chapters, offering both encouragement and helpful criticism. I owe special thanks to Jennifer Mattison, layout designer, and Linda Benedict, who read certain chapters and offered numerous suggestions as to style and content. Gregg Black, John Dodge, Tom Lehman, Richard Perkins, Brad Stamm, Lisa Surdyk, Greg Wilkinson and several anonymous reviewers read chapters and provided thoughtful suggestions. Al Black also read several chapters and offered helpful ideas and encouragement throughout the project. Matthias Hess, Jessica Spear, Kristina VanDyk, and Heather Walts each read a number of chapters and made significant editorial comments.

I also owe special thanks to Nathan Birky, publisher, Aimee Williams and Bobbie Sease, editors, and Lyn Rayn, graphic designer, for their encouragement and significant contributions to the final product.

The Hoselton Chair of Private Enterprise and Ethics provided significant financial support for this project in its early years. The Houghton College Faculty Development Fund and Academic Vice President's Office also provided funds and institutional support. For all of this, I am very thankful.

Finally, I owe many thanks to my family. My children were very patient with me during the writing project. Laura prayed, Jesse assisted, Sara and Susanne served, and Andrew encouraged. And finally, I am particularly grateful to my wife, Patricia, for her patience, encouragement, and support, and for giving me "release time" to work extended hours, often late at night or early in the morning.

Robert A. Black
March 2004

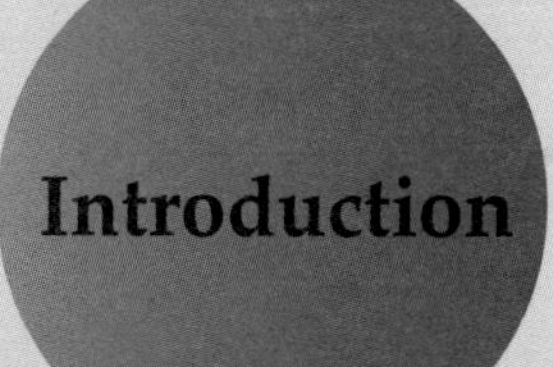

Faith and Learning

Integrating Christianity and Economics

What this chapter will help you think about:

1. What does integrating faith and learning mean?
2. Why is integrative learning valuable?
3. What are the history and causes of the secularization of education?
4. How do secular thinkers view religious ideas?
5. When did the discipline of economics emerge as distinct from moral philosophy?
6. What are the preconceptions of a Christian view?
7. How can we apply Christian belief to economics?
8. What key economic ideas emerge from studying the Bible?

- **Integration of faith and learning:** education "in the light of Christian revelation"; ideally it prepares students to think in new ways about new problems

Christian higher education is committed to **integration of faith and learning**. What does this mean and why bother? Although students should certainly interact with church doctrine, Arthur Holmes in *The Idea of a Christian College* (Eerdmans 1975) contends that the purpose is not merely to indoctrinate the student into church doctrine. Rather than merely giving selected answers to the problems and controversies of the past, the Christian college or university should educate the student to think in new ways about new problems "in the light of Christian revelation" (15). Let's explore what this means.

Integrative Education

- **Integrative thinking:** to combine diverse ideas so that they form a cohesive whole

To integrate means to weave distinct elements into a cohesive whole. Christian education seeks to make students' training whole or complete, providing them with an understanding of literary, historical, and scientific knowledge, tempered by spiritual understanding and moral sensitivities. **Integrative thinking** does not simply throw the parts together, but forms diverse ideas into a logically related set.

Why Integrative Christian Education?

- **Secular learning:** education in ideas that are not religious or otherworldly

Ideas emphasized in most state and non-religious colleges and universities are **secular** and deal with the natural world, but not with spiritual or otherworldly ideas. College students could seek supplemental religious training as an adjunct to their usual training in the secular disciplines of college or university. Shouldn't we keep secular education and spiritual training separate? Holmes notes that it would be less expensive (15). Were average students able to bring the different ideas together in their minds, putting them into a coherent whole on their own, this approach could work. The task of the teacher, however, is to show the way by putting disciplinary training in spiritual perspective. For example, how do new institutional ideas about economic growth and ideological commitments to moral principles compare with the patterns of economic growth in historically Christian Western Europe and the United States? We are freer to treat this topic in an integrative setting than in an educational environment dominated by the scientific method of gathering social-scientific facts.

If students were able to integrate religious and secular ideas by themselves, they also wouldn't need teachers in any of the secular disciplines themselves or for purely spiritual training either. Holmes, however, contends that the role of the teacher is crucial in modeling enthusiastic integrative scholarship and in critically evaluating students' performance (100).

Moreover, the very idea of separating knowledge into secular and spiritual compartments poses intellectual problems for atheist and believer alike. If there is no God, then all knowledge is secular, even if we label certain myths and beliefs as religious. If, however, God exists as Christians and others believe, then all knowledge is His and there is no purely secular knowledge. Whatever your belief system, it is incoherent if it completely separates the secular and the sacred.

Secular Views of Religion: Naturalism

Many secular teachers do provide a running critical commentary on the nature of religion. Those who hold a naturalistic philosophy about human existence are especially critical. For example, **naturalism** rejects belief in supernatural phenomena such as God, angelic and demonic activity, and heaven and hell as real places or states of existence. According to natural philosophy, when you die, you die. Humans are not eternal beings.

- **Naturalism:** rejection of the supernatural, and of the influence of divine or demonic forces in the world

As a result, believing students in secular universities have reported that certain of their atheist or agnostic teachers roundly criticize and belittle religious texts and beliefs, so that the students feel shamed in front of their peers. Other teachers politely tolerate dissenting views that express religious convictions, but make clear that this is not the prevailing view in the academy.

More sophisticated teachers offer less demeaning but nevertheless intellectually critical secular explanations of the rise of religion and its social purposes. As Expansion Point I.1 shows, naturalistic thinking has led to a **functional view of religion**, as expressed by Emile Durkheim and Karl Marx. The purely secular

- **Functional view of religion:** social-scientific studies show that humans create religious beliefs to serve human functions, such as giving life meaning and exerting control over others

Expansion Point I.1: Emile Durkheim and Karl Marx on the Functions of Human Religion

Eighteenth-century sociologist Emile Durkheim provided a functionalist theory of religion. Humans create religious rites, beliefs, and organizations for the following functions: to knit people together in peaceful solidarity, to give their lives meaning, to promote social control over them, to provide each with an identity and with psychological comfort, and to assist in valuable social change.

Karl Marx, widely cited by sociologists, also held a functional view of religion. More radical than Durkheim, Marx described religion as the "opiate of the masses." Capitalist bosses manipulated and used religious ideas such as the promise of the hereafter to numb the laboring class to the pain of exploitation by the production-for-profit system. The threat of eternal punishment for sins such as stealing property and committing murder further reinforced the dominance of the minority capitalist class.

These functional theories of religion are useful when comparing various religions. Expressing a functional perspective is not necessarily inconsistent with religious belief. Many functionalist sociologists, however, dismiss religious belief by reducing religion to *merely* secular functions that humans have couched in sacred terms. It suggests the inference, especially to uncritical students, that supernatural explanations *cannot* be true, an assertion that social science (by its own rules) is unable to prove or even discuss.

Biologists commit a similar reductionist fallacy, Christians believe, when they say that humans are merely a collection of certain chemical compounds and that thinking is merely a combination of chemical reactions and electrical impulses firing across neural synapses. Such a description fails to admit the possibility of a spirit that could survive the death of the body, again a proposition that science cannot prove.

Source: John Farley, *Sociology*, 3rd ed. (Englewood Cliffs, NJ: Prentice Hall, 1994), 404-08.

expression of functionalism is that religion is a human creation for merely human purposes. References to the supernatural are convenient devices to increase compliance.

The naturalistic philosophy of human existence certainly ought to be discussed in college. Perhaps we *are* merely flesh and blood and have no spirit. Such a statement, however, is a matter of faith and is never scientifically verifiable. To be fair, secular scholars must admit this rather than assume that it is fact. They also ought to examine their own presuppositions and faith commitments such as the naturalistic philosophy, and they should state them clearly. That is honest and transparent scholarship, which is what integrative learning intends to be.

- **Two steps to integrating faith and learning:**
  1) admit faith commitments
  2) show how faith applies to discipline

Integrating Christian Belief

Christians who integrate their faith and learning effectively do so in **two steps**. They first make their faith commitments obvious, especially when they impact their interpretations of facts and theories. Christians believe, for example, that to interpret human behavior (as economists and other social scientists do) requires an understanding of human nature. The Christian will interpret facts in light of a belief in the sinful nature of people.

They next demonstrate how to apply their faith commitments to their disciplines. The task of believing scholars is to infuse their disciplines with a believer's insights so as to increase understanding, not distort it. Their insights into truth about the world (as opposed to the ability to state facts in sequence) require the instruction of the Holy Spirit (Holmes 1975, 25). Only with such divine insight, especially into the meaning of Scripture, can we accurately comprehend the world around us. Christians also believe, however, that none of us is capable of knowing all truth or even most of it, and our integrative scholarship should be suitably humble.

Tradition vs. the Prevailing Secular View

The dominant view today of intellectuals in the United States and even more so in Europe is that religious education and other disciplinary training should be kept separate. While the consensus for this view is weakening, it still influences many people to think as follows: schools and colleges should educate youth for five days a week, and let those who want spiritual training seek it through religious organizations on the weekends or at least after the school day is over. The rise of state-supported and mandated education in the United States, with a tradition of separation of church and state, ensured education's gradual secularization. Religious education is still offered in secular schools, but as social history or from a radical-critical perspective of the texts as myth.

Religious Basis of American Colleges

Secularization of education is not an ancient practice. The longer tradition in America and Europe has been to integrate the two. The first American colleges, including those considered to be elite today, were dedicated primarily to training pastors. Their divinity schools carry on, but the universities have otherwise been thoroughly secularized. Yet the tradition of higher education until the late 1800s and early 1900s was to integrate religious and moral training into the curriculum.

That tradition continues more or less in certain liberal arts colleges (mainly in the United States) that remain connected with specific denominations or with the broader membership and organizations of the Christian church. Schools of the Coalition of Christian Colleges and Universities, for example, and various Catholic universities maintain a Christian atmosphere. At schools where the tradition is more vigorous, many classes and the general milieu of the campuses promote particular Christian traditions such as Catholic, evangelical, fundamental, reformed, or Wesleyan. At those schools where the tradition is ebbing and less vigorous, religious training is restricted to a few courses that are added on to the main body of secular disciplines and professional tracks.

Why the Current Separation of Secular and Spiritual?

The scientific revolution and the increasing influence of

• **Enlightenment:** eighteenth-century philosophical movement emphasizing human reason, not religious tradition or divine revelation, as the source of knowledge

• **Scientific method:** system of gaining knowledge about the world; when a problem arises, the researcher formulates a hypothesis to explain it, gathers systematic evidence, and tests the hypothesis, repeating the process as needed

enlightenment philosophy caused educators to segregate secular education and spiritual. Science emphasizes the study of facts that can be empirically verified, while it discredits ideas of religious "truth." The **Enlightenment** was an eighteenth-century philosophical movement to free human reason from religious restrictions. As Expansion Point I.2 notes, economics followed this secular line of thinking in the late 1800s, becoming a social science after having been a branch of moral philosophy.

In a strictly **scientific education**, religious ideas and "God talk" are inadmissible. Scientists tend in their professional talk at least to be atheistic (unbelieving) or agnostic (not knowledgeable) about religion. The idea of a Creator is not susceptible to laboratory experiments or systematic collection of empirical data. Closer inspection of certain data about the physical environment in the late twentieth century, however, called the purely atheistic view into question. According to Diogenes Allen (1993), that the universe will sustain life only within certain narrow physical parameters lends support to a creation hypothesis. Such precise tuning could hardly be expected by random chance alone.

Expansion Point I.2: Economics Emerges from Moral Philosophy

The rise of economics and other social sciences as individual university disciplines is rooted in the secularization of education. When Adam Smith lectured at Scottish universities in the mid to late 1700s, political economy was a branch of applied moral philosophy. Economics emerged as a separate social science in the U.K. in the 1870s and 1880s, around the time that Cambridge University eliminated its requirement that faculty hold orthodox Christian beliefs.

Also in the late 1800s, certain U.S. economists began to draw a sharp line between the disciplines of economics and ethics. Expressing the secular trend, American economist Simon Newcomb wrote in 1886:

> [We] may analyze the desires and appetites of men, investigate their various good and evil tendencies. . . . This, however, is not the object of Political Economy, but of Moral Science.
>
> Taking the desires and appetites just as they are, and regarding them merely as forces that impel men to action, we may investigate the laws of human activity to which they give rise. In other words, having been given a community of men moved by certain desires, we trace out the laws that govern their efforts to gratify those desires. This and this alone is the object of Political Economy as a pure science.

Mainstream economists today contend that they should investigate "what is" before considering "what ought to be." They claim to investigate the state of economic nature from a morally neutral perspective. Policies about what ought to be in the economy are more effective if first informed by the relevant economic facts.

Critics contend that economists' claims of scientific neutrality are a myth. Their very choices of which hypotheses to test in the search for facts will be influenced by their prior beliefs, including their morals. Their preconceptions about the world will also influence their interpretations of the evidence they collect.

Source: Simon Newcomb, "The Basis and Method of Economic Science," in *Principles of Political Economy* (New York: Harper & Brothers, 1886), 11.

Scientism, the extreme emphasis on scientific proof, also discredits moral ideas that arise from religious belief until research establishes their usefulness as scientific fact. As an example, social critics rejected religious morals about abstaining from sex outside of marriage in mid-twentieth century America. The empirical efficacy of abstinence, however, reemerged with the medical evidence about incurable, sexually transmitted diseases (STDs) that impaired human health or threatened life itself. AIDS and other STDs that had no immediate antidotes curtailed the philosophy of promiscuity made popular during the sexual revolution of the 1960s. Even so, every moral principle of the past remains suspect until certified by science as useful.

• **Scientism:** the belief that scientific method is the source of all knowledge

Indicting the Church and the Human Heart

Theologian Herman Bavink wrote that "the endless division of the Church gives the world cause for joy and derision, a reason for its unbelief" (cited in Berkouwer 1976, 46). Similarly, we may hold the Christian church guilty of contributing to Enlightenment skepticism. The Church has been guilty at times of provoking warfare other than spiritual, of advocating for the rich and powerful rather than the poor and downtrodden, of defending slavery rather than freeing the captives, of defending and justifying the king's faults rather than defending the pure faith, of storing up treasures on earth rather than in heaven, and of majoring on minor matters of personal behavior while ignoring the "weightier matters of the law." Enlightenment thinkers such as David Hume were skeptical of subjecting their reasons to revealed religious dogma. While each of us bears responsibility for our spiritual beliefs, the Church bears responsibility for the quality of its witness.

Nevertheless, according to Christian belief, the Enlightenment philosophy of heaven on earth by reason of humanity also expresses the desire of humans to define and rule themselves. The Enlightenment expresses a natural tendency of fallen humans to rebel against God. To understand this, we should investigate Christian belief in more detail.

Christian Faith

Christianity begins with a person, Jesus Christ, who is also one with God and who is God. Christianity takes seriously Jesus' distinctive teachings about God the Father and His unique relation to the Father. The Bible records personal accounts of His life, death, Resurrection, and teaching, and therefore is also integral to the faith. His disciples' belief that He was the Messiah, God's Son sent to redeem sinners, rested on Jesus' own testimony and their experiences with Him.

Believers ever since have put their faith in Jesus based on the biblical record of the disciples' eyewitness testimony and on

subsequent preaching about His death and Resurrection. As John Stott explains (1982, chap. 1), the preaching of the biblical account of Jesus has been central to the Christian traditions—from the early Christians, to the Preaching Friars of the Roman Catholic Church such as Francis of Assisi, to the Reformers such as Martin Luther, John Calvin, and Hugh Latimer, and to eighteenth-century Evangelicals such as John Wesley and George Whitfield.

Yet Christians also hold that the Holy Spirit's work in their hearts and minds gives life to their belief. The Holy Spirit is the third person of the Godhead, as revealed in the Bible. His activity in our lives is supernatural, not explained by any appeal to natural processes. As Jesus described the life-changing work of the Spirit to the Pharisee Nicodemus, "The wind blows where it wishes and you hear the sound of it, but do not know where it comes from and where it is going; so is everyone born of the Spirit" (John 3:8 NASB).

Christianity as described here rests on faith commitments that are clearly at odds with Enlightenment presuppositions and naturalistic thinking. The Christian faith includes a different worldview, a high view of the source and reliability of Scripture, and a distinctive view of human nature.

Worldview: The Sovereignty of God

God is Sovereign Creator of the universe, as well as personal Redeemer and Lord (Holmes 1975, 87). He exists as one God in three persons. Humans are fallen and sinful, yet God desires a personal relationship with us. God's Son Jesus was born into our world, fully human and fully divine, in order to reveal the Father and His purposes, and to reconcile sinful humans to God, giving us hope of regeneration by the Holy Spirit.

The unified worldview proceeding from these beliefs contrasts starkly with the fractured worldview of many atheists and agnostics. Christian intellectuals see a world given meaning by its Creator. Belief in a loving God who has fashioned all things for a purpose gives coherent meaning to the Christian's intellectual and personal service to God and to others. Understanding human sin, a Christian also understands evil in the world.

Secular intellectuals, however, are caught between contradictory visions. The scientist claims that the world has rational, naturalistic meaning independent of human will, while the existentialist philosopher concludes from the naturalistic view that all is meaningless, except for the meaning that each individual creates by an act of the will (Holmes 1975, 58). Therefore, the secular scholar seeks intellectual coherence by piecing together diverse facts, while desperately trying to create meaning in a personal life of self-actualization and in relations with others that have little meaning outside of a search for pleasure. The existence of evil dashes all rational hopes for ever improving human relations, while feeding feelings of existentialist despair. As Brian Griffiths (1984, 36) put it, the Enlightenment philosophy "worships reason and makes a virtue of science, and yet is at heart anti-rational, nihilistic, and materialist."

A High View of Scripture

A Christian belief is that God reveals Himself in Scripture. He has used human writers of the Bible to reveal the story of creation, the fall, and redemption through Jesus the Christ (Greek term) or Messiah (Hebrew term). A further belief is that the Bible is authoritative for guidance about personal living and about the corporate life of God's people. This describes a **high view of Scripture** (without entering into various debates about it).

The Bible is in two parts, the Old and New Testaments. The Old Testament describes God's several covenants with individuals such as Adam and Abraham and the people of Israel. The Old Testament also contains books of law given by God to the Hebrew people (descendants of Abraham). The New Testament describes a new covenant made in the blood of Jesus between God and believers in Jesus, who are the members of the Christian church (also called the bride of Christ). A biblical covenant is a "permanent" agreement between unequals, a "gracious undertaking entered into by God for the benefit and blessing of man, . . . specifically those who by faith receive the promises and commit themselves to the obligations which this undertaking involves" (Osterhaven, in *Evangelical Dictionary of Theology* 1984, 276-78).

• **High view of Scripture:** sees the Bible as God's revelation of Himself, and an authoritative communication to humans of His truth; as such, it must be reliable

Using the Bible effectively to integrate faith and disciplinary learning requires that we both interpret and apply the meaning. (See Fee and Stuart 1982, especially 12-13.)

Exegesis vs. Eisegesis

Because the Bible is God's revelation, the Christian is advised to handle it carefully in order to understand what it means, aided by an understanding of what the text meant when written. Reading for an author's original meaning, however, is not always easy or straightforward. Unwary readers often fall into **eisegesis**, or reading meaning from their own life setting into the text. For those who believe that the original intent of the biblical authors is not crucial to the Christian faith, how they read the text is not so important. The interpretive challenge only arises if the text's original meaning is crucial. Bringing one's own experiences, cultural expectations, and beliefs to the text before understanding the original setting would then interfere with a correct understanding.

• **Eisegesis:** reading meaning into a text, based on one's own cultural and historical context and knowledge

To read Adam Smith's *Wealth of Nations* (1776) as an

explanation of advanced industrial capitalism, for example, would be a mistake since the Industrial Revolution had hardly begun in 1776. Smith wrote in the midst of the "patent revolution" that preceded it (Blaug 1985). Similarly, reading biblical uses of numbers in light of modern standards of numerical precision is also mistaken. Biblical writers lived when recording time to the tenth of a second was impossible, and they did not refer to a day as a precise twenty-four-hour period (Fee and Stuart 1982).

• **Exegesis:** reading meaning out of a text, based on understanding its language, its cultural and historical contexts, and its author's knowledge

Reading meaning out of the text, which is **exegesis**, is the appropriate approach to understanding an author's intent. Reading a text repeatedly helps, but exegetical methods require more than just careful reading. They also require intimate knowledge of the language in which the author wrote, the culture in which the author lived, and the knowledge that the author possessed while writing. Thus, integrative scholars consult commentaries, Bible dictionaries, and other helps written by biblical experts.

Hermeneutics: Bridging the Gap

• **Hermeneutics:** the art of applying the meaning of a text to the reader's life

The art of applying the knowledge of a text to our lives today is called **hermeneutics**. Effective application, of course, requires effective interpretation. Once we understand as well as possible what a text meant, we can apply it more effectively. The Old and New Testaments both pose hermeneutical challenges. Expansion Point I.3 illustrates a problem in applying a proverb from the Old Testament to today. The story of Jesus cleansing the temple of traders illustrates a New Testament problem.

Jesus in the Temple: Anticommerce or Antitrust? John 2:13-22 tells how, using a whip, Jesus chased money changers and dealers in sacrificial animals from the Temple at the beginning of His three years of recorded ministry and preaching (see also Luke 19:45). A hermeneutical question is: should a preacher today speak out against the general evils of all commerce and how traders exploit the buyer, or should the preacher speak against a particular kind of problem that is less obvious? Knowing the answer requires that we understand whether Jesus was against commerce in general or whether He had a particular concern with the Temple traders. Robert Solomon (1993, 355) states a prevailing view:

> Jesus chased the money changers from the Temple, and Christian moralists from Paul to Thomas Aquinas and Martin Luther followed his example, roundly condemning most of what we today honor as "the business world."

The Bible, however, does not record any occasions outside the Temple when Jesus disrupted trading in coins or sacrificial animals. Was this because money and animals were traded only in the Temple? Archaeologists have unearthed what appear to be kiosks (booths for trading) located at the base of the Temple mount, and therefore outside the Temple. An older scholar, Alfred Edersheim (1898), reported that the same traders who sold in

Expansion Point I.3: Without a Good Plan, the People Perish?

In preparation for a new building program, the pastor quotes Proverbs 29:18 from the King James Version of the Bible: "Where there is no vision, the people perish." What the congregation needs, he says, is a clear vision of a plan for reaching the neighborhood with new outreaches. The new facilities are a key aspect of that vision.

The business consultant, in a secular context, warns her clients that a strategic plan is crucial to a successful business. She also quotes the proverb: "Where there is no vision, the people perish." The saying is so well known that it has currency even in a corporate setting . . . especially in a corporate setting, given the recent emphasis on strategic planning.

In 1992, presidential candidate Bill Clinton quoted the proverb in his criticism of President Bush's perceived failure to articulate a vision for national economic recovery.

Are any of these applications based on an accurate exegetical understanding of Proverbs 29:18? In a word, no. Significantly, none of them quoted the second part of the proverb: "but he that keepeth the law, happy is he."

The writer of this Proverb would have understood a lack of vision not as a failure to make human plans or to follow a human visionary, but as a failure to understand the law of God and *His* purposes. One rewording of the proverb is: Without an understanding of how God expects them to behave, the people act immorally. The reference to the law in the second part then makes perfect sense. In addition, an understanding of the law and Word of God required a prophet to deliver that message to the people.

A more appropriate application of the proverb would go something like this: If you people don't pay attention to what the Word of God says and His will for you, you will loosen your morals and end up spiritually dead in sin and in a famine for His Word. But if you listen to His Word, you will be blessed with a good life.

Many Bible verses are well suited to inspiring a church group to organize lively programs and a suitable building plan. They encourage us to organize our business or personal life, or to administer a nation's economy effectively. Proverbs 29:18 is not among them.

Sources: Robert Black, "Without a *Strategic Plan* the People Perish?" *Journal of Biblical Integration in Business* (Fall 1998): 124-37.

Jerusalem also pitched tents in the regions around Jerusalem during the weeks before the holy days when people went to the Temple. They would have sold coins and animals to those who were planning ahead. Jesus then was not necessarily against commerce in general, or we might have heard about other events or about a more general condemnation of traders and of people who don't arrange for their own sacrifices.

Instead, Jesus focused on two abuses in the Temple itself. First, the hustle and bustle of trade defiled the Temple, and second, it crowded out Gentile worshippers. According to this view, trade is not evil in its place and time, but Temple worship is neither the place nor the time. We can speculate with Edersheim that Jesus was also upset because the representatives of the High Priest were abusing their authority to regulate activity in the Temple. Edersheim imagines that their approval would have been required to trade within the Temple, and economic experience tells us that such a

privilege could have been worth a handsome payment to those who allowed it. We should recognize that the Temple authorities may have thought it genuinely beneficial to allow traders to provide the means for paying taxes and offering sacrifices where the Jews needed them. The crucial problem, however, was that the traders were operating in the outer court, which was the only place Gentiles were allowed to worship God.

Our lesson from the cleansing of the Temple, therefore, should not be about the general evils of exchanging money or trading commodities. While certain traders today do commit fraud and abuse, this text does not speak to the general evils of commerce. Jesus' cleansing of the Temple applies more to the things that crowd out our worship, whether interfering with corporate worship in the church or interfering with personal worship (the believer's body being the temple of God).

Try reading and applying Scripture exegetically yourself. First read 2 Corinthians 8 several times. Then read Expansion Point I.4, a case study in Christian stewardship in the Church. Have the leaders described in the case made an appropriate decision based on the text they cited in their fund-raising campaign?

The Postmodern Criticism. Postmodernism is a twentieth-century philosophy that rejects modern rationalist approaches to how we know. Postmodernists therefore reject the preeminence of the scientific method. Their criticism of modernism also extends to literary interpretation. They assert that, among other things, a consistent reading of an ancient text for the original intent of the author is not just difficult, but impossible.

How does this affect biblical interpretation? The postmodern belief in the subjectivity of all knowledge means that we all will come to quite different conclusions about a given text. Cultural differences among readers today will lead to widely different readings. As a result, the postmodernists say we should abandon the search for original meaning and be content to read into and out of the text whatever meaning that we choose. Communities of readers who share common traditions may seek to make of the text what they will as a group.

Exegetical interpretation, however, is beyond the ability of even the best scholars. The gap between our culture today and the authors' is too great. Their efforts are like circular reasoning. They cannot help but read into the text what is already in their minds. The exegete gets caught in a hermeneutical circle.

Exegetical scholars respond that the criticism is well taken but too extreme. With care, we can spiral in and approach the original meaning of the texts. In the end, Christians believe that biblical interpretation relies on faith in God's help in bridging the centuries-old hermeneutical gap.

Expansion Point I.4: First to the Lord Campaign, A Case Study

In mid-1988, First Avenue Baptist Church in suburban Philadelphia decided on a two-million-dollar capital campaign to build an addition to its church building. The current building included a large sanctuary, fellowship hall, and assorted offices and classrooms. Sunday attendance was high, seminary classes met in the building and used the offices, a preschool operated during the week, and other groups including a Korean church used the building regularly.

The church had been serving the local community very well. At the time of the campaign, it counted about six hundred members and regular adherents. Members organized a number of ministries in the church and around town, such as Boys Stockade, Pioneer Girls, and ministries in prisons and nursing homes. The church served the local Christian community with three or four annual sacred concerts and had two services each Sunday morning. Sunday school was full, even bursting at the seams.

Church leaders felt that adding classrooms and a larger foyer would improve the church building and the ability of the church to meet the needs of its people and guests. Some leaders and church members wanted to consider a community building with a gymnasium, although a local public school had one about a quarter of a mile away.

The Philadelphia-area economy thrived during the period, but the 1987 tax increase and the stock market crash in October 1987 created an uncertain economic future. Church leaders said that they saw the Lord work in a successful campaign during the troubling period of the late 70s and early 80s, so they decided to ignore the possibility of a weakening economy.

Leaders of First Baptist hired consultants from Atlanta to help in fund-raising. For $50,000, this Christian organization would assist the church with advice, themes, methods, and materials in a campaign called "First to the Lord." The campaign title comes from 2 Corinthians 8:5, which says, "but first gave their own selves to the Lord" (KJV).

The context of the verse is that the Apostle Paul is encouraging Corinthian believers to take a collection each week to send to the church in Jerusalem. In Acts 4 and 5, as the early church grew in Jerusalem, the members met each day to worship in the Temple. Those with wealth gave to a common pool of funds so that all could eat. Those with property sold it and gave the proceeds to the apostles (although Ananias and Sapphira lied when they held back a portion of their proceeds, and paid with their lives). Now the Jerusalem believers were living in relative poverty.

First Baptist kept informed about Christians around the world. It had a three-minute "Focus on the World" segment each week in its worship service to bring global spiritual concerns to the body. One missionary had recently visited from the Philippines and had asked the people there to help with constructing a cinder-block church building for a group that had lost its building in a hurricane. Another Christian, president of a seminary in the Far East, visited and spoke, saying that for a dollar a day or $365 a year, Asian Christians could keep one evangelist in mainland China.

One church member suggested that the leaders should fund similar outreaches overseas, constructing buildings in impoverished areas. The church members already supported a number of mission groups and families in domestic and overseas work. The leaders did not agree that this campaign should divert funds to more mission work. The membership voted to support the capital campaign and to make additions to their church building. Within a few years, the project was complete.

By the mid-1990s, however, the church was embroiled in the "New Era" scandal, a Ponzi scheme that took advantage of nonprofit fund-raisers. The church lost land in the aftermath, and numbers declined for several years.

(This is the author's fictionalized account of an actual case, for discussion only. Names have been changed or deleted, and no judgments are implied about the suitability of decisions made in the case.)

Human Nature

God created humans in His own image. Within limits, they have power to be creative themselves. God calls humans to use their creative abilities in their work. But sin shatters the image.

The Fall

The human decision to choose to do wrong is referred to as the **Fall of Man**. This is recorded in Genesis 3 as the story of Adam and Eve in the Garden. Deceived by the serpent, they chose to follow their own preferences and eat the fruit of the tree of knowledge of good and evil, because it looked "pleasing to the eye" and good for food. They rejected the path of obeying God's commandment to abstain from eating the fruit of that tree.

- **The Fall:** original sin of Adam and Eve; caused all creation to become fallen (afflicted with the effects of sin)

The Fall afflicted all humans and even all of creation. The Bible therefore describes human nature as always beset by a tendency to sin. As the prophet Isaiah wrote, "All we like sheep have gone astray" (53:6 KJV). And the Apostle Paul wrote that "all have sinned and fall short of the glory of God" (Romans 3:23 NIV).

Regenerated in Christ

People inhabit one of two possible states, either unregenerate and unrepentant or regenerated in Christ and repentant of past sins. The sinful state is referred to as being "dead in sin." The unrepentant nonbeliever continually sins. **Regeneration** refers to spiritual renewal, or being brought back to life. To repent means to turn in the other direction or to turn from sin. The repentant believer is not sinless, yet does not continually sin. Regeneration changes a Christian's thinking. Paul encourages the believer not to be "conformed to this world" but to be "transformed by the renewing of your mind" (Romans 12:2 KJV), and to have the mind of Christ (Philippians 2:5). Paul also refers to bringing every thought captive to Christ (2 Corinthians 10:5).

- **Regeneration:** spiritual renewal of the person who has turned away from sin

The Christian life is described as beginning with a crisis experience like childbirth, and then progressing. We become conscious of our sinful state and separation from God. We are "born from above," as Jesus put it (John 3), empowered supernaturally to appropriate the grace of God. Grace is His unmerited favor or gift, by which we are saved from sin, through faith in Christ Jesus (Ephesians 2:8). As an infant grows and matures, the believer also grows in grace and knowledge of the Lord through reading the Bible, prayer, fellowship, and other disciplines. With perseverance through life's trials and temptations, led by the Holy Spirit, the believer has the promise of eternal life with the Father.

Integrating Christian Belief and Economic Thought

This particular expression of the Christian faith seems so far removed from the economy and economic thought. Why bother to integrate spiritual issues into the economics curriculum? As stated above, intellectual honesty requires us to investigate presuppositions and faith commitments. We also integrate ideas to allow people who believe in God to remain true to their spiritual commitments and religious traditions, and people who do not to understand the faith more completely. Furthermore, we integrate to explore the influences of our worldview. Our faith shapes our worldview, and the worldview shapes our explanations of certain aspects of economic behavior and appropriate economic policies.

A more humble purpose of faith integration is to investigate the economic aspects of common morals. As explained below, moral behavior has economic consequences, and religious instruction is inextricably bound together with teachings about right and wrong behavior.

How then does Christian belief interact with the study of economics? Since the influence runs both ways, we can study the two directions of influence. Belief in Jesus and knowledge of Scripture and Church tradition help us to evaluate economic theories and policies, while knowledge of economics helps us to interpret the Christian life. A third approach is to compare where Scripture and economic theory seem to have arrived at similar conclusions.

Economic Lessons of Scripture

Economics concerns the production, distribution, and consumption of goods and services. What does the Bible have to say about these important topics? Christian economists have found certain ideas in common and have been exploring the implications of the biblical worldview.

Four Key Conclusions

John Tiemstra (1993, 227-47) has identified four key conclusions about which most Christian economists agree (see also Surdyk 2002, 69-98).

Creator and Owner vs. Steward. God is the Creator and we are His stewards. Stewards are responsible to care for the wealth entrusted to them. Our stewardship places limits on our notions of property and self-determination in economic affairs. It would be improper to conclude, however, that stewardship demands socialized ownership of all resources. Deuteronomy 3:12-20 states that God divided the land among the tribes of Israel, to be

- **Four key economic lessons of Scripture:**
  1) God is Creator and Owner, and humans are stewards.
  2) God cares equally for rich and poor.
  3) God condemns the love of material things in place of worshipping Him.
  4) God calls man to regular work and to Sabbath rests.

used by individual families for their property, as against the claims of other people (Joshua 13–21). The full implications of stewardship, therefore, remain to be explored.

God Cares for the Poor. Poverty is not necessarily a curse from God. The books of law in the Bible demand that those with wealth and power show concern for the poor. The law of Leviticus 19:9, for example, limited a property owner's use of the land. It required the owner not to reap the fringes of the field, but to use them for the poor. The prophets warned and condemned those who gained wealth by taking unfair advantage of the poor. Isaiah the prophet wrote, "'What do you mean by crushing my people, and grinding the faces of the poor?' declares the LORD, the LORD Almighty" (3:15 NIV).

God's concern for the poor does not mean that He condemns all rich. God doesn't want anyone to perish. Yet Jesus indicates that the "rich man" was condemned for failing to help the poor man, Lazarus (Luke 16:19-31). And Jesus indicated that wealthy people will have trouble getting into heaven (Matthew 19:23). Even so, God extends grace to those who trust Him at all income levels.

Love of Material Things Condemned. God calls people to love Him and other people, not material possessions. God saw that creation was good (Genesis 1), but worshipping creation is bad. The rich young ruler who would not give up his wealth to follow Jesus could not enter the Kingdom of God, even though he had kept the commandments (Luke 18:18-30). Love of possessions over all else, like any other ungodly devotion, is idolatry.

Work and Sabbath Mandates. The fourth commandment has two aspects: work six days, and rest on the seventh. For what purpose did God mandate this rhythm of work and rest? Commentators note that, contrary to other leaders of His time, Jesus lent nobility to work by laboring as a carpenter. Then when Jesus spoke on the Sabbath law, He made clear that the purpose was for people's benefit, not for mere religious form: "The Sabbath was made for man, not man for the Sabbath" (Mark 2:27).

To the Christian, work is an honorable calling, but we are free to rest without worry that we will fall behind. We are not slaves to work. This contrasts with modern conceptions that, while work is a rat race to be escaped, we dare not take a break from it lest we lose our place to those more dedicated.

Worldviews in Conflict

Biblical theology emphasizes three key events of a Christian worldview: creation, the Fall, and redemption in Christ. Belief in the stewardship of humans follows from this view, but so does an emphasis on human sin. The effects of sin influence our interpretation of economics as an Enlightenment science. One target is the emphasis on human rationality, another is the emphasis on efficiency, and a third is the emphasis on economic freedom.

Rational Humans? Mainstream economists emphasize two aspects of human rationality. First, people make reasoned decisions about what to buy, what to produce, and so on. On average, people will make optimal decisions. Second, economists can use their reason, unguided by any sort of divine inspiration, to determine the principles of economic behavior.

The Christian perspective, however, contends that human reason is fallen. Therefore, economists' assumptions that actual behavior is optimal and that reason will lead us to understand this behavior are flawed. Some Christian economists believe that they should engage their inspired intellects to rewrite the principles of economics in accord with scriptural truth (see Hocksbergen 1994, 126-42). Yet other Christian economists find important truths *in* mainstream ideas (see Lunn and Klay 1994, 143-63). Moreover, the sin that inhibits economists' reason hampers their critics too, which is especially important because Christian critics at many points are merely reflecting the ideas of secular critics.

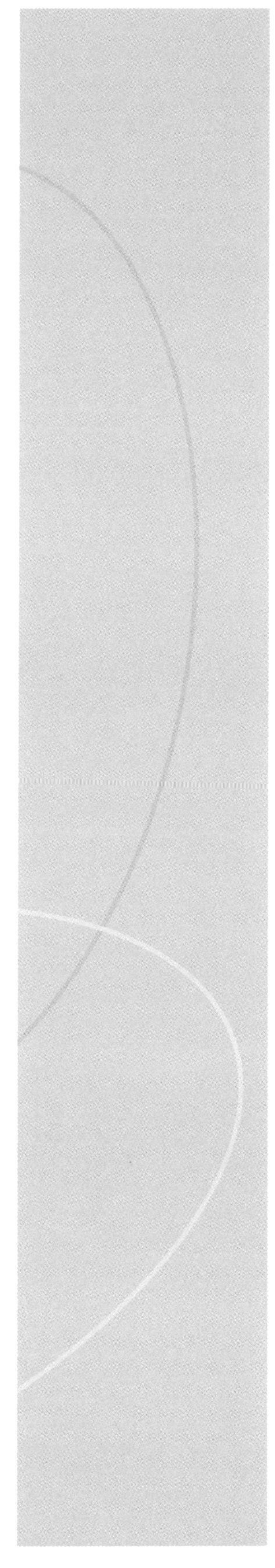

Efficiency as a Tool or Goal? Mainstream economics focuses on the concept of economic efficiency as a tool of analysis. Certain Christian economists complain that the tool of efficiency has become the goal. Instead of pursuing appropriate goals such as a moral distribution of income in an efficient way, economists prefer the existing distribution of income because it is determined by free markets, which in theory maximize a particular measure of economic efficiency. That reasoning confuses means and ends.

As Brian Griffiths notes (110-111), efficiency is not a sufficient criteria for judging what is best. Morality, for example, is also important. John Mason (1993) makes precisely this point when he contends that a prior economic goal for Christians is helping the poor, as Scripture commands. If government welfare policies that help the poor are inefficient, then this is a cost of doing what is right. Market efficiency is not a biblical priority.

Even so, economists very well may have valuable thoughts about helping the poor efficiently by, for example, using lump-sum subsidies (cash payments) when possible, instead of subsidies that lower the price of one good (and thereby distort people's decisions). Policy makers also would be wise to consider economic theories of the disincentive effects of certain welfare policies. Economic ideas are not useless.

Ideology of Freedom. Libertarians hold to a worldview in which economic and political liberty are either the highest good or are necessary for people to achieve the highest good. Griffiths

(105-106) asserts that such an ideological commitment to liberty in defense of capitalism conflicts with a Christian view. While defending capitalism from a decidedly Christian perspective, Griffiths rejects the libertarian ideology because it promotes the individual to first place in making moral decisions. He also rejects an ideological commitment to natural harmony or the equilibrium of forces of unregulated free human choice, although the equilibrium method affords keen insights into economic activity.

Griffiths (116) justifies market economies because Scripture encourages wealth creation, and the market system is most effective at creating wealth. The Christian perspective, however, puts limits on human freedom in pursuing market activity. A Christian worldview also emphasizes worship of God, stewardship, service to others, life in community with others, and commitment to justice (122). This is not to say that rejecting the ideology of freedom ratifies radical collectivism.

Economic Lesson or Spiritual Homily?

While a scriptural worldview has economic implications, certain texts may mislead. A biblical text may seem on the surface to be commercial in nature, but have a spiritual meaning. Jesus told about the vineyard owner who went out in the morning, afternoon, and evening looking for workers (Matthew 20:1-16). In the end, he paid all workers the same wage. Those who had labored all day complained bitterly. The owner answered that he had kept his agreement and that he could pay the others as he chose.

Does this parable state a biblical theory of wages that an employer could cite today? Under the view that parables have one spiritual meaning, probably not. This parable seems to promise instead that all who enter the Kingdom of God, whether early in life or at the last hour, will earn the full reward of eternal life.

Other lessons in Scripture are both economic *and* spiritual. Read Expansion Point I.5 about paying taxes to Caesar as a case study in economic *and* spiritual interpretations of Scripture.

Economic Insights into Christian Beliefs

Economics, with its emphasis on scarcity, efficiency, complex patterns of human behavior, and rigorous analysis of direct and indirect effects of policy on that behavior, is a unique perspective in the social sciences. Used wisely, economic insights allow us to interpret Scripture and to evaluate social policy more effectively.

Interpreting Scripture

Many biblical events and parables have uncertain economic significance. A keener understanding of commercial activity and economic concepts helps with the interpretation of those details. The discussion earlier of Jesus cleansing the Temple of the traders

Expansion Point I.5: Whose Image Is This?

Jesus' ministry and popularity threatened leading authorities of His day, so much so that He united bitter political rivals. Herodians and Pharisees, for instance, were political enemies. The Herodians supported the rule of the Roman Caesar who allowed King Herod to rule in Galilee (see Luke 23:5-7). The Pharisees were religious zealots who resisted Roman rule.

Matthew 22 records that one day late in Jesus' ministry, the disciples of the Pharisees went with a group of Herodians to confront Him. The Pharisees' students put this question to Jesus:

> "Teacher, we know that You are truthful and teach the way of God in truth, and defer to no one; for You are not partial to any. Tell us therefore, what do You think? Is it lawful to give a poll tax to Caesar, or not?" (vv. 16-17 NASB)

They had Jesus on the horns of a dilemma. If He answered no, as the Pharisees secretly hoped He would, He was in rebellion against Caesar and risked death. If He answered yes, as the Herodians preferred, then He would lose favor among the people, who resented Roman rule, and would be recognizing a power greater than the God of the Jews. Jesus, however, turned their question against them.

> But Jesus perceived their malice, and said, "Why are you testing Me, you hypocrites? Show me the coin used for the poll-tax." And they brought Him a denarius. (vv. 18-19)

Why were the disciples of the Pharisees hypocrites? We are left to speculate. One commentator suggested that they were caught holding the coin of the very empire they detested. They did not want to pay taxes to Caesar, but they were willing to use his coins to carry out the trade that enriched them. And the Roman roads and the peace that Roman soldiers enforced, while harsh, would have encouraged commerce in the region and with it economic prosperity. Whatever the hypocrisy, Jesus came to the point.

> And He said to them, "Whose image and inscription is this?" And they said to Him, "Caesar's." Then He said to them, "Then render to Caesar the things that are Caesar's, and to God the things that are God's." And hearing this they marveled, and leaving Him, they went away. (vv. 20-22)

We too can marvel at the parallel that Jesus suggested. The coin bore Caesar's image. We bear the image of God. The clear implication is that we ought to give ourselves to God, even as we pay our taxes to the government that issues the money we use.

Source: John Peter Lange, *Commentary on the Holy Scriptures,* trans. and ed. Philip Schaff (Grand Rapids, MI: Zondervan, 1960).

illustrates this point. An economist understands what may be an overly fine distinction to others: the difference between criticizing all commerce and criticizing traders who are benefiting from a monopoly status. Not all traders are monopolistic and exploitative, contrary to popular opinions. An economist also understands the influence of power in allocating valuable space in the Temple.

A fine line exists, however, between a careful application of informed opinion to the text and an imposition of preconceptions on the text. Temple leaders may have had other reasons for

allowing traders inside the walls. The text itself gives no direct support. Why speculate then? To show that perhaps Jesus was not merely anti-commerce, as stated above.

Evaluating Public Policy

Since Scripture expresses God's concern for the poor, many Christians propose various schemes to help the poor. One approach is to mandate programs of poor relief that establish a minimum safety net for individuals and their families. Another is to redistribute the wealth of the rich equally among all people.

As suggested above when discussing worldviews, economists can contribute several important principles to such discussions. While agreeing with the benefits of a social safety net, economists who have studied their actual impact also will note their social and economic costs. Over and above the costs of providing relief, a safety net encourages the wrong kind of behavior. Incentives matter, economists say, and programs that aid the legitimate poor also encourage others to adopt lifestyles that qualify for the relief.

In the United States, policy makers tried to avoid the disincentives of welfare programs by refusing to provide relief for women and children if an able-bodied man was present in the house. This created an incentive for poor women with children to separate or not to marry. The program also reduced the felt need of the children's fathers to provide support. The end result was wholesale destruction of American families. In 1996, for example, 13.7 percent of people in the United States lived in poverty, but 35.8 percent of people living in households headed by women lived in poverty (U.S. Bureau of the Census 1999, 480).

Scripture Predates Recent Economic Ideas

Scripture includes many moral lessons about economic activity. Christian economists who focus on the larger questions of economic justice for the poor and stewardship often dismiss these moral lessons as not really true integration of faith and learning. Recent research, however, has highlighted the economic significance of just those simple moral virtues that Scripture promotes, including a good reputation, honesty, and hard work. Scripture predates these recent "advances" in economic theory.

The Value of Reputation

Proverbs 22:1 says, "A good name is to be more desired than great wealth, Favor is better than silver and gold" (NASB). This version (as compared to the NIV) doesn't say that a good name is more desirable, but that it "is to be more desired." The first half of the proverb is a command, while the second asserts the value of being favored. Desire a good reputation instead of great wealth, and you will find that a good reputation is itself great wealth.

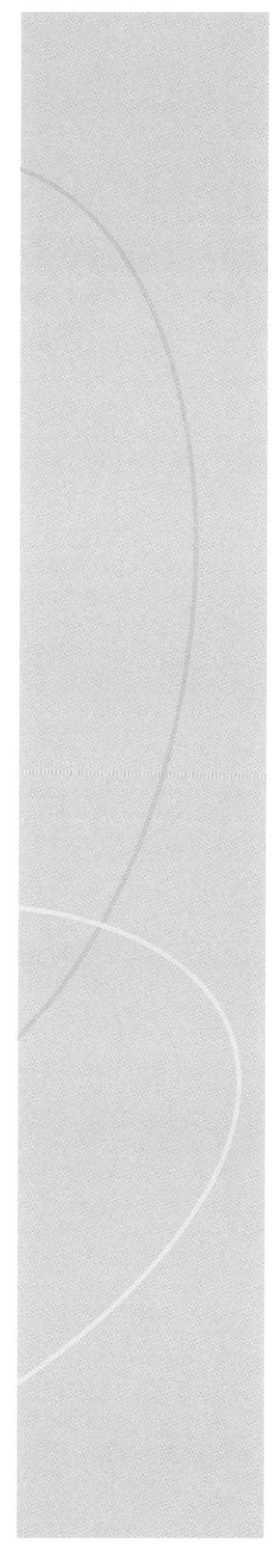

Several thousand years later, professional economists were also concluding that reputation had great value in commercial trade. Daniel Klein's volume on *Reputation: Studies in the Voluntary Elicitation of Good Conduct* (1997) includes various economists' thoughts on the value of reputation. An article by Bruce Benson on the Law Merchant (1997, 165-190), for example, says that the loss of reputation due to bad business behavior by a medieval European trader meant the loss of his commercial connections and the loss of his livelihood. A good reputation assured an established trader continued access to credit and increased the possibilities for maintaining a steady flow of commerce and of gold and silver as income. After divorcing themselves in the late 1800s from the shackles of medieval religious and ethical traditions, economists are learning from medieval traders how ethics and economics are intertwined.

The Value of Honesty

Honesty is a simple virtue that promises a reward. Deuteronomy 25:13-15 commands honesty in commerce:

> Do not have differing weights and measures in your bag–one heavy and one light. Do not have differing measures in your house–one large, one small. You must have accurate and honest weights and measures, so that you may live long in the land the LORD your God is giving you (NIV).

In other words, be honest and have integrity in your commercial dealings with others. When selling grain, don't weigh out a full pound for a friend, but then use a fraudulent weight to give only a part of a pound to a stranger.

The reward for just weights and measures is to "live long in the land." We can interpret this as an economic blessing rather than a mere promise of a long life, for they were to be in the "land of promise" with its economic blessing. Since Deuteronomy was written as a covenant between God and all Israel, we can reasonably take this particular part of the code to have communal meaning. All of Israel was to remain honest so that all might be blessed together. Curiously, Jeremiah 5:1, anticipating the fall of Jerusalem to foreign conquerors, quotes the Lord as saying, "Go up and down the streets of Jerusalem, look around and consider, search through her squares. If you can find but one person who deals honestly and seeks the truth, I will forgive this city" (NIV). None is found and the city is besieged and eventually falls.

The Value of Hard Work

Hard work is another simple virtue of Scripture that promises a reward. As Proverbs 14:23 says, "All hard work brings a profit, but mere talk leads only to poverty" (NIV). The reward from industriousness would seem to accrue to the worker, but the proverb does not limit the benefit to the worker. It may be that the benefits of our hard work spill over to other people as well. The "wife of noble character" of Proverbs 31, for example, benefits her entire

household through diligent commerce as she makes and sells "linen garments" and "supplies belts to the tradesmen" (v. 24 NASB).

What is the economic significance of these simple virtues of honesty and hard work? Nobel Prize winner Douglass North in his *Institutions, Institutional Change, and Economic Growth* (1990) asserts that honesty and hard work are essential informal institutions that promote economic growth and the wealth of nations. "Traditions" of honesty and hard work lower the costs of doing business and encourage the trade and investment that lead to higher standards of living.

Assuring honesty in weights and measures is part of the commercial codes of many nations. Even before the covenant in Deuteronomy, the king of Babylon standardized weights and measures around 2,500 years before Christ (Fowler 1996). Federal and state governments today have bureaus of weights and measures that set and enforce standards in commerce, monitoring scales, price scanners, and labels for accuracy. Published standards reduce uncertainty in trade and the costs it imposes on traders.

Assuring honesty and punishing dishonesty in commercial agreements through contract law, legal advisors, and numerous civil and criminal lawsuits each year is costly. The economic importance of ethics stems from the efficiency of traders who keep their word without forcing others to resort to the law and courts.

Looking Ahead

Christian economists hold diverse views on integrating Christian belief and economic learning. Some want to overturn the secular mainstream, while others work comfortably within it. This text presents the secular mainstream of economic thought as offering important lessons. Even when wrong or inadequate, it *is* the mainstream and is worth studying as such. To understand its critics requires understanding its ideas.

The text does address inadequacies of the mainstream from secular and Christian perspectives. You will read about how the theory of individual consumer demand ignores social effects on consumption. You will read about strategies of self-control in consumption that hit at the heart of mainstream belief in stable (as opposed to wildly shifting) consumer preferences. The alert reader will note that unstable preferences are consistent with the Christian view of imperfect human control.

The text makes no attempt to build a separate Christian economics. But the reading "What Should Christian Economists Do?" (in the chapter on the history of economic thought) does compare the views of Christian economists. It contrasts those who wish to build a separate Christian economics with those in the mainstream. The comparison builds upon a critical assessment of the utilitarian and positivist underpinnings of the mainstream "neoclassical" theory.

More than most economics texts, this one addresses topics of concern to a Christian, such as: the perfectibility of humans vs. sinful human nature, Ebenezer Scrooge as a repentant sinner compared to a radical-socialist interpretation of Dickens' "A Christmas Carol," U.S. "blue laws" and the Sabbath rest, early Church views on private property, Jeremy Bentham's secular utilitarian view of law vs. William Blackstone's view of the divine source of law, and the debate between Christian socialists and Christian capitalists.

The text also treats topics of general moral and religious interest, such as: student complaints about dorm food and the relativity of thankful attitudes, the economic significance of moral capital, economic effects of opportunistic behavior (immorality) in commerce, whether economists and their students are more selfish than others, moral criticisms regarding economists' emphasis on GDP, the role of religion in culture as a balancing force in democratic capitalism, the causes of wealth and poverty, whether capitalism corrupts culture, and the Soviet squelching of culture.

CHAPTER SUMMARY

1. Integration of Christian faith and learning combines disciplinary knowledge with revealed truth so as to give coherence to a student's understanding of facts and theories. The goal is intellectual honesty and remaining true to one's spiritual faith commitments.

2. For the atheist or the believer, a strict segregation of ideas into secular and religious is logically incoherent. If there is no God, then even human religion is one of the facts of life to be explained. If there is a God as Christians and others believe, then all truth is God's truth and the divided mind makes no sense.

3. Naturalistic philosophy explains religious belief and its rites as human creations with functions that serve human needs for individual meaning, social control, solidarity, and so on.

4. Higher education in the United States traditionally did not separate faith and disciplinary learning. Enlightenment emphasis on human reason over divine revelation as the source of knowledge, scientism as the belief that scientific method is the source of all knowledge, and the rise of state-supported education with a tradition of separation of church and state contributed to the current division of secular learning and religious belief. The Church may be guilty of causing the rise of secularized education, but a human desire for autonomy and a rebellion against God is at work too.

5. Christian faith begins with Jesus Christ and the belief that He was both fully God and fully human. He came to this world to reconcile sinners to God. The Christian emphasis on the sovereignty of God conflicts with a secular worldview. Many Christians traditionally have held a high view of Scripture and its authority. Understanding what it meant when written is necessary to properly interpret it and apply it today. Christian belief holds that humans are fallen, but that they have the hope of regeneration by God's grace (gift) through faith in Jesus.

6. Integration of Christian faith and economic learning can proceed in several directions. Scripture teaches lessons about economic topics such as production, distribution, and consumption of goods and services. Economic understanding gives insight into the interpretation of Scripture. And in many of its simple moral lessons, Scripture anticipates important current research in economics.

Problems for Practice

I.1 What are the logical inconsistencies in a radical separation of intellectual scholarship in the various academic disciplines and scholarship on religious beliefs? Does the inconsistency depend on whether you believe in God or are an atheist? How do atheists view religion?

I.2 What are the reasons given for and against integrating religious faith into disciplinary learning?

I.3* Do you agree with the economist's assertion that the study of "what is" should precede the study of "what ought to be" in the social sciences? What are the issues? See Expansion Point I.2.

I.4 What are the differences between the following words: exegesis, eisegesis, and hermeneutics? What is your view of the appropriate way to read the Bible? Should we read it like other literature?

I.5 According to the explanation in this chapter, what are two possible interpretations of Jesus' cleansing the Temple of money changers and other traders? Which do you tend to support (or are there other interpretations)? How would you apply this text to the Church today? First, read the text for yourself in John 2:13-22. You may want to consult a commentary.

I.6 How has a Christian worldview affected the interpretation of modern secular economic theories?

For your portfolio:

I.7* Write a one-page-maximum reaction to the First to the Lord Campaign explained in Expansion Point I.4. Base your reaction on a thorough reading of 2 Corinthians 8. Use Scripture first. Consult commentaries as secondary references after you have read the chapter itself four or five times. Many college libraries have excellent commentaries in their reference sections and in the stacks (consult computer catalog). Electronic copies of the Bible and commentaries are available online at www.crosswalk.com.

You have two writing tasks. First, answer the question: Is the "First to the Lord" campaign a proper use of Scripture, according to reasonable exegetical and hermeneutical principles? Second, in your conclusions, briefly express your convictions about the responsibilities of local churches regarding collecting and using offerings.

I.8* Choose one of the following topics and apply the exegetical approach to understanding the Scripture that is listed with it. How would you apply the Scripture to the question raised for the topic? Write a one-page paper, citing sources from online or library commentaries and other references.

a. American companies are prevented by U.S. law from paying bribes to foreign officials when competing for foreign contracts. Bribes are legal in many other countries, and U.S. companies are put at a disadvantage in foreign competition. Should the U.S. change the law, as some leaders suggest, so that U.S. companies must merely abide by laws of the nation where they are competing? Apply the following verses: Exodus 23:8; Deuteronomy 27:25; Proverbs 6:35; Ecclesiastes 7:7; Isaiah 5:23; Amos 5:12. Hint: These mainly discuss accepting bribes. What do you conclude about *paying* bribes?
b. Christian socialists today contend that Acts 4:32-36 shows that the early Church lived communally. They contend that the Jerusalem believers had no private property, sharing everything in common. They contend that Ananias and Sapphira died because they did not share with others (see Acts 5:1-11). Other Christians contend that the sin of Ananias and Sapphira was that they lied, and that these verses do not condemn private property among Christians. What is your interpretation and application for Christians today? Should all live in communes?
c. If you are wealthy, you cannot be a good Christian. God really loves the poor (1 Samuel 2:8; Isaiah 14:30). Wealthy people cannot get into heaven (Matthew 19:23-24). Should every Christian give away all personal wealth in order to be a true believer? Also consult Proverbs 19:17, Luke 19:8, and 1 Timothy 6:17-19.

For class discussion:

I.9 Based on statistical research, economist Laurence Iannaccone (2002) has concluded that nations that have a state church have very low rates of participation in regular religious services (some in the range of two or three percent of the population). Nations that hold to strict separation of church and state, such as the United States, have much higher rates of religious participation (fifty percent or more). Applying standard economic theory, he concludes that free competition encourages religious participation and monopoly power restricts the output of religious services (as in goods and services). How would you respond to such an application of secular economic thinking to religious topics? How would you explain his findings?

See Answer Key for hints/answers to starred (*) questions.

SECTION I

Introduction to Scarcity, Economy, and Economic Method

All economic activity and economic analysis start with a human problem: scarcity. People and their economic systems have always struggled against scarcity. Economic analysis studies the efficient use of resources to push back the limits of scarcity.

Chapter 1 defines the problem of scarcity and reviews the methods humans use to overcome scarcity. The next four chapters take a detailed look at the economy and economic analysis. Chapter 2 introduces economic analysis of scarcity, price, efficiency, and cost. Chapter 3 tells the history of the idea of economics, from stewardship to the science of individual and public choice. Chapter 4 reviews theories and actual examples of economic behavior. Chapter 5 introduces the methods of microeconomics and macroeconomics.

The next four chapters take a broader view of the economy and economic analysis. Chapter 6 asks, "What Is an Economy?" and focuses on economies as systems. Chapter 7 shows that any economy is endowed with natural, technical, and human resources, as well as human organizations and institutions. Chapter 8 examines the meaning and nature of individual wealth and poverty, while Chapter 9 explains the causes of economic growth and the wealth and poverty of nations, showing the importance of particular institutions. Chapter 10 explains the powers and economic roles of government.

Chapter 1

SCARCITY

The Essence of Economics

What this chapter will help you think about:

1. What is scarcity and why is it the primary economic issue?
2. How do humans and their governments battle scarcity?
3. What is rationing and how does it affect economic efficiency?
4. What are the various approaches to rationing?
5. What are the different measures of economic efficiency?

Agrarian peasants struggle to survive a year of drought and famine. A family spends the last of its monthly income five days before the end of the month. Elected politicians fiercely debate how many tax dollars to spend on military arms, social welfare programs, or national infrastructure like canals, highways, bridges, and airports. A child chooses which toy to buy with a small allowance. These examples illustrate the effects of the economic problem of scarcity, the reason for all economizing and economic analysis. Economizing is doing the best we can with what we have. Economic analysis explores how best to accomplish this.

Scarcity: The Economic Problem

• **Scarcity** arises due to limited resources and unlimited wants.

Scarcity, economists teach, is the fundamental economic problem, arising because our wants are limitless while our resources are not. Much of our individual and communal lives are devoted to solving problems of scarcity. Most family, societal, and political problems have their roots in scarcity.

Something is scarce if its price is greater than zero. People will pay money or trade other valuable goods or services for something that is scarce. Normal air is not scarce because you do not have to work or pay for it. Normal air under pressure, however, is a scarce good because someone must work with a pump to fill a tank. Pure oxygen is also a scarce good, because someone has to work and use resources to separate and collect it. Food is scarce, even when we have plenty of it, because its price is positive.

To test whether something is scarce, ask any number of people if they would like one free. If you have more buyers than you have items to give, you can sell it at a positive price because the good is scarce. So two indicators of scarcity are either a market price above zero (the price established in free exchange of goods), or a waiting line for the good if it is arbitrarily given away free.

A sign of generalized scarcity is that we pay for most goods we use each day, either with money, time, or other goods. Very little is free. We pay for meat and milk, houses and furniture, books and classes, and cars and plane rides. The price of each is in large part a measure of the scarcity of the good.

Even if a good's price happens to be zero, does that prove that it is not scarce? No, it may indicate a subsidized price. If lunch at a soup kitchen is advertised as free, economists point out that someone paid for it. Someone paid for the vegetables, meat, and spices. Someone took time to prepare and serve it. Using this reasoning, economists of the Chicago School of Economics have long been known to say, *"There is no such thing as a free lunch."* Charity does not eliminate scarcity. The key to scarcity is the market price of a good, set by free exchange, not by artificially established prices.

We see evidence of scarcity in human relations and morality. Scarcity encourages a range of human feelings from normal acquisitiveness to greed, from normal comparisons of economic status to outright envy, and from personal responsibility for providing for one's needs to dependence on others. Scarcity causes individuals either to give to others charitably or steal from others selfishly. Scarcity causes people either to compromise or to fight. Marriage counselors and financial advisors know that money problems, especially heavy debt and binge spending, are common causes of divorce.

Scarcity is an enduring and pervasive problem. Human history gives no indication that scarcity has ever been permanently overcome in any economic system. Overcoming scarcity would require a miracle. Indeed, the Bible records miracle stories in which scarcity is temporarily overcome. Miracles, however, are attributed to divine intervention rather than to the cleverness of human technology or organization, leaving us little hope that we can overcome scarcity in the world. As Jesus said, "The poor you will always have with you" (Mark 14:7 NIV). So too scarcity is always with us.

Scarcity Imposes Limits

With limited resources, people confront numerous limits in their personal, business, and political lives. Families confront a limited income, also called a **budget constraint**. Businesses confront limits to their ability to raise funds and therefore to gather resources for their work. Governments confront budget constraints too: they cannot spend more money than they can raise in taxes, borrow, and print.

• **Budget constraint:** the effects of limited income on consumption possibilities

Public policy makers, by the way, have from time to time incorrectly assumed that printing money to pay for more spending somehow would break the bonds of public scarcity. Printing money to pay government bills only shifts purchasing power from households and businesses to government. The extra money also inflates prices, if the economy is otherwise working normally and if productive capacity is the same.

• **Production possibilities:** maximum output of a nation's goods and services when resources and technology are fully used

A nation's **production possibilities** are limited by its resources, its available technology, and how fully resources and technology are being used. While it is hard to describe all possible combinations of products, limits exist. A traveler can, for example, fly from New York City to London, England, in under four hours, but not under four minutes. The technology does not exist yet for such speedy regular passenger travel. An American farmer can, on average, feed over 35 people, but not over 350. Once again, agricultural technology has limits. Furthermore, society can't simply pass a law demanding more products than its resources will produce.

Scarcity and Choices

• **Tradeoff:** choosing one option means foregoing another

Limits to production possibilities force societies to choose among alternatives. Economists call such choices **tradeoffs**, meaning if you want more of one good, you will have to trade and have less of another. If a nation's economy is fully employed, it can have, for instance, more consumer goods today for immediate consumption or more productive equipment to expand future production, but not more of both. A state legislature can spend extra tax revenues for, say, 500 miles of new road or 30 new schools, but not both. Tradeoffs abound in public and private life.

Production Possibilities Curve

Economists illustrate tradeoffs with what they call a production possibilities curve. Exhibit 1.1 shows a simple production possibilities curve for a nation that can produce arms (military weapons) or food. The quantity of arms is illustrated on the vertical axis, and the quantity of food is illustrated on the horizontal axis. Moving from the origin—the (0,0) point—toward the upper right corner means increasing production of both arms and food. The curved line illustrates that the nation faces limits to production possibilities, where resources and technology are constant but are used fully. When the nation is at maximum production possibilities, having more arms means having less food.

The production possibilities curve in Exhibit 1.1 illustrates the tradeoffs facing all nations and their governments. Let's restate the conclusion about production-possibility tradeoffs. **If a nation's resources and technology are being used fully, having more of one good thing means having less of another.** If a nation wants its government to produce more social services with

Exhibit 1.1: Production Possibilities of Arms and Food

The nation represented here can produce arms and food. The production possibilities curve connects the extremes of producing all arms and no food (point A) or all food and no arms (point F). The points on the curve in between (B, C, D, and E) show the tradeoff between arms and food. The nation can only produce at one point at a time, somewhere on or inside the curve. For an idea of several nations' relative expenditures on arms, consider that, in the 1980s, we would place Japan at about E, the United States at D, and the Soviet Union at C.

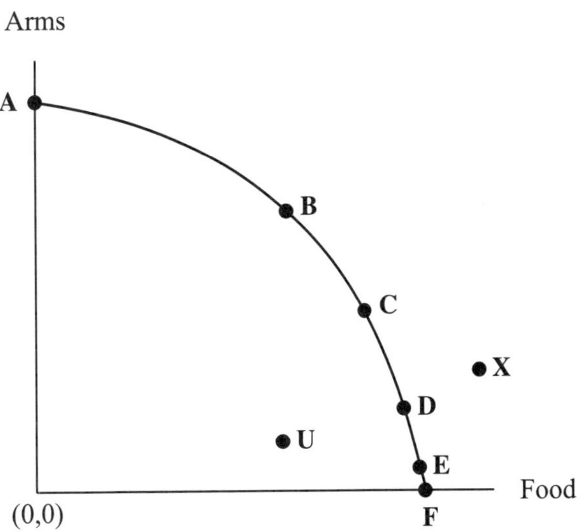

Point X, with more arms and food, is not possible given current resources and technology. It will be available only if the economy grows. Point U represents less-than-full use of resources, a situation involving unemployment or underemployment of labor and equipment. At point U, the nation can increase both arms and food until it is fully employed. Once fully employed (on the curve), however, the nation can have more food only at a cost of having fewer arms.

a fixed budget, then it will have to give up other government goods or services such as military power, law enforcement, or education. If society wants more of all these government services, then it must sacrifice private goods and services.

Household and Business Tradeoffs

Families also must choose how to spend a limited income. Should I buy a sweater, a sweatshirt, or a pair of jeans? Do we take a vacation or trade for a new car? Americans love to have choices or "options" among different colors, styles, price ranges, and so on. Scarcity limits our options. We can't have all we want, let alone have it in the color we want. We must choose how to spend our limited income and use our limited time. Should I watch a television program or exercise? Will you read a novel, take a walk, study, work a second job, or spend more time with family?

Businesses must choose which investment projects to begin and which old projects to continue. Managers must budget limited investment funds among almost limitless investment projects. Managers also must budget their time. Many books teach the busy office manager how to prioritize work, process mail and papers efficiently, and eliminate time wasters. For examples, see Expansion Point 1.1: Time-Management Tips.

Expansion Point 1.1: Time-Management Tips

Here are eight tips for effectively managing time in business, as well as in the home and at school:

1. Rule your time, don't just plan your use of it. Decide what are the first things in your life (take the long-run view) and do the first things first. Planning your day should come after planning your life and setting short-term priorities.

2. Make lists. Once your life goals and short-term priorities are set, make lists of tasks to complete and keep your lists in one book, checking them off as completed.

3. Fight procrastination by rewarding yourself for success, dividing huge tasks into little ones, setting your own deadlines, and perhaps delegating unpleasant tasks to others who may enjoy them more!

4. Avoid unnecessary interruptions by making yourself unavailable. Shut the door. Hide in the library. And don't constantly interrupt others.

5. Limit meetings. Don't waste your time or other people's time. Go only when you have to. Invite only those who need to know or can help. Meet standing up to keep it short. Always begin on time.

6. Control your telephone time; don't let it control you. Keep conversations short. Make all your return calls at the same time each day.

7. Read effectively. Cut your reading list as much as possible. Read only when needed. Tear out articles that you want to read and file for later use, tossing the rest of the magazine (but only if it is yours, and not the library's).

8. File it or toss it. Handle papers only once. Make your decision where they go the first time you pick them up or quickly put them in a "Hold for Later" folder.

Sources: Stephen R. Covey, A. Roger Merrill, and Rebecca Merrill, *First Things First: To Live, to Love, to Learn, to Leave a Legacy* (New York: Fireside/Simon & Schuster, 1994).

Stephanie Winston, *The Organized Executive: New Ways to Manage Time, Paper, People, and the Electronic Office*, rev. ed. (New York: W. W. Norton, 1994).

Battling Scarcity

Human progress has been a continuous battle to find new techniques of production and distribution and new forms of commercial and social organization, so as to satisfy more wants with less human effort. To **economize** is to make the best use of available resources in pursuit of economic goals such as a higher standard of living. Expansion Point 1.1 lists only a few of numberless economizing strategies. Economic historians can document thousands of years of human efforts against the limits of scarcity.

• **Economize:** make the best use of available resources in pursuit of economic goals

How have people and their governments reacted to scarcity? Mixing competition and cooperation, they have adopted at least six broad strategies: exchanging, rationing, stealing, increasing production, innovating, and revolting. Exchanging, rationing, and stealing simply reshuffle existing supplies of things that satisfy wants and needs. Producing more and innovating don't reshuffle existing supplies; they add to them. People's utopian dreams and peaceful or violent economic revolutions have not always lived up to expectations, especially when hopes were unrealistic.

Exchanging Goods

Because of the benefits of voluntary exchange, people push back the limits of scarcity by exchanging goods and services. A practice as old as human civilization, exchange is the usual method of distributing scarce products and resources. Adam Smith (1776, bk. I, chap. 2) called it a human "propensity to truck and barter." Even if modified or outlawed by government, exchange is rarely if ever eliminated entirely. While held captive in World War II prison camps, Allied soldiers developed systems of exchange, with cigarettes as money and prices of other goods rising when cigarette supplies dwindled.

Benefits of Exchange

The potential benefit from exchange lies in a simple idea that **trade is a positive-sum game**. If two traders value two goods differently, voluntary exchange can improve the economic welfare of both. When you go to the store to buy food, you value the food more than the money because you have too little food and relatively more money. On the other side of the exchange, the merchant values the money more because inventories of goods must be sold and bills paid. You value the convenience of not having to grow food or negotiate with farmers and processors yourself. The merchant develops valuable connections and expertise, and also earns discounts by buying in volume, increasing benefits to you.

• **Trade is a positive-sum game:** both parties can benefit from voluntary exchange that moves goods to more valuable uses

Even with a middleman, **trade creates value**. In theory and assuming no adverse effects on third parties, voluntary exchange increases both traders' senses of well-being without making anyone else worse off. Exchange increases economic efficiency by moving output to its most valuable uses. The historical rise of specialization in production in village and city-state economies, for example, led to individual and regional surpluses and shortages of goods and services. Exchange enabled traders to make themselves better off by giving up part of their surplus in exchange for what was in short supply.

• **Trade creates value:** voluntary trade makes scarce goods more valuable

Barter Exchange

Barter is the direct or "bilateral" exchange between two traders of one good for another. Bilateral simply means two-way exchange. Exhibit 1.2 illustrates barter between a farmer and hunter in a village society. The grain farmer has extra wheat but not enough meat, so he trades or "barters" with the cattle farmer who has too little wheat and more than enough meat. Each trader values greatly what is lacking, and values less what is plentiful. When wants and surpluses match, both can benefit from exchange.

• **Barter:** trading one product for another, without money

Yet the benefits of barter are limited because barter requires a **double coincidence of wants**. Each trader must want what the

• **A double coincidence of wants** is required for barter exchange.

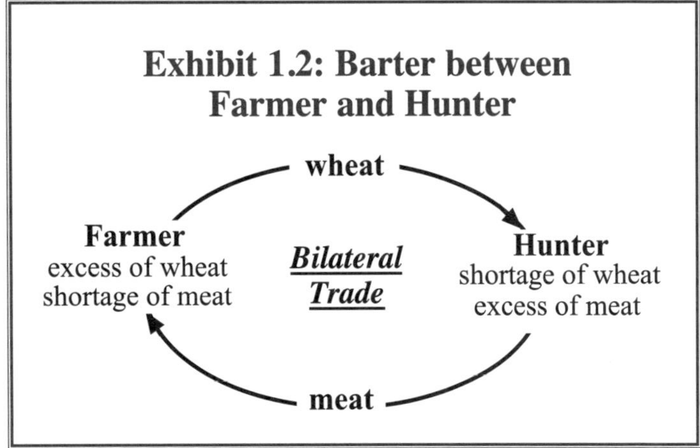

other has to offer, which is less likely than a complex pattern of surpluses and shortages. If the hunter needs wheat but the farmer raises grain and *also* fishes and raises chicken for meat to eat, barter no longer benefits both because their wants do not coincide.

Market Exchange with Money

Market exchange with money is more efficient than barter, creating more value by facilitating even more trades. Buyers and sellers continually bid and recontract to balance product and resource supplies and demands.

- **Money:** a widely accepted means of payment in exchange

- **Market exchange:**
  1) creates incentives to produce more
  2) moves goods to most valuable uses

As a **widely accepted means of payment**, money makes a double coincidence of wants unnecessary. Exhibit 1.3 shows a simple circular flow of money where households and businesses meet for exchange in product and resource markets. Consumer spending flows to businesses, and comes back as household income (solid line). **Real flows** of products (goods and services) and resources move in the other direction (dotted line).

Exchange has two benefits besides creating value. First, it **creates incentives** that encourage more production. Profit, for example, motivates producers. Second, as discussed in the next section, trade at market prices is one method of rationing limited goods to offset scarcity's effects. Each buyer's willingness to pay determines who values a product the most. As a result, exchange in a well-functioning market not only moves goods to *more* valuable uses (as does barter), but in theory a price system also **allocates goods** to their ***most* valuable uses**.

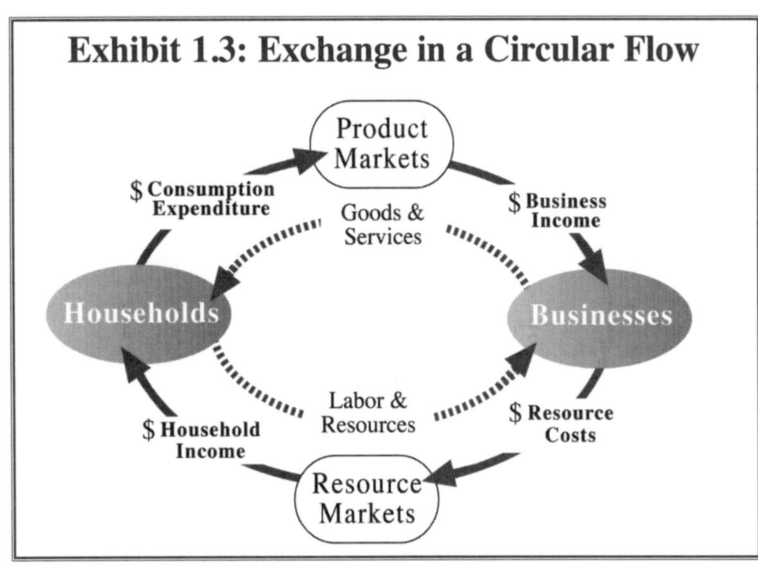

Rationing

- **Ration:** to divide resources, goods, and services among various uses

When confronted with limited quantities of resources, goods, and services, people must carefully ration what is available. To **ration** means to divide available goods or services among competing individuals, groups, and uses. People may divide products based on fairness, or on the receiver's rank. To promote freedom and stimulate current and future production, people may allow free exchange. Individuals and families ration in their daily lives, dividing time and money among different uses. A parent dividing food at dinner or handing out money allowances is rationing.

Each economic group and nation develops various institutions (economic rules and agreements) and organizations to ration available resources. Through them, the nation answers these **fundamental questions:** (1) What will be produced? (2) Under whose direction will production occur? and (3) Who will receive the available goods and services and how much? Individuals answer the questions with their own enterprise and buying choices. Governments answer the questions in part when they collect taxes and divide public income and wealth to meet various goals. When a government restricts uses of a war material, for example, rationing is at work. When a government allows free markets to work, however, rationing is by the market system, according to individual work effort, voluntary exchange, and the influence of changing prices and wages.

- **Fundamental questions:**
  1) What to produce?
  2) Under whose direction?
  3) Who gets the product?

Four Methods of Rationing

Rationing output, an important aspect of what is called "distribution" in economic theory, can be accomplished in at least four ways: (1) a leader makes arbitrary decisions, (2) individuals organize markets in which rationing is decentralized (largely outside the control of a central government), (3) each person gets an equal share, and (4) first-come, first-served at a zero price. Political power, social values, and property rights will influence what mix of these methods a society uses to ration products.

- **Four methods of rationing:**
  1) arbitrary choice
  2) market rationing
  3) equal shares
  4) first-come, first-served

Arbitrary Rationing by Government. When political and economic power is centralized and not subject to veto, arbitrary rationing is more likely to occur. Arbitrary rationing causes inefficiencies in economic activity and also generates many complaints. When a sovereign rations goods and services by will and whim, the end result is not always justice. More often, a privileged elite benefits and the sovereign gains their support.

- **Rent seeking:** petitioning government for special privileges

In democratic societies, governments also arbitrarily ration certain goods, causing people to plead for a portion. Economists call this **rent-seeking behavior**, when citizens petition the government for a special privilege or share. Since pleading for a share of redistributed output produces no added output, rent seeking is an inefficient method of rationing.

Decentralized Rationing by Market Exchange. Where political and economic power is decentralized, voluntary exchange in free markets arises spontaneously. Rationing then occurs by market exchange. Sometimes these markets are **fixed-price markets** and sometimes they are **flexible-price auctions**, as explained in Expansion Point 1.2.

- **Fixed-price markets:** prices don't adjust often; they are set in menus, in catalogs, and by large corporations
- **Flexible-price markets:** prices constantly adjust

How do markets perform? Economic theory and history demonstrate their efficiency. Markets do not, however, tend to distribute goods equally, complain the critics. Yet advocates say that, with rules of the game properly applied, market exchange can allow for equality of opportunity. Arbitrary government decisions generally do not.

Critics also complain that buyers and sellers must compete in auction market and that this competition is socially harmful. As a result, they call for more economic cooperation. People compete, however, in most activities, not just commerce and production for profit. People compete for mates, they compete to be the best dressed, most popular, or smartest, and they compete in athletic contests. Therefore, government rationing of resources does not eliminate competition, it alters the form of competition. Instead of competing in markets, people compete for favors from rulers or bureaucrats.

Equal Shares. When people want to ensure apparent fairness in rationing, they generally consider equal shares. Socialistic

Expansion Point 1.2: Rationing by Flexible-Price and Fixed-Price Markets

Fish-market auction

The markets for autos, dinner at a restaurant, and catalog sales are usually fixed-price markets, in which prices are fixed by "list prices," menus, and catalogs. Markets for gold, stocks, government and corporate bonds, fish, wheat, and other agricultural commodities, however, are auction markets, in which prices change minute by minute.

In certain markets, apparently fixed prices adjust often enough to approximate auctions. Menu prices at a restaurant may vary by time of day and for age of the customer. Prices are higher at dinner than at lunch and lower for the young and old. Companies with fixed catalog prices may still give some discounts. Steel prices in the United States are posted but discounting still occurs, especially in times of weak demand. U.S. automobile prices are also discounted, although the percentage discount has fallen since the 1960s.

When demand is variable and unpredictable, fixed-price markets are not as efficient as auction markets. Unusually high demand with fixed prices creates shortages, so that some people who value the good very much cannot buy it. Shortages do, however, create opportunities for traders to make a profit by starting an auction that can satisfy unmet demand. Unusually low demand with fixed prices means that existing supplies will not be fully used. In contrast, an auction market allows prices to fall so that supplies are used. In short, flexible prices help to match supplies of goods with varying customer demands, making auction markets a popular method of rationing in free societies.

Market analyst James Cash (*Nightly Business Report,* PBS, February 10, 1999) has predicted that online auctions would develop in a variety of consumer goods, just as they are rapidly developing in commodities markets and markets for producer goods. Among the first consumer goods to be auctioned on the Internet in the 1990s were airline tickets.

programs emphasize equality of outcomes. A slight variation is to give shares equal to each person's need. Critics of socialist programs complain that providing for each person's needs destroys important incentives for individual work and initiative. Advocates for socialist schemes contend that basic human justice requires such fairness. A compromise solution is that society may provide for an equal *minimum* level income or standard of living. Critics still complain that too generous a minimum turns a social safety net into a hammock.

First-Come, First-Served. Another approach to fairness is that a product or resource be distributed on a first-come, first-served basis. At public campgrounds in the United States, a portion of the campsites will be set aside for those who arrive first (with no reservations allowed). The same is true for spaces in many parking lots. Except for certain reserved spots, most places are available to those who arrive first.

Changing and Mixing Rationing Systems

Societies change systems of rationing from time to time. During war, governments often confiscate goods and ration them to promote the war effort. In World War II, the U.S. government fixed prices of consumer goods and then rationed the goods to families by issuing coupons for rubber tires, gasoline, butter, meat, and so on. **Price controls** of the early 1940s were called General Max (for General Maximum system of prices). The war effort required the government to buy huge quantities of these goods. Controlling prices and rationing kept the cost of the war lower and forced consumers to bear the war's cost through reduced consumption rather than increased taxes. At war's end, the United States returned to rationing the controlled goods mainly by markets.

- **Price control:** government-imposed maximum price (price ceiling) or minimum price (price floor)

No society uses only one method of rationing goods at a time. In fact, goods and services such as college football tickets are rationed in quite complex ways that involve all four of these methods. See Expansion Point 1.3 for more details about distributing tickets. Most economies also have a mixture of rationing by free-market exchange, arbitrary decree, and fairness methods.

A nation's primary system of rationing depends on the system of property rights prevailing at the time. **Private property rights** (the rights to hold, use, sell, or give away property) encourage and permit voluntary market exchange. Public ownership of property, on the other hand, requires rationing through government plans and agencies. Most modern nations rely heavily on the market system for many goods, but also legislate significant government interventions for health care and for programs related to poor relief, national defense, and education.

- **Private property rights:** the legal rights to hold, use, and sell or give away property

Expansion Point 1.3: Rationing College Football Tickets

Tickets to college football games provide an example of the complex methods of rationing. At a university with a winning program, seats in the football stadium often sell out and must be rationed among potential fans. Students are usually treated with fairness in mind. At some schools, all students who want to attend have equal rights to get in free. Every student may have equal access to student seating, except that during a popular game, when student attendance is high, seating may be first-come, first-served. Late students must stand.

At other schools, students must pay for a ticket just as alumni and guests do. Ticket prices for alumni and guests are set high enough to generate substantial revenue for the university, but low enough to fill available seats each week. This is a fixed-price market in the short run, although price is adjusted each year. The school will set a lower price for students because they have less income and are less able to pay.

Rather than charge more for the best seats, the school can choose to make the best seats available to wealthy contributors to the college, or to loyal fans who buy season tickets for many years. Seniors and graduate students may get better seating than first-year students, with sophomores and juniors in between.

When a game is particularly popular, and football tickets are in high demand, first-come, first-served operates alongside equal shares: the first fans to apply get the tickets, but each fan may be limited to eight or ten tickets to assure fairness. Football players get an equal share of tickets set aside for them and can arbitrarily give tickets to whomever they choose. The school will also arbitrarily set aside tickets for guests of the school, including politicians, dignitaries, and prospective athletic recruits.

For fans who arrive outside the football stadium without a ticket, vigorous free-market auctions may be taking place. "Scalpers" who have bought a number of tickets in advance and others who simply have more than they want will be selling tickets at prices that can be quite high for popular games. Scalpers intend to buy at a low price and sell at a high price. However, if too many tickets are available for the game, scalpers must sell their tickets at a loss. Scalping prompts ethical debates and complaints, but those who can buy tickets at the last minute are often quite happy to find a ticket auction.

When will scalpers find it profitable to operate? First, the college must have a fixed price for its tickets rather than a price that adjusts with changing demand. Second, the college game must be sold out so that no tickets are available at regular prices. These conditions suggest an interesting conclusion about scalping and markets in general: when an auction market is not planned by authorities and demand is high, humans will tend to innovate to create an auction.

Rationing and Social Welfare

Rationing affects social welfare by influencing economic efficiency and economic equity. Efficiency in rationing is defined by how well the rationing scheme meets human needs and wants. A more efficient system of rationing will increase social welfare. Equity in rationing determines how equally human wants and needs are met, and whether minimum needs are met.

Rationing is sometimes referred to as "dividing the pie." How we divide the pie has important effects on economic welfare. Each approach also affects various groups differently, causing people to differ on their perspectives on the fairness of each.

Those who favor giving out equal shares tend to believe that free-market exchange is unfair because the wealthy receive more income than the poor. Their critics respond that the wealthy earn more than the poor because they are more productive. This conflict of views has created one of the more vigorous economic debates in history.

A problem with everyone receiving equal shares, however, is that while it seems fair, it is not efficient. In terms of a pie, some people like bigger and some like smaller pieces, while others want none. Inflexible redistribution systems that don't recognize people's varied preferences may end up being neither fair nor efficient. Efficiency requires getting tickets, food, and pieces of the pie to those who value them most. That is best done with voluntary exchange at market prices. Setting arbitrarily low prices tends to cause people both rich and poor to eat more and waste food.

Rationing systems affect another aspect of economic efficiency: productivity. How big will the pie be and how many pies will be produced in the future? Gathering all the food produced and then distributing it equally may seem fair, but such a rationing system can drastically reduce future food production. As some socialist governments have discovered, farmers will refuse to plant and harvest crops when they are not adequately compensated for them. After liberation from colonialism in the mid-1900s, revolutionary African governments chose to pay their farmers less-than-market prices for agricultural products. The goal was to raise money for industrial development by selling the food internationally at market prices. The actual effect was to significantly reduce food output because farmers decided that it was no longer sensible to produce as much for such low prices.

Remember this about rationing scarce goods: first, scarcity makes rationing necessary; second, power, property rights, and social goals affect rationing decisions; third, the system of rationing affects economic efficiency and perceived fairness.

Theft and Wars

A second human reaction to scarcity is theft. People steal from one another, from businesses, and from governments to increase their consumption possibilities. Governments also steal to increase land holdings and access to raw materials and labor. At times, governments take wealth from their citizens by threat and overt force. They also make war to do so. History records humanity's thievery and warring, and its costly defenses against these actions.

In the United States, theft or stealing is probably the most common intentional criminal act. Theft takes many forms, and the law has many distinct words for it, such as: *burglary* for breaking and entering, *rustling* for theft of livestock, *embezzling* for stealing entrusted funds or property from an employer, *pilfering* for

stealing bit by bit over time, *shoplifting* for stealing goods for sale in a retail store, and *robbery* for theft by force. While *theft* refers to taking property against the owner's will, *fraud* is taking something with permission but by means of deceit.

Storytellers have made heroes of many thieves throughout history. Robin Hood stole from the rich to give to the poor. Jesse James and Bonnie and Clyde stole money from banks. While we enjoy the stories, theft is costly and is a drag on economic activity. In 1996, the estimated value of stolen property in the United States was more than $15 billion (Federal Bureau of Investigation 1997). The high cost, about $1,300 per crime in 1996, compels people to devote significant money and effort to preventing theft, insuring themselves against it, and finding and prosecuting those who steal. Using scarce resources to police against theft does not directly produce more goods. Were it not for thieves, society could apply these resources to more productive work. Theft also reduces economic initiative. We spend money and considerable thought devising strategies and technology to protect against theft, as explained in Expansion Point 1.4.

Individuals have difficulty protecting against government theft. Communist revolutionaries in Eastern Europe used military force to confiscate the land and property of wealthy farmers, merchants, and industrialists. Returning confiscated land is also challenging. When the revolution ended in 1990, questions arose as to who owned what. Had the revolutionary confiscation been legal or illegal? Who were the true heirs of former property owners? To prevent inappropriate confiscation of property, citizens may demand that governments pass and abide by laws limiting the government's power to seize private property. In democratic nations, citizens have insisted on **due process** (including a court hearing about the government's need for the property) and **just compensation** (at fair market value) for the confiscated property.

•**Due process and just compensation** protect citizens against unjustified seizure of property by government.

Governments also take from other governments by threat or open military aggression. Governments have fought wars over scarce resources such as land, coal, and oil. Japan invaded China in 1931 partly to secure supplies of Chinese coal. Germany invaded the agriculturally rich Sudetenland in 1939 at the start of World War II. Iraq invaded Kuwait in 1990 partly due to conflicting claims on oil fields under their common border.

The threat of military aggression leads nations to prepare costly defenses against it. Though nations see them as necessary, such military expenditures tax social resources because they are not productive. Nations having no major defense expenditures can enjoy a relatively higher economic living standard. After World War II, for example, the Allies prevented Germany and Japan from rebuilding their militaries, but this restriction freed

Expansion Point 1.4: Theft and the Games People Play

People protect themselves against theft with a variety of simple yet cunning strategies. Business partners keep joint bank accounts requiring two people to sign each check. The banker has safe deposit boxes that must be opened with two keys: the banker keeps one and the customer keeps the other.

Even in small matters, schemes are cunning. You and a friend own equal shares of a piece of cake. Your friend agrees to cut. You want to split it equally, but if the cutter chooses first, he may cut the cake unevenly and you will be cheated. You can ensure a more equal cut by the rule that "one cuts and the other chooses." The cutter will then slice so that both pieces are about equal.

Wealthy individuals contemplating marriage rely on detailed prenuptial agreements specifying who gets what property in the event of a divorce. Such agreements protect their wealth against unscrupulous partners who would marry and then divorce them in order to win a settlement for half of the joint property. Love is blind, as is justice, but lawyers keep watch over a lover's wealth.

Businesses that hold valuable stocks of goods and equipment pay people to watch them day and night and then pay others to watch the watchers. Retailers watch customers like hawks through one-way mirrors, with cameras, and with their own security staff dressed as shoppers to catch those that shoplift.

The New York Federal Reserve Bank protects a good part of the world's stock of monetary gold in an airtight vault built into solid rock. America's own gold is mainly housed in a reinforced, concrete underground bunker at Fort Knox, Kentucky. The Buffalo Branch of the Federal Reserve prevents theft by assuring that no one is tunneling underneath. Its cash vault stands on pillars and is therefore exposed on all six sides. Using angled mirrors placed along the foundations, guards can look down one side, see under the vault, and out the other side.

precious resources to help them rebuild their civilian economies more quickly. For their part, the Allies decreased their individual defense expenditures by forming an alliance for joint defense, the North Atlantic Treaty Organization.

Given that people will steal and governments make war, effectively policing against theft and military aggression has beneficial economic effects. Protection and policing make people more willing to work harder and smarter to accumulate wealth to meet their wants and needs. Political scientists who hold **statist views** emphasize how important the military and political umbrella of a strong nation state is for world trade. They cite how commerce and economic development flourished under the *Pax Romana* of 2,000 years ago, the *Pax Britannia* of the nineteenth century, and the *Pax Americana* of the middle and late twentieth century (*pax* is Latin for peace). Sailors, for example, are more willing to carry freight on the oceans when a peaceful nation's navy rules the seas, deterring aggression by pirates and pirate nations.

• **Statist view:** a strong nation provides an umbrella for world commerce

• **Specialization** increases worker productivity by dividing complex work into simple tasks, with each worker assigned to a particular task.

Human Work

A third approach to scarcity is human labor. People enhance supplies of scarce goods and services by making more. The earth provides food, natural shelter, light, and heat, but not enough for everyone. To make resources more valuable for meeting needs and wants, workers change their form and location. As Adam Smith noted in *Wealth of Nations* (1776, bk. I, chap. 1), workers multiply their efforts by **specialization** and the division of labor. Each worker specializes in one of the many tasks into which they divide a complex job.

Do people naturally want to work hard or must they be enticed or coerced to offer more labor? Although some volunteers work without pay, most laborers demand pay. Certain nation states, in contrast, have allowed and even thrived on forced labor. Slave plantations in southern American states used forced labor until the Civil War ended in 1865. Russian dictator Joseph Stalin forced political prisoners to work as slaves, mining metals and minerals in Siberia during the 1930s. By the end of World War II, though, Stalin discovered that paying Soviet workers bonuses to migrate east and do the work was more efficient. China has been accused of using prison labor to produce low-cost goods for export, a practice that infuriates American companies that make the same goods with more expensive non-captive labor.

For whom will we work? Different economic systems allow people to work for different employers, whether themselves, a business owner, a corporation, a cooperative, or a government agency. From 1917 to 1990 in the Soviet Union, a growing government-planned bureaucracy employed more and more workers. Yet, during that time Russians also worked for themselves, especially producing food in their own dacha gardens. At the same time in Hong Kong, an island state off the southeastern coast of China, a growing free-enterprise economy employed most of its workers in private businesses. During the later part of that period, the kibbutz or communal living and working arrangements became increasingly popular in Israel. In the United States, independent family farms were the main source of food at the beginning of the 1900s, but they competed more and more with large commercial farms toward the end of the century.

The human urge to work can become excessive, making us greedy or compulsive "workaholics." While greed and workaholism can be channeled to the benefit of others, they can be personally destructive. These issues lie outside the narrow mainstream economic view of work, requiring that we also view work through psychological, social, and moral lenses.

In any event, people in industrialized nations today do less manual labor than before. However, they must continue to meet their growing needs and wants with physical and mental effort. They devote that effort increasingly to learning new techniques, building more machines, and inventing new ways to increase the productivity of labor.

Human Skill and Invention

Human skills, tools, machines, and improved methods and materials are important substitutes for unskilled human effort. Therefore, humans battle scarcity with a fourth approach: they try to increase human productivity through education, capital accumulation, and invention. Specialization often requires or leads to more skill at the job. Breaking work into simple tasks also encourages development and use of special tools, as well as mechanization. More tools and machines increase worker productivity. Human specialization and capital accumulation, therefore, contribute to pushing back the limits of scarcity.

Throughout history, workers have sought to make their labor easier and more productive by **worker** education and **training**. General schooling equips workers with transferable skills such as reading, writing, and computing. The apprentice system of on-the-job training passes along worker knowledge and particular skills from one generation to the next. Europe's apprentice system of the medieval period was by no means the first. In Babylon, as early as the eighteenth century B.C., Hammurabi required that craftsmen train young workers.

• **Worker training:** general training gives transferable skills; on-the-job training often gives skills suited to a particular work site

An important issue in the twenty-first century for American workers is whether or not they will have the skills to meet job requirements and make their firms competitive in the world economy. Even manufacturing jobs increasingly require that workers know statistical analysis in order to implement quality assurance methods.

Creative people use their education and experience to do more than just work. Inventors see a problem and solve it by developing better tools and techniques. Inventors generally build on the work of others. Some new ideas, however, bear no fruit for many years. As explained in Expansion Point 1.5, human ingenuity turned fire and water into a steam engine in the first century A.D. Practical use of steam, however, came 16 centuries later and steam lasted as a prominent source of power for about 200 years.

• **Innovation:** incorporating inventions and new ideas into a production process

Innovation, the process of applying new machines or ideas to actual production, still takes time. The digital computer was invented in the 1940s and was essential in big business by the 1960s and 1970s. By the 1980s, most businesses and many families had a microcomputer. As computers become more powerful, businesses find new ways to use them. Economists attributed a surge in labor productivity in the United States in the 1990s to the computer revolution. For example, after Wal-Mart computerized and reengineered its ordering of disposable diapers, it was selling them before it had paid for them (Hammer and James 1993, 60-62).

Incorporating an invention into production may require that inventors develop other technologies first. Richard Trevithick, for instance, built the first steam locomotive in 1804, but the heavy machine broke the brittle iron rails at the Penydarren tramway in South Wales. Steam trains first required improvements in the refining of iron for track. Solar cells to convert sunlight to electricity were available commercially in the 1960s, but their widespread use in automobiles requires development of lightweight, high-capacity storage batteries.

Historians mark industrial and commercial revolutions by their dominant inventions. Developing steam power for commercial use marked the Industrial Revolution of the 1800s. Similarly, the digital computer marked an information-services revolution of the late 1900s. Some economic revolutions, however, are more violent than others, seeking to sweep away the existing economic system with its alleged artificial limits on production and its unfair system of distribution. They may be based more on utopian dreams than on practical ideas for economic innovation.

Utopian Dreams and Revolutions

• **Socialism:** an economic system with publicly owned productive equipment

Utopian dreamers, complaining about the system of private property with its unequal distributions of income and wealth, have from time to time proposed schemes to reduce the effects of scarcity. In the eighteenth and nineteenth centuries, they proposed that **socialism**, an alternate system for organizing society with publicly owned industrial equipment, would make the human condition better. For instance, Welsh philanthropist and industrialist Robert Owen tried his socialist communes in England and America. Owen was a peaceful reformer and eventually earned the respect of other English reformers because he risked his own wealth to fund his ideas. His communes, however, had mixed success.

Marxist Economics

• **Capitalism:** an economic system with privately owned productive equipment, a profit motive, and wage labor

Karl Marx and Friedrich Engels, in their *Communist Manifesto* (1848), advocated the violent overthrow of what Marx called **capitalism**. In the economic system of capitalism, private owners of machinery hired wage labor to produce goods and kept the profit for themselves. Marx's dream was that, if control of productive equipment could be taken from the capitalist class (the bosses) and given to councils (or *soviets*) of workers, scarcity of goods would disappear. Since bosses were restricting output in order to make an economic profit, eliminating bosses would

Expansion Point 1.5: Applying Steam Power (Slowly, Part by Part)

In the first century A.D., Hero of Alexandria developed a steam engine, one version of which was called an "aeolipile." Hero's invention was not practically applied for over 1,600 years, until Thomas Savery used steam power to raise water out of mines. In 1698, Savery received a patent on a pump with hand-operated steam valves that raised water when cooling steam contracted and created a vacuum. Fourteen years later, in 1712, Thomas Newcomen introduced a piston to the steam engine, with the steam driving the piston up and down while the piston moving in a cylinder created a vacuum to pump water.

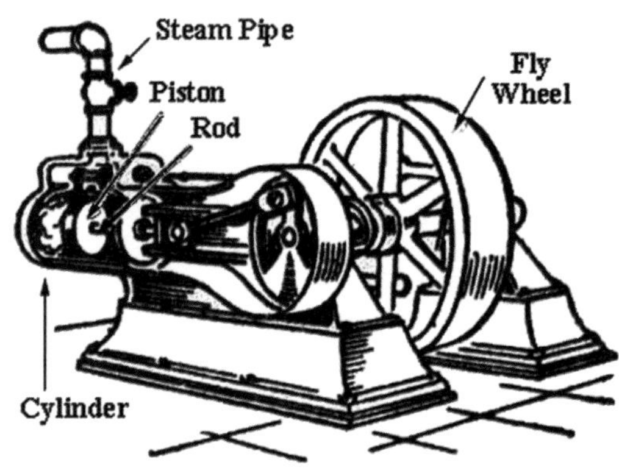

Steam Engine

Newcomen's design was inefficient because the piston had to be heated and cooled on each stroke. In 1865, just over a century and a half later, James Watt dramatically increased the steam engine's efficiency by cooling the steam outside the piston chamber in a separate "condenser." Watt also invented another engine part, a wheel turned by the reciprocating piston to convert back-and-forth motion into rotary motion. Now steam engines not only could pump water, but could also turn a shaft and run the industrial machines that would soon be invented. Steam transformed the English textiles industry by supplying power for carding, spinning, weaving, and printing.

In 1769, for example, Frenchman Nicholas-Joseph Cugnot applied steam power to a road carriage. By the first decade of the 1800s, water and rail transport also used steam. William Symington built a steam-powered tugboat in Scotland in 1802 and Robert Fulton built a steam-powered passenger ship in America in 1807. In South Wales in 1804, Richard Trevithick put a steam-driven locomotive on tracks used for horse-drawn carriages.

About 1,700 years passed between the invention of a steam engine in Alexandria and its widespread application in the Industrial Revolution, first in England, and then in America, Japan, and elsewhere. About 100 more years passed before the internal-combustion engine replaced the steam engine.

Source: "Steam Engine," *Encyclopedia Britannica*. CD-ROM, 1999.

supposedly eliminate artificial scarcity. When the Marxist dream was realized in its Soviet form, workers did not respond as predicted. Even under a system of social ownership, they still required material incentives to increase productivity.

While Marx didn't spend much time explaining how socialism would work, he imagined that a socialist state with public ownership of equipment would arise and then fade. As it withered, state socialism would be replaced by communism, where each contributed according to his ability and took according to his need.

•**Perfectibility of man:** changing the economic system, providing education, or simply the passing of time will improve people's moral behavior

Utopian Philosophy and Its Critics

Utopians and socialists of the 1700s and 1800s believed in the **perfectibility of man**. Socialists thought that people would no

longer steal and cheat each other if the private property system were eliminated. By changing the economic conditions under which workers strive, their behavior would improve.

Utopian reformers thought that people would gradually get better, eventually making many older institutions such as families, the laws of property, police, and the courts unnecessary. As a result, Robert Owen believed that, under the existing system, humans were not responsible and could not be held accountable for their actions. Human behavior, especially bad behavior such as stealing, was due to circumstances beyond their control, especially the private-property system. Yet Owen's own experiment in America failed after his partner defrauded him.

Traditional Christian believers consider themselves to be more realistic about human nature, believing that sin afflicts the natural human condition. It holds no hope of perfectibility in this age. Moreover, people are individually and collectively responsible for sin.

Mainstream economists, of course, do not talk in terms of sin, but they consider themselves similarly realistic. Economists contend, without moral judgment, that people are self-interested in their choices and are responsible for them. Even people who commit crimes do so rationally, weighing potential costs and benefits. An economist would therefore predict that, with no laws against theft and no police to protect property, stealing would increase, not decrease.

Mainstream economists simply disagree with utopian schemes to overthrow economic systems that mix private property and moderate government reform and regulation. Anyone, for that matter, who understands the universality of scarcity will be skeptical of idealistic economic schemes that promise an easy end to want and economic deprivation. Scarcity poses a very real and significant barrier to utopian dreams because political and economic revolution cannot remove limits to our resources. Socialist revolutions that have been won in the streets and halls of political power have afterward been defeated soundly in socialized factories and on collectivized farms.

Neither traditional Christians nor mainstream economists, then, wait for a new economic system to make all humans selfless. Yet, as Expansion Point 1.6 explains, Charles Dickens expressed hope in his nineteenth-century piece *A Christmas Carol* that, while some capitalist bosses were greedy, significant change in character is possible without social revolution.

Expansion Point 1.6: "Gain" and Economizing in Dickens' *A Christmas Carol*

Ebenezer Scrooge was an old economizer. The main character of Charles Dickens' tale *A Christmas Carol,* Scrooge dedicated himself to business. Yet, rather than praise him as a wise steward of time and money, Dickens called him a "tight-fisted hand at the grindstone, Scrooge! a squeezing, wrenching, grasping, scraping, clutching, covetous old sinner!" Despite his wealth, Scrooge contributed to no charity except through mandatory taxes that supported public poor relief.

A few commentators say Scrooge was a product of his capitalist environment, "Mr. Laissez-Faire, . . . an allegorical example of all that Dickens hated in the free competition system" (Goldberg, 1972, 33). But did "exploitative" nineteenth-century English industrial capitalism really make Scrooge a greedy boss? Would eliminating private property change the motives and reform the sinner? The text itself implies different conclusions.

Wealthier than most, Scrooge nevertheless felt the pain of scarcity, living a life more miserable than the working poor around him. He was cranky and unloved, while his underpaid, overworked employee Bob Cratchit was joyful and beloved. Scrooge's counting-house fire burned low to conserve coal, and he saw to it that the fire near Cratchit's desk burned even lower. Scrooge's house was poorly lit and poorly heated too: "He was obliged to sit close to [the fire], and brood over it, before he could extract the least sensation of warmth from such a handful of fuel" (chap. 1). Near the needy Cratchit family's "four-roomed house," however, "the brightness of the roaring fires in kitchens, parlours, and all sorts of rooms, was wonderful" (chap. 3).

Scrooge's home and office also contrasted sharply with the warehouse of his former master. On an earlier Christmas Eve, when Ebenezer served as apprentice to old Fezziwig, the warehouse was filled with joy and festivities. Fezziwig provided a wonderful party for his family and workers. "There was negus, and . . . a great piece of Cold Roast, and . . . of Cold Boiled, and there were mince-pies." Sharpening the contrast, Dickens adds that "fuel was heaped on the fire; and the warehouse was as snug, and warm, and dry, and bright a ball-room, as you would desire to see on a winter's night." While Fezziwig had spent only "a few pounds of . . . mortal money," the "happiness he [gave was] quite as great as if it cost a fortune" (chap. 2).

Scrooge, though, had no parties. He had no time to visit his nephew's home for Christmas (chap. 1). He also had no wife, having once chosen money over love. In a vision, Scrooge's fiancée of earlier years, Belle, described their engagement and how he had changed:

> His face had not the harsh and rigid lines of later years; but it had begun to wear the signs of care and avarice.
>
> "It matters little," she said softly. "To you, very little. Another idol has displaced me . . . A golden one. . . . I have seen your nobler aspirations fall off one by one, until the master-passion, Gain, engrosses you. . . . But if you were free to-day [from your earlier marriage commitment] . . ., can even I believe that you would choose a dowerless girl—you, who in your very confidence with her, weigh everything by Gain; or, choosing her, if for a moment you were false enough to your one guiding principle to do so, do I not know that your repentance and regret would surely follow? I do; and I release you. With a full heart, for the love of him you once were. . . . May you be happy in the life you have chosen."
>
> She left him, and they parted (chap. 2).

In his dream, Scrooge began to see more to life than work and wealth, and began to fear for his soul. In the end, Scrooge was not changed by a renunciation of his profession, his wealth, or the economic system in which he lived, but by a revelation. He repented and became liberal in his giving in the very same economic and social setting in which he had once been miserly (chap. 5). His heart and behavior changed, not society nor its material conditions.

Sources: Charles Dickens, *A Christmas Carol*. An Online Library of Literature. Accessed July 29, 1999 at http://www.literature.org/authors/dickens-charles/christmas-carol/html.

Michael Goldberg, "A Philosophy of Christmas," *Carlyle and Dickens* (University of Georgia Press, 1972), 32-33.

Chapter Summary

1. Scarcity is pervasive and enduring. It results from limited resources and unlimited wants and needs.

2. A good is scarce if people want more of it than is available free. An indicator of the scarcity of a good, service, or resource is its market price.

3. Scarcity requires people to make choices among various uses of limited resources. Economic choices among goods involve what economists call tradeoffs.

4. The Production Possibilities model illustrates that scarce resources imply limits to production of goods and that scarcity forces society to trade one good for another. When scarce resources are fully employed, the cost of choosing more of one good equals the amount of another good given up.

5. People battle scarcity by exchanging and rationing available resources, goods, and services, and by increasing their supplies of goods and services with more labor, education, tools, and technology. Certain people also steal and make war to gain command over more resources. Others adopt utopian and revolutionary philosophies in the hopes of increasing the supplies of needed and wanted goods.

6. The method a society uses for rationing goods affects economic efficiency. Rationing systems alter the ability of a given supply of goods to satisfy wants and the incentives to supply more goods in the future. Exchange is efficient but outcomes are not equal.

7. Although people are always engaged in the struggle, no economic system or new technology has completely conquered scarcity.

Problems for Practice

1.1* How would you react to the following argument about the irrelevance of economic analysis of scarcity in our present world?

> The technological revolution has made economic analysis of scarcity meaningless. Computers and the free flow of information on the Internet have created the potential for a new world where goods and services can be supplied in sufficient numbers to eliminate unmet wants. While economic analysis, with its emphasis on rationing goods, may have been relevant to the old age of agrarian and industrial economics, it is no longer useful.
>
> In fact, it is the economists, the bankers, and the capitalist bosses who stand in the way of progress. They don't eliminate scarcity; they create it to increase business and financial profits. The new era will allow for enough goods and services for all humans when we take control of the economy and put technology to its best uses.
>
> Therefore, we should "abolish economics and make way for the economy of abundance." Abundance will then flow from the new technology available to us. But first we will have to call a conference of experts and "users of the electromagnetic radio frequency spectrum" because now there are few if any available new frequencies and slots for satellites in outer space.

Explain your reactions and give examples to support your views. (Source: Kevin Kelley's interview with "futurist" Hazel Henderson, in *Wired*, February 1997.)

1.2* Rationing goods by voluntary exchange is efficient but causes a conflict with people's ideas of fairness. Why doesn't the U.S. government gather up all the milk produced in the nation each week and give it out equally to all people in the United States? Wouldn't this be fair? What other effects of such a policy could you expect now and in the future?

1.3* This chapter contends that human history is the story of the battle against scarcity. Use your knowledge of local, regional, national, and global history to challenge or support this assertion. Build your case with up to five different historical examples.

1.4* How is food rationed in the United States? Answer this question with the complexity that reality

See Answer Key for hints/answers to starred (*) questions.

demands. Consider how families, businesses, and governments ration food.

1.5 Have you ever bartered for anything? Explain for what and with whom. Do you think both parties gained from the exchange? Explain your answer.

Economics in Film and Literature:

1.6 Read the O. Henry story entitled "The Gift of the Magi." Discuss the role of scarcity and the choices the main characters made.

1.7 Sudden changes in the conditions of life can drastically alter relative scarcities. View the film *The Flight of the Phoenix* and discuss how the relative scarcity of resources changed dramatically after the plane crashed. Discuss the new conditions the survivors faced and how they coped. How did goals change? Was time scarce anymore? Was money important? Which goods were scarce? How did they ration scarce goods?

For your portfolio:

1.8* Find an article which discusses some aspect of scarcity as economists define it. The author need not use the word "scarcity," but you should identify where the writer is confronting one or more of the symptoms of scarcity: people making choices, paying prices, or rationing available supplies. Note whether the article is specifically about a shortage of a good. Photocopy the article and highlight key sentences and paragraphs. Write several marginal comments.

For class discussion:

1.9 Be prepared to discuss your views and examples in answer to 1.1.

1.10* Do you agree or disagree with the following statement? Explain and support your view from your own learning and experiences.

"All of human history is the history of scarcity and people's attempts to overcome it. All interesting questions of human current events are economic at root."

Does the text support or refute this statement? Cite the evidence for your conclusion from the text.

1.11 With which of the following statements do you agree more fully? Explain.

"Governments impose restraints on themselves regarding due process and just compensation and prosecute cases of private theft because:

a. Confiscation and theft of property do not create wealth, they merely redistribute it . . . or
b. Confiscation and theft are simply wrong, violating the eighth commandment and widely accepted standards about property."

1.12* Evaluate the truth or falsity of the following: "The rate at which people work and their productivity is fixed within certain limits. People can work longer hours each day but they otherwise can't enhance their individual ability to push back the limits of scarcity."

1.13 What is the difference between invention and innovation? What is their significance to the battle against scarcity? Under what economic conditions would you expect them to flourish?

1.14 How do Marxists and other socialists differ from capitalists in their view of the causes of and cures for scarcity?

1.15 How does the socialist view of the perfectibility of man differ from the traditional Christian view of human behavior and the mainstream economic view of human behavior? Why is this issue important?

1.16 Do you believe market exchange is socially beneficial, as this chapter explains?

1.17 Do you agree with the following statements? Support your view. Does the textbook agree or not? Cite evidence from the text. Explain.

a. "Rationing is wrong! People should be free to consume what they want without artificial limits."
b. "The precise method of rationing is not really so important to human economizing, because they each have the same effects on social welfare."
c. "It is not usually possible for methods of rationing to be working simultaneously in the supply of any particular product."

1.18* Assume that your teacher gives a group of students a bag of cookies. [Perhaps you can convince the teacher to actually try this!] How would the cookies be divided? How should the cookies be divided? In how many different ways could the cookies be divided? Which method is most efficient? Most fair?

Chapter 2 SCARCITY AND ECONOMICS

Analysis of Price, Efficiency, and Cost

What this chapter will help you think about:

1. What is economic analysis?
2. How is price related to scarcity and economic analysis?
3. Why is the demand and supply model important in economics?
4. What are the forces that bring a market price to equilibrium?
5. What are the different measures of economic efficiency?
6. Why are only opportunity costs relevant to good decisions?

How do economists contribute to the historical human struggle against the limits imposed by scarcity? Since the time of Scotsman Adam Smith's writing of *An Inquiry into the Nature and Causes of the Wealth of Nations* (1776), economists have systematically analyzed how best to push back these limits. This chapter more carefully defines economic analysis and then introduces three key economic ideas: (1) market price as a measure of scarcity, (2) economic efficiency as a measure of success in the struggle against scarcity, and (3) opportunity cost as the appropriate measure of economic costs. In doing so, this chapter also introduces demand-and-supply analysis of market price and output, and distinguishes among various concepts of economic efficiency.

What Is Economic Analysis?

• **Economics:** the study of using resources efficiently to meet unlimited wants

Economics is the study of the efficient use of scarce resources to best meet unlimited wants and needs. Economists first must be able to measure the degree of scarcity of various resources and products. As mentioned in the first chapter, market price is a measure of scarcity. Second, economists must be able to give concrete methods to evaluate the efficient use of resources. Market prices also play important roles in gauging economic efficiency.

Economic analysis has employed two approaches: the scientific method and the legal-historical method. Economics as science attempts to test hypotheses to disconfirm or lend support to theories about economic cause and effect. Science depends on studies that are replicable. Not all economic activity is replicable.

Therefore, economics also has relied on the legal-historical method of gathering eyewitness accounts of one-time-only economic events. Both the scientific and legal-historical study of scarcity, though, require a theoretical framework. What follows is a brief introduction to the theoretical relationships of price, efficiency, and cost to scarcity.

Market Price and Scarcity

Economists have labored to explain how **the market price of a good is a measure of its scarcity**. A market price is established by voluntary, unrestricted exchanges, where many buyers and sellers can participate. Price is a measure of how much individuals value a good, service, or resource.

•Price is:
1) a measure of a good's scarcity;
2) a basis for comparing market values of various goods; and
3) a measure of *marginal value,* the value of the *last* unit of a good sold, but not the total value of a good.

Price, Value, and Scarcity

You have heard it said, "You can't compare apples and oranges." This is not exactly true because the market prices of apples and oranges provide an effective basis for comparing how much people like them. If apple prices per pound are higher than orange prices per pound, people have a relative preference for a pound of apples. So you can compare apples and oranges, but you can't be sure why their market values differ. A higher price for apples could be due to a current short supply of apples, not just a love for them. Nevertheless, price allows us to compare preferences for apples and oranges.

Scarcity of a good is generated by a difference between the quantity demanded and the quantity supplied. Since the price of a good in free exchange varies with changing conditions of demand and supply, price is a useful measure of scarcity. A high price for diamonds, for instance, indicates that diamonds are relatively scarce. A low price of water indicates that water is relatively less scarce.

Smith (1776) referred to this difference in the prices of water and diamonds as the diamond/water paradox. Water was more necessary to life than diamonds, but water had a much lower price. Price therefore did not seem closely related to usefulness of a good.

Another English economist, Alfred Marshall (1890), resolved the paradox by noting that diamonds were relatively scarce and water was plentiful. As a result, people's demand for diamonds was not as well satisfied as their demand for water, and the prices reflected the different levels of unmet desire. The next diamond that society could get was worth more because it brought more satisfaction than the next glass of water. Market price reflects the added or **marginal value** of the last unit of diamonds or water, not the total value of diamonds or water.

In short, market prices help economists to compare the relative scarcity of products offered for sale. Market prices are not, however, measures of either the total value of a good to society or the intrinsic or moral values of goods.

Demand and Supply Determine Market Price

• **Quantity demanded (Q_d):** the amount a buyer or group is willing and able to buy at a *specific* price

If scarcity is the fundamental economic problem, demand and supply is the fundamental tool of economic analysis. Demand and supply explains how various factors interact to determine prices in actual markets. Any market price for a product or resource is determined by the forces that affect either demand or supply.

• **Demand (D):** the various amounts a buyer or group is willing and able to buy at *various* prices

The Demand and Supply Model

This will be only a brief introduction to the economist's model of demand and supply. You will understand it best by repetition and by adding details in stages, so we will return to it regularly. More insights and applications appear throughout the text.

Demand. The demand for a product summarizes a buyer's willingness and ability to purchase various quantities of a product or resource at various prices. If your family is willing and able to buy 10 gallons of milk per month at a price of \$2.50 per gallon, 10 is your **individual quantity demanded**. Perhaps all families in the region would buy 80 million gallons of milk at a price of \$2.50. The sum of quantities demanded for all families in the region would be the **market quantity demanded (Q_d)**.

• **Law of demand:** as price increases, quantity demanded decreases

Demand summarizes various combinations of prices and quantities demanded. If price falls to \$2.00, perhaps your family would buy 11 gallons a month, and quantity demanded in the market might increase to 90 million gallons. If price rises to \$3.00, perhaps your family would buy only nine gallons a month, and quantity demanded in the market might decrease to 70 million gallons. **Market demand (D)** summarizes all such combinations of individual or market prices and quantities demanded.

• **Quantity supplied (Q_s):** the amount a seller or group is willing and able to sell at a *specific* price

Panel A of Exhibit 2.1 illustrates the market demand for milk. The demand relation assumes that as price rises, quantity demanded falls. This inverse relation between price and quantity demanded is the **law of demand**.

• **Supply (S):** the various amounts a seller or group is willing and able to sell at *various* prices

Supply. The supply of a product summarizes the willingness and ability of sellers to sell various quantities of a product or resource at various prices. If a farmer is willing and able to sell 3,200 gallons of milk per month at a price of \$2.50 per gallon, 3,200 is the farmer's **individual quantity supplied**. Perhaps all farmers in the region would sell 80 million gallons of milk at a price of \$2.50. We call the sum of quantities supplied for all farmers in the region at that particular price of \$2.50 the **market quantity supplied (Q_s)**.

• **Short-run law of supply:** as price increases, quantity supplied increases

Market supply (S) summarizes various combinations of prices and quantities supplied. If price falls to \$2.00, perhaps the farmer would only sell 2,800 gallons a month, and market quantity supplied might decrease to 65 million gallons. But if price rose to \$3.00, perhaps the farmer would be willing to sell 3,400 gallons and market quantity supplied might be 95 million gallons. Supply summarizes all such individual or market prices and quantities supplied. We are assuming that farmers can adjust short-run output by altering the mix of feed, hormones, and so on. In practice, quantity supplied may be less responsive than is shown here.

Panel B of Exhibit 2.1 shows the market supply of milk. As price rises, quantity supplied increases. This direct relation between price and quantity supplied has in the past been called the law of supply. Today, we can qualify that and call it the **short-run law of competitive supply.**

Market Equilibrium. Offsetting forces of demand and supply cause price to move toward equilibrium. Equilibrium price is where quantity demanded equals quantity supplied and where there is no tendency for price to change.

In Panel C of Exhibit 2.1, \$2.50 is the **equilibrium price (P^*)**. Market quantities of milk bought and sold at \$2.50 are both equal to 80 million gallons per month. We call this the **equilibrium quantity exchanged (Q^*)**.

Actual markets never come to complete rest. Factors affecting price are always changing, causing market prices to fluctuate.

Exhibit 2.1: Demand and Supply in the Market for Milk

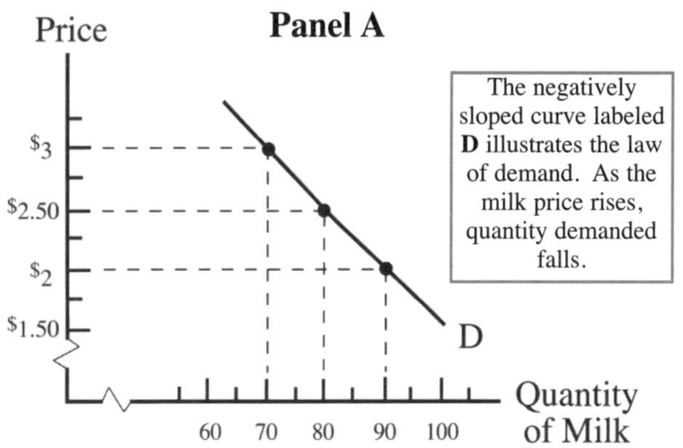

Price	\$2.00	\$2.50	\$3.00
Quantity Demanded	90	80	70
Quantity Supplied	65	80	95

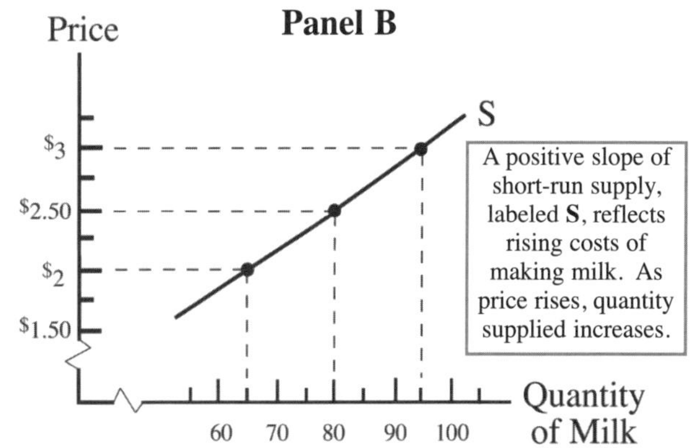

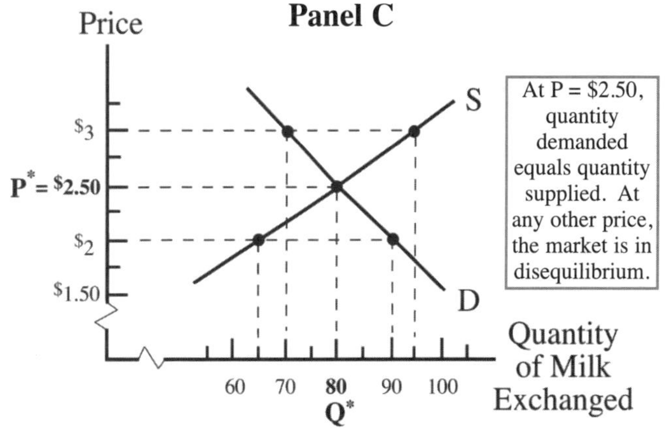

Exhibit 2.2: Demand and Supply Equilibrium and Disequilibrium

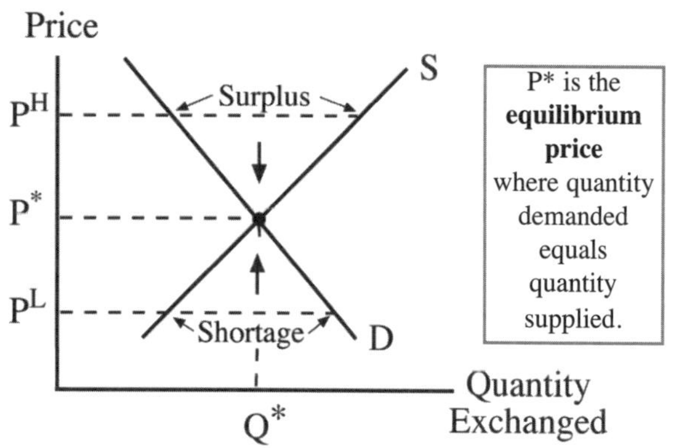

At any price other than P*, the market is in **disequilibrium**.

At a higher price, P^H, quantity supplied exceeds quantity demanded, causing a **surplus**.

At a lower price, P^L, quantity demanded exceeds quantity supplied, causing a **shortage**.

The two arrows pointing to equilibrium price illustrate that markets are **self-adjusting**. A shortage causes price to increase, and a surplus causes price to decrease, re-establishing equilibrium.

Nevertheless, economists find that the concepts of equilibrium price and output are most helpful in explaining the reasons that market prices do change.

Market Disequilibrium. At any other price than equilibrium, the market is in disequilibrium. The two disequilibrium conditions are a shortage or a surplus. Because of the fundamental principles of the law of demand and the short-run law of supply, the forces of disequilibrium tend to move the market toward equilibrium.

Exhibit 2.2 illustrates an equilibrium of demand and supply at a price P* and quantity Q* in the market for any resource or product. The graph has no numbers, but do remember that price increases when we move up and quantity increases when we move to the right.

If market price is higher than equilibrium price, say at P^H, a **surplus** will prevail. A surplus occurs when quantity supplied is greater than quantity demanded. A surplus causes the market price to fall toward equilibrium.

- **Surplus:** market price is higher than equilibrium, and quantity supplied exceeds quantity demanded
  ($Q_s > Q_d$)
- **Shortage:** market price is lower than equilibrium, and quantity demanded exceeds quantity supplied
  ($Q_d > Q_s$)

If a market price is lower than equilibrium price, say at P^L, a **shortage** will prevail. A shortage occurs when quantity demanded is greater than quantity supplied. A shortage causes the market price to rise toward equilibrium.

Economists contend that markets **adjust automatically** toward equilibrium. A market price below equilibrium price causes a shortage that raises price. A market price above equilibrium price causes a surplus that lowers price.

Will equilibrium price be a socially desirable price? The short answer is that, under ideal conditions of competition and full information about economic costs and opportunities, market prices do tend to be socially desirable. In the long run, the market equilibrium price of a product will tend to just cover economic costs of making it. But critics say that actual markets are rarely ideal, beset as they are by monopoly power and other problems.

Two other important questions about markets are: how long does it take for full long-run adjustments in the market price, and how close to the economic ideal are actual markets? Supporters of markets contend that adjustment is relatively rapid and that markets operate close to the ideal. Critics disagree. People who believe in the general efficiency of markets tend to rely on free markets to ration goods. But when the critics prevail, governments impose selective or general price controls.

- **Self-adjusting markets:** a surplus causes P to fall and a shortage causes P to rise. Disequilibrium forces, therefore, move market price back toward equilibrium
- **Price floor:** a legal minimum price
- **Price ceiling:** a legal maximum price

Government-Controlled Prices

Government can intervene in markets and establish legally controlled prices. In the United States, for example, federal, state, and local governments have established and regularly adjusted minimum wages for low-income workers. They have also at times established minimum prices for farm products. City governments have instituted maximum prices for apartments to keep urban voters happy. The U.S. government has at times held down prices of gasoline and natural gas.

A minimum legal price, established above equilibrium, is a **price floor**. Panel A of Exhibit 2.3 shows the effect of making P^f the legal minimum price. A price floor causes a surplus because quantity supplied is greater than quantity demanded. Critics of a legal minimum wage, for example, complain that while it helps those who remain employed, it also reduces the demand for low-wage workers, causing layoffs.

A maximum legal price, established below equilibrium, is a **price ceiling**. Panel B of Exhibit 2.3 shows the effect of making P^c the legal maximum price. A price ceiling causes a shortage because quantity demanded is greater than quantity supplied. This is why Americans waited in line for gasoline in 1979, when the government maintained below-market price ceilings.

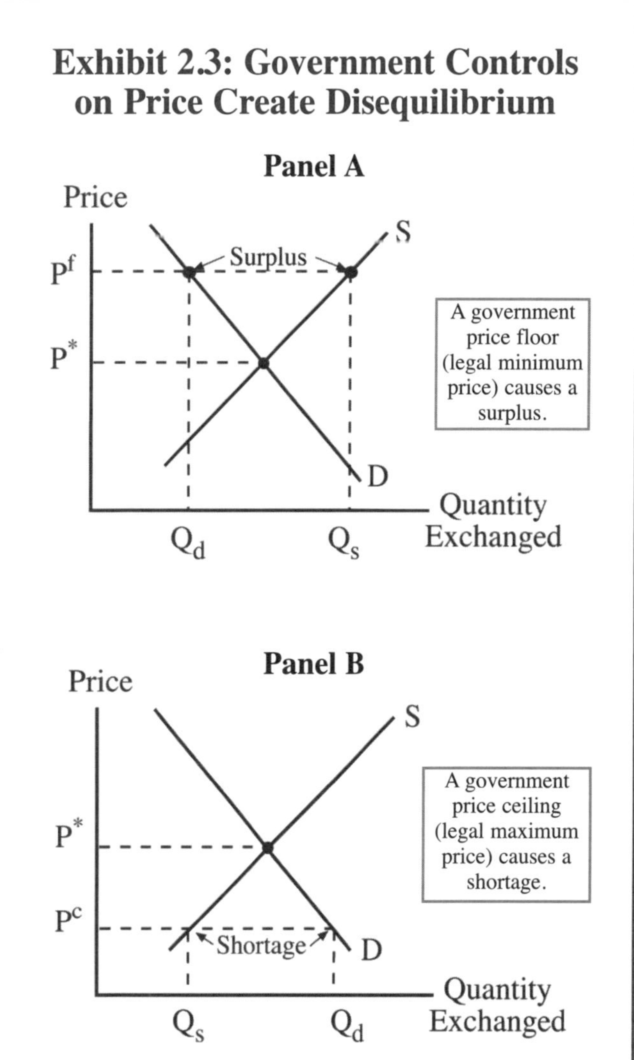

Government price controls do not repeal the forces of demand and supply. While controls prevent market prices from prevailing, market *forces* remain in play, causing surpluses or shortages.

Consider what happened in the market for milk. Until the late 1990s, the U.S. government instituted a price

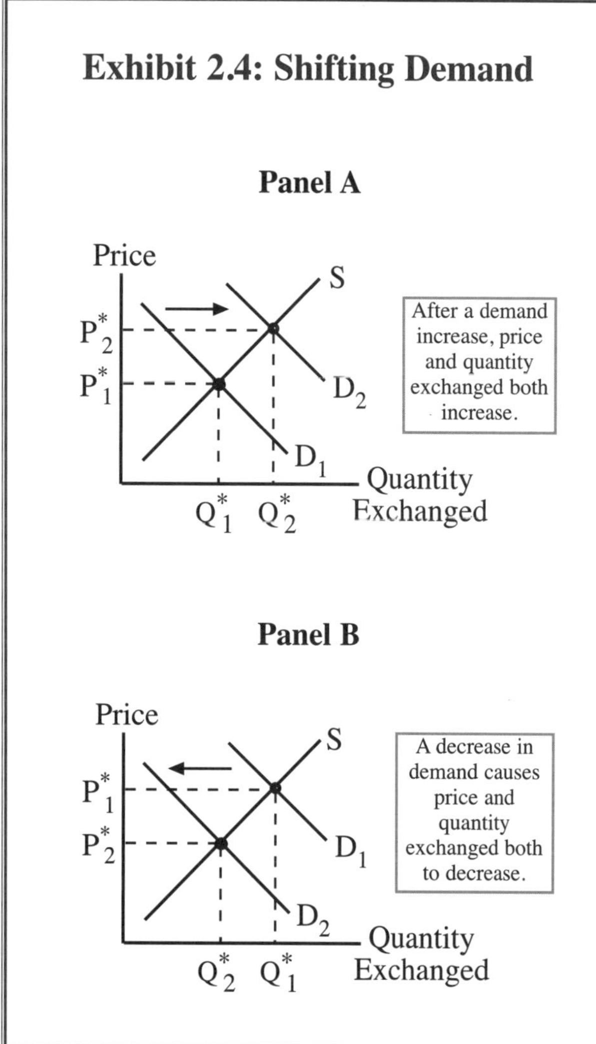

floor on the price of raw milk. As expected, this encouraged dairy farmers to increase the quantity supplied of milk. Higher prices for raw milk, however, also increased the retail price of a gallon of milk, decreasing sales.

Shifts in Demand or Supply

Demand and supply for resources and products are always shifting because of changing economic factors. Such shifts then alter market prices and the quantities exchanged. To analyze shifts in demand, we will focus on the effects of seasonal swings in demand for vacations, and cyclical fluctuations in income and the demand for electronic equipment such as computers. To analyze shifts in supply, we will consider the effects of seasonal fluctuations in the supply of agricultural commodities, and anti-competitive effects of a merger on the supply of airline tickets.

An **increase in demand**, on the one hand, will generally cause an increase in market price and quantity exchanged. Every summer in Atlantic-coastal states of the United States, for example, rental prices for apartments and houses at various ocean beaches rise. The reason is that demand for vacation rentals is higher during the summer than in the winter. Rental prices rise to a peak in July and August, the height of vacation season, and then fall through September and October. Panel A of Exhibit 2.4 illustrates such an increase in demand and the resulting increase in price and quantity exchanged.

A **decrease in demand**, on the other hand, will generally cause a *decrease* in market price and quantity exchanged. If household and business buyers of computers, for example, experience falling incomes in an uncertain economy, they will decrease their demand for computers. As a result, computer retailers and manufacturers will suffer losses and will cut prices to eliminate excess inventories. Panel B of Exhibit 2.4 illustrates such a decrease in demand and the resulting decline in price and quantity exchanged.

An **increase in supply**, on the one hand, will generally cause a decrease in market price but an increase in quantity exchanged. In North America, the price of tomatoes falls in summer because they are growing locally at that time, and are in greater supply when they mature. Apple prices traditionally reach their lowest levels a bit later in the fall because they are maturing then. Panel A of Exhibit 2.5 illustrates an increase in supply and the resulting decline in price and increase in quantity exchanged.

A **decrease in supply**, on the other hand, will generally cause an *increase* in market price but a *decrease* in quantity exchanged. Lawyers in the Antitrust Division of the U.S. Justice Department complained of the possible anti-competitive effects of a merger between two major airline corporations in 2001. Any merger of airlines that serve many of the same cities would reduce the supply of airline services in those cities. Such a decrease in the supply of tickets would increase prices and violate antitrust laws. The new airline would earn higher profits at the expense of customers who paid the higher prices or were prevented from flying. Panel B of Exhibit 2.5 illustrates this decrease in supply and the resulting increase in price and decrease in quantity exchanged.

Exhibit 2.5: Shifting Supply

Panel A

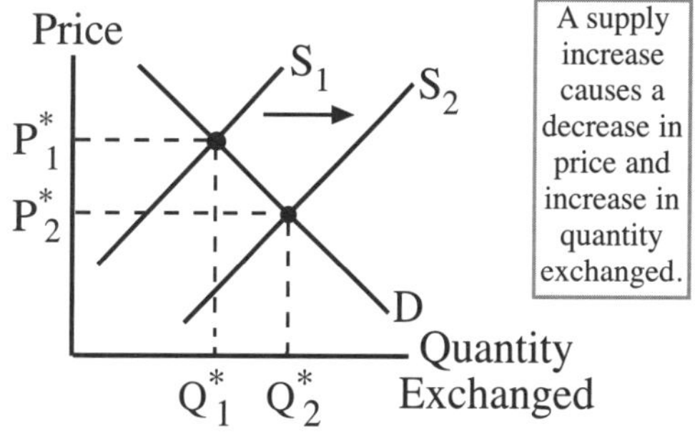

Panel B

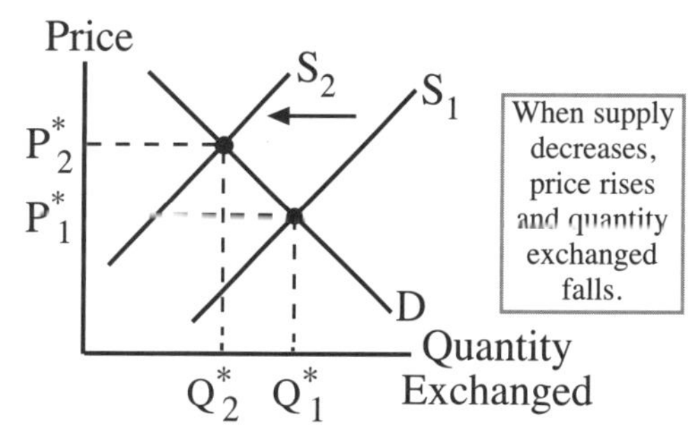

Market Process and Market Failure

A benefit of learning demand and supply analysis is that we learn to think about markets not as a time and place where buyers and sellers meet, but as a process by which buyers and sellers exchange. Through the market process, people ration available supplies, signal wants and desires, and gain important information on relative scarcities of products and resources. Price information directs private individual decisions about buying and working, businesses in their productive activity, and government policy makers in their regulatory oversight.

As with any process, the market process does not work perfectly. Markets, for instance, tend toward failure when information is poor and when risks of loss are high, or when economic power is unequally distributed between buyers and sellers. With limited information on possible risks and returns of market activity, for example, businesses often choose to produce what they might have bought in the market. When consumers are unsure of the quality of a product such as a used car, they may choose not to buy very many used cars in the market. And when just one or a few producers dominate the supply of a product, markets fail to deliver their full theoretical efficiency and social benefits. Markets also do not treat all people equally, favoring those who have the most wealth or the most ability to produce it.

- **An Increase in Demand** causes a higher market price.
- **A Decrease in Demand** causes a lower market price.
- **An Increase in Supply** causes a lower market price.
- **A Decrease in Supply** causes a higher market price.

- **Market Price and Efficiency:** economic concepts of efficiency rely on the market prices of resources and products

- **Productive Efficiency:** the combination of resources that minimizes average cost of production

- **Average Cost:** total cost divided by total goods produced

Scarcity and Efficiency

Since economics is about an efficient battle against scarcity, a careful definition of **efficiency** is in order. Then we can compare the efficiency of different ways of producing goods and services, using resources, and organizing an economy. Take note that, as measures of the values of resources, goods, and services, **market prices** provide important information about certain measures of economic efficiency. Let's consider seven concepts of efficiency.

Productive Efficiency

Productive efficiency refers to using the best combinations of equipment, labor, and other resources in production. As shown in Exhibit 2.6, productive efficiency means minimizing the cost of producing each unit of a good or service. **Average cost of production** is the measure of productive efficiency. Production costs reflect the market prices of resources that the firm uses in production. As the following equation shows, average cost is total cost of production divided by total goods produced.

Average Cost = Total Cost / Total Goods Produced

Exhibit 2.6: Productive Efficiency as Minimum Average Cost

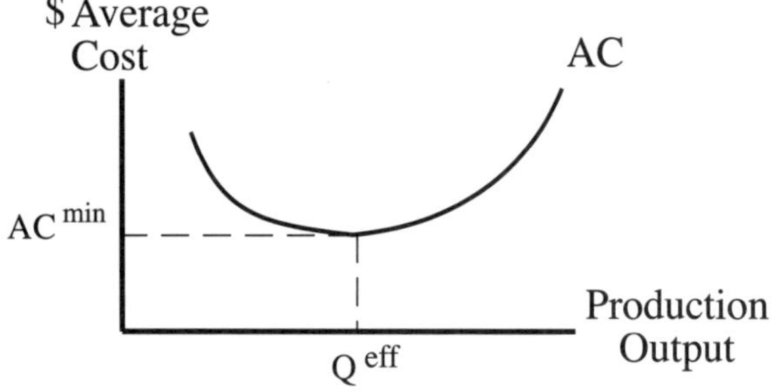

This graph shows an important aspect of many productive activities. With a given size of plant and equipment, average costs of production will first fall and then rise as quantity produced increases. The minimum of average cost, $\mathbf{AC^{min}}$, indicates the most efficient level of production, $\mathbf{Q^{eff}}$. Costs of production reflect relative scarcities of the inputs used to make the product.

You can compare the efficiency of different methods of production and different forms of organization by calculating their average costs. If two methods of producing steel each create 1,000 tons of steel and the total cost of the first is $40,000 while the total cost of the second is $50,000, which is more efficient? The first method is more efficient because its cost per ton of steel, $40 = $40,000/1,000, is $10 per ton less than $50, the average cost of the second.

Productive efficiency varies with the costs of labor and machines. Since labor and machine costs vary widely between India and the United States, for instance, what is productively efficient in India will not necessarily be efficient in the United States. In India, where labor wages are relatively less expensive than machinery, labor-intensive methods of production

Expansion Point 2.1: Average Costs of Stamping Parts on Different Presses

Economic analysis does not have to be complex. Sometimes simple calculations lead to valuable gains in productive efficiency. A senior economics student of mine wanted to do an internship at a machine shop nearby. This machine shop produced parts for its customers in large lots on machine presses of various sizes. One press might be rated at five tons while another was rated at 10 tons. While these machines were interchangeable, a bigger press might be more expensive to use on parts that did not require the larger capacity.

By measuring the efficiency of each machine when making several parts, the student provided valuable advice to the firm about scheduling which machines to use for which parts. His method was simple: calculate and compare the average costs of parts when produced on each of the different machines. He used information about numbers of parts produced in each run along with the labor time, machine time, and labor and machine costs to calculate average cost.

For example, on a run of 3,500 parts on a 10-ton press, the average cost might have been $0.32. On a run of 2,400 parts on a 5-ton press, average cost for the same part might have been $0.19. With such information, the firm can make important decisions about scheduling which machine to use in the future, and about the proper mix of machines it wants when it considers future purchases of machine presses. Lower costs per part that result from this analysis can improve the machine shop's profits, lower its prices when it bids for future jobs, and contribute to overall efficiency in the economy.

will tend to be more efficient than machine-intensive methods. Therefore, in India, low-paid workers dig ditches with picks and shovels. In the United States, where wages are high and machinery costs low, one skilled worker with a backhoe on a tractor digs the ditch, but at a lower cost than having a crew of laborers do the work.

Productive efficiency varies with energy costs too. When oil prices rose in 1974, energy-intensive production methods were less efficient. Heating homes in winter, for example, was accomplished by putting more insulation in ceilings and walls and by burning less fuel.

Productive efficiency is a relatively simple concept. Choose the process that minimizes average cost of production. Such a simple principle can be helpful in managing a factory, as is illustrated in Expansion Point 2.1, where an economics student did the calculations for a business.

Allocative Efficiency

Allocative efficiency refers to distributing society's resources among their best possible uses so that the value of output is maximized. For example, allocative efficiency provides information about whether we have too many automobiles and not enough rapid

- **Allocative Efficiency:** distributing resources to their most valuable uses transit systems in the nation, too much wheat and not enough barley or oats, or too much electricity and not enough pollution-control equipment. If land, labor, equipment, raw materials, and other resources are being put to their highest valued uses, the answer to these questions would be no.

Efficiency in Exchange

• **Efficiency in Exchange:** distributing output to its most valuable final uses

• **Pareto Efficiency:** no one can be made better off without making someone else worse off; the existing distribution is as good as it gets

Efficiency in exchange, a special case of allocative efficiency, refers to the effectiveness of the distribution of output among individuals and families. Do barriers to exchange prevent output from reaching its most valuable final uses? Cultural or government restrictions, for example, can reduce efficiency by restricting trade. Costs of shipping goods to market also can restrict trade. If people are able to exchange goods freely and if exchange costs are low, then voluntary exchange should be efficient. **Pareto efficiency** is another term for efficiency in exchange. A Pareto-efficient distribution of available goods and services is one where no trade could be made that would make at least one person better off without making another person worse off. That implies that the existing distribution is as good as it gets.

• **The Indicator of Allocative Efficiency in Exchange:** prices of resources or products are equal in all uses

An **indication** that exchange is allocatively efficient is that prices for the same good are the same in different locations. If wheat is selling for $2.50 a bushel in the eastern United States, but for $8.50 a bushel in the West, this would not be efficient. The reason is that, because wheat is much more valuable in the West, people in the East are wasting valuable wheat. Efficiency would improve if traders moved wheat from east to west. A commodities dealer could offer to buy wheat in Ohio at, say, $3.50 a bushel and ship it to California to sell at $7.50 a bushel. Assume that the cost to ship a bushel was only $1. Eastern farmers get more money for their wheat, western consumers pay less and eat more, and initially the dealer earns a profit of $3 per bushel.

Eventually moving grain from east to west would equalize prices on both coasts, with a difference remaining for shipping costs. Exchange is most profitable, then, when the existing distribution of goods is least efficient. Exchange also tends to increase efficiency in the uses of goods by equalizing prices and eliminating inefficient use of a good where it is less valuable.

Institutional Efficiency

• **Institutional Efficiency:** the effects of a nation's or organization's choice of commercial rules and customary practices and agreements on the costs of transactions

Institutional efficiency, a concept related but not identical to efficiency in exchange, results when a society's or organization's choice of rules minimizes the costs of commercial transactions. This concept is more familiar to students of what is called institutional economics. The idea is especially important in explaining the factors that promote a nation's economic development.

The formal and informal rules of the game and how individuals and organizations structure their interactions are important to both the efficient operation of a nation and its business and government agencies. High standards of living require extreme specialization of workers and highly complex patterns of commercial trade. Such trade involves many millions of transactions among pairs of buyers and sellers. Each transaction imposes a cost on the traders. The higher the costs of such transactions, the less commerce traders will undertake and the lower will be the nation's average standard of living. Institutions matter because certain rules and practices are more likely to lower transactions costs and encourage trade.

Dynamic Efficiency

Technological changes in production allow society to use existing resources more efficiently. In its use of both electricity and space, the transistor radio was more efficient than older vacuum-tube radios. Capturing solar energy holds the promise of one day being more efficient than burning coal or oil.

- **Dynamic Efficiency:** speed of adapting to new technology and other economic changes

Dynamic efficiency assesses how effectively an economic organization or system promotes technological change and adapts to new technology introduced by others. Researchers say that a less authoritative, more encouraging form of business governance tends to encourage innovation. Economic systems that rely more on free enterprise and less on coercive central planning also tend to promote dynamic efficiency.

Macroeconomic Efficiency

Macroeconomic efficiency concerns how fully a regional or national economy employs its labor, machinery, and resources. Market economies experience fluctuations in economic output and employment. We can measure macroeconomic efficiency by the rate of unemployment or by the difference between actual output of goods and services and estimated full-employment output. The rate of unemployment is the number of workers unemployed in a given week divided by the total number in the labor force.

- **Macroeconomic Efficiency:** how fully a nation employs its resources

Productivity of Labor

A final measure of efficiency, the **productivity of labor**, is helpful in evaluating a particular firm or an entire economy. Productivity of labor can be calculated in real or money values. To measure real productivity, simply divide the total real output of a firm by the number of workers who produced it. Money values are needed when averaging productivity of many different goods that cannot be easily compared in real terms. Simply divide the dollar value of total output in the nation for one year by the total number of workers employed that year.

- **Productivity of Labor:** total output divided by number of workers employed; or the dollar value of output divided by the number of workers

Expansion Point 2.2: Comparing National Productivity

The U.S. economy was strengthened in World War II (1941-45), while the German and Japanese economies were devastated by bombings. During the next three and a half decades, however, West German and Japanese economies made incredible advances. The chart below uses calculations of the productivity of labor in each country in 1980 to illustrate their resilience. Productivity of labor is calculated as the value of its output divided by the labor force. By 1980, these nations had average productivities of labor that rivaled the United States. In some manufacturing sectors, especially automobiles, German and Japanese worker productivity exceeded that of American workers.

The 1970 values of labor productivity, shown in the far right-hand column, illustrate how the productivity gap was wider a decade earlier. The comparison of productivities shows that, from 1970 to 1980, U.S. productivity per worker grew by only 5.2%. With compounding, that is less than a half percent a year. West German productivity grew 22.8% and Japanese productivity grew 34.4% over the decade! Since wage increases are generally tied to productivity growth, the slowdown in U.S. productivity growth in the 1970s was a major concern to economists and policy makers in the early 1980s.

By the 1990s, U.S. productivity was growing more rapidly again. For more practice on using labor productivity to compare economic performance, see Problem 2.7 at the end of the chapter. The results there for Japan and the United States are much different.

Mathematical Note:

Percentage change in productivity over the decade can be calculated as [(New Value - Old Value) / (New/2 + Old/2)]*100. This is just the change in labor productivity divided by the average productivity times 100. For West Germany, the number is: [($41,269 - $32,813) / $37,041] * 100 = 22.8%.

		1980 Data		(1970)
Nation	**Number of Laborers**	**Value of Output***	**Productivity of Labor**	**Productivity of Labor**
West Germany	27,260,000	$1,125,000,000,000	$41,269	$32,813
Japan	55,740,000	$1,797,000,000,000	$32,239	$22,787
United States	106,940,000	$5,063,000,000,000	$47,344	$44,944

* Real gross domestic product in 1996 U.S. dollars for comparison.

Source: "Selected OECD Countries: Economic Profile," Organization for Economic Cooperation and Development. Found at http://www.odci.gov/cia/publications/khies97/c/tab7.htm and http://www.odci.gov/cia/publications/khies97/c/tab16.htm.

• **Productivity growth:** percentage change of labor's productivity from year to year

Economists compare **productivity growth** by calculating the percentage change of labor's productivity from year to year. Expansion Point 2.2, for example, compares labor productivity and productivity growth in West Germany, Japan, and the United States. It also illustrates that U.S. productivity grew very slowly between 1970 and 1980.

To summarize this section, economists evaluate efficiency with multiple measures and concepts:

- Productive efficiency requires the least-cost combinations of labor, machines, and other resources inside the firm.
- Allocative efficiency is an ideal distribution of resources among competing uses in the whole economy.
- Exchange efficiency moves society's goods and services to their most valuable uses.
- Dynamic efficiency is the flexible and rapid adjustment to new technology and changing prices.
- Macroeconomic efficiency requires a full employment of economic resources.
- Institutional efficiency involves efficient rules and play of the commercial game.
- Productivity of labor is measured as the real or money value of output per worker.

Someone once said it is silly to double your speed when you don't know where you are going. Remember that efficient economic activity is a means to an end, not the end itself. Choosing economic goals, though, lies outside the scope of pure economic analysis. People must apply ethical principles to determine for what purposes they will efficiently use their resources. Maybe that is what Philip Wogaman (1986) meant when he said, "Economics is too important to be left to economists."

Scarcity and Opportunity Costs

Choosing efficiently generally involves measuring costs. Efficient decision making requires evaluating all costs of each decision, not just explicit money costs. Economists prefer to measure the **opportunity cost** of one choice as the value of the benefits from the best alternative choice that you have to forego in order to make the first choice. Opportunity costs include more than simply the out-of-pocket money expenses of consumption or production. They also include the costs of time spent to buy, use, or produce goods and the value of your own resources that you used (resources for which you paid no money at the time).

• **Opportunity cost** of a choice is the value of the best alternative choice that you must give up.

If you watch one television movie on your own set, except for a small charge for electricity used, the out-of-pocket cost is zero. The full opportunity cost of watching the movie, however, could be the value of knowledge you would have gained by watching a documentary or reading a good book. Or it might be the value of the income that you would give up because you could not work during that time. If you could have painted walls for a neighbor at $7 an hour, the opportunity cost of watching a two-hour movie is $14. As Expansion Point 2.3 makes clear, the accurate calculation of **economic profit** must account for opportunity costs.

• **Economic profit** is over and above all opportunity cost.

Expansion Point 2.3: Yard-Sale Profits or Losses?

The idea of opportunity cost forces us to be more careful about how we use the word "profit." Those who hold yard sales in summer may report that they "made" $100 profit during the sale. The total revenues from the sale, however, can hardly be called a profit when opportunity costs of time are included. A yard sale may involve three to five hours of work at pricing and organizing goods. Another four to eight hours may be expended in managing the sale itself. Sometimes two or more people put in a total of 10 to 20 hours altogether on the sale. If revenues were $100 but the yard-sale enthusiasts also could have used the 20 hours to paint houses for $7 an hour, they lost $40 on the sale. The opportunity cost of time was (20 hours @ $7 per hour) equals $140.

Understanding opportunity cost of time can lead to a better decision about time use. The revenues from any sale must first pay for labor invested. A potential seller whose wage in a regular job is high will be more likely to forego the sale, pack up the goods, and donate them to a charitable enterprise. If a charity will pick up the goods, that would be even better.

Opportunity Costs and Economic Analysis

Opportunity cost applies everywhere in economic analysis. For instance, the principle that "there is no such thing as a free lunch" is a logical conclusion. A student, who says, "I got a free CD with my music text!" fails to understand that there is no such thing as a free CD. First, producing the CD and its contents used scarce resources. Second, the $85 price of the text probably included the price of the CD. Although companies do give free samples, in each case the company has to pay the costs of the sample. It also probably charges those costs to advertising expenses, which paying customers eventually fund.

Opportunity Costs vs. Sunk Costs

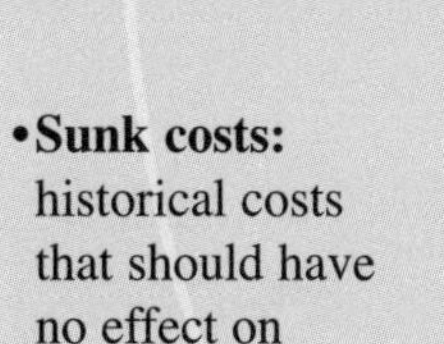

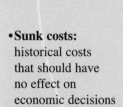

• **Sunk costs:** historical costs that should have no effect on economic decisions

Opportunity costs are the basis for another economic principle: **"sunk costs" or "historical costs" are irrelevant to good economic decision making**. If a pharmaceutical company has spent $5 million researching a new drug and has not had any success, it is improper for the project head to complain that the project should not be scrapped because that would waste $5 million of effort. Such a comment assumes that the $5 million has been stored in a bank and bringing the product to market will give access to the money. This is a faulty analogy, however. It may be that the $5 million was fully or partially wasted. In any event, the money already spent is a sunk cost. The firm should ignore sunk costs and focus on future opportunity costs and benefits. Perhaps bringing the drug to market would cost $3 million more but, because of project delays, expected revenues may be less. Perhaps due to a competitor's progress with a similar drug, the project might now generate only $2 million in revenue. If so, the firm would expect to lose $1 million more by continuing the project. It should cut its losses, scrap the project, and forget about the $5 million of sunk costs. Only if the company expects the extra revenue to be greater than the extra cost of $3 million is continuing the project economical.

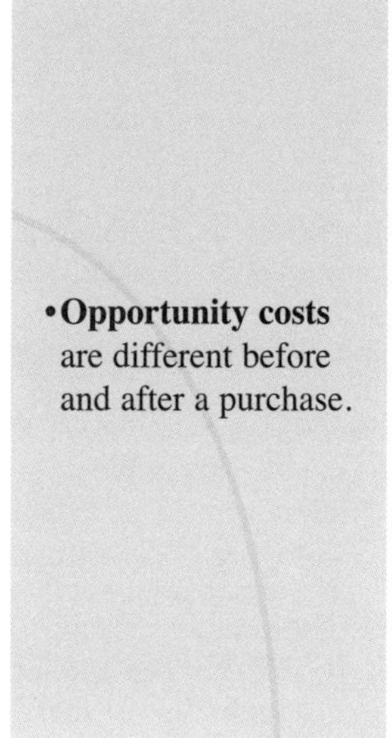
• **Opportunity costs** are different before and after a purchase.

Opportunity costs are **different before and after** making a decision. In calculating costs of driving a car, insurance costs and license-plate fees are sunk only after you buy the car. When deciding whether to buy a car, insurance costs and license fees should be considered. When deciding whether to drive a car you already own, insurance costs and license fees should not be considered since they are now sunk costs. (See Grant and Ireson 1987, 54-62.)

CHAPTER SUMMARY

1. Economists study the efficient use of scarce resources to meet our unlimited wants and needs.

2. Economics has tended to combine scientific analysis with legal-historical analysis of past and present economic conditions. Both approaches benefit from the theoretical framework of demand and supply and the concepts of efficiency and opportunity costs.

3. Market prices reflect relative scarcities of resources and products. A relatively higher price indicates relatively more scarcity.

4. The model of demand and supply explains how economic factors affect market price and quantity exchanged. Market price of a product or resource tends toward equilibrium price, where quantity demanded equals quantity supplied.

5. A market price greater than the equilibrium price causes a surplus, with quantity supplied greater than quantity demanded. A market price less than equilibrium causes a shortage, with quantity supplied less than quantity demanded.

6. Governments impose price controls in certain markets. A price floor is a legal minimum price that is set above equilibrium price and that causes a surplus. A price ceiling is a legal maximum price that is set below equilibrium price and that causes a shortage.

7. Changes in economic factors can change demand or supply and thereby influence market price and quantity exchanged. An increase in demand or decrease in supply leads to a higher price. A decrease in demand or increase in supply causes a lower price.

8. Economists identify six measures of economic efficiency. Productive efficiency is the efficient combination of labor, machines, and other resources inside the firm that minimizes average cost of producing a good. Allocative efficiency considers how effectively resources are used by competing industries in the whole economy. Exchange efficiency, a special case of allocative efficiency, measures whether goods and services are being used for their most valuable purposes. Dynamic efficiency compares the flexibility and speed of an economy in adjusting to new technology and changing prices. Macroeconomic efficiency measures how fully an economy employs all its resources. Institutional efficiency refers to having the set of economic rules and commercial practices that minimize the costs of transactions.

9. The average productivity of labor (real amount or dollar value of output divided by labor input) is an important practical measure of efficiency in production or in a nation as a whole.

10. Opportunity cost is the economic measure of costs. The opportunity cost of an activity is the value of the best alternative that a person gives up to do the activity. Opportunity cost includes money cost, time cost, and lost income from using one's own resources.

PROBLEMS FOR PRACTICE

2.1* What is economic analysis? Why is market price important to economic analysis? Why is a precise definition of efficiency also important?

2.2* Which of the following will tend to cause an increased market price and which will cause a decrease in market price for each product or resource?

a. a surplus of wheat at the current price
b. an increase in demand for gold
c. a flood of new imported cars in the auto market
d. a shortage of gasoline
e. the end of the legal minimum wage
f. a drop in demand for microcomputers
g. an interruption in the global supply of oil

2.3* Analyze the following hypothetical news reports as to whether the effect on price and output was probably caused by an increase or decrease in either demand or supply. Graph the effects of the story, using demand and supply.

a. "Prices of tomatoes are higher this summer due to heavy rains in the coastal growing regions. The rains are causing the fruit to rot before it matures, leaving tomato lovers facing lower stocks in wholesalers' warehouses and on retailers' shelves."
b. "Recently, heavy job layoffs in the Philadelphia region have caused many families to abandon plans for vacations. As a result, ocean resorts have fewer visitors and rental prices for apartments are lower on average this year."
c. "Medical research now suggests that regular consumption of cow's milk may tend to raise children's IQ's. As news of the research spread last fall, the average price of a gallon of milk in the region rose 17 percent."
d. "The arrival last year of two discount airline companies at the Buffalo regional airport has increased competition. The average price per mile for tickets has fallen 23 percent during the past 12 months."

2.4* Explain what you know about the effects on equilibrium price and equilibrium quantity exchanged of each of the following:

a. The demand for houses is higher this year than last, but the supply of houses is also higher this year due to recent increases in lumber imports.
b. Interest rate increases have reduced the demand for large-screen televisions at the same time that economic troubles in Asia have caused increases in the supply of large-screen televisions in the United States.

2.5* Which of the three production processes described below is productively most efficient?

Process	**A**	**B**	**C**
Quantity Produced	100	110	90
Labor Cost	$800	$300	$700
Land Cost	$100	$100	$100
Equipment Cost	$200	$850	$300
Materials Cost	$450	$350	$400
Total Cost	$1550	$1600	$1500

Does a government commitment to using more labor-intensive techniques influence which method is considered to be efficient? In terms of the three methods described, what would be the clearest indication that labor-intensive methods are indeed more efficient?

2.6* Assume that the exact same wall-to-wall carpeting is selling for $20 a square yard in Bristol, TN, and $30 a square yard in Atlanta, GA. Are there any reasons that selling costs should be $10 more in Atlanta? If not, what do you conclude about economic efficiency in the buying and selling of carpet? Explain how this situation might be changed by shrewd traders.

What if the same carpet sells in Honduras for $80 a square yard? How would you explain such a high price in such a poor country, where people do not generally have the high incomes to buy such carpet? Think in terms of any processes that interfere with the efficient rationing of carpet.

2.7* The two charts below show statistics for the number of workers and the dollar value of output of the United States, China, and Japan in 1995 and 1990. Which nation had the highest and lowest productivity in the earlier year? Did the rankings of nations change between the first and second year?

1995 Data

Nation	Number of Laborers	Value of Output†	Productivity of Labor
China	623,880,000	$3,535,000,000,000	?
Japan	65,990,000	$2,885,000,000,000	?
U.S.	132,300,000	$7,397,000,000,000	?

1990 Data

Nation	Number of Laborers	Value of Output†	Productivity of Labor
China	567,400,000	$2,061,000,000,000	?
Japan	63,050,000	$2,687,000,000,000	?
U.S.	125,840,000	$6,739,000,000,000	?

† Real gross domestic product in 1996 U.S. dollars.

Source: "Selected OECD Countries: Economic Profile." Profile of Organization for Economic Cooperation and Development accessed from CIA Web site: http://www.odci.gov/cia/publications/khies97/c/tab7.htm (*and* tab16.htm).

2.8*a. Assume that a business flyer has a choice between a three-hour trans-Atlantic flight on a supersonic Concorde and a six-hour flight on a standard airliner. The economizing traveler will consider the opportunity cost of both time and money for tickets. Assume that the flyer's wage represents the opportunity cost of time in the air. If the price of a Concorde ticket is $3,000 and the price of a standard ticket is $600, at what wage will a flyer be indifferent to the gap between the higher price of the Concorde and the longer standard flight?

b. Many people will fly because time is scarce and money for an airplane ticket is less valuable than the time. Why do certain people who value their time still take the bus or train when each takes longer than a plane for many trips?

2.9* Your friend comes back from a yard sale saying, "I only paid $5 for this beautiful flowered dress. What a steal!" Meanwhile, at the house of the yard sale, the wife is saying to the husband, "We did pretty well today. We made over $200 profit. I even sold that old flowered dress of mine for $5. Imagine that!"

a. Who stole what from whom? Explain in terms of the economic analysis of exchange.

b. Do you agree that the $200 should be considered profit from the six-hour yard sale?

For Your Portfolio:

2.10* Work on this in small groups. Construct a brief survey with questions asking whether the responder thinks that government agencies are more or less efficient than private businesses (or equally efficient). Write two or three questions and decide how best to ask them: in person, on the phone, or by e-mail.

Then have each group member survey five people. Bring survey results back to the group and analyze the data. Draw conclusions about your survey and explain.

Group Discussion:

2.11 Economics is about means and ends: how to efficiently use scarce resources (means) to meet needs and wants (ends). A complicating aspect of the distinction between means and ends in economics is that economic freedom is both a means to an end and an end in itself. Economic freedom is a goal for libertarian economists such as Milton Friedman. It is also a means to achieving productive, allocative, exchange, and dynamic efficiencies (the jury is still out on the relation between freedom and macroeconomic efficiency). Should economists and social theorists speak of economic freedom as a means to economic efficiency or as an end?

See Answer Key for hints/answers to starred (*) questions.

Chapter 3

What Is Economics?

A Brief History of Economic Thought

What this chapter will help you think about:

1. How is the term "economics" derived from the Greek word for household steward?
2. What did economics or stewardship mean to the Greeks and early Christians?
3. How is "economics" now related to the interests of the state, party, or individual?
4. What are the various schools of economic thought from the 1600s to the present?
5. When did economics become a science?
6. In what sense can public-choice theory be considered a return to stewardship?

Economics was a "household" word when its Greek root was used by Plato in his *Republic* (417 A, 498 A, 407 B) and by others in ancient Greek literature. Once the French physiocrats and the Scotsman Adam Smith presented systematic explanations of economic activity, the term economics began to take on a range of meanings, from political economy to scientific analysis, from individualist to collectivist theories, and from abstract, deductive, mathematical analysis to historical, inductive methods. I hope you enjoy this lightning review.

Ancient Economics

Economics had a narrow meaning to classical Greek writers and to members of the early Christian church in Asia Minor. The writings of the Greek philosophers Plato and Aristotle, for example, do anticipate some of the modern economic debates about private or public property and the role of the individual and state. Nevertheless, economics was clearly understood in the context of scarcity of household food and supplies, and the proper management of the household.

Greek Stewardship: Economics at Home

The Greek terms *oikos* and *oikovoμous* are the sources for our term "economics." [In Greek, ν (nu) is the n sound and μ (mu) is an m sound.] *Oikos* refers to a household, usually composed of father, mother, family, servants, and slaves. *Oikovoμous* refers to the steward of the household, who managed various supplies according to the master's orders. The steward dispensed food among the servants, giving each the portion indicated by the master. Thus, to the Greeks, economics meant "getting it right," or following the master's instructions regarding scarce resources.

•**Greek stewardship:** the steward distributes resources according to the household master's orders

Homer's *Odyssey*, an epic Greek poem, contains strong themes about Odysseus' wife Penelope's "stewardship" of his household while he is gone. Not only does she keep their home intact during his ten-year wandering return from the Trojan War, but she also preserves the spiritual integrity of the house against the pressures of her many suitors to dispense her love in unauthorized ways.

Christian Stewardship: Economics in God's Kingdom

In the Bible, the Apostle Peter includes an encouragement to Christians around the ancient world to "Be good economists of the grace of God" (1 Peter 4:10). Texts of English Bibles say, "Be good stewards," but the word in the Greek text is *oikovoμous*. This call to stewardship of God's gifts is a good description of God's place in the Christian's view of all aspects of life, including the economic. God is the owner of the house and believers are His stewards or "economists" in the Greek sense of *oikovoμous*. They are to follow instructions in the use of the gifts of God.

•**Biblical stewardship:** when making decisions, a good steward attends to the will of God, as recorded in Scripture, and to the Holy Spirit's leading

Economic analysis had roots in theological thought that addressed the secular as sacred. Expansion Point 3.1 explains how the church fathers and medieval scholastics examined economic issues by interpreting the meaning of the commands and condemnations of God about poverty and wealth, lending at

Expansion Point 3.1: Early Church Views on Private Property

Preaching Political Economy

Early Christian theologians treated economics in terms of God's ownership and man's stewardship. John Chrysostom, a Greek living about 347 to 407, "praised the economy of God" and considered private property to be a cause of strife. Augustine, prominent in the North African Church at the time, "declared wealth to be a gift from God." While agreeing that wealth caused problems, private property was to be avoided but not eliminated. Augustine reasoned that, while the earth belongs to the Lord, emperors or kings, who ruled at the Lord's will, instituted private property, giving it legitimacy in this world.

Medieval "Scholastic" Thomas Aquinas (1225-1274) later offered what was a "complete and authoritative statement of medieval economic thought" and what became "official Catholic philosophy" on economic topics. Aquinas reasoned that private property was consistent with "natural law," but he also favored Old Testament restrictions on property. Stopping short of calling for equal distribution of all property, Aquinas nevertheless emphasized the stewardship of wealth and an individual's responsibility to share with others, especially those in dire need.

Source: Henry William Spiegel, *History of Economic Thought*, 3rd ed. (Durham, NC: Duke University Press, 1991), especially 44-59.

interest (usury), and "buying low" in order to "sell dear." The idea of a just price, for example, linked product pricing to moral duty, even in the event of natural disasters and shifts in demand or supply that would otherwise influence the market price.

More recently, a group of Christian economists has taken up the combination of theological and economic issues. Beginning with Douglass Vickers, a number of Christian economists writing in the later 1900s have attempted to explain economics in light of their faith. While largely refusing to condemn lending at interest or buying low and selling high, they have returned to a stress on the stewardship aspect of economizing. We are to conserve that which God owns and which God has entrusted to our care. But how can Christian economists ignore clear biblical commands not to lend at interest? See Expansion Point 3.2 for a comparison of Christian and Islamic responses.

This, of course, is not the secular meaning of economics today, because secular thought tends to be atheistic or at least agnostic about the divine (an atheist doesn't believe in a supernatural God, and an agnostic says we can't know and perhaps should not care). Moreover, somewhere between the ancient Greek and biblical use and the modern secular uses of economics, its meaning has changed. The basis for deciding how to conserve scarce resources has shifted from obeying a master's orders to satisfying individual wants and preferences or, in other cases, to pursuing the interests of the state or political party.

Early Political Economy

The modern period in Europe, the rise of reason and scientific inquiry, began in the 1500s. At that time, merchant capitalism was spreading across Europe. The nation states of Europe were also emerging more clearly from the feudal system. As merchant capitalism developed, national rulers required some economic policies to turn the benefits of commerce to their own account. That led to the rise of **political economy**, the rules by which a nation's resources ought to be administered for the benefit of the King, the state, the nobles, and in a few instances, the people.

•**Political Economy:** the rules by which a nation's resources ought to be administered for the benefit of sovereign, nation, and people

In the seventeenth and eighteenth centuries, English and French scholars showed special interest in policy economics. A group called mercantilists were economic advocates for restrictive national policies. A group called French physiocrats advocated for freedom.

Mercantilists as Economic Advocates

In the seventeenth century, **mercantilist** pamphlet writers on the subject saw political economy as the practice of designing government policies to benefit the particular special interest which

Expansion Point 3.2: Is Lending at Interest a Sin? Christian and Islamic Views

Interest is a payment for using someone else's money or for owing a debt. If you borrow $100 this month and pay back $110 next year, the $10 extra dollars is interest and you have paid a 10 percent rate of interest.

The Old Testament condemns charging interest. The psalmist wrote of a person who walks with "integrity" and does "righteousness": "He does not put out his money at interest" (Psalm 15:2, 5, *NASB*). The law of Deuteronomy condemns charging interest to a fellow Israelite:

> "You shall not charge interest to your countrymen: interest on money, food, *or* anything that may be loaned at interest. You may charge interest to a foreigner, but to your countrymen you shall not charge interest, so that the Lord your God may bless you . . ." (Deuteronomy 23:19, 20)

> ***"You shall not charge interest to your countrymen: interest on money, food, or anything that may be loaned at interest."***
> *Deuteronomy 23:19 NASB*

Medieval Christian teachers upheld the prohibition against interest. Modern capitalism, however, arising as it did in predominantly Christian Europe, poses a historical contradiction to this law. Capitalism depends on a financial system that rewards savers with interest and charges interest to borrowers. Modern capitalism appears to be pragmatic and scientific, rather than Christian, in its philosophy, and surely more so today. The rise of merchant and industrial capitalism, however, coincided with the rise of the Protestant Reformation. Max Weber has even attributed the rise of capitalism to the spread of Calvinism, with its emphasis on following Scriptural principles. There is at least an apparent contradiction in Weber's "Christian" capitalism that rests on a bedrock of financing business investment at interest paid to Christian savers.

If Protestant capitalism is supposed to conform to biblical principles, how do Christians get around the prohibition on interest? Some don't. They simply condemn capitalism and take a more idealistic and socialistic view of what economy can be. Others see that the prohibition was limited and accept interest from a bank but charge their family no interest. Still others simply ignore such laws, holding to less dogmatic and less literal beliefs.

The religion of Islam has a similar conflict but takes another approach to resolving it. Islam is not antagonistic to commerce and yet, like the Old Testament, the *Qur'an* (Koran) prohibits *riba* ("increase") or interest.

How do Muslims avoid borrowing and lending at interest? Islam allows for *qirad*, or the sharing of profits from an enterprise. Ideally, a lender asks for no interest from a commercial loan. Instead, the lender is a partner in a business and agrees to share its profits or losses. *Qirad* promotes commerce without lending at interest and without violating the law in principle. But, in practice, complain Islamic economists, some partners hide the true extent of their profits and thereby defraud their partners.

Certain biblical scholars take a different view of interest. They look more carefully at what the text meant in the day it was written and what it therefore means today. This is called the exegetical method, in which the scholar reads meaning out of the text rather than into it. Lending in the Old Testament period was mainly for poor relief, not for productive investment where risk was involved. Exodus 22:25 shows that the law is to be understood in this context of lending to the poor: "If you lend money to My people, to the poor among you, you are not to act as a creditor to him; you shall not charge him interest. If you ever take your neighbor's coat as a pledge, you are to return it to him before the sun sets, for that is his only covering" (*NASB*).

Since lending for productive investment to otherwise adequately supplied people was not in view, the Old Testament law does not on the surface condemn modern capitalist banking. The law, however, has another application in a capitalist setting. It still condemns those urban money shops and loan sharks who exploit the poor and their immediate needs for money and who charge excessive interest rates.

Source: J. Barkley Rosser and Marina W. Rosser, *Comparative Economics in a Transforming World Economy* (Chicago: Irwin, 1995), 114-120.

• Mercantilists: pamphlet writers who supported special interests, surplus of trade, and accumulation of precious metals

they represented. Mercantilists were not systematic students of economics; they were lobbyists in the court of the sovereign, having roles similar to lobbyists in U.S. federal, state, and local governments. The mercantilists practiced **economic advocacy**, always writing to take a side favorable to their patrons. But they also had to show clear benefits to the sovereign and the national treasury.

Mercantilists wrote in an age of national rivalries, when exporting gold to pay for imported goods from another country would seem to add to the wealth of one's rival and diminish wealth at home. Therefore, they discouraged imports from other nations and promoted imports of raw materials from one's own colonies.

In that setting, Thomas Mun was an advocate for the British East India Company. Mun's *England's Treasure by Foreign Trade* (first posthumous edition, 1664) argued that sending gold and silver out of the country in the East India trade was actually valuable to England. Instead of paying much higher prices to Turkish traders, England was buying spices and cloth at a sharp discount in India and employing its own fleets and sailors to bring back the treasures. Furthermore, precious metals exported to India were more than offset by resale of imports to other nations. Authorizing the East India Company to export silver and gold would eventually bring more money back into the country. In short, Mun was arguing that, while the general prohibition on exporting gold and silver might be nationally beneficial, an exception should continue to be made in the case of the East India Company.

Physiocrats as Advocates

• Physiocrats: eighteenth-century French economists who believed that land is the only productive resource; they favored individual liberty and *laissez-faire* (limited government)

In the mid 1700s, French physiocrats Francois Quesney, Anne Robert Jacques Turgot, and others began writing about **land as the sole source of wealth**, compared to the "sterile" classes of industrialists, merchants, ministers to the court, or clergy. **Physiocrats**, as their name implies, were advocates for the importance of land and the agricultural sector. And yet they only lobbied for taxes on land because they thought it was the only productive sector. They also argued against harsh, restrictive French mercantilist policies.

Influenced by Enlightenment ideas of the 1700s, the physiocrats favored individual liberties. A French finance minister and physiocrat, Turgot advocated and briefly implemented economic policies favoring peasants and the working class. He repealed a law that required peasants to put in several weeks a year working on the French roads. Had Turgot's more liberal policies not been reversed shortly after he implemented them, the French Revolution might have been avoided (Oser and Brue 1988).

An important idea coming from the physiocrat Vincent de Gourney was *laissez-faire*, or let it alone. The French government should free businesses from restrictions on internal and external trade and "leave it alone" (Oser and Brue, 35).

An advocate takes up one side of an issue. The mercantilists and physiocrats, then, were both **national advocates** but with different themes. Mercantilist writers operated within the environment of the crown's restrictions on economic activity for the benefit of the state. To them, economic analysis was special pleading to advance a special interest with attention to the interests of the state and its sovereign.

Physiocrat writers sought efficiency in taxation, but also sought freedom from economic restrictions by the crown and, therefore, took an individual perspective. The physiocrats advocated economic liberty and tax reform with the larger objective of promoting the wealth of the French state. Yet, as Spiegel (1991, 199) says, the physiocrats were advocates for a natural order that included "surprisingly modern" ideas beside medieval ones, such as the primacy of land, and they also advocated for the "ancient regime" of France that was about to fall in the revolution.

English Political Economy: Discovering Economic Laws

In the late 1700s and early 1800s, English writers on political economy called **classical economists** began to write more systematically about economic theory, policy, and institutions. Classical political economy began with the work of Scottish moral-philosophy lecturer Adam Smith and later included Parson Thomas Malthus, stockbroker David Ricardo, philosopher John Stuart Mill, and others. Most but not all classical economists were English—J. B. Say was one exception.

• **English classical political economy:** tended toward a philosophy of *laissez-faire*, analytical and deductive in method

Classical economists by and large advocated policies of *laissez-faire*, or limited government involvement in the market, following ideas of the French physiocrats. Government control in England and France was often quite harsh and stifling. A mix of mercantilist and feudal restrictions and taxes smothered initiative and commerce. As a result, these writers advocated a political economy in which the government regulated the economy very little. The minimum tasks of government were protecting life and private property, providing a national defense, regulating the money supply, and providing a few "public goods" that the free market could not. Even so, the classical school attempted to discover the laws that governed economic behavior and to design economic policy accordingly.

Adam Smith's Optimism

Adam Smith's book, *An Inquiry into the Nature and Causes of the Wealth of Nations*, published at the start of the American

Revolution in 1776, was one of the first clear statements of these ideas. Individual initiative, private property, and free-market exchange promoted a nation's wealth most effectively. The resources of society would be put to their best use when government restrictions were lifted, with individuals acting in their own self-interest. The "invisible hand" of the price system was to be the coordinating mechanism. By providing signals about scarcities, shortages, and profitabilities in commerce, the price system would direct individuals who were mainly promoting their own self-interests to promote the interests of others.

Smith believed in a natural harmony of human interests. Economic interests of the individual and the state, for example, were not necessarily at odds. The wealth and economic interests of the state would flourish, Smith optimistically contended, under a system of "**natural liberty**." His critics, however, accused Smith of proclaiming a "gospel of greed" and pursuing a "science of egoism." Whether Smith actually preached that greed is good is discussed in Expansion Point 3.3.

Smith rejected Quesney's emphasis on agriculture as the sole source of wealth in a nation. Living in industrially active Scottish cities of Kirkaldy and Glasgow, Smith easily saw "the wealth being created at every hand in workshops and factories of craftsmen" (Heilbroner 1967, 45). Smith did take from the physiocrats the importance of the circulation of money as a stimulus to the productivity of workers.

Other Classical Economists

While Smith was an optimist, **Parson Thomas Malthus** thought that an unregulated economy might tend to have severe economic crises. He wrote about overpopulation and inadequate food supplies. He also wrote about the potential for a **general glut** (excess supply) **of goods on the market**.

French classical economist **Jean-Baptiste Say** was more optimistic about the market's ability to regulate itself. Say's Law of Markets tended to dominate classical thought about the largely unexplored ideas of macroeconomic instability. Say said that when goods are produced, the people pay money to buy them; in short, "**Supply creates its own Demand.**" A general glut of goods could not persist due to the flexible adjustment of prices, wages, and interest rates, which eliminate surpluses in product, labor, and credit markets.

David Ricardo was also pessimistic about the English economy. He feared that it might eventually **stagnate**, having no further outlets for profitable investments in agriculture due to "diminishing returns to labor." His cure was to increase economic freedom in grain markets, allowing a free flow of imports into

Expansion Point 3.3: Did Adam Smith Teach That Greed Is Good?

One of the best known quotes from Adam Smith's *An Inquiry into the Nature and Causes of the Wealth of Nations* (1776) is about self-love:

> It is not from the benevolence of the butcher, the brewer or the baker that we expect our dinner, but from their regard to their own interest. We address ourselves not to their humanity but to their self love, and never talk to them of our own necessities but of their advantages (26-27).

A number of commentators interpret this very negatively. Here is the smoking-gun proof that Smith advocated greedy behavior. How else could the passage be read? The passage, however, actually seems to contain quite a different meaning.

In this second chapter of *WN*, Smith was writing that, while spaniels beg for their dinner, humans would do better not to beg. The very next lines are: "Nobody but a beggar chooses to depend chiefly upon the benevolence of his fellow-citizens. Even a beggar does not depend upon it entirely." If comments about begging are the context of Smith's statement about self-love, what does it mean?

Smith seems to be saying that it is better to try to get our dinner by *addressing ourselves to* the self-love of the merchant. We ought to be kind and offer to pay them for our dinner, rather than beg for it. It is most selfish to beg and unselfish to pay for what you want or need.

You might find it elsewhere in Smith's *Wealth of Nations*, but you won't find the smoking gun of greed in this passage. It is quite benign and yet informative about how markets socialize people at great distances, encouraging them to cooperate so that each will have just what he needs for dinner.

Sources: Adam Smith, *An Inquiry into the Nature and Causes of the Wealth of Nations,* Glasgow ed. Edited by R.H. Campbell and A.S. Skinner (Indianapolis: Liberty Fund, 1981). Originally printed in 1776.

England. Eliminating the protectionist **corn laws** would lower grain prices, lower labor's wages, and increase farmers' profits, delaying stagnation. Neither Ricardo nor Malthus, though, foresaw dramatic increases in agricultural mechanization and productivity.

English political economy, then, tended to be **cosmopolitan**, emphasizing cooperation across borders, not national economic competition. A nationalist has political interests narrowly focused on a home state. A cosmopolitan has international interests.

Economic analysis for the English was therefore a search for **universal economic principles** rather than nationalistic policies to advance the interests of one state or another. Just as Enlightenment scientists sought laws of physical motion, such as the law of gravity, the classical economists were seeking the laws of economic behavior. We can see this tendency in the laws they claimed to discover, like the iron law of wages, the law of diminishing marginal product, and the law of comparative advantage.

The classical method was to examine **individual behavior** and its conclusion was to increase individual **economic freedom**. While some "popularizers" of *laissez-faire* theory leaned toward extremism, the major classical economists, Smith and Mill in particular, maintained some sense of balance on the importance of government. In spite of this balance, the classical economists had their critics in Britain and elsewhere, who accused them of methodological errors and narrow perspectives.

Critics of Classical Economics

A number of writers on economics did not agree with the individualism and analytical deductive nature of English political economy. They also rejected capitalism, more or less. We will review historicists, institutionalists, literary critics, and socialists.

German Historicists and American Institutionalists

•**German historical economists:** nationalist and protectionist in philosophy; historical in method

The **German historical economists** contended that classical thought ignored the role of institutions and the interests of the state, as against those of the individual. German historicists of the mid-1800s were quite **nationalistic**, rather than individualistic or cosmopolitan. Recognizing that Germany lagged behind England in industrial development, their focus tended toward building the German economy. Individual interests would have to be secondary to the interests of the state.

•**American institutionalists:** disciples of German historicists; analyzed economic institutions

The later **American institutional economists** followed the historical approach, emphasizing the evolution of economic institutions. **Thorstein Veblen** was a more critical institutionalist, while **John Commons** was more constructive. Veblen criticized the system of managing commercial factories for profit. Instead, he preferred a communist model of having a soviet (committee) of engineers operate plants at full capacity for the social welfare of all. Commons examined the legal and commercial **transactions** of capitalism, accepting capitalism but recognizing that most economic transactions did not follow classical models of atomistic competition with many buyers and sellers.

Both the historical school and the later institutional school rejected classical views about how the price system would automatically harmonize self-interests. For both schools, economics was the study of the evolutionary economic progress of nations and institutions. Their methods were "inductive" and "historical," and they rejected the classical emphasis on deducing "economic laws" that supposedly applied at all places and in all times. Expansion Point 3.4 provides a brief review of deduction, induction, and the scientific method.

Neither the historical economists nor the more critical institutionalist economists produced a clear program of historical or institutional economics. In other words, much of their work was not very different from what historians do—it lacked economic

Expansion Point 3.4: Should Economics Be Inductive or Deductive?

Which is the best way to learn about an economy: inductive or deductive reasoning? Deduction involves reasoning from general principles to specific conclusions. Deduction is pure thought, like the man at the left. Induction, on the other hand, involves observing the world and recording data, like the woman to the right. Then we reason from particular observations to general conclusions.

Here is an example of deductive thinking from the general to the specific:

General Principle: The law of demand is true—as the price of any product goes up, quantity demanded will fall.

Deductive Conclusion: If the price of wheat rises, people will decrease the quantity they demand.

The law of demand is assumed to be a timeless, general statement that applies anywhere. Deductions about wheat prices and purchases should hold, whether the price of wheat increases in Dusseldorf, Germany; Cardiff, Wales; or Bombay, India.

Here is a plan for inductive analysis of demand that begins with specific observations about individual events, and then moves to general conclusions about all such events:

Observations: Monitor the actual trade in wheat in Dusseldorf, Cardiff, and Bombay. Record quantities traded at various prices and note whether quantity demanded falls when price rises. If this is true, other things equal, then a conclusion is warranted . . .

Inductive Conclusion: If the price of wheat rises, the quantity demanded will fall.

In our observations of the wheat trade, we might find that all other factors are not equal. We might observe an exception where a city government had fixed the price of wheat no matter what the conditions of demand and supply. Without variation in price, we could not confirm a negative relation between price and quantity demanded in that city, but we would have another principle that government can and does interfere with the market for wheat. We also might find that any illegal wheat trade obeys economic law even when it is in contempt of city law.

In practice, scientific analysis in economics includes a circular or spiraling process of reasoning that combines inductive and deductive methods:

1. A problem in our daily life causes us to search for an explanation;
2. An informed guess leads to a tentative general principle;
3. From the tentative principle we derive a **testable hypothesis**;
4. We test the hypothesis with data from systematic observations;
5. The test tends to support or disconfirm the general principle; and
6. If confirmed, we continue to test under different situations or, if disconfirmed, we return to step two and form a new general principle.

Deduction occurs at step three while induction occurs at steps two and five. Since the reasoning process is imperfect, we will further test and retest various hypotheses. Others may join the testing process, the nature of science being to conduct **replicable experiments**.

Even though both induction and deduction are necessary to human reasoning, debates about inductive versus deductive method have continued throughout two centuries of economic analysis. Not until American economist Irving Fisher began "econometric" testing of the hypothesis that money increases cause price increases, did economists take seriously the need to test economic conclusions rigorously.

distinctives. Spiegel contends that Wilhelm Roscher succeeded as a historical economist precisely because he combined a historical approach with a survey of classical theory (1991, 420).

Mainstream economists toward the end of the twentieth century tended to reject both purely deductive analytical theory that had no empirical content and purely historical analysis that had no body of economic theory. Professional journals in economics began to insist that theoretical ideas be subject to empirical testing and that empirical analysis have a "rigorous" theoretical basis.

Literary Critics

The German historical economists were not the lone critics of classical economics in the mid-1800s. Several English **literary critics**, especially Thomas Carlisle and John Ruskin, offered pointed comments about the cold, calculating nature of economic behavior as described by David Ricardo and the "Manchester School" of economics. They rejected what they assumed to be an overemphasis on selfishness and greed as motivations for economic activity, and a tendency to ignore human altruism. Even Cambridge economist Alfred Marshall agreed that these critics had a worthy point. Ricardo, living as he did in the London world of stockbrokers, may have been too familiar with the sharp practices of financiers and too ignorant of the communal practices in rural districts (see Marshall's *Principles of Economics*, 1890).

Ruskin, in *Unto This Last* (1862), argued against the classical economists' partial view of human behavior. As he saw it, self-interest was equivalent to "avarice" and "covetousness." He understood the classical economists to have said that the self-interest motive was more regular than "inconstant . . . social affections" such as charity. Therefore, classical political economy seems to say, in Ruskin's words, "Let us eliminate the inconstants, and, considering the human being merely as a covetous machine, examine by what laws of labour, purchase, and sale, the greatest accumulative result in wealth is obtainable. Those laws once determined, it will be for each individual afterwards to introduce as much of the disturbing affectionate element as he chooses."

As Ruskin complained, classical theory is like studying the human body as if it were only a skeleton. Though the deductive laws of classical political economy may be logical, they are of no interest because they are irrelevant to actual human experience. In daily life, humans are flesh and bones, as well as self-interest and social affections intermingled.

Ruskin was an **advocate for the poor** and for their equitable treatment in distributing society's output. As a result, *Unto This Last* was more like a sermon to the English middle and upper classes. His criticism of political economy was powerful in its day, but the ability of the self-interest model to explain everyday human behavior is also powerful. Ruskin's criticism and the object of it both survive to this day.

Socialist Critics

Karl Marx and the **socialists** also contended that classical political economy ignored the interests and exploitation of the laboring class. Marx especially advocated for industrial workers of the world, while other socialists advocated more broadly for the working and non-working poor. For socialists, private ownership of the means of production was to blame.

Marxism

For Marx, political economy was the study of the rise and eventual fall of capitalism under its own exploitative weight. To him, the central issue of capitalism was the exploitation of workers in the **wage-labor system** of production in which capitalists owned the equipment or means of production, and hired laborers at a market wage. Laborers' wages were less than the value of goods they produced. The difference, which Marx called **surplus value**, accrued to the capitalist as unearned profits. Marx's example in *Das Kapital* (1867) suggests that a capitalist's profits would equal the wages he paid to all labors. Expansion Point 3.5 assesses the realism of his example with U.S. data.

- **Marxists:** advocate revolution against capitalism, state socialism, and eventually communism

Marx's **dialectical materialism** emphasized how the material conditions of production—the class conflict between capitalists (thesis) and laborers (antithesis)—would lead to a revolt of the laborers (proletariat) and to a new economic "synthesis" in state socialism. Eventually communism would arise, once the state had "withered away."

Marx did contribute to economic thought as one of the first to analyze the business cycle. Marx thought that cycles of boom and bust were inherent to capitalism. Growing power of the financial sector would make the cycles worse, as more and more wealth became owned by or mortgaged to banks. This stage of history he called "finance capitalism." But key questions remain about Marxism. Are profits really unearned? Doesn't allowing for profits derived from wage labor benefit society and even laborers themselves, especially compared to state socialism? And is the fall of capitalism really inevitable?

Leninism

Vladimir Lenin continued the Marxist tradition by contending that capitalist ventures into international trade and colonialism were **exporting the exploitation of labor**. Lenin prompted the more recent criticism of multinational corporations with his ideas that capitalists in developed nations would use foreign investment to exploit developing countries.

Expansion Point 3.5: Are Capitalist Profits Really Equal to Wage Payments?

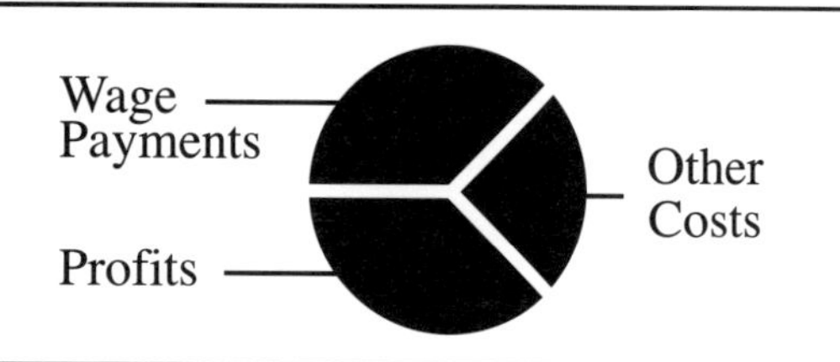

Functional Distribution of U.S. National Income, 1998

	Billions of $'s	Percent of Total
National Income	$6,646.5	100.0
Wages & Salaries	$4,687.2	70.5
Proprietors Income	551.2	8.3
Rental Income	158.2	2.4
Corporate Profits	817.9	12.3
Net Interest	432.0	6.5

In his critique of capitalism, Karl Marx used examples of the spinning business to suggest that the profit of a capitalist boss would equal what he paid his laborers. If the firm paid workers $10,000 a month in wages, the boss would take home $10,000 in profit over the same period. This implies a 50 percent rate of exploitation (it is not exactly a 50 percent rate of profit because Marx's example also included payments for worn-out spindles and materials to make yarn).

When I discussed this with a Russian instructor of economics, he said that, yes, they were taught in school that the rate of profit under capitalism was 50 percent. How accurate is this assumed rate of profit?

If Marx's example were accurate, profits would equal payments to workers in a capitalist economy. Data for U.S. national income divided into its components of wages and salaries, rents, profits, and interest tell a different story. The following table gives the breakdown of national income for 1998.

The data show clearly that in the U.S. economy profits are far less than payments to workers. Marx considered rent and interest to be part of profits, so we should include them in an aggregate value for Marxian profit. Yet, even if we sum proprietors income, rental income, corporate profits, and net interest income, the total of $1,959.3 billion is still only 41.8 percent of wages and salaries and only 29.5 percent of total national income.

Marx's example of the textile industry was provocative and memorable, but it was not an accurate representation of an advanced capitalist economy such as that of the United States. Wages and salaries in the United States in 1998 were fully 70.5 percent of national income.

Sources: Karl Marx, "Profit Is Made by Selling a Commodity at Its Value," *Value, Price and Profit*, ed. by Eleanor Marx Aveling, 1865, http://csf.Colorado.EDU/psn/marx/Archive/1864-IWMA/1865-VPP/.

"Gross Domestic Product: Fourth Quarter 1998 (Preliminary)," BEA News Release, February 26, 1999, http://www.bea.doc.gov/bea/newsrel/gdp498.htm.

Lenin's ideas about capitalist imperialism, however, seem to be contradicted by evidence that most of the direct foreign investment by multinationals from advanced capitalist nations occurs in other advanced capitalist nations. The evidence suggests that the capitalist nations have been growing rich by exploiting one another.

Summary of Marxism/Leninism

For Marx in the mid-1800s, economic analysis was a tool for exposing the supposed inherent flaws in capitalism that would lead to its eventual collapse. The supposed flaw was that capitalism required the **increasing immiseration of labor** through higher and higher rates of surplus value and exploitation. Past some point, increasing exploitation will necessarily lead laborers to revolt against the capitalist bosses.

For Lenin, economic analysis was applying Marxist principles to two tasks: (1) designing a socialist command economy without reliance on production for profit, traditional law, ethics, religion, or a market economy, and (2) explaining how laborers' rising standard of living in capitalist nations must be due to the "export of capital" and exploitation of other workers by direct foreign investment in developing nations. For both Lenin and Marx, economics was useful as a tool for pursuing the **class interests of industrial workers** and the **interests of the Communist Party** worldwide.

Neoclassical Microeconomics of Optimization and Balance

In the late nineteenth century, what is now part of mainstream or **neoclassical economics** became a separate university discipline. Economics became increasingly precise and mathematical. Political economy, the art of making economic policy, became **economics**, the **science of decision making**. By the 1890s, you could major in economics in English universities, the time at which universities were freeing themselves from requiring church membership and doctrinal statements of religious belief from their professors. This change promoted the complete secularization of Adam Smith's branch of moral philosophy.

•**Neoclassical economics:** the mathematical, deductive, individualistic mainstream of economics in the twentieth century, especially of microeconomics; neoclassical theory:
1) made economics into the science of decision making, distinguishing it from policies of political economy
2) separated economic analysis from moral theory

Economists of the neoclassical tradition devoted themselves to writing rigorous statements of how a market-directed economy was efficient and beneficial to society. They also investigated market imperfections and how government interventions might cure them. They largely ignored economic institutions, focusing on mechanistic economic principles. From the mid to late nineteenth century, many of the principles of **microeconomics**—what we call neoclassical **price theory**—were developed. Neoclassical economists accepted the classical mechanistic Newtonian view of the world. But they corrected some minor and major analytical errors of their predecessors.

Marshall's Economics

Alfred Marshall is an important neoclassical economist. His *Principles of Economics* (1890) set the standard for economics courses for many years. His book did *not* include the phrase "political economy" in its title, as previous English economists had, because it was not so much about proper government economic policy as it was about describing the principles by which households and businesses use scarce resources and trade products.

Marshall developed demand and supply analysis to analyze how consumer wants and producer costs *both* influence prices of products in the market. Demand and supply analysis showed that market prices were set by a balancing of opposing forces, an **equilibrium of interests** of buyers and sellers.

J. B. Clark

The first American economist to be well known as such in Europe was John Bates Clark, a neoclassical economist of the late 1800s. Clark used economic theory to show how in theory the competitive market system would lead to a fair distribution of the output. Each worker, for example, would be rewarded according to the amount that he contributed to output. This was called the **marginal productivity theory of distribution**.

Critics of neoclassical theory later called this the J. B. Clark fairy tale because it depended on what they thought were very precise assumptions. Working with the same mathematical tools of analysis, critics noted that if firms got more efficient when they got larger or if firms advertised to promote differences in their products, the results of pure competition would not hold.

Neoclassical Welfare Economics

In the early 1900s, several neoclassical economists began to consider the unequal distribution of wealth and evidences of market failure. Monopoly power and spillover costs in production, such as the effects of pollution on those outside a business, are examples of market failures. Based on their studies, they advocated government policies in individual markets that could improve society's welfare. As a result, this theory was called **welfare economics**. It considered how redistribution programs might address inequalities and how taxes might correct market imperfections that we call externalities (e.g., pollution).

•**Welfare economics:** study of policies that will increase general welfare; it considers redistribution policies to reduce poverty and taxes to correct market imperfections

Commentary on Neoclassical Theory

As the dominant method today but also the target of significant criticism, neoclassical economics deserves careful assessment. To sum up the method, it examined **rules for getting the most value out of the scarce resources** available to society. The general rule is that **balancing extra costs** and **extra benefits** leads to a maximum of net benefits. Neoclassical economics also examines with rigor Adam Smith's idea that a competitive market system can efficiently allocate resources to various industries. It also pursues Smith's analysis of the harmful effects of monopoly. Important assessments and criticisms of the method follow.

It Ignored Macroeconomics

Neoclassical economic theory during the period from 1880 to 1930 ignored questions about aggregate or macroeconomic outcomes. Neoclassical economists dismissed unemployment as a temporary phenomenon, and ignored the roles of capitalist and government institutions in causing unemployment. When the Great Depression came in 1930, this omission from neoclassical theory appeared as a major defect of the discipline.

Its Philosophy Is Utilitarian and Positivist

Neoclassical theory expresses mathematically an individualist version of Jeremy Bentham's "**utilitarianism**." Pain and pleasure measured by market prices are the basis for choice. Neoclassical micro theory in standard principles of economics courses emphasizes individual decision making. Consumers maximize utility; producers maximize profits. Both economize based on self-interest, without apparent regard for others.

While Bentham focused more on public law-making that would encourage increases in utility for all, neoclasscial economics focuses on individual choice. Even so, Bentham's principle of utility has been increasingly influential in economics and law, as Expansion Point 3.6 notes.

Neoclassical inquiry also has come to rest on the philosophy of **positivism**. August Comte, a social scientist of the mid-1800s, taught that social scientists should consider only observable (positive) data from the human senses to determine matters of fact. Comte refused to consider theological ideas, for example, in describing the world.

Demand and Supply as Positive Value Theory. As positivism, the mainstream neoclassical theory of value describes how actual market prices are determined—prices that can be observed. They refuse to consider metaphysical (unobservable) ideas such as intrinsic value. The model of demand and supply described in detail in this text is, therefore, positivist in philosophy. Don't fret about ultimate values, they urge, but be content to describe what resources and products market activity reveals to be valuable based on willingness to pay and cost to produce.

Positive economics can describe religious behavior, such as the observable fact that middle-aged men attend religious services less frequently than younger and older men. Positivism, however, does not consider the truth or falsity of religious belief. Middle-aged behavior can be explained by observing that their wages are higher and their time more valuable than men of other ages. Middle-aged beliefs cannot be directly observed.

Positive Analysis vs. Normative Analysis. Mainstream economic analysis believes positive analysis is prior to normative policy making. Before saying what we ought to do, we should decide what is true about our world. Or to paraphrase, we *ought* to say first what is. Critics of logical positivism say that a careful analysis of values is morally superior to descriptive methods, because the methods cause their own bias.

"Stewardship" Is Lost

Note how the meaning of economics has moved far away from the idea of stewardship, away from the idea of "getting it right." In theory, an individual could have collectivist, benevolent, or

•**Utilitarianism:** laws and morals should be based on policies that bring the greatest good for the greatest number

•**Positivism:** matters of fact are decided based only on observable (positive) data

•**Positive vs. Normative Analysis:** the distinction between describing "what is" and "what ought to be"; positive analysis comes first, say mainstream economists

Expansion Point 3.6: Jeremy Bentham's Utilitarianism in Secular Law and Economics Today

Jeremy Bentham's *Principles of Morals and Legislation* (1780) began dramatically:

> Nature has placed mankind under the governance of two sovereign masters, *pain* and *pleasure*. It is for them alone to point out what we ought to do, as well as to determine what we shall do. On the one hand the standard of right and wrong, on the other the chain of causes and effects, are fastened to their throne. . . .
>
> A measure of government . . . may be said to be conformable to or dictated by the principle of utility, when in like manner the tendency which it has to augment the happiness of the community is greater than any which it has to diminish it.

Bentham was rejecting contemporary English notions that law was revealed divinely and in nature, and directly contradicting popular legal ideas of English jurist William Blackstone. Compare, for instance, Blackstone's conception of the law from his *Commentaries on the Law:*

> Man, considered as a creature, must necessarily be subject to the laws of his creator. . . . And . . . he should in all points conform to his maker's will. . . . This will of his maker is called the law of nature.
>
> And if our reason were always . . . clear and perfect, unruffled by passions, unclouded by prejudice, . . . we should need no other guide [to natural law] but [reason]. But every man now finds . . . that his reason is corrupt, and his understanding full of ignorance of error.
>
> [Therefore, divine provision] . . . hath been pleased, at sundry times and in divers manners, to discover and enforce its laws by an immediate and direct revelation. The doctrines thus delivered we call the revealed or divine law, and they are to be found only in the holy scriptures. . . .
>
> Upon these two foundations, the law of nature and the law of revelation, depend all human laws; . . . no human laws should be suffered to contradict these.

Do you see parallels in language and yet the sharp contrasts in beliefs about law? For Blackstone, laws and morals depend on the revealed will of God. For Bentham, laws and morals depend only on human calculations of pleasure and pain. Having abandoned ideas of divine law, Bentham advocated a utilitarian calculus that is now summarized in modern theories of consumer behavior that emphasize individual maximizing utility. Bentham's principle of diminishing marginal utility of money became the basis for governmentally enforced redistribution of wealth to increase general welfare.

In law, the "positive" legal theory of the Chicago school follows from Bentham's utilitarian notions of law by teaching that laws should be designed to maximize wealth in society, where wealth measures general welfare. Late twentieth-century movements to decriminalize prostitution and homosexuality as "victimless crimes," and therefore not crimes at all, also follow Bentham's prescriptions for redesigning law. If an act brings only pleasure and no pain, it is not a crime according to utilitarianism. Critics cite injured bystanders in supposedly victimless crimes, such as the spouse and children in many instances of prostitution or adultery. Even so, Bentham's ideas are still influential today.

Sources: Jeremy Bentham, *An Introduction to the Principles of Morals and Legislation* (1780).

William Blackstone, *Commentaries on the Laws of England* (1765).

otherwise pure preferences, but that was never the assumption of economists. Realistically, utilitarian economic analysis contributed to freeing individuals from the bonds of traditional constraints on selfishness and lasciviousness, allowing them to pursue their own desires ("do your own thing" or "do it till you're satisfied," as popular expressions go).

The utilitarian perspective has certainly not been bound by traditional morality generally, or Christian morality in particular. Critics in the 1980s and 1990s, such as Amitai Etzioni and

Amartya Sen, contended that extreme individualism could have socially undesirable consequences, marked by a declining sense of social duty and responsibility.

It Ignores Imperfect Competition

Other economists in the 1920s used neoclassical economics, but questioned assumptions that markets are either purely competitive or purely monopolized. Writing theories of **imperfect competition**, Joan Robinson (1933) and Edward Chamberlain (1950) listed theoretical reasons and actual evidence that many markets were partly (but not fully) monopolistic rather than purely competitive. Their analysis of **market structure** argued for appropriate **government regulation**. Economic theory was starting to address potential incompatibilities of private and social interests.

In spite of its many critics, neoclassical economics, modified to allow for departures from pure competition and strict adherence to a policy of *laissez-faire*, continued to be the core of mainstream economics in the United States in the twentieth century. Neoclassical thought had strong competition, though, from other schools such as the Austrians and Keynesians, to whose work we now turn.

Twentieth-Century Responses to Neoclassical Economics

The ideas of Adam Smith and the economic models and methods of Alfred Marshall comprise much of what is taught as principles of microeconomics in the United States today. Yet other streams of thought have responded to neoclassical thought and contributed significantly to current economic ideas.

Austrian Economics of Individualism

A school of Austrian economists arose in the middle and late 1800s, led by Carl Menger, Friedrich von Weiser, and Eugen von Bohm-Bawerk, all professors at the University of Vienna. Austrian economics continued into the twentieth century and recently experienced a resurgence. Austrians tend to be less willing to abandon ideas of *laissez-faire* than neoclassical theorists, but share the individualistic emphasis in their method.

Nineteenth-Century Austrian Marginalists

Carl Menger engaged members of the German historical school in a great debate over economic method. The Austrians were individualistic and deductive, though not so mathematical as neoclassical economists, while the Germans were historical and nationalistic. The Austrians analyzed individual decision making based on diminishing marginal utility and marginal thinking in general. **Friedrich von Weiser** introduced the concept of opportunity cost as appropriate for efficient decision making.

•**Austrian economics:** individualistic in method and philosophy

Austrians rejected not only German-historical nationalism but

also Marxist socialism and communism. For his part in defending individualistic capitalism and the payment of interest as a legitimate earned income, **Eugen von Bohm-Bawerk** was labeled the "Dean of bourgeois economics" by his critics. Bohm-Bawerk justified interest as a reward for people who would postpone consumption in order to lend money and goods to those who value present consumption even more highly. He also charged that the main complaint of socialists was not really with capitalism but with the human condition of scarcity, "with which socialism would have to cope just as capitalism did" (Spiegel 1991, 539).

Twentieth-Century Austrians

The Austrian tradition continued into the 1900s, as did the debate with socialists. Ludwig von Mises, Joseph Schumpeter, and Friedrich von Hayek are the best-known Austrian economists of the 1900s. They wrote against a growing tide of socialism in economic scholarship and in government policy in Europe.

Ludwig von Mises complained that socialist planners could not set prices of resources and products correctly without capitalist free markets and, therefore, could not achieve efficient allocation of resources. He was most dogmatic in his rejection of any government intervention, even in the regulation of banks and the supply of money. Von Mises was most concerned with studying actual human action rather than with devising socialist dreams.

Friedrich von Hayek described England's coming socialist experiment as *The Road to Serfdom* (1944), comparing it unfavorably to the start of socialist enterprise in Soviet Russia and Nazi Germany. Hayek noted that kind-hearted visionaries start socialist movements, but the worst rise to power because they alone are willing to exercise the brutal power needed to force individuals to adopt the collective vision. He also raised questions about who will plan and choose for whom under socialism. Whose vision will rule?

Joseph Schumpeter emphasized the role of the capitalist boss as an entrepreneur, rather than an exploiter of labor. The entrepreneur innovates, devising industrial and commercial applications for inventions and new ideas. While entrepreneurs destroy the strongholds of existing capitalist bosses, they at the same time create new opportunities for investment and consumption. Capitalism is therefore a continual process of **creative destruction**. Schumpeter warned, though, that capitalism would begin to fail as it destroyed the social relations that had earlier nourished it, particularly under the control of "absentee stockholders" and "salaried" workers (Spiegel 1991, 544-45).

Austrian economics emphasizes individual freedom and begins economic analysis as the deductive study of individual choice. While reaching conclusions similar to English classical and neoclassical political economy, the Austrians avoid mathematical economic analysis. For Austrians, economic analysis is the study of individual behavior and how it varies under changing economic conditions. The Austrians, especially von Mises, stress a method called praxeology, the study of actual human behavior (or practice). They reject the socialists' theoretical speculations, saying they don't understand human behavior.

Keynesian Macroeconomics

In the 1930s, the **Great Depression** and 25 percent unemployment caused economists to begin to think much more about aggregate economic issues. **John Maynard Keynes** presented new ideas in his 1936 book, *The General Theory of Employment, Interest and Money*. He contended that a collapse of private spending for consumption, initiated by a collapse in private business investment, led to the Great Depression. Business people stopped investing because of the stock market crash of 1929 and the subsequent decline in expected profitability of new investment.

Falling investment then set in motion **expenditure-multiplier effects** on income and spending. An initial drop in investment caused a greater drop in national income. Low demand for investment goods such as buildings, machines, and inventories caused employers to lay off workers in those industries. Due to the layoffs, worker income fell, causing them to buy less. Falling consumer spending then caused further layoffs of workers and further declines in income. As the cycles of layoffs, income cuts, and spending cuts continued, the initial decline in investment was multiplied into greater declines in national income and employment.

Keynesian economics started **macroeconomics**, which examines causes of unemployment, inflation, and the business cycle. Keynesians believe that the free market is unstable, and has no automatic adjustment mechanisms such as Say's Law. Keynesians advocate heavy government intervention to stabilize the economy at full employment. Fiscal and perhaps monetary policies could offset fluctuations in the market economy. With the economy stabilized at full employment, free markets could once again allocate scarce resources.

For Keynes, economic analysis was an instrument for demonstrating the inherent **macroeconomic instability of market economies**, the value of government stabilization policies, and mild programs of redistribution of wealth that would still leave control of wealth largely in the hands of private individuals.

Monetarism

In the 1940s and 1950s, Milton Friedman led a resurgence of neoclassical ideas that government should keep out of markets. He also gave a macroeconomic response to Keynes' explanation

- **Great Depression:** collapse in global economic activity in the 1930s; unemployment in the U.S. reached 25% of the labor force

- **Keynesians** believe that changes in aggregate spending are the most important determinants of economic activity.

- **Expenditure-multiplier effects:** an initial shock to private spending leads to greater eventual declines in national income and employment

• **Monetarist:** an economist who believes changes in the money supply affect economic activity in the short run and the price level in the long run

of the Great Depression. Friedman and other **monetarists** blame the Federal Reserve's (also know as the Fed) restrictive monetary policies for the severity of the Great Depression. Friedman and Anna Schwartz (1960) concluded this by examining minutes of the Fed's own Board of Governors' meetings for evidence. Their finding was that government policy, not private investment or consumption, destabilized the market economy. Most importantly, the Federal Reserve had failed to carry out its chief function in a banking crisis of being a lender of last resort for failing banks. Moreover, the Fed Governors did not understand the multiple effects that a $1 drop in bank reserves would have on total money supply. They therefore misunderstood the importance of offsetting currency drains from the banking system as fearful depositors panicked and withdrew their deposits.

Friedman also complained about the redistributional effects and inflationary effects of increasing the size and scope of government in the United States during the Great Depression and after World War II. The federal government's growing regulation of the economy shifted resources from a productive private sector to an inefficient public sector. When the federal government funded spending for new programs with Treasury debt instead of tax increases, the Federal Reserve steadily monetized the new debt until 1979. Monetizing the debt means that the Federal Reserve issued new money in order to buy U.S. Treasury bonds that had been sold to the public. Monetizing all of this new debt each year, Friedman contended, led to faster and faster inflation with no long-term effect on output or productivity.

To monetarists, then, the quantity of money is a crucial determinant of the level of economic activity in the short run and the level of inflation in the long run. **Money matters**! While Friedman and the monetarists were ascendant in the 1970s when inflation was a major economic problem, their influence waned in the 1980s. For monetarism to guide central bankers, money must have a stable relation to the level of economic activity. After 1982, however, the previously stable relation ended.

Chicago School

Neoclassical and Austrian economics have been fused in twentieth-century economic thought of the Chicago school, whose best-known member is **Milton Friedman**, a contributor to price theory as well as monetarism. For Friedman, economic analysis should apply **methodological individualism** to blunt the socialist criticisms of free-market economies. Methodological individualism studies individual choices to understand the economy. Milton and Rose Friedman's book *Free to Choose* (1980) asserted that allowing individuals to be "free to choose" is efficient, while government intervention in economic activity is not. Critics find the book simplistic, but commend it for its power to persuade.

George Stigler and Gary Becker also made important applications of methodological individualism to economic analysis. Stigler advanced price theory and the economic analysis of information. Becker contributed to the economic analysis of household decisions, race, and investments in human capital. All three of these Chicago economists are Nobel Laureates in economics.

Both the Austrian school and Chicago School promote a libertarian philosophy, especially of economic liberty. They do not assume, however, that humans always act as extreme individualists. A common theme among these writers is that free humans will spontaneously form their own associations that promote both individual and group interests. Such voluntary organizations are in fact found in any free society. A criticism of the libertarian philosophy is that it promotes freedom to the highest human goal. It seems to idolize individual choice, rather than use freedom as an instrument, along with other instruments, to achieve goals such as justice and mercy.

Public-Choice Theory

During and after the Great Depression in the United States, the role of the federal government in the market economy expanded, encroaching on the private sector's traditional tasks. But redistribution programs were not effective in eliminating poverty and seemed to cater more to special interests than to the needy in general. Economic statistics of administrative costs of social welfare programs showed that more than half of federal dollars for poor relief did not actually reach the poor, but were spent creating federal bureaucracies to administer welfare. In addition, social welfare programs subsidized the wealthy and middle class as much as or more than the poor. Critics said that the minimum wage supported incomes of mainly middle-class youth more than incomes of heads of poor households, who generally either did not work or worked at wages above minimum. Subsidies to college students helped the middle class as well as the poor. Agricultural farm-price supports for such things as sugar transferred money, not from the rich to the poor, but from those who had little political organization and power to those who had much. Government regulation also began to stifle initiative, as it had in the Mercantilist period.

In the 1960s and 1970s, a few economists began to question the role of government as a benevolent, all-knowing dictator. **Public-choice theory** arose to study how government officials supply public money in response to the demands of their constituents. It assumes that **politicians seek to maximize their own utility** rather than society's welfare. Maximizing votes for reelection is their goal. Politicians' decisions, for example, reflect a built-in **bias** toward public-budget deficits because voters prefer increasing government spending to raising taxes. Politicians also cater to **special interest groups** to get their votes, spreading the costs of these gifts

• **Public-choice theory:** politicians supply public spending to voters who demand it; politicians act in their own interests, seeking to maximize votes

among a general population that does not know what it is buying with taxes or new debt. Individual voters stay **rationally ignorant** because informing themselves about politics and government seems to have no significant effect at the ballot box.

Public-choice economists stress the **importance of rules**, especially constitutional rules that constrain public policy and individual decisions of politicians and bureaucrats. Rationally ignorant voters cannot be expected to provide guidance. Yet giving responsibility for directing government to lobbyists and their special interests is like appointing the fox to guard the chicken coop. Nor can politicians be expected to use their own reason to govern in the general interest. Therefore, economists such as **James Buchanan** have shifted attention away from the "rule of reason" and have begun to focus on the "reason for rules."

Emphasizing **constitutional rules** seems to return to the Greek notion of economics as getting it right. Public-choice theory applies economic analysis of self-interested behavior to the actions of politicians and bureaucrats in order to show how their behavior must be constrained to promote the public welfare. A constitution is the written direction of the people, as masters, to the politicians elected to serve as stewards.

Other Recent Integrative Schools

A key distinctive of the various other schools emerging in the later half of the 1900s is that each seems to integrate ideas from at least two of the schools listed above. Expansion Point 3.7 reviews these other schools very briefly. The one mentioned most in this text is the new institutional school of thought, which has made the most innovative contributions to economics in the past few years.

Is There a "Christian Economics"?

At the start of the chapter, you read about a movement of Christian economists who have been reviving the idea of economics as stewardship of God's resources. Does a distinctly Christian approach to economic analysis exist?

"No," say certain Christian economists. The positive facts and methods of economics are universal and don't vary depending on the economist's particular religious or moral beliefs. A rising price caused by a decrease in supply due to a drought is a fact, and the method of demand and supply is a logical system of ideas, neither of which are especially religious or sacrilegious. Expansion Point 3.8 presents the views of several Christian economists who have adopted this view, including Paul Heyne and J. David Richardson.

And yet our use of positive economic analysis is never completely value neutral, other Christian economists say. As an abstract method, economic analysis may filter out important

Expansion Point 3.7: Strands of Economic Ideas in Late Twentieth-Century Schools of Thought

From the major schools of economic thought arose several twentieth-century hybrids. For instance, three schools emerged by combining the Keynesian tradition with other schools. Certain **Post-Keynesians**, such as Joan Robinson, interpreted Keynes through the lense of Marxist exploitation of labor. They see the inflation process as a "wage-price" spiral due to class conflict between labor and capital. Post-Keynesians emphasize nationalization of industry and income redistribution. Many institutionalists in the late 1900s were also Post-Keynesians. Economic analysis for the Post-Keynesians continues a moderated Marxist criticism of capitalism.

Economists of the "**neoclassical synthesis**," such as Paul Samuelson, took ideas from Keynes that are more compatible with individual freedom in markets. They combine a Keynesian view of macroeconomic instability of market economies with a Marshallian view of the efficiency of the market system with its dependence on coordinating decentralized decisions of individuals through the price system.

In the 1980s and 1990s, economists with a resurgent interest in Keynesian theory took the label **new Keynesians**. They say that human expectations depend on imperfect information and are irrational. New Keynesians also say that prices and wages adjust sluggishly to aggregate economic shocks such as oil-price increases and food shortages, causing recessions to be longer than they need to be, unless government policy stabilizes the macroeconomy.

Out of the classical emphasis on automatic adjustment comes **new classical economics** and its analysis of the macroeconomic effects of people's "rational expectations" about the future. New classical economists believe that business cycles are primarily created by real economic shocks such as droughts or oil shortages. They use mathematics to extend classical analysis of human rationality in economic decisions and classical criticism of government policy. New classical economics changed thinking in the 1980s about the power of government to actually influence economic activity in the long run.

The 1980s and 1990s also saw renewed interest in the institutions of capitalism. Following ideas of John R. Commons and Ronald Coase, **new institutionalists** applied rational-choice theory to studies of transactions costs, various forms of economic organization (called the "new microeconomics of the firm"), and the institutional underpinnings of market economies. Commons investigated the legal basis for market economies. Coase, a Chicago economist and Nobel Prize winner, explained that hierarchical firms exist in a market economy to minimize transactions costs. Another Nobel Prize winner, Douglass North, cited neoclassical economics for ignoring the historical institutions of market economies. While not antagonistic to economic freedom, the new institutionalists see economic analysis as the study of the rules and play of the game (as in the rules of baseball and the managers' and players' strategies for play).

information and therefore may induce an ethical bias. Designing economic policies also requires prior moral principles to rank economic goals such as freedom, equality, or minimal living standards. John Tiemstra (1993) and Roland Hocksbergen (1994), therefore, urge a rejection of mainstream neoclassical economics (see Expansion Point 3.8).

Economic debates often center on whether efficiency or equity should be the standard by which to judge economic policies. Christian stewardship includes both standards: we should ensure

Expansion Point 3.8: What Should Christian Economists Do?

Articles in *Christian Scholar's Review* and the Association of Christian Economists' *Bulletin* have expressed various views on the possibility of a distinctly Christian economics and about what Christian economists should do. Here are summaries of various perspectives.

Gerald Brock: "The government policy context offers an ideal opportunity to mix Christian value judgments with formal economic analysis." Like Daniel of the Old Testament, we should be "diligent" in studies, "especially honest," tactful with authority (even when mistreated), and ready to give "wise advice." ("The Christian Economist as Dream Interpreter," *ACE Bulletin*, [Fall 1994]: 5-8.)

Earl Grinnols: Since Christian belief should make a difference in action, investigate how such beliefs should make an economic difference. Discover how to test a hypothesis such as the following: "A society of guileless individuals will outperform a society of dishonest individuals." ("Panel Discussion: What Should ACE Do?" *ACE Bulletin* ([Fall 1994]: 34-36.)

James Halteman: Compare secular economic systems to find the one that does the least damage to Kingdom values. Encourage Christians to live accountable lives in community with one another, rather than materialistic lives directed by individual decisions. Submit economic decisions such as buying a house or car to one another. ("An Anabaptist Approach to Economic Systems," *ACE Bulletin* [Fall 1990]; and *Market Capitalism & Christianity* [Grand Rapids, MI: Baker Books, 1988].)

Paul Heyne: No "distinctly Christian way of doing economics exists." Searching the Old Testament for principles to apply to current policy is fruitless because Christians are not under the law. "[L]ive together as if we were justified by nothing but the Grace of God, . . . invite others to join the community." ("Passing Judgments," *ACE Bulletin* [Spring 1994]: 9-10.)

Roland Hocksbergen: Neoclassical theory has fallen victim to a postmodern criticism of science and positivism. Christian economists should build a new distinctly Christian economics based on "wholistic meaning, rather than economic 'causality.'" ("Is There a Christian Economics?" *Christian Scholar's Review* 24, no. 2 [December 1994]: 126-42.)

John Lunn & Robin Klay: Utility is a broad concept, not narrowly selfish, and the neoclassical model predicts Christian and non-Christian economic behavior at the margin. Use it. ("The Neoclassical Model in a Postmodern World," *Christian Scholar's Review* 24, no. 2 [December 1994]: 143-63.)

John Mason: Apply moral principles of Scripture to public policy. U.S. welfare policies to help the poor should recognize biblical principles that, for example, the family is worth preserving, even if the policies are inefficient. Also, Christian economists should inform those who write on economics and know theology well but who don't know economics. ("Panel Discussion: What Should ACE Do?" *ACE Bulletin* [Fall 1994]: 36-39; "Biblical Teaching and the Objectives of Welfare Policy in the U.S.," *ACE Bulletin* [Fall 1993]: 7-30.)

J. David Richardson: Do mainstream economic analysis. Perform standard statistical tests of economic hypotheses, but with a sensitivity toward Christian values and beliefs. Don't abandon the discipline for theology or mere economic commentary. ("What Should [Christian] Economics Do? . . . Economics!" *ACE Bulletin* [Spring 1994]: 12-15; "Frontiers in Economics and Christian Scholarship," *Christian Scholar's Review* [June 1988]: 381-400.)

John Tiemstra: Abandon the positivist, utilitarian, scarcity model of neoclassical theory, recognize our stewardship, and use other approaches such as institutional and post-Keynesian economics. Don't ignore beliefs. What we know as Christians helps us to understand the economy. ("What Should Christian Economists Do? Doing Economics, But Differently," *ACE Bulletin* [Spring 1994]: 3-11; "Christianity and Economics: A Review of Recent Literature," *Christian Scholar's Review* [1993]: 227-47; Tiemstra et al., *Reforming Economics* [Lewiston, NY: Mellen, 1990].)

minimum living standards while also eliminating waste in resource use. As a result, strict insistence on either efficiency or equity imposes an ethical bias. John Mason (see Expansion Point 3.8) contends that an economist's positive emphasis only on efficiency in public welfare programs is wrongheaded. Since welfare programs are notoriously wasteful, making efficiency a primary goal can interfere with the biblical mandate to care for the poor.

Chapter Summary

1. Economics has meant various things at different times and places in history, from doing the right thing to pursuing the economic interests of the individual, state, or political party.

2. The Greek notion of *oikovoμous* meant stewardship of a household's resources, following the directions of the master of the house.

3. The biblical notion of stewardship followed the Greek idea, in which God is the Master who sets rules for living and using resources. The church fathers and medieval Christian theologians who wrote about economic ideas and Church doctrine adopted this stewardship idea.

4. Mercantilist pamphlet writers of the 1600s and 1700s were economic advocates for special interests, but they gave heed to the economic interests of the crown. They assumed that a nation's wealth consisted mainly of precious metals in its treasury.

5. The French physiocrats of the 1700s advocated for individual interests so as to promote the overall interests of the nation. The term physiocrats referred to their belief that land was the source of all wealth.

6. Classical English political economy from 1776 to 1870 adopted a more cosmopolitan approach to economic analysis. By promoting individual interests and the freedom to trade, wealth in various nations could grow simultaneously. Adam Smith advocated a system of natural liberty in which specialization and division of labor would automatically promote a nation's wealth, through a harmony of interests. This wealth was not gold and silver in the treasury, but the productive capacity of a nation's people and their accumulated machinery and skill.

7. Critics of English political economy included the German historical school, American institutional economists, Karl Marx and other socialists, and the English literary critics.

8. Austrian economists, critics of the critics, emphasized individual choice in capitalism, and opposed German nationalism and Marxist state socialism.

9. Neoclassical economists used mathematical, deductive analysis to refine and explain classical principles of the market economy. They focused primarily on what is called mainstream microeconomics, a study of individual maximizing choices, and a balancing of forces that tend toward equilibrium. Neoclassical theory, therefore, is positivist and utilitarian in philosophy, controversial characteristics that have generated significant criticism. Positive economic analysis of "what is" should precede normative analysis of "what ought to be." It ignored macroeconomic problems and ethical concepts like stewardship.

10. Welfare economists examine the ability to improve social welfare with redistribution policies and with taxes on production methods that impose external costs such as pollution. They also show the welfare effects of imperfect competition.

11. Keynesian economics introduced depression economics and the general field of macroeconomics. Keynes believed in the instability of income and employment in market economies, due to multiplier effects. Initial shocks to investment spending and production after the stock market crash of 1929 were multiplied into greater shocks because of circular effects of falling income on consumption and falling consumption on income. These multiplier effects on spending and employment led to the severity of the Great Depression, Keynes thought.

12. Milton Friedman and monetarist economists emphasized the powerful effects of money on economic activity and prices, and the stability of free-enterprise market economies. Government was a major source of instability in the Great Depression, especially through the Federal Reserve's monetary policies. The Fed failed to offset currency drains from the banking system, they contend, leading to falling money supply and economic activity.

13. Public-choice theory treats politicians and bureaucrats like any other humans: they make decisions based on their own self-interest. Politicians don't promote the general welfare; they use political power to promote their own power and reelection. Public-choice emphasis on the "reason for rules" is a return towards an economics of stewardship for public officials.

14. Recent hybrid schools include Post-Keynesians, neoclassical synthesis, new classical economists, new Keynesians, and new institutionalists.

15. There is no distinct Christian economics, but there is a growing literature that seeks to bring a Christian perspective on stewardship to the evaluation of economic analysis.

PROBLEMS FOR PRACTICE

3.1 List the various views of what economics has meant for different writers and schools of thought since the time of Plato's *Republic*.

3.2 What exactly did Adam Smith say in the *Wealth of Nations* about the role of "self-love" in a market economy? Did Smith preach that greed is good?

3.3 What was the controversy in the history of economic thought about deductive and inductive economic analysis? How has the conflict been resolved, if at all, by mainstream economists?

3.4 What was Karl Marx's criticism of capitalism? Did Marx have an accurate example of how the revenues of the firm are split among capitalist owners, their workers, and other income earners? Explain.

3.5 Did the early institutional economist Thorstein Veblen have the same view toward capitalism as the more recent new institutionalists?

3.6 Are Keynesian and monetarist views of the causes of the Great Depression similar or different? What about their views of the stability of a market economy and the need for government intervention to stabilize the macroeconomy?

3.7 When did economics become a science? What change in thinking accompanied this change?

For your portfolio:

3.8* Choose three of the schools of thought explained above, or particular writers from three different schools, no more than two from one century. Read about the schools or writers in a history of economic thought book. Learn more of the details of each one. Identify what other issues they covered. For specific writers, find their original works and read a chapter or two. Write a brief summary of your research for each one. It is not important to learn everything about each one; just learn something well and write about it. If assigned, do this problem together with 3.9.

3.9* For three economic schools of thought or writers, one each from the eighteenth, nineteenth, and twentieth centuries, find a history book that gives some of the background of the period in which they wrote. You may want to read an economic history text for historical analysis of economic ideas and economic analysis of history. What was happening in those countries when the schools or writers were active? If assigned, do this question in conjunction with 3.8.

For class discussion:

3.10 Who do you think are the top five economists since the 1600s? Base your answers on this chapter and anything else you know about economic thought.

3.11 Discuss Bentham's utilitarian views of the appropriate basis for law and morals. Is it possible, as the text suggests, that traditional morals could be consistent with Bentham's ideal of the greatest good for the greatest number? Bring specific evidence about the topics to bear in presenting the different views on this question. To prepare, you might read a bit more about utilitarianism.

3.12 With which two economists or schools of thought in the main body of the text do you most agree, and with which two do you least agree? Explain why.

3.13 With which late-twentieth-century economist or school of thought in Expansion Point 3.7 do you most agree, and with which do you least agree? Explain.

3.14 With which Christian economist in Expansion Point 3.8 do you most agree, and with which do you least agree? Explain.

3.15 What biblical or other moral principles, if any, do you think can and should be integrated into economic analysis? Are there dangers of such integration? Explain.

See Appendix A for hints/answers to starred (*) questions.

Chapter 4

Economic Behavior

Rationality, Costs, and Benefits

What this chapter will help you think about:

1. What are the principles of rational human choice?
2. What are the implications of assuming rational human choice?
3. Were Nazi political appeals to German voters rational?
4. What are the major criticisms of rational-choice theory?
5. What other aspects of human behavior broaden our view of economic activity, and how do they address the criticisms of rational choice?
6. Are economists more selfish than other people?

To understand economic activity in general requires that we understand individual behavior and the social, legal, and natural constraints on that behavior. This chapter introduces important ideas about human economic behavior.

Mainstream Assumptions about Human Economic Behavior

What distinguishes economic analysis from other social sciences? Is it that economists study the economic activities of consumption, production, distribution, and related commercial and regulatory activities, while other social scientists do not? No, this is not the distinctive of economics. All social sciences examine these activities more or less. Mainstream economics distinguishes itself through its assumptions that human behavior is **rational** and that people choose their actions thoughtfully. To understand the discipline and its critics requires understanding rationality.

- **Rational choice** is self-interested, and optimal.

Individuals Choose Rationally, Within Limits

- **Limits to optimizing behavior:** limited knowledge, transactions costs

Rationality implies that humans are self-interested calculating optimizers. **Incomplete information**, however, limits people's ability to optimize. The **transactions costs** of making otherwise beneficial exchanges also impose limits. While mainstream economists assume rational behavior in their theories, most do not assume that people always act rationally. Economists generally understand human imperfections, but they believe that assuming rationality is helpful in predicting average economic behavior. The principles of rational behavior follow.

People Are Self-Interested

What does it mean to assume that people are **self-interested**? Acting on self-interest sounds disgraceful, but it has a broader meaning than being selfish. Pursuing self-interest means attending to your own concerns, whether they are about selfish interests or higher aspirations. Perhaps you run a business ruthlessly like Scrooge, without regard to others, scraping and gouging for every bit of profit that you can get. That does sound selfish. Perhaps, however, you manage a soup kitchen and your "self-interest" is to find the best price and quality you can when you buy the groceries to feed 300 people a day.

- **Self-interested behavior:** attending to your own concerns, but not necessarily selfishly

People Optimize

When making economic decisions, humans will **optimize** (do the best they can). That is, people will maximize benefits, minimize costs, and balance various competing interests. For example, business owners maximize profits, and consumers maximize their own satisfaction. People try to minimize the costs of achieving their goals. Managers optimize the productivity of resources by balancing the mixes of those resources—capital, labor, energy, and so on—in various production processes. In simple terms, optimizing humans do the best they can with what they have.

- **Optimize:** to maximize or minimize a value, or to balance competing interests and generally do the best you can

People Have Limited Knowledge

Knowledge about economic opportunities is valuable, especially knowledge of the locations of the best price and quality of goods and services. Because **knowledge is scarce**, no one is fully informed about the exact state of their world and the opportunities available to them. Optimizing behavior implies, however, that consumers endeavor to make themselves knowledgeable about the relative costs and benefits of their alternative choices in consumption, production, and exchange.

- **Knowledge is scarce:** as with other resources, information is limited and costly to obtain

People Search for Information

Since searching for information is costly, people will spend time and money to gather only the information that they need. They will search, for example, for information on product prices, availability, and quality. They will not search for all possible information. They will balance the cost of learning more against the expected benefits of the extra information. The last time you shopped, how many stores did you search before buying clothing? Most likely, you did not search every possible store. You may have checked the newspaper advertisements, however, for current sale prices.

Because people demand information, others will supply it at a price. The scarcity of knowledge creates a market for information about many things, including knowledge of the weather (which is very valuable to farmers), job opportunities, items for sale or rent, and saleable skills. The newspaper classified advertisements create a market for information, as do bookstores that carry do-it-yourself books and other instruction manuals.

People Seek to Reduce Transactions Costs

A recent addition to our understanding of rational choice is that people will arrange their public or private affairs as best they can to reduce transactions costs. They do so by setting rules, making agreements with others, and following customs about what is or is not appropriate economic behavior.

Government rulers, for example, will set tax-collection rules to minimize the costs of gathering revenues, as in the rules that force U.S. businesses to pay employees federal and state income taxes before giving wages to the workers. Business managers will reduce the likelihood of losing money in a deal by paying lawyers to write contracts that protect their interests. People will agree to drive on the right side of the road where that is the legal convention to reduce the possibility of having a costly accident.

These principles form the core of rational-choice theory. People are self-interested. They do the best they can. Their knowledge is limited, but they shop in the market for information so long as it is beneficial. And they arrange their affairs and follow conventions so as to reduce transactions costs.

Implications of Rationality

- **Implications of rationality:** Individual people
  1) know what is best,
  2) form rational expectations,
  3) compare costs and benefits, and
  4) decide deliberately.

What are the economic implications of the assumption that human behavior depends on rational, optimizing, informed choices? Assuming rationality raises at least four questions. Who should decide for the individual? How do people form expectations about the future? Do people really make logical comparisons of costs and benefits? And are individual choices always deliberate? Economists' answers generate controversy.

People Generally Know What Is Best for Themselves

Normally, individuals who are rational and well informed will know what meets their needs best and what they want most. Economists who hold this view don't want a paternalistic government to make choices for the individual. The role of government is to solve problems of social choice when individuals' interests directly conflict, and when one individual's decisions have negative effects on others.

When government does try to choose for individuals, bureaucrats often design programs that fail to recognize the variety of needs and wants of individuals. One size does not fit all. Martin Feldstein has said that the nationalized British health-care system, for instance, lacked a process to let individuals trade for more or less health care. The system of free health care could not cater to individual desires without forcing them to pay to visit fee-for-service health-care providers outside the system (Feldstein 1995, 28-31).

People's Expectations of the Future Are Rational

The future is unknown, but humans can benefit by making a best guess. Economists ask, how do people form expectations about it? Do they, for example, rely entirely on the past? People do use past knowledge, but they also use knowledge of the present as an indicator of future changes. By learning about their present economic system, they form **rational expectations** of the future that are correct on average. Assuming rational expectations is not the same as assuming that people always forecast correctly. Rationality allows for surprises.

- **Rational expectations:** on average, people are correct in their estimates of future economic conditions

An important implication of rationality is that very few "hot tips" about the stock market will make you rich, as explained in Expansion Point 4.1. Critics of the theory of rational expectations point to speculative fevers in stock markets and real estate as evidence that markets are not always priced properly.

Rational-expectations theory also contributes to our understanding of how people make loan contracts. For example, when making loan contracts, borrowers and lenders must each predict what the rate of inflation of prices will be over the term of the loan. This enables them to know what a reasonable interest rate will be. An interest rate of six percent per year when prices

Expansion Point 4.1: Can You Make Money On a Hot Stock Tip?

Your friend calls to tell you that, if you act fast, you can profit from a great opportunity to invest in the stock of a new company that makes revolutionary inflatable packaging. Soon everyone will be using it. He read about the company's announcement in the morning newspaper and thought you would want to know. He tried to call before noon but could not get through. Should you get on the Internet and place an order for the stock?

If expectations are rational and the information is already in the news, market watchers will know that this price is about to head higher. How long do you think it would take for informed market participants to place enough buy orders to bid up the price of the stock? The theory of efficient markets suggests that, because stock markets efficiently incorporate all new information, it will take no time at all. If the announcement were in the early morning edition of today's newspaper, the news must have broken first the previous day on the electronic news. Since many market investors watch these news services, if the announcement came by 1:30 P.M., the market price of the stock may well have reflected the good news by 1:35, if not sooner. By the time you bought, you would be paying the stock share's full value, which would reflect the higher expected future earnings of the firm.

Efficient markets suggest that you can't make money on hot tips that are really lukewarm. If you are far from the source of the news, and if you do not act immediately, you will not, *on average*, profit by the news. You might still profit by any "excessive exuberance" of later investors who drive the stock price well above its sustainable level, but you must know when to sell before the price returns to a reasonable value.

Critics of rational-expectations make light of the theory with a joke. If you see a $10 bill on the ground, they say, you should not stop to pick it up. If it were really a $10 bill, someone else would have picked it up first.

are rising at 12 percent per year is great for the borrower, but will cause the lender to lose money. If past annual inflation has been three percent for ten years, people might naively expect that inflation would be three percent in the coming year. Rationally formed expectations also will consider whether the central bank is changing its policy and rapidly increasing the money supply and volume of credit. Such expansionary monetary policies would lead to higher future inflation. The prudent lender must therefore charge higher interest rates. Lenders who don't understand central banking may be fooled once, but they will then learn to watch the central bank and will do better the next time.

People Compare Extra Costs with Extra Benefits

Rationality implies that people compare expected costs and benefits of various activities before making choices. A rational person, though, does not merely compare total costs and benefits. A rational person compares extra costs and extra benefits. Economists call the extra costs of one more unit of a good, service, or resource the **marginal cost** and the extra benefits of an extra unit the **marginal benefit**.

- **Marginal cost:** extra costs of one extra unit of a good, service, or resource
- **Marginal benefit:** extra benefits from one extra unit of a good, service, or resource

Marginal benefits and marginal costs are different for the buyer and the seller in an exchange. Let's say that you buy one more pair of shoes at a price of $40, but you were willing to pay up to $60 for them. The price you pay of $40 is the marginal cost, and the value you expect from them is the expected marginal benefit. In this case, since you would have paid up to $60, we can assume that the marginal benefit to you of the shoes equals $60.

When a shoe store sells you the shoes, however, the $40 price is the store's marginal benefit of the sale. The store's marginal cost of the shoes is the extra expense of selling them to you. Extra expense includes factory or wholesale price of the shoes and the sales commission. Perhaps marginal cost might be $32.

Since people compare benefits and costs, changes to perceived benefits or costs will alter human behavior. This principle is the basis for most mainstream economic analysis today. It is summarized in the statement, "**Incentives matter**." Economists believe that, on average, they can predict responses to changing incentives using economic theory.

- **Incentives matter:** people compare extra costs and extra benefits of an activity; benefits are an incentive and costs are a disincentive to action

Every Human Action Is Rational

Rational-choice theorists believe that every human action is rational. People do not generally stumble into decisions, even those that turn out badly. Their assessments of costs and benefits may be mistaken or focused only on the short run, but their decisions are deliberate, informed, and self-interested.

What seems like irrational behavior may actually be a result of careful planning with occasional mistakes. A plane leaving an airport gate without enough fuel to complete its flight might seem to be the result of irrational airport fuel policies. Why not just fill up the tanks? Yet, as Expansion Point 4.2 explains, the present fueling process balances costs and benefits, even though it increases the risk of errors in calculating fuel loads for each flight.

Rational-choice theory proposes controversial motives for human behavior. A donor, for example, actually engages in a form of exchange when giving a "gift." The donor is either deliberately creating an obligation to be fulfilled at a later date, or is paying an obligation created by receiving an earlier gift. In other words, there are no purely selfless gifts.

A provocative application of this theory is that inheritances from parents are not pure gifts to their children. Parents supposedly use the promise of an inheritance and the threat of disinheritance to control their children. For more discussion and evidence about a rational-choice explanation of inheritances, see Expansion Point 4.3.

In long-term-care psychiatric hospitals, economists have tested the extent to which changing costs and benefits matter for people who appear to behave "irrationally." Researchers first established reward systems for patients. Make your bed to earn three coupons. Refrain from hitting your roommate during the day to earn five coupons a day. Patients could use coupons to buy candy, soda, and other items at a hospital store. After establishing a mini-economy, researchers then changed the wages and prices. Patients responded

Expansion Point 4.2: Fill 'er Up? Not at That Price! Why Airplanes Fly on Half-Empty Fuel Tanks

Between 1986 and 1995 at U.S. airports, 39 airplanes left their gates without enough fuel to make their flights. Sixteen of them actually took off. How could airport maintenance workers forget to fill up these planes? If tanks were routinely topped, there would be no worry about running out in midair.

Under airline policy, however, pilots order only enough fuel to make their flight, plus a set margin. Why? Because the cost of fuel is the second largest expense of running an airline. A U.S. airline might buy 2 to 3 billion gallons of jet fuel a year. With tanks filled, takeoffs and flights would cost even more, as jets burned extra fuel to lift the fuel itself. To conserve, pilots carefully calculate fuel loads. Occasionally, due to weariness, distractions, or hurry, pilots do miscalculate and their planes make unscheduled landings. The process of taking on a partial load, however, is intentional, helping to keep ticket prices low.

Source: Julie Schmit, "Study Shows Jets Running on Fumes," *Rochester Democrat and Chronicle*, Tuesday, April 4, 1995:1A (Gannett News Service).

Expansion Point 4.3: Rational-Choice Theory on Leaving an Inheritance

The Hebrew proverb says that leaving an inheritance results from righteousness and perhaps a sense of duty: a good parent leaves something behind for grandchildren. Rational-choice theory, however, ignores the difference between a good and bad parent and the concept of duty. It explains inheritances in terms of the parent's self-interest.

> ***"A good man leaves an inheritance for his children's children."***
> *Proverbs 13:22 NIV*

According to one explanation, inheritances are the residual from a rational calculation of the benefits and costs of saving money for retirement. The wise saver will have extra funds at death because of a rational plan not to run out of retirement funds before death. Leaving an inheritance for children is a statistical accident.

The empirical evidence about bequests in the United States, however, created a problem for rational-choice economists. Inheritances left over after people died were too big, on average, to be fully explained by a desire not to run out of money before they died. Parents seemed to be intending to leave money to their children. Rational theorists then developed an alternative explanation: a parent's gifts were really part of an exchange. Parents who left large bequests were using potential inheritances to control their children's behavior.

Rational choice does seem on the surface to explain one recent change in U.S. saving behavior—an increase in retirees' investments in annuities. An annuity pays a constant amount of money until death, at which time the investment company that paid the annuity, not the heirs, owns the funds. Rational-choice theorists say that this supports their view that parents are really interested in providing for retirement till death, not in leaving an inheritance. Buying an annuity, however, is also consistent with a parent's desire not to run out of retirement funds so as not to be "a burden to the children." Furthermore, recent psychological experiments have shown that humans do indeed act benevolently at times, apart from narrow calculations of self-interest.

rationally. At higher prices of candy bars, patients bought less candy. Given greater rewards for making the bed, patients made their beds more often, and so on (Nicholson 1993).

A more controversial implication of rational-choice theory is that people's decisions to join the Nazi Party in Germany in the 1930s were rational. Recent evidence suggests that Germans who joined did so for economic reasons, such as increased job security due to Nazi promises of protectionist trade policies. While not justifying the Nazi horror, Expansion Point 4.4 explores this controversy and the nature of the evidence in more detail.

Property Rights Affect Costs and Benefits

The right to hold private property gives individuals, businesses, selected state agencies, and other organizations the right to own, use, and transfer ownership of possessions. Free enterprise relies on private property rights. Socialism, on the other hand, denies many private property rights, especially the right of individuals and businesses to hold the equipment, land, and other resources that produce goods and services. In socialism, property can be held communally or by the state. Under communal property, since everyone owns it, no one really owns it. Under state property, a state agency holds property and individuals do not have common or joint property rights; the agency acts as an individual owner with discretion how to use and dispose of the property.

Property Rights as an Incentive. Compared to communal property rights, private property rights assure that people will consider the full costs of using resources today and the benefits of saving resources and maintaining them in good repair. In Tsarist Russia, peasant farmers were reluctant to make improvements to the land they worked because they did not own the land. Even after emancipation in 1861, peasants held their land collectively. To be fair, strips of land rotated among different families from year to year. Therefore, a family could not reap all the future benefits of making improvements to a strip of land, such as removing rocks or stumps. Lacking communal agreements, only an unusually gracious family would forego a year's harvest and let a field lie fallow to renew its fertility, since the next family would reap the benefits of the crop rotation. In contrast, on a privately

Expansion Point 4.4: Was Membership in the Nazi Party a Rational Economic Decision?

Why did Germans in the 1930s vote Adolph Hitler and his Nazi party into power, supporting their evil policies to come? One explanation is in the economic disaster of the Weimar Republic, during which the German economy was destroyed by hyperinflation and the burden of paying reparations for World War I. Economic turmoil led people to accept any strong leader without careful thought.

Another explanation is that the Nazis' rise "was a lower-middle class phenomenon." Primarily uneducated, unthinking "Archie Bunker" types supported Hitler. [Archie Bunker was the bigoted, ignorant main character of a 1970s American television situation comedy.] A third explanation was that Germany's experience with nationalism in the middle and late 1800s predisposed its people to accept fascism. A less precise explanation given by some who lived through it was that Nazism was just "craziness."

European historian and Jewish scholar William Brustein has come to a much different, and to other academics, shocking conclusion that the rise of Hitler was a rational economic response. Evidence uncovered by others in the early 1980s from German voting records had suggested that people from various economic classes voted for Hitler, invalidating the "Archie Bunker" hypothesis. Brustein's work after 1988 offered an economic explanation for observed patterns of Nazi party membership, one that focused less on Germany's past or on mere craziness, and more on economic rationality.

Early in their administration, the Nazis emphasized nationalist policies of tariffs and quotas to protect German agriculture and other industries from foreign competition. Brustein found, not surprisingly, that those who joined the Nazi party were more likely to be working in industries that benefited from such protectionism. Workers who would not have benefited from protectionism, such as those in export-oriented industries, were less likely to join the party. Even so, Nazi brutality remains another matter.

Source: Ellen K. Coughlin, "Rational Fascists? Sociologist Probes People's Motives for Supporting the Nazi Party," *The Chronicle of Higher Education* (June 23, 1995): A10.

owned farm, those investing time and money to improve the land by adding fertilizer, rotating crops, or clearing large rocks reap the benefit through higher future yields.

Property Rights and Conservation. Private property rights can actually encourage environmental conservation. A communally owned lake or field is called a common resource or simply a "commons." The **tragedy of the commons**, due to overuse of publicly owned resources like forests or fisheries, arises precisely because rights to resources are held in common. When a forest is held in common, trees will be cut faster because the individual cost to each woodcutter of taking a tree today is zero! While the cost to society is a lost tree, the individual says, "If I don't cut this today, it will be gone next year because someone else will cut it." If, on the other hand, the woodcutter owns the stand of trees, then cutting a tree today has a positive individual cost, the lost use of the tree next year. Private landowners will consider the future of the forest when preparing to cut a tree today. They will also be more willing to plant trees for the future, as lumber companies now do on their own land. They know that they will be able to reap the benefits of their investment in 20 to 40 years. The same is not true for communally owned forests. If the woodcutter plants a tree, anyone has a right to cut it any time.

• **Tragedy of the commons:** the exploitation of resources occurring when a lake, forest, field, or other resource is owned communally rather than privately

Criticisms of Rational-Choice Theory

Rational-choice theory is provocative, especially to intellectuals outside mainstream economics. The critics are too numerous to mention, but they raise at least two key objections. First, rational-choice theory gives a too-narrow psychology of economic behavior. Second, people's decisions are not purely rational.

A Narrow Psychology: Human Motives

Do people actually focus only on their own interests? Or are they capable of benevolence as well? While economists seem comfortable with a stark view of human decision making, other scholars, particularly those in the humanities, rebel against this too-narrow psychology. They also fault economic instruction.

• **Criticisms of Rational-Choice Theory:** 1) a narrow psychology of human behavior 2) teaches individualism 3) defends behavior of greedy capitalists

Individualist or Communalist?

Do people really make choices purely as individuals, based on their own preferences and goals, independently of others? Critics, especially sociologists, contend that our thoughts and decisions are socially determined. We always act with regard to others. Even selfish people may choose to appear to be generous to avoid the condemnation of others. Our assessments of what is valuable also depend on what others consider to be valuable.

Socio-economists such as Amitai Etzioni go further. They wish to teach students to have communal sentiments. Etzioni wants to include in the economist's concept of "utility maximization" decisions that make us feel better by helping other people rather than ourselves (Etzioni 1988). This was always possible but rarely done.

Teaching Selfishness?

Teaching that people *actually* behave as self-interested individuals is different from teaching students to behave selfishly. Yet, does the one lead to the other? As explained in Expansion Point 4.5, critics of rational-choice theory now have evidence from a research study that economics students act more selfishly than other students when playing in cooperative games.

Critics also complain that a free-market system encourages greed in profit-oriented business owners and managers. This is more accurate as a criticism of all human behavior. Yearly, the news media report that leaders of *charitable* organizations have earned excessive incomes or have embezzled funds. We also read of exceptions. When a U.S. factory burned in the 1990s, its capitalist owner continued to pay workers without legal obligation to do so.

Expansion Point 4.5: Are Economists and Their Students More Selfish than Others?

If the local firefighters came through your neighborhood asking for donations for a new fire truck, would you give a significant contribution? Or would you say, "Sorry, but the budget is really tight this month." A "free rider" is one who refuses to contribute voluntarily, knowing that others will help pay for the truck and that it will be there when they need it.

When several researchers (Marwell and Ames 1981) tested for free-riding behavior among academics, they found that economists were more likely to refuse to cooperate than non-economists. Critics of rational-choice theory cited this result frequently in the 1980s and 1990s.

WARNING: Studying economics may be hazardous to your moral health.

Voluntary contributions to a common cause are only one form of cooperative behavior that people choose or refuse. Researchers can structure the rules of experimental games to test whether players tend to compete as individuals or cooperate with others. One such study (Frank et al. 1993) found that college students specializing in economics courses tended to be less willing to cooperate than other students. Once again, the critics blamed the economic theory of self-interested behavior for the observations of higher levels of uncooperative behavior.

Interpreting these results is more complex than that. Perhaps learning about self-interested behavior *does* cause more selfishness. Perhaps, however, causation works differently, and selfish people are simply more attracted to the study of economic theories of self-interest and acquisitiveness. If so, then the research studies are subject to what is called a "self-selection bias" where selfish people choose to be economics students and teachers.

Students of economics may want to ask whether or not their course work poses a threat to their moral health.

Sources: Robert H. Frank et al., "Does Studying Economics Inhibit Cooperation?" *Journal of Economic Perspectives* 7 (1993): 159-71.

G. Marwell and R.E. Ames, "Economists Free Ride, Does Anyone Else?" *Journal of Public Economics* 15 (1981): 295-310.

A Faulty Psychology: Human Irrationality

A further criticism of rational-choice theory is that it ignores irrational aspects of economic behavior. People choose based on more than accurate assessments of economic costs and benefits. Daniel Kahneman shared the 2002 Nobel Prize in economics for his psychological research into economic irrationality.

Evidence of Irrationality

What evidence points to irrational economic decisions? A recent study showed that, between 1982 and 1997, share prices at 26 international stock exchanges made larger average gains on sunny days than on cloudy days (Hirshleifer and Shumway 2001). Unless an economic link between sunshine and commercial prospects exists, such results are not purely rational. They show that human emotions and moods may influence stock-market evaluations independent of economic factors.

If people on average prefer getting $100 today to $150 one week from today, they should also prefer getting $100 fifty weeks from today over getting $150 fifty-one weeks from today. However, Matthew Rabin, a 2000 MacArthur Foundation Genius Award winner for his work in irrationality, says that people will tend to choose the $100 today but the $150 fifty-one weeks from today. He attributes this to an irrational self-control problem in choices involving immediate costs or benefits (Ainsworth 2000).

Effects of Irrationality

How does irrational economic behavior affect our understanding of commercial behavior? Non-economic factors distort economic decisions. Management decisions about whether to compete vigorously with new entrants to their market may be motivated by non-economic factors such as pride, competitive spirit, and anger rather than by strict calculations of expected profitability. Consumer decisions may be distorted by vanity and short-run biases toward temporary pleasure.

Broader Principles of Economic Behavior

Alongside rational choice are other natural human behaviors with economic significance. Among them are the tendencies to associate, to compete, to innovate, to choose between opportunism and self-restraint, and to play strategic games. Rather than threatening our belief in human rationality, the explanation of each weakens the case of the critics. For example, the fact that reasonable individuals cooperate pokes fun at the criticism that individual choice is *selfishly* individualistic.

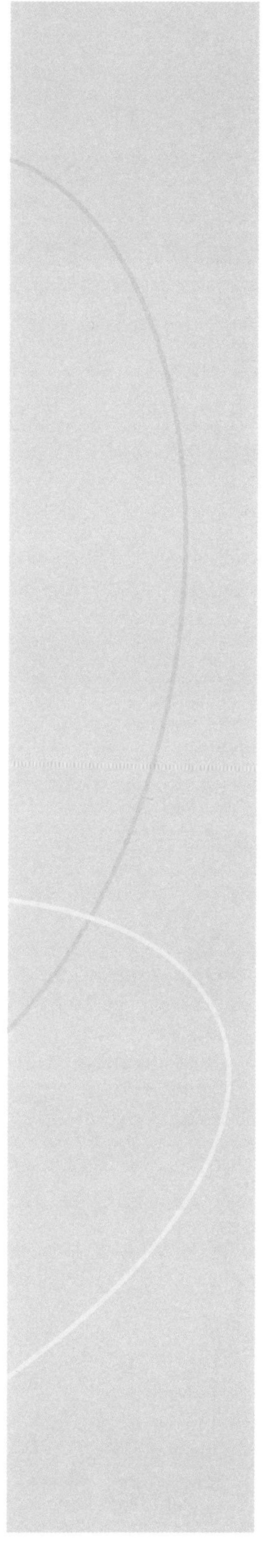

Individuals Associate Voluntarily

Rational individuals are not necessarily radical individualists. First of all, to teach that individuals will make their own choices based on costs and benefits is different from teaching that individuals should or will always choose to act alone. Second, evidence shows that people voluntarily form numerous business, social, political, and religious associations. Rational individuals understand when collective action will promote their own interest.

Evidence of Voluntarism

In the United States, evidence suggests that collective civic action has been declining. Data show that Americans' willingness to associate in PTAs, bowling leagues, and other social activities peaked in the 1940s and has been declining since. After dismissing other causes, Robert Putnam (1995, 65-78) attributes the decline in social connectedness to the rise of television.

Nevertheless, Americans take advantage of the political and economic freedom to associate, including in charitable enterprises. In 1995, 48.8 percent of adults in the United States worked as volunteers for organizations for an average of 4.2 hours per week. About 26 percent did religious work, 17.5 percent helped in education, and 15.4 percent helped in youth development (U.S. Bureau of the Census 1998). In addition to doing volunteer work, Americans' willingness to buy corporate stock or mutual-fund shares, form partnerships, attend religious services, and participate in PTA, Little League, and other associations demonstrates that free individuals will choose to associate.

Naive critics of individualism mistakenly assume that voluntary associations are generally socially beneficial. Collusive businesses, however, cooperate to fix prices at high levels, against the public interest. In undemocratic alliances, business leaders and government officials conspire against the public interest.

Implications for Government Action

Society, therefore, cannot justify government coercion (restraining or compelling by force) by an assumed unwillingness of rational individuals to band together. Society must justify coercive government actions on other grounds, such as protecting life and private property, preventing the powerful from trampling rights of the powerless, or augmenting insufficient voluntarism.

Individuals and Their Organizations Compete

Competition extends beyond commerce. People compete not only for products and for shares of market activity, but also for mates, for social and political power, and for public handouts.

Critics of competition abound, but their efforts to eliminate all competition ignore the social benefits of competition that stimulates productive activity. Competition in the computer and electronics industry created incredible technological advances and made them available at increasingly lower prices. Competition among political parties makes government more responsive to the public. National economic competition, expressed as protectionism in foreign trade, and competition for government handouts, however, can reduce economic efficiency. Ironically, critics of market competition often favor such inefficient interventions. A government seeking economic efficiency, therefore, should promote beneficial commercial competition, avoid wasteful competition, and maintain a system of political competition.

Individuals Innovate

Individuals with adequate economic and political freedom will innovate. They will develop technical improvements, new methods of associating, and their own rules for guiding commercial conduct. People will devise many innovations so they can legally or illegally circumvent government constraints on their behavior. For instance, because government tax agents have a tougher time tracing cash income and cash sales, tax evaders ask to be paid in cash rather than with more easily traced checks.

How innovative are government bureaucracies? Rondo Cameron (1993, 31) concludes that the first large centrally commanded civilizations seem to have been responsible for few if any technological increases in the productivity of labor. "Almost all the major elements of technology that served ancient civilizations—domesticated plants and animals, textiles, pottery, metallurgy, monumental architecture, the wheel, sailing ships, and so on—had been invented or discovered before the dawn of recorded history."

• **Opportunism:** pursuing one's own interests without regard for others; taking immoral advantage of circumstances

People Choose to Act Opportunistically or to Exercise Self-Restraint

While mainstream economic theory largely ignores the morality or immorality of human behavior, a realistic account of commerce cannot. We regularly observe people in business who act opportunistically or with moral restraint.

• **Moral self-restraint:** refusing to exploit unequal power, information, or loop-holes

An **opportunist** takes advantage of circumstances to pursue his own interests without regard to moral principles or the negative effects on others. Opportunism in business may arise from unequal distributions of power or information. The only seller of a new life-saving product might exercise monopoly power by raising its price well above its cost of production. The seller of a defective used automobile might know about its faulty brakes, but not disclose this to a buyer. Opportunism also arises due to loopholes in regulations or provisions of a contract.

A shopper could buy a television for one night to watch the season's final ball game, and then invoke the store's liberal return policy to ask for money back.

The opposite of opportunism is **moral self-restraint**. Those who exercise self-restraint refuse to exploit unequal power, unequal information, or loopholes. Commercial self-restraint may lower a trader's immediate gains from exchange, but also may encourage trust and a profitable long-term business.

Exercising full power when negotiating a contract is a minor form of opportunism. American economist John Commons (1924) taught that individuals negotiating contracts to buy and sell would choose whether to exploit or restrain their bargaining power. In a wage bargain, for example, an employer could exercise hiring power by paying a very low wage, or the employer might exercise restraint and pay a higher wage than the minimum needed to hire the worker.

An example of industrial opportunism is the **holdup**, where one party to a contract gains economic power and asks to renegotiate a more favorable contract. If Ajax Hose is presently the sole supplier of hoses to Beta Engine Manufacturing, Ajax could hold up Beta and increase prices of its hoses. Firms facing such a threat can protect themselves. If the threat is credible, Beta's managers can contract with several suppliers in defense. Alternatively, Beta's managers can buy Ajax Hose to avoid the holdup.

•**Holdup:** using economic power to renegotiate a more favorable contract; threats of such reneging affect the conduct and organization of firms

Self-restraint—refusing to act opportunistically—cultivates trust and promotes long-term relations that have value to businesses. Abiding by the rules of fair commerce is an important example of self-restraint. As long as business competitors follow appropriate rules of the game, competition in production and exchange leads to economic efficiency. Free market advocates recite Adam Smith's belief in the harmony of self-interests that the price system of a market economy creates. Opportunistic behavior in a market economy threatens that harmony. Self-restraint and the trust it promotes encourage it.

People Play Strategic Games

•**Strategic game:** a contest (such as industrial competition) in which a player's strategic pursuit of a goal influences and is influenced by an opponent's strategy; players decide to compete or cooperate

People play **strategic games** involving behaviors described above: association, competition, innovation, opportunism, and self-restraint. Any game of strategy has at least two players, each with a goal. In a **zero-sum game**, when one player wins, another player loses. In such a game, the strategy must be to compete, trying to reach the goal while preventing the other players from reaching their goal. Strategies account for and neutralize other player's strategies. Alternatively, players can seek cooperative strategies that create a **positive-sum game**, where both can win.

Expansion Point 4.6 illustrates a well-known strategic game, the Prisoner's Dilemma. Economists use similar strategic games to model the interdependent plans of two or more competing or cooperating firms. One firm's strategy to win market share will affect the market shares of its rivals. In such games, planning alone is not adequate. Each firm must anticipate a rival's reactions to the plan, and must then decide whether cooperation or competition will bring a greater reward.

Commercial Games

Traders' choices to compete or cooperate are crucial to commercial progress. A merchant who chooses to cooperate and play fairly with others will more likely gain repeat business and promote beneficial exchange. A merchant may, however, compete with his trading partners in order to capture all of the gains in each trade. Such strategies include always driving a hard bargain, or taking complete advantage of others through opportunism, as when a thief decides to run with the goods *and* the money. Both behaviors discourage further trade.

Business cooperation, however, may evolve into collusive schemes against the public, often to raise prices and profits. While traders benefit, they do so at the consumers' expense.

Expansion Point 4.6: The Prisoner's Dilemma

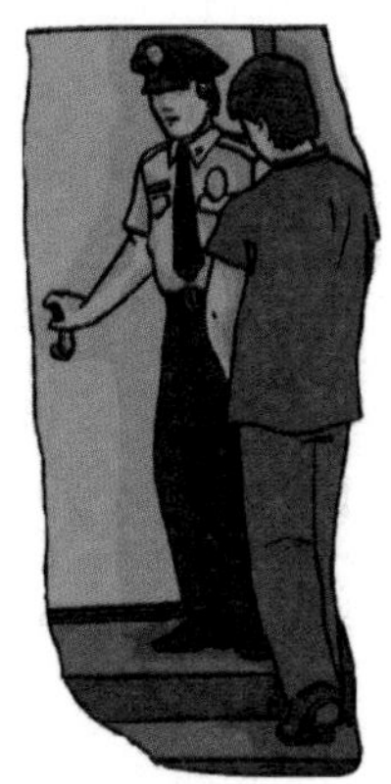

Imagine that you and a friend are caught by police who suspect you of a serious crime against the state. Let's assume that you are both not guilty, and that the police only have evidence against each of you for a minor crime, which will land you in jail only for a year.

To get evidence of the more serious crime, the police offer each of you the same deal. If you testify against your friend but he refuses to testify against you, you go free and your friend spends 20 years in jail. Of course, if both of you implicate each other, you will both be found guilty. For your cooperation against your friend, you will receive only a five-year sentence.

This is the prisoner's dilemma: to defect against your friend or to be faithful to your friend. The choices and payoffs to each combination of choices are as follows:

		You	
		Testify	**Keep Silent**
Your Friend	**Testifies**	Each gets 5 yrs.	You get 20 yrs. Friend goes free
	Keeps Silent	You go free Friend gets 20 yrs.	Each gets 1 yr.

If the prisoners don't trust each other, each will likely testify, and both will get five years. Otherwise, each risks getting 20 years. They will only receive the minimum one-year sentences if each trusts the other not to testify, or if both hold strong beliefs such as "never rat on a friend" or "never tell a lie."

Commercial agreements involve decisions related to the prisoner's dilemma. Two traders agree to exchange jewels for gold. Each can either keep the agreement or defect. If both keep their word, both earn a modest profit. If one defects and successfully steals the other's wealth, the thief earns a greater profit and imposes a big loss on the other. If both try to steal, both lose.

Industrial and Retail Games. Industrial competitors play strategic games over market share. A competing firm can cut price to gain share. Yet, if its competitors also cut price, each suffers lower profits, but none gains greater share. Firms may learn to collude tacitly by refusing to cut price (a cooperative solution). Increasing advertising to increase market share may spark an advertising war. Once again, market share changes little, unless one campaign is especially good, but advertising costs increase.

Shoppers and retail salespeople play strategic games too. Salespeople often have flexibility to offer lower prices to buyers who are less willing and able to pay. Sales representatives will therefore try to assess a buyer's income and wealth, looking carefully at a customer's clothes. When wealthy people learn the game, they may go shopping in their oldest clothes.

How Long Will the Game Last? Strategic games are either **one-period** or **multi-period** games. Commercial trading relations in market economies are normally multi-period games. Cheating among traders is lower when commercial relations are ongoing. A fly-by-night opportunist might succeed in playing a series of single-period games by moving from town to town. The opportunist will not, however, thrive in normal commercial games that are played repeatedly by the same merchants. The other players will devise methods of sanctioning the immoral player.

The end of a multi-period game is like a one-period game. Therefore, an end-game strategy will be nothing like a mid-game strategy. An opportunistic employee who plays strategic games with his employer will vary strategies over time. While planning to stay employed, he will behave well and maintain high productivity to keep his job. After accepting a new job offer and giving two-weeks notice, however, his productivity on the old job may fall. He may even steal company secrets to assist in his next job. For this reason, an employer may ask a worker not to come to work after accepting a new job. The behavior of workers to be laid off or fired may also deteriorate during the notice period, and therefore the employer may ask them to clear out their desks and hand over their keys immediately.

Regulatory Games

Government regulators must play strategic games with innovative businesses. Consider the banking industry. In the 1930s, to eliminate destabilizing competition among banks and to keep banks' costs of acquiring funds low, the U.S. government imposed interest-rate "ceilings" (a legal maximum rate that a bank may pay depositors). In the 1960s, when market interest rates rose higher than ceiling rates, the policy had an unintended effect. Bankers offered non-money gifts of toasters, china, or silverware to encourage depositors to save with them, thus negating the desired effects of the ceilings.

In the 1960s, regulations allowed depositors to hold certificates of deposit (CDs) at market rates of interest, but checking accounts earned no interest. By the mid-1970s, corporations were buying overnight CDs to earn interest on their checking account balances. In the early 1980s, government regulators finally quit the game and repealed interest rate ceilings.

• **Loophole mining:** searching for a method of avoiding the effects of a rule without breaking the rule

Economists call such innovative behavior **loophole mining**. Government imposes rules, the private sector innovates by finding a loophole, government closes the loopholes or relaxes the rules, the private sector seeks other innovations, and so on. Demonstrating that the banking example is not unusual, Expansion Point 4.7 describes a strategic game between the U.S. government and sugar importers in the 1980s.

Expansion Point 4.7: Playing Games with Sugar Importers

In 1982, the U.S. government imposed quotas (limits) on imports of sugar into the country. American food processors, which bought most of the sugar used in the United States, preferred the less expensive foreign sugar to more expensive domestic sugar. The quotas, however, reduced processors' access to the lower-priced imported sugar.

Importers immediately began to play games with the government quotas, taking advantage of two loopholes. First, the quotas regulated only imports that contained more than 94 percent sugar. Second, Canada had no sugar quotas. Consequently, certain Canadian firms that imported sugar added 6 percent corn syrup and reexported the "non-sugar" to the United States. After 350 million pounds of non-sugar crossed the border, the U.S. government outlawed these shipments.

Then Canadian firms sent in sugar-laden cake mixes, high-sugar content cocoa mixes, and maple syrup products, from which American firms could extract less-expensive sugar. These Canadian products were also banned, but, because the amendments applied only to Canadian abuses, companies in other countries began sending in high-sugar-content. Candy imports also increased, because they were made with sugar that was much less costly than the sugar American firms had to buy. To squelch each of these innovations required additional U.S. government decrees.

Source: Anne Krueger, "The Political Economy of Controls: American Sugar," in *Empirical Studies in Institutional Change*, ed. Lee J. Alston, et al. (Cambridge: Oxford University Press, 1996), 194-97.

Chapter Summary

1. Economists assume that humans choose rationally. Human rationality implies self-interested, optimizing, knowledgeable decision making.

2. Human rationality is limited by incomplete information. People's optimizing behavior is also limited by transactions costs.

3. Individuals will search for information to make better decisions, and they will also reorganize private and public activities to reduce transactions costs.

4. People generally know what is best for them. Their expectations of the future are also rational, informed by past and current information, and by knowledge of the systems in which they operate. People cannot be fooled continually.

5. Seemingly irrational behaviors often have a rational explanation, even when the behavior is sometimes in error.

6. People compare costs and benefits of their actions and respond to incentives and constraints that alter those perceived costs and benefits.

7. Property rights affect costs and benefits of using and conserving resources. The tragedy of the commons occurs because people overuse a property that is held in common.

8. Critics contend that rational-choice theory is too narrow a view of human behavior.

9. A broader review of economic behavior recognizes that: individuals associate voluntarily to cooperate; people choose to act opportunistically or to exercise self-restraint; individuals and groups compete; individuals innovate to circumvent regulations on their behavior; and individuals play strategic games with each other.

10. A player in a strategic game must consider the actions of rivals, and must decide whether to compete or cooperate. Traders play one-period and multi-period commercial games differently.

Problems for Practice

4.1 What are the three characteristics of rational economic thought? What are several economic implications of rational thought?

4.2 Economists say that consumers will search the market for information. How many stores did you search before buying clothing the last time you shopped? Could you be absolutely sure that you paid the lowest price? Did it matter? Explain.

4.3* List and explain one of your own examples for each of the following ideas from the text:

a. Individuals associate voluntarily.
b. Individuals innovate to circumvent regulations on their behavior.
c. Seemingly irrational behaviors often have a rational explanation, even when the behavior is sometimes in error.
d. Property rights affect individual costs and benefits of conserving and maintaining property.
e. People act opportunistically in commerce.
f. People act with restraint in commerce.
g. Individuals play strategic games with each other or with government regulators.

4.4 To show mercy and allow for a student's occasional off day, some teachers offer "retests" to students who do poorly on their first try at an exam. What do you think will be the long-run effects on study habits of this policy?

For your portfolio:
4.5* Find an article or other source of an example of your answers to 4.4. For example, research a case where people or businesses play a strategic game with each other, or a case of innovative behavior, strategy, and loophole mining in the face of government regulation. Write up to a page summary.

For class discussion:
4.6 Critics of economic thought complain that humans are capable of benevolence. Based on your own experience, would you agree that humans actually do choose what is in the best interest of others and ignore their own interests? Or would you tend to agree that humans are self-interested? Give evidence.

4.7 What do you think of the rational-choice explanation of inheritances and annuities? In light of your thoughts, how would you evaluate the proverb that a good parent leaves an inheritance for grandchildren?

4.8* Some people don't like competition, including economic and athletic competition. They suggest, for example, that basketball be played as a game in which both teams can win by simply adding the scores of the two teams. How do you think this would change basketball? What are your views about competition? Can you refute this negative view of competition?

4.9 We can conceive of trade as a game. Let's say you and a friend play a trading game. If you both agree not to cheat the other, you both make $10. If either one cheats the other, the cheater makes $15 and the one cheated loses $10. If both cheat, each loses $5. Analyze the outcome of trade under different assumptions about people's behavior. First assume that traders will only play a one-period game. Then assume that traders will play the game repeatedly so long as both agree.

See Answer Key for hints/answers to starred (*) questions.

Chapter 5

Economic Method

General Principles

What this chapter will help you think about:

1. What are the challenges of explaining economic causality?
2. How do we assess regular but uncertain economic effects?
3. What are the important features of microeconomic analysis?
4. What are the key ideas of macroeconomic analysis?
5. How do methodological individualism and wholism differ?
6. How do marginal and aggregate analysis differ?
7. How does partial-equilibrium analysis differ from general-equilibrium analysis?

Economic method has several important features that distinguish it from other social sciences. In chapter 4, you read that economists assume that human behavior is rational. Two other distinctives of economic method are that (1) it is more mathematical and scientific than other social sciences, and (2) it incorporates both of the two broad philosophies of social science, methodological individualism and methodological wholism, in its two branches of microeconomics and macroeconomics. Microeconomics explains individual behavior, while macroeconomics explains aggregate behavior, or economic outcomes in the whole.

Overview of Economic Method

Mainstream economists favor highly mathematical theories of economic relations. They also tend to use statistical analysis to test theoretical relations. Behind all the math and all the statistics, though, are a few key principles about their method. Let's begin with the main goal of all the math and statistics: explaining causality.

Economic Analysis Seeks to Explain Causality

Economists seek to describe economic behavior in terms of event causation: one event causes another event. A higher interest rate causes borrowing for investment and consumption to decline. A lower price of gasoline causes more driving. Economists explain causation based on two types of reasoning. First, they offer theoretical explanations of causation using the logical principles of economic behavior. Second, they seek empirical evidence that one event does indeed follow its cause.

Complexities of Causality

Economic thinking is complicated because the direction of causation between two events can sometimes go both ways, a situation called **two-way causation**. For example, a change in prices causes a change in consumption, but a change in consumption also causes a change in prices. More specifically, gasoline prices and the amount of driving people do affect each other. As stated above, a higher gasoline price can cause less driving. More driving, however, can cause a higher price. Increased driving during summer vacations will cause gasoline prices to go up as consumers compete for a scarce resource. Then again, if gasoline producers expect more summer driving, they may produce so much extra gasoline in the spring that prices are lower when families are driving more.

- **Two-way causation:** for variables X and Y, a change in X causes a change in Y, but a change in Y also causes a change in X

As with other social sciences, economic thinking involves **causal chains**, which are sequences of causal events. Higher government spending (holding taxes constant) causes more government borrowing. More government borrowing causes higher interest rates. Higher interest rates cause less borrowing for consumption and investment. Less consumption and investment spending mean more layoffs of workers and lower incomes. Therefore, higher government spending and borrowing stimulate production of goods and services the government buys, but they can cause layoffs and falling incomes in industries whose customers are sensitive to interest-rate changes.

- **Causal chains:** a change in X causes a change in Y that causes a change in Z . . .

Short-Run and Long-Run Effects

Economists also emphasize that short-run causal effects often differ from long-run effects. The **short run** is a period during which full adjustment to an economic change is not possible. In the **long run**, decision makers will have made all adjustments to the economic shock. In hiring labor, the short run is the time until management and labor can negotiate a new wage contract. In agriculture, it is the time until a new crop can be harvested or planted. In factory production, the short run is the time until more equipment can be bought and larger buildings built. In consumption, it is the time until consumers can change their buying habits.

- **Short run:** time is too short for all economic adjustments to be made
- **Long run:** time is sufficient for all economic adjustments to be made

If buyer demand for wheat rises, for example, the price of wheat and profitability of producing it will rise in the short run, but will fall back in the long run. In the short run, stored wheat and acres of wheat already planted are fixed, thus limiting the short-run ability of supply. Since quantity of wheat cannot respond to the increase in demand, the price of wheat responds. In the long run, these limits are not binding and quantity can expand to meet demand, allowing price to fall back to a level that covers farmers' costs of producing wheat.

A second example from international trade will show the generality of differing short-run and long-run effects. If the value of a nation's currency falls against other currencies, the short-run effect is that its people will have to pay more for goods they buy from other countries. As a result, a lower currency value causes more money to flow out of a country. If the U.S. dollar falls in value against the Japanese yen, Americans must pay more dollars to meet the yen price of Japanese cars. This short-run explanation assumes that buyers will want the same quantity of foreign goods. In the long run, however, a portion of U.S. buyers will decide to buy a domestic car instead. If enough Americans substitute domestic for Japanese cars, the lower value of the U.S. dollar will cause the amount of money leaving the country to fall (not rise) in the long run. This process is called the "J-curve" effect.

- **Positive statistical correlation:** two variables tend to increase and decrease together

- **Negative statistical correlation:** when one variable increases, the other tends to decrease

Correlation Is Not Necessarily Causation

Two economic variables are positively correlated if, when one variable increases, on average the other tends to increase. They are **negatively correlated** if, when one increases, on average the other tends to decrease. Economists use statistical correlations among variables to test theories of economic causation.

Statisticians warn, however, that **statistical correlation does not prove causation**. If driving decreases after the price of gasoline goes up, that does not conclusively demonstrate that one caused the other. It merely supports a hypothesis that quantity demanded and price are inversely related. Nevertheless, economists assume that causal relations exist among economic relations. These relations are regular enough to be dependable, but they are also subject to uncertainties.

Economic Relationships Are Regular Enough

Economists believe that the causal relations among economic variables are regular enough to be represented algebraically and graphically. Consider an important relation in the economic analysis of consumption, the demand relation (introduced in chapter 2). If the price of a product such as a can of soft drink increases, economists think that on average, and holding other important factors constant, the quantity of cans per day that consumers demand will go down. Economists represent this **law of demand** as a negatively sloped line on a graph with quantity-demanded on the horizontal axis and price on the vertical axis.

- **Law of demand:** if price increases, quantity demanded of a good or service decreases

Exhibit 5.1 shows such a demand relation for the number of soft drinks sold every hour at a soft-drink machine. At \$0.40 per can, for instance, nine cans are bought per hour. At \$1.00 per can, though, only three cans are bought per hour. Oversimplifying so as to use simple algebra, economists represent the demand relationship with a linear equation:

$$\textbf{Quantity Demanded} = \textbf{a} + \textbf{b} * \textbf{Price} \qquad (b < 0)$$

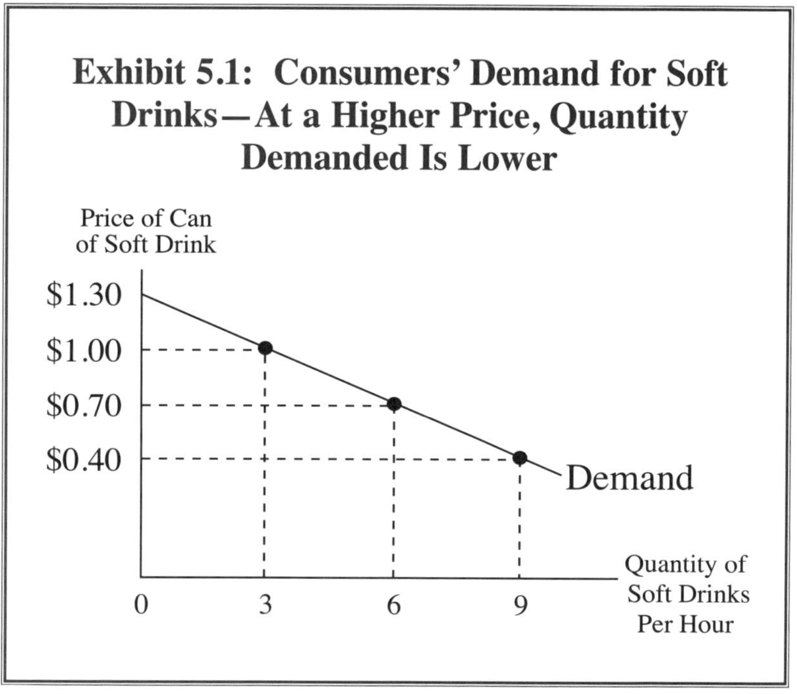

In a demand equation like this, the slope (b) would be negative to reflect the law of demand. A similar equation for quantity supplied would have a positive slope (d):

$$\textbf{Quantity Supplied} = c + d * \textbf{Price} \qquad (d > 0)$$

To represent the equilibrium condition, we would set quantity demanded equal to quantity supplied:

$$\textbf{Quantity Demanded} = \textbf{Quantity Supplied}$$

So when economic variables are related to each other in predictable ways, we represent this with graphs and algebra. In the case of demand and supply, we can represent the market for a product with three equations.

Economic Relationships Also Have Uncertainty

In Exhibit 5.1, the demand line was an exact relation, drawn with certainty. More advanced economic analysis allows for uncertainty in demand and other relationships. Prices or quantities demanded change due to both known and uncertain influences. Uncertainty arises from random errors and unknown systematic influences. To allow for uncertainty in economic relations, economists use probability theory and statistical analysis.

Statistical Experiments in Economics

We can illustrate a few key ideas about uncertain economic relations by pursuing the soft drink example and a hypothetical

• A change in an **independent variable** causes a change in a **dependent variable.**

• **Scatter diagram:** plot of points showing correlation between two variables

• **Regression line:** average relation between an independent and dependent variable

statistical experiment. Let's say that the owner of a number of soft-drink machines decided to let his daughter do an economics experiment with one machine. He will let her vary the price of cans every week for fifty-two weeks. She plans to use prices of $0.60, $0.80, $1.00, and $1.20, and to measure changes in weekly sales. With four prices and 52 weeks in the year, she will have 13 weeks of quantity-demanded data for each price. In this experiment, price is the **independent variable**, which the researcher controls, and quantity demanded is the **dependent variable**, whose changes are caused by changes in the independent variable.

Exhibit 5.2 illustrates a plot of a portion of the 52-week price and quantity combinations that the economics student might have observed in an uncertain world. Each point on the graph represents one week's combination of price and quantity demanded. Observations are scattered at each price, showing random variations in the quantities demanded. Exhibit 5.2 is a **scatter diagram** like those commonly used in statistical analysis. Notice that the scatter of points does follow the general pattern of demand: as price rises, the average number of cans bought falls. The light gray line running through the middle of the points represents the average demand relation. Statisticians call this a **regression line.**

Interpreting the Results

Why would the number of cans of soft drink demanded each week vary over the course of a year, even when price is the same? Because other variables matter. Weather and season of the year might affect sales. On hot days, people need to replace more

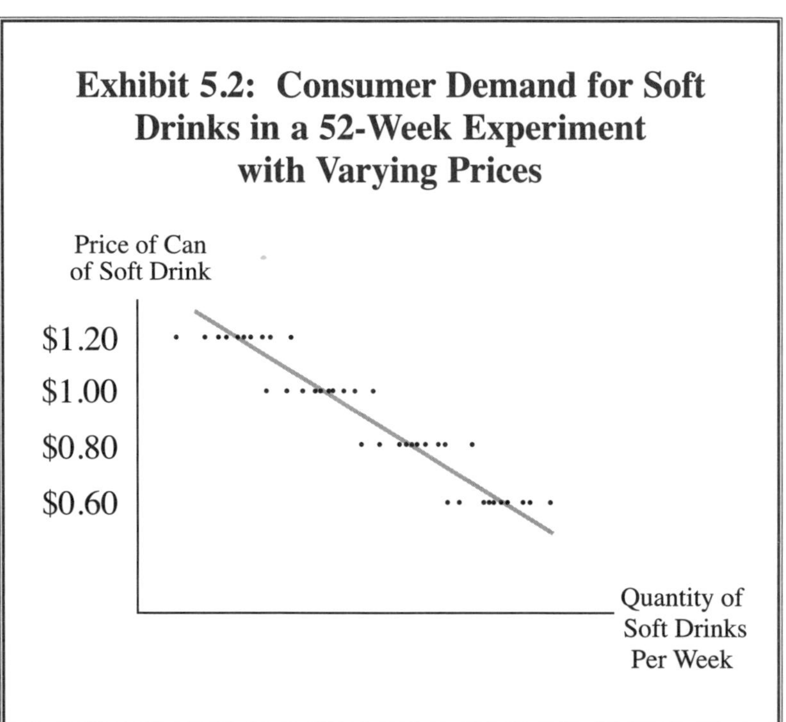

Exhibit 5.2: Consumer Demand for Soft Drinks in a 52-Week Experiment with Varying Prices

fluids each day and might drink more of everything, including soft drinks. If the machine were in a school, the school calendar would affect sales. During the weeks when school was out, the machine would sell fewer cans. Many other factors would affect quantity demanded at each price each week.

In the limited analysis of demand illustrated so far, causation runs from price to quantity demanded. A change in price causes a change in quantity demanded. The statistical data in Exhibit 5.2 would tend to support, though not prove, such a causal relation.

Principles of Microeconomic Analysis

Economics is a distinct social science because of its distinct method, rather than its content (which all social sciences address). One distinction is that economics uses more mathematics than sociology, political science, or anthropology to express its assumptions and conclusions about human behavior. Microeconomics also tends to be individualistic in its methods and its conclusions. In fact, to a great extent, the method of microeconomics is to observe and quantify individual behavior.

Methodological Individualism

Economists often conclude that individual choice is efficient. Preachers and social critics, however, sometimes assert that economists teach selfishness. The critics regularly condemn the supposed evils of teaching economic "individualism." The method of microeconomics, however, is subtly different. It is called **methodological individualism**.

• **Methodological individualism:** studying individual decision making so as to understand overall economic activity

What Is Methodological Individualism?

Microeconomists begin by analyzing how individuals behave and how they will react to changing economic conditions. In studying the movements of market prices, for example, economists first want to know how an individual consumer and an individual producer will react to a higher price of the product. If the price of gasoline goes up, will the average consumer buy less and will the average producer be willing to sell more?

Once economists understand the behavior of individual buyers and sellers, they can predict what will happen in the overall market for gasoline when price increases. A rising price of gasoline will cause a surplus of gas if all other factors affecting consumer demand and producer supply are unchanged. Economists can further predict how the rising gasoline price will affect overall activity in the economy.

Applications of Methodological Individualism

Methodological individualism can be used to examine human behavior in any economy, not just in a market economy emphasizing individual choice. Several examples in this text explain how individuals reacted to changing policies in socialist economies. For example, Expansion Point 6.2 will explain how individual Russians reacted in unplanned ways to higher taxes of a socialist government. Individual behavior is the key to economic analysis, even in economies dominated by a collective philosophy.

Economists also examine individual behaviors of government politicians and bureaucrats in a democratic market economy. When a food and drug regulator in the United States keeps a new drug off the market, for example, Milton and Rose Friedman (1980, 193-200) explain that the bureaucrat is acting in his own interests, and not necessarily for the common good. Here again, methodological individualism is useful in an apparently social, rather than individual, context. Economists of this persuasion are convinced that, even in communal settings, economic outcomes depend on the cumulative effects of individual decisions.

Assume That Other Things Are Equal

- **OTBE assumption:** in economic relations, the assumption of other things being equal

An important assumption in the analysis of economic relations, especially in microeconomics, is that other things are held equal. The relation between the quantity demanded and the price of a product, for example, assumes that many other factors are held constant. For example, if prices of clothes are increasing from one year to the next, but family income is also rising during the same period, the family may buy more clothing at higher prices. While this seems to violate the law of demand, it does not. The law of demand assumes that price is varying with **other things being equal (OTBE).**

The student of laboratory science will recognize that the OTBE assumption is consistent with the scientific method of allowing only one causal factor to vary at a time. Many misunderstandings about economic method and policy result from failure to understand or apply the OTBE assumption.

Microeconomic Analysis Is Marginal Analysis

- **Marginal analysis:** making decisions by comparing extra benefits against extra costs

Marginal analysis means that, to optimize, decision makers compare extra benefits of an activity with extra costs. Marginal analysis refers to analyzing *extras*, rather than *totals*. To understand why analyzing extras is better, let's compare total and marginal thinking about pollution.

Consider an extremely high level of pollution, where fish die from poisoned water, house paint peels prematurely from acid rain, people grow sick from breathing polluted air, and others die from living near solid-waste dumps. The total costs of extreme levels of pollution will be greater than the total benefits of allowing the economic activity that causes such pollution. Total thinking, therefore, would lead to eliminating all pollution and all the economic activity that creates it because the costs of pollution are greater than the benefits. The problem with such total thinking is that no pollution means no economic activity at all—no horses that leave waste when providing transportation, no fires that smoke when providing heat, and so on. The cure is worse than the problem.

Marginal thinking, on the other hand, is consistent with reasonable thinking: reduce pollution until the extra benefits of another unit of pollution reduction are equal to the extra costs of lost economic activity. The public-policy problem is to find the balance between lost economic activity and a higher environmental quality. The best balance, however, requires that decision makers include all costs and benefits in the calculations. Environmentalists, for example, insist on estimating or at least considering future costs and benefits to future generations of present economic policies. Any hidden costs or benefits, or any exaggerated costs or benefits, will make decisions less than optimal.

Marginal thinking relies on two key economic assumptions. The first is **increasing marginal costs**: as the level of any activity increases, its extra costs per unit eventually rise. The second is about **decreasing marginal benefits**: as any activity increases, its extra benefits per unit eventually decrease. A unit of an activity refers to economic activity such as buying pounds of meat, producing numbers of cars, or trading pounds of fruit. Marginal thinking concludes with the **equi-marginal rule**: the maximum of net benefits (total benefits minus total costs) occurs where extra benefits equal extra costs. In economic terms, the maximum occurs where marginal benefits equal marginal costs.

- **Increasing marginal cost:** as the level of most activities increases past some point, the marginal cost tends to increase
- **Decreasing marginal benefit:** as the level of most activities increases past some point, the marginal benefit tends to decrease
- **Equi-marginal rule:** the optimal level of any activity is the level where marginal costs equal marginal benefits

Everyone Thinks Marginally

Economists assume that people already are marginal thinkers in their daily decisions. They don't need to be taught. Let me illustrate with the following money offers in a game of exchange. If I promised you $10 in exchange for $2, would you take the deal? If I promised you $8 in exchange for $4, would you take that deal? If I offered $6 in exchange for $6 would you agree? If I offered to give you $4 in exchange for $8, would you agree to that deal? If your answers to the four questions were yes, yes, it doesn't matter, and no, you already understand the basics of marginal analysis.

To prove that marginal thinking maximizes net benefits of such a game, examine the numbers. Assume that you start this game with $2. At which offer will you maximize your net benefit from exchange? Your net gain is $8 on the first exchange, $4 on the second, $0 on the third, and -$4.00 on the fourth exchange. So the maximum of the total gain is on the second or third exchange.

Exhibit 5.3: Maximizing Net Benefit from an Exchange Game

Trade Number	0	1	2	3	4
Marginal Benefit	0	$10	$8	$6	$4
Marginal Cost	0	$2	$4	$6	$8
Money Holdings	$2	$10	$14	$14	$10

Exhibit 5.3 summarizes your marginal costs, marginal benefits, and total money holdings at each point in this game. You have the most money from the game if you stop trading on the third trade, where marginal benefit equals marginal cost of another trade (you could stop after the second trade, but you would not know if this is best until the third trade is offered). This conclusion is true because, in the example, marginal costs are rising and marginal benefits are falling.

Marginal Thinking and Running Laps

Actual economic decisions are rarely as easy to analyze. Nevertheless, the marginal method applies to all decisions. Exhibit 5.4, for example, illustrates marginal thinking applied to an athlete running laps. The two lines on the graph represent rising marginal costs and falling marginal benefits of running an extra lap. Running the first few laps costs little because the time to run them is short, the burden on the joints is not great, and the muscles are able to burn stored food efficiently. At higher numbers of laps, however, each lap costs more because time is more precious, joints ache more, and muscles work less efficiently. Extra benefits of the first few laps are high but begin to fall at higher numbers, representing a diminishing return to more of the same exercise.

Runners don't need to draw a graph for each workout, but the best runners do optimize their mix of exercises and activities. Optimizing means to balance competing uses of exercise time. The maximum number of laps that a runner can physically complete may not be the best if running takes away from health, diverts time from other valuable exercises like weight training, and reduces time for studies. Different runners' individual decisions will differ. For the long-distance runner, more laps may be better, but for the sprinter, only a few may be needed to warm up.

Reducing Pollution Again

Extra benefits fall and extra costs rise in almost all individual and public policy choices. This includes the earlier example of pollution reduction. Eliminating the first unit of pollution is less

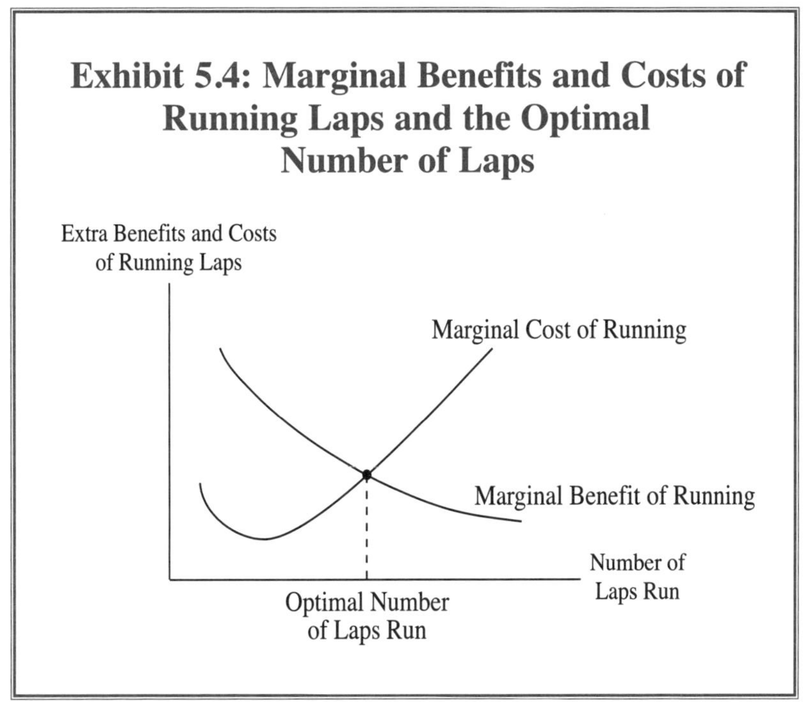

costly than eliminating the last. One study concluded that giving one in ten U.S. cars a better tune-up—the one in ten cars that were found to be very badly tuned—would reduce pollution at a very low cost. The better gas mileage in those cars would pay for their tune-ups over time. Redesigning all cars to eliminate all remaining pollution from automobiles, however, would be very costly and not very beneficial. The health benefits of reducing pollution are much greater for the first unit than the last.

A similar use of marginal thinking occurred in 2001 when environmental advocates wanted to increase the average fuel efficiency of and reduce pollution from all automobiles. One proposal recognized that the greatest gain could be won by regulating the least efficient automobiles, the sport-utility vehicles.

Willingness to Pay Measures Marginal Value

As mentioned in chapter 1, prices are very important in assessing economic efficiency. Prices measure the value that consumers, producers, and others place on scarce goods, services, and resources. The concept of willingness to pay, as opposed to the equilibrium price a buyer actually pays, measures the marginal value of each unit of a good.

Consumer Surplus and Willingness to Pay

"Willingness to pay" is helpful in assessing the benefits of exchange. For example, the difference between a consumer's willingness to pay for a product and the price she actually pays is a measure of the net value to that consumer of using resources to

make the product. English economist Alfred Marshall called this net value **consumer surplus**.

In an airport, people may pay $2.00 or more for a 12-ounce can of soft drink and then complain about the high price. This complaint, however, doesn't mean that a product bought voluntarily has no net value. A person's willingness to take time to pay $2.00 for a can implies that the can was more valuable to the buyer than $2.00. Yet the buyer is annoyed that airport vendors, through their monopoly power, captured more of the consumer surplus than the buyer would have liked.

We can illustrate the calculation of consumer surplus with the example of a machine selling soft drinks. If a buyer is willing to pay $1.00, but only has to pay $0.70 to a machine, the buyer reaps a small consumer surplus of $0.30. This is the difference between willingness to pay and the actual price paid.

Exhibit 5.5 illustrates the consumer surplus from buying soft drinks using a hypothetical demand line for soft drinks and the price at a given machine selling cans. The machine price is $0.70 per can. The demand line shows that people will buy six cans per hour, the buyers being willing to pay between $0.70 and $1.20 per can. The consumer surplus for a person willing to pay $1.00 but actually paying $0.70 equals $0.30. The shaded area represents total consumer surplus per day. The dollar value of this area equals the sum of the six people's net benefit from exchange.

Exhibit 5.5: Consumer Surplus From Buying Soft Drinks

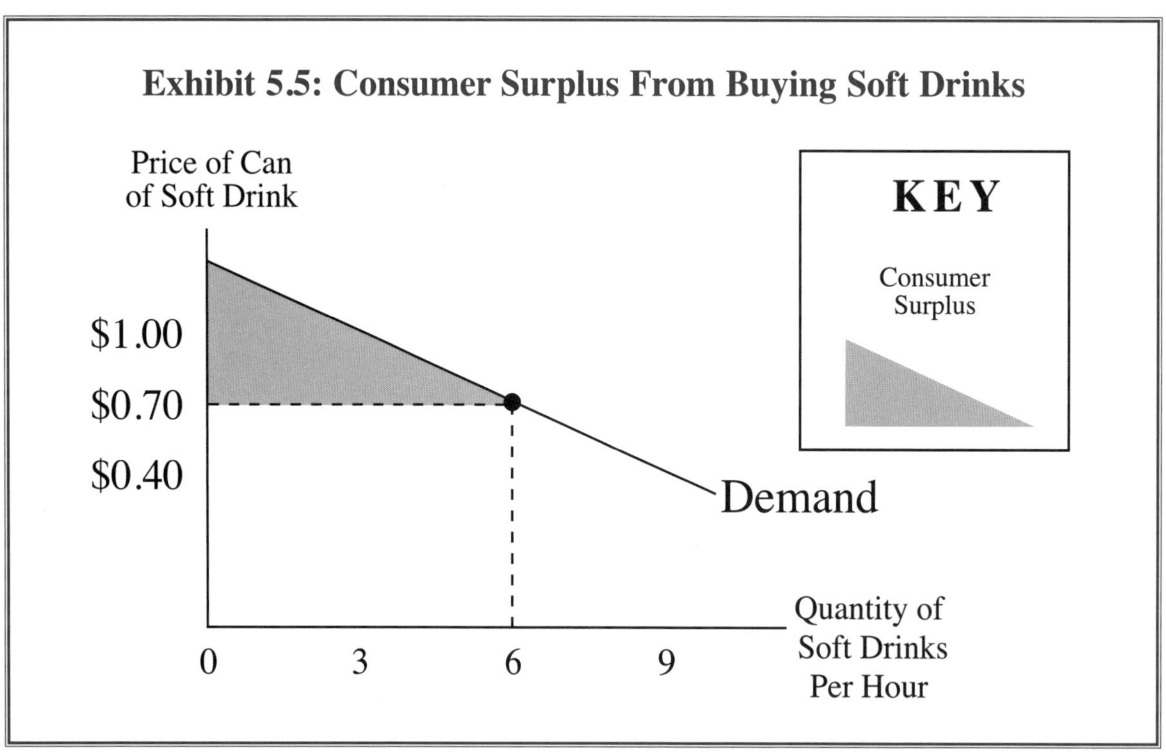

Exhibit 5.6 shows in more detail that a consumer surplus results from subtracting costs from benefits. Consumer surplus is the total value to consumers of six cans of soft drink minus the payment for sodas purchased. The consumers' total value from the six cans is represented as the sum of the prices they would be willing to pay. This sum equals ($0.70 + $0.80 + $0.90 + $1.00 + $1.10 + $1.20) or $5.70.

The rectangle with dimensions of $0.70 per can times six cans and an area of $4.20 represents the total payment that the machine will earn per hour. Consumer surplus, the area under the demand curve and above price, is ($5.70 - $4.20) = $1.50 every hour. This is not an incredible amount, but then this is a small-scale example.

Implications for Social Welfare

A more detailed theoretical analysis would show that, under ideal circumstances of competition and full information among buyers and sellers, **market exchange maximizes the value of consumer surplus**. If government would restrict the sales of cans of soft drinks, then the value lost would be greater than the value gained. On the other hand, if government encouraged consumers to buy more by paying part of the $0.70 cost of soft drinks, the additional value of the extra cans past six per day (in this example) would be less than the total cost to buy the cans. Market exchange under competitive conditions brings consumers to a level of consumption where extra costs exactly equal extra benefits, and this is the level where consumer surplus, a measure of social welfare, is at a

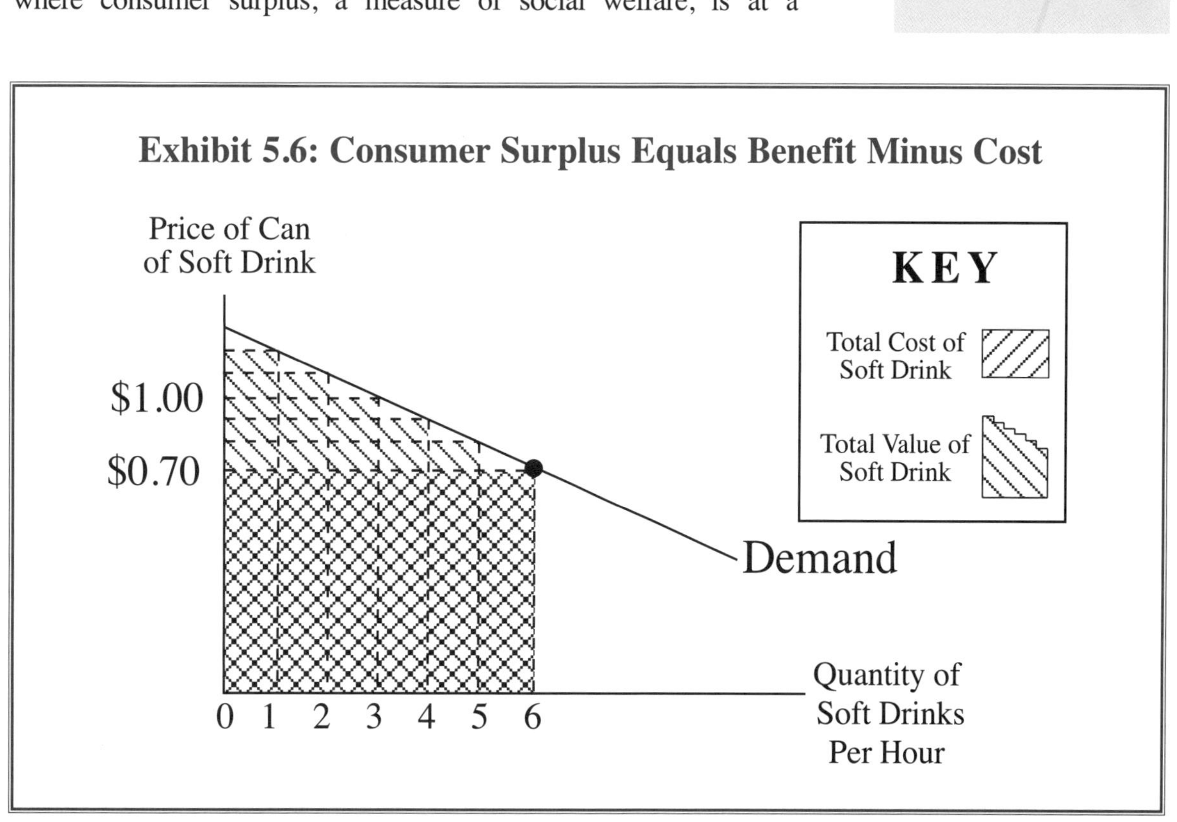

maximum. Critics of market economies will note that market conditions are rarely ideal. Market advocates say that the market system performs closer to the ideal than any other system can.

Principles of Macroeconomic Analysis

• **Macroeconomics:** analyzes aggregate or overall economic behavior; it is wholistic in method, focusing on economic totals

The method of **macroeconomics** is to measure and explain aggregate economic behavior. It therefore has a very different philosophical basis than microeconomics. A key difference is that macroeconomics applies wholistic methods. Furthermore, macroeconomics cannot hold other things constant in its analysis, nor is it marginal analysis, focusing instead on totals or aggregates.

Methodological Wholism

Macroeconomists largely ignore individual economic choices and instead focus on overall economic activity. While macroeconomic theory has to have firm microeconomic foundations, macro analysis emphasizes that the whole is not simply the sum of the parts. Thus, the perspective of macroeconomics is wholism.

What Is Methodological Wholism?

The wholistic perspective refutes an implication of methodological individualism, that understanding individual behavior is all we need to understand human behavior overall. Market prices, for example, are influenced by more than the sum of purely individual decisions. An individual buyer considers not only personal tastes, but also what others buy and what others think of what the individual buys.

Students of sociology will recognize that the wholistic view is the sociological view. While psychology, for example, and microeconomics examine individual behavior, sociology, the hybrid field of social psychology, and macroeconomics examine the big picture and how larger social and economic structures and processes modify the sums of individual decisions.

• **Fallacy of composition:** what is true for an individual is not true for the group

If you have studied logic, you will know that wholistic thinking highlights the **fallacy of composition**. What is true for the individual is not necessarily true for the larger group. A well-known example is that, in a theater fire, if one person runs to the exit, he may get out faster. If everyone in a large group runs, however, chaos follows and very few may get out alive. Here are economic applications to illustrate the point.

Applications of Methodological Wholism

A controversial application of wholistic thinking is John Maynard Keynes' idea of a "paradox of thrift" (Samuelson 1958, 237). In theory, if an individual family saves more of its income, it will have more purchasing power in the future. In Keynes' macroeconomic theory, however, if all families save more, the overall level of consumer spending will fall, causing businesses to produce less. Falling production will cause all families' incomes to fall. Therefore, higher saving may *not* lead to more purchasing power in the future. Critics contend that this paradox ignores long-run effects of saving on interest rates and business investment, but the paradox does illustrate wholistic thinking.

Agricultural market activity provides another example of wholistic thinking. As households increase their demand for products using soybeans, for instance, the price of soybeans will usually rise in the short run. If only one farmer plants 200 more acres of soybeans for the coming season, that farmer's income should also increase. If, however, many farmers plant millions more acres of soybeans, then soybean prices may decrease so much that overall farm income from soybeans could actually *decrease*.

Assume That Nothing Is Constant

While microeconomic analysis assumes that other things are held equal, macroeconomic analysis must assume that everything is free to vary at the same time. In microeconomics, when we study one market at a time, we apply **partial-equilibrium analysis**. We ask, for example, what happens to the price of lettuce if the wages of farm workers rise, holding family incomes and other factors constant.

• **Partial-equilibrium analysis**: studying equilibrium in one market at a time, assuming that prices and outputs in other markets are constant

In macroeconomics, however, we cannot assume that the family incomes are constant while the price of labor is rising. Simple logic shows that family incomes in the overall economy depend directly on the level of worker wages. In macroeconomics, overall economic activity cannot be analyzed without allowing for all decision makers to react to the decisions of everyone else.

Macroeconomics Is General-Equilibrium Analysis

Macroeconomic models of market economies, therefore, apply what is called **general-equilibrium analysis**. In analyzing product markets, labor markets, money markets, and other financial markets, macroeconomists recognize that prices and quantities sold in one of these markets have powerful effects on prices and outputs in each of the other three.

• **General-equilibrium analysis**: assuming that prices and quantities sold in one market can affect prices and quantities in all other markets

Everything Affects Everything Else

In macroeconomic analysis, everything affects everything else! As illustrated in the circular-flow model introduced in chapter 6 ("What Is an Economy?"), activity in financial markets affects outcomes in product and resource markets as well. For example, interest rates are determined by demand and supply of financial assets in money and other financial-asset markets. And yet, through their effects on consumption, saving, government borrowing, and business investment, interest rates also affect equilibrium wages, family incomes, and a number of other macroeconomic variables. Then, after interest-rate changes have their effects, changes in wages, incomes, and so on will have feedback effects on financial markets and interest rates.

• **Aggregate:** the sum or total of individual parts, as in aggregate income or aggregate consumption

• **Gross Domestic Product (GDP):** a measure of aggregate economic activity

Macroeconomics Emphasizes Totals

While marginal analysis emphasizes extras, macroeconomics emphasizes totals. Therefore, macroeconomics analyzes aggregate economic activity, rather than individual activity. To **aggregate** means to sum all the individual parts into a total. Mainstream macroeconomists gauge the health of an economy by measuring its aggregate level output. Specifically, they measure **gross domestic product** (GDP), which is the total output of goods and services for final consumption. To explain changes in GDP, they also measure aggregate consumption, aggregate income, aggregate imports and exports, and other totals that summarize the levels of activity in parts of the economy. As Expansion Point 5.1 shows, however, GDP has its critics.

Expansion Point 5.1: Technical and Moral Criticisms of GDP

Critics of macroeconomic analysis raise a number of technical and moral questions about summing up economic activity. Technically, GDP ignores the value of economic activity in the home. It only measures market transactions at market prices. Production in the home is unpaid and therefore unmeasured. If we paid each other to clean and cook for us, GDP would go up, but economic efficiency might go down.

In addition, chasing material wealth each year imposes costs in the form of market activity that GDP counts as benefits. Working more increases stress and the costs of ill health. We also buy the means to earn higher incomes, including gasoline and auto repairs for transportation, and work clothes to play the role. We eat out more while busy making more money to pay to eat out more. More health care, more clothes, more gasoline, and more meals out contribute to GDP. But they are for many a cost of creating wealth, not wealth itself.

Philip Wicksteed, an English Unitarian economist of the 1800s, complained that economic method may lead us to confuse ends with means. We measure GDP as if it summarized the end goal of economic activity. Yet, if GDP is rising, are we all really better off? GDP is an imperfect measure of only a portion of the means to make us happy. A rising value of aggregate output of bread has the potential to make us better off, but as Jesus said, "Man does not live on bread alone" (Matthew 4:4 NIV). And most religions reject the materialistic philosophy that a rising supply of goods and services is the ultimate end of all human activity. In answering the question, "What is the chief goal of man?" the Westminster Confession, for example, answers, "To glorify God and enjoy Him forever." At times, GDP can obscure any higher view of human purpose than market sales.

• **Aggregate demand and supply:** a model explaining the levels of overall output and price

Aggregate Demand and Supply Determine the General Levels of Price and Output

How do we explain how high GDP will be and how high the general level of prices will be? Economists use the model of **aggregate demand and aggregate supply**. Aggregate demand is the relationship between the general level of prices and a measure of the overall economic output that people are willing and able to buy. Aggregate supply shows how changes in the general level of prices affect the overall economic output that factories and businesses are willing and able to supply. Just as demand and supply determine the price in an individual market, aggregate demand and supply determine an economy's output level and general price level. And just as an individual firm has an efficient level of output, so the economy has an efficient overall level of output.

•**Real GDP:** the money value of economic output, controlling for changes in prices so as to measure only on changes in real output

Macro Equilibrium

Equilibrium of aggregate demand and supply determines the levels of output and price, as shown in Exhibit 5.7. Equilibrium output is Q^*_1 and equilibrium price is 1.0. The details of market demand and supply and aggregate demand and supply are not identical. Aggregate output, for instance, is the *money value* of output of all goods and services controlling for price changes, or **real GDP**, rather than the output of any one good such as automobiles. The general principles, however, are the same.

Exhibit 5.7: Equilibrium of Aggregate Demand and Supply

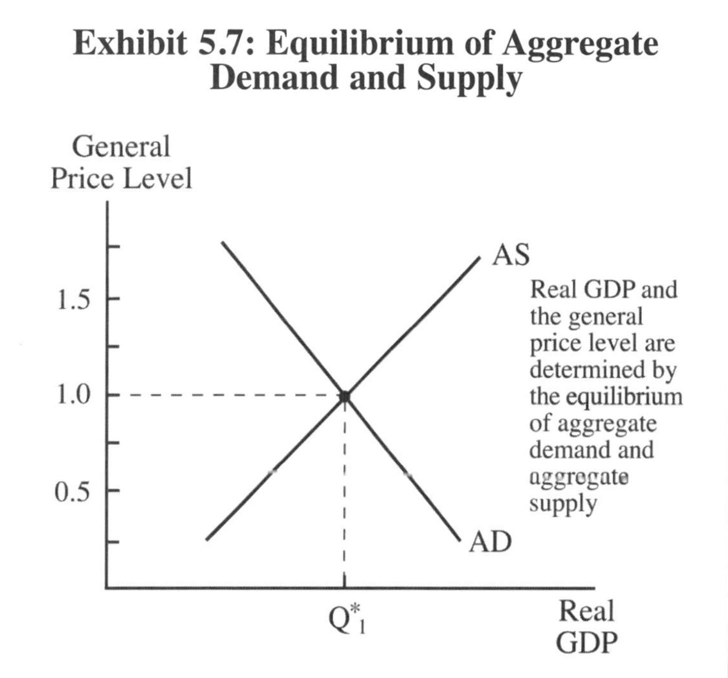

More helpful for the student than examining a single equilibrium is to examine the effects of a shift in aggregate demand or aggregate supply, when equilibrium output and the general price level change. Here again, the graph and explanation are much the same (up to a point) as market demand and supply.

Increases in Aggregate Demand

An increase in aggregate demand, for example, causes higher output in the short run and a higher price level too. The effects of an increase in aggregate demand are illustrated in Exhibit 5.8.

What macroeconomic events would cause aggregate demand to rise? Here is a partial list: an increase in the money supply, a cut in taxes or an increase in government spending, an increase in demand for exports of goods and services to other countries, and an increase in consumer spending or business investment due to more optimistic expectations about future economic activity and future income. Each would cause an expansion in economic activity, at least in the short run, and a rise in the general level of prices.

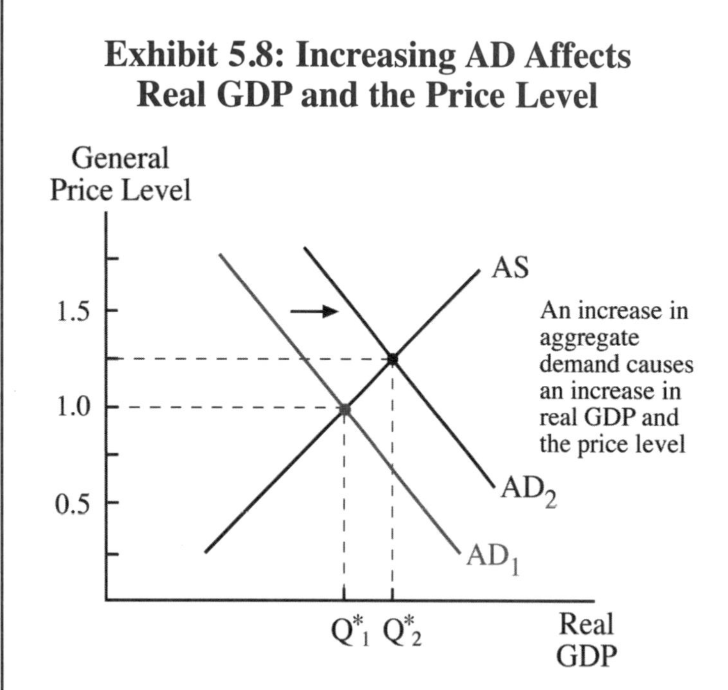
Exhibit 5.8: Increasing AD Affects Real GDP and the Price Level
General Price Level
1.5
1.0
0.5
AS
An increase in aggregate demand causes an increase in real GDP and the price level
AD2
AD1
Q*1 Q*2
Real GDP

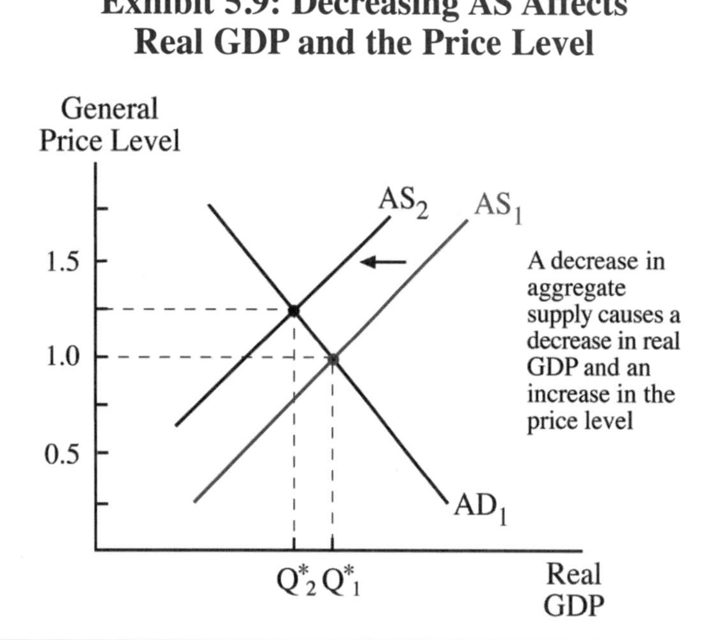
Exhibit 5.9: Decreasing AS Affects Real GDP and the Price Level
General Price Level
1.5
1.0
0.5
AS2
AS1
A decrease in aggregate supply causes a decrease in real GDP and an increase in the price level
AD1
Q*2 Q*1
Real GDP

Exhibit 5.8, then, illustrates an economic expansion that is caused by increasing aggregated demand. Real GDP is rising, but the expansion may also cause a problem of inflation of prices. Obviously, a decrease in the money supply, a rise in taxes, or a decrease in exports, consumer spending, or business investment will cause a decrease in aggregate demand, a contraction in economic activity, and a lower general level of prices.

Decreases in Aggregate Supply

A decrease in aggregate supply would also cause a recession and a higher general level of prices, as illustrated in Exhibit 5.9. If all firms simultaneously reduced their willingness to supply goods and services, the economy would suffer, as shown by output falling from Q*1 to Q*2 and price rising from 1.0 to about 1.25.

A rise in oil prices or a widespread drought and higher food prices could cause a recessionary decrease in aggregate supply, because energy and food prices affect the entire economy. Aggregate supply would also fall if workers demanded higher wages and businesses demanded higher prices. Lower oil and food prices or lower wage and price demands would have the opposite effects.

Chapter Summary

1. Economists explain economic activity in terms of cause and effect. Causal difficulties include different short-run and long-run effects and reverse causation. Causal relations among economic variables are regular enough, but they are also subject to uncertainty. Economists use algebra and geometry to explain regular economic relations, and statistics to measure uncertain economic relations.

2. Microeconomics uses methodological individualism. To understand overall economic activity, first analyze individual decisions.

3. People compare costs and benefits of their actions and respond to incentives and constraints that alter perceived costs and benefits.

4. Microeconomic analysis is marginal analysis. Optimizing behavior means choosing the level of any activity that equates the extra costs with the extra benefits of an extra unit of that activity.

5. Willingness to pay measures the value of extra product. Consumer surplus is the net value of output, subtracting actual price paid from the buyer's willingness to pay. Under competitive market exchange, consumers maximize their surplus value.

6. Macroeconomic analysis is total analysis. It begins by measuring and explaining changes in economic aggregates, such as gross domestic product (GDP) and aggregate consumer spending.

7. Critics complain that GDP ignores non-market work, while including certain costs as well as benefits of market work. GDP may confuse ends with means and ignore spiritual aspects of life.

PROBLEMS FOR PRACTICE

5.1 Explain in your own words what it means for economists to try to explain economic causality. What patterns of causation and what causal relationships over time do they observe? Give examples.

5.2 Is economic analysis of behavioral relations the same as the analysis of statistical correlations among variables? Are the two related at all? Explain by making reference to the analysis of demand for and supply of a good such as cans of soft drinks. Explain how we use algebra and graphs to explain the regularity and uncertainty of economic relationships.

5.3 What are the principles of microeconomic analysis? Restate them in your own words, adding your own examples as you are able.

5.4* Describe an activity in your own life not explained in the text in which extra benefits of the activity fall and the extra costs rise as the level of activity increases. Do you really think marginally, or is it all or nothing for you in your personal decisions?

5.5* In Exhibit 5.6, what would be the effect of requiring that only four cans per hour be sold at that machine? Is net value to society increased or decreased by this rule?

5.6* The Jones family pays an average of 25 percent of its income as income taxes. Because tax rates are higher as income rises, the Jones family pays $0.40 on the last dollar that it earns. Therefore, it pays a "marginal tax rate" of 40 percent. If the Jones family is considering the contribution to its standard of living of the last few thousand dollars of gross income, which tax rate is more useful—the average tax rate of 25 percent or the marginal tax rate?

5.7 What is consumer surplus and what does it measure? Tell in your own words how market activities create or destroy consumer surplus and the implications for social welfare.

5.8* Assume that the demand and supply equations for bushels of wheat are as follows:

$$Q_d = 15 - (3 * P)$$
$$Q_s = 1 + (4 * P)$$

Also assume that, in equilibrium, $Q_d = Q_s$. Solve for equilibrium price by setting quantity demanded equal to quantity supplied. What is the disequilibrium condition at prices of $1.50 and $2.50?

5.9 How does macroeconomic analysis differ from microeconomic analysis? What questions does macroeconomics consider?

For class discussion:

5.10 What factors will cause aggregate demand to increase, and what will be the effect on economic output (real GDP) and the general level of prices? What factors can cause aggregate supply to increase, and what will be the effect on economic output (real GDP) and the general level of prices? Which would a tax increase cause? A money supply decrease? Be able to illustrate the various cases of shifting AD and AS.

5.11* What other factors might cause quantity demanded for soft drinks to vary each week (in addition to the two discussed for Exhibit 5.2)?

5.12 Do students study their books as hard as they possibly can? If not, is this evidence that students do not optimize and therefore do not act rationally? Think marginally.

See Answer Key for hints/answers to starred (*) questions.

Chapter 6

What Is an Economy?

Economy as System

What this chapter will help you think about:

1. What is an economy?
2. What are the three fundamental economic activities?
3. Why should we view an economy as a system?
4. How does the economy interact with government and culture?
5. How does the circular flow express economic complexity?
6. What are four actual types of economic systems?
7. How do these systems differ?

- **Economy:** a system of social, commercial, political, and legal institutions by which people use their resources to produce, distribute, and consume goods and services

An **economy** is a system of social, commercial, political, and legal institutions and organizations by which people use their scarce resources to produce, distribute, and consume goods and services. Four distinct ideas are important in this definition. First, an economy involves three fundamental activities: **production, distribution, and consumption**. Other economic activities support those three. Second, an economy is a **system** with interrelated subsystems, such as financial markets, resource markets, and a legal network. Third, an economy has **resource endowments** of labor, tools, equipment, minerals, and so on. Finally, an economy is endowed with particular **institutions and organizations**. Institutions are its rules and customary behaviors such as property laws, commercial codes, social conventions, and moral beliefs regarding economic goals. Economic organizations are the administrative structures and associations of people that monitor and direct commercial, governmental, and social activity.

This chapter focuses on economies as systems. Any system has a set of goals, and the goal of an economy is to make, distribute, and allow people to use goods and services. To explain different aspects of the economy as a system, we will review two models: first, a three-sector model of the balance between economy, government, and culture; second, the circular flow of income and spending. All economies are the same or similar. This chapter concludes with a brief introduction to four historical types of economic systems: democratic capitalism, Soviet state socialism, the social-welfare state, and neo-mercantilist economies. A general overview of the two other aspects of an economy—its resource endowments and its institutions and organizations—will follow in the next chapter.

Fundamental Economic Activities

Certain human activities are decidedly "economic" and a few are fundamental. **Production, distribution, and consumption** are three fundamental economic activities of any tribe, village, or civilization. In every culture, at every time in history, people have attempted to meet their needs by combining brute labor with other scarce resources such as land, available tools, human knowledge, and raw materials from animals, plants, and minerals. They exchange any surplus products for other goods and services, increasing their ability to meet needs and wants.

• **Three fundamental economic activities:**
1) production
2) distribution
3) consumption

Producing, Distributing, and Consuming

Consuming goods and services sustains life, provides pleasure or alleviates pain, and allows us to pursue other goals, whether noble or not. Most goods and services that we consume first must be made or produced—thus the name "products." People must then distribute these products to consumers, whether by voluntary "market" exchange or command planning.

Production can be as simple as using garden tools, a few seeds, fertilizer, yard space, and hard work to grow vegetables. Or production can be as complex as assembling a computer with parts produced all over the world. Whether simple or complex, production combines resources of labor, human knowledge and skill, tools and machines, materials, and land to make goods or services. In brief, production transforms inputs into outputs.

• **Production:** Combining resources (inputs) to make goods and services (products or outputs)

Distribution involves the division of output among all members of society. Think of distribution as splitting a pie among people who want "their share." The distribution question is usually on their minds when people call for economic fairness. Yet distribution also influences economic output. How society distributes output today influences what will be produced and consumed tomorrow.

• **Distribution:** Dividing the economic pie into shares for different people and groups

Chronologically, **consumption** is the final act of this three-act play. Consumption is also the most important because it motivates production and distribution. Consumption is always the goal of production and distribution for a majority of the people a majority of the time. Other goals may interfere at times, and leaders may redirect production and distribution toward pursuing wars, personal glory, or ideology, but ordinary people's attentions usually center on production and distribution for the purpose of consuming to meet needs and wants.

• **Consumption:** Using products to meet wants and needs, the goal of production and distribution

Finance, Government, and International Commerce

Other economic activities are closely related to the three fundamental activities. Financial activities of saving, investing,

and borrowing, for instance, are closely related to consumption, production, and distribution. Saving is a decision not to consume. Investing is a decision to put savings to productive use by creating more equipment, building a new building, or buying more inventories of goods. If you do not have your own savings set aside, you must then borrow other people's savings for any investment or any consumption that exceeds your income.

Government activities can also affect what is consumed and produced and how economic output is distributed. Taxes, for example, reduce household income and consumption, and business income. In addition, government spending and transfer payments (government gifts) alter what is produced and who receives the output. Government redistribution of income, for example, can shift income from the rich to the poor or from the politically weak to the politically powerful.

International trade, shipping goods and selling services across national borders, is another economic activity that can enhance a nation's consumption possibilities. International trade influences patterns of production in the world and the global distribution of income. When American firms shift production to Indonesia, for example, Americans temporarily lose jobs, Indonesians gain jobs, and eventually total jobs in the world may increase. Government interventions in international trade can also alter global and national patterns of consumption and production. When the United States protects domestic automobile makers, the companies earn higher profits and U.S. auto workers have more jobs, but U.S. consumers pay more for their cars and foreign auto makers lose sales and jobs.

This brief review of fundamental and other important economic activities illustrates an important economic principle: the parts of an economy are interrelated, and changes in one sector impact other sectors. This is a major theme of this chapter, and for emphasis you will see it repeated several times, especially in our discussion of an economy as a complex system.

Economy as a Complex System

An economy is a complex system of money flows, legal relationships, organizations, and governmental interventions that affect economic activity by establishing incentives for and restraints on human behavior. The economy of any industrialized nation, whether socialist or free market, is too complex to be quickly understood in all its details. The global economy is even more complex, composed of its own intricate subsystems. International trade creates commercial linkages among various national economies, and causes national currencies to flow through global financial markets. International trade also involves multiple levels of government taxes, regulations, and subsidies.

Understanding Economic Systems

If they are so complex, why is it important to understand economic systems? The complexity of the system **links** the **welfare** of others to our economic decisions and our welfare to their economic decisions. In *The Logic of Failure*, Dietrich Dorner makes this point about economic, ecological, and political systems:

> The modern world is made up of innumerable interrelated subsystems, and we need to think in terms of these interrelations. In the past, such considerations were less important. What did the growth of Los Angeles matter to a Sacramento Valley farmer a hundred years ago? Nothing. Today, however, aqueducts running the length of the state make northern and southern Californians bitter competitors for water. Of what concern to us were religious differences in Islam forty years ago? Apparently none. The global interrelations of today make such dissension important everywhere (1996, 5).

• **Economic complexity** links others' welfare to our decisions and our welfare to their decisions.

Individuals may fail to understand the economic subsystems in which they make decisions. Jane Bryant Quinn (1999), for example, has explained how a stock-market investor using the Internet can go into debt online without intending to do so and without even realizing it. For an explanation, see Expansion Point 6.1.

Government policy makers also fail on occasion to understand systemic economic relationships, especially how policies and regulations can change individual and group behavior. They often forget a simple economic principle: in all economic systems, the

Expansion Point 6.1: How to Go Into Debt in the Stock Market Without Really Trying

Oops!

Beware! Buying stocks over the Internet may be hazardous to your balance sheet. If you don't understand the trading system, you can go into debt very quickly and not even know it.

If you have an online account at an investment firm, you might put in an order to buy a highly volatile technology stock when its price is $10. Let's say you want to buy 2,000 shares of stock with $20,000 that is already in your investment account. Before the order to buy is executed, however, the stock's price rises to $14. When the stock is bought, the broker pays $28,000 for the shares and bills them to you. Since your account has only $20,000, you are indebted to the investment firm for $8,000! To avoid triggering such a loan, put in a "limit order" stating the highest price you will pay for each share.

Another error is to get impatient when an order doesn't register immediately on the computer screen. If you think your order did not go through, you may click again. But if the trader's computer system is merely running slow, you may have just doubled your order and overspent your account again, triggering another loan.

Source: Jane Bryant Quinn, "Investors Buying Stocks on Margin Online Are Best Positioned to Hear 'Crack of Doom,'" *Buffalo News*, Sunday, April 4, 1999, C-13.

• **People respond** to policy changes in ways that protect *their* wealth and meet *their* needs and wants.

people will respond to policy changes with decisions that reflect their desires to acquire and keep wealth and to meet their own needs and wants. Expansion Point 6.2 reviews two historical examples of a political leader's failure to fully understand economic systems and the resulting policy mistakes.

It is not possible to describe here all aspects of an economic system. It is possible to describe particularly important aspects of economies as systems, using simplified models of economic activity. Here are two helpful models. The first is a model of how economic activity is embedded in a broader social setting. The second is a model of the complexity of flows of money income and expenditure in modern economies.

Expansion Point 6.2: Effects of Failing to Understand Economic Systems

Government officials who impose policy changes and moral constraints on economic activity often regret the effects. The reason, as illustrated in the following examples, is that they often fail to fully understand the system that they want to change, and how people will react.

1. A policy error that unravels quickly can be repealed before it is enacted. On Tuesday, November 12, 1991, President George Bush said that credit card interest rates were too high. Hearing Bush's comments, Senator Al D'Amato proposed legislation to limit interest rates to 14 percent.

By Thursday, Citicorp could not sell its credit card related securities in financial markets. By Friday, investors had became fearful that regulation would cause falling profits in domestic banking.

During the day, share prices of U.S. bank stocks plummeted. Understandably, the Senate put aside the proposal to limit rates.

2. The United States is not the only country afflicted with policy mistakes. Before his death in 1953, Soviet leader Joseph Stalin's economic policies also went awry. During World War II, Stalin heavily taxed peasant holdings of property to pay for the Russian war effort.

When the war ended, Stalin continued the heavy taxation, partly because he disliked the peasants and partly to direct their efforts away from private farming and toward collective farm work. Stalin levied a tax on each cow and fruit tree, for example, to capture some of the value that flowed from such private wealth.

Between 1943 and 1951, the tax rates increased about 50 percent. What did the peasants do? They slaughtered their cows and chopped down their fruit trees to reduce their tax liability. Private holdings of cattle were 29 million in January 1950, but only 23.2 million in January 1952.

Source: Alec Nove, *An Economic History of the U.S.S.R.* (New York: Penguin Press, 1969), 301.

The Economy in Balance

Economies always operate within political and cultural systems. To understand a nation's economic activity requires that we understand the political and social forces that encourage, direct, or restrict it. A short explanation and pictorial model will illustrate.

In describing the ideal of **democratic capitalism**, Michael Novak explains the interrelatedness of the economic, political, and social (or cultural) spheres of influence.

> What do I mean by "democratic capitalism"? I mean three systems in one: a predominantly market economy; a polity respectful of the rights of the individual to life, liberty, and the pursuit of happiness; and a system of cultural institutions moved by ideals of liberty and justice for all. In short, three dynamic and converging systems functioning as one: a democratic polity, an economy based on markets and incentives, and a moral-cultural system which is pluralistic, and, in the largest sense, liberal. Social systems like those of the United States, West Germany, and Japan (with perhaps a score of others among the world's nations) illustrate the type (Novak 1982, 14).

Exhibit 6.1 illustrates the main point, that economic activity occurs in a larger social context where government and cultural forces may intervene. Each sector of this model—economy, government, and culture—deserves further explanation.

The **economy** is the free-enterprise sector for production, distribution, and consumption of products. The economy includes three key freedoms: to hold, use, and assign the use of private property; to voluntarily exchange resources and products at fluctuating market prices; and to cooperate and contract with one another in various enterprises, whether for private profit, for mutual aid, or for civic betterment. Economic freedom promotes innovation and productive activity.

The **government** sector is authorized to use coercive force. Ideally, its agents exercise that power to improve public welfare. Government can improve economic efficiency by establishing and administering the rules of the game for private

- **Democratic capitalism** is a balance of:
  1) free-enterprise,
  2) coercive government, and
  3) pluralistic culture

- **Economy:** the free-enterprise sector with
  1) private property,
  2) voluntary exchange at market prices, and
  3) freedom to cooperate and contract with others

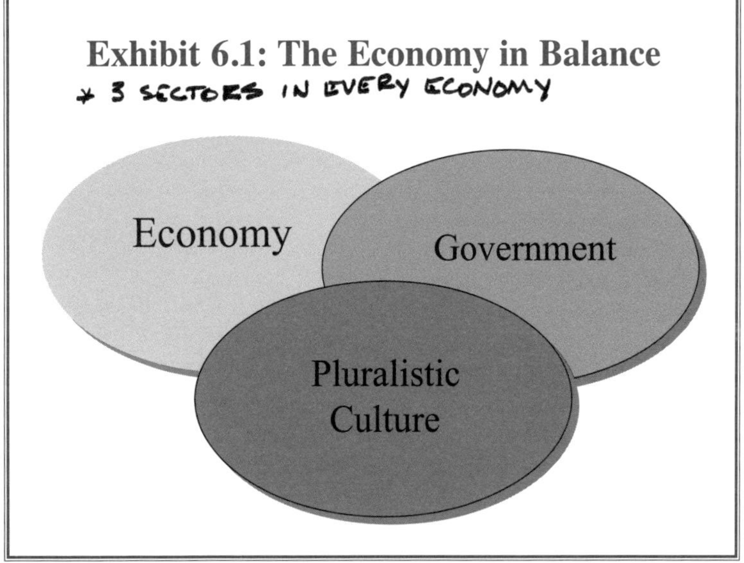

- **Government:** the coercive sector that:
  1) exercises its power to improve public welfare;
  2) sets and enforces rules for private and public action; and
  3) provides other services such as a regulated money and national defense
- **Pluralistic culture**: non-commercial, non-coercive sector that:
  1) expresses moral, religious, artistic, intellectual, and social interests and aspirations;
  2) emphasizes freedom of ideas; and
  3) is embodied in formal and informal social institutions

and public action, supporting a police force and a justice system to restrict harmful private impulses. In the classical English political economy of Adam Smith (*Wealth of Nations* 1776), the government also would provide minimal additional services such as regulating the money supply and providing for national defense.

A **pluralistic culture** reflects the noncommercial moral, religious, artistic, intellectual, and social interests and aspirations of a people. Being pluralistic, the sector lacks the coercive power of government and is distinct from it in emphasizing tolerance and freedom of beliefs. Government can enforce cultural freedoms and can force people to abide by their legal contracts in the cultural sphere.

A people's culture expresses itself in formal and informal institutions and organizations of religion, education, art, and ethnicity. A tolerant culture need not declare all views to be equally valid. It does allow different views to compete in a marketplace of cultural ideas. An effective pluralistic culture will nevertheless influence commercial and governmental structures and outcomes.

Implications

Novak's analysis of democratic capitalism suggests an important principle about economic activity in any setting. Economic theories that ignore the pervasive influence of government and culture will tend to be sterile and not very helpful in educating people about how economic activity actually proceeds. For example, using the mainstream economic measures of productive and allocative efficiency (introduced in the first chapter), we could label all actual economic activity inefficient. While such analysis can be helpful, it also can be misleading when it ignores the constraints imposed by governmental and cultural institutions. In former communist economies, for example, allocative efficiency is not practically attainable without time-consuming changes in government and commercial culture. In short, the theoretical ideals of free-market economic efficiency are not always practically attainable without addressing influences from the other two sectors.

While economic, governmental, and cultural spheres may seem to operate independently, in practice people experience significant overlap. This is true, not only for national policy, but also for individual choice. Social conventions of appropriate dress usually shape individual decisions of what clothes to buy. Cultural attitudes about humane treatment of animals now influence sales of fur coats. Rules such as "no shoes, no shirt, no service" in restaurants regulate individual decisions about what to wear. Governments also regulate, in the public interest, the sale of flammable clothing, influencing the cost of clothing. Therefore, simplified models of consumer choice that treat all household decisions as purely individual, while *quite* helpful for analyzing certain aspects of individual choice, tend to ignore such constraints.

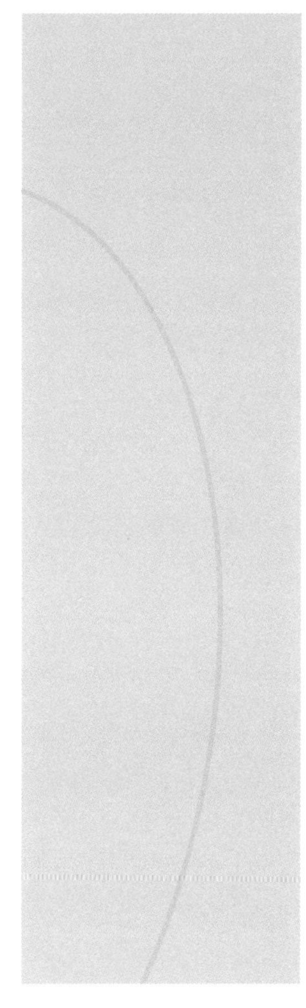

Imbalances

Novak's model suggests that a society out of balance will suffer either slower economic progress or severe economic inequities. Perhaps other benefits accrue, but historical evidence suggests that sectoral imbalances have negative effects overall. Of course, each national economy strikes its own balance among the three sectors. And within each sector, structures and operations vary across nations. Certain democratic economies such as the Japanese and the French, for instance, attempt more government economic planning but offer less government welfare to families than social-welfare states such as Britain or Germany.

Nevertheless, we can identify instances in which the free economy, the coercive government, or the church with a cultural monopoly have dominated. Exhibit 6.2 illustrates the imbalances and lists several examples. In the case of cultural imbalance, the word "church" is used in the general sense of a dominant religious institution, as in the distinction between church and state (not just in the sense of the Christian institution). In each case, history suggests the ill effects of the imbalance.

Dominant Church. The Christian church in southern Europe repressed economic freedom in the sixteenth century. Persecutions during the Spanish Inquisition (after 1478) caused many Jewish and Muslim artisans, professionals, and skilled workers to flee Spain in the ensuing years. On the eve of the scientific and capitalist industrial revolutions, intolerance drove wealth, knowledge, and innovative thinking from southern to northern Europe and elsewhere (Landes 1999, 179-81). Historians

Exhibit 6.2: Economic, Governmental, and Religious Imbalance

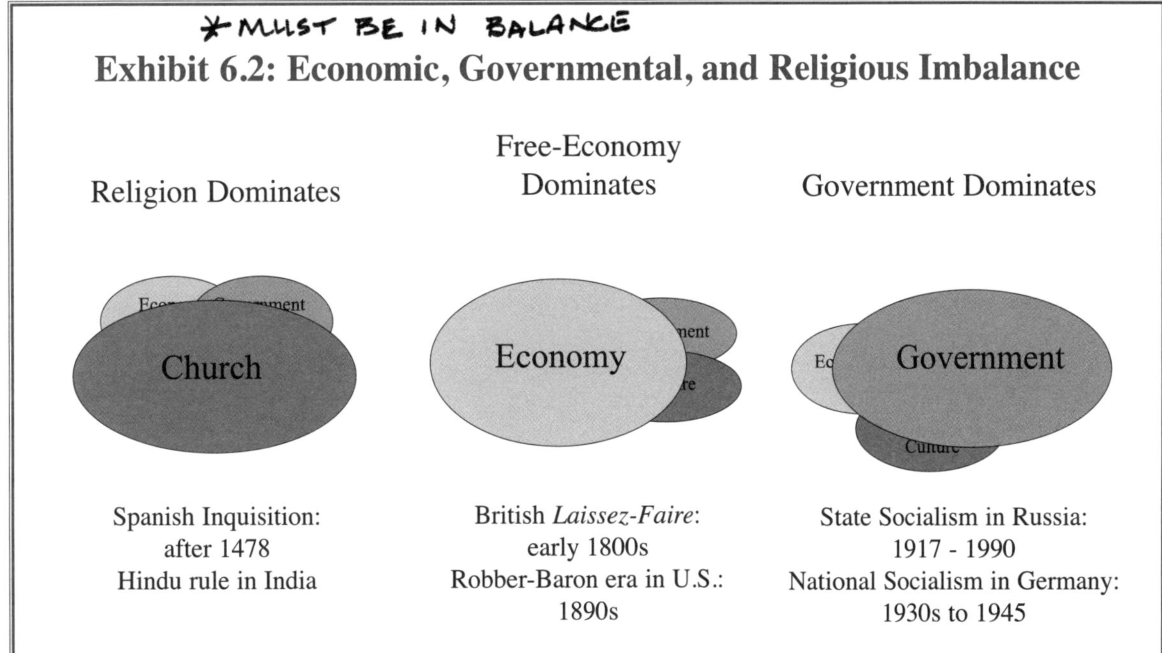

Spanish Inquisition: after 1478
Hindu rule in India

British *Laissez-Faire*: early 1800s
Robber-Baron era in U.S.: 1890s

State Socialism in Russia: 1917 - 1990
National Socialism in Germany: 1930s to 1945

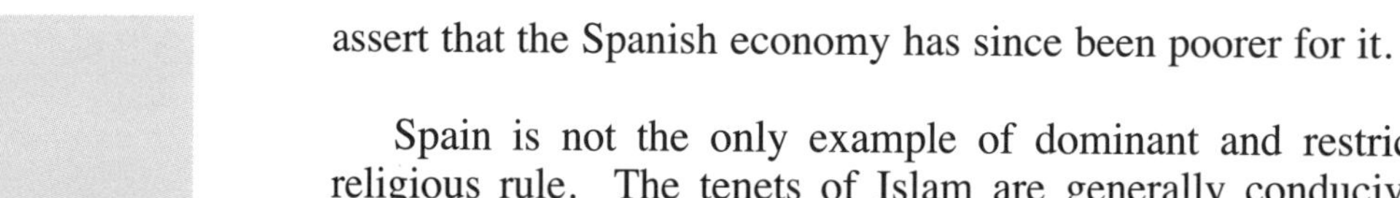

assert that the Spanish economy has since been poorer for it.

Spain is not the only example of dominant and restrictive religious rule. The tenets of Islam are generally conducive to commercial activity, yet Muslim clerics in Iran in the twentieth century imposed such strict religious rule that economic progress was affected. Hindu belief, however, is generally less conducive to commerce. India's economic progress has suffered as a direct result of Hinduism's religious preference for the welfare of cows and other animals, as compared to concerns for the welfare of humans, especially those in the lowest castes. A philosophical fatalism also requires Hindu believers to accept rather than better their economic status.

Dominant Economy. Historians blame *laissez-faire* in Britain in the nineteenth century for economic inequities and excesses such as child labor in coal mines and factories (although British culture must also shoulder a share of the blame). The minimal-government philosophy prevented Parliament from supplying rapid relief to victims of the Irish potato famine in the 1840s.

Dominant Government. The Soviet planning system that ruled Russia and other communist nations in the twentieth century thoroughly squelched free-market activity and non-communist culture. While underground markets thrived and the Russian Orthodox Church persevered through great difficulties, the extremes of Communist rule also squelched innovation and economic growth after the 1950s.

National Socialism in Germany was more successful at promoting economic growth, in part because it maintained the free-market framework in spite of heavy government direction. Yet Nazi rule so thoroughly squelched the spiritual and humane influences of the German Lutheran Church, and it turned the German economic machine to such aggressive military purposes that other nations rose up and defeated the system.

Conclusions

We draw two conclusions, then, from Novak's model. First, economic activity is constrained by government and social institutions and organizations. Second, a society out of balance is at risk. While not everyone will agree with Novak's ideal conception of democratic capitalism, current discussion centers on shaping the mix of sectoral influences.

Novak wrote *The Spirit of Democratic Capitalism* (1982) as a reaction against certain Catholic theologians who claimed that the socialist ideal held the moral and religious high ground. Novak contended that the Christian faith was consistent with a proper understanding of capitalism. In the 1970s and 1980s, the intellectual conflict between socialists (those pursuing their ideals of social justice) and economic liberals (those favoring capitalist liberties) was vigorous. Expansion Point 6.3 compares socialist and democratic-capitalist ideals and reviews these Christian perspectives at odds. Today, however, with the failure of socialist-oriented state economic planning, debate centers on how to shape democratic capitalism to balance the ideals of both economic liberalism and social justice.

Expansion Point 6.3: Who Holds the Moral High Ground? Christian Socialists vs. Christian Capitalists

Socialism

1. *Emphasizes cooperation and sharing.*
2. *Condemns capitalism's individualist greed.*
3. *Condemns class system and class conflict.*
4. *Promotes equality of outcomes.*
5. *Expresses hope for social justice.*

Democratic Capitalism

1. *Rejects totalitarianism.*
2. *Encourages individual initiative.*
3. *Channels greed productively.*
4. *Rejects sin of envy as a basis for policy.*
5. *Upholds eighth commandment against stealing.*

With which of these ideals are you more comfortable? Theologians and economists with moral sentiments have argued both sides of the debate from the same Scriptures. Christian socialists, for example, have used the Bible to show that God is concerned for the poor and against the greedy and the rich who trample the poor for their own gain. Therefore, they conclude, God favors socialism.

Christian capitalists, however, also have used the Bible to show that God condemns envy, covetousness, and the taking of other people's property, even if for supposedly noble purposes. Therefore, God must favor the freedom of a market economy with private property.

Michael Novak's idea of a balance of forces in democratic capitalism is consistent with what many Christians believe to be three important tenets of the faith.

(1) God made man and woman in His own image. As image bearers, people should be free to be creative and to make their own decisions.

(2) But man and woman sinned and all creation is now fallen. So, God ordained governing officials and structures to restrain and punish evildoers.

(3) Even so, Jesus Christ came to reconcile sinful humanity to a righteous God. Therefore, an active Church that proclaims the message of forgiveness and makes disciples to be salt and light in the world moderates excesses of free commerce and coercive government.

The task of Christian theologians and economists has moved beyond the moral and religious aspects of the capitalist/socialist debate. According to Stephen Smith, "the question of what *kind* of market system is best is now more important than ever, and, in fact, underlies many of the most contentious public policy debates in the U.S. today."

In retrospect, the Bible supports neither pure capitalism nor pure socialism (as Marx described it), and knowing this could have saved much rancor. First, pure capitalism is based on the unassailable rights of property and the pure freedom of contract. Scripture, however, claims that God is the sovereign and His people are the stewards of His property, setting limits on our "rights." Scripture recognizes no complete freedom of contract. Instead, it mandates limits on rights to sell land, to charge interest for loans to the poor, and to reap all one's grain (commanding that landowners leave the fringes and not reap twice so that the poor could glean behind them). Second, pure socialism condemns hiring of wage labor for profit, but the Bible nowhere condemns this per se. Yet the question of appropriate balance remains.

Sources: Michael Novak, *The Spirit of Democratic Capitalism* (New York: Touchstone, 1982).

Stephen L.S. Smith, "Integration and Differentiation: Economics at Christian Colleges," *Bulletin of the Association of Christian Economists* (Fall 1994): 9-23.

Complexity of the Circular Flow

Another helpful visual model of economic activity is the circular flow of income and expenditure. A portion of the model to be developed in the macroeconomic section of this text is reproduced in Exhibit 6.3. This is not the place to explain it fully, but we can use it to highlight the complexity of economic systems.

The circular flow shows that households and businesses interact in product, resource, and financial markets. Consumption spending and income payments are the two main flows in the model. Households and businesses also meet in the public square of government, adding to the complexity. Just as government affects economic activity in the three-sector model above, government taxing, spending, and borrowing constrain and subsidize households and businesses here.

Simultaneous Causation

How would you answer the question, "What causes what in the circular flow?" For example, does a change in household income cause a change in household consumer spending, or does a change in consumer spending cause a change in income? The model makes clear that income and consumer spending influence each other simultaneously.

According to the economic theory of John Maynard Keynes (1936), this **simultaneous causation** (or feedback) between income and consumer spending contributes to the instability of the level of employment and income in market economies. The circular flow, therefore, is helpful in teaching about the business cycle, those recurrent fluctuations in economic activity.

- **Simultaneous causation (feedback) between income and consumption:** changes in consumer spending cause changes in income, and at the same time changes in income cause changes in consumer spending

Interdependence of Markets

More generally, activity in one market affects activities in the other three. A change in financial market conditions leading to higher interest rates, for example, will influence consumer saving and borrowing, and, therefore, consumer spending. Higher rates will also reduce business borrowing for investment, while increasing the cost of government borrowing.

In addition, Exhibit 6.3 shows that a nation's economy combines domestic commerce with international trade. Therefore, increases in domestic consumer spending will, for example, stimulate foreign imports and production in other countries.

As you can see, economic activities in various sectors and markets are interdependent. What causes what in this model? Everything causes everything else in the circular flow. We will explore the circular flow in more detail in a later chapter. Let's turn now to a brief review of four types of economic systems.

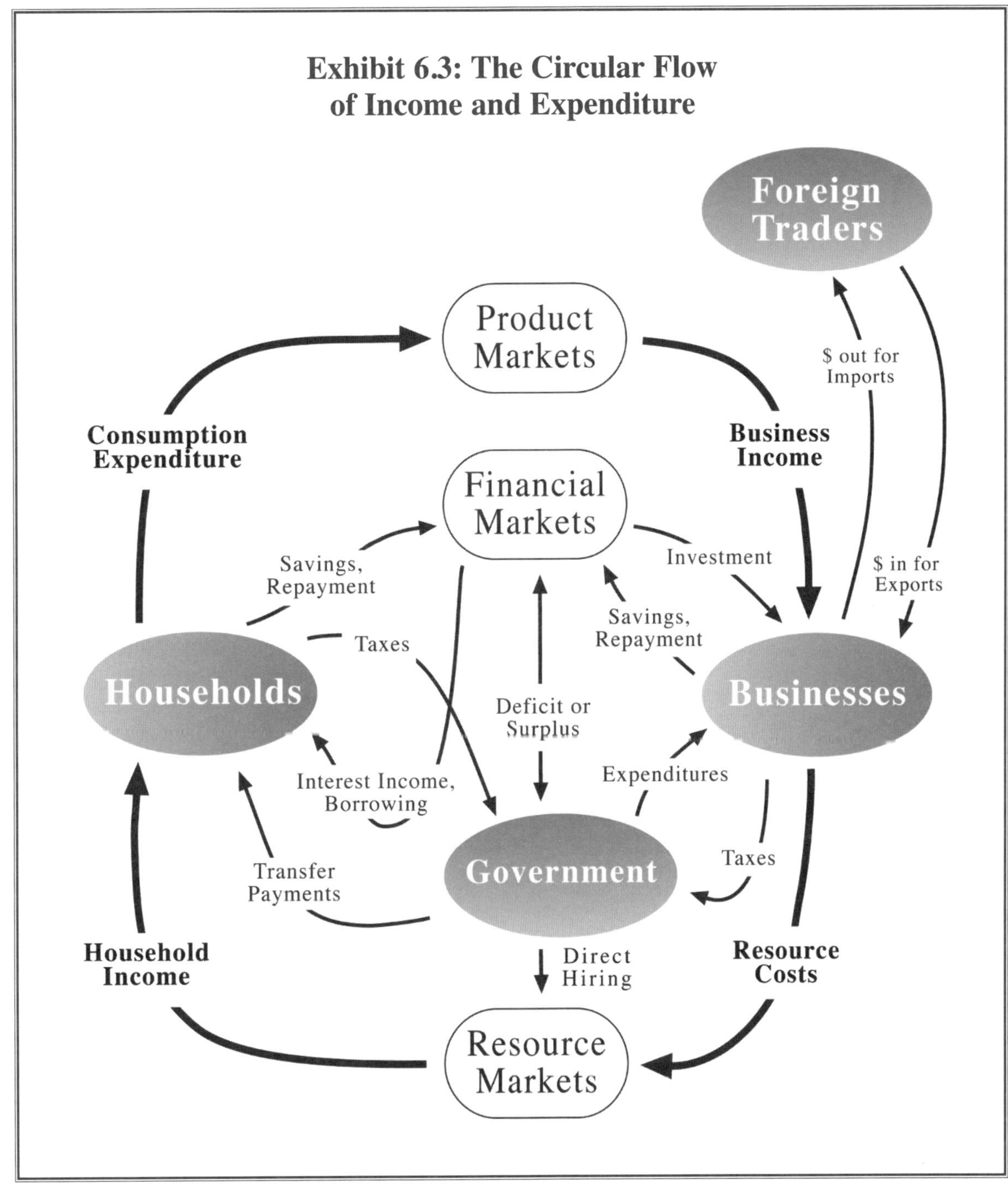

Comparing Twentieth-Century Economic Systems

Prominent twentieth-century national economies tended toward one of four types: capitalism with its preference for free enterprise, state socialism with its central plan, the social-welfare state with its concern for economic equality and family security, and the neo-mercantilist state with its concern for national economic security.

Actual national economies blend the essential elements of these four systems. Yet each tends toward one type. For example, we see democratic capitalism in the United States, state socialism in the Soviet Union, the social-welfare state in Sweden, and neo-mercantilism in Japan. The four types are explained both historically and in terms of abstract extremes.

First, we define the essential features of each system, focusing on economic goals and policies. Then we will briefly compare and contrast the primary tendencies of each.

Capitalism

Adam Smith's *Wealth of Nations* (1776) described a system of "natural liberty" in which individuals would be free to pursue their own interests with the support of government but with minimal interference. England's Parliament gradually adopted the philosophy of *laissez-faire* (French for "leave it alone"), where it prevailed in the first half of the nineteenth century. The United States tended toward a *laissez-faire* ideal from the early 1800s to the 1920s.

Franklin D. Roosevelt's interventionist policies and the philosophical attack on *laissez-faire* by John Maynard Keynes and others held sway in the United States through the middle of the twentieth century. Milton Friedman, however, thrived as a leading twentieth-century advocate of economic freedoms, and by the 1980s the capitalist philosophy was increasing in popularity.

In *The Road to Serfdom* (1944), Friedrich Hayek's condemnation of Soviet state socialism in Russia and National Socialism in Germany under Nazi rule also helped make the philosophical case for capitalism. The cruelty to humanity of both and the dynamic inefficiency of Soviet central planning, as well as budget problems in the social-welfare states boosted capitalism to first place by the beginning of the twenty-first century.

Economists and policy makers still debate the appropriate mix of capitalist freedoms and government regulation. Here, though, you may contrast capitalist freedoms with state socialism and more interventionist forms of mixed capitalism.

Capitalism

- **Goal:** freedom
- **Policies:** promote free markets, private property rights, and the rule of law; limit government intervention and welfare redistribution

Goals of Capitalism

The primary goal of capitalism is to promote economic freedom, secured through political freedom. Advocates for capitalism assert that developing individual initiative and good moral character is both a goal of and a requirement for maintaining economic and political freedoms. And economic and political freedoms promote related goals of cultural and religious freedoms.

Economic Policies of Capitalism

Economic production and distribution are directed by prices established in markets where buyers and sellers meet voluntarily.

Business profits are not necessarily immoral, but are often rewards for innovation and good management. Profits and high prices signal other businesses to come into an industry, while losses and low prices drive firms out.

The rule of law is central to the success of free enterprise. Government interventions in the market must be minimal so as to preserve as much freedom as possible. Although Marxists complain that production by wage laborers, hired by capitalists, exploits the workers, government must not interfere in the labor contract unless the imbalance of bargaining power is excessive.

Because social-welfare policies require taking wealth from the rich, such policies are considered immoral or at least inefficient when they cause disincentives to work and wealth creation. Government must defend private property rights and enforce the laws of contracts among equals.

Problems of Capitalism

Critics of capitalism raise at least five charges against it. First, market economies tend to foster more inequality of family income and wealth than other systems. Second, the profit and other monetary incentives that drive capitalism may do more than channel greed; they may encourage antisocial, selfish behavior. Third, market economies also have been historically more unstable than planned economies. Fourth, individuals with economic power, especially capitalist bosses and other wealth holders, can unduly influence government policies and the administration of laws in their favor.

Successes of Capitalism

Capitalism in Britain, the United States, and elsewhere in the last 200 years has been phenomenally successful in raising the standards of living of people at all economic levels. Furthermore, statistics show that in the last two decades of the twentieth century nations with more economic freedom tend to have higher rates of economic growth.

Economic benefits have their costs, though. Growing income inequality, for example, accompanied economic growth in the United States in the 1980s and the 1990s. And as Expansion Point 6.4 notes, the degrading effect of capitalism on culture is another issue for debate.

Expansion Point 6.4: Does Capitalism Corrupt Culture?

Capitalism debases culture, critics charge. Freedom means pornography, for instance, and competition causes a race to the bottom. Increased competition with the three major networks in U.S. broadcast television from cable television, for instance, seems to have led the networks to devalue their products.

Furthermore, the critics say, global capitalism and the media spread the debased culture into other countries.

Without doubt, economic and political freedom have their costs and their seamy side. Family, church, and other social groups share responsibility. For this reason, Jesus encouraged His disciples to be salt and light in the world.

Yet the efficiency of capitalism has democratized access to culture, whether good or bad. More people than ever may have their music (whether Bach or MTV), or art, or education.

State Socialism

After the Bolshevik revolution of 1917, Vladimir Lenin moved Russia toward state socialism. Joseph Stalin imposed central planning starting in 1928. Until 1989, the Soviet economy in Russia demonstrated the feasibility and yet the severity and eventual limits of a command economy.

Russia industrialized rapidly under Stalin's forced collectivization of agriculture in the 1930s to promote the economic and military might of state socialism. While industrialization required extreme force, Russia's rapid economic progress attracted attention from other strong leaders. In the 1950s, Mao Tse-tung invited Russian advisors into Communist China to promote Soviet-style industrialization. Communist North Korea also adopted the Soviet model of command and control. Certain African leaders implemented parts of the Soviet system when colonialism ended and economic development began in the 1960s.

Market-style reforms in China in 1984 and the collapse of the Communist Party in Russia in 1989 brought a sudden end to the hope that economic control from the center could deliver continual economic development. Even so, studying state socialism provides a valuable contrast to other economic systems. It also shows likely costs and benefits of central command in any organization.

State Socialism

- **Goal:** advance interests of industrial workers, Communist Party, and the state; foster economic equality and security
- **Policies:** implement a central plan to produce and distribute goods; control the economy's commanding heights

Goals of State Socialism

The goals of Soviet-Russian state socialism were to promote the interests of industrial workers, the Communist Party, and the state. It also sought to promote economic equality and security.

Economic Policies of State Socialism

Under state socialism, the party and its central government direct most aspects of production and distribution. Party officials and government bureaucrats direct the economy through a central plan. Government interventions in production and distribution must be thorough in order to implement provisions of a central plan. Market prices are allowed to allocate goods only in marginal sectors of the economy.

To facilitate control, the state generally owns the means of production, the factories and equipment for making goods and services. The onset of state socialism has been marked historically by successive programs to nationalize industry. First, this occurs in the "commanding heights" of the economy: steel and concrete manufacturing; electricity, natural gas, and other utilities; and agriculture.

Problems of State Socialism

The history of state socialism lists at least two important indictments against it. First, enforcing collectivization of property and agricultural land entailed brutality to the point of mass starvation and elimination of political enemies of the state. Whether such policies were necessary or not is less important than that totalitarian rulers were unimpeded in using or allowing these tactics in the Ukraine and Kazakhstan in the 1930s, China in the late 1950s, and North Korea in the 1990s. As noted in Expansion Point 6.5, central planning also interfered with cultural expression. It severely limited other personal freedoms too. State socialism failed to achieve the highest moral ideals of socialist theory.

Second, central planning was productively, allocatively, and dynamically inefficient. Planners created a system of incentives that led in the short run to misallocation and misuse of the means of production and distribution. A truck-transport agency might be rewarded for miles traveled, leading drivers to take longer, not shorter, routes. Price controls on consumer goods led to chronic shortages of desirable goods and services. Central planning also hindered innovation and economic growth in the long run. The planning system demanded conformity and rarely rewarded efficient modifications of methods or materials. A change of routine in a pipe-manufacturing plant, for example, caused planners great difficulties, since it required changes in the plans of the many plants that supplied it with materials and that used the pipe.

Successes of State Socialism

Incomes in Soviet Russia were more equal than in the United States or other capitalist nations. Studies before and after the end of Communism in Russia suggest the same effect. Before the end, the average income among the top 10 percent of families was just three times the average income in the bottom 10 percent. After the introduction of market-style reforms, the difference grew to 10 times. These studies may not consider the added access that party officials had to prized Western goods, at below-market prices. Yet, while state socialism stifled increases in standards of living, incomes tended to be more equal.

The planning system also insulated Russians from painful business-cycle fluctuations. The planning system, for all its inefficiencies, ran at about the same pace each year compared to the last or the next. For instance, during the 1930s, the United States and other Western capitalist economies experienced a severe economic collapse in the Great Depression. Russians, however, were in the midst of an industrial boom, insulated from cyclical fluctuations in the West.

Expansion Point 6.5: Socialist Culture

Soviet state socialism directed cultural expression in art, music, and society toward the goals of the state. Allowing opposing cultural views would hinder the interests of the party and state. Religious belief, for example, threatened state control because it demands allegiance to God and to goals other than the state's. Skills of artists, playwrights, and musicians were another cultural element directed by the state.

As a result, state-socialist leaders squelched religious fervor and natural artistic expression. Believers, artists, and musicians were among those who suffered Stalin's purges in the 1930s.

As with capitalism and with any human endeavor, the successes of state socialism entailed costs (other than its brutality). For example, finding a job was, in one sense, no problem for university graduates. While in the United States, availability of jobs was fluctuating with the business cycle, Russian students always had a state job upon graduation. And yet, the job might require one to move away from home and go to a city thousands of miles away, perhaps east of the Urals, in Siberia. The penalties for refusing a state job meant that students had to be creative in earning a legal exemption. To stay in her home city, a woman could gain a legal exemption and retain her state job benefits by marrying a city worker and conceiving a child.

The Social-Welfare State

The Inca civilization in South America offered the benefits and imposed the requirements of social-welfare policies at least a thousand years ago. More recently, historians credit Otto von Bismarck with creating a modern social-welfare state in Germany in the 1880s. In order to keep German laborers from favoring socialist revolution, Bismarck initiated an old-age pension, unemployment compensation, and disability insurance for workers.

The social-welfare state emerged in other nations in the twentieth century. Britain adopted social-welfare-state policies after World War II as part of a plan to rebuild its economy. Sweden also committed to income redistribution and social-welfare policies and, by the 1970s, was known as "socialism with a kind face." Even the United States adopted weaker forms of social-welfare protections from the 1930s to the 1970s.

Democratic governments in Europe and the United States were, however, promising more than they could necessarily deliver in the long run. By the 1990s, economists in these nations were projecting that they could not fund their welfare-state programs very far into the twenty-first century at current rates of taxation and economic growth. Yet people's desires for economic security are strong, and social-welfare policies will probably survive.

Social-Welfare State

- **Goal:** economic equality and security for the family
- **Policies:** redistribute wealth with progressive income tax and inheritance tax; implement social security, national health care, minimum wage, unemployment compensation, and worker's compensation

Goals of the Social-Welfare State

The primary goal of a social-welfare state is to promote economic security and equality for its people as individuals and families (as opposed to security of the state). Economic security means freedom from concerns about loss of income due to unemployment, injury at work, or poverty in old age. Economic equality refers to more or less equality of income and access to economic opportunities, and to balancing economic power.

Economic Policies of the Social-Welfare State

The social-welfare state requires policies to redistribute income, especially a progressive income tax. Unlike state socialism, the social-welfare state does not require social ownership of productive equipment. In Britain, increased nationalization and social-welfare policies did arrive together after 1946. In Sweden, however, the government imposed high tax rates on incomes and redistributed the revenues through social programs, but it did not own much of the industrial base.

The social-welfare state establishes programs that ensure economic security. Most important for workers are a social security system (old-age pension), unemployment insurance, and worker's compensation (disability payments for workers injured on the job). A national health-care system is also crucial, ensuring that every person has access to hospitals, doctors' offices, and medicines. Other programs that welfare states have imposed include nationalized housing and, of course, universal education.

Problems of the Social-Welfare State

The welfare state falls prey to **three systemic problems**: disincentives to good behavior, rent-seeking behavior, and loss of information in the bureaucracy (Morse 1995). All three stem from the specific methods of implementing and administrating government programs.

• **Three problems with social-welfare policies:**
1) disincentives
2) rent seeking
3) lost information

First, programs to support low-income individuals and families reduce the incentive to work hard. Furthermore, even if bureaucrats have little discretion to give out funds, the programs increase incentives to cheat and appear to be poor to meet program conditions. The more generous the programs, the greater the disincentives to good behavior.

Second, in gathering and redistributing a large share of a nation's resources, the state encourages individuals and interest groups to waste resources as they lobby for funds for their favored programs. They petition politicians, who decide state and national budgets. They also petition bureaucrats with the discretion to redirect funds to them. Economists call this "rent seeking" because it does not create any additional resources (just as the demand for agricultural land and the willingness to pay land rent does not create more land). Time and other resources spent in rent seeking are therefore unproductive and inefficiently used (the resources could have been used to create goods and services).

Third, the welfare-state bureaucracy sets standards and makes discretionary decisions without the information that local individuals and agencies would have. This is an advantage, for example, that local faith-based welfare organizations have over central government's agencies. The bureaucracy doesn't know what individual needs are legitimate or how local scarcities and wants vary. "All the tacit information about a person's specific situation and character is lost to the system" (Morse 1995, 6).

Sweden's social-welfare successes faded in the 1980s and 1990s, partly because special interest groups competing for increasingly larger pieces of the pie fractured its once-strong national consensus about the system's purposes. Ending or revising the system, however, poses significant political challenges because people adapt to and come to depend on the state subsidies.

Successes of the Social-Welfare State

Europeans who travel to the United States report that they do prefer their own welfare-state systems. The benefits are readily apparent and fundamental to their lives. People enjoy a state-mandated free college education, free health care, an assured pension, and generous vacation and personal days each year.

- **Two reasons for persistence of social-welfare policies:**
  1) risk aversion
  2) relativity of happiness

Two psychological reasons apparently cause people to enjoy the benefits of the social-welfare state, despite the high rates of taxation and the disincentives engendered. First, people tend to be **risk averse** and government social-welfare programs are one method for people to share their risks. Second, **happiness is relative**. People assess their own welfare in relation to their neighbor's living standards. Studies show that people are no happier in countries with the highest income levels. Apparently, people can adjust their expectations to various levels of income and feel happy, so long as they do not feel that they have fallen well below the visible living standards of others.

As with capitalism and socialism, however, the benefits have their costs and conditions. Social-welfare state successes led to rising federal budget deficits, increased government borrowing, and rising interest rates (think in terms of interdependence in the circular flow of Exhibit 6.3). Higher interest rates cause reduced private investment and therefore a lower rate of economic growth into the future. The welfare state has been, to a certain extent, borrowing from the future for its current benefits. Another conditional aspect of social-welfare successes is that they seem more feasible in nations with more homogeneous populations.

Neo-Mercantilism

The mercantilist system arose in the 1600s in western Europe when kings and queens recognized that national power depended on successful merchants who exported products and brought gold and silver into national treasuries. The sovereign needed precious metals to fund a standing army and navy that would assure national military and economic power.

A mercantilist philosophy of protective tariffs emerged later in the United States in the 1790s under Alexander Hamilton's economic leadership of the U.S. Treasury. It also arose in Germany after the unification of the 39 states in the 1870s. German nationalist sentiments peaked in the Nazi period in the 1930s and

40s. The Nazis rose to power by promising mercantilist-style protection of industry. Expansion Point 4.4 explains how the Nazis appealed to certain voters' economic rationality with such policies.

Japan adopted a militaristic mercantile philosophy until the end of World War II. Afterward, Japan pursued non-militaristic mercantilism, a system called neo-mercantilism here. The astounding success of the Japanese economy until the 1980s is as notable as its astounding economic difficulties in the 1990s.

Goals of Neo-Mercantilism

The primary goal of neo-mercantilism is to promote the economic security of the state. As with historic mercantilism, the goal is to ensure a positive balance of trade, with exports exceeding imports. Other goals are to assure a ready supply of raw materials for domestic industry and to promote export markets as well.

Neo-Mercantilism

- **Goal:** state security
- **Policies:** develop an **industrial policy** to subsidize favored industries, promote exports of finished goods, and manage imports of raw materials

Economic Policies of Neo-Mercantilism

Since neo-mercantilism is a variant of capitalism, economic production and distribution are directed mainly by market activity. The state, however, intervenes systematically for national purposes. Japan, for instance, promoted exports by its steel industry and development of computer manufacturing, while defending its farmers from foreign agricultural competition.

Systematic **industrial policies**, in which government planners choose which industries are winners and are targets for state subsidies, mark neo-mercantilism. So does a close cooperation between industry and government officials. In Japan, the Ministry of International Trade and Industry (MITI) coordinates industrial policies and cooperates with industrial leaders.

Problems of Neo-Mercantilism

Neo-mercantilism falls victim to the same inefficiencies of any form of state planning. Government officials tend to protect their cronies in industry. In Japan in the 1990s, for example, critics charge that financial regulators did not properly force private bank officials to write bad debts off their books. Such strict enforcement of banking rules would have harmed these banks and brought shame to their managers. Whether this financial regulatory restraint is prudent or not, the problem gave neo-mercantilism the name of "crony capitalism."

Critics also charge that industrial planning leads to ongoing subsidies for inefficient businesses and unprofitable industries. Studies have shown that Japanese subsidies for its steel industry, for example, earned very low rates of returns compared to private investment standards. The desire to insure industrial power has had the ill effect of weakening certain industries by shielding them from foreign competition. This happened in the United States as well, where protection for the steel industry led to higher-than-average industrial wages and declining efficiency.

Successes of Neo-Mercantilism

The Japanese economy grew quite rapidly from 1946 to 1989. By the 1980s, U.S. managers were traveling to Japan to learn from their managers and to improve worker productivity and product quality. Whether Japanese economic success was due to industrial policies or other cultural factors, MITI officials appeared to be economic geniuses. Optimism about neo-mercantilist planning, however, declined as Japan bogged down in recession during the 1990s. Once again, economic successes are conditional. The benefits of business and government cooperation soon gave way to the costs of an inflexible system that didn't adjust rapidly to changing economic conditions.

Comparing the Systems

Exhibit 6.4 illustrates key differences between the four economic systems. Each economy makes decisions about its support for two key goals: individual economic security and equality on the one hand, and state economic security on the other. The model shows a nation's commitment to economic equality and security for families on the horizontal axis, and to economic security for the state on the vertical axis.

Each system occupies a corner of the graph. Capitalism has a weak commitment to individual and state *economic* security. State socialism strongly commits to both. The social-welfare state favors individual security, while neo-mercantilism favors state security. You might complain that the United States is capitalist, and yet it defends the steel and automobile industries to maintain military readiness, and provides for individual security. True enough, but these are democratic concessions to mercantilist and social-welfare sentiments.

Exhibit 6.4: Concern for Individual and State Security in Economic Systems

High
Neo-Mercantilism
State Socialism
Government Attention to the State's Economic Security
Capitalism
Social-Welfare State
Low
Government Attention to Individual Economic Security
High

This picture oversimplifies the comparison. In practice, each national economy is an extremely complex web of human relations, of economic rules and commercial conventions, and of government, business, and social organizations. The next chapter addresses these additional complexities.

Chapter Summary

1. An economy is a system of social, commercial, political, and legal institutions and organizations by which people use their resources to produce, distribute, and consume goods and services.

2. The three fundamental economic activities are consumption, production, and distribution. Other important activities include finance, government interventions, and international trade.

3. An economy has interrelated financial, legal, and other subsystems that can be quite complex. To effectively implement policy, leaders must understand the complexity of the economic system.

4. Each society has three sectors: the private market economy, government as the coercive sector, and the cultural sector that reflects a people's religious, social, intellectual, and artistic views. Each sector influences the others, but imbalances are harmful.

5. The circular-flow model represents the money flows of income and expenditure in a market economy. Changes in income and consumer spending cause each other simultaneously and, in fact, a change in any flow can cause all others to change.

6. Four major economic systems of the 1900s were capitalism, state socialism, the social-welfare state, and neo-mercantilism. The welfare-state emphasizes individual economic security. Neo-mercantilism seeks economic security for the state. State socialism emphasizes both, while capitalism emphasizes economic freedom, not economic security.

Problems for Practice

6.1 "Managing a contemporary household involves all of the fundamental economic activities. Even principles of government and international trade are involved at home." Explain whether you think this statement is true or not. Use examples.

6.2* Briefly explain a time when a decision maker in a home, business, or government made a policy change without fully understanding the system involved. Explain the undesirable effect of this policy change.

6.3 Give two of your own examples of the interdependence of markets and money flows in the circular-flow model.

6.4* Consider five policies of your home country and five other nations in the news. Identify where you would locate each policy and nation in the scheme of Exhibit 6.4. Explain your reason.

Economics in film and literature:
6.5 In your library or local video store, borrow the movie *Stalin* with Robert Duvall in the lead, or the documentary movie *Harvest of Shame* about collectivization of agricultural lands in the Ukraine in the 1930s. See also the book *Harvest of Sorrow* by Robert Conquest on the Ukrainian tragedy.

For your portfolio:
6.6 Research one of the nations (other than your home country) mentioned in the review of four economic systems. Write a brief review of the economic successes or failures at that point in history. Explain in terms of the ideas presented here. Is this nation fully committed to one system or another? When did its commitment change and how?

6.7 The United Nations' *Human Development Report* ranks nations according to quality of life. Research the top three nations and classify them according to degree and type of government intervention in the market economy. Which type of economic systems seems to be the best? Would other factors affect the rankings?

For class discussion
6.8 Critically evaluate the model of three-sector balance in society. First, what factors, if any, are ignored? Second, how would you strike an appropriate balance?

6.9 What moral ideals should an economic system uphold? Are any ideals contradictory? How do you strike a moral balance among competing ideals? Be ready to defend your view, using the concepts and models explained in this chapter and in other sources.

See Answer Key for hints/answers to starred (*) questions.

Chapter 7

Economic Endowments

Resources, Organizations, and Institutions

What this chapter will help you think about:

1. With what kinds of natural, physical, and human resources is any economy endowed?
2. How do endowments of resources affect economic activity?
3. Which resource and environmental problems are a threat to economic progress?
4. What are institutional and organizational endowments?
5. How are economic organizations important to economic activity?

• **Economic resources:** land, labor, tools, capital equipment, raw materials, and entrepreneurial ability

Every economy is endowed with **resources** of land, labor, minerals and other raw materials, tools, capital equipment, and entrepreneurial ability. Every economy is also endowed with economic **organizations** and **institutions** shaped by culture and developed over time. Organizations are the administrative structures and associations of people. Institutions are the rules and customary behaviors of a people, including its laws, commercial practices, and moral beliefs.

This chapter provides an overview of these endowments of an economy. The first part explains its resource endowments and their importance. The second explains organizations and institutions, with institutional theory treated in detail in the next chapter.

Resource Endowments

Economic resources are the inputs to the production processes that transform them into goods and services. Every economy is endowed with its own particular natural resources, a stock of tools and mechanical equipment that embody some level of technology, and human skills and the educational systems for passing them on. Ukraine, for example, has excellent soil for farming, while Greece has rocky soil less suited to farming. Greece, though, has access to the sea, and is home to many shipping companies. In 1850, England was an industrial powerhouse. Germany, Russia, Japan, and other nations are known for excellent educational systems that train workers well for technical jobs in industry, while many countries still struggling to develop their economies have inadequate educational systems. Such natural, mechanical, and human endowments are crucial to a nation's economic activity.

Exhibit 7.1: Economic Endowments

Natural Resources
- Geography (waters, forests, and terrain)
- Climate (rainfall, sun, and temperature)
- Fuels and Minerals
- Soil (sandy, silty loam, clay, and so on)

Capital Equipment and Technology
- Amount, condition, and technology of equipment
- The rate of accumulation of capital equipment
  (rates of saving and investment)
- The rate of improvement of technology
  (rates of research and development and assimilation of foreign technology)

Human Resources
- Population size and its age distribution
- Education of the population
  (technical, ethical, and literary training)

Organizations and Institutions
- Laws, commercial practices, and cultural attitudes
- Stock of moral and cultural capital
- Commercial associations and businesses
- Governmental, educational, religious, and cultural agencies

Natural, technical, and human factors that have shaped economies throughout history are listed in Exhibit 7.1. The list is not detailed. The text itself gives more details about each group.

Natural Endowments

Natural resources are important to a nation's economic growth. Saudi Arabia has developed rapidly because it is a dominant exporter of crude oil. South Africa used its exports of gold and other minerals to fund its economic growth. The United States is a major exporter of agricultural products because, in part, its regions have the soils and climates suited to producing a variety of foods.

Endowments or Access?

Naive theorists think that an abundance of natural resources like minerals, fuels, water, and fertile soil must lie within a nation for it to be prosperous. The resource-poor but very wealthy island economies of Hong Kong and Singapore, however, demonstrate that this is not necessarily true. A nation must have **access** to resources for industrialization. Access depends on factors such as waterways, ports, development of other forms of transportation,

and a commercial inclination. In other words, international trade provides access to other nations' resources, making it one of the more important economic activities in addition to consumption, production, and distribution.

Nevertheless, natural-resource endowments, especially waterways, shape regional and national economic development. Having rivers and seaports for domestic and foreign trade has been important to all civilizations because shipping by water is usually less expensive than shipping over land. That explains why, during the Roman Empire, much commercial trade went by river and sea, not by the famed Roman roads (Cameron 1993). Where rivers were not adequate for shipping, men, animals, and machines dug canals. In the mid-1800s, for example, the Erie and Genesee Canals in upstate New York connected "western" farmers to urban markets such as Albany and New York City. The Panama and Suez Canals connected pairs of oceans to give even longer service as important shipping routes. Even though jet transport is available today, water-born trade continues to flourish because the cost of shipping heavy items is still lower by water than by air.

Climate and Geography

A region's climate can define an economy and determine its economic progress. The cold climate and short growing season around Hudson Bay in Canada meant that trapping was more profitable than farming. Representatives of the Hudson's Bay Company, however, could only ship furs back to England during warm months when the bay was not frozen. The moderate climate of Florida makes it suitable for grazing cattle or growing oranges, while the climate of Nebraska makes it unsuitable for oranges but good for cattle or wheat. Florida's warm climate also makes it popular for winter tourists from farther north, while Colorado's snows make it a haven for those who love winter sports.

Geography also shapes patterns of economic development. The geography of New York State, with the Mohawk River cutting a narrow valley between the Adirondack Mountains to the north and the Catskill Mountains and northern Appalachians to the south, made the Erie Canal technically feasible. Because of good deep water ports, with easy access to the Atlantic Ocean, Boston, New York City, Philadelphia, and Charleston grew as regional commercial centers and ports for international trade. And, while skiers come in winter, hikers and climbers also come to Colorado's mountains in summer.

Even **soil conditions** in a region have economic consequences. Sandy soils in southern Europe allowed a simple, lightweight plow to scratch the ground in a crisscross pattern. Heavier clay and loam soils in northern Europe required development of a "heavy-wheel plow" that could cut deeper and turn over long furrows of the heavier soil (Cameron, 52). Greece's mountains are partly responsible for it being home to many worldwide shipping companies. After beginning as agrarian farmers, Greeks quickly became great sailors and traders like the Phoenicians, because the "rocky, mountainous character of their adopted homeland . . . soon drove them to the sea. . . . Their excellent natural harbors and the numerous islands of the adjacent Aegean Sea also encouraged this departure" (Cameron, 33).

Resources and Economic Change

The coming of age and later economic decline of a natural resource can dramatically change global and regional income and power distributions. Arabian oil made billionaires of nomadic sheepherders. Soviet control of Asian oil fields helped to support world Communism. Russian Soviets subsidized Cuba's economy by trading its oil for Cuban sugar on terms very favorable to Cuba. Welsh coal deposits around the Pennines made Cardiff in South Wales the most important coal-shipping harbor in the world until the coal veins were emptied. Coal still can be found in the hills of West Virginia, where it was mined throughout the twentieth century. The economic value to the U.S. economy of West Virginia fluctuated as the price of oil, a substitute fuel, rose and fell. When oil prices rose in the 1970s, for instance, West Virginia coal was king again. But when oil prices fell in the 1980s, coal was less in demand as a fuel and the regional coal economy suffered as a result.

Environmental Concerns about Resource Limits

Since the 1960s, economists and policy makers have confronted the concerns of environmentalists. We can identify two potential problems in resource use. The first is the rate at which resources are being exhausted. The second is pollution generated in the use of certain resources.

Limited Resources. Remember that the fundamental economic problem is limited resources. Environmentalists have focused special attention on the rates at which industrial economies use resources. Resources can be put in at least **three categories**: nonrenewable, renewable, and inexhaustible. Rates of usage of the first two should concern us.

• **Types of natural resources**:
1) nonrenewable
2) renewable
3) inexhaustible

Nonrenewable resources are those which are fixed in supply, such as the total supply of copper ore and naturally occurring crude oil. Once they are gone, we will have to find **substitutes**. Environmentalists suggest that industrial economies may be exhausting these nonrenewables, with dire consequences to follow. Economists emphasize the importance of innovation and the supply of substitutes.

Renewable resources such as trees and fish in the sea will not necessarily run out, but they are replaced in nature at a rate that may be slower than the use rate in an economy. This is not only a problem of industrial economies, but of preindustrial systems as well.

Deforestation and depletion of soil fertility are ancient problems. Industrial economies simply accelerated the rate of use and the breadth of the problem. Experts, however, can carefully manage forests and seas, and large corporations are often at the cutting edge of these techniques when managing their own resources.

The Role of Property Rights. The tragedy of the commons, explained in chapter 4, arises under public ownership of resources. One of these tragedies is the overfishing of international waters around the globe. When all corporations may fish the open seas at no cost, it is no longer in any one company's interests to conserve fish. A solution is for nations to agree to limits and then to enforce them with their own corporations. Dividing property rights to the oceans among nations would help solve the problem, but this is highly unlikely.

The Role of Prices and Resource Markets. Economists note that the price system will play an important role in encouraging conservation of scarce resources and development of substitutes. As Exhibit 7.2 shows, when the supply of a resource is decreasing while demand is increasing, its price increases.

Exhibit 7.2: A Rising Price Conserves Scarce Resources

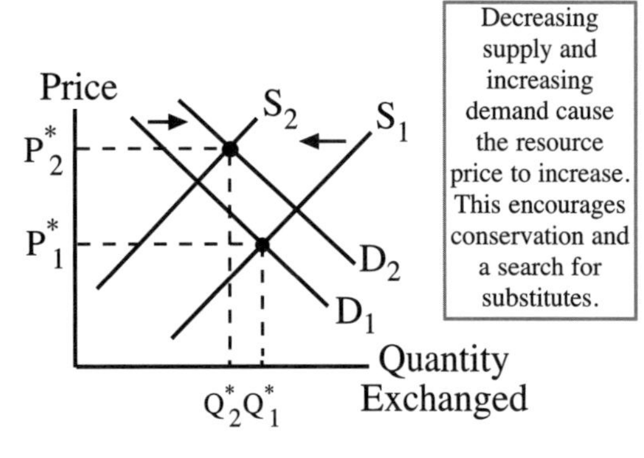
Price
P^*_2
P^*_1
S_2
S_1
D_2
D_1
Quantity Exchanged
$Q^*_2 Q^*_1$
Decreasing supply and increasing demand cause the resource price to increase. This encourages conservation and a search for substitutes.

As the price of a scarce resource rises, innovators will find it profitable to search for substitutes. We have synthetic materials such as nylon, rayon, and latex because of the rising costs of natural products such as cotton, wool, and rubber. When the prices of crude oil and gasoline rise, substitutes such as natural gas from coal and gasoline additives from corn are more reasonable to develop.

The critics worry, of course, that we may not act in time, depleting resources before finding adequate substitutes. No one knows what the future holds. And yet economists continue to put faith in rising prices.

The Role of Inexhaustibles. Environmentalists encourage rapid development of technologies to use resources that cannot be exhausted. For example, wind power, solar energy, and geothermal power are apparently inexhaustible sources of energy.

Here again, price matters, and market economists take a more relaxed approach to these technologies. When the prices of exhaustibles increase high enough, these technologies will be economical and the market will quickly develop. In 2000 and 2001, for instance, the price of electricity increased dramatically in the United States. At higher rates per kilowatt hour, the news began to report that windmill generators and solar cells were now more economical than ever. Higher natural gas prices at that time also prompted more exploration and drilling for new wells.

What If We Are Wrong? An important issue is whether we are discounting the interests of future generations too steeply. A related concern is whether we are depending too much on future technological improvements to meet the needs of our children and grandchildren to come. How guilty should we feel about our rate of current resource use and our level of concern (or complete lack of concern) for the future?

Environmental Concerns about Pollution

Air, water, and soil pollution are not new in the industrial age. They are, however, now more widespread. Pollution is an unwanted consequence of producing goods and services, as a materials-balance approach to understanding production in Exhibit 7.3 shows. Production generates not only economic goods and services but also economic bads. Since the total amount of material input must equal the total amount of material output, waste in production processes is inevitable.

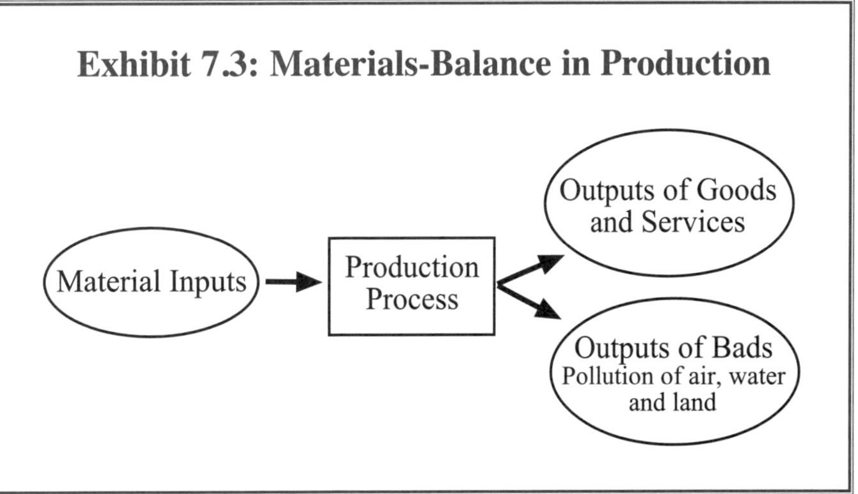

The bads simply can't be destroyed. We may be able to change the form of the pollution and/or to control it somewhat, but more production generally means more pollution. Even so, more efficient production processes may reduce waste and recycle scrap. A factory that trims metal or plastic can remelt the waste and reuse it, and the good news is that rising prices for landfill and stricter limits on pollution do encourage such measures.

Pollution as an External Cost. Pollution is production of unwanted by-products, and those who produce them often ignore their effects, passing the problem on to others. Economists say that, left unchecked, pollution creates costs that are external to private production, or **externalities** for short.

When an electric power plant in Ohio burns coal, pollutants from the smokestacks drift for hundreds of miles into Pennsylvania and beyond. There the pollutants cause harm to plants, house and automobile paint, and people's health. People in

Pennsylvania bear the costs but get none of the benefits of electricity used in Ohio. People in Ohio pay a lower price for electricity than they would if the power plant had avoided polluting.

We represent the effects of external costs of pollution as two supply curves for electricity. One reflects only the private costs that the power plant bears. The other reflects the private costs plus social costs of damage done by the pollution. Exhibit 7.4 illustrates the effect in the electricity market. Users in Ohio pay a lower price (P^*_1) than would be optimal to cover all costs of production (P^*_2). Users also buy more electricity (Q^*_1) than they would at the higher, optimal price.

Exhibit 7.4: Pollution Imposes External Costs on Others

Price | $S_{\text{Private \& Social Costs}}$ | $S_{\text{Private Costs Only}}$ | P^*_2 | P^*_1 | D | Q^*_2 | Q^*_1 | Quantity of Electricity

P* is too low, Q* too high when electricity supply does not reflect full social cost of pollution.

The regulatory solution proposed by welfare economists is to tax the electricity company for every kilowatt hour it produces. The tax should equal the external social costs of production. This tax would lower the firm's willingness to produce and would provide a fund to compensate those harmed by the remaining pollution. A difficulty with compensating individuals is determining who has been harmed and how much.

A private solution to the problem is to write laws that make it illegal to pollute and allow those harmed to sue in civil court for damages. A similar difficulty with the private solution is that transactions costs for people to prove harm and litigate a case would be high. Damages from pollution may be hard to discover, taking many years to reveal themselves in property damage or higher rates of mortality or ill health.

- **Market for pollution rights:**
  1) a firm has rights to pollute up to a limit
  2) a firm that can reduce pollution at low cost may sell pollution rights to a firm that can reduce pollution only at high costs
  3) this system increases pollution-reduction efficiency

Regulatory Challenges. Two challenges face regulators seeking to limit pollution. First, how can it be done most efficiently? Second, how can it be done comprehensively?

Efficiency requires that we encourage industry to undertake the lowest-cost pollution measures first. If we wish to reduce particulate in the air from smokestacks, imposing across-the-board limits will not be efficient. One firm may be able to reduce particulate emissions by a much lower cost per ton than another firm. Economists recommend that firms be allowed to sell pollution permits. Creating a **market for pollution rights** encourages those firms that can reduce pollution more cheaply to sell their rights to firms that find it more costly.

This thinking applies the marginal method and the principles of allocative efficiency introduced in earlier chapters. The marginal cost of reducing pollution in one factory will be equal to the marginal cost in another factory, not by imposing across-the-board limits but by allowing a market to develop.

A **comprehensive program** is also important. If one nation imposes strict pollution controls, it will find that industry will move to nearby nations and pollution may drift back with the winds or water currents. The Kyoto Treaty on global pollution reduction, for all its political and economic challenges, attempts a comprehensive solution to the pollution problem.

• **Comprehensive pollution controls:**
1) limits must extend beyond regional and national borders to be effective; and
2) limits must cover air, water, and soil pollution to prevent pollution tradeoffs

Comprehensive air, water, and soil controls are also needed. If a city imposes only strict limits on water pollution, for example, industries may simply convert the pollution into air or soil pollution. Chemicals that a factory would discharge into the river may be burned or dumped at a landfill instead. Comprehensive controls prevent firms from exploiting such pollution tradeoffs.

As noted above, another important tradeoff exists between economic activity and environmental regulation. Restrictions on logging drives up lumber prices and causes regional unemployment. Restrictions on pollution drive factories to other regions. A great concern in negotiating the North American Free Trade Agreement in the 1990s was that factories would move equipment and jobs to Mexico where pollution restrictions were less severe or weakly enforced. Environmentalists also note, however, that pollution regulations do stimulate pollution-control industries and research into advanced technologies that may have certain economic benefits.

Capital Endowments

Economists call productive equipment **physical capital** or capital equipment. Especially important in determining a nation's economic progress are the degree of **mechanization** of agriculture and industry and the level of **technology** in the machines. Why are machines and technology economically important? More machines and better industrial technology tend to increase the productivity of a nation's labor force, allowing for a higher average national standard of living.

• **Physical capital**: the buildings and equipment that labor uses in production; capital increases the productivity of labor

Through mechanization of agriculture and biological and chemical advances in seeds, fertilizers, and pest control, the United States needs fewer and fewer farmers to feed more and more Americans and, through grain exports, many other people as well. In 1850, 63.7 percent of American workers labored in farming. By 1990, only 2.5 percent of workers were farming, and yet the United States was the leading world exporter of corn and wheat, and the number-two exporter of rice behind Thailand (*World Almanac and Book of Facts: 1995*, 136, 141). This means that one U.S. farmer in 1990 produced enough raw materials to feed about 40 Americans.

Capital Moves to Markets or Resources

Markets attract capital, but so do resources. Factory location is an economic decision that weighs the costs of shipping resources to the factory against the costs of shipping finished products to the market. Products that need a heavy resource added at the end of production (**weight-gaining products**) locate near markets. Soft-drink bottlers locate factories close to urban markets, since water is usually available. Cement requires adding much sand and water, and so cement factories also locate close to final users.

- **Production of weight-gaining products** is located closer to markets to save costs of shipping final product.
- **Production of weight-losing products** is located closer to raw materials to save costs of shipping materials.

Industries locate close to their sources of raw materials when production requires heavy or specialized raw materials, but especially when weight is lost during production (**weight-losing products**). Local resource endowments such as mineral deposits or natural harbors may also attract industrial and commercial development. For example, because the processes to turn bauxite into aluminum must be tailored to the specific character of the local bauxite deposits, and because much weight is lost in production, aluminum-smelting facilities are located right at the bauxite pits.

Capital Makes Resources Valuable

Mechanical and industrial technology can make otherwise useless natural-resource endowments very valuable. Before the oil industry boom of the late 1800s, only a few people such as the Seneca Indians living near what is now Cuba, New York, knew the benefits of crude oil. To the nomads of Saudi Arabia, crude oil was a troublesome tar sticking to their sandals.

Scientific and industrial developments in the chemical industry, however, separated crude oil into its components of gasoline and other valuable hydrocarbons. The chemical and industrial technology to refine crude oil into gasoline, kerosene, and other usable products turned desert tars into gold. More recently, technological advances in recycling paper, plastics, metal, and glass allow industries to convert trash into treasure.

Technological Change Can Make or Break a Region

Changing technology can exalt one region and bring another low as it alters the type of equipment and raw materials needed. One example is the iron, timber, and coal industries. Early iron furnaces were located in the deep woods because charcoal (partly burned wood) was the fuel. By the mid-1800s, however, iron furnaces tended to be located near coal fields because coal was the fuel for the newer blast furnaces. Technology to burn anthracite (hard coal) developed new coal fields. As Expansion Point 7.1 explains, iron making in eastern Pennsylvania in the 1800s shifted from heavy woods west of Philadelphia to the anthracite coal beds beneath Scranton and Wilkes-Barre to the north.

Steam-power development also affected regional economic progress due to its use as a power source in textile factories, other

Expansion Point 7.1: Iron Smelting Technology, Fuel Supplies, and Iron Furnace Location

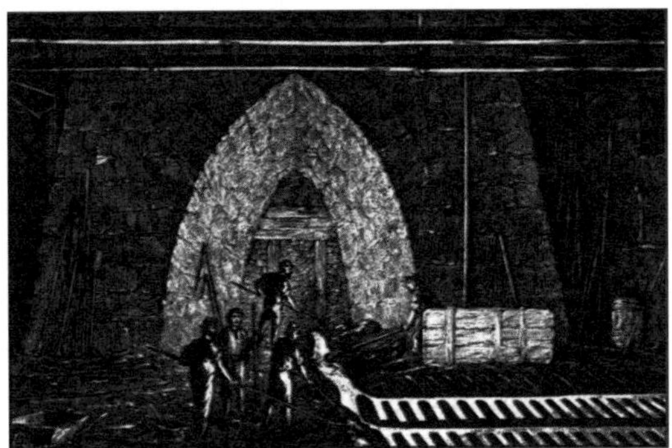

In Pennsylvania, you can still visit historical sites where iron ore was smelted into iron in the 1700s and 1800s. The revolutionary-era Hopewell Furnace, a U.S. national historical site, is located in a heavily wooded area of Pennsylvania, approximately 50 miles west of Philadelphia. The furnace made cannons for the American Revolution of 1776.

Scranton, Pennsylvania's iron furnaces, on the other hand, sit beside Roaring Creek in the very middle of a large industrial city. Operating from the mid-1800s, these furnaces made iron track for the growing railroads, and bridge beams and other castings for a growing industrial nation.

Why are these iron furnaces situated so differently, one in the deep woods and the other in a city? The reason is the changing technology of iron smelting, from charcoal smelting to anthracite smelting. Iron is refined by melting the ore (rock) that contains it, with the help of limestone. Iron furnaces, therefore, need access to iron-ore and limestone deposits. But iron furnaces also consume huge quantities of fuel for melting the rock and, therefore, are usually located close to fuel supplies.

Early on, iron was produced in the United States in furnaces fired by wood charcoal, explaining Hopewell's rural location. After the 1830s, smelting iron with anthracite coal quickly replaced smelting with wood charcoal. Anthracite (hard coal) required much hotter temperatures and a "blast furnace" technology where air was pumped into the furnace to make it hotter. But smelting with anthracite was much more efficient than with wood charcoal. When available in the United States, the new technology changed Scranton and nearby Wilkes-Barre into nineteenth-century industrial centers for iron making, because those cities were in a valley containing huge formations of anthracite coal.

Both cities eventually fell into economic decline in the late 1900s. Iron use declined, and coal was more expensive to remove as the miners moved to lower seams of coal. Eventually the lowest shafts flooded when the Susquehanna River burst through the ground into the mine.

Histories of the iron industry in the United States, then, show us how technology and resource endowments affect industrial development. Hopewell Furnace was intentionally built far from the major city of Philadelphia, in the woods but also near deposits of iron ore and limestone. Scranton's Roaring Creek iron furnaces were not, however, built in the middle of a great industrial city. They were built on top of a huge deposit of anthracite coal and the city built up around them. The later growth of iron and steel production in Pittsburgh at the other end of the state is also related to resource endowments. Pittsburgh sits on the Monongahela River just north of the bituminous coal fields of West Virginia, and within modern shipping distance of the iron ore fields beside the western Great Lakes.

light manufacturing, and in rail transportation. In colonial America, New England was the leading industrial region because its rivers were particularly well suited to turning waterwheels to run factory machines. The advent of steam power in the 1800s and then electric power freed industry to concentrate elsewhere in the nation. Steam locomotives made canals obsolete, moving grain farming out of western New York and into the Midwest.

Human Endowments

A national economy is endowed with people with various education levels and skills. It has an education system and a stock of cultural ideas about education that either promote or inhibit industry and commerce. Population size, worker skills, the education system, and cultural influences all affect potential economic output and standards of living.

Economic Effects of a Changing Population

Demography is the study of the social and economic effects of changing population characteristics. A growing population, for instance, has two opposing effects on economic welfare. Rising population means more mouths to feed, but also more potential workers to produce goods and services.

Economic development, in turn, has two opposing effects on population and economic welfare in less-developed nations of the world. The growth rate of a nation's population depends on the nation's birth and death rates. Historically, economic development has first caused a decrease in infant mortality and an increase in life expectancy. During that period, total national output may be increasing slowly, but per capita incomes will be falling because population is growing more rapidly.

• **Per capita income:** total national income divided by population; a measure of economic development

Per capita income is total income divided by population. For per capita incomes to rise, national income must grow faster than population. After several decades of falling death rates, economic development then leads to falling birth rates, as birth control becomes more common. At that point in the pattern of development, per capita income begins to rise.

Slowly rising populations or falling populations can also have notable national economic effects. In the 1960s, a popular place for Philadelphia-area teenagers to work and spend their summers was in hotels, shops, and restaurants on the barrier islands of the South Jersey shore (Ocean City to Wildwood, New Jersey, for instance). By the 1980s, though, live birth rates in the United States were falling and affluence was rising, and fewer teens were available for summer work. The shortage of workers forced the owner of two Ocean City amusement arcades, for example, to hire youth from Ireland.

Shifting population patterns in the United States are also threatening the viability of U.S. Medicare and Social Security systems for the elderly. In the first two decades of the twenty-first century, fewer young workers will be available to support the aging baby-boom-era adults when they retire. Baby boomers are those Americans born in large numbers during the 20 years after 1946, give or take. After the mid-1960s, U.S. birth rates declined dramatically. Fewer workers will support more retirees than in the past.

The Significance of Human Capital

Human capital refers to a person's stock of vocational skills and technical knowledge. Labor power is the strength and endurance to move dirt from one place to another. Human capital is the ability to build, equip with fuel, and operate a backhoe to dig the dirt. Formal and informal systems of education contribute to human capital. Declining education standards can cause a nation's stock of human capital to decline. To understand the value of human capital and the difference between unskilled and skilled labor, see the story about an expensive auto repair in Expansion Point 7.2.

Expansion Point 7.2: The Meaning and Value of Human Capital

Sam's car was running rather roughly as he drove to town one day. He stopped at Fred's auto mechanic's shop, barely making it in the drive before the car stalled. Fred opened the hood and then told Sam to start the engine up again. With a screwdriver, Fred adjusted two screws on the carburetor until the engine purred smoothly. Fred took only five minutes to get Sam back on the road. Driving away, Sam shouted, "Send me a bill, Fred."

When Sam received Fred's bill for $22.50, however, he was angry. The next day, he took the bill back to the shop and shoved it in Fred's face, shouting, "You charged me $22.50 for turning two screws!" Fred grabbed the bill and quickly scribbled a breakdown of the charges. "For turning two screws, $2.50. For knowing which two screws to turn, $20.00."

The **skill** and **education level** of a people are among the most important determinants of a nation's economic welfare, much more important than the availability of natural resources. An educated workforce can overcome lack of natural resources by negotiating their supplies from other peoples.

As said above, Hong Kong and Singapore have flourished in spite of a lack of natural resources because they had access to resources. Japan is another island economy that flourishes on an even bigger scale, yet without great endowments of natural wealth. Japan imports coal, oil, and some other raw materials and intermediate goods to use in its industrial economy. How do Hong Kong, Singapore, and Japan gain access to needed raw materials? All three depend on well-educated and commercially astute citizens to make necessary trade connections.

An educated workforce also can impact an economy in other ways. Educated people tend to have lower birth rates and to be better able to develop or adopt new technologies from abroad. Education even can contribute to reducing water pollution in developing countries, as explained in Expansion Point 7.3.

Expansion Point 7.3: Education and Pollution Reduction in Developing Countries

Education can have dramatic economic effects, and surprising environmental effects too. Water pollution afflicts some nations that have not yet industrialized because of water run-off from farm fields. Andrew Steer of the World Bank reports that these water pollution problems in developing countries, however, tend to decrease with increasing literacy rates for women.

The reason is that, in developing countries, women do most of the agricultural work, but are usually not taught to read. As a result, the women who use the fertilizer brought in by development organizations cannot read the instructions and apparently overfertilize the soil in many cases. Excess fertilizer then runs off into streams and rivers, increasing algae growth, and polluting the water.

Recent development programs have increased efforts to educate girls as well as boys in less developed nations. When they are able to read directions on bags of fertilizer, women agricultural workers are then able to avoid overfertilization. Water pollution is reduced as a result.

Today many industrial workers must be very well educated. Consider the skills needed to run an automated steel factory or a computer-operated automobile production line. In the early 1900s, managers made most decisions about factory operations. In the early 2000s, workers and managers will plan work cooperatively, improving production processes and ensuring product quality. Manufacturers also will increasingly expect line workers to perform statistical process control.

Global trade and investment have accelerated the shift in demand from low-skilled to high-skilled workers in the United States. Auto corporations, for example, now send factories that employ lower-skilled workers to upholster seats and injection-mold plastic parts to Mexico and Asia, where wages are lower. At the same time, U.S. corporations are creating high-skilled financial-services and computer-oriented jobs.

Organizations and Institutions

• **Economic organizations:** ongoing human associations that influence economic activities; they are cooperative and hierarchical in nature

Just as the skill and education of individuals have powerful economic effects, so too the social learning and structure of a people help shape the rate of economic growth and the adaptability to change. Social learning and structure are reflected in the nation's economic organizations and institutions.

An **economic organization** is an ongoing association of people that engages in joint production, consumption, and distribution of goods and services or other economic activities. Mutual savings banks, for instance, are an economic association, as are farmers' cooperatives that flourished in the nineteenth and twentieth centuries in the United States. In fact, advanced economic activity in the United States is associated with a multitude of very complex organizational structures such as commercial partnerships, corporations, government regulatory agencies, and nonprofit agencies.

An **economic institution** is any law, persistent rule of behavior, or custom that influences the type of economy and its activities. Any economic system, whether tribal, village, manorial, communist, city-state, or nation-state, will include specialized institutions for production and distribution. To understand economies throughout history is to understand their institutions.

Although a complete list would be too long, Exhibit 7.5 summarizes important types of economic organizations and

• **Economic institutions:** laws, rules, customs, and agreements that influence economic activities and distinguish economic systems from one another

Exhibit 7.5: Economic Organizations and Institutions

Economic Organizations

Political Organizations:
- political parties
- regulatory agencies
- systems of income redistribution
- state planning and production systems
- political lobbies

Commercial Organizations:
- legal partnerships
- corporations (for-profit and not-for-profit)
- FASB—Financial Accounting Standards Board
- Better Business Bureau
- ISO 2000–International Standards Organization
- labor unions
- business and professional organizations

Financial Organizations:
- private or state banks
- associations of banks for clearing checks
- stock and bond market exchanges
- private or state insurance and pension funds
- mutual funds
- central bank
- financial regulatory agencies

Civil Organizations:
- voluntary groups promoting civil society
- hunger relief organizations
- Kiwanis and Rotary
- nonprofit lobbies
- other nongovernment organizations (NGOs)

Economic Institutions

Legal and Political Heritage:
- rule of law versus rule of king or party
- common law, Magna Charta
- Ten Commandments and the Jewish Law
- Marxist idea that law is a capitalist tool
- Democracy with political competition or Totalitarian rule

Commercial Laws:
- property, contract, patent, and copyright laws
- legal forms of commercial institutions
- Marxist/Leninist laws against profit and wage labor
- rate, route, safety, and social regulations

Commercial Institutions:
- other private commercial codes
- GAAP (Generally Accepted Accounting Practices)
- networks of traders and buyers and sellers

Civil Institutions:
- spirit of civic duty
- spirit of volunteerism

Social and Moral Institutions:
- religious economic teachings
  - concern for the poor
  - paying tithes and giving gifts
  - laws against lending at interest
- attitudes on work, thrift, and honesty
- attitudes toward commerce

institutions. Recognizing the potential overlap of these categories and the incompleteness of the list, let's review a few details about economic organizations.

Types of Economic Organizations

Economies are endowed with various legal, political, financial, commercial, civil, and social organizations. Each augments, modifies, or restricts economic activity in its own way.

These groupings can conceal the fact that certain institutions cross boundaries. For instance, a nation's central bank is both a legal and a financial institution. In addition, a central bank is necessarily political, sometimes suffering inappropriate manipulation by politicians. And a central bank always owes its existence to and is accountable to the government. In spite of the overlap, the groupings are instructive.

Legal, Political, and Regulatory Organizations

An economy's legal organizations create, adapt, and enforce laws, the official rules enforced by government. The legal system rests on a specific institutional ideology, such as the rule of law, the divine right of kings, or the political supremacy of one party. The legal foundation, particular rules, and regulatory processes that emerge shape a nation's political and economic progress.

Politics concerns itself with making public policy (as opposed to administering it). Democratic nations are endowed with particular political parties that compete to exert influence over laws and regulatory activities through their grass-roots and high-level organizations. These organizations and their beliefs develop over time, gaining and losing strength as events unfold.

Parties operate in legislative organizations established by law. Their political decisions are always essentially economic, either promoting private economic activity by establishing and enforcing rules for private property and free exchange, or by redistributing resources and products for private or public uses. Political decisions can also impose constraints or incentives on private or public economic activity.

After politicians make public policy, bureaucrats and civil servants administer it. The existence and structure of administrative agencies helps to determine the efficiency and equity of economic and regulatory activity. Views about the value of regulatory agencies differ. Workers may favor the safety regulations imposed by the Occupational Safety and Health Administration (OSHA), while businesses may complain that OSHA rules raise their costs and reduce competitiveness of U.S. businesses.

Polity and bureaucracy influence each other. If political action institutes powerful laws but creates weak or underfunded bureaucratic organizations, the laws are less likely to be fully applied. The existence of bureaucratic organizations also creates political pressure to maintain funding for them, because bureaucrats vote and also lobby politicians.

Commercial Organizations

A nation's economic capability depends on the commercial organizations that develop to produce goods and services. Organizational form matters too. The size and international reach of modern corporations is a controversial feature of capitalism. The legal difference between for-profit and not-for-profit businesses ensures adequate provision of various kinds of products, including educational services that are more suited to the not-for-profit form.

Very important to maintaining the health of capitalism are the commercial associations that businesses form to regulate themselves. A beneficial philosophy of government regulation is to allow business to try first to regulate itself. This is the purpose of the Financial Accounting Standards Board (FASB) and its rulings that guide public accountants who provide information to investors about publicly traded businesses. FASB's challenge is to regulate accountants without becoming captured by the corporations whose books they affect. Businesses also form associations to reduce their own costs by, for example, creating industry standards. This is the function of the International Standards Organization (ISO).

Financial Organizations

Banks, credit unions, insurance companies, and pension funds are financial institutions. Private financial institutions help savers who want to earn interest avoid the risks of finding their own borrowers and eliminate extra costs of arranging a loan. The ready availability of financial services in all regions of a nation encourages productive investment.

Regulation is particularly important in financial markets because bankers and financiers are often risking much more of other people's money than their own. Government organizations such as a central bank and other regulatory agencies also affect the stability of the money supply and financial system as they oversee private banks, insurance companies, pension funds, stockbrokers, and mutual funds.

Civic Organizations

Political scientists and economists use the phrase "civil society" to refer to those organizations that perform public duties but are outside the direct control of government or for-profit businesses. The more ineffective government and commercial institutions are at efficiently and equitably distributing goods and

• **Civic organizations:** perform civil (public) duties and attend to the needs of those outside their group services, the more important are civic institutions. Civic institutions are also important when private oversight of economic activity is preferable to the more forceful hand of government.

Many local civic organizations perform public services outside the scope of government. Civic clubs such as Kiwanis and Rotary provide not only fellowship among members, but also charitable and civic services. Parent Teacher Associations are voluntary organizations to promote local education. The list of all local civic organizations in the United States would be quite long. Their chief characteristics, though, are that they are voluntary or not-for-profit organizations that pursue the public interest without government coercion.

Business organizations engage in civil society when they voluntarily regulate themselves and their members. The Better Business Bureau operates as a nonprofit source of information about business behavior, and also acts as mediator in disputes between consumers and the public. The American Institute of Certified Public Accountants is an example of a professional association that has served a civil function by regulating public reporting of corporate financial information in the United States. Its creation, the Financial Accounting Standards Board, now sets private standards (as opposed to government rules) for reporting transactions in publicly held U.S. businesses.

Civic organizations also operate internationally. The International Red Cross, Salvation Army, World Relief, and other emergency aid organizations perform charitable duties as global citizens. For example, with Kosovo refugees on the verge of starvation in parts of Yugoslavia and Albania in April 1999, the nonprofit relief agency Mercy Corps organized an airlift of food. Other civic groups regularly provide relief services in cities and towns in the United States itself. In general, such charitable civic institutions have been most needed and effective where the rules of law and efficient commerce are absent.

Social Organizations

• **Social organizations**: cooperative organizations that pursue the interests of individuals within the group

The term **social organizations**, as used here, refers to cooperative efforts to pursue the interests of individuals within a group (in contrast, civic organizations attend to the needs of those outside their group). A school board, for example, is authorized to meet the educational needs of students in its community, not students all around the world. A religious group generally pursues the interests of its members, even though it may try to add to the membership. Certain "faith-based organizations" do perform civic duties, providing social services to people outside their groups, but that is not true of all churches, mosques, and synagogues.

Families and other informal and formal social organizations pass a people's **culture**, a set of beliefs and social expectations, from one generation to the next. As Thomas Sowell makes clear in his book *Race and Culture* (1994), cultural attitudes and practices have long-lasting economic effects. Cultural attitudes create powerful economic institutions, affecting the acquisition of wealth, the sense of responsibility for charity, and the importance of education, saving, and hard work. Such cultural traits persist for generations. The willingness to accept the risk of being an entrepreneur, for example, varies among different cultures, as do certain economic skills in farming, commerce, and even piano making (Sowell 1994).

• **Culture**: the set of beliefs and social expectations, passed from one generation to the next, that create powerful but informal economic institutions

Cultural beliefs may constrain or otherwise affect economic systems. The academic culture in the United States, for example, generally is critical of capitalism, claiming that it nurtures greed. Business professors and students regularly complain that professors and students in other disciplines attempt to shame them. This could have the perverse effect of directing morally sensitive students away from capitalism, leaving the field open for those who do indeed choose the field of business out of greed. If capitalism nurtures greed, however, surely socialism nurtures human envy. A climate of envy can have negative economic effects, stifling productive effort. Envious people resist anything, even beneficial economic innovation and commercial activity, if it makes someone else wealthier than they are.

Harsh social attitudes about race led to racial segregation in the United States and apartheid in South Africa. Racial discrimination causes economic harm to those out of favor, while benefiting those favored. Discrimination limits economic opportunities for disadvantaged groups, leading to lower income. The privileged class gains an abundant low-cost supply of labor due to its ability to limit educational and employment opportunities for others. In spite of moral questions, supporters preserved segregation in part due to these economic advantages.

Economic Institutions

Institutions are the laws of government, the rules governing various organizations, and the social conventions governing less formal associations. The next chapter reviews economic theories of institutions in detail. Here you will find only a brief introduction to the idea that various laws, rules, customs, and commercial agreements can encourage or discourage economic activity.

Institutions Affect Commerce

Commercial activity in any nation is rarely carried out entirely by spontaneous market activity. Even a seemingly spontaneous farmers' market in the center of a town will have underlying rules and conventions that shape traders' behavior. Commercial activity flourishes best under a set of rules that define how the game shall be played. Well-written formal and informal laws, rules, and customary behaviors can reduce the costs of doing business.

Commercial rules include government laws of property, contracts, and torts (damages). Merchants also develop their own rules for trade and sanctions for those who break them. Their private rules historically have developed into formal legal codes. Commercial customs of late medieval European traders, for instance, became part of European civil law.

A nation's endowment of economic institutions and organizations affects economic progress because certain legal systems, social practices, customary commercial behaviors, and organizational structures are more economically efficient than others. Some rules and organizations promote economic activity, while others discourage it. For example, rules restraining government from taking property without just compensation and due process will encourage commerce.

Furthermore, laws that restrict free enterprise will drive able **entrepreneurs** out of the country, while systems encouraging enterprise will attract them. Entrepreneurs are the skilled organizers of commercial activity and risk takers that make commerce go. Without organizers and risk takers, a nation's commerce and living standards will not progress.

- **Entrepreneurs:** organizers of commercial activity who take risks in the hope of a future return

- **Moral capital:** a people's collective understanding of appropriate rules of moral restraint and its skill and persistence in applying them

Moral Capital and Institutions Matter, Too

A nation's **moral capital** is its collective understanding of appropriate rules of moral restraint and its skill and persistence in applying them. A collective memory about not stealing and not cheating promotes economic activity. Economic activity also depends critically on moral sentiments, those informal social and moral institutions that allow commerce and promote work effort. In short, an adequate stock of moral capital allows trust to flourish, and trust promotes trading relations among merchants, industrialists, workers, and consumers.

Moral capital also reflects a learned sense of public duty. In the United States, this responsibility has been passed from one generation to the next as a moral obligation to do one's **civic duty** to vote, volunteer in public service, and generally attend to public as well as individual interests. In Europe, obligations of the nobility to act with the honor and generosity implied by their rank and wealth has been called **noblesse oblige**, although the term is out of favor due to its elitist implications. Soviet Russian leaders created the idea of "socialist man," the ideal to which Russians should aspire in their dedication to the state and to the cause of world socialism.

Education, Society, and Moral Training

A nation's education system, whether formal or informal, is responsible for a people's moral education. Families, religious groups, schools, sports leagues, and other associations train students in the rules and in attitudes toward them. For instance, schools and organized athletics both train students for market competition and political action.

Schools can teach the acceptance of commercial competition or the use of political processes to overturn existing commercial structures. Community sports leagues teach children about the rule of law and attitudes toward it. Little League Baseball, for example, can teach children to play by the rules while playing competitively, or coaches can teach children to bend or break the rules to "win at all costs." For that matter, teachers can too. To improve their students' performance on standardized tests, teachers have sometimes broken rules and given test questions to their students for practice before the exam. Whatever philosophy teachers and coaches impart, they inevitably teach youth how to act in commerce and in the public square.

Religious leaders also teach rules, reinforce or alter customs, and influence attitudes about economic activity. They may support or reject the institutions of, for example, private property rights, for-profit commerce, socialism, or government redistribution of wealth. Religious organizations also institute among their members principles of general morality. In doing so, they contribute to the nature of a people's moral capital.

Moral education now will have economic consequences later. Recently, commentators in the United States have reported the economic and social effects of moral education. Abandoning traditional moral education in schools may be causing rising rates of crime and illegitimate births. If true, eroding morals have future economic implications, affecting government and private spending on crime prevention, prisons, and support for fatherless families.

Effects of Special Religious Institutions

Religious organizations also teach and promote their own special rules, customs, and beliefs. Certain religious institutions can have important economic effects. Religious organizations are themselves supported by such practices as tithing and offerings, institutionalized religious behaviors that support a host of church and religious organizations. To **tithe** is to pay a mandatory tenth of family income to the church. An offering is a voluntary gift. The *Zakat* is an Islamic counterpart to tithes and offerings.

- **Tithe**: paying a tenth of one's income to the church

Religious institutions can also directly encourage or restrain market commerce. On the one hand, a salt-fish industry in Canada thrives on a Roman Catholic tradition of eating fish during Lent. On the other hand, church-supported **blue laws** limited Sunday commerce and recreation in the United States, and kept retailing businesses and amusement parks closed involuntarily. Religious institutions also can lose their economic influence as society becomes more secular. United States blue laws, while dominant for about two centuries, gradually lost force after the 1950s. See Expansion Point 7.4 for more details on the blue laws and the Sabbath idea as a religious institution.

- **Blue laws**: originally printed on blue paper, they restricted Sunday commerce and recreation in the United States until the 1950s

Expansion Point 7.4: The Sabbath, U.S. Blue Laws, and the Economy

Hebrew books of the Law report that in the fourth of the Ten Commandments the Lord instituted a Sabbath day of rest. Originating in New England in the 1700s and printed on blue paper, blue laws were enacted in the United States that restricted Sunday labor, commercial activity, and amusement. The Jewish Sabbath is Saturday, the seventh day of rest in the Genesis account of God's creation. Christians, though, observe Sunday, the day the Lord rose from the dead, as a Sabbath.

A Sunday Sabbath influenced commerce for two centuries duc to a consensus about the value and propriety of a day of rest, but also due to a threat of fines for violators. As long as most U.S. shop owners agreed to suspend business for the day, all shop owners could refrain from Sunday commerce without fear of losing business.

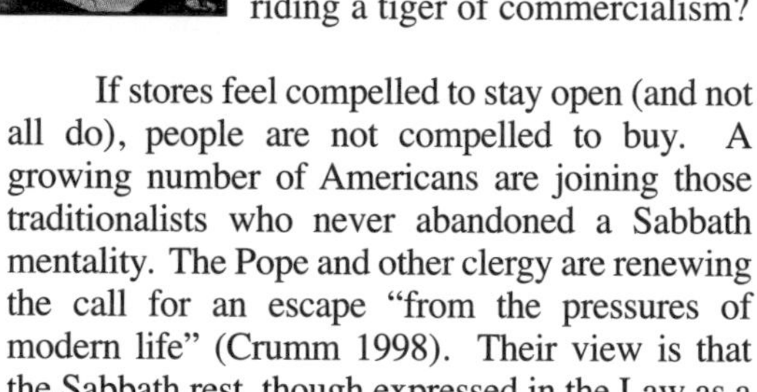

The U.S. Supreme Court never invalidated a commercial Sabbath, refusing to overturn Sunday-closing laws in *McGowan v. Maryland* (1961) and *Braunfeld v. Brown* (1961). When the religious consensus broke down, however, retailing stores found it profitable to open on Sunday in violation of the law and simply pay a fine. Extra revenues from serving Sunday shoppers more than compensated for the fines. Eventually, police refused to enforce the laws, and most state and local governments repealed them. As a result, Sunday commerce is now much more common in the United States. People working six days a week or using Saturday for play, can now shop on Sunday for food, clothing, and other goods. Yet some employees who don't want to work on Sunday must work anyway.

Craig Gay and others lament the end of a commercial Sabbath. Gay, for example, contends that "business and commerce" in a market economy "have not only threatened the observance of the Sabbath, but they have often become the object of idolatrous devotion and worship" (1994, 193). Gay contends that "adopting a Sabbath attitude . . . would help . . . put economic life in perspective."

Economists can reasonably argue that restoring Sabbath rules against commerce would reduce economic activity and standards of living. Why shouldn't retailers who do want to observe a Sabbath simply stay closed? Without a cultural consensus, however, a retailing firm could lose customers to competitors by *not* opening on Sunday. A Chinese proverb says, when you ride the back of a tiger, it is hard to get off. To what extent are we riding a tiger of commercialism?

If stores feel compelled to stay open (and not all do), people are not compelled to buy. A growing number of Americans are joining those traditionalists who never abandoned a Sabbath mentality. The Pope and other clergy are renewing the call for an escape "from the pressures of modern life" (Crumm 1998). Their view is that the Sabbath rest, though expressed in the Law as a duty, is a privilege, not a jail sentence.

Sources: "Sunday Closing Laws," *Oxford Companion to the Supreme Court* (Cambridge: Oxford University Press, 1992), 847-48.

Craig M. Gay, "On Learning to Live with the Market Economy," *Christian Scholar's Review* (December 1994): 180-195.

David Crumm, "In a Restless World, Families Strive to Heed Their Religions' Call to Remember the Sabbath," *Buffalo News*, Saturday, September 5, 1998, A-11.

Chapter Summary

1. An economy is endowed with natural resources like favorable climate, geography, soil, minerals, ports and waterways.

2. Industrial development causes environmental problems, including rapid rate of resource use and air, water, and soil pollution. Resources are nonrenewable, renewable, or relatively inexhaustible. Critics question whether nonrenewable resources are being used too fast by industrial capitalism.

3. Economists contend that rising resource prices promote conservation and the search for substitutes.

4. The materials-balance model shows that pollution is inevitable in production when output of goods weighs less than inputs. Unwanted by-products result.

5. Pollution is a by-product that businesses ignore, creating an external cost for others in society. When the producer doesn't bear the cost of pollution, product price is too low and quantity exchanged too high, compared to a social optimum. A tax on pollution could cause producers to raise prices toward the socially optimal level.

6. A nation's capital stock includes tools and productive equipment that embody various technologies. Capital and technology move to markets or toward resources. Capital also develops previously unusable resources. Changing technology can make or break a region's economy.

7. A nation is endowed with a population that has skills, education, and attitudes toward work, saving, and other economic activity. Human knowledge, tools, and equipment are crucial to economic development. Resources can be acquired elsewhere.

8. People create and modify economic organizations and institutions to direct and alter economic behavior and activity. Economic organizations are the ongoing cooperative, hierarchical associations of people. They include legal, political, financial, commercial, civil-society, and social organizations.

9. Economic institutions are laws, rules, agreements, and customs that direct economic behavior and activity. A nation's institutional structure tends to either promote or discourage entrepreneurs, commercial activity, and overall economic progress.

10. Culture and moral capital matter in economic development. Moral capital is collective learning about and ability to abide by moral rules. Attitudes toward commerce, the rule of law, and political action affect future economic activity. Families, schools, religious leaders, and so on can build moral capital and do transmit attitudes about economic institutions.

11. Certain religious institutions such as the tithe, Zakat, and Sabbath have important economic effects.

Problems for Practice

7.1* What are the special economic endowments of the region within a 25- to 50-mile radius of your home? What are your own endowments of human capital?

7.2* Explain with a graph how pollution imposes social costs that are not reflected in product price, and the effect on market price and output of the good.

7.3* Explain why a market for pollution rights is efficient. Would you support a proposal to let one business sell its pollution rights to another business?

Economics in film and literature:
7.4* Borrow the video *How Green Was My Valley*, starring Walter Pidgeon and Maureen O'Hara. The movie is about the life of a family of Welsh coal miners and how it changed with shifting economic conditions caused by closings of nearby mines.

For your portfolio:
7.5* Write a one-page history of the rise and/or fall of a city or region due to changing institutions, technology, patterns of trade, or patterns of resource use. Expansion Point 7.4 is your model.

7.6* Write a brief description of your *own* examples of a religious institution with economic effects.

For class discussion:
7.7 Do you agree or disagree with the assertion that human capital is a more important national economic endowment than natural resources?

7.8* Are you as confident as those economists who think that rising resource prices will solve most problems with limited resources? Do you have as much faith in technological progress as they do? Explain.

7.9 Very few mainstream economists include moral or religious ideas in their list of factors that promote economic growth. (Check old texts and see.) Who is correct—mainstream or institutional economists?

7.10 In capitalist economies, associations of accountants and businesses regulate themselves. Do you favor this system? Do you see any advantages or potential problems? Explain.

7.11 Do you think that the general intellectual attitudes on high school and college campuses tend to favor or reject commercial activity? Does it matter?

See Answer Key for hints/answers to starred (*) questions.

Chapter 8

WEALTH AND POVERTY

Explaining Varying Living Standards

What this chapter will help you think about:

1. What is wealth and does it differ from income?
2. How do absolute and relative poverty differ?
3. How do we measure levels of poverty and standards of living?
4. What causes poverty?
5. What approaches have people taken to alleviate poverty?
6. How does the functional distribution of wealth differ from the household and family distributions of wealth?
7. How are income and wealth distributed in the United States?

- **Distribution question:** Which people will get how much of the output of goods and services produced?

In 1500, most of your forebears lived in absolute poverty, a "hand-to-mouth" existence. Soft manufactured cotton cloth did not exist, wheat bread was a luxury, and most people had ill health, ate poorly, and wore clothing made of burlap and other rough cloth. Wealth versus poverty was mainly a matter of royalty versus commoner and landed gentry versus peasant. Very limited social mobility made escaping poverty a mere dream.

By the twenty-first century, billions of the offspring of commoners, yeomen farmers, peasants, and paupers had escaped into middle and upper-class lives of relatively great wealth and opportunity. Yet, billions of people remained in desperate poverty. The stark contrast today between rich and poor forces us to confront the nature and causes of poverty and wealth.

Defining Wealth and Poverty

Who is poor and who is wealthy? Is a family with a color television, cable service, six-year-old sedan, videocassette player, refrigerator, and microwave poor? Or is a family with 20 cows, a mud-and-grass hut, and none of the conveniences of a modern home poor? In America in the twenty-first century, the answer to the first question may well be yes, while in sub-Saharan Africa, the answer to the second question may well be no.

Answers to important public-policy questions hinge not only on how much we care, but also on how we define and measure wealth and poverty. We will begin by defining wealth and income. Then we will compare relative and absolute concepts of poverty.

Wealth

Derived from middle-English, **wealth** refers to all those things outside us that make us well. While the meaning is simple enough and seems clearly to be associated with the good life, wealth has come to be highly controversial in economics and religion. Most controversial to economists is whether privately held wealth is more or less moral and efficient than publicly held wealth, and whether the distribution of wealth is more or less important than the creation of wealth. Expansion Point 8.1 compares socialist and classical-liberal economists' views on these issues. People of faith and others who reflect on life's meaning also question the relative importance of accumulating wealth as one's life goal. Expansion Point 8.2 takes up these moral and religious questions. Meanwhile, we should explore in more details what wealth is.

• **Wealth:** those things that make us well

Expansion Point 8.1: Competing Economic Perspectives on Wealth

Socialists and classical liberals offer very different economic perspectives on wealth and, therefore, on the economic role of government.

Socialists and the Distribution of Wealth
Socialists question the distribution of existing wealth in society. They highlight the poverty of workers compared to others' wealth. To them, economics is about how we divide the pie. Following Karl Marx, socialists attack the laws of private property that undergird market economies. Socialists advocate holding productive wealth in common, and look suspiciously on private wealth.

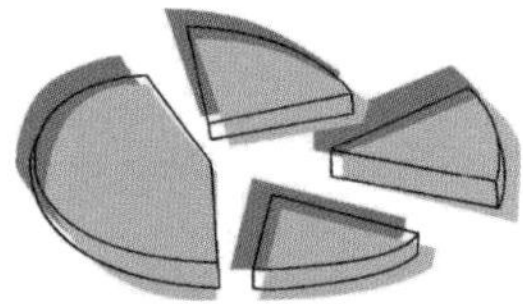
Dividing a given pie

Socialists advocate more progressive tax systems that apply much higher tax rates to the wealth and incomes of the rich. Government's economic task is to design social-welfare policies that redistribute wealth and income, and equalize flows of goods and services to all people.

Socialists say that unequal distributions of wealth and income caused the Great Depression of the 1930s. Because the wealth of the rich grew faster than the wealth of all other groups during the 1920s in the United States, aggregate consumption was too low in the 1930s to sustain economic growth. Other economists doubt this simplistic explanation of a complex event, but socialists recommend it as a cure for economic stagnation.

Classical Liberals and the Creation of Wealth
Classical liberals such as Adam Smith and Jean-Baptiste Say were free-market economists who emphasized economic liberty and the creation of wealth more than the distribution of wealth. For them, economics is about explaining how to bake new and bigger pies. (David Ricardo, with his emphasis on the distribution of national income among land owners, farmers, and laborers, is a notable exception.)

Baking new pies

Classical liberals complain that socialists take a static view of wealth and assume that the size of the economic pie they redistribute is fixed or will grow at a fixed rate. Redistributing wealth and socializing productive wealth, however, alter economic incentives. High tax rates on income and wealth curb people's incentives to be productive and to accumulate productive wealth, causing the pie to grow more slowly or not at all.

Free-market advocates praise the incentive effects of a system of private wealth, while condemning any more than a bare minimum of public taxing of private wealth. They see redistribution programs as weapons in an inefficient and destructive class warfare that socialist politicians wage in order to gain the votes of the poor. The chief roles of government are to protect the interests of property and to assure economic freedom.

Expansion Point 8.2: Is Wealth Good or Evil?

Is wealth good or evil? Utilitarian economists hold wealth to be good by definition because it promotes human welfare. Yet certain followers of the "dualist" philosophy of Aristotle and Thomas Aquinas believed that the spiritual life was supreme and the material world was to be shunned (Adie 1984, 1160). Today, few if any mainstream philosophical or religious traditions teach that material wealth is intrinsically bad (none say that what is good is bad). Yet most religious traditions do instruct in proper attitudes toward wealth. Here are key issues.

Is the highest human goal to pursue a good material existence or a good spiritual life? Your answer follows from your ranking of the importance of material wealth. Most religious traditions teach that other goals are more important, especially revering God and helping others. Jesus, for example, taught His followers, "Seek first his kingdom and his righteousness, and all these [material] things will be given to you" (Matthew 6:33 NIV). This verse demands caution regarding personal wealth.

An ascetic life expresses extreme caution about material wealth. For example, Ignatius of Loyola, founder of the Jesuit monastic order of the Roman Catholic Church, together with six fellow seminarians at the University of Paris in 1534, took vows of poverty before entering missionary work. They were not declaring material goods to be evil. Each merely agreed to forsake personal property, and to hold goods in common.

Asceticism has led many Christians into an austere lifestyle, without ostentatious displays of wealth but short of taking vows of poverty. Earning wealth is not bad, but flaunting it is. The Protestant ethic of European Calvinists (as described by the German sociologist Max Weber) encouraged hard work and wealth accumulation as a sign of one's divine election, but the ethic emphasized thrift rather than pleasure or lavish consumption. The Shakers of nineteenth-century America, while very productive, lived a simple lifestyle (except for the dance) and also held most of their goods in common.

Sharing wealth with those in need expresses another moral view toward wealth. For Israelites of the Old Testament, this meant sharing with the priests through tithes and offerings and sharing with the poor through charity. Islam has taught a similar concern for the poor and a duty to share one's possessions with them. More strictly, Jesus called His disciples to give to the poor privately, and not announce their giving "with trumpets" (Matt. 6: 1-4). He called the "rich young ruler" to discipleship by first demanding extreme charity: "Go, sell everything you have and give to the poor . . . Then come, follow me" (Mark 10:21).

What dangers does wealth pose? A preoccupation with wealth diverts our attentions from more noble ideals. That is why Jesus said, "How hard it is for the rich to enter the kingdom of God" (v. 23). The lure and promise of wealth may pervert our decision making, as in a judge who accepts bribes. Another person's wealth may cause us to covet or steal, both sins in the Old Testament law. Or we may come to trust in our own wealth.

Individual wealth, however, may also be an opportunity for service to God and to other people. (Adie, 1159) The biblical view of wealth is that, since God created all things useful to people, wealth cannot be intrinsically bad. Yet we are stewards of the wealth God has entrusted to us, both individually and communally.

Source: D.K. Adie, "Wealth, Christian View of," *Evangelical Dictionary of Theology*, ed. Walter Elwell (Grand Rapids: Baker, 1984), 1159-63.

Technical Aspects of Wealth

To be precise, wealth is a stock of tangible or intangible things that are useful for meeting needs and satisfying wants, and that therefore have exchange value. Let's examine the **four aspects**: wealth is a stock, wealth is either tangible or intangible, wealth is useful, and wealth has money or barter exchange value.

Wealth is a stock existing at a point in time. A bank account may hold $45,000 on a given day or a family may own two cars at a point in time. Wealth is not the same as income, which is a flow of value per period of time. Having a million dollars in the bank is different from earning a million dollars a year.

Wealth enables humans to meet basic needs for food, clothing, and shelter, and to satisfy wants over and above basic needs. We usually think about wealthy people as being able to satisfy any whim or fancy, but wealth includes the most modest tools and savings. Wealth that produces other wealth or a flow of income is **capital**. Stocks, bonds, and bank certificates of deposit are financial capital. Machinery and factories that produce goods or services are physical capital.

Wealth includes not only tangible factories and equipment, but also intangible assets such as a brand name, a patented idea, the code for a computer software program, or a musical score. People's knowledge and skills that have market value—such as the ability to build cabinetry or to write computer software—are called **human capital**. A good credit rating gives an individual or a company access to other people's money, and a sterling commercial reputation ensures a steady flow of customers to a business; both are also intangible wealth. Wealth now resides in electronically coded accounts and rides around the globe on electronic waves. It grows within the mind, expressed as an author's carefully written thoughts that sell millions of books, or an athlete's expert muscle movements that win a multimillion-dollar free-agent contract.

Since useful things have value to others, wealth will have a monetary or exchange value. Evidence of monetary value is the ability to sell something at a positive money price in a voluntary transaction. Exchange value is also evidenced in an ability to swap one form of wealth for another, as in barter trade.

The value of wealth is culturally determined and depends on what we know about it. What is valuable in one time or culture may have little value in another. Ancient Buddhist temples that had value to their builders years ago and to many in the world in 2001 were, in the estimations of Taliban leaders in Afghanistan, worthy only to be destroyed. Changes in tastes and desires affect the value of wealth. A painter's art is valued by cultural fashion.

Changes in our knowledge about what is true, safe, or acceptable also affect the value of wealth. Shares of stock in the United States, for example, fell in value in May, June, and July of 2002 only after news that the accounting books of various companies did not accurately reflect their previous income and debts. In the 1970s, a factory making asbestos-based home siding would have had less value after publication of research showing that exposure to asbestos could cause cancer.

- **Wealth is**
  1) a stock of things,
  2) tangible or intangible,
  3) that are useful for meeting needs and satisfying wants, and
  4) that therefore have exchange value.

- **Capital:** wealth that produces other wealth or a flow of money income

- **Human capital:** intangible wealth that people hold as their knowledge or skill

- **Income is**
  1) a flow of money or resources over time,
  2) from wealth or labor services,
  3) having a real value that depends on the general level of prices.

Income Flows from Wealth or Work

Income and wealth are closely related but they are not the same. Consider **three aspects** of income: it is a flow of money or resources over time, it arises from wealth or labor services, and its real value depends on the general level of prices.

Income is a flow per period of time of money or other value goods or services (while wealth is a stock). When we say, "My friend makes a lot of money," we really mean, "She has a high yearly monetary income."

Income flows out of a stock of wealth. At five percent annual interest, $50,000 in a bank certificate of deposit pays $2,500 interest income per year. The wealth stored in a retail business or a coal mine may yield a profit each year. Income also arises from labor services. At $15 an hour, 40 hours of work earns $600 of income a week. We may get our income from our own wealth or labor or from other people's wealth or labor. Even welfare payments flow from the general wealth of the nation.

The real value of your family's income depends on the prices that you pay for the goods and services that you buy. If prices have risen 20 percent over the past five years, the real value of a fixed income of say $40,000 has declined by about 16 percent. That is, $40,000 today will buy only 84 percent of the food, housing, and other goods and services that it bought five years ago. While your nominal income (your income "on the face of it") is still $40,000, your real income is only $33,333 (which is $40,000 divided by 1.2 to account for the 20 percent rise in prices).

- **Social vs. private and public wealth:**
  1) social wealth is a net value that considers offsetting obligations
  2) private wealth is held by an individual or group of individuals apart from official state ownership
  3) public wealth is held by the state or state-authorized agencies

Social vs. Private and Public Wealth

Social wealth is the total value of all the wealth of a group. It includes wealth held privately by individuals, families, and other partnerships, wealth held in common by corporations, communes, and cooperatives, and public wealth held by the state. Let's distinguish private wealth, which is held by private individuals and groups, and public wealth, which is held by the state.

Consider **two aspects** of social and private wealth. First, social wealth is the *net* value, not the total value, of all wealth. One person's financial wealth may be another person's debt. Second, private wealth creation occurs cooperatively and competitively. Wealth creation by one individual, business, or government may either augment or reduce the wealth of another. Let's explain.

Social Wealth as Net Private and Public Wealth. Total social wealth is not simply the sum of all wealth, which would involve double counting. Let's say a family owns a house worth $200,000, but the bank owns a mortgage against that house for the family's debt of $120,000. The family's wealth is the value of the house less the family's debt, or $80,000, and the bank's stake is

$120,000. Otherwise we mistakenly calculate total wealth of the family and bank as $320,000.

Modern accounting recognizes these offsets to wealth when keeping the books of a family or business. When accountants add the value of a truck or other equipment as an asset on the books of a firm, they also balance this by entering any corresponding liability, such as a bank loan or an issue of stocks or bonds to raise money to buy it. Accountants then calculate the business's **net worth** as its assets minus liabilities. **Total social wealth** then is the sum of all private and public net worths.

- **Net worth:** assets minus liabilities
- **Total social wealth:** the sum of all private and public net worths

Exhibit 8.1 shows the Census Bureau's estimates of the combined balance sheets for U.S. households and nonprofit organizations from 1980 to 2000. The data show two important aspects of measuring wealth: the secular effects of economic growth and inflation, and the cyclical effects of a recession. First, net worth of households and nonprofits more than doubled between 1980 and 1990 and again between 1990 and 2000. These increases are due to a growing U.S. economy in both decades and to rising prices during that time. Second, net worth of households and nonprofits fell from 1999, the peak of the business cycle, to 2000, the first year of the Clinton-Bush recession. The recession's full effects had not yet been felt in 2000, but households had been stung by declining financial wealth due to falling stock-market share prices.

Exhibit 8.1: Combined U.S. Household and Nonprofit-Organization Balance Sheet

Year	1980	1990	1999	2000
Assets*	$10,989	$24,315	$49,218	$48,978
Liabilities*	$1,455	$3,747	$6,958	$7,560
Net Worth*	$9,533	$20,568	$42,260	$41,418

* in billions of current dollars

Source: "Table No. 689: Household and Nonprofit Organization Sector Balance Sheet, 1980 to 2000," *Statistical Abstract of the United States: 2001*, U.S. Bureau of the Census, Section 13: Income, Expenditure, and Wealth. Found at http://www.census.gov/prod/ 2002pubs/01statab/statab01.html

Wealth Creation in Cooperation and Competition. Wealth creation may either augment or threaten another person's wealth. If you own a rural home and the state improves the road past the property, creating the road may increase the value of your property. Yet competitive wealth creation may also destroy wealth. When one city promises to build a new sports stadium to lure a team from another city, that competition can lower the value of existing stadiums in other cities. If my pharmaceutical company holds a patent on a drug to cure the common cold, the patent is my private wealth since it creates profit for me, and it is also public wealth since it creates a net health gain to society, the value of curing colds. If, however, you invent and patent another drug that does the same and that costs the same to make, you create value for yourself, but your discovery reduces the value of the first patent. Competition causes people to be willing to pay a

lower price for the first drug. Wealth is redistributed from my company to yours (but it is not possible to say for sure whether social wealth increases, decreases, or remains the same).

Government Policies and Social Wealth

Ideally, all government policies would create net social wealth or at least would not reduce social wealth. In practice, government falls far short. Because politicians and bureaucrats often choose what is politically best over what is economically efficient, certain inefficient government actions will destroy social wealth.

Absolute Poverty

• **Absolute poverty:** a lack of minimal wealth and income needed to sustain health or even life itself

To maintain good health, people require minimal amounts of food, shelter, and clothing. Without the minimums, a person dies or his health deteriorates. A person in **absolute poverty**, therefore, does not have the minimum wealth and income to sustain good health or even life itself.

Income Poverty

• **Income poverty:** the usual meaning of poverty, a flow of income and resources that is inadequate to assure a minimally good life

Development experts refer to the most obvious problem of being poor as **income poverty**, the lack of an adequate flow of money and resources each year. World income poverty is staggering, especially given the wealth accumulated in the United States and other industrialized nations. At the beginning of the twenty-first century, over 46 percent of the 6 billion people in the world subsisted on less than $2 per person per day (*World Development Report 2000-2001: Attacking Poverty*, 3). For a family of four, this means living on less than $2,920 a year. Twenty percent struggled with incomes below a dollar of income per person each day (p. 3).

• **Subsistence wage:** the wage that is just adequate to assure that a family has a minimally good life

We can call the break point between a wage that leads to absolute poverty and a wage that provides an adequate standard of living the **subsistence wage**. In the 1800s, several English classical economists thought that wages of the mass of unskilled workers would automatically tend toward the subsistence level, as explained in Expansion Point 8.3 on the "iron law of wages."

Health and Educational Deprivation

• **Health poverty:** poor health caused by lack of access to basic health services

Ralph Waldo Emerson said that "the first wealth is health." The poor fall rather easily into **health poverty**, characterized by poor health that reduces quality of life and is caused by a lack of access to basic health services.

Income and health poverty are obviously related because a lack of income restricts access to health care, and ill health further limits a poor worker's ability to continue to earn income. Paying for needed health care further drains income. The cost of health care may involve time a person takes from work to walk several days to a free clinic. Ill health also leaves families deeper in poverty.

Expansion Point 8.3: The Iron Law of Wages

English classical political economists David Ricardo and Thomas Malthus believed in a principle called the "iron law of wages." They asserted that agricultural workers' wages would tend toward the subsistence level. This is the break point between absolute poverty and a standard of living able to sustain life. In the iron law of wages, you see one good reason why the English considered economics to be the "dismal science."

The theory was simple. If wages rose above subsistence, family life would be so good that enough newborn babies and children would live to adulthood to increase the labor force. But an increasing labor force would, by the laws of supply and demand, press wages down below subsistence as the workers bid up the price of the limited supply of food. Due to lower wages and higher food prices, fewer newborns and children would then survive to become adult workers, the labor supply would fall, and wages would rise toward subsistence as food prices declined.

Adam Smith's economic ideas were much more optimistic because he allowed for increases in the productivity of workers due to increases in capital equipment and technological improvement. Smith's *Wealth of Nations* (1776) includes historical remarks about the progress in laborers' productivity and their living conditions. Indeed, throughout the 1800s, gradual and then rapid mechanization led to dramatic increases in the productivity and wages of agricultural and industrial workers.

In the 1850s, Karl Marx's theory of exploitation of industrial workers by factory owners borrowed heavily from English classical explanations of the subsistence wage. By 1900, however, industrial wages in the United States and Britain were above subsistence and rising, and the iron law of wages had thoroughly rusted through. Since then, economists have relied on variations in the theory of demand and supply to explain different wages in different occupations. Yet, even the theories of demand and supply and of wage differentials follow from the earlier work of Smith in *Wealth of Nations*.

Sources: "Subsistence Theory of Wages," *The Encyclopedic Dictionary of Economics*, 4th ed. (Guilford: CT: Duskhin Publishing Group, 1991), 237.

Adam Smith, *An Inquiry into the Nature and Causes of the Wealth of Nations*, Glasgow ed. Ed. R.H. Campbell and A.S. Skinner (Indianapolis: Liberty Fund), 1981 [1776]. See especially bk I, ch. 7 on demand and supply, and ch. 8 on wages.

In most regions of the world, good health for the poor starts, not with access to CAT scans and the latest surgical and medical care, but with improved water sources and sanitation (sewer) facilities. Yet, even in these basics, great disparities exist in the global distribution of water and sanitation facilities. In the 1990s, all of the people in the Netherlands, Norway, and the United Kingdom, for example, had access to improved water sources and sanitation works. In Ethiopia, however, only 27 percent had access to improved water and only eight percent had sanitation works (*World Development Report 2000-2001*, 286-87).

The health-care failures facing the poor can be disturbingly simple problems. In Africa, operations are canceled because physicians and nurses have exhausted the supply of rubber gloves (Shao 2001, 22). In other cases, problems are monumental. In Russia, the end of the Soviet system threatened publicly funded health care. While hospital beds and doctors might be available for a burn victim, for example, in the late 1990s families themselves had to buy medicines that were in short supply. For poor families, costs could be excessive and injured loved ones might do without.

Further complicating their poverty, the poor generally have low education. When work is available, low education keeps wages low, and poverty then contributes to low education of successive generations. Low education also hurts farm yields. In Vietnam, a study in 2000 by Alberto van de Walle showed that irrigation projects yielded lower benefits where adults were less educated (see *World Development Report 2000-2001*, 78).

Relative Poverty

- **Poverty line:** official government-determined levels of income below which families of various sizes are in relative poverty
- **Relative poverty:** having less than the usual or socially accepted levels of income and wealth

According to government statistics, millions of people in industrialized nations such as the United States live below the official **poverty line**. Yet other statistics regarding their standards of living show that many of them are not in absolute poverty. The poverty line, however, refers to a point of **relative poverty**, meaning when people don't have "the usual or socially-acceptable amount of money or material possessions" (*Webster's Ninth Collegiate Dictionary*). The poverty line is a socially, not biologically determined minimum standard of living. The U.S. government sets the poverty line at about 40 percent of the median income of a family of a given size.

A difficulty with the poverty line is that the number of people vary by different measures of income. While not considered in the official U.S. definition of income for poverty considerations, taxes reduce disposable income, and noncash government transfer payments such as food and housing subsidies for the poor raise income. Capital gains from the sale of appreciated assets and the Earned Income Tax Credit for the working poor also raise income, although they too are ignored in the official definition of income. As Exhibit 8.2 shows, when taxes, income from capital gains, and the EIC are considered in income, over one million people are no

Exhibit 8.2: How Taxes, Capital Gains, EIC, and Noncash Transfers Affect Measures of People in Poverty, U.S. 2000

Measures of Income	Number of People below Poverty Line	Percent in Poverty
Official definition	31,054,000	11.3%
Official less taxes plus net capital gains and EIC	29,914,000	10.8%
Official less taxes plus EIC and all noncash transfers	26,336,000	9.5%

Source: "The Marginal Effect of Taxes and Transfers on Poverty Estimates: 2000," U.S. Census Bureau, based on a November 2001 correction. http://www.census.gov/hhes/poverty/poverty00/tablef.html.

longer in poverty in the United States. Adding non-cash transfers (but ignoring capital gains) lowers the number in poverty by nearly five million Americans. If we also included the implicit value of services that flow from houses that people own, millions more people (especially elderly who own their homes) would escape "poverty."

Causes of Poverty

While defining poverty and wealth, we have hinted at the causes of poverty. Let's explicitly list and briefly explain various causes, citing a few supporting statistics. First a key distinction.

Particular vs. Systemic Causes

An individual may have a low income due either to particular causes or to systemic causes. **Particular causes** of poverty operate within the individual's own personal situation, for the most part independently of what is happening with other individuals. Not working at a job that pays an adequate wage or salary because of ill health or lack of training, for example, are particular causes of poverty. Conservative defenders of free enterprise tend to focus on the particular causes of poverty over which the individual has control, such as education decisions and personal work ethic.

- **Particular causes of poverty:** affect an individual or family independently of other people, often depending on individual decisions or special circumstances

Systemic causes of poverty operate due to forces outside the individual's personal situation and largely outside the individual's control. They affect groups of people, not just individuals. Not working because the economy has collapsed in a depression is a systemic cause of poverty. Not working because of discrimination is a systemic cause. Liberals tend to emphasize the systemic defects of market economies such as business cycles, while conservatives emphasize the systemic problems arising from government, such as the disincentives of poor relief and the weak institutions of non-market economies.

- **Systemic causes of poverty:** operate due to forces outside an individual's control, affecting groups of people due to major events and general circumstances in society and the political economy

Yet, sociologists complain, what seem to be particular problems may have systemic roots. A worker may have few skills because he was born into a poor family and had inadequate nutrition in formative years. An unemployed worker may be poor because he dropped out of high school, apparently an individual decision. Perhaps, however, the decision was rooted in a family culture that goes back generations to earlier times, when the family's people were dominated by another ethnic group that deprived them of educational opportunities in order to keep them in subjection.

So Why Are People Poor?

Recognizing these analytical complexities, we will list important causes of poverty. The list includes causes for which individuals might be responsible (such as refusing to participate in

a voluntary pension plan) and those over which they have no control (such as being hurt in an industrial accident caused by others). The causes reflect competing economic and social perspectives.

Low Productivity on the Job

A general cause of low income for an individual is low productivity at work. Employers will normally pay a worker no more than the worker contributes to the revenues of the business. This common-sense principle leads to the following causes of poverty.

Lack of Education. In the United States, average personal income is directly correlated to average levels of education for both men and women, for all age groups, and for all ethnic groups listed. In 2000, an American with a college degree could expect to earn $53,457, while a person with less than a ninth grade education could expect to earn only $14,149. (U.S. Census Bureau, 2000) The lower income would keep a single person out of relative poverty, but not a family of four. The Census Bureau's poverty level for one person under age 65 in 2000 was $8,959. For a family of four, however, the poverty level in 2000 was $17,463. The same effects are true internationally: education is crucial to wealth creation.

Increasingly technical aspects of work today require higher levels of education than for industrial and clerical workers a century ago. Low levels of education pose special problems for developing nations, because the learning deficit is so widespread compared to the technical demands in agriculture and industry. Creating human capital is essential to development.

Lack of Advanced Capital Equipment. Workers are more productive if they have equipment. Capital that embodies the latest technology will further increase worker productivity (assuming the worker has adequate education and training). In nations and regions where capital investment has been lacking, workers will use older, less productive methods and more primitive equipment, leading to lower incomes and standards of living.

Exhibit 8.3 shows such a correlation between economic development and three indicators of levels of technology: consumption of traditional (versus modern) fuels as a percentage of total energy use, kilowatt hours of electricity consumption per capita, and research and development expenditures (R&D) as a percentage of gross national product (GNP). As expected, traditional fuel use is high, electricity consumption per person is low, and research and development is relatively low in low-income nations.

Defective Work Ethic. A defective work ethic affects a person's ability to learn in school and to be productive at work. In the twentieth century, economists as scientists tended to avoid such a value judgment, preferring to discuss a person's work-leisure

Exhibit 8.3: Indicators of Technology and Levels of National Economic Development

National Rank	Traditional Fuel Consumption ('97)	Electric Cons. Per Cap. Kilowatt hrs. ('98)	Research & Devel. as % of GNP ('87-'97)
High Income	3.4	8,406	2.4
Middle Income	7.3	1,370	1.0
Low Income	29.8	362	0.9

Source: *Human Development Report 2001: Making New Technologies Work for Human Development* (New York: Oxford University Press, 2001), 55 and 203.

tradeoff. Economists as social commentators, however, have recently been more willing to assess the economic effects of varying cultural attitudes toward hard work. Thomas Sowell, for example, in *Race and Culture* (1994) asserts that the cultural and educational elite's disdain for hard work limits certain nations' economic progress. Other cultures promote notable work ethics, and immigrants from those countries have gained commercial power in those countries where the elite refuses to take up the work of business management (Sowell 1994, 34-36).

Disability. Certain people remain in poverty because they are unable to acquire skills or work. The primary reasons are physical, mental, or emotional impairment. One tragedy is that otherwise healthy children born into poor families may fail to get adequate nutrition when young, leading to a lifetime of disability, limited skills, and low productivity even in menial jobs. Another chronic problem in the labor market has been the disability associated with old age. Without adequate pensions, manual laborers who fail to acquire other skills tend to suffer decreased physical ability, lower productivity, and low income in old age.

Poverty promotes poverty. Poor health care and poor nutrition associated with long-term poverty increase the probability of disability at any age, but especially in old age.

Restricted Access to Work

Certain people who otherwise could work productively do not have *access* to education, jobs, and adequate incomes. The reasons are both individual and systemic, as the following list will show. Each could involve either relative or absolute poverty.

Discrimination, Domination, and Retribution. Racial, ethnic, religious, and gender discrimination have contributed to the poverty of many individuals and groups over the years. A systemic problem, discrimination prevents its victims from gaining higher education and landing preferred jobs that pay

higher wages. Discrimination may work informally or through formal governmental institutions that deny access to one or more groups. Discrimination against blacks in the United States was both formal and informal, as is discrimination by Arabs against black Africans in the Sudan. In Ireland, Anglo-Irish domination contributed to centuries of poverty for Irish Catholics.

Discrimination and the political disenfranchisement that often attend it have not always meant poverty for their victims. In the United States, Asian immigrants have experienced severe discrimination and yet their ethnic group has used an entrepreneurial spirit and close-knit culture to earn above-average incomes over time (see Sowell 1994.) Even so, in the United States in 1999, blacks were about two and one half times as likely to be poor as were whites (23.6 percent of blacks versus 9.8 percent of whites, according to *Statistical Abstracts of the United States 2000*, Table 679). Critics of the U.S. system attribute this outcome to racism.

Government officials can formally or informally punish those against which they choose to discriminate. In Soviet Russia, certain middle-class merchants, factory owners, Christian believers, and others were sent away from their more lucrative jobs in cities to work in agricultural communes and to live in relative poverty. In the mid-1930s, the Nazis prohibited Jews from holding civil-service jobs. The Nazis eventually killed millions of European Jews, gypsies, and others in the 1930s and 1940s.

Divorce and Out-of-Wedlock Childbearing. Divorce and out-of-wedlock childbirth in the United States have led to the "feminization of poverty." As the usual primary caregivers for children, single mothers and their children tend to experience more poverty than single men. Due to child care responsibilities, single mothers have limited access to both education and to high paying jobs. In 1999 in the United States, the average income for a family with a female head (no husband present) was $23,732. A male householder with no wife present had an average income of $37,626 (*Statistical Abstract of the United States: 2000*, Table 673).

Employer Power. The power of employers who dominate particular labor markets to depress wages can be a cause of relative poverty. A monopsonist is the only buyer of a good or service, enabling the buyer to depress the price or wage below competitive market levels. In the United States, workers in Appalachian coal fields and in Southern textile mill towns have allegedly been victims of the mine and factory owners' monopsony power in the past.

Disasters. Social, political, and natural disasters cause affected families to be poor until economic systems and structures can be rebuilt. Wars, civil unrest, political mismanagement, floods, earthquakes, droughts, and tornadoes impose economic hardships. They interrupt food production, transportation, and distribution. Those disasters that damage houses, roads, bridges, utility systems, and other infrastructure cause lasting poverty.

Even in natural disasters, poverty begets poverty. Floods, earthquakes, and other disasters tend to cause greater relative harm to living standards in already poor nations. Hurricanes in Honduras and Nicaragua in the 1990s, for example, revealed that houses there were less able to withstand the battering of winds and water than houses in the United States. Poor people build less sturdy structures with weaker foundations and in riskier locations, such as on the sides of unstable hills. The same tends to be true regarding resistance to earthquake damage. While earthquakes damage buildings everywhere, those in less developed regions are more susceptible to damage and collapse, with greater immediate loss of life and long-term economic harm.

Business Cycles. Trade cycles in a market economy cause fluctuations in unemployment. When business activity declines, workers have more difficulty finding and keeping jobs. Without government assistance or private charity, these spells of unemployment throw more families into poverty. In the United States, the percentage of families below the poverty level rises during recessions and falls during economic expansions. The U.S. economy experienced a recession in 1980 to 1982 and again from 1990 to 1991. The data in Exhibit 8.4 tend to confirm that recessions in these years contributed to increased rates of poverty. Cycles in developing nations can have even more severe effects on the poor.

Exhibit 8.4: Families in Poverty and the Business Cycle in the U.S.

Year	1978	1980	1982	1984	1986	1988	1990	1992	1994
% U.S. Families in Poverty	9.1	10.3	12.2	11.6	10.9	10.4	10.7	11.9	11.6
Stage of Cycle	Expansion	Recession	Recession	Expansion	Expansion	Expansion	Recession	Recovery	Expansion

Source: U.S. Bureau of the Census, *Statistical Abstract of the United States 2001*, Table 685. Found at www.census.gov.

Weak Economic Institutions. Access to jobs that provide high standards of living requires an institutional setting that promotes job creation. Commercial institutions include rules protecting and promoting private property, efficient contracts, and responsibility in the safe and fair uses of property. Nations and cultures with traditions of strong institutional support for honest and productive commerce tend to generate more jobs and wealth. Nations with weak institutional traditions tend to have weak commercial sectors, with limited job creation and more poverty.

Other Causes of Poverty

Economists and other social scientists have identified other causes of poverty besides low productivity and restricted access to work. We will list important ones here.

Lack of Wealth Due to a Low Rate of Saving. People without a job can still live well from their own wealth. Those without accumulated wealth, however, will live in poverty when they don't have jobs, especially in old age. The chief reason for lack of wealth individually is a low rate of saving out of income.

Extreme poverty means a hand-to-mouth existence for many families that prevents them from saving for the long run. Paternalistic employers and governments have in the past reacted by imposing mandatory pension systems. In the United States, the federal system is called Social Sccurity. Government revenues in less developed nations are either inadequate to fund poor-relief programs or are directed toward other purposes, such as support for the military and the governing elite.

Financial crises and weak financial-system institutions for protecting savers can cause people to lose what savings they have. In the Depression of the 1930s, lack of private or public deposit insurance when the banking system collapsed caused many who had saved for retirement to live their later years in poverty. Even after the Depression, pension funds have not always been stable. Due to economic problems, financial fraud, or a combination of both, many workers have discovered that their firm or union has lost or stolen their pension funds. In 2001, Enron employees lost most of their pensions due to restrictive rules requiring that they invest in the firm's own stock.

Unanticipated inflation also will threaten savings. In the United States in the 1970s, gradual price inflation slowly eroded the purchasing power of fixed pension and Social Security payments, pushing more and more elderly into poverty. In Russia in the summer of 1998, sudden inflation of prices eroded the value of people's private savings and government pensions.

- **Intergenerational income mobility:** the ability of children to move into an income class different from their parents

Limited Intergenerational Income Mobility. Children of the poor are usually less upwardly mobile. Poor families are less able to give good education and good health care to their children. They live in poor neighborhoods with poor schools, fewer good job opportunities, and poor transportation systems to areas where jobs are available. Poor families also may pass along the culture of poverty: defective attitudes toward education and work, for example, or dependency on government welfare that traps successive generations. Notable exceptions abound—a dedicated parent works several jobs and saves to give a child a better life. But evidence suggests that the culture of poverty does trap others. As a result, poverty persists from generation to generation.

Alleviating Poverty

Anti-poverty programs take various forms. We will review three: working directly with and for the poor, reforming the economic system, and providing a safety net.

Working Among the Poor

Churches, mission agencies, nongovernmental organizations (NGOs), and selected government agencies such as the Peace Corps, the World Bank, UNICEF, and USAID work directly with the poor. Here are the types of programs they offer.

Helping Individuals with Essentials

Traditional missionaries, Peace Corps workers, and certain NGOs such as Compassion International, the Red Cross, and Mercy Corps feel burdened to help the poor directly. They provide food, medical supplies, doctors, and teachers to meet pressing physical needs. Compassion, for example, arranges for families in the United States to sponsor poor children in other countries, meeting their long-term needs for food, clothing, shelter, and education. Red Cross, Mercy Corp, World Relief, and other agencies also provide disaster relief.

Providing Spiritual Encouragement

People expect that mission agencies and local churches will address people's spiritual needs as part of a wholistic development process. Expansion Point 8.4, however, reviews the World Bank's surprising involvement with African churches. What led to this unusual alliance of secular and sacred?

Expansion Point 8.4: The World Bank and African Churches

The Council of Anglican Churches of Africa cooperated with the World Bank in a March 2000 Conference on Alleviating Poverty in Nairobi, Kenya. Although the World Bank is "necessarily nonconfessional," its president James Wolfensohn and the Archbishop of Canterbury George Carey agreed that the Bank and the churches are "partners." They recognized "an important area of common ground between faith and development. . . . religious leaders are close to the poor . . . Faith communities offer health services, education, and shelter to the vulnerable and disadvantaged." Furthermore, "spiritual ties" help bind "societies otherwise rent by . . . discrimination, conflict over resources, and violence."

Editors of conference papers identified important spiritual and moral themes as: the need for effective African leadership, the roles of bribes and violence in corrupting and disrupting leadership, "the church's key role in training servant leaders of integrity," the importance of reducing gender inequality, the promise that care from the Church and "Christian living" are answers to the problem of HIV/AIDS, and the role of microenterprise lending.

Source: Deryke Belshaw, Robert Calderisi, Christ Sugden, eds., *Faith in Development: Partnership Between the World Bank and the Churches of Africa* (Washington, D.C.: World Bank, 2001).

When economists advocated technical approaches to development in the 1950s, they and governmental experts largely ignored spiritual aspects of development. Late in the twentieth century, however, experts began to acknowledge that faith-based organizations were successful in solving social problems, including poverty. A growing literature now examines various sides and aspects of the topic (search "church AND economic development").

Providing Microenterprise Loans

• **Microenterprise lending:** making very small loans to poor people to fund start-up businesses such as bakeries and taxi services

Recently, development experts have also recognized the contribution of **microenterprise loans** to the poor. In nations where poor people's access to financial markets and business loans is severely limited, relief organizations make loans of from $25 to $1,000 to small groups of people with good ideas but little collateral or income to support a normal bank loan. Recognition is relatively new, but the concept is not. Opportunity International began making loans in Latin America in 1971 and now operates globally. Grameen Bank began in Bangladesh in 1976. Other agencies such as World Hope International have also begun to provide loans.

Expansion Point 8.5 explains how lenders have adapted institutions to the special requirements of microenterprise loans. The rapid increase in the size and number of organizations making microenterprise loans illustrates their practical success in helping people escape poverty as they promote productive commercial activity.

Developing Infrastructure

Many of the same agencies that develop programs to help individuals also see the wisdom of longer-term projects to develop infrastructure. The World Bank, for example, has undertaken rural electrification in Nicaragua, road maintenance in Thailand after the Asian crisis of 1997 and 1998, and sanitation projects on the Indian subcontinent. Other less complex projects by mission groups and other aid agencies include digging wells for water, clearing and leveling fields for an airstrip, and building block structures for schools and medical clinics.

Organizing and Empowering the Poor

While microenterprise lending empowers the individual poor for commercial activity, other programs seek to empower the poor socially and politically. Empowerment programs seek to build networks and organize the poor in self-help groups, equipping them with external seed money and start-up expertise, and promoting self-government. The World Bank sponsors empowerment programs that emphasize imposing the "rule of law" in favor of the poor, increasing state responsiveness to the poor, "decentralizing" government control to encourage self-rule among the poor, building "pro-poor coalitions," addressing "social stratification"

Expansion Point 8.5: Adapting Banking Institutions to Problems of Microenterprise Lending

Private banks in industrialized market economies have carefully developed the institutions (rules, customs, and commercial practices) of lending to individuals and businesses. Loan contracts are complex documents that protect the lender's interests against opportunism by the borrower. Banks also screen borrowers carefully, normally extending loans to customers with whom they have an ongoing deposit and borrowing relationship. Another customary practice is to require that the borrower put up collateral to back a loan (Mishkin 1998). Cars and houses themselves back auto loans and housing mortgages. Business inventories back the lines of credit that finance the inventory investment. Banks also carefully monitor the performance of provisions in their loan contracts to assure that borrowers use the funds as agreed.

The challenges in microenterprise lending are great. How do lenders, often from another culture, screen prospective borrowers to eliminate opportunistic borrowers, while meeting the credit needs of those who are honest and likely to repay? How do lenders require collateral of loan customers with otherwise good prospective, but who are poor and have no collateral to offer?

Microenterprise lenders adapted their practices, designing new institutions for screening customers and ensuring repayment. They lend, not to individuals, but to groups of six or more customers at a time. Furthermore, each member of the group agrees to repay debts of any member who defaults (refuses or is otherwise unable to repay the loan). These practices use the borrowers' knowledge of each other as a screening device. They are unlikely to agree to borrow with people whom they know to be untrustworthy or whom they believe are likely to fail in business. They also meet in groups to discuss prospective business ideas, selecting which seem likely to succeed or fail and helping each other to shape their business plans. Group members also help each other in times of unexpected distress.

How successful are these adapted lending practices? World Hope International claims that microenterprise repayment rates are sometimes "better than in mainline banking systems in the United States."

Sources: Frederic S. Mishkin, *Money, Banking, and Financial Markets*, 5th ed. (Boston: Addison-Wesley, 1998), 198-99, 206, 245-248.

"Microenterprise: Ministry Overview," World Hope International, August 2003. Accessed at http://www.worldhope.net/microenterprise/micro.htm.

and "fragmentation," and "building social institutions and social capital" (chapters 6 and 7, *World Development Report 2000-2001: Attacking Poverty*).

Recent studies claim successes over the past three decades. Grameen Phone project, for example, is empowering rural poor people with cell-phone "connectivity" in Bangladesh (Camp and Anderson 1999). The World Bank has been applying its community-driven development strategy in Brazil since the mid-1970s, decentralizing federal programs and bringing control to state and local agencies (World Bank 2001). Also ahead of the trend, the U.S. Catholic Bishops began a Campaign for Human Development in 1969 to fund self-help programs among America's poor (Pope John Paul II 1979).

Revising the Economic System

During the nineteenth and twentieth centuries, three anti-poverty approaches advocated dramatic revisions to the economic system. While quite different in philosophy, each sought to eliminate poverty's systemic causes.

Fomenting Marxist-Leninist Revolution

Marxism-Leninism swept the world with revolutionary fervor after the emergence of Communist rule in Russia in 1917. Expansion Point 8.6 explains that the functional distribution of income, the split of income between laborers and owners, concerned Marx and Lenin. Capitalist market economies, featuring private ownership of the means of production (factories,

Expansion Point 8.6: The Functional Distribution of U.S. Income

People in an economy have different functions as suppliers of either labor, land, capital equipment, or entrepreneurial ability. The **functional distribution of income** refers to the distribution of shares of a nation's income among people grouped according to their economic functions. The functional shares include payments of wages, rent, interest, and profit respectively.

Karl Marx and his disciples believed that laborers do not get a fair share of income and output of goods and services. One difficulty with using labor's share as a measure of how well laborers are doing in the supposed battle over economic shares is that labor's share can go up when times are very bad. In the Great Depression, for example, labor's share of national income went up, even though 25 percent of workers were unemployed. The reason was that, while wages and salaries fell during the Depression, company profits plunged proportionally more than total wages and salaries.

The exhibit below presents data on the functional distribution of income in the United States. It lists shares of national income in dollar and percentage terms for wage and salary earners, proprietors, those earning rent, and corporate profits. Interpreting the data is difficult, but several points are clear. Labor in the United States tends to get between 65 and 75 percent of national income. Corporate profits are nowhere near 50 percent, a common but uninformed opinion due to Marx. Ten percent is a normal share for before-tax corporate profits. After removing taxes, profits drop closer to five percent of national income. Rental income is quite low, at between one and two percent. Proprietors' income, at between eight and nine percent, includes both wages and profit of those owning their own firms or partnerships.

Functional Distribution of Income in the United States

Year	National Income	Wages, Salaries & Supplements	Proprietors' Income	Rental Income	Corporate Profits
1977	1638	1183	147	23	184
	100%	72%	9%	1.4%	11%
1987	3813	2758	350	45	273
	100%	72%	9%	1%	7%
1997	6647	4687	551	158	818
	100%	70%	8%	2%	12%

Source: National Bureau of Economic Research, *Economic Report of the President 1999,* 358-59. Accessed at http://www.nber.com.

equipment, and land), allegedly caused poverty for those who worked for capitalists in the factories and fields. The solution to poverty was not gradual piecemeal reform of the market economy, but overthrow of capitalism and construction of state socialism.

State ownership of productive property in Russia after the 1920s did increase economic equality, but it did not generate lasting economic growth that would solve the problem of widespread poverty. Nor did economic revolution elsewhere end poverty. One difficulty is that economic revolution in Africa, for example, meant military and political revolutions that destabilized national agriculture and increased poverty for many.

Building a Social-Welfare State

Economic freedom in a market economy leads to unequal incomes and unequal wealth. As Expansion Point 8.7 shows, the distributions of income and wealth in the U.S. market economy show inequality. The goal of the social-welfare state is to reform the market economy with aggressive government programs to **redistribute** wealth and income, and to equalize access to goods and services.

• **Redistribution:** government uses taxes and subsidies to shift income and wealth from rich to poor or among other groups

Britain's social welfare state nationalized industry, housing, and medical care. Sweden avoided widespread nationalization of industry, but used high income tax rates to redistribute income. The Swedish social-welfare state more successfully eliminated economic inequality. The British system tended to preserve privilege for the elite. Overall, however, the European social-welfare state reduced levels of poverty and inequality when compared to the United States.

The chief problem attending social-welfare policies has been that they thwart economic vitality by creating disincentives to saving, investment, and work effort. They also can create increased dependency on the state and encourage, especially in Sweden, a balkanization of social groups as they compete for benefits from government programs. Toward the end of the twentieth century, the European welfare states experienced slower economic growth as the U.S. economy boomed. A stagnating economy and a revision in ideology prompted England to follow Margaret Thatcher's free-market reforms in 1979. Following a prolonged economic slump in the early 1980s, England's economy began to strengthen and even led Europe for a time in the 1990s.

Reforming Institutions for a Market Economy

The World Bank and the U.S. government believe that voluntary market exchange, supported by institutions of private property and private contracts, promotes economic growth in the long run. Called the **Washington consensus** by its detractors, this view sought to restructure economic institutions. If development

• **Washington consensus:** view held by the World Bank and U.S. Government that encouraging the rule of law in a market economy, with transparent government, is the best development program

Expansion Point 8.7: U.S. Distribution of Income & Wealth

The **household distribution of income** measures how individual households share national income. Statisticians group households (people living in the same house) into income classes from rich to poor, usually in five (quintile) or ten (decile) groups. They calculate the percentage of national income each group receives. In a nation with exactly equal income, with no rich or poor, each group gets exactly the same share of income. In nations with highly unequal income distributions, the top fifth of income earners will have much more than 20 percent of total income in the economy, while the bottom fifth will earn much less than 20 percent.

The following exhibit shows the household distribution of income in the United States for 1975, 1985, and 1995. The data are for quintiles of the population. The share of income among households in the top quintile has been rising, while the share of income in the bottom quintile has been falling.

U.S. Household Distribution of Income

Year	Lowest 20%	Second 20%	Third 20%	Fourth 20%	Highest 20%
1975	5.6	11.9	17.7	24.2	40.7
1985	4.8	11.0	16.9	24.3	43.1
1995	4.4	10.1	15.8	23.2	46.5

Source: U.S. Bureau of the Census, *Statistical Abstract of the United States: 1998*, Table No. 747, 473.

Is economic freedom under capitalism necessarily to blame for unequal income? Perhaps, but other factors such as gender equality and divorce can also contribute to income inequality. Increasing workplace opportunities for women, for example, can raise the income of rich families, and lower the income of poor families, if women who get high-paying jobs and men who get high-paying jobs tend to marry each other. A divorce can split one family with average income per person into two families, one with the wife and children who have less income and the other with the husband who has more income.

The **distribution of wealth among families** (related people living together) is another way to assess economic equality. The complaint about the U.S. market economy that "the top 10 percent of families own 90 percent of the corporate stock" is politically powerful, but not necessarily accurate. It makes no mention of the biggest group of holders of stock, financial institutions, such as mutual funds, insurance companies, and pension funds. Through shares and contracts with such companies, many other families and pensioners indirectly hold stock. Furthermore, investment advisors warn families with less wealth against holding risky stocks.

Not surprisingly, though, families in the United States with the highest annual incomes tend to be the wealthiest families too. The following exhibit shows the relation between household income and household wealth in the United States in 1995. Families were grouped by their level of income, with the median wealth calculated for each group. The chart also lists the percentage of families in each group.

Average U.S. Family Wealth for Different Income Classes

Income*	<$10K	$10K to $24.9K	$25K to $49.9K	$50K to $99.9K	>$100K
Median Net Worth*	$4.7K	$30.0K	$53.4K	$121.1K	$482.0K
% of Families	16.1%	26.9%	30.6%	19.8%	6.5%

* All data are in thousands of dollars, for 1995.
Source: U.S. Bureau of the Census, *Statistical Abstract of the United States: 1998*, Table No. 767, 482.

•**Import substitution:** programs to limit imports and subsidize domestic manufacturing

programs promote the rule of law, private property rights, and transparent government, free enterprise will supposedly cause commerce to flourish, standards of living to rise, and poverty to recede.

These reforms targeted Soviet-style economic programs initiated in the 1960s and 1970s in Africa. They had curtailed free markets in agriculture and industry and promoted state planning. Related targets of reform were programs of **import substitution** that had been popular in Latin America since the 1930s. Import substitution encourages domestic industry with import barriers.

Critics complain that the Washington consensus promotes U.S. and Western domination of world trade. Evidence, though, suggests that recent World Bank initiatives have helped the plight of the rural poor in Africa. Yet free market policies have also subjected industrial workers to global economic fluctuations, as in the Asian crisis of 1997 and 1998. And the United States had its own crisis of free-market institutions in the accounting and financial scandals of the late 1990s and into 2002.

Even so, the U.S. economy largely eliminated absolute poverty. Exhibit 8.5 shows that the access of the poor in the United States to household appliances has increased dramatically in recent years. Such consumption data indicate less poverty than levels of income. According to Daniel Slesnick, only two percent of U.S. families were poor in 1989 regarding consumption expenditures, down from 13 percent in 1965 and 31 percent in 1949 (Cox and Alm 1999, 16). Official U.S. income statistics, however, placed 10 percent in poverty in 1988. (See Exhibit 8.3.) The data should not lessen our concern for the poor, but they do challenge those who complain that the U.S. economy worsens the condition of the poor.

Exhibit 8.5: Percent of U.S. Families in Poverty Who Own Appliances

	1984	1994
Washing Machine	48.2%	71.7%
Refrigerator	95.8%	97.9%
Microwave	12.5%	60.0%
Color TV	70.3%	92.5%
Videocassette Player	2.4%	59.7%

Source: W. Michael Cox and Richard Alm, Table 1.2, "Even the Poor Have More," *Myths of Rich and Poor* (New York: Basic Books, 1999) 15.

Providing a Safety Net

A social safety net attempts to assure not economic equality, but minimum standards of living. It provides economic security for those who have not insured themselves and for those who have experienced such severe disasters that they have exhausted private insurance benefits. The United States tends to favor this approach: mild programs for redistributing income and wealth, as opposed to more radical programs to equalize incomes and wealth. Food stamps, Aid to Families with Dependent Children (until 1996), the minimum wage, unemployment compensation, and disability insurance place a net under those who falter economically, while allowing for economic freedom and its incentives toward growth.

Disincentives

A welfare safety net, however, creates disincentives to work similar to those in the social-welfare state. Critics warn against making the net too comfortable. As a result, poor relief in the

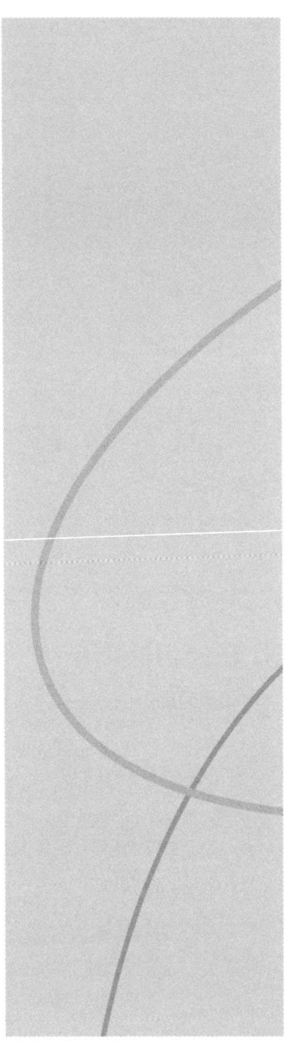

United States is not an easy life. The U.S. Congress, for example, keeps the minimum wage low enough that a family of four cannot be comfortable if only one worker in the family is earning it. At $5.50 an hour, the minimum wage in 2002 would yield only $220 a week, or $11,440 for a year. And in 1996, the Congress and President Bill Clinton overhauled the federal welfare system, replacing the Depression-era Aid to Families with Dependent Children with the Temporary Assistance to Needy Families program. One goal was to reduce the disincentives for the poor to work. When the new program set lifetime limits of five years of relief, welfare rolls fell significantly, aided by the economic boom of the 1990s.

Milton Friedman on Redistribution

In democracies, voters can redistribute wealth from rich to poor. Moral decency requires that those who are able should ameliorate the pain of the poor. If we are to help, what is the correct attitude? Nobel Prize winner Milton Friedman (*Free to Choose* 1980, ch. 5) highlights several important distinctions. First, equality of opportunity is more desirable than equality of outcome because equality of outcome requires coercive power. Equalizing incomes under Communism in Russia and China, for example, took a terrible human toll measured in freedoms and lives lost. Even then, incomes never were equal.

Second, voter attitudes toward redistribution bear watching. Redistributing income can help equalize opportunities for the poorest of the poor, and as Friedman notes, the United States has a traditional willingness to help the poor, both publicly and privately. But a 90-percent majority voting to tax itself to give to the poorest 10 percent is radically different from an 80-percent majority voting to tax the top 10 percent to help the bottom 10 percent.

Chapter Summary

1. Wealth is what makes us well. More technically, wealth is a stock of tangible or intangible things that are useful for meeting needs and satisfying wants, and that therefore have exchange value. Income is a flow of money and resources out of wealth or due to labor.

2. Social wealth is the total net worths of individuals and organizations. It recognizes the balancing of assets and liabilities and the effects of cooperation in enhancing wealth and competition in destroying and transferring wealth.

3. Absolute poverty is the lack of access to income and resources that are sufficient to maintain life and minimal well-being, health, and education. Relative poverty means having inadequate income and resources to meet usual or socially acceptable living standards.

4. Causes of poverty are either particular to an individual or family or systemic and outside the individual's control. Causes of poverty include: low productivity at work due to poor education, lack of advanced capital equipment, defective work ethic, or disability; restricted access to work due to discrimination, divorce and out-of-wedlock childbearing (the feminization of poverty), employer monopsony power, government retribution, disasters, business cycles, and weak institutions; and other causes such as inadequate wealth due to a low saving rate or financial crises and inflation, and limited intergenerational income mobility.

5. Approaches to alleviating poverty include: working among the poor by helping with essentials, giving spiritual encouragement, making microenterprise loans, building infrastructure, and organizing and empowering the poor; revising the economic system by fomenting a Marxist revolution, building a social-welfare state, or strengthening institutions of a market economy; and finally, building a social safety net.

6. Many democratic market economies redistribute income with taxes and subsidies. Disincentive effects limit a government's ability to redistribute income. Social welfare programs reduce productive effort and encourage competition for subsidies.

7. The functional distribution of income measures how income is shared among the different suppliers of resources: wage and salary for labor, profit for entrepreneurs, interest for owners of machinery or financial capital, and rent for landowners.

8. The distribution of income among households in the United States is less equal than in other countries with more aggressive redistribution programs.

Problems for Practice

8.1* Are you wealthy? Is your family wealthy? Or are you poor? Define the terms and explain your situation in two ways. First, show that your family is wealthy. Then, show that you are poor. Finally, explain how two different answers are possible.

8.2 What are the political and economic perspectives on programs to redistribute income? What are some of the limits to redistribution?

8.3 What are the political and economic perspectives on wealth creation? Who favors this perspective and what do they think about income redistribution?

8.4 What three approaches to alleviating poverty advocate revising the economic system? Which is the Washington consensus? Which did Sweden use? Which did Russia try? Explain the results.

8.5 What are the differences between the functional distribution and the household or family distributions of income? What do data for the United States show about each? Are income and wealth correlated? Which families tend to hold the wealth in the United States?

For your portfolio:
8.6 Research more recent statistics on the U.S. distributions of income and wealth. Do new data continue to support the conclusions expressed here? See the U.S. Census Bureau's Web site and look especially for the most recent *Statistical Abstract of the United States*.

Class discussion:
8.7 Your math teacher has promised to allow you to vote on what system of distributing grades she will use in the course. The first is traditional: you will each work independently and will each receive your individual grade based on individual performance on the usual tests. The second is more cooperative: you will study together, you will take exams individually, and you will earn the average class test grade. In each case, though, the average grade will be an 80%.

Which system would encourage more individual effort? What would the hardest working students think about this system? What will the lazier students think? How do your conclusions about this apply to programs that redistribute income?

8.8 The Shakers, a religious sect, formed communes in the 1800s in the United States, some of which lasted into the 1900s. Each person who entered signed a contract to contribute to production and to take an approximately equal share of output while living there. According to a study by John Murray (1995, 217), the number of people joining Shaker communities who could sign their own names declined throughout the 1800s. He assumed that this meant they were less literate, and he inferred that new entrants were less productive over time as well. What would explain the decline in literacy and the productivity of new entrants into the commune?

8.9 Consuming food is necessary for life, as are clothing and shelter in most regions of the world. Do you think that the government should control production and distribution of these necessities? Explain your reasons in detail. Are your answers based on principles of morality or economic efficiency?

8.10* In its *Human Development Report 1998*, the United Nations complained that the richest 20% of the world's people consume nine times more meat than the poorest 20%. The richest also consume 80 times more automobiles and goods made with paper than the poorest do. How would you explain this unequal distribution of consumption patterns and the underlying unequal distributions of income? Does it matter whether you view redistribution as having to do with dividing a fixed pie or a pie whose size can be increased by human effort and ingenuity? Does redistribution affect productivity? How do limits to nonrenewable resources affect your thoughts?

See Answer Key for hints/answers to starred (*) questions.

Chapter 9

Economic Growth

Why Are Some Nations Rich and Others Poor?

What this chapter will help you think about:

1. How do economists measure economic growth?
2. What are the historical theories of economic growth and the difficulties with each?
3. How do institutions promote trust among traders and why is that significant?
4. Which three institutions are crucial to economic activity?
5. Why are certain nations rich and others poor?
6. What have we learned about corporate piracy in the United States?

The twentieth century gave us two economic surprises. The first was how rapidly wages of workers in certain industrialized nations rose so far above mere subsistence. The economic success of the United States and other Western nations is astounding, as are the economic recoveries of war-devastated West Germany and Japan since 1946. Recent economic successes in South Korea, Thailand, Malaysia, and elsewhere in Asia are even more remarkable, requiring half a century or less to convert nations of peasant farmers into industrialized economies. The rise of these Asian tigers has caught the attention of those nations that long for but have not achieved rapid development.

A second, related surprise is why wages have not risen above subsistence throughout most of the rest of the world. Rising productivity of labor and industrial wages in the United States, England, Germany, Japan, and elsewhere have created an expectation that industrialization and rising wages would spread. As Exhibit 9.1 shows, per capita national products varied greatly around the world in 1995. Given the wide availability of technical information on how to industrialize, why do billions of people still live in absolute poverty with low levels of productivity? Perhaps it has been the oppressive system of international trade and investment through which the rich nations exploit the poor nations and keep them poor. If so, how did the Asian tigers rise so quickly?

- **Economic institutions:** laws, rules, contract agreements, social customs, and moral beliefs that influence economic activities and distinguish economic systems from one another

This chapter reviews the measurement of economic growth and the history of economic thought on the causes of national wealth and poverty. A final section then explains an emerging new institutional view of economic progress.

Exhibit 9.1: International Comparison of Gross National Products Per Person, 1995

Nation	Per Capita Output (U.S. $ Equivalents)	Nation	Per Capita Output (U.S. $ Equivalents)
Japan	$41,160	Russia	$4,478
Germany	$26,190	Brazil	$4,084
United States	$25,550	Thailand	$2,806
Finland	$17,921	Croatia	$2,068
New Zealand	$17,473	Algeria	$1,365
Argentina	$7,909	El Salvador	$1,671
Saudi Arabia	$6,815	India	$348
Hungary	$6,519	Congo	$114
Turkey	$5,682	Ethiopia	$96

Source: "Gross National Product, by Country," *Statistical Abstract of the United States: 1998,* Table 1354 (Lanham, MD: Bernan Associates, 1999), 835.

Data are in constant (adjusted-for-inflation) U.S.-dollar equivalent.

Assessing Economic Growth

Before discussing theories of economic growth, let's consider how economists measure and evaluate economic growth. For instance, to understand the numbers in Exhibit 9.1 above, you also need to understand potential statistical and interpretive problems with such numbers. Furthermore, not all economists have the same perspectives on the benefits of economic growth as measured with these numbers.

Measuring Economic Growth

To gauge a nation's economic growth, we can apply some variant of the following approach. First measure the value of the nation's output of goods and services each year. Then calculate the value of output per capita each year. Finally calculate changes in total output and per capita output, assessing whether growth has been positive and how the rate of growth compares to a standard such as 3 percent per year. A key to humane economic growth is a rising average standard of living.

- **Measuring economic growth:**
  1) measure the value of national output of goods and services;
  2) calculate per capita output; and
  3) calculate the percentage change from year to year of total output and per capita output

Value Gross Product

Economists calculate the value of gross national product (GNP) or gross domestic product (GDP) as the market value of final output of goods and services produced in a given year. Final output means for final use by the end consumer, not for intermediate use by a business to produce other goods and services. In theory, calculating gross product is simple. We multiply market prices by market outputs and sum the totals:

Value of Gross Output = Sum for all products of (Price * Quantity)

Gross national product (GNP) considers nationality of the producers. GNP is the value of final goods and services produced by *a nation's citizens and registered corporations*, even if part of the output is produced in foreign countries. Gross domestic product (GDP) considers domestic geographic boundaries. GDP is the value of goods and services produced *within a nation's boundary*, even if it is by foreign companies and foreign individuals. GNP and GDP can vary by 3 percent or more in a given year.

Calculate Per Capita Output

Per capita means per head or per person. Per capita output is simply the value of total output divided by the number of people. Per capita output is a better measure of people's standard of living than total output. After calculating GNP or GDP for a nation, divide the value of output by its population in that year. For GDP, the formula is:

Per Capita GDP = GDP / Population

In Exhibit 9.1, you see per capita GNP for various nations. Additional statistics for India and Thailand will show how different the results are when comparing total GNP and per capita GNP. For India in 1995, GNP was $326 billion (in constant U.S. dollars), a great deal of money. Per capita GNP in India, however, was only $348 because India had nearly one billion people! (All data in this section are from U.S. Bureau of the Census, *Statistical Abstract of the United States: 1998*, Table 1354, p. 835.)

Thailand, a seemingly less productive economy, had a GNP of only $167 billion in 1995. That is about one half of India's GNP. With a population of less than sixty million people, however, Thailand had a per capita GNP of $2,806. This is eight times India's per capita GNP.

Calculate a Rate of Economic Growth

We can calculate a growth rate of GDP in percentage terms as follows:

$$\textbf{Rate of Economic Growth} = [(GDP_{1995} - GDP_{1990}) / GDP_{1990}] * 100$$

This is approximately the approach used to report annual growth rates in the United States and other nations. Quarterly rates can be multiplied by four to get an annualized rate.

This formula also can be applied to per capita output. It would show very rapid increases in the standards of living of people in Thailand and other "Asian Tigers" in the early 1990s. Between 1990 and 1995, the growth of per capita GNP in Thailand was 39.5 percent or about 7 percent per year. [To calculate an annual rate exactly, find the fifth root of 1 + 0.395 and then subtract the one. The precise annual rate is closer to 6.88 percent.] Three percent real growth would be rather good. For the United States during that period, the per capita rate of growth was +3.7 percent or less than 1 percent real growth per year. Why so low? The United States experienced a recession in 1990 and 1991 and a slow recovery through the first half of 1992.

Not all nations had growing standards of living in the 1990s. In various countries, wars, droughts, depressions, and rapid population growth caused per capita output to fall. The Democratic Republic of Congo (formerly Zaire), for example, has suffered the afflictions of wars and revolts. And in 1994, over a million refugees fled there from civil war in Rwanda. Applying this formula to Congo's per capita GNP reflects the turmoil. Per capita economic growth was -50.4 percent between 1990 and 1995, partly due to the greater population. Russia suffered a depression from 1990 to at least 1995, after the fall of communism.

Comparing Economic Growth Rates

To compare the economic growth among nations, economists must adjust the GNP and GDP numbers from each country. The market value of India's output normally would be measured in rupees, while market values are in rubles in Russia and in dollars in the United States. For ease of comparison, economists must convert the output values for each nation to a common currency. Let's compare the benefits and costs of two widely used methods to convert to a common currency.

Using Market Exchange Rates

Exchange rates provide a simple, low-cost conversion of market values to a common currency, such as the United States dollar. Each nation's currency trades against the dollar at an exchange rate. The exchange rate is the ratio of either United States dollars per foreign currency or foreign currency per United States dollar. To go from other currencies to the dollar, we want the dollar value in the numerator.

Here is how to convert Japan's GDP into United States dollars. Find the value of Japan's GDP in yen (•) and the (dollar/yen) exchange rate ($ / •), and multiply the two together.

Japan's GDP in $ = Japan's GDP in • * ($ / •)

While simple, this method is subject to undue influence by wild fluctuations in exchange rates that don't reflect the purchasing power of the two currencies. In 1995, for example, when the data in Exhibit 9.1 were converted to U.S. dollars, the $/• rate was distorted by such wild fluctuations. Because the dollar's value had fallen dramatically, the value of Japan's output

measured in dollars was inflated dramatically. As a result, Japan's economy appeared to be more productive in 1995 than it would have in 1994 when the dollar value was much higher.

Considering Purchasing Power Parity

Using exchange rates to convert currency values assumes purchasing power parity of exchange rates. Parity means that 100 U.S. dollars, when converted at market exchange rates into various currencies, will buy the same amount of goods and services in any other country as it will buy in the United States. In 1995, many Americans played golf in the United States for $10 to $50 a game. If parity held, you should be able to take $50, convert it to yen, and then play a game of golf in Japan for that approximate amount of yen. In Japan, however, golf would have cost the equivalent of $100 to $300.

Many goods and services such as certain foods, golf games, haircuts, and automobile service are not traded internationally. Exchange rates do not take into account the wide variations in prices of nontradable goods. This is why purchasing power parity rarely holds in the short run.

Because the Japanese economy has many restrictions on imports, purchasing power parity in the yen/dollar exchange rate is less likely. At exchange rates current in May 2001, for example, it would have taken $138 to buy in Japan what only $100 would buy in the United States (U.S. Bureau of the Census, *Statistical Abstract of the United States: 2001*, Table 1346, online version, www.census.gov).

The Japanese case was extreme in 2001, but few exchange rates reflect purchasing power at a given time. In Australia, for example, $73 would buy what $100 could buy in the United States as of May 2001 (*Statistical Abstract of the United States: 2001*).

Given the significant departures of market exchange rates from parity of purchasing powers, simple comparisons such as in Exhibit 9.1 are not helpful for precise comparisons. We *can* be sure that the difference between per capita GNP in Japan and India is not due to a departure from purchasing power parity of the rupee/yen exchange rate. If, however, we want to know with more certainty whether Japan or the United States is more productive per capita and in total, we require a more precise conversion. Expansion Point 9.1 explains purchasing power parity adjustments.

Conceptual Problems with Growth Measurements

Even when statistically accurate, measures of economic growth contain additional problems. They ignore a number of factors, including the distribution of output within a nation and the many factors not captured in market prices.

A measure of per capita output is an average. A high per capita output can hide great inequality of the distribution of the benefits

Expansion Point 9.1: Purchasing Power Parity Adjustments to GDP

To adjust for differences in the prices of nontradable goods, economists create currency conversion ratios that attempt to establish purchasing power parity of two currencies. Let's say that you took $100 (U.S.), converted it to yen, and shopped in Japan. A purchasing-power-parity exchange rate (PPP) would enable you to buy in Japan with that amount of yen what $100 would buy you in the United States. You would be able to buy the same amounts of food, clothes, haircuts, golf games, and so on.

To adjust for the departure from purchasing power parity of two currencies, we would substitute the PPP conversion ratio for the simple exchange rate. The changes to comparative values of GDP and GNP when using PPP exchange rates can be dramatic. The exhibit below shows the effects of two different calculations of per capita GDP for 1995.

Since the U.S. dollar is the base currency, its GDP does not change. Australia's and the United Kingdom's GDPs go up with the PPP rates, meaning that their currencies are undervalued at prevailing market exchange rates, compared to purchasing power parity.

The effect on Japan's GDP is most dramatic, but in the opposite direction. Because Japan's nontradable goods tend to be so expensive compared to nontradables in the United States, and because the U.S. dollar was relatively undervalued in 1995, exchange-rate conversions make the Japanese economy look more productive than PPP calculations. With exchange-rate transformations, output in Japan was over $42,000 per person, more than 150 percent of U.S. GDP per capita. After adjusting with PPP rates, however, Japan's output per capita is just under $22,000, or only 78 percent of U.S. GDP per capita. No transformation of the value of economic output is perfect, but you can see how wildly different the comparisons can be. When done correctly, PPP transformations are superior to unadjusted market exchange-rate calculations.

1995 GDP Comparisons Using Simple Exchange Rate Transformations vs. Purchasing Power Parity Adjustments

Nation	Per Capita Output (Exchange Rates)
Australia	$19,174
Japan	$27,821
United Kingdom	$18,109
United States	$23,784

Nation	Per Capita Output (Purchasing Power Parity)
Australia	$20,376
Japan	$23,235
United Kingdom	$18,636
United States	$27,821

Sources: For exchange-rate calculations at 1995 prices and exchange rates, see U.S. Bureau of the Census, 2002. *Statistical Abstract of the United States: 2001*. "Table No. 1340: Gross Domestic Product [GDP] by Country: 1995 to 2000." Found online at www.census.gov.

For purchasing power parity calculations, see U.S. Bureau of the Census, 1999, "Table No. 1355: Gross Domestic Product, by Country, 1980 to 1997: *Statistical Abstract of the United States: 1998* (Lanham, MD: Bernan Associates), 836.

of production. This is especially true in oil-producing nations, because the benefits of oil production are often captured by a small minority of the nation's population. Oil production has few linkages to the rest of a nation's economy. Therefore, measures of the distribution of income and of basic services are also helpful in evaluating how broad the effects of economic progress are.

Market prices do not reflect all of the economic activity in a nation. Very low per capita output in a developing nation will not reflect the significant effort of many people in their own homes and fields. GDP and GNP do not capture the values of goods and services that are not exchanged and are therefore not priced or reflected in income and sales data.

Market values also do not capture certain costs of production that are off the books. Costs of pollution, for example, may be hidden for many years. Therefore, the GDP in 2000 may not reflect all the costs of ill health, premature death, and other damages from chemicals dumped in the air, ground, or water.

We want to value and assess the net benefits of economic activity. Yet GDP, GNP, and related calculations ignore certain benefits and costs of production. While popular with economists and the media, these statistics are far from perfect. Now let's turn to the less-than-perfect theories of the causes of economic growth.

Historical Theories of the Wealth and Poverty of Nations

Concentrations of severely impoverished people in less developed nations, and the wide and growing gap between these nations and the industrialized nations force us to ask: Why are some nations rich and others poor? What causes economic growth?

The history of economic thought includes several well-known explanations of the wealth and poverty of nations. Our review starts with Adam Smith. It will contrast the optimism of classical and neoclassical theory with the dismal views of David Ricardo and Thomas Malthus, the radical perspectives promoted by Karl Marx and Vladimir Lenin, and the view that geography and culture matter. Note the shortcomings of each view.

Classical and Neoclassical Optimism

Classical economic theory arose in England and on the European continent in the late 1700s and early to middle 1800s. Neoclassical theory arose after 1870 and dominated mainstream microeconomics throughout the 1900s. The classical theory of Adam Smith in particular and neoclassical theory are both relatively optimistic about the potential for economic growth.

Adam Smith on the *Wealth of Nations*

Adam Smith devoted his best-known book, *An Inquiry into the Nature and Causes of the Wealth of Nations* (1776), to the question of what makes a nation wealthy. His answer was straightforward. Wealth is the productive capacity of a people, not its stock of gold. Productivity increases with specialization and

the division of labor, an increasing stock of capital, and technological improvements. Voluntary exchange within a system of "natural liberty" directed by the "invisible hand" promotes wealth creation. Government interference, monopolies, and other restraints on commerce inhibit wealth creation.

Smith also wrote *The Theory of Moral Sentiments* (1759). His ideas on free markets presumed an ethical foundation in society. Smith assumed, for instance, that enlightened individuals were able to act as "impartial spectators," judging what was morally appropriate even when personally involved in a situation.

Assuming a moral base and asserting that morality matters are, however, quite different from explaining precisely how commercial morality affects exchange, and few commentators on Smith have explained the connection in any detail. Moreover, when the moral status of a society is changing over time or is simply defective, assuming that a positive moral climate prevails is unhelpful. We need a more careful development of Smith's ideas in *Lectures on Jurisprudence* (1766), largely ignored until recently. (See Klein 1997, 2, 17-20, and a discussion of it below.)

Neoclassical Growth Theory

Neoclassical economics is a late-nineteenth and twentieth-century mathematical revision of many of the principles of Adam Smith's *Wealth of Nations* and the rest of classical economics. Neoclassical economists assert that economic output depends on the level of technology and the amount of labor and capital available. The implication is clear: a growing labor force and a high rate of saving that leads to a high rate of capital accumulation will promote economic growth. Innovations and technological change will further enhance the productivity of capital and labor.

The key to national standards of living is productivity of labor. Labor's wage depends directly on productivity, measured as quantity of output per laborer (Q/L). Productivity of labor increases as capital per worker increases and technology improves. Standards of living grow fastest in those countries with the highest rates of saving, capital investment, and technological innovation because productivity of labor will grow the fastest in them.

Nobel Prize winner Kenneth Arrow, however, has noted that the naive neoclassical analysis of resource flows doesn't square with the facts of international development. (See rear cover of North 1990.) Capital will supposedly move to where it is scarce, for that is where capital will earn the greatest profit. If capital is highly mobile and if technology can be adapted, why did capital and technology not move to the nonindustrialized nations during the twentieth century? The coexistence for so long of poor and rich nations disproves the automatic adjustments of neoclassical theory.

Classical Pessimism

Not all classical economists were optimistic about economic growth. David Ricardo gave us a theory of economic stagnation and Thomas Malthus gave us a theory of the limits to growth due to scarcity of food. Both writers are responsible for economics having the label "dismal science."

Richard T. Gill (1963, 23-24) states that Ricardian and Malthusian growth theory stems from two ideas. First, population grows whenever wages rise above subsistence (the iron law of wages). Second, the economy will stagnate as population grows. Their dismal prediction: England's economy would stop growing.

Malthus' explanation is well known. Food supplies would fail to keep pace with population growth. The ensuing food crisis would limit economic growth. Ricardo's explanation is less well known. Using England's fixed supply of land more and more intensively would lead to diminishing returns to labor in agriculture. Diminishing returns would mean a falling rate of profit, decreasing incentives for further investment and expansion. The result would be economic stagnation.

The major criticism of Malthusian and Ricardian economics is also well known. Both failed to account for dramatic increases in productivity of labor due to technological advances in agriculture and industry.

The Radical Critics

What prevents the movement of capital and the transfer of technology needed to make poor nations wealthier? Radical economists of the late twentieth century continued to blame the capitalist economic system and private property, with property and power concentrated among the industrialized nations.

Karl Marx

In the mid-1800s, Karl Marx labeled as capitalism the system of private ownership of the means of production and hiring of wage labor in production. Marx developed a stages-of-growth theory that emphasized who controlled the means of production (Gill 1963, 22). For Marx, capitalism is one stage in history.

While Marx admitted that capitalism led to accumulation of great productive capacity, to him the question of rich versus poor nations was less relevant than the distribution of output within each nation (in this sense, Marx was Ricardian). In Marx's theory of the exploitation of labor, the important questions are, why are capitalists rich and laborers poor, and what are laborers to do about it?

Vladimir Lenin

Rising living standards for industrial workers in capitalist nations between 1850 and 1900 forced Vladimir Lenin to rethink Marx's explanation of capitalism's inevitable downfall. He developed a theory of capitalist imperialism. Capitalists in industrialized nations, Lenin reasoned, were delaying the collapse of capitalism by exploiting people in poorer countries through the "**export of capital**" (Lenin 1939/1991, 90-93).

•**Export of capital:** Lenin's phrase for direct foreign investment by capitalists, through which they exploit workers of other nations

Dependency Theory

In the 1960s, **dependency theory** arose along the lines of Lenin's economic theory of capitalist imperialism. The system of world trade allows capitalists in the developed nations to continue to exploit the less developed countries, maintaining poor nations in a dependency status. Direct foreign investment by multinational corporations is especially damaging, and expatriation of profits to corporate headquarters in the developed countries is alleged proof that the multinationals take out more than they put in. Developing countries export mainly primary commodities (minerals, agricultural products, etc.). To benefit themselves, industrialized nations turn the terms of trade (real prices of commodity exports) against the developing nations.

•**Dependency theory:** developing nations are kept in poverty by the capitalist system of world trade through which capitalists in industrialized nations manipulate the terms of trade and exploit host nations with direct foreign investment

Theotonio Dos Santos summarized the implications of dependency for economic growth as follows:

> From this cursory analysis we see that the alleged backwardness of these economies is not due to a lack of integration with capitalism but that, on the contrary, the most powerful obstacles to their full development come from the way in which they are joined to this international system and its laws of development (Dos Santos 1970/1991, 144-52).

Criticizing the Radical Critics

Just as Marx incorrectly predicted the increasing immiseration of labor, Lenin's theory of imperialism and the later theory of dependency run counter to certain facts. Multinational corporations in capitalist nations such as the United States tend to invest most heavily in other capitalist nations. The greatest amount of direct foreign investment from the United States, for example, goes to Canada. Apparently, industrialized capitalist nations are exploiting each other, with rather good success.

While dependency theory was a popular explanation of poor economic performance in Latin America, the multinational presence there is not as significant as in industrialized nations. Furthermore, recent evidence suggests that those Latin American nations that have been most dependent on foreign trade and investment have grown the fastest (Kaufman, Giller, and Chernotsky 1975; cited in Harrison 1985, 154).

As to the perils of exporting primary products, the United States is currently the world's largest exporter of such goods. And being exporters of primary products did not hinder the economic progress of the United States, Canada, and Australia in the 1800s. Furthermore, each of those countries welcomed and benefited from British foreign investment in their times of early industrial development (Harrison 1985, 152).

Although nations that participate in global trade grow faster than those that refrain, the critics of capitalism persist. Commercial misbehavior is never acceptable, but capitalism per se is not guilty of all the charges leveled against it. Expansion Point 9.2 provides an example of seemingly unfounded charges against the system of global international trade.

Geographical Determinism

Geography seems to have influenced the historical economic progress of nations. In a chapter entitled "Nature's Inequalities," David Landes (1999, 5) asserts the obvious but painful truth that "the rich nations lie in the temperate zones, particularly in the northern hemisphere; the poor countries, in the tropics and subtropics." This is not a racist theme based "on membership in a [biological] group" of people, he says. Rather it is based on climate, the biology of disease, and human habits and institutions.

Heat, Disease, and Rainfall

Tropical heat discourages vigorous labor, no matter what one's race. "In general, the discomfort of heat exceeds that of cold" (Landes, 6). Tropical heat, especially the lack of frost, also fails to limit harmful insects and the diseases they carry (Landes, 7). Had inland farmers in Africa, for example, grown cash crops for export, transport to the coast would have been made overly expensive due to the threat of disease to animal or human porters.

Tropical rainfall is not well suited to cultivating many crops. Torrential downpours destroy a portion of the crops, while seasonal drought destroys much of what remains (Landes, 13). Alternating monsoon and dry seasons shorten the growing season.

More Than Geography

Historical patterns of economic progress cannot be attributed fully to geography. It is at most a necessary but not sufficient condition for growth. Why did commerce and technology develop so rapidly and dominantly after 1500 in one part of the temperate region, in Western Europe? And why did earlier economic progress in China and the Middle East stall?

Expansion Point 9.2: Blood in Our Sugar from World Trade?

A colleague sent an article critical of global capitalism. He wanted a response to David Shrock-Shenk's complaint that he wouldn't be giving thanks to God that year for all his material blessings because he no longer believed that God had blessed Americans with their great wealth. Specifically, the author would not give thanks for the sugar that he uses to can peaches. Here is part of his Thanksgiving complaint.

> **Why I Won't Thank God** . . . Once we met a young woman [in the Philippines] who stopped to buy supper for herself and her three children at a small grocery store—a small tin of sardines and a half-pound of rice with the 25 cents she had earned for hoeing sugarcane for twelve hours in the tropical sun.
>
> Standard economic theory calls this a fair price. . . . But this woman with little education and no other job skills was "willing" to work all day for 25 cents only because if she did not, her children would starve.
>
> **Blood in Our Sugar**. The sugar I used to can peaches this year may have been grown by the woman I met in the Philippines. . . . [A]re my cheap peaches a "blessing from God" when the woman who raised the sugar I used to preserve them doesn't earn enough to buy decent suppers for her children?
>
> The main reason I am wealthy is not that God has blessed me, but . . . largely because wealth has flowed into this country from around the world for centuries. Goods we buy are cheap in great part because people who make them receive less than an adequate wage. . . .
>
> **What I Will Not Do**. So I will not thank God for money in my bank account that results from an unjust and sinful economic system.

How would you respond to this criticism? Here are a few thoughts.

(1) The United States is not as dependent on foreign trade as are many other nations. We import about 11 percent of our GDP, up from about 5-7% in 1960±. Our wealth comes mainly from the fact that we trade with each other in the United States. Moreover, most of U.S. foreign trade is with other industrial nations, such as Canada, Great Britain, Germany, Japan, Singapore, and Hong Kong.

(2) The global system of free trade has taken South Korean peasants of the 1950s to a very high standard of living in the twenty-first century. Nations that chose to abandon free trade and develop their own industry, such as Sri Lanka, have had much less success in achieving higher living standards for their people.

(3) Refusing to eat sugar, bananas, and so on would hurt these poor workers more than eating lots of them. If they truly have no alternative but to work for an evil landowner, then losing that job might be worse. In any event, there are better responses than refusing to buy the products.

(4) The strongest criticism of this complaint is that the U.S. government *limits* sugar imports. Perhaps the poverty of sugar cane workers is due, not to free trade, but to government policies that will not let farmers in other nations sell as much sugar to the United States as they want. Perhaps such prayers of thanksgiving are doing more damage to workers of the world than free trade played according to humane rules (about which people in the United States ought to be concerned).

Historically, plantation owners (in the Caribbean, for example) have used slave labor to grow sugar cane because the work is difficult. Even so, we need to explore how we can help these poor people in the Philippine cane fields and elsewhere, rather than attacking a system that is more complex than simplistic criticisms allow.

Source: David Shrock-Shenk, "Why I won't thank God for all my things this Thanksgiving,"*Mennonite Brethren Herald* 37, no. 11 & 12, June 12, 1998.

Culture Matters

Cultures vary, and certain cultural traits may influence economic progress. As opposed to dependency theory, a cultural explanation suggests that factors *internal* to a nation contribute to poverty or wealth.

The idea is widely accepted that some cultural *attitudes* promote growth and others do not. The view that some *cultures* are inherently hostile to growth, however, seems to some to be racist. Lawrence Harrison, an exponent of the cultural view, rejects the racist label. Racist explanations are genetically rooted and imply immutable differences. Cultural differences can be seen in countries whose people share the same racial background. Culture is neither intrinsic nor immutable (Harrison 1985, 166).

Harrison reviews several cultural explanations of national wealth and poverty. Gunnar Myrdal, for example, investigated what he considered to be the myth that poor cultures are more just and caring. W. Arthur Lewis examined cultural factors that produce relatively more entrepreneurs. Max Weber, Joseph Schumpeter, and David McClelland also investigated the role of entrepreneurs in stimulating economic growth. (See Harrison 1985, chapter 2, "What Others Have Said.")

Yet the question remains to be answered: what key characteristics of societies promote growth? About neoclassical growth we asked, which societies will save and invest more in future productive capacity and technological development? About culture we ask, which characteristics promote growth and encourage entrepreneurs to take risks?

New institutional economists claim to have a theoretical framework that answers these questions in the context of rational economic behavior. We will examine this theory in detail, paying particular attention to its analysis of business morality.

- **Two ideas of new institutional economics:**
  1) economic growth requires complex patterns of voluntary commerce; and
  2) complex patterns of commerce require formal and informal institutions that promote freedom and efficiency (lower transactions costs) in investment, production, and exchange

New Institutional Economics and the Wealth and Poverty of Nations

All historical systems of social and political institutions are not economically equal. Certain nations have efficient institutions that promote commerce, and others have inefficient institutions that promote the interests of the powerful and that discourage trade.

The new institutional view rests on **two ideas**. First, economic growth and rising standards of living require the complex patterns of voluntary commerce that we find in advanced industrialized market economies. Voluntary trade among free and informed people creates value by moving goods and resources from where they are valued less to where they are valued more. Advanced commerce involves specialized investments, lengthy and highly technical production processes, and sophisticated transactions. Second, these complex patterns of market commerce require certain formal and informal economic institutions that promote freedom and efficiency in investment, production, and exchange. Those nations with institutions that encourage complex patterns of mutually beneficial trades, sophisticated commercial innovation, and productive investment in specialized tools, equipment, and education will tend to prosper.

Preliminary Concepts

You will need a few preliminary concepts to understand new institutional explanations of economic growth. They include the distinction between an exchange and a transaction, the meaning of an economic institution, and the potential for opportunism in commerce. You will want to know why transactions costs matter because economic institutions can lower the costs of transactions that are subject to opportunistic behavior by commercial traders.

Transactions Costs Matter

New institutional analysis has revived John Commons' idea that complex personal **transactions,** rather than simple impersonal exchanges of goods and services, dominate market commerce. Commons' view, stated in *Legal Foundations of Capitalism* (1924, 187), contrasted with Adam Smith's idea of market exchange as atomistic competition, noted in *Wealth of Nations* (1776).

• **Transaction:** involves complex agreements and promises to buy and sell in the future; a transaction is more complex than exchange at a point in time

How Does Market Exchange Differ from a Transaction? An exchange is an instantaneous swap of products for other products or money. Smith wrote primarily about such highly impersonal exchanges of goods and services among large numbers of people in, for example, an agricultural marketplace. Exchange at a point in time is not particularly costly to complete, and the mechanism of demand and supply determines prices.

In a transaction, traders agree to exchange goods, services, money, or other assets *over time*. Transactions involve the legal technicalities of writing and enforcing contracts that may cover long time periods, during which risks of default or fraud increase. In short, in a simple exchange we swap money, goods, and services, while in a transaction we swap promises regarding future exchanges. Simple exchanges involve relatively low costs. Due to the costliness of transactions, however, traders have developed complex institutional arrangements. Product price depends on institutional efficiency. The theory of transactions costs explained here complements a demand-and-supply theory of exchange.

What Are the Costs of Transactions? Since a transaction is a promise to exchange over time, buyer and seller must guard against the costs of broken promises. Transactions with a high probability of success may require costly searches of the market for a trustworthy buyer, seller, borrower, or lender. Successful investors, producers, and traders must pay to write and enforce legal agreements that protect themselves against fraud and theft.

• **Transactions costs:** costs of protecting against broken promises, fraud, and theft; they include costs of writing and enforcing contracts, and monitoring workers and suppliers

Transactions costs include, therefore, the costs of writing contracts that protect buyer and seller or borrower and lender. They also may include added costs of enforcing contracts. They involve costs of preventing and prosecuting fraud and outright theft of merchandise and services. Transactions costs include not only the private costs of a lawyer, but also the social costs of maintaining police and justice systems that promote private property and enforce contracts and liabilities. Taxes pay for such services.

How important in commercial activity are transactions costs? Economics texts teach that the major economic costs are costs of production, including wages for labor, a return to capital, and money spent for raw materials and intermediate products. Institutionalists contend that the major costs of commerce are those involved in completing transactions. John Wallis and Douglass North, for example, "found that more than 45 percent of national income was devoted to transacting" (North 1990, 28; citing Wallis and North 1986).

Opportunism Is Costly

Opportunism and the mere potential for it give rise to most transactions costs. **Opportunism** means taking advantage of circumstances through unprincipled, immoral, or illegal behavior, without regard to the effects on others. In trade, once a contract is made, a party to the transaction may benefit by failing to keep promises. If you lend a friend who has no conscience $1,000, the friend may feel better off by simply not repaying the debt. If two traders agree to meet in a certain remote location to trade goods for gold, one trader might see benefit in planning to steal the gold, or the other trader might see benefit in stealing the goods.

• **Opportunism:** taking advantage of circumstances with unprincipled, immoral, or illegal behavior; acting without regard for effects on others

Costs of Breach of Contract. Consider the costs of opportunism with an example of breach of contract. Assume that Jones agrees on Monday to sell a car to Wilson for $15,000. The trade will occur on Friday, allowing Wilson time to shop for and negotiate an auto loan. By Thursday, the bank has approved Wilson's loan, but since then Miller has offered Jones $15,600 for the car. If Jones accepts Miller's offer, his breach of contract is opportunistic and perhaps illegal, depending on how he concluded the initial agreement with Wilson.

What are the costs in such a breach? First are opportunity costs of time if Wilson does nothing to contest the breach. Both

Wilson and the bank officer have foregone other profitable uses of their time to pursue these sale and loan agreements. Next are possible legal expenses if Wilson seeks a legal remedy for the breach. To enforce the agreement, Wilson will undertake a costly lawsuit to take possession of the car or to recover costs and damages. Jones' opportunism may cost more than his $600 gain.

Adam Smith on Reputation in Trade: Assuming Away Problems of Opportunism. In his *Lectures on Jurisprudence* (1776), Adam Smith considered the problem of opportunism. Once a contract is made, what is to keep one party to the bargain from reneging on the deal or cheating? Smith answered that those who trade most frequently will be least likely to cheat.

> Whenever commerce is introduced into any country, probity and honesty always accompany it. These virtues in a rude and barbarous country are almost unknown. Of all the nations in Europe, the Dutch the most commercial, are the most faithful to their word. The English are more so than the Scotch, but much inferior to the Dutch. . . . This is not at all to be imputed to national character, as some pretend . . . It is far more reducible to self interest . . . A dealer is afraid of losing his character . . . When a person makes perhaps twenty contracts in a day, he cannot gain so much by endeavoring to impose on his neighbors, as the very appearance of a cheat would make him lose. Where people seldom deal with one another, we find that they are somewhat disposed to cheat, because they can gain more by a smart trick than they can lose by the injury which it does to their character. (Smith 1776, *Lectures on Jurisprudence;* reprinted in Klein 1997, 17-20.)

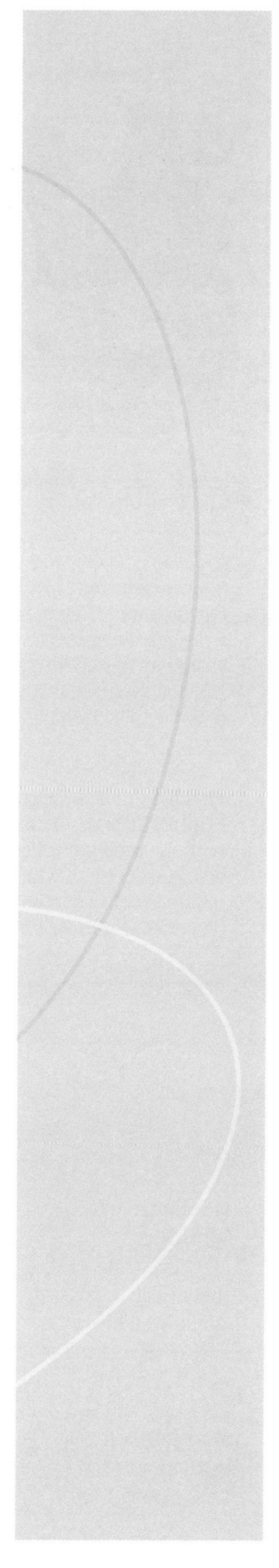

Ignoring the nonscientific nature and the startling frankness of Smith's sociological comments, consider his economic insight. Because merchants gain a living from frequent trades, they must act so as to assure a steady supply of deals. A self-interested concern for maintaining their valuable commercial reputation automatically increases their honesty.

While unprofitable in Smith's simplistic theory, opportunism may in specific situations be a preferred strategy. Expansion Point 9.3 details when cheating in commerce is the rational strategy.

Smith's analysis of cheating does not explain the rise of commerce, but simply assumes that commerce exists. If Dutch commerce increased Dutch honesty, what factors promoted the Dutch interest in and ability to conduct commerce? Smith also takes for granted that the Dutch trade more than do the "barbarians." Why wouldn't rational people in *all* nations see that it is in their self-interests to conduct more trade and to conduct it honestly? An institutional explanation of the rise of trade and honest dealing among commercial peoples through history seeks to understand which institutions promoted commerce as a profitable enterprise.

Expansion Point 9.3: When Are Traders More Likely to Cheat?

Adam Smith said that a merchant's self-interest would make him more honest. Yet commercial bad behavior abounds, and cheating is more likely under certain conditions.

The likelihood of cheating increases as the expected number of future trades with the same person decreases. For example, before retiring from a business or before moving on, a trader may decide that swindling is now consistent with self-interest. Fly-by-night operators who regularly roam to new markets plan to do so in order to benefit from cheating. They have no long-term customer goodwill to protect (Black 1994). Established merchants who plan to stay in a location thrive by not cheating.

A customer is more likely to cheat a merchant than a merchant is to cheat a customer (Tullock 1985). A customer has fewer meetings with a merchant compared to a merchant's continual contact with customers. A single buyer or single seller of a product, however, has market power that allows for more cheating. Where else can dependent buyers go? In large numbers of both buyers and sellers, cheating is less likely (Tullock).

A business with a valuable brand name or trademark to protect will tend to refrain from bad behavior that would damage its reputation. Facing bankruptcy due to poor economic conditions, however, even a business with a brand name may resort to bad behavior to maintain profitability (Black).

A merchant who knows more about product quality than the buyer, such as an appliance repair person, is more likely to cheat. The highly technical nature of the work makes detection less likely. The complexity of various financial transactions and accounting statements of the Enron Corporation in the 1990s, for example, made detection of fraud more difficult. Increased likelihood that experts such as journalists are monitoring cheating and will publish the findings, however, will cause such tendencies to cheat to decrease.

Sources: R. A. Black, "John Commons on Customer Goodwill and the Economic Value of Business Ethics...," *Business Ethics Quarterly*, vol. 4, no. 3 (1994): 359-365.

Gordon Tullock, "Adam Smith and the Prisoner's Dilemma," *Quarterly Journal of Economics* (1985): 1073-81; reprinted in *Reputation: Studies in the Voluntary Elicitation of Good Behavior,* ed. Daniel B. Klein (Ann Arbor: University of Michigan Press, 1997).

The Role of Institutions in Commerce

An **economic institution** is any law, persistent rule of behavior, agreement, or customary practice that influences the type of economy and its activities. What must institutions do to promote commerce? Since voluntary exchange raises standards of living, widespread fear of opportunism will decrease the volume of trade and reduce standards of living. Therefore, an important economic role for institutions is to promote trust among traders so that they all undertake beneficial trades. Let's consider why and how.

• **Economic institution:** any law, persistent rule of behavior, agreement, or customary practice that shapes an economy and its activities; efficient institutions promote trust among traders

Institutions Must Promote Trust. To encourage economic growth, commercial rules, customs, and arrangements must promote trust among merchants. They must trust in the willingness and ability of people to refrain from cheating on their agreements. They must trust that government authorities will not confiscate their wealth and will only tax it moderately and fairly. They also must trust that thieves and robbers will not steal their wealth, or will be punished to inhibit future threats.

A reputation for good conduct promotes trust. Adam Smith's vision of the spontaneous development of trust among frequent traders seems, however, a bit idealistic. In commerce, we find conscious arrangements intended to promote good behavior, monitor reputation, and punish bad behavior. Traders, for example, adopt certain customs and practices that allow them to pose **credible threats** of punishment to others who threaten commercial stability. Other institutions, such as commercial connections (networks among traders), allow them to pose **credible commitments** to keep their word. For more details, see Expansion Point 9.4.

- **Credible threat:** creates an expectation that cheaters will be punished
- **Credible commitment:** creates an expectation that a negotiator will keep his or her word and perform agreed duties

A History Lesson: Transition to Markets in Eastern Europe. In the 1990s, mainstream economists received a surprise tutorial about how important economic institutions are to the structure and progress of market economies. Economic texts in the 1960s contained mostly mechanistic, neoclassical

Expansion Point 9.4: The Role of Credible Threats and Credible Commitments in Commerce

Which institutional arrangements promote trust among people who exchange goods and services? Those that enable traders to offer credible threats to punish public or private opportunism. And those that enable traders to offer each other credible commitments not to behave opportunistically.

Being able to offer a credible threat to punish those who steal and cheat encourages restraint and builds trust on which commerce thrives. A tale from medieval history will illustrate. When invading bands from Hungary stole and murdered their way through medieval German farms and villages, they retarded regional agricultural and commercial progress. Why accumulate excess goods, crops, and herds if bandits would soon return to steal them? But then certain German villagers and farmers plotted a response. When they successfully captured a group of invaders, put out the eyes of all but one, and had the fortunate one lead them back to their homes, the Germans showed that they could offer a credible threat to the marauding Magyars. This encouraged people of both regions to settle into more peaceful agriculture and commerce.

Being able to offer a credible commitment to those who are considering a promise to buy or sell also builds trust. Swapping hostages is one way for warring tribes to build such trust. If chieftains swap sons, each has greater assurance that the other will not launch a further assault. Holding hostages, their commitments to live peacefully are more believable, creating conditions favorable to production and trade.

Developing long-term **connections** or **networks** of traders also promotes trust, particularly when the traders share cultural, religious, or ethnic bonds Being a member of a successful trade network offers lower cost access to profitable trades. The network enhances both credible threats to punish cheaters and credible commitments to keep one's promises. The network can more easily punish those who cheat because its members know each other, will communicate about breaches of ethics, and will be able to deny access to profitable trades to an offending trader. The network, by virtue of its long-term character, can also recognize and reward a trader's good reputation. Being honest is not as valuable as being known to be honest.

microeconomic theory of market demand and supply with Keynesian macroeconomics, but they offered very few historical or institutional details. Now, however, economics texts are more likely to contain significant institutional detail. What changed?

Collapsing communist-party leadership in Russia and conversion from centrally planned socialist economies to market economies showed professional economists that market economies have been shaped by their legal institutions, such as property rights and the rule of law, and by their commercial practices, such as accounting systems and networks of traders. Expansion Point 9.5 gives more details about the role of connections among traders. Now to the point: which institutional conditions make some nations wealthy and others poor?

Institutions That Make a Nation Wealthy

Douglass North won the 1993 Nobel Prize for research into the economic institutions of market economies. As early as the 1960s, North had begun to publish historical accounts of the growth of the English and American economies. His work claimed that market economies depend on certain legal and social institutions, including those that promote economic freedom and private property, and those that promote self-enforcing contracts.

Don't mistakenly think that government automatically sets the rules of the game by which traders must play and that government then enforces the rules. This naive view is only partly correct. At least **three types of institutions** are crucial. Since governments don't always behave themselves, the first duty of national law is to *constrain the government*. Second, governments do provide laws, police, and courts, but these are only effective as symbols and as last resorts. Finally, an efficient private commercial system operates on its own rules, on trust, and on informal institutions that reduce costs of making transactions by promoting self-enforcing contracts.

- **Three types of economic institutions:**
  1) constitutional constraints on rulers;
  2) formal commercial laws and agreements; and
  3) informal morals, customs, and behaviors

Constitutional Rules Develop Trust

Market economies arose in which constitutional rules constrained the coercive powers of government. The sovereign (king, queen, or other national government) must respect property rights and refrain from confiscating property. Confiscatory policies drive out entrepreneurs and stifle the complex commercial trade that promotes economic progress. When governors act with restraint, tax responsibly, and honor private property rights and other commitments, commerce proceeds.

A written constitution is not sufficient, however. Traders must trust that their rulers will keep their word. Therefore, constitutional government encourages commerce only if the governed can offer credible threats to retaliate when governors break the rules and act opportunistically. The threat of removal from office will suffice.

Expansion Point 9.5: From Socialism to Free Markets and the Institutions of Capitalism (Connections Matter!)

Communism's collapse and the transition to market-oriented economies in the 1990s in Russia and in Eastern Europe illustrated the critical role of economic institutions in a market economy. Politicians can change their economic theories overnight, but they cannot immediately create the new institutions to support them. This in a nutshell is why the transition to market economies was very painful throughout the 1990s, especially in Russia. It meant replacing a comprehensive central planning system with institutions that did not yet exist there on a large scale. Free-market banks and the accounting systems of production for profit were just emerging. Managers and workers lacked training for operating within markets.

For years, mainstream economists in the United States and elsewhere had preached about the efficiencies of market economies and the inefficiencies and inflexibilities of socialist central planning. Until 1990, though, they had written little on how to change from socialism to free markets. The collapse of party control in communist nations taught them how difficult it was to change quickly. The institutions of capitalism took years to develop in democratic-capitalist economies. Stock markets, public accounting rules, a banking and insurance industry, laws of property and contracts, and courts with experienced judges cannot be created overnight. Neither can emerging market economies instantly create the commercial connections that develop among traders over time. The value of such connections is not yet well understood by free-market economists, but it should be.

The fastest way to replicate these institutions is to import them through existing free-market businesses that bring in connections, expertise, and conventions. Foreign companies, however, will want a stake in domestic firms. Those nations, therefore, that were more willing to embrace foreign financial capital, such as Poland and Hungary, adapted their economies more quickly. China's market sector had already begun to develop rapidly after 1984, and the main channel was the ethnic and cultural connections it had in industrialized capitalist nations. Chinese merchants and industrialists in Hong Kong, Taiwan, and around the world hastened to invest in China's mainland when it opened to capitalist ventures. They brought valuable commercial connections to technical experts, resource suppliers, politicians in Washington, D.C., and retailers in global markets for finished goods.

When Russia, on the other hand, converted to a market economy in 1991, it lacked several of these advantages of other emerging market economies. Unlike the Chinese, Russia had no extensive global network of ethnic Russian merchants and industrialists poised to bring financial capital and connections to its newly opened markets (although these connections are likely developing now). Unlike Hungary and Poland, Russian Slavic nationalism was less willing to allow Western control of industry into its country. This nationalism is a tradition that goes back centuries and involves the historic split between the Russian Orthodox Church and the Roman Catholic Church, and also Russia's more recent commercial divorce with the West due to the Cold War. The lesson is that institutions matter, especially the commercial connections among traders.

Rulers also must be able to offer credible commitments to keep their promises. The benefits to government of a growing economy and increasing flow of tax revenues from commerce allow leaders to make credible commitments. Even a tyrant has an incentive to exercise restraint in taxation and confiscation because of the benefits of a prosperous nation. Fifteen percent of 100 is better than 50 percent of 10. Constitutions that fund rulers adequately further encourage credible commitments. As Expansion Point 9.6 explains, the English and American Constitutions provide for such credible threats and credible commitments to wayward rulers.

Formal Commercial Institutions

Formal commercial institutions include written public laws and private contracts that have the force of law. **Three kinds of commercial laws** are crucial. Property law establishes the rights and responsibilities of private ownership. Contract law asserts rights and responsibilities of parties to voluntary contracts. And tort law specifies liabilities for negligent behavior that causes a tort (damage) to other persons or their property.

- **Three kinds of commercial laws:**
  1) property law
  2) contract law
  3) tort and liability law

Two considerations are key. First, commercial efficiency requires more than written laws; it requires effective enforcement. Second, effective enforcement is costly.

Formal Enforcement Must Be Thorough. To promote trade, a formal justice system must enforce commercial laws thoroughly and effectively. This requires a fair and responsive police force,

Expansion Point 9.6: Constitutional Rule in England and the United States

England and the United States both have constitutional forms of government that are notable for restraining rulers and granting economic and political rights to subjects and citizens. England developed a constitutional form of government when William and Mary agreed to the Bill of Rights and came to power in 1689, after the Glorious Revolution of 1688 had deposed James II. North and Weingast (1989) asked, why would William and Mary agree to limit their discretionary power over property?

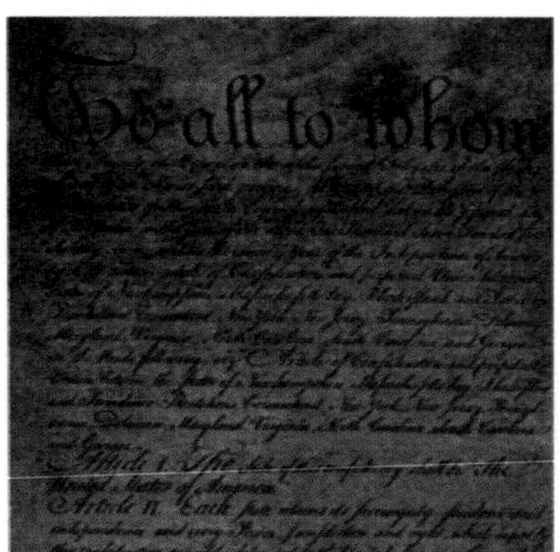
U.S. Constitution

First, the English people posed a credible threat of revolt. In 1215, English nobles had successfully forced King John to sign the Magna Charta, establishing their rights to privileges previously granted. In the 1640s, Oliver Cromwell led a successful Puritan revolution against Charles I. In 1685, a Protestant Parliament revolted against James II, inviting William to invade England from the Netherlands. History gave William and Mary evidence of a credible threat to retaliate against any opportunism.

What made the sovereign's promise in England to refrain from taking property for royal use credible? Because the new constitutional system provided regular funding for the crown's needs. The constitutional bargain included incentives compatible with peaceful, law-abiding rule.

The U.S. Constitution also includes credible threats to the power of the president or Congress, should they fail to play by the rules that limit their ability to tax and govern. Competing political parties and regular elections serve as a check on any power structure that might develop. The threat of impeachment further threatens a wayward president.

Source: Douglass North and Barry Weingast, "Constitutions and Commitment: The Evolution of Institutions Governing Public Choice in Seventeenth-Century England," *Journal of Economic History* 49, no. 4 (December 1989); reprinted in *Empirical Studies in Institutional Change,* edited by Lee Alston, Thrainn Eggertsson, and Douglass North (Cambridge: Oxford University Press, 1996), 134-65.

court system, and penal system. Weakly enforced laws will fail to provide a credible threat to those who violate commercial laws. Weak official enforcement means higher transactions costs for traders who wish to protect themselves with private police, security systems, and so on.

Formal Enforcement Is Costly. As with private security, effective formal enforcement of the law through police action and court decisions is expensive. Taxes to fund formal enforcement will raise the costs of making transactions. Widespread opportunism may even overwhelm formal systems of enforcement and dispute resolution. Thus, formal institutions can, at best, only support what must be an informal, unofficial set of institutions.

Informal Institutions Rule

The informal moral principles and attitudes that people pass along either encourage or discourage trade and economic progress. How? Moral rules that promote trust among entrepreneurs and traders attract capital investment, increase the productivity of labor, and further promote economic progress.

Informal Institutions Cut Costs. North attributes great importance to the role of informal institutions that shape the moral character of a people. Which informal institutions are economically efficient, and how do they work? North states a surprisingly simple conclusion:

> Effective traditions of hard work, honesty and integrity simply lower the costs of transacting and make possible complex, productive exchange (North 1990, 138).

Internally motivated workers are more productive and less costly to monitor. Honest workers and traders with integrity also require less monitoring. Honest employers attract and retain the most honest and productive employees, and workers have more trust when agreeing on work contracts. Negotiating with suppliers and other associates who have integrity and keep their word requires less costly defenses against cheating and less effort to enforce contracts because the probability of a breach is lower.

An example will illustrate the effect of good morals on the willingness to invest, produce, and trade. You are considering investing $100 million of your own and other investors' money. You plan to build a furniture factory, to hold inventories of raw materials and finished products, and to develop a network of suppliers and customers. Where would you rather invest? Your first choice is a region where people work hard, workers won't steal your inventory, suppliers keep their word about contract prices and delivery dates, and customers pay their debts. Your second choice is a region where people are lazy and prone to steal from their bosses, suppliers go back on their word when it suits them, and customers rarely pay bills on time. Where will transactions costs be lower?

Self-Enforcing Contracts Are Key. Investors and entrepreneurs prefer settings where contracts are **self-enforcing**. In a self-enforcing contract, parties to the agreement keep their word and correctly expect others to keep theirs as well. When traders know that workers, suppliers, and customers will behave themselves and meet their obligations, writing, monitoring, and enforcing contracts costs less. Expansion Point 9.7 examines whether the good moral behavior that leads to self-enforcing contracts arises from an evolutionary process of institutional change, or from religious teaching that demands certain behaviors even when unprofitable.

- **Self-enforcing contracts:** people keep their commitments and meet contractual obligations without costly third-party enforcement

Institutional Barriers That Keep Nations Poor

In neoclassical theory, national wealth depends on a high saving rate and technical progress. Yet, in a world where capital is highly mobile and technology is easily available, why do most of the people in many nations remain poor? The automatic adjustment mechanism of neoclassical theory ought to bring balance to national wealth and the productivity of labor. Capital should flow to where it is scarce, raising productivity of labor, wages, and standards of living. Self-interest should ensure good morals.

Instead, automatic adjustments have failed. Why? While the developing institutional structures in the economies of England, Western Europe, Japan, and the United States encouraged economic progress, the inefficient economic institutions of many other nations discouraged productive activity and encouraged redistributive activity (with wealth flowing not from rich to poor, but from the politically weak to the politically powerful). Without effective constitutional constraints on their rulers, without formal enforcement of commercial laws that promote economic freedom and responsibility, and without informal institutions promoting hard work, honesty, and integrity, economic exchange is costly and economic stagnation more likely than progress.

In the absence of institutional development, many nations remain poor (North 1990, 136). Three reasons for the poverty of nations emerge: (1) many nations are simply pirate economies; (2) opportunism is pervasive because it is a natural state; and (3) economic progress is path dependent.

Pirate Economies Don't Grow

Geography aside, inefficient institutions govern poor nations. To put it most simply, investors will not accumulate or invest capital and advanced technology as readily in a pirate economy as they will in a just economy. The world is not divided neatly into good and bad nations. America, for instance, is not totally just. The recession of 2000-2002 exposed the work of corporate

Expansion Point 9.7: Evolving Good Behavior or True Belief?

Institutional economics asserts that self-enforcing contracts are crucial to commercial progress in market economies. According to North (1990), informal institutions that promoted hard work and honesty in nineteenth-century America were economically efficient, encouraging education, productive activity, and accumulation of capital. Do the good behaviors required for self-enforcing contracts arise from an evolution of self-interested human behavior or from religious ideological commitments? Are commercial ethics in America rooted in pragmatic self-interest or in religious conviction?

A secular understanding of economic progress holds that, through the interaction of self-interest and human ingenuity, certain nations have developed efficient legal traditions, principles of good business behavior, and enforcement mechanisms that could pose credible threats to rogue traders. Even the secular view, however, allows for ideological influences on economic behavior. An ideological commitment means that people hold to their moral principles even when doing so seems not in their self-interest. Religious tradition, of course, is a major source of such convictions, and commentators outside the secular tradition emphasize the economic importance of religious teaching.

On the one hand, Americans borrowed a common-law tradition that developed over centuries in English courts. And its great commercial center in New York arose with a thoroughly secular and pragmatic commercial philosophy, rather than with a religious fervor.

On the other hand, although America has never been universally or officially Christian, various Protestant churches of Europe, the Anglican Church, and the Roman Catholic Church, as well as Judaism and other religious traditions have influenced its culture. Each tradition has helped promote strong moral teachings about honesty, integrity, and hard work. The McGuffey *Readers* of American grammar-school education in the 1800s, for instance, reflect a Judeo-Christian influence (with direct biblical quotes and readings in early editions). They focused on reading as well as on moral training, especially in lessons such as, from the *First Reader*, "The Good Girl," "The Kind Boy," "Good Advice," and "The Little Boy Who Told a Lie," and from the *Second*, "The Little Idle Boy," "The Greedy Girl," and "The Diligent Scholar."

Economists as scientists tend to ignore economic behavior's religious roots and focus on secular evolution. Students of economic and cultural history, however, cannot ignore religious influences on the development of morals. This is not to say that Judaism or Christianity are either necessary or sufficient for economic progress. Asian traditions have also developed strong ethical traditions that promote hard work and honesty and, therefore, promote commercial progress. The point is that the religious roots of economic progress deserve scholarly consideration.

Sources: Douglass North, *Institutions, Institutional Change, and Economic Performance* (Cambridge: Cambridge University Press, 1990).

Douglass North and Barry Weingast, "Constitutions and Commitment: The Evolution of Institutions Governing Public Choice in Seventeenth-Century England," *Journal of Economic History* 49, no. 4 (December 1989); reprinted in *Empirical Studies in Institutional Change,* edited by Lee Alston, Thrainn Eggertsson, and Douglass North (Cambridge: Oxford University Press, 1996), 134-165.

William H. McGuffey, *Eclectic Readers* (Fenton, MI: Mott Media, 1982, [1836]).

pirates, as Expansion Point 9.8 documents. Even so, the abstraction of just versus pirate economies will show how relatively unrestrained opportunism hinders economic progress.

In a **just economy**, informal cultural institutions that transmit high moral standards promote self-enforcing agreements, moral

Expansion Point 9.8: Corporate Pirates and Good Institutions Gone Bad in the United States

In 2001 and 2002, the news told of corporate pirates caught looting financial markets. Falling stock prices magnified their abuses of otherwise useful business practices. Here are details.

CEOs Cashed Out Their Options

As investors were buying stock at the peak of the market boom, corporate officials were selling. A more serious charge is that various companies used accounting tricks to inflate corporate earnings so as to prop up stock prices in the short run, while insiders cashed in their shares.

Stock **options** are institutional responses to a principal-agent problem: managers may act in their own interests rather than in the interests of the firm. Stock options are designed to reconcile a manager's interests with the shareholder's interest, which is to maximize the value of shares. A firm may give its CEO an option to buy 100,000 shares of its stock at $15 one year later. If the stock is now worth $12, the CEO can benefit from the option if he increases the firm's profitability and boosts the stock price to, say, $20. The CEO can then buy shares at $15 and sell at a $5 per-share profit (or hold for a future profit).

A CEO who finds the company in trouble has a perverse incentive to lie about the firm's true condition. Top officials may conspire to inflate the revenues of the firm or inflate its net worth until cashing their options. Unaware of the company's true condition after examining its income statement and balance sheet, investors may buy stock that is worth much less than they paid. The firm has committed fraud because a good institution (stock options) has gone bad.

Accountants Cooked the Books

Two valuable commercial institutions are: (1) a banking practice to advance a firm its future earnings, called a prepay, and (2) a legal entity called a subsidiary, a separate company owned by a corporation. Accountants at the failed energy company, Enron, allegedly used both methods to artificially inflate its earnings. Ignoring guilt or innocence, consider how to do this.

Banks earn income by agreeing to **prepay** future sales revenues to a firm, which may gain tax benefits. This is legitimate and useful when recorded honestly. But a bank and a troubled company might use a fictitious sales account to create a prepay that is actually a loan, thus hiding debt from investors.

A troubled company could also create a **subsidiary** to hide debt. As a separate entity with separate books, a subsidiary can legally isolate more risky investments from less risky ones. Investors in each company then take on levels of risk that they choose. But a parent firm also can hide debt by shifting loans to the subsidiaries' books. Or it can inflate its assets by recording an inflated value of the subsidiary on its books. Each of these causes the parent company to appear to be more profitable than it really is.

External Auditors Also Consulted

Hiring independent auditors is a core institution of financial accountability in advanced market economies. Outside auditors certify the truth of a firm's income statement and balance sheet. Trouble developed, however, when accounting firms that served as auditors also sold consulting services to the same corporations. Auditors were no longer independent, and evidence suggests that they failed to properly serve investors.

Stock Analysts Inflated Reports

Major brokerage houses underwrite new issues of stock for corporations (buying initial stock offerings to sell them at retail at a profit). They also provide analysis of stocks for investors. Although each can be valuable commercial practices, doing both in the same firm creates a conflict of interest. Should the analyst report honestly or promote stock that the firm has underwritten? Analysts apparently gave overly optimistic assessments of stocks that their firms were underwriting, even joking about the practice in emails.

Sources: Mike France and Wendy Zeller, "Enron's Fish Story," *Business Week*, Feb. 25, 2002, 39-40.

John A. Byrne, *et al.*, "How to Fix Corporate Governance," *Business Week*, May 6, 2002, 68-78.

Mark Gimein, "You Bought. They Sold," *Fortune*, Sept. 2, 2002, 64-74.

Julie Creswell, "Banks on the Hot Seat," *Fortune*, Sept. 2, 2002, 79-82.

restraint, and economic efficiency. Lower transactions costs in a just economy make investments more profitable and more inviting to entrepreneurs. A culture of good behavior promotes the restraining influence of formal institutions.

In a **pirate economy**, people are opportunistic and even predatory, and the nation fails to thrive. Informal institutions may encourage opportunism as a way to get ahead, increasing transactions costs for traders, who must defend themselves against opportunism. Formal institutions may reward opportunism, as when bribes are legal and expected or when governmental confiscation and redistribution of wealth reward the politically powerful. Confiscatory tax rates make investment less profitable.

Entrepreneurs avoid the pirate economy, preferring to invest in a just economy where costs are lower. This is why most direct foreign investment from one developed nation tends to go to other developed nations, not to less developed nations. The risks due to opportunism overwhelm the returns to scarce capital.

This is not to say that all people living in poor nations are lazy, lying thieves. Evidence suggests that while a people may work hard and be honest, a nation's leaders can impose inefficient taxes and economic controls. Pirates in power pursuing their own interests may be the problem. Or, lacking *any* "controlling legal authority," warring factions may dominate an area.

Opportunism Is Natural and Pervasive

If inefficient institutions impede economic growth, why do they persist in poor nations? Won't the police and the courts restore order and encourage good behavior? Sadly, opportunism is pervasive. North (1990) contends that inefficient institutions, opportunism, and predatory behavior are the normal state. The police and court officials in such a culture will often tend toward opportunism, demanding bribes and playing favorites instead of promoting justice and economic efficiency.

Pervasive opportunism implies that efficient systems may not last. While the U.S. economy, for example, grew fabulously in the 1800s and 1900s, North (1990) is not certain about the stability of its institutions into the future. People must guard and continue to cultivate efficient institutions. South American nations adopted market-oriented institutions and grew rapidly after independence in the 1850s. Yet they abandoned those institutions in the 1930s, and their controlled economies failed to thrive for decades.

Economic Progress Is Path Dependent

Economic progress is **path dependent**, which means that initial conditions matter and institutional change is gradual. "You can't get there from here" exaggerates the point a bit, but not much. A nation becomes locked into a rigid institutional structure. Economic progress cannot be prompted, managed, or forced

- **Just economy:** an abstract ideal; a culture of high moral standards in which most contracts are self-enforcing, and in which other formal commercial institutions and constitutional rules are economically efficient

- **Pirate economy:** a culture in which opportunism is normal, government policies are confiscatory, and other economic institutions are inefficient, failing to discourage opportunism

- **Path dependency:** initial conditions limit current choices for economic development, and institutional change occurs only gradually

without careful reworking of that structure. For instance, Russia's hope in 1990 for a rapid conversion from state socialism to mature capitalism proved impossible. Economic institutions are bound up in the habits of a people, not simply written into law.

CHAPTER SUMMARY

1. Economists measure economic growth with GNP and GDP, the market values of economic output. They adjust for population by calculating output per capita. They compare national outputs by converting to a common currency with market exchange rates or with adjustments for purchasing power parity.

2. Adam Smith and neoclassical economists were optimistic about economic growth. Thomas Malthus and David Ricardo were pessimistic, foreseeing economic stagnation. Karl Marx and Vladimir Lenin developed a theory of exploitation of workers and exploitation of less developed countries that eventually became dependency theory. The facts of economic progress don't support naive neoclassical ideas about the mobility of capital or dependency theories that trade stunts the growth of developing countries. Cultural theories and geographical explanations of economic progress are only partially correct.

3. Institutional economic theory begins with transactions cost. This is a revival of John Commons' idea that the personal and costly transaction is more common in capitalism than standard theory recognizes. In a simple exchange, we swap money, goods, and services, while in a transaction we swap promises regarding future exchanges. Not only demand and supply, but also institutional efficiency determine prices.

4. Institutions that promote trust among traders and investors are efficient because they reduce transactions costs. Self-enforcing contracts, formal commercial rules, and constitutional limits on government promote trust and efficient exchange.

5. Institutions of self-enforcing contracts include: (a) credible threats such as hostage exchanges, a history of persistence in retaliation for opportunism, and a formal legal system; and (b) credible commitments resting on reputation or moral ideology.

6. Effective constitutional limits require credible threats of retaliation for breach of the law and credible commitments by rulers to keep their word.

7. North and Weingast (1989) explained that economic progress in England accelerated as the sovereign accepted constitutional limits on the arbitrary power to confiscate wealth. Economic progress in America in the nineteenth century seems also to be associated with informal institutions of "hard work, honesty, and integrity" (North 1990).

8. At least **three types of institutions** are crucial to economic progress. First, a market economy requires constitutional rules and supporting institutional arrangements that constrain the opportunism of rulers. Second, formal rules and enforcement mechanisms must set the broad parameters of market behavior and serve as a last resort against public and private opportunists. Third, informal institutions that reduce costs of making transactions by promoting self-enforcing contracts are essential.

9. The collapse of communism in Eastern Europe and conversion to market economies there illustrated that capitalism depends on commercial institutions such as the historic networks of traders.

10. Nations with efficient formal and informal institutions tend to be rich and those with inefficient institutions tend to be poor. The contrast between a just economy and a pirate economy is overly simple but instructive. Institutions develop in a just economy to minimize transactions costs. Not all institutions, however, are efficient. Institutions in a pirate economy promote the interests of the powerful.

11. The United States experienced the work of corporate pirates toward the end of the 1990s. Implicated were institutions gone awry, including the stock options of managers, auditors compromised by their work as consultants, stock analysts and their inflated reports, and the devious use of prepays and subsidiaries to hide debts and inflate revenues and net worth.

12. Economic history also shows that economic progress is path dependent. Initial institutional conditions matter. And institutional change is gradual and uncertain.

Problems for Practice

9.1 How do economists measure economic growth? Explain the statistics they use. In Exhibit 9.1, how did the United States compare with Japan, Finland, Russia, and Ethiopia?

9.2 Explain why economists who want to compare the values of gross output in different nations make a correction to exchange rates to adjust for purchasing power parity. In Expansion Point 9.1, how did the United States compare with Japan once this adjustment was made?

9.3 In your own words, explain each of the historical economic theories of national economic growth. Then briefly explain for each: is it mainly an incomplete or an untrue explanation of economic growth?

9.4 Explain how formal constitutional constraints and formal commercial laws promote economic progress. Use the preliminary ideas that you learned about new institutional theory to explain their roles.

9.5* Explain how an ethic of hard work, honesty, and integrity contributes to economic progress. Do you think this is truly central to economic progress? To what extent are a just economy and a pirate economy helpful ideas in explaining economic growth?

9.6* Explain whether each of the following statements is consistent with new institutional analysis of what causes economic growth.

a. "The higher the proportion of swindlers in a nation, the more costly transactions will be as traders expend effort and money to protect themselves."
b. "The chief function of a constitution is to restrain those who would overthrow the government."
c. "We understate the importance of moral training in economic analysis. As the country music song goes: 'This world turns on lessons learned.'"

9.7 The emerging market economies in the formerly communist nations of Eastern Europe illustrated that economic theory and ideology were not the only difference between capitalism and socialism. What did this transition reveal about the importance of commercial connections and traders among networks?

For your portfolio:

9.8 Investigate one of the following cultures and write a paragraph on how and why it flourished in a certain period and another paragraph on why it did not continue to progress economically after that period. What were the sources of its economic advantages and eventual disadvantages? Which institutional factors mattered? Consult texts such as David Landes, *Wealth and Poverty of Nations*, and Rondo Cameron, *A Concise Economic History of the World*.

a. Sumerian riverine civilization (2000 B.C.)
b. traders of the Indus Valley (after 3000 B.C.)
c. earliest Chinese civilization (from 500 B.C.)
d. the Incas (before A.D. 1500)
e. the Aztecs (before A.D.1500)
f. Islam and Arabic influence (A.D. 750 to 1100)

9.9* Investigate the economic rise of one of the following European nation states between A.D. 1200 and 1700. What were the sources of its economic advantages? Which institutional factors mattered? Again consult texts such as David Landes, *Wealth and Poverty of Nations*, and Rondo Cameron, *A Concise Economic History of the World*.

a. Portugal
b. Spain
c. Italy
d. the Netherlands (Dutch)

9.10 Investigate the issues of Expansion Point 9.8 further. What institutional changes have been proposed by the U.S. Congress and the president, the Securities and Exchange Commission, the New York Stock Exchange and the NASDAQ, associations of shareholders, and any other private or public groups?

For class discussion:

9.11 Which of the explanations of economic growth seem most accurate to you? Which, if any, seem least helpful? Pick the two best and the two worst explanations, and explain why you chose them.

9.12 Soviet Russia industrialized very rapidly in the 1930s with a communist philosophy that recognized the ultimate power of the state and rejected traditional moral training as exploitative tools of capitalist oppression. How did those experiments go? Do you think that economic development can be promoted today without attention to constitutional constraints and moral training?

9.13 What are the actual and likely future effects on U.S. financial markets and U.S. economic growth of the financial fraud revealed in 2001 and 2002? See Expansion Point 9.8, and read other articles on Enron, Global Crossing, Adelphia, and related cases.

See Answer Key for hints/answers to starred (*) questions.

Chapter 10

GOVERNMENT

Powers and Functions

What this chapter will help you think about:

1. What sources of government power affect economic outcomes?
2. What is the "rule of law" and what are its historical roots?
3. How does abiding by the rule of law promote commerce?
4. What specific provisions of the U.S. Constitution involve economic activity and how has their interpretation by the Supreme Court influenced economic activity?
5. What are the general economic functions of government and by what types of policies do governments pursue them?
6. What are the key perspectives on the nature of government?

Economic activity among real, imperfect people will inevitably require government oversight. People's interests clash. They dispute ownership of property. They seek protection from each other and seek a set of rules and institutions to make commercial activities less risky. At times, people develop adequate rules and resolve disputes privately, but not always.

• **Government:** officials, rules, and organizations by which authority over a people is exercised; it is distinctive as the only social organization authorized to use **coercive power**

Government is defined by its officials, rules, and methods of exerting its authority. Rules define acceptable and unacceptable behavior, and officials enforce rules and regulate behavior to protect rights. If conflicts arise, government determines guilt or innocence, and punishes wrongdoers. Because rules may conflict and may provoke different interpretations, governing agencies—the courts or judiciary—adjudicate disputes about the rules.

Government Power

How is government different from normal commerce among individuals, businesses, and other groups? Government alone has the legitimate power to use **coercive force** to levy taxes, appropriate property, and enforce behavior. Individuals, businesses, and non-government organizations do not. Private activity must rely on voluntary cooperation among parties to an agreement.

The Basis for Power

What gives government the right to coerce its people with force? Philosophies of government have varied in human history.

A **divine right** of the king or queen to rule is perhaps the first to be clearly articulated. Christian kingdoms of Europe required the blessing of the Church to retain the appearance of divinely granted authority—without the blessing, kingdoms were more subject to subversion.

The power to rule by **sheer might** is quite a different idea and resides in the ability to command and control humans. When a people acknowledge the authority of unrestrained power, they generally do so either out of fear or out of a sense that a strong fist is needed to keep order. In the Russian economic crises of the 1990s, many Russians supported the return of a strong fist. Similarly, in the political upheaval of the late 1960s, Richard Nixon appealed to the American sense of a need for "law and order," even though his methods of enforcing order—such as keeping secret files on dissident Americans and breaking in to steal information—were themselves unlawful.

The democratic philosophy of government assigns authority to the people. Through a **social contract** that they make with government, the people give it authority over them to improve the welfare of all. The social contract, as imagined by the English philosopher John Locke, can be renegotiated as needed. It is essentially an economic instrument that tries to balance the costs and benefits of individual autonomy and collective action. Thus, a social contract trades away economic as well as political freedoms in exchange for public peace and justice.

• **Social contract:** an agreement among people establishing a government with limited powers and a citizenry with prescribed responsibilities

Limiting Government Power: The Rule of Law

The rule of law is the idea that all governors—politicians, bureaucrats, kings and queens—are subject to the law. The rule of law limits the power of government to steal private property, for example, and is therefore fundamental to economic progress. Most economies have laws and legal organizations, but not all governments operate under the rule of law. Laws made arbitrarily by a dominant political party or by the crown or military dictator are inconsistent with the rule of law.

A legal system under the rule of law starts with a set of first principles about the law, expressed in a constitutional form of government. These principles may be derived from divine revelation or some other expression of religious ideas, the idea of natural law, or social custom. The people, however, must approve the first principles and must record them to serve effectively as a basis for more detailed laws. Each new law can then be reviewed as to whether it is consistent with those first principles.

As Expansion Point 10.1 explains, the U.S. Constitution follows in a long historical tradition of establishing the rule of law. A brief history of the relation of the U.S. government to the U.S. economy will illustrate the economic importance of constitutional rules.

Expansion Point 10.1: The Rule of Law in Historical Perspective

The rule of law is an ancient institution found in the Jewish Torah, the books of the Law. Deuteronomy 17: 18 commanded that when the king of Israel took the throne, he was "to write for himself . . . a copy of this law" (NIV). This demanded that he should both remember and be subject to the law. The people were also to show respect for the judge or priest who applied the law and to abide by their decisions or be put to death (Deuteronomy 17:8-13). Youth were to "write [the commandments] on the tablet of your heart" (Proverbs 7:3).

Reproduction of the *Magna Charta*

In the *Magna Charta* of 1215, English nobles demanded that the tyrant King John respect their rights, particularly those previously granted to them by the sovereign. These included the right to a trial of their peers, and the rights to hold property and collect duties previously assigned to them.

In his book *Lex Rex* ["Law is King"] (1644), the Scotsman Samuel Rutherford boldly stated the general principle established in the *Magna Charta*, that the law is king rather than the king law. The English legal tradition was further strengthened by the development of the common law, based on the decisions of judges in civil suits throughout England.

Establishing the rule of law promoted English commercial and industrial development, because it encouraged consistent application of rules of contract and trade. In the *Magna Charta*, for instance, article 41 established that:

> "All merchants shall be able to go out of and come into England safely and securely, . . . for buying and selling by the ancient rights and customs free from all evil tolls, except in time of war. . . ."

With such protections, merchants could depend on a fixed set of rules, and could expect that their property would be free from seizure and unjust taxation. This reduced the costs of trade, encouraging commerce and increasing standards of living.

The U.S. Constitution contains similar assurances that the government cannot take property without due process or just compensation. This made industrialists and merchants more willing to accumulate productive wealth in America, knowing that they could reap the fruits of their efforts and risk taking. A correlation between high living standards and support for the law around the world lends support to the claim of its economic importance.

The U.S. Constitution and the American Economy

The U.S. Constitution is an economic document with a significant impact on the American economy. This economic impact, however, has changed in the past two centuries. The histories of constitutional law and of government interventions in the U.S. economy show that government's role and reach have gradually extended as the courts have reinterpreted the constitutional rules.

Nevertheless, the U.S. Constitution and the attached Bill of Rights and other amendments established the rule of law in economic and political activity. Since the U.S. Constitution was ratified by vote of elected state representatives, the system of government it creates is the product of a social contract.

Constitutional Rules

The Constitution contains the rules listing and restricting the federal government's powers. While it grants specific economic and political powers to government, it also limits those powers directly and indirectly.

On Taking Private Property

The right of the government to take property is a good example of how constitutional rules both grant and limit that power. Governments have the power of **eminent domain**, the right to force you to give over to government your property or partial rights to it. If you resist, governments can compel you with a threat of force to do so. Government powers to take property, however, are limited in the United States. Although the Constitution assumes the government's power of eminent domain, it explicitly restricts that power in the "**takings clause**" of the Fifth Amendment.

• **Eminent domain:** the right of government to take property or rights

When government condemns and takes property under the power of eminent domain, it must give "**just compensation**." If government and the property owner cannot agree on what is just compensation, they must appeal to the courts to assess a fair market value of the property. The U.S. Constitution also explicitly forbids one individual the right of eminent domain over another.

• **Just compensation:** a limit on government's right of eminent domain, requiring payment of fair value for property seized

The power of eminent domain is used today to gather property rights needed to build roads and bridges, just as it was in England in the few hundred years before American independence. The power is also used to regulate private property for a public purpose without actually taking ownership. The government must compensate for such **regulatory takings,** but it is sometimes difficult to know what are reasonable land-use restrictions and what are "takings" requiring compensation. As explained in Expansion Point 10.2, a recent Supreme Court decision in a land-use case in Oregon, *Dolan v. City of Tigard,* took up this question of the extent of a local government's power to restrict a private property owner's right to use her land as she saw fit.

• **Regulatory takings:** government regulation has the effect of seizing property *value* without taking title to the property

On Separated Powers

Constitutional rules about making laws express clearly the intent to limit governmental powers by separating and checking them. In the United States, federal laws are enacted jointly by a representative legislature and an elected executive, the president, and are reviewed by the Supreme Court. A **separation of powers**, among other things, helps to limit the arbitrariness of government interventions in the economy. The **federalist** structure of government, dividing powers among local, state, and national

Expansion Point 10.2: Land for Bike Paths and Green Space? The Supreme Court Speaks on "Takings"

How did John and Florence Dolan's ordinary application in 1991 to the City of Tigard, Oregon, for a building permit to expand the size of their plumbing supply store end up in the U.S. Supreme Court in 1994? The reason is that the City of Tigard gave the Dolans an unusual response. The city agreed to approve the permit *if* the Dolans would dedicate 10 percent of their land to be used for a bike path, green space, and improved drainage.

> ***"...nor [shall any person] be deprived of life, liberty, or property without due process of law; nor shall private property be taken for public use, without just compensation."***
>
> Fifth Amendment to the U.S. Constitution

Since the city was not offering to pay fair market value for use of the land, Florence Dolan (taking up her late husband's suit) complained that this regulatory confiscation of her property violated the takings clause of the Fifth Amendment to the Constitution. Her suit contended that the property was worth $30,000. The city contended that granting a permit was a fair exchange for the parking and drainage problems that development might cause. Their study, following state land-use guidelines, found that the building project would indeed have some effect on traffic and drainage, though they did not specify the dollar value of the effect, nor did they show clearly that the bike path would solve traffic problems.

If you were a judge, would you favor the property owner's rights or the city's interest in protecting itself against too much local traffic and the risk of more flooding? Would you agree that the city's power of eminent domain justified the taking of property and that the permit was just compensation?

Here is how the Supreme Court ruled. By a slim majority of 5-4, the Court ruled in favor of the private-property owner. It said that the permit was not just compensation for the taking of land. It set down a general rule that compensation must be roughly proportional to the value of the property taken for public use.

Commentators noted that this was the first time in a half century that the Court had strongly asserted the primary importance of private property rights. The Court was firm in saying that individual property rights rank right up there with free speech, freedom of religion, and other featured civil rights. Governments must be more cautious in imposing on a few owners of private property the burden of improving social welfare.

Sources: Theodore J. Boutrous, Jr., "Rule of Law: The Supreme Court Remembers Property Rights," *Wall Street Journal*, Jun 29, 1994, A17.

Robin Franzen, "Oregon's Takings Tangle," *Planning* 60, no. 6, June 1994, 13.

- **Constitutional rules that limit or disperse federal economic power:**
  1) just compensation
  2) separation of federal powers
  3) powers reserved to the states
  4) political competition

entities, also disperses power. Sometimes the courts must resolve overlapping jurisdictions and outright legal contradictions.

Powers not delegated specifically to the federal government by the U.S. Constitution were left to the states. Even so, the Constitution allowed the federal government to regulate interstate commerce, and through that clause the courts have extended the reach of the federal government to most commerce in the United States. Advocates of **states' rights** want to resist this encroachment on state powers over commerce, and the history of U.S. commerce is in part a history of conflict over federal versus states' rights to regulate economic activity. Federalism does, however, subject individuals and businesses in the United States to different regulations and taxes at each level.

Encouraging Political Competition

By allowing more than one political party to rule, the constitutional rules promote healthy **political competition**. The United States maintains a strong two-party system of Republicans and Democrats, with only occasional competition from "third parties" and independents. Many democratic nations today, though, have multiple parties. Under majority rule, a multi-party system requires coalitions of parties to form a ruling government.

One-party rule does not require leaders to build political coalitions, but it does cause other serious problems. Just as a commercial monopoly can exploit its customers, so a monopoly party can rule with impunity over its people. Communist nations claimed that the Communist Party was adequate to represent workers, and it allowed no other parties to compete. A one-party system did stabilize the economy over time. And, in the economic turmoil of the 1990s after the collapse of communist rule, many Russians longed for that stability. Yet, the majority of Russians voted against a return to the totalitarianism of one-party rule.

As in business and sports, political competition improves performance when it is done within the rules of the game. A second difficulty with the Communist Party in Russia especially was that it was dedicated to advancing the economic and political interests primarily of industrial workers. With one-party rule, Russian peasants had inadequate representation in political decisions.

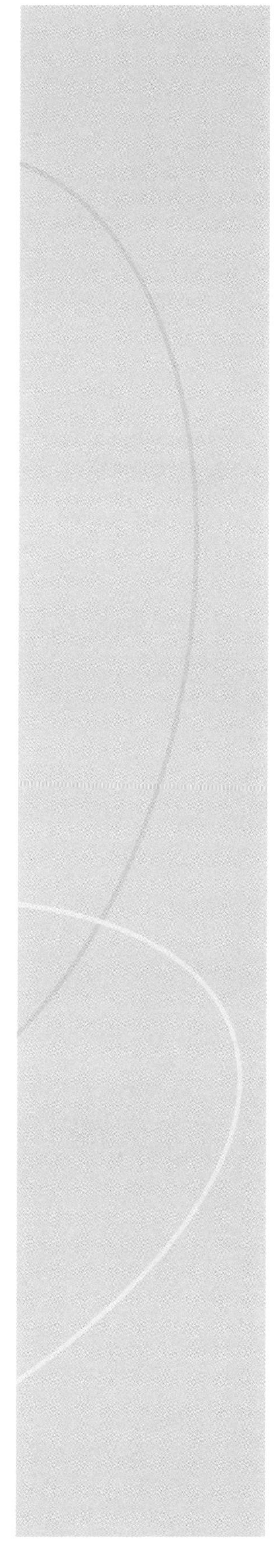

Changing the Economic Rules

Several other important constitutional rules are notable for how the courts have modified their interpretations over time. The United States began as a market economy with minimal government intervention, as a rebellion against excessive interference from the English crown government. Federal economic power, however, has gradually expanded. The cases that come before the Supreme Court reflect the changing interpretations of several key clauses of the Constitution. As a result, our federal, state, and local governments do much more today and require many more economic resources than they did when they were first empowered.

Laissez-Faire Constitutionalism in the United States

Early on, the federal government conducted foreign affairs, defended the nation from foreign aggression, regulated foreign trade and taxed imports, regulated interstate commerce, and protected life and property. The Constitution also gave it the power to regulate the supply of money, but the government did this only indirectly until the twentieth century.

In the beginning, the U.S. government did intervene in the free economy, imposing tariffs on imports as its primary source of revenue. Secretary of the Treasury Alexander Hamilton provided the justification for tariffs, urging in his *Report on Manufactures* in 1793 that the government use tariffs to protect its emerging manufacturing sector from tough competition by English factories.

- **Laissez-faire:** "let it alone," meaning minimal governmental intervention in a free economy

In the nineteenth century, however, the United States generally followed the philosophy of ***laissez-faire***, or minimal governmental intervention in economic activity. As suggested by English political economist Adam Smith, the government saw its functions as primarily providing for **national defense**, a **legal system**, a **stable money supply**, and certain **public goods** that free markets did not adequately provide.

- **Minimal functions of government** provide for
  1) national defense,
  2) a legal system,
  3) a stable money supply, and
  4) public goods.

From the 1860s until the 1930s, certain justices of the U.S. Supreme Court played along with an explicit judicial philosophy of *laissez-faire* constitutionalism (see *Oxford Companion to the Supreme Court* 1992, 492-493). Gradually, however, the Court eroded *laissez-faire* policies on many fronts. This erosion occurred in several ways. The Court expanded existing constitutional powers of government, such as those expressed in the commerce clause. Court decisions also circumvented constitutional limits on government powers, such as those contained in the contracts clause. The Court also invented new powers in an evolutionary development of the economic role of government. Expansion Point 10.3 explains the details of evolving constitutional law and its economic effects.

Evidence of Government's Growing Influence

Estimates of the share of government activity in the economy demonstrate the expanding economic role for government. Since the 1930s were a critical period in the expansion of government's economic role, Exhibit 10.1 provides data on government's share of the U.S. economy for selected years, beginning in 1929. It shows that all government expenditures, including spending for defense, other goods and services, salaries, and payments of transfers to individuals, increased from 10.1 percent to 32.5 percent of economic activity. Notice how dominant the government was in 1944 during World War II, primarily due to federal spending to purchase armaments and mobilize the armed forces.

Since 1930, much of the growth of government spending as a portion of total economic activity has come because of an increase in government transfer payments. Transfers are payments for which the government gets no good or service in return. As a result, the United States is now referred to as a "transfer society." This phrase highlights how the government has turned from its traditional functions of protecting life and property, and providing a national defense, to providing poor relief, equalizing income distribution, and pleasing special interests. The majority of transfer payments in the United States, though, do not go to the poor. Government supports middle and upper income families

Expansion Point 10.3: Constitutional Law and Widening U.S. Federal Powers in the 1900s

The U.S. Supreme Court building

The history of the U.S. government's widening powers is the history of more expansive Supreme Court interpretations of certain clauses in the U.S. Constitution, especially the commerce clause. These more expansive interpretations led to less emphasis on other clauses, especially the contracts clause.

The **commerce clause** of the Constitution, allowing the federal government to regulate interstate commerce, was originally restricted by court decisions. As late as 1918, the Supreme Court ruled in *Hammer v. Daggenhart* that the Congress could not regulate children's work hours even if the goods that they made were shipped interstate. The Court relied on a historic distinction between commerce—shipping across state lines—and manufacturing that is wholly within one state.

By the end of the Great Depression in the 1930s, the court had abandoned the distinction between commerce and manufacturing, and had expanded greatly the regulatory powers of the federal government so that its reach extended to local economic activity.

The **contracts clause** (article 1, section 10, clause 1) prohibited state governments from interfering with rights and obligations of contracts. People were bound to do what they had lawfully agreed to do, or to pay the stated penalties, including losing their property. Fundamental to commercial activity, the right of free contract has been restricted as the legislatures and courts agreed that other social interests sometimes outweighed it. Restrictions on child labor violate the letter of a right to free contract, but most Americans agree with this infringement.

Another important imposition on the right of free contract came when the Supreme Court in *Ogden v. Saunders* (1827) said that states could write their own bankruptcy laws (a power that had been reserved to but unused by the federal government). In 1898 and again in 1978, the U.S. Congress passed bankruptcy laws that specified more liberal conditions under which debtors could seek relief from their creditors. "Relief" meant that they would not have to give up everything they owned if they were deemed bankrupt—if their debts were greater than their assets. Other impositions on rights of free contract include a minimum wage and government restrictions on hours of adult labor.

The commerce clause gave the federal government power to regulate the rates and routes of "common carriers" working across state lines. A common carrier is a firm that offers transport services to the general public. Therefore, government regulated water and rail traffic in the 1800s and later trucking and air traffic in the 1900s. This was traditional economic regulation or **rate and route regulation**.

Less clear was the extent to which the federal government had a constitutional right to regulate health and safety conditions, and to impose economic equality. Broad authority could be found in the constitutional grant of the "Power to . . . provide for . . . the general welfare of the United States," but for many years the courts held in check the implied **police powers** in respect of rights of private property and constitutional reservations of powers to the states. Nevertheless, during the middle and late 1900s, the federal government increased its oversight of occupational health and safety, consumer product safety, and environmental quality. The federal government also increased its control of health care for the poor and elderly, through Medicaid and Medicare. Furthermore, it mandated equal pay for equal work.

Source: *Oxford Companion to the Supreme Court* (Cambridge: Oxford University Press, 1992), citing several articles.

Exhibit 10.1: Government Expenditures as a Percentage of Total U.S. Economic Activity*

Year	1929	1944	1959	1974	1989
All Government Expenditures	10.1%	54.3%	25.8%	29.5%	32.5%
Government Transfer Payments	0.9%	1.4%	5.5%	10.4%	11.9%
Government Defense Spending	-	46.3%	8.9%	5.2%	5.5%
Non-defense Gov't Purchases	-	4.8%	10.2%	13.7%	13.3%

*Total U.S. economic activity is measured as gross domestic product, the sum of all public and private spending.

Source: James Gwartney and Richard Stroup, *Introduction to Economics: The Wealth and Poverty of Nations* (New York: Dryden, 1994), reporting on the *Economic Report of the President*.

with, for example, student loans and other tuition assistance. It also supports businesses with subsidies and tax breaks.

Exhibit 10.1 shows, for instance, that government spending on national defense became relatively less important in the U.S. economy over time. World War II inflated defense spending for 1944, but more recently defense spending has fallen from about 10 percent of economic activity in the 1960s to about 5 percent in the 1980s and 90s.

Economic Functions of Government

People's opinions of the economic functions of government tend to fall into three rough groups: idealistic, realistic, and cynical. Idealists about government think that it has superpowers to correct all economic wrongs and promote the social interest, if only the right political party or economic system is in place. Cynics, at the other extreme, express primarily negative views about the evils of government excess and its tendency to promote its own interests rather than the public interest.

The realistic view assesses government's true potential to promote social welfare and its tendency to be corrupted for private gain. A realist recognizes the need for government, while watching to ensure that its power is directed toward and limited to appropriate functions.

Government's functions can be grouped as follows into **six categories**: protecting, mediating, regulating, distributing, supplementing, and stabilizing. Not all economists or policy makers agree that each category deserves equal consideration, but let's consider them all here.

Protecting

Government **protects the people** by defending individual life, policing property laws, and defending the nation from foreign aggression. It also may protect workers against unsafe work conditions or the public against the pollution of a private firm. The U.S. federal government also has protected the civil rights and safety of minorities against the unconstitutional laws of a state and the power of a dominant majority. An important environmental consideration is that the government is responsible for protecting people against pollution that spills outside the control of business and onto the general public.

- **Six governmental functions:**
  1) protecting
  2) mediating
  3) regulating
  4) redistributing
  5) supplementing
  6) stabilizing

Mediating

While policing the economy, government also **mediates disputes**. A mediator hears disputes and reconciles the interests of the parties involved with existing law. It is one thing to prosecute a thief by gathering evidence of a crime and reaching a verdict, or to award a settlement when one person has caused obvious damage to another's property. It is quite another to mediate a dispute about who owned the property in the first place or whether a damage or injury occurred at all. Civil courts mediate disputes about contracts, property rights, and responsibility for damages.

A democratic government also mediates disputes among interest groups and parties in the nation as to which policies to pursue. Government must mediate among the interests of racial groups, between those who desire economic freedom and those who desire economic equality and security, and between those who want a strong or a weak national defense. Government also mediates disputes between owners and workers, ending strikes when needed.

Can Government Mediate and Protect Fairly?

Cynics question whether government can ever mediate fairly between interest groups. In the 1970s and 1980s, a group of critical legal scholars, writing from a radical political perspective, raised the question in articles published in U.S. law school journals. Following Marx, they claimed that legislatures write laws and the courts interpret them to protect property interests. Furthermore, their studies showed that poor people get less than equal justice under the law, suffering more severe punishment in criminal courts, for example, than people with more wealth.

The ideas of Judge Richard Posner and others in the Chicago tradition of law and economics opposed the critical legal scholars' perspective. They argued that the common law has certainly developed over the years to protect the interests of property. Contract, property, and tort laws are written to maximize the value of wealth, which benefits all of society by preventing activities that destroy socially beneficial private wealth.

Must Government Alone Mediate and Protect?

The rise of private arbitration and private security services in the United States shows that free people do not always rely on government. Recent work in economic history shows that formal private arbitration actually arose in Europe during the growth of commerce in the late medieval period. Many contracts today include provisions that disputes will be resolved by private arbitrators. Corporations, private colleges, apartment buildings, and gated communities all routinely hire their own security services.

Why not rely on government to mediate disputes and protect people? Because government services may be inefficient and slow, judges may be ill-informed about the details of technical commercial disputes, and local police may be overworked and underfunded. A lengthy delay in a court case or in a response of public police forces impose their own costs on those affected. Under such conditions, the benefits of private mediation and security may outweigh the costs.

Regulating

Mediating disputes sometimes means **regulating certain commercial activities** to protect the interests of one group against another. Governments regulate utilities such as electric and telephone companies, banking and finance, and nuclear-energy use. Governments also regulate all commerce in broader ways such as through fair-trade laws and restrictions on child labor.

The SEC and FASB

The Securities and Exchange Commission (SEC) has responsibility for regulating activity in stock and bond markets. Yet it exercises its power with restraint, preferring to allow financial firms to regulate themselves through the work of internal auditors and certified public accountants. Public accountants regulate themselves through their own professional associations and through their rule-making body, the Financial Accounting Standards Board. When such private self-regulation breaks down, the SEC steps in to impose appropriate financial reporting and conduct in stock and bond exchanges.

OSHA Under Fire

The Occupational Safety and Health Administration (OSHA) regulates the workplace with responsibility for eliminating threats to employee health and safety. OSHA established regulations for air quality in coal mines and forced companies to install ventilation equipment. It sets and enforces safety standards in factories, such as requiring that presses for stamping out parts have safety doors and double-start buttons to prevent harm to workers by keeping their hands free from the machine's moving parts.

Critics, however, have calculated the costs of OSHA's regulations and have found, for instance, that the costs to save a life through safety regulations are excessively high. A study found that benzene regulations probably saved a few lives each year, but, after forcing firms to pay for the safety measures, the cost was about $33 billion dollars per life (Rhoades 1985; reprinted in *Annual Editions Microeconomics* 1993, 8). How many more lives could have been saved by diverting the $33 billion in safety expenses to programs providing prenatal care to poor mothers and health care and food to their babies?

Redistributing

Democratic governments, in reconciling the interests of the rich and poor, regularly decide to **redistribute income and wealth**. Policies increase equality or establish a welfare safety net. Property owners tend to resent government's distributive function because it conflicts with the function of protecting their property rights. Redistributing income also has long-run effects on work effort and overall economic efficiency. Designing redistributive programs that don't reduce work effort is a challenge.

Government Activism

The philosophy of redistribution rests on a **liberal progressive view** that government should intervene in the market when it can make people better off overall. Taking a dollar from a rich person and giving it to a poor person will in theory hurt the rich person only a little and help the poor person greatly. The liberal progressive view encourages government activism in redistribution and regulation. Critics of such activism say that it often bends or breaks constitutional limits on the federal government's powers.

Government as Parent

The redistributive and protective functions of government may lead it to adopt a **paternalistic attitude**, protecting individuals from themselves. As an example, the U.S. government restricts how support for the poor may be used. Government subsidies to the poor may be used to pay for food and housing, but not for beer and cigarettes. In fact, the government restricts which foods a food stamp recipient can buy, excluding for example certain imported foods. (The government also taxes some behaviors that it thinks individuals would be best to limit. Taxes on cigarettes and alcohol have been known for years as "sin taxes.")

Supplementing

A fifth function of government is to supplement the functions of the free market. As Expansion Point 10.4 explains, government provides for certain **public goods**, or what Adam Smith called "public works." A market economy may not provide a sufficient quantity of such goods because private suppliers cannot recoup their costs, since their benefits are hard to contain or are difficult to price for a private profit. Public goods like roads and canals have **two attributes** that distinguish them from other goods: non-rival consumption and nonexclusive consumption.

- **Liberal progressive view of government:** policy should actively intervene in markets to increase overall social welfare, including regulating commerce and redistributing income

- **Government paternalism:** government acts as parent to its citizens, trying to protect them from their own bad decisions

- **Two attributes of public goods:**
  1) non-rival consumption
  2) nonexclusive consumption

Broadcast television signals illustrate both of the characteristics of a public good. First, consumers are not rivals competing for a scarce supply of the signal. If I put up an antenna and receive the signal, this does not reduce the amount of television signal available to your house and to others. Second,

Expansion Point 10.4: What Did Adam Smith Say about Public Works?

In his *Wealth of Nations* (1776, book V, chapter 1, part 3), Adam Smith explained that the government was responsible to provide for a certain class of goods. These few quotes tell what he meant and tell a bit about how such works should be financed to best provide for their upkeep.

> The third and last duty of the sovereign or commonwealth is that of erecting and maintaining those publick institutions and those publick works, which, though they may be in the highest degree advantageous to a great society, are, however, of such a nature, that the profit could never repay the expence to any individual or small number of individuals, and which it, therefore, cannot be expected that any individual or small number of individuals should erect or maintain. The performance of this duty requires, too, very different degrees of expense in the different periods of society.
>
> After the publick institutions and publick works necessary for the defence of society, and for the administration of justice, both of which have already been mentioned, the other works and institutions of this kind are chiefly those for facilitating commerce of the society, and those for promoting the instruction of the people.

What institutions and works would promote commerce but not be profitable for private investors? Smith singled out projects such as "good roads, bridges, navigable canals, [and] harbours." Those projects that would require ongoing, careful maintenance should, Smith thought, be built at public expense but then operated at a profit by a private person, not a public commissioner. The reason was that private operation would provide the needed incentive to keep the work in repair.

> In several different parts of Europe the toll or lock-duty upon a canal is the property of the private persons, whose private interest obliges them to keep up the canal. If it is not kept in tolerable order, the navigation necessarily ceases altogether, and along with it the whole profit which they can make by the tolls. If those tolls were put under the management of commissioners, who had themselves no interest in them, they might be less attentive to the maintenance of the works which produced them.

Since a "high road" was not usable if its maintenance were neglected, Smith thought that high roads should not be left in private care because the "proprietors . . . might neglect altogether the repair of the road, and yet continue to levy very nearly the same tolls."

Where trade requires protection from thieves, Smith thought that the government ought to promote the commerce by providing the means for defense. Costs of the defense should be passed on in the form of a tax to the traders who benefited. Smith said that the first tariffs on imported goods supposedly helped to pay for such defense: "The protection of trade, in general, from pirates and freebooters, is said to have given occasion to the first institution of the duties of customs."

Source: Adam Smith, *An Inquiry into the Nature and Causes of the Wealth of Nations*, Glasgow ed. Edited by R.H. Campbell and A.S. Skinner (Indianapolis: Liberty Fund, 1981 [1776]).

the broadcast company originally had great difficulty excluding anyone with an antenna and television from receiving the signal. Now they can scramble signals if they choose, but without such equipment, the television company could not effectively exclude those who did not want to pay for it.

The two peculiarities of public goods cause two effects that limit their profitability and encourage government intervention: **free-riding behavior** of people asked to pay for a public good, and **spillover benefits** in production of a public good. These two problems lead certain economists to claim that government should provide them and pay for them with taxes. That was Adam Smith's point with canals and other "public works" (Expansion Point 10.4). Building them was the government's job to be paid for with taxes, but maintaining them was more of a private good, payable by tolls. Here are more details on these effects.

• Two reasons for government to provide public goods:
1) free-riding behavior
2) spillover benefits

Free Riders

Non-exclusivity of the public good gives rise to the free-rider problem. If a private company, for example, were to ask who wanted to pay for a public good such as national defense, many people would seek a free ride on others. They know that if the company does raise the funds to pay for defense, the company cannot defend everyone but them.

Free riding, a form of opportunism, is reduced if people have a strong moral commitment to sharing common burdens and to doing their civic duty. If, however, free riding is as extensive as many economists suspect, then the amount of money raised from contributions to the project will not be adequate to pay for the socially desirable level of the good. Then, government can use its coercive power to tax people to pay for the public good.

Spillover Benefits of Public Goods

Another way to describe the non-rival aspect of consuming public goods is to say that they provide **spillover benefits**. If you buy a traditional liberal-arts education for yourself, all of society will benefit from your increased self-control, learning, and enhanced moral and civic character traits. You can't capture and charge others for all of the benefits that your education provides, because some benefits spill over into society.

• Spillover benefits: producing certain goods for one person creates benefits that spill over to other people at zero or very low extra cost

Just as spillover costs of pollution lead to a price that is too low and an output that is too high (see chapter 7), spillover benefits of non-rival consumption lead to a price that is too high for the individual consumer and an output that is too low. Government can help in theory by, once again, taxing people and providing more education and other public goods with spillover benefits.

The State-Socialist Solution to Market Imperfections

In socialist nations, the government does not just supplement the market. It replaces market functions partially or fully by nationalizing industry and agriculture. The theory of socialism is that the market is so defective that merely supplementing it will not correct its fundamental defects. Therefore, command socialism, for instance, takes over most functions of the market, including production, pricing, and distribution of output.

The Free Market Solution

Chicago-school economists such as Ronald Coase contend that institutions of the free market can overcome the difficulties of free-riding behavior and spillover benefits. Lighthouses provide a public good (non-rival and nonexclusive consumption of the light). Yet in England's past, private lighthouses have operated successfully.

Honey bees provide spillover benefits to apple orchard owners, fertilizing trees. Orchards also provide spillover benefits to beekeepers. Yet government is not needed to arrange for apple orchards and beekeeping. Orchard owners contract with beekeepers to have the hives located in the orchards where the bees can pollinate the tree flowers and the trees can provide nectar.

Stabilizing

- **Business cycle:** fluctuations in economic activity, employment, and income

The sixth function of government is to stabilize the economy when it is subject to macroeconomic fluctuations. The macro-economy is the overall economy, measured by summing the money value of national economic activity. The **business cycle** is the tendency of output, employment, and income in market economies to fluctuate over time. Stabilization policy requires that government use control of the money supply, taxes, and spending to reduce economic fluctuations. This perspective is called Keynesian economics, a hotly disputed idea since its introduction in 1936 (see more on John Maynard Keynes in chapter 3).

Exhibit 10.2 illustrates the business cycle and the stabilizing function of government. Left to itself, a market economy will supposedly grow unsteadily along the fluctuating path. The ideal government stabilization policy will allow the economy to grow along a smooth path, without the fluctuations.

Critics of this view, such as Milton Friedman, contend that government itself contributes to the instability of an otherwise stable market economy. Policy lags in curing a contraction in economic activity, for example, may not stimulate the economy until it is already recovering on its own. Friedman contended that such lags in government policy *aggravate* the cycle.

The controversies over stabilization policy and the other functions of government point to deeper philosophical debates about the nature of government. Let's conclude this introduction to government in the economy by reviewing the major viewpoints.

Exhibit 10.2: The Business Cycle and Stabilization Policy

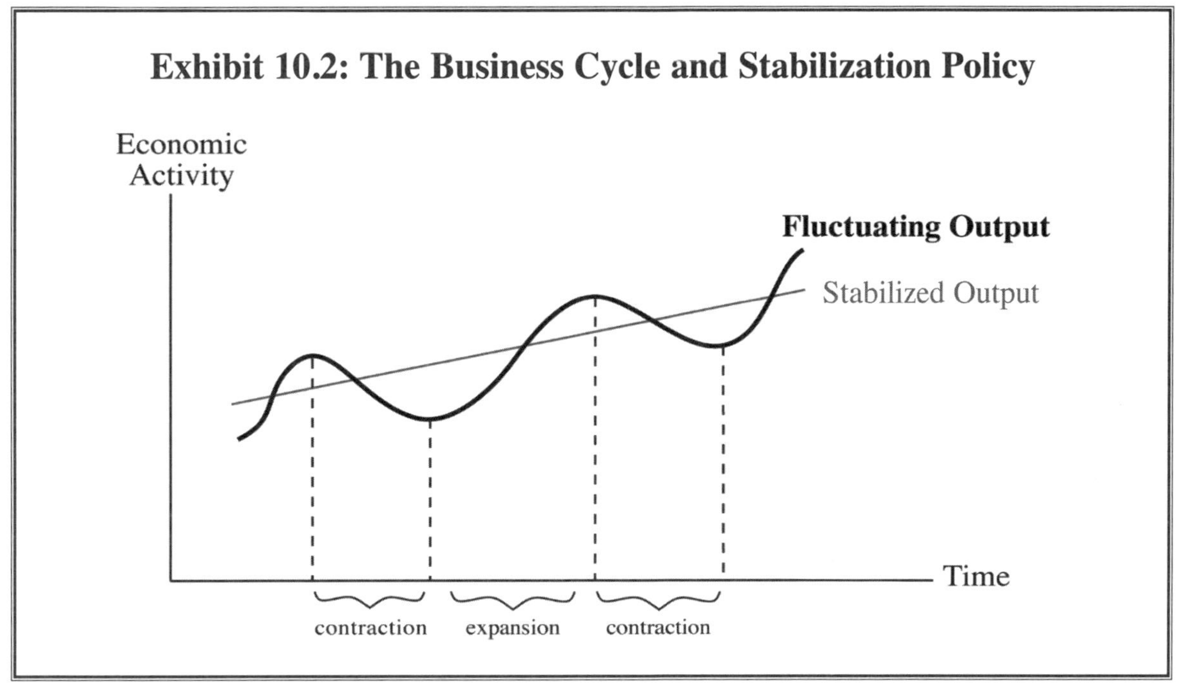

On the Nature of Government and the Economy

On the surface, the debate about the economic effects of deficit spending seems like a mere technical debate about how the economy works. In truth, it is part of a broader, more philosophical, and more important debate about the nature of government itself. Here is a brief review of several important perspectives.

Public-Interest View

Those who are most idealistic about government take a public-interest view of government. They assume that government can (1) understand the problems afflicting society, (2) design and implement policies to correct those problems, and (3) maintain the stance of a benevolent dictator who will always act in the public interest. While the market economy has many defects, government can reform the market economy.

- **Public-interest view:** politicians and bureaucrats understand social problems, implement effective policies, and always act in the public interest

In the United States, those labeled as "liberals" and "progressives" tend toward the public-interest view. They rely on government policy to solve problems of racial inequality, poverty, and income inequality, while rejecting the libertarian emphasis on economic freedom. Progressives have found a popular theme with their emphasis on increasing economic security. While most Americans surveyed in 1999 did not like the idea of more government programs in general, they did favor specific programs such as Medicare and Social Security. Americans resist government restraints but they welcome government-funded insurance.

Many liberals and progressives who are steadfastly realistic and even pessimistic about human nature in private business take an idealistic view of government. Yet, in many countries, including Japan and the United States, people who run private for-profit businesses also take turns in public service. Does public service change their orientation from self-interest to the public interest? The public-choice view says, "No."

Public-Choice View

• **Public-choice view:** politicians and bureaucrats pursue policies that promote their own interests

Public choice refers to the government policies that determine how public funds, as opposed to private household or business funds, will be gathered and spent. Special interest groups demand public programs and politicians supply them in exchange for votes and campaign contributions. Public-choice theory expresses one of the more pessimistic views of government because it applies the principle of self-interested behavior to private citizen and public servant alike.

According to public-choice theory, the politicians who direct government as public servants are, in fact, not serving the general public well at all. Public-choice theorists describe politicians as selfish opportunists who will take what they can get, give away to friends what they are able, and provide what they must to special-interest groups to win their support during elections. Government bureaucrats are no better, making decisions that are always in their own best interests but rarely in the public's best interest.

Why is it that self-interested behavior is so beneficial in private enterprise but so damaging in public service? It is because of the tremendous power that government coercion gives to politicians and bureaucrats. In private enterprise, exchange is voluntary. Public officials can compel payments and participation.

Political Processes

Public-choice theorists highlight the details of the processes by which politicians make public policy and bureaucrats conduct it. Special-interest groups petition their representatives, and politicians trade votes through pork-barrel politics and logrolling. That is how government makes public choices in a democracy. **Pork-barrel projects** are those expenditures that benefit a particular political district. **Logrolling** is the process by which politicians agree to trade votes for each other's pet projects.

• **Pork-barrel projects:** public expenditures that benefit a particular political district

• **Logrolling:** politicians agree to trade votes for each other's pet projects

What's Wrong with Pork?

What is wrong with politicians voting public funds for projects that benefit narrow interest groups or particular regions of a state or nation? Here are several reasons. First, because power is distributed unequally in the government, pork-barrel projects are often distributed unequally. Senators who lead or serve on powerful committees can assure that projects are directed to their states. Many defense contractors chose to locate near Atlanta,

Georgia, allegedly because of the ability of former Senator Sam Nunn to deliver defense appropriations to them. Senator Robert Byrd publicly promised and delivered multimillions of dollars in federal spending to West Virginia.

Second, even if pork-barrel projects were evenly distributed, they would not necessarily be economically efficient. Efficient public spending requires that benefits from a project at least outweigh the costs. Let's say, as an example, you would like a recreational lake near your town. Let's say that the lake would bring a total value of $700,000 to the area, as economists measure economic value. The lake is a bad economic value because its cost is greater than its benefits.

You, however, decide to advocate for the lake because it would benefit you personally. A lake would increase the revenues you earn in your local business that is near the proposed recreation area. Through political pressure, you and others persuade your Congressman and two Senators to propose a matching federal grant of $500,000. With their combined clout, Congress passes a bill with your pet project attached. Together with local funds, the federal grant will build a $1 million lake that will be worth only $700,000 to the region. But people in the region will be thrilled because their local government paid only $500,000. Locally, the lake is economically sound. Nationally, money is wasted on projects whose costs may regularly outweigh their benefits. Who pays the extra costs? Taxpayers in other districts.

New Institutionalist View

New institutionalist economists are more realistic about government than those holding the public-interest view and less pessimistic than public-choice theorists. They examine the historical development of governmental institutions and find that certain governments and rules promote economic efficiency, and others discourage efficiency. For example, Andrew Stone, Brian Levy, and Ricardo Paredes (1996, 95-128) found that Brazil's formal commercial rules were much less efficient than Chile's.

• **New Institutionalist view:** certain constitutional systems and policy rules are efficient, promoting economic progress, while others are inefficient

According to the new institutionalist view, one defect of the public-interest and public-choice views of government intervention is that they explain the reasons for regulation without regard to historical change. The U.S. government, for example, instituted tariffs on sugar imports to provide public revenues, not to protect special interests, as the public-choice view would suggest. Anne Krueger (1996, 169-218; see also the editors' comments, 166-168) contends that no great sugar interest even existed for the government to protect with the first tariff in 1796. A public-choice explanation confuses cause and effect and confuses the current policies to continue sugar protection with previous policies to implement them. Sugar-tariff protections promoted the rise of a U.S. sugar industry, and bureaucratic experts, not a powerful sugar lobby, now control the program.

Institutionalists contend that market activity and informal commercial institutions will adjust to make the best of existing formal institutions. Krueger (1996), for example, found that U.S. sugar tariffs induced the market to develop substitutes for sugar, such as artificial sweeteners and high-fructose corn syrup. If producers need sweeteners, the market will supply it despite government interventions. Stone, Levy, and Paredes (1996) found inefficiency in Brazil's formal government institutions, but they also found that informal private institutions of commerce adapted. While Brazilian justice against business customers who write bad checks is slow and not as strict as Chilean justice is, the garment industries in the two countries are nearly equally efficient. Brazilian garment firms readily extend credit to business customers through a private system of credit reports that relies on the value of good reputation, rather than on the remedies of the courts. The dominant institution is an informal rule that vendors should always protect their credit reputations. Private networks of traders will impose private constraints that encourage traders to limit their opportunism, even when government cannot.

Marxist-Radical View

Karl Marx, a vigorous critic of nineteenth-century capitalism, argued that the ruling class of capitalists controls law and government. Capitalists use law and government to exploit labor. Through law, capitalists justify their ownership of the means of production. Through government, capitalists enforce their control of productive equipment and suppression of the working class.

- **Marxist-Radical view:** government serves the ruling capitalist class, keeping laborers in subjugation; reform of existing forms is useless; change requires revolution

Marxists have not favored progressive reforms of democratic capitalist governments. Such a system, they believe, is improperly founded on the rights of property and the interests of capital. They favor, instead, revolution and violent overthrow of the existing power structure. In its place, a socialist state would initially impose public ownership of productive equipment. The Marxist hope, however, was that the state would later "wither away." The history of Marxism has so far shown this to be only a dream.

Libertarian View

A libertarian perspective emphasizes economic, political, religious, and other liberties as the highest goals. While Marxists believe that coercive economic control will usher in an ideal communist society, libertarians hold to an opposite extreme. Government coercion rarely can be justified, except in protecting private liberties and property.

An extreme libertarian perspective also rejects the view of liberal progressives who think that they can increase social welfare with paternalistic and coercive government policies. Liberal progressives want government to liberate people from the slavery and insecurity of a purely private market economy. Libertarians believe that government intervention in the economy enslaves people, as suggested by the title of Friedrich Hayek's book, *The Road to Serfdom* (1944).

Libertarians believe that to increase social welfare, government policy should be based as much as possible on voluntary participation by citizens. To believe in voluntary assessment and payment of taxes, however, seems far-fetched. The libertarian perspective seems to idealize the individual, ignoring a propensity toward opportunistic behavior. Libertarians respond that they have faith in voluntary arrangements among free individuals, coupled with private methods of agreement enforcement. What they fear most is the unconstrained power of a coercive government, which also will tend toward public opportunism.

Chapter Summary

1. Government is distinctive because it can legitimately use coercive force. The basis for government power has varied historically from the divine right of the sovereign and sheer might to the social compact.

2. The rule of law limits the coercive power of government to those uses formally prescribed in a constitution. The *Magna Charta* was an early example.

3. The American government is constitutional in form. The U.S. Constitution, the Bill of Rights, and other amendments specify the powers of and limits on the federal government.

4. Economic powers of the U.S. government include eminent domain, but the government must give just compensation under the takings clause of the Constitution. Other limits on government powers include the separation of powers among the three branches, the reservation of unspecified powers to the states, and political competition.

5. Government intervention in the U.S. economy has gradually increased. Especially from the 1860s to the 1920s, *laissez-faire* constitutionalism ruled Supreme Court decisions. After the 1920s, government powers increased with an expansive reading of the commerce clause, and a narrow reading of the contracts clause.

6. Between 1929 and 1989, government's share of economic activity in the United States has grown from about 10 percent to about 32 percent. Much of the growth in government spending has actually been for transfer payments, which buy no goods or services.

7. The functions of government include protecting life and property, mediating disputes, regulating commerce, redistributing income, supplementing the market economy by providing public goods, and stabilizing the macroeconomy.

8. Justifying government activism in the economy relies on a liberal-progressive philosophy and the peculiar nature of public goods (non-rival and nonexclusive consumption).

9. All economists do not favor pursuing all six goals. Milton Friedman and other economists of the Chicago school have argued that voluntary cooperation in the market solves many problems, while government intervention causes many more.

10. The public-interest (liberal-progressive) view of government competes with public-choice, new institutionalist, Marxist, and libertarian views. Each draws different conclusions about the potential for government intervention to increase social welfare.

PROBLEMS FOR PRACTICE

10.1 "All governments have power. A democratic, constitutional government has authority in certain matters, a king has dominion, a socialist government planning agency has command, and the local magistrate has jurisdiction." Use a collegiate dictionary or a thesaurus to evaluate how accurate this statement is. Have the various words for government power been used correctly?

10.2* How can imposing the rule of law increase economic efficiency? Why would placing limits on government's ability to intervene in the economy make economic outcomes better? What perspective do answers to these questions assume?

10.3 Did the Supreme Court's ruling in *Dolan v. City of Tigard* (Expansion Point 10.2) expand or contract a government's power of eminent domain in the United States? Explain the legal principles that decided the case.

10.4 Rank the functions of government by importance, according to your view. Explain your ranking, including what you think government should do and why. If you make moral arguments for government, be sure to explain the foundation for your moral prescriptions. If economic efficiency is important, explain how it can be achieved.

10.5 How is a public good different from other goods? Which aspects of a college education (lecturing, memorizing, testing, discussing, tutoring, and advising) are public goods and which are private?

10.6 What are the contrasting views of liberal-progressive activism in the economy and Chicago-school preferences for voluntary cooperation in the free market to solve various economic problems? Review the commentary on all of the functions of government and create a list of the two perspectives. List activist reasons for government to intervene and where. Then list Chicago-school responses.

10.7 In your own words, explain the different perspectives on the nature of government (public-interest, public-choice, Marxist, etc.). Your answer will expand on your understanding of the last question.

For your portfolio:.
10.8 Find a copy of one of the following and examine it for its economic implications: (1) Deuteronomy in the Bible, (2) the *Magna Charta* (1215), (3) Samuel Rutherford's *Lex Rex* (1644), (4) the Declaration of Independence, or (5) the U.S. Constitution. All but Rutherford's book should be available on electronic encyclopedias. Write or type your comments on one side of a sheet of paper.

10.9 Research the various perspectives about the nature of government and the economy. Interview teachers, friends, and family as to their personal perspective and why they hold it. Find readings on each view and briefly summarize key ideas.

For class discussion:
10.10 Has the evolving constitutional basis for government intervention been beneficial to the U.S. economy overall? Has it increased efficiency or equity?

10.11 Be prepared to discuss answers to 10.4. Also, which functions do you feel are inappropriate? Why?

10.12 Which of the perspectives on the nature of government do you favor most and which do you favor least? Explain in comparison to the other views.

See Answer Key for hints/answers to starred (*) questions.

SECTION II

Introduction to Microeconomics

Consumption, Production, and Price Theory

Microeconomics explains individual behavior. It is the foundation for explaining market activity. In this section, we review only a few of the details of the principles of microeconomics. Chapter 11 explores consumer choice in spending a limited budget on various goods and services, as well as the factors that influence those choices. Chapter 12 explains the nature of production as the creation of wealth. Chapter 13 reviews details of price theory, including the causes of changes in market prices and quantities exchanged, the meaning and significance of elasticity of demand and elasticity of supply, and the influence of market structure on the determination of market price and quantity.

Chapter 11

Consumption

Buying and Using Products

What this chapter will help you think about:

1. In what way is consumption the most important economic activity?
2. What is the consumer's budget constraint?
3. What are the sources and uses of household income?
4. How do consumers economize?
5. What is the relationship between diminishing marginal utility and consumer demand?
6. What is the utility-maximization theory of rational consumer behavior and what are its implications?
7. What are some of the psychological and social aspects of consumer behavior?
8. What are some of the controversies about consumer behavior?

Consumption is the fundamental economic activity, motivating to a great extent all other economic activities. In an ideal world where fruit falls from trees, grains and vegetables grow wild for each person to harvest, climate is mild, and people's wants constrained, production or distribution need not be extensive. Given their need to eat to live, however, humans could not inhabit such a world without consuming the fruits, grains, and so on.

Consuming goods and services means using them to satisfy wants and needs. When you eat a hamburger, you are consuming beef, wheat, tomatoes, and the direct services of someone's labor (perhaps your own) and cooking equipment. You are also consuming indirectly the services of countless other people on the farm, over the road, at the slaughterhouse, and at the local store.

- **Consumer preferences** summarize people's desires and expectations about how useful goods will be in satisfying needs and wants.

Our **preferences** rank our various needs and wants according to importance. Our preferences specify what we like about each good and service available to us, and how useful we expect the products to be in satisfying our needs and wants. We have needs for food, but we may have preferences for steak over chicken, and so on. People's preferences for consumer goods and services are shaped by their personality, family status, and a host of other economic, psychological, and social factors. Scarcity, however, always constrains our ability to satisfy our preferences. A family case study will illustrate.

Consumption and Scarcity: Cutting Costs with the Jones Family

Economists assume that the goal of human consumption is to maximize utility. The **utility** of goods and services is a theoretical measure of how well they meet needs and satisfy wants. Since needs and wants can be defined in many ways, utility is a fairly flexible concept. When economists assume that consumers maximize utility, they reflect their belief that consumers carefully consider what they buy, why they buy it, and how happy it makes them. Utility-maximizing consumers will act rationally, based on their own individual preferences.

• **Utility:** a theoretical measure of how well products satisfy needs and wants

Scarcity affects consumption activity and forces consumers to economize. While consumers would like more of many goods, they face limits on their abilities to get and use them. A hypothetical study of the Jones family's budget will illustrate the limits and economizing choices facing consumers. Not all families are as traditional as the Joneses, but all confront scarcity and choices.

Scarcity Imposes a Budget Constraint

Scarcity imposes limits on a family, called a **budget constraint**. In a monetary economy, the family has limited income, limited savings from which to draw funds, and limited ability to borrow for present consumption. With these limited funds, it wants to buy seemingly unlimited products at prices that the family cannot directly change. The family hopes that these products will make its members happier (but that of course is subject to debate). A simple equation summarizes the budget constraint:

• **Budget Constraint:** consumers have limited income to buy products at given prices

Income - Saving + Borrowing = money available to buy products

Family income depends upon its earnings from selling labor services and other resources. Money paid for each product equals the price of that good times the quantity bought. Adding up all these amounts for the year equals annual **consumer expenditures**.

Consuming a good differs from making a consumer expenditure. Buying a new refrigerator is a consumer expenditure. Using the refrigerator every day provides a flow of consumption services. **Consuming** the refrigerator is using it. Buying an ice-cream cone happens at the same time as consuming, making them harder to distinguish—if you don't eat fast, the ice cream melts. Since economists have more data on consumer expenditures than on actual consumption, they analyze expenditures more thoroughly, using them to measure consumption indirectly.

• **Consuming goods:** using products

• **Consumer expenditure:** buying products

While the above equation helps us to understand the budget constraint, families don't usually write out their economic problem with algebra. But they don't ignore the budget constraint.

• **A family budget** shows sources and uses of income.

Most express it as a **family budget**, showing yearly or perhaps monthly sources and uses of income. Exhibit 11.1 shows a sample budget for the Jones family of four, earning $44,900 per year.

The Jones family earns income from wages and salaries, and from interest on savings (but it has no shares of corporate stock that pay dividends). It also receives a transfer payment from Social Security for a disabled child. A government transfer does not pay for any services rendered by the family. It redistributes income, in this case to a family with special needs as defined in the Social Security law.

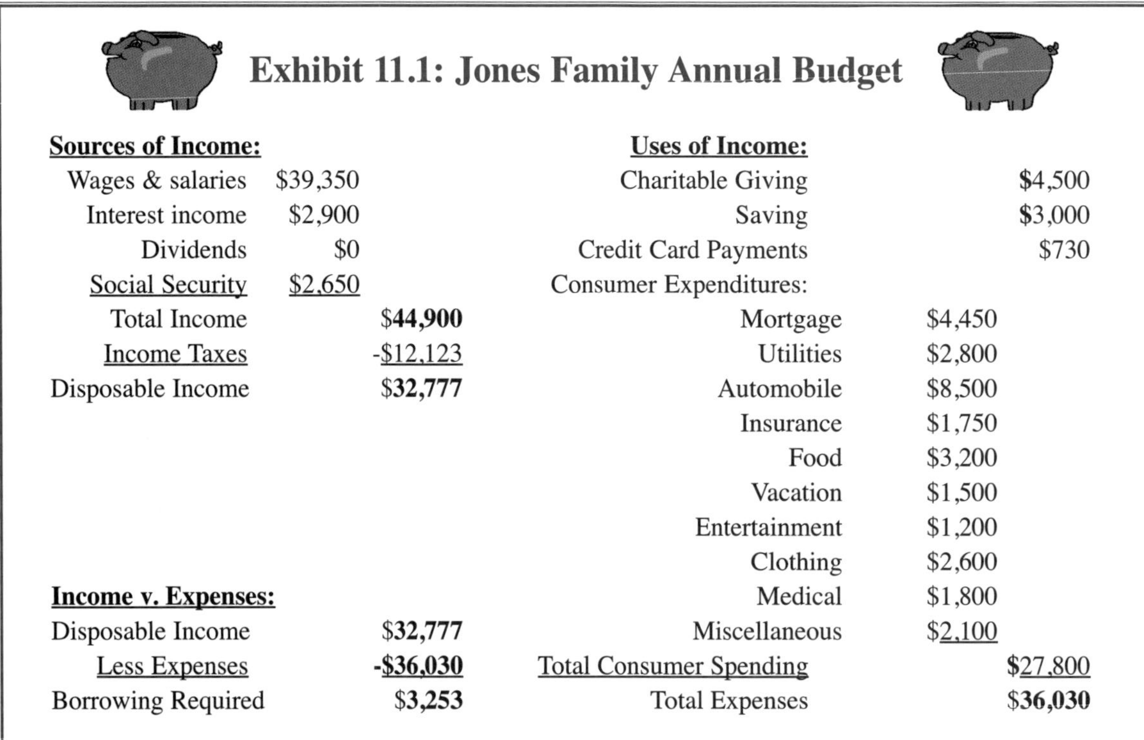

Exhibit 11.1: Jones Family Annual Budget

Sources of Income:		
Wages & salaries	$39,350	
Interest income	$2,900	
Dividends	$0	
Social Security	$2,650	
Total Income		**$44,900**
Income Taxes		-$12,123
Disposable Income		**$32,777**
Income v. Expenses:		
Disposable Income		**$32,777**
Less Expenses		**-$36,030**
Borrowing Required		**$3,253**

Uses of Income:		
Charitable Giving		$4,500
Saving		$3,000
Credit Card Payments		$730
Consumer Expenditures:		
Mortgage	$4,450	
Utilities	$2,800	
Automobile	$8,500	
Insurance	$1,750	
Food	$3,200	
Vacation	$1,500	
Entertainment	$1,200	
Clothing	$2,600	
Medical	$1,800	
Miscellaneous	$2,100	
Total Consumer Spending		$27,800
Total Expenses		**$36,030**

On the expenditure side, the Jones family follows its religious convictions by planning to give about 10 percent of its income to the religious organization to which it belongs and to other charities. Islam calls such charitable giving *Zakat*, referring to how gifts to the poor "purify" the giver. Judaism and Christianity call it "tithes" and "offerings." Tithe refers to giving a tenth of income.

At one time, paying the tithe to a church was more common than it is today. European nations began enforcing the tithe during the sixteenth century. The legal practice lasted in France until 1789 and in England until 1836. The average American family does not give 10 percent to charity, but many do give. Most private colleges, for example, depend on charitable giving to educate students, whose tuition payments cover only a fraction of the costs of college.

The Jones family's planned consumption expenditures are only about 62 percent of its before-tax income. Taxes alone take 27 percent. Saving, paying back debts, and charitable giving take up 18 percent (with borrowing accounting for the excess 7 percent, for those who are still counting).

The Jones family's expected income does not fully cover expected taxes, savings, gifts, and planned expenditures. They must borrow $3,253 to cover the shortfall of income. If the family borrows now, it will have less money to spend in the following years, as it pays back its consumer debt. If the family chooses not to borrow, it will have to economize now. What should it do? Cut spending? Take on a part-time job or work overtime to increase income? Let's analyze the economizing decisions that they face, recognizing that this is an idealistic example of an American household, with many families facing far more severe choices.

Economizing to Stay within Budget

When the Jones family meets to discuss its annual budget, on the agenda are several decisions they can make: work more, buy fewer things, buy more intelligently, and reassess saving and giving. Their discussions will illustrate just a few important aspects of the economic analysis of consumption, such as the work-leisure tradeoff, brand loyalty, and substitutability in consumption.

Work-Leisure Decisions

Decisions about work and leisure directly affect household income. Mr. Jones offers to work overtime, but the rest of the family complains that he is already too busy. While they would like the extra money, Mr. Jones needs more time with the family and needs more leisure to reduce stress in his life.

Mrs. Jones has been thinking about returning to work as a part-time realtor, a job she quit eight years ago to have and raise her three children. That, however, would require buying an extra car, hiring household help when she is out, especially for cleaning and child care in the spring and late summer, when the real estate business is more active. She would also need new clothes, a home office, and a second phone line. They all begin to wonder whether the extra costs would outweigh the benefits, a question addressed in Expansion Point 11.1.

Brand Loyalty and Generic Substitutes

Consumers often act out of habit, going to the same stores, doctors, dentists, and restaurants. When we regularly buy the same brands of all various products, our **brand loyalty** can create tremendous economic value in the popular brands. Henry Sidgwick (1883) commented that such commercial habits save us time by freeing us from the compulsion to waste it shopping around. After a while, though, habit turns to laziness, and we may

Expansion Point 11.1: Are Two Incomes Really Better than One?

The U.S. Labor Department has estimated that a two-worker family with average income loses about 67 percent of its second income to work-related expenses. This does not include child care. What are the extra expenses? Taxes of course, but also costs of paying housekeepers, time lost in getting ready for work and commuting (when you could be working at home instead of paying someone else), money costs of commuting such as having an extra car, costs of clothes for work, and costs of eating out more because of busy schedules. Add to that any child care costs and the extra income disappears rather quickly.

If a family adds $20,000 per year for an extra 40 hours a week for 50 weeks a year, the wage seems to be a respectable **$10 an hour** ($20,000 / 2,000 hours). Actual time worked, however, should also include the 10 extra hours of preparation and commute per week. Now the hourly wage is down to **$8 an hour** ($20,000 / 2,500 hours). That is not all, though. Taxes and money expenses of work eat up 67 percent of the extra income, leaving only $6,600 per year of net income. Then $2,000 of that goes for very modest child care expenses for before-school and after-school care. Now the net wage is down to **$1.84 per hour!**

This same effect occurs when we are working at a second job. I once calculated the gross and net wage for a college teacher who traveled 60 miles a week to teach a night course at a regional university. Earning $2,000 for a course requiring only 45 hours of class contact, the gross wage would have been a surprising **$44 per hour**. Taking out taxes, and adding in travel time, course-prep time, time to read exams, and costs of driving his own car, the wage was more like **$11 per hour**. That is rather low for a professional. Based on this information, the professor decided that time with his family was more important than earning such a modest extra income.

What is the lesson here? When calculating the benefits of earning extra income, you must also calculate the full costs. Consider the direct time on the job *plus* the indirect time as well. You must also make your decision based on net income, not gross income. Good decisions require that you calculate all the relevant costs of an activity and measure whether extra benefits really do exceed extra costs, and by how much.

Source: Andy Dappen, *Shattering the Two-Income Myth* (Brier, WA: Brier Books, 1997), 4-5.

overlook better quality products or lower prices because of ignorance. Once we are offended by a product, however, we may refuse to buy it again and may warn others against it.

Brand-name value can spring from the superior quality of a product, or merely from the habits of customers who buy their usual brand without thinking or who perceive higher quality that does not really exist. Many manufacturers of brand-name products, for instance, make the exact same product, but package it under a different label. According to people who have worked in such companies, this is true of apple juice, disposable diapers, mattresses, and carpet. Ask family and friends to see how common this practice is. Sometimes manufacturers package the exact same product as more expensive “premium brands” *and* less expensive “store brands.” Buying such store brands, therefore, can cut food bills by 20 percent or more, without necessarily sacrificing quality.

When the Jones family deliberated about their shopping habits, they too realized that better comparative shopping might help cut their food bills. Brand-name boxes of raisin bran cereal cost $3.49, while store-brand boxes cost only $2.29 with little or no loss of quality. If they were less picky about buying only brand-name goods, the Joneses estimated that they could save about $640, or about 20% of their budgeted expenses for food.

When it came to buying off-brand clothes, however, the two children were less agreeable. The wrong shoes, for example, could get them laughed out of school, they complained. Mom and Dad suggested that the children should at least watch for sales on the brand-name products they liked. Demand for clothes is higher in season and prices then fall as each season winds down. If they could also time their purchases well and guess what clothes they would be needing next year, they could shop at end-of-the-season sales. This would be easier for the adults to do than the children, because the children were still growing. Their hope was to save perhaps 15 percent of their $2,600 clothing budget, which would be $390.

The economic principle is that consumers can **substitute** one good for another in certain situations, though not always. The more willing consumers are to substitute one good for another, the more responsive they will be to a change in the price of either good. For those who are indifferent between Way Better Peanut Butter and Mr. Peppy Peanut Butter, a higher price of Mr. Peppy will cause them to substitute a jar of Mr. Way Better for Mr. Peppy. A lower price of Mr. Peppy will cause them to buy it again.

• **Substitution:** consumers will switch brands or products when price or quality changes

Necessity or Luxury?

When forced to cut back, most families will cut luxuries first and cut necessities only as a drastic last resort. Of course, what exactly is a necessity is a matter of great debate in American society. Nevertheless, some expenditures are relatively more necessary than others.

Economists know that consumers will also react differently to a price change for a necessity or luxury. If the price of medicine for chronic illness rises, a family will not tend to buy less of such a necessity. If the price of fresh shrimp rises, though, the family may decide that it will cut that luxury. It will also adjust how often it buys products. Maybe a haircut once a month is a necessity, while a haircut every week is a luxury.

The Jones family's next task, then, was to discuss what was necessary and what was a luxury in the budget. They focused first on their planned vacation, two weeks at the seashore in a rented apartment costing $850 for the two weeks. The remaining $650 was for eating out, taking a day cruise on a boat, and other entertainment. They decided that they needed the vacation at the shore in order to relax and have time together, but be away from the demands of work around the house. They would, however, eat out less and trim spending on other extras, cutting the vacation budget to $1,250, and saving $250.

Postponing Consumption

- **Durable goods** provide a flow of services over time.
- **Nondurable goods** are consumed quickly.
- **Services** are intangible products.

Economists divide products for consumption into three categories: durable goods, nondurable goods, and services. **Durable** goods such as automobiles, refrigerators, tools, and televisions provide a flow of services over a longer period of time. **Nondurable goods** are consumed all at once or in a short period of time. Some nondurable goods are perishable, like milk, fresh fruits and vegetables, and fresh meat. Other nondurable goods, such as household chemicals and paper products, are nonperishable and are able to be stored. And finally, **services** are intangible products provided by humans, such as maintaining, repairing, operating, or teaching about tangible products. Teachers who instruct, barbers who cut hair, or financial experts who advise about retirement investments provide services to consumers.

Consumers more easily can **postpone** buying durable goods than buying nondurable goods. The Joneses have to restock the refrigerator every week or two, but they can wait to buy the new refrigerator. The Joneses have been saving for several years to replace the cabinets and appliances in their kitchen. They devote $1,200 of budgeted savings per year to the future kitchen project. While savings for retirement and emergencies are necessary, the Joneses conclude that perhaps they can postpone part of the remodeling project. The old range and dishwasher look a bit out of date, but they are still serviceable. Buying a more efficient refrigerator, though, will save enough electricity to pay for the change. Changing cabinets is a luxury and is definitely postponable, but the refrigerator is a good investment now. They decide to cut savings for the kitchen by $800 this year, delaying most of the project another year or two.

As an investment for the future, they will investigate which appliances perform best at a reasonable cost and which have the lowest rates of repairs over the past ten years. Certain consumer groups conduct tests and publish their product reports. The Joneses will subscribe to a consumer group's magazine to see which appliances have the best repair records, based on owner surveys.

At this point, the Joneses have cut budgeted expenditures by $2,080. Initially, their excess spending was $3,253. Now their budget deficit is only $1,173. As a result, they decide that they will not seek additional work outside the home. Instead, at a future meeting they will trim planned expenditures further. Expansion Point 11.2 lists popular tips for consumers that the Joneses also may want to consider. They decide not to cut charitable giving. Finally, they agree not to add to their debt, but to repay it at an even faster pace.

Expansion Point 11.2: Tips for Cutting Consumer Spending

Here are some tips for reigning in an unruly family budget. A question at the end of the chapter will ask you which economic ideas are being applied here. (These are only examples of popular suggestions, and no guarantee of suitability for any particular situation is implied in this listing.)

1. Food shop only when you are not hungry, and buy only items on your shopping list (except for bargains on items you use regularly).

2. Enjoy the leftovers. People who eat leftovers generally spend less on food each week.

3. Avoid impulse buying, especially on more costly items. As a family, set an upper limit, such as $30, for any spending that has not been discussed in advance. Also examine your motives for spending on impulse. Are you truly in need, or are you sad, frustrated, angry, or keeping up with others?

4. Save regularly. To assure that you do, sign up to have savings deducted automatically from your paycheck at work before you are able to spend it.

5. Value your time. Before driving across town or to the city for advertised bargains, consider the cost of driving and the cost of your time. At $0.32 per mile for gas, oil, and wear on your car, a 50-mile trip costs $16. Since the trip will take an extra hour of driving, consider the value of your time that cannot be spent doing other important tasks.

6. Avoid costly consumer credit. If you can't pay your credit card balance in full each month, tear up the card. Credit card interest on unpaid balances is expensive. If you qualify, find a card with low regular rates of interest and low fees.

7. Know the full cost of using and keeping what you are buying. A travel trailer, for example, may seem like an inexpensive way to a dream vacation, until you consider the costs other than the trailer itself. You will also pay for regular upkeep (painting the top every year and adjusting trailer brakes every 3,000 miles on some) and added wear and tear on the tow vehicle. And the cost of a campsite can be half the price of a nice motel. For another example, a dog, even one that is initially free to you, will impose potentially significant yearly costs for food, occasional boarding at vacation time, and health care.

The Economics of Consumer Behavior

This brief survey of the Jones family's budget calculations reflects the prevailing view of economists that consumers act rationally. Whatever the structure of the household, economists believe that consumers will behave predictably. Before turning to several criticisms and comments about the economists' perspective, let's briefly summarize the key ideas. The first idea is a psychological assumption about consumer preferences for more of a good. The next set of ideas explains the implications of rationality for consumer behavior. The most general are that informed consumers will seek to balance their spending.

Extra Satisfaction from Extra Consumption Diminishes

Economists recognize one important psychological aspect of consumption: **diminishing marginal utility**. This simply means

• **Diminishing Marginal Utility:** as a consumer uses more and more of a good, the additional satisfaction from each extra unit of the good diminishes

that extra measures of a good give us less and less additional satisfaction. You want food very badly in the morning when you first get up. Then, as you eat, your extra pleasure from each bite begins to diminish until you want no more. At some point, to eat another bite would make you sick.

Diminishing marginal utility is the usual theoretical explanation for the law of demand. Consumers are willing to buy more of a good only at lower prices because each additional unit of food provides less satisfying power. This relationship is illustrated in Exhibit 11.2 as the diminishing marginal utility of food and the law of demand applied to food.

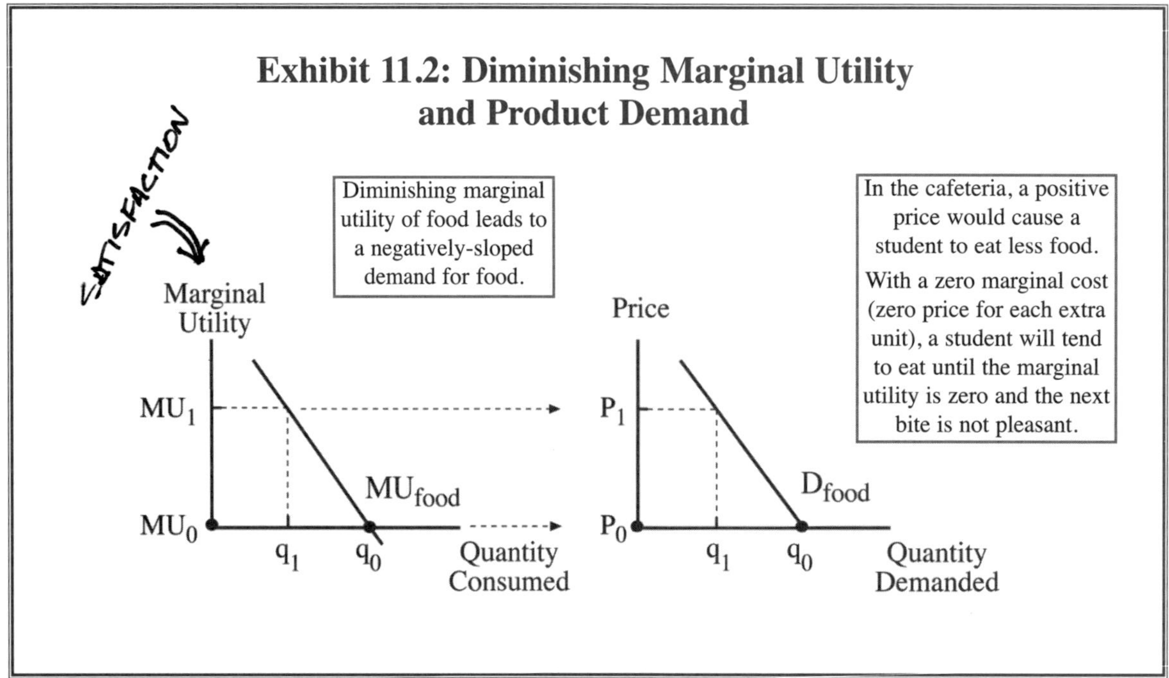

Diminishing marginal utility provides a novel explanation for why college students don't like college cafeteria food. In spite of dramatic increases in variety and quality of food—for example, sandwich and taco bars; hot meals or cold cereal; and ice cream and other desserts—students continue to complain. While cafeteria food may not be just like food at home, the pricing of the food and the failure to place limits on how much students eat well could contribute to the problem.

If a student had to pay a positive price for each cup of drink, vegetable, entree, salad, or dessert, then the price would regulate the student's consumption. The student would leave feeling that the next bite of food would have had a positive marginal utility. This outcome from a positive price is shown in Exhibit 11.2 at the price of P_1, quantity of q_1, and a marginal utility of MU_1.

Cafeteria food often is distributed at a zero marginal cost to the student. Students pay a flat fee for the semester under this meal plan, and then they may eat as much as they want. But when each additional bite of food is free and quantity is unlimited, the student consumes more food at each sitting, until the marginal utility of food is zero. At that point, students leave the cafeteria feeling as if another bite would make them just a bit sick (negative marginal utility). This is illustrated in Exhibit 11.2 at the outcome P_0, q_0, and MU_0.

No wonder they complain about the food. Changing the pricing scheme would solve part of the problem of complaints about the cafeteria. For further thoughts on the psychology of cafeteria food, see Expansion Point 11.3 later in this chapter.

Rational Consumer Decisions

Consumers seeking to maximize utility while facing a limited budget will increase quantity demanded at a lower price. The level of household income and individual preferences are key determinants in buying decisions. Consumers will borrow more or less and save less or more as interest rates decrease or increase. They will watch the prices of substitutes and complements and act accordingly as relative prices change.

Consumers will seek the amount of information that balances the benefits of more information with the costs of getting it. Their brand loyalty will be based on reasonable information about product quality and available alternatives, not on blind obedience to marketing pitches. Consumers also will forecast future prices based on available information about changing market conditions.

In the mainstream theory, the consumer is not especially concerned about helping others, nor at all worried about what others think about his decisions. By definition, the rational consumer is unaffected by irrational fears.

In general, a rational consumer balances consumption, allocating income efficiently, so that the last dollar spent on each good gives equal additional satisfaction. (In theory, if this condition is not met, a reallocation of spending could make the consumer better off. Simply spend less where extra satisfaction per dollar is lower, and spend more where it is higher until balance is restored. You shouldn't fret this technical detail, but economists do.)

If you find this description a bit unrealistic, you are not alone. Therefore, we will consider criticisms of the theory and mainstream responses to them. This theory is a powerful tool for analyzing market activity, where people do tend to pay close attention to their own interests, making informed decisions on average, especially over the long run. At least, that is the mainstream economists' story, and they are sticking to it.

- **The Rational Consumer:**
  1) knows personal preferences;
  2) has limited income and seeks to use it to maximize utility;
  3) considers product price, other prices, and interest rates when buying;
  4) considers interest rates when saving and borrowing;
  5) buys information as needed;
  6) gives little heed to irrational fears or to others' needs or viewpoints; and
  7) seeks an optimal balance in spending and saving.

Psychological and Social Aspects of Consumption

Economics, psychology, and sociology are separate fields of study in school, but economic and psychosocial effects on consumption are intertwined in the economy. Consumer tastes and preferences that influence consumption are obviously mental calculations and, therefore, are subject to psychological influences before they influence the economy.

Preferences are also formed in a social setting. As a result, what others do affects how we evaluate the expected utility we will derive from goods. Here is a brief and partial review of some of the psychological and social aspects of forming preferences and acting on them in the economy.

The Relativity of Consumption

Relative levels of consumption affect who feels satisfied and who doesn't. While poor Americans today may live better lives in many ways than royalty of two hundred years ago, the poor may not feel so well off compared to what they see on television. Wealthy people in a relatively poor country may feel wealthy compared to their fellow citizens, but not feel very wealthy compared to what they see on Western television.

A middle-class American college student who travels to a developing nation may suddenly feel not only blessed, but also incredibly rich, as discussed in Expansion Point 11.3. Feelings of wealth and satisfaction are relative.

Habits Influence Consumer Perceptions

Habits affect consumer preferences and perceptions about happiness. We judge our standard of living not only by what others have, but also by what we have recently had. That means that initial conditions matter when we evaluate our current level of income. It matters whether we arrive at a given current income on the way up or down.

How well off would you feel about an income of $20,000 this year? You would feel happier about it now if last year you had an income of only $15,000 (as opposed to $25,000). We also grow accustomed to patterns of consumption, and breaking them can be painful. If you are in a habit of having cereal with milk and banana in the morning, you may not appreciate any change in your routine, no matter how much others might like a different menu such as an egg, toast, and bacon.

Force of habit is so strong that when a downturn in economic activity lowers household income, consumers will struggle to

Expansion Point 11.3: Preferences for Cafeteria Food Are Relative

How do college students evaluate cafeteria food? They compare it to what they have known, and often grumble that it is not as good as food at home. A few students, though, travel overseas and get an opportunity to compare their food with what people eat in lands where standards of living are low.

One American college student spent a summer in Romania in the mid-1990s. While there, she ate what the people of that nation ate each day. Being a former communist nation, Romania was in a painful and incomplete transition to a market economy and food was not plentiful. When she returned to college, the student was invited to describe during chapel her experience overseas. Her strongest comment was an exclamation of how thankful her fellow students should be about the food they had to eat.

The food now available to students in the dead of winter at some of the higher latitudes in North America would astound their great grandparents. With a foot of snow on the ground and the howling winds blowing from the north, these students could eat as much as they wanted of fresh vegetables at a salad bar. They were free to drink whatever they wished and as much as they wished of sodas, fruit juices, coffee, tea, and milk. They could choose a main dish from a sandwich bar, stir-fry bar, taco bar, or the regular line. How amazing it is to be able to eat all the cake, fruit, or ice cream that they could possibly want for dessert.

Quality in the cafeteria does vary from day to day and may not be just like home cooking, but our assessments of cafeteria food are thoroughly conditioned by the abundance we have experienced throughout our lives. What economic system created so much abundance that we are so unmoved about having so much food?

To test ideas about attitudes toward food relative to its abundance or scarcity, a student surveyed other college students. She asked them three questions:

(1) How do you like the quality of food in the cafeteria?
(2) How do you like the quality of food in your own home?
(3) How do you think a person your age from another country whose family lived on $1,500 per year would answer 1?

Possible answers were: Very Good—4; Good—3; Neutral—2; Poor—1; and Very Poor—0. The mean response for each question was as follows:

Question Number	**Average Response**
1	2
2	3.8
3	3.8

[Number of students surveyed: 32]

Cafeteria food was significantly less popular than food at home, but students also thought that someone with much less income would rate the cafeteria food significantly better. We can't say for sure that people with substantially less income would actually like the cafeteria food. That idea would require separate testing. The survey shows, however, that students do *believe* that tastes are relative to past experience.

The fact that students preferred home food to cafeteria food could be interpreted at least two ways. Either habit matters in forming preferences and the cafeteria food was inconsistent with previous habits, or the food at home actually is better. By the way, *no* student favored cafeteria food over home food, and none thought they were even equal.

protect the lifestyle to which they are accustomed. They will borrow and withdraw savings to continue to buy the same goods and services and to maintain the same housing and automobile. A permanent decline in income and standard of living will force painful lifestyle changes for all but the most flexible who have learned with the Apostle Paul "to be abased" *and* "to abound" (Philippians 4:12 KJV).

Culture Shapes Preferences

Human preferences about consumption are also culturally determined. What is desired in one culture may be detested in another. Some people like snails or ants as food, but do you? Recently, animal-rights activists in the United States have protested using animal fur as clothing. Many Americans don't buy furs now, but this was not always so and is not so today in all nations.

Since popular culture can change rapidly, preferences change rapidly too. Fads in clothes, music, and fun come and go, influencing consumer buying in waves. Are wide ties "in" now or "out"? What's up with platform shoes and bell-bottoms? Those who said goodbye to them in the 1970s were surprised to see them back in the 1990s. A sought-after color of cloth or automobile 10 years ago may be quite unpopular today, but what about a decade from now? First earth tones are in, then pastels, neons, and eventually back to basics with the primary colors.

Fear Influences Buying

Fears, real or imagined, can keep people from accepting new products. Grandmother once said, "Please don't put those earphones on me. I don't like electricity around my head." She may have been recalling the introduction of electric wiring into houses many years before, when people feared that electric current would harm them. Now, though, we have evidence that high-power lines near the home may do just that! True or not, such news makes homes near power lines less popular and therefore less valuable.

Fears of the harm that escaping radiation might do also slowed the introduction of microwave ovens. As fears (and prices) declined, microwave use increased. Here again, though, pregnant women are now warned not to stand too close to working microwaves that could be leaking.

Controversies about Consumer Theory

Not all scholars embrace the theory that consumers' objectives are only to maximize their individual utility and satisfy wants. Criticisms vary, but they tend to suggest that the model is too narrow and does not realistically explain all consumer behavior.

Critics, for example, challenge the amorality of economic analysis, the assumption of narrow individualism, the assumption that consumer preferences are stable, and the assumption that consumers are well informed. What follows is a survey of these four criticisms and a final comment about what they imply about whether or not government needs to protect consumers. Alongside the criticisms you will read a few of the responses of economists who support the mainstream model.

Moral Criticism of Consumer Theory

Amitai Etzioni (1988, and other recent books) calls the utility maximization theory the "me-first" model of economic behavior. He and others complain that economists are teaching students to act selfishly when they teach that people do so. This makes people think more about their own wants than about their social duties and the legitimate needs of others who are less well off. Defenders of the utility theory say that it is an effective method of predicting how normal humans will make consumption decisions, because most humans are not constantly overwhelmed by either a sense of duty or benevolence.

Critics emphasize the distinction between consumer needs and consumer wants. Needs of everyone ought to be met first, then we can proceed to worry about wants. John Kenneth Galbraith (1958/1979) in the 1960s advanced this argument by claiming that consumer wants are created by marketing departments and the advertising campaigns of large corporations. Marketing experts, he alleged, sell consumers what their companies can make most profitably, rather than what consumers actually need. Friedrich A. Hayek (1961/1979, 7-11) responded to Galbraith: since *all* consumer wants are socially created, why are the wants that marketing experts create necessarily bad? Hayek feared a government monopoly on ideas about what consumers should want, more than he feared competition among corporations for consumer attention.

• **Bandwagon effect:** our wants depend positively on what other people want

Sociological Criticism of Consumer Theory

Another criticism of utility theory is sociological rather than moral. It relies on a technical criticism of the theory of individual choice. Harvey Lebenstein (1950/1979, 12-30) noted that two social aspects of consumption—bandwagon and snob effects—are inconsistent with utility theory, in which individuals know their own minds and shop accordingly. The **bandwagon effect** suggests that we may not like a new style of clothing until we see others in our social group wearing it. After seeing a style on people we admire, we jump on the bandwagon. This contradicts the idea that consumers make up their own minds. For Veblen, product demand was socially determined.

• **Snob effect:** we don't want what everyone else wants

Due to a **snob effect**, we may not want to be caught dead wearing the same clothes as other people, except those in a higher social group. Our snobbery makes us unwilling to eat and shop with those from the "lower classes." We may even refuse to buy a product that is "popular," fearing it would mark us as too common. We may therefore prefer higher to lower-priced goods and services. If true, this contradicts the law of demand. The snob may demand a higher rather than lower quantity at a higher price. Once again, individual demand is socially determined.

Defenders of the utility theory say that bandwagon effects simply illustrate that consumers watch each other to gather information about what is a desirable product. They also respond that in competitive markets where price equals average cost, price may indeed be an indicator of quality. Those who want higher quality will see a lower price as a signal of low quality.

Are Consumer Preferences Really Stable?

Another controversy about consumer theory concerns the stability of preferences: do our preferences about goods and services change wildly, or are they rather stable? Maximizing utility requires that individual preferences are worth considering, and therefore must not shift wildly. If preferences shift moment by moment, then maximizing utility really has no consistent meaning. A decision you make about what to buy for dinner at 3 P.M. cannot be optimum if your tastes in food have changed radically by 5 P.M.

Who Is to Judge Tastes?

Stability of preferences also has implications for defining moral behavior. If preferences are stable, then we might as well not try to change each other's preferences. This view is reflected in the translation of a Latin saying, "There is no disputing tastes." As a result, say some economists, we cannot argue with a drug addict about personal preferences. Doing drugs is how addicts "maximize their utility" and we ought to leave them to it as long as they do no harm to others.

A problem arises with the philosophy of social *laissez-faire* in consumption, however, when some drug users claim to want to quit but can't. If our tastes are highly variable, fluctuating from day to day and susceptible to bad habit and influence, then we can and should try to reshape our own tastes and exhort others to conform to more acceptable and healthy patterns.

Self-Command in Consumption

Economist Thomas Schelling (1984, 1-11) has cited evidence about shifting preferences from everyday life: humans often restrain themselves from doing things that they really like to do. Paying not to eat food and joining Alcoholics Anonymous are two examples. To Schelling, these attempts to defeat their own preferences provided evidence that consumers have two minds about what they want and sometimes try to defeat one set of wants.

For a review of the evidence that humans have conflicting preferences and use a variety of strategies to rule their preferences, see Expansion Point 11.4. If humans do have conflicting preferences and try to defeat some of their wants, what does it mean to say that consumers should be left alone to maximize their utility?

Expansion Point 11.4: Ulysses and the Sirens, and Other Tales of Conflicting Preferences

People's preferences can be quite unruly and even inconsistent. Some want very much to eat, but want to be healthy and good-looking too. Others like to drink alcohol in the evening, but also want a clear head in the morning and no regrets for bad behavior. We want to watch television, but we also want to study, read, exercise, or work around the house more. The worst conflicts arise when what we want most on the spur of the moment is not what we will want to have wanted as we look back later. You may want to sit around doing nothing now, but next week you will wish that you *had* wanted to study for exams more thoroughly. Facing such conflicts, some people adopt a philosophy of "just do it," while others seek to rule over their preferences so as to **minimize future regrets**.

How do humans rule such unruly preferences? They make **strategic precommitments**, binding themselves to have only what they want to want, scheming so that unwanted wants will be hard to gratify. Ancient Greek literature contains a tale of such a strategy. In Homer's epic poem *The Odyssey,* the Sirens' sweet song often tempted sailors to their deaths. Ulysses' advisor Circe warned him, but also gave him a plan by which he could hear the music and still defeat his desire:

> "If anyone unwarily draws in too close and hears the singing of the Sirens, his wife and children will never welcome him home again, for they sit in a green field and warble him to death with the sweetness of their song. There is a great heap of dead men's bones lying all around, with the flesh still rotting on them. Therefore, pass these Sirens by, and stop your men's ears with wax that none of them may hear; but if you like you can listen yourself, for you may get the men to bind you as you stand upright on a cross-piece half way up the mast, and they must lash the rope's ends to the mast itself, that you may have the pleasure of listening. If you beg and pray the men to unloose you, then they must bind you faster." (250)

We do similar things today. I like apple pie so much that I don't buy it at the store. Fred likes to watch too much television, so he puts it in the closet. Betty wants a natural childbirth, so she tells the doctor in advance, "I don't want pain killers, no matter what I say then." George likes food so much that he goes away to a ranch (or "fat farm") and pays people to withhold extra food from him for days at a time. Because Nancy loves to sleep in each morning, she puts her alarm clock on the far side of the room so that she will have to get out of bed to shut it off. Alice and Dave use their credit cards too much, so they cut them up. These are strategies for avoiding gratifying preferences that we prefer not to prefer.

For certain people, then, exercising self-control means complete abstinence. The temperance movement in the United States, for example, traditionally advocated abstinence from alcohol. If you look up the meaning of temperance, though, you will see that it means "moderation," implying that a little drinking would be okay. How did moderation in drinking come to mean abstinence? It is because some people have very imperfect self-control, so that deciding to have "a drink" generally leads them to drunkenness. Drinking alcohol distorts decision making, and they consume more than they had initially planned. A student of mine in 1987 conducted an informal study at a Bar Mitzvah and found that, indeed, guests on average did consume a bit more than they had planned. Similarly with food, having a single piece of pie may quickly lead to having a few more. For those with imperfect self-control, moderation may require abstaining.

Sources: Homer, *The Odyssey,* trans. Samuel Butler in Encyclopedia Britannica Great Books series, 1952.

Thomas Schelling, "Self-Command in Practice, in Policy, and in a Theory of Rational Choice," in *American Economic Review: Papers and Proceedings* (May 1984): 1-11.

Jon Elster, *Ulysses and the Sirens: Studies in Rationality and Irrationality* (Cambridge University Press, 1985).

R.A. Black, "Endogenous Demand for Alcohol and Self-Command: A Model of the Temperance Solution," *Handbook of Behavioral Economics* 2B, 1991, 453-72.

Are Consumers Well Informed?

A final complaint about consumer theory concerns consumer information: just how knowledgeable are people about what they buy? For example, do you know how many rat hairs are in the canned food you eat? The government has set upper limits on the number of rat hairs, mouse feces, and other foreign matter that an inspector can find in canned food before rejecting the lot. Would you buy a can of food if you knew it was close to any of these limits? A bread factory worker in the late 1960s told about workers who would spit into the dough as it was being mixed. Would you pay $1.50 for such a loaf of bread? In fact, most people don't know about these difficulties, but would care if they did.

Critics of the assumption that consumers are well informed note that they are also rather ignorant of what chemicals are in their food and how pure their water is. State laws now require local water systems to test for bacteria, lead, and other contaminants and to make corrections to the systems. Would consumers demand this level of testing on their own, and are the tests really cost effective? When information about product quality is available, most consumers don't seem to be interested. Critics note that less than five percent of Americans, for example, regularly read magazines devoted to unbiased reporting of tests of product quality and durability.

Do Consumers Need Government Help?

To what extent do consumers need government's help to protect them from unsafe products and fraudulent advertising claims? Critics of the utility model of individual choice tend to support more government intervention on behalf of consumers. Government must be the watchdog, eliminating unsafe products from the market and punishing or limiting those who take advantage of consumers. In the 1960s and 1970s in the United States, Ralph Nader was the best-known consumer advocate. He is credited with forcing General Motors to remove its Corvair automobile from the market because it was *Unsafe at Any Speed*, as the title of Nader's book put it.

Friedman on Freedom vs. Regulation

Professor Milton Friedman from the Chicago School of Economics is a popular critic of more government intervention. Friedman contends that government itself does not serve the consumer well, especially in those activities in which it has a monopoly, such as the Post Office. He further contends that food and drug regulators are too slow to allow new products on the market, because it is not in their own interests to do so (see chapter 7, "Who Protects the Consumer?" in *Free to Choose*, with Rose Friedman 1980). The regulator gets no extra benefit from letting a successful drug on the market early, for example, but must bear the costs of letting a dangerous drug on the market before its danger is fully known. The regulator therefore has a personal bias toward overly lengthy testing of new drugs and foods.

Regulatory Waves

The ebb and flow of the consumer-protection debate expresses itself as waves of regulation and deregulation in the U.S. economy. More recently, the debate has swung toward realism about the limited ability of government to achieve the lofty goals of its idealistic advocates. Many economists would agree, however, that government has benefited consumers by passing labeling regulations. By compelling manufacturers to inform buyers about product contents, volume, and price, and about safety hazards of using a product, the laws enable consumers to spend their incomes more efficiently and to either avoid dangerous products or use them appropriately.

Summary

In spite of the criticisms, the mainstream neoclassical view of consumer behavior is durable, primarily because it is useful in predicting market behavior. The wise economics student would do well to understand both the theory and its limitations.

Chapter Summary

1. Of the three fundamental economic activities, consumption is primary. The desire of humans to consume draws forth production and leads to some system of distributing output.

2. Consuming goods means actually using goods, while buying goods is called consumer expenditure. You don't consume a refrigerator when you buy it; you consume it over many years.

3. A family budget shows that scarcity imposes limits and forces the family to make choices about work and leisure, income-tax strategies in consumption, substituting lower-priced goods, and deciding what is necessary and what is postponable or a luxury.

4. Certain products are durable goods, others are nondurable goods (both perishable and non-perishable), while still other products are services.

5. Diminishing marginal utility of additional units of a good being consumed explains the law of demand. It also suggests why students complain about cafeteria food that is available at a zero price.

6. Before buying, a consumer checks the price of a product and compares it to prices of other goods. Consumers also consider their limited incomes and their preferences as they try to maximize utility.

7. In buying products, consumers also consider factors such as the prices of other goods, interest rates, government regulations, and expected future prices.

8. Psychological and social effects on consumption suggest that tastes and preferences are relative to past levels and what others have, are influenced by habits, are culturally determined, and are shaped by fads and fears.

9. Critics of the utility theory of consumption complain about the emphasis on one's own pleasure, rather than on others' needs and one's own benevolence and duty. Critics have also challenged the individuality of preferences and the law of demand, because of bandwagon and snob effects. Other critics challenge the assumed stability of consumer preferences and the assumed knowledge of the consumer. Milton Friedman, however, contends that economic freedom benefits the consumer more than government control does.

PROBLEMS FOR PRACTICE

11.1* Which of the three fundamental economic activities is primary and why?

11.2* During a downturn in business activity, also called a recession, family incomes and levels of consumption fall. Which do you think would fall more in a recession, the demand for durable or nondurable goods? Explain.

11.3* You buy a box of copy paper, a heavy-duty paper stapler, and two boxes of staples for use in your home office, from which you operate a real estate business.

a. Is the stapler a durable or nondurable good?
b. Are staples a durable or nondurable good?
c. Is this stapler a consumer or investment good?

11.4 List five different examples of rational behavior by consumers. Then list what you might consider to be five examples of irrational behavior by consumers. Are there underlying reasons for such apparently irrational behaviors?

11.5* Why do some families give gifts to leaders of churches, synagogues, and mosques? Do they do it to "maximize utility" or to do their duty? If it is their duty, what does it mean to say, as Christian teachers do, that God wants people to give with a cheerful heart? As part of the answer to this question, review the meanings of giving a "tithe" versus giving an "offering," "gift," or Islamic Zakat.

11.6* Two college students receive checks in the mail. The first student expected a check from home for $100 but only got $25. The second student expected $10 but actually got $25. Which one is better off in terms of purchasing power? How will these students feel about their gifts? Is this "rational" thinking, as you understand the term?

11.7* What do the popular tips for wise shopping and budgeting listed in Expansion Point 11.2 say about the factors that influence consumer behavior? What economic principles and ideas from this chapter and the previous chapters (especially chapters 4 and 5) are illustrated in each of the tips?

11.8* List several strategies that you, your friends, or others have used to keep yourselves from getting what you want. This question could apply to shopping or consuming goods already bought, or to decisions about using your time and other resources. Explain in each case what the goal is.

For your portfolio:
11.9 Briefly research one or two of the criticisms of utility theory or the psychological and social aspects of consumption. Write a one-page summary of your results.

11.10 Working in groups of two (married without children) or three (with one child), make a family budget based on an income of $40,000 per year, living in your area. Make needed assumptions about housing, utilities, taxes, and other needs. Discuss and debate vacations, autos, and so on. Then remake the budget for $25,000 per year, assuming that one spouse quits or loses a job. Where must you cut and where do you feel that extra spending is needed? Do you both or all agree on everything?

For class discussion:
11.11* Exhibit 11.1 shows a family that is planning to go further into debt in the next year unless changes are made. Discuss what you think are good reasons for going into debt. For example, should the family be borrowing to take a vacation? Should it be giving gifts and offerings when it is going into debt? Should it be going into debt? If not, how would you trim expenditures or increase income? How would you go about balancing the Joneses' budget?

11.12 Is consumer ignorance or lack of self-control an acceptable reason for government to intervene in the market economy? To what degree and with what interventions do you think the government might help the hapless consumer? List any examples already in practice.

11.13 What are the benefits and costs of consumer freedom? Should the government limit itself to providing consumers with information? Should government control production and distribution of consumer products?

11.14 Do you agree with the analysis in Exhibit 11.2, that diminishing marginal utility and a zero marginal cost for food help explain why students complain about cafeteria food? Explain your reasons.

11.15 How do we know when enough consumption is enough? Should our appetites alone be our guides? Can economic analysis per se answer such a question?

See Answer Key for hints/answers to starred (*) questions.

Chapter 12

PRODUCTION

Creating Wealth

What this chapter will help you think about:

1. What is production?
2. What roles do entrepreneurs play in production?
3. What risks do entrepreneurs take?
4. What are the goals of production?
5. How do the books of a firm reflect these goals?
6. What are five key principles of the economics of production?
7. How do legal aspects affect production and efficiency?
8. How is production organized and why does it matter?

• **Production:** creates wealth by transforming inputs of land, human labor and skill, capital equipment, and raw materials into useful outputs of goods and services

Before we can consume wealth, we must create it. **Production** creates wealth by using tools and knowledge to transform and relocate materials for valuable uses. Until the twentieth century, the vast majority of people on earth were engaged in the hard work of producing basic necessities by tilling soil, sowing seed, reaping harvests, spinning, weaving, cutting trees, digging clay and minerals, and various other activities for producing food, housing, and clothing. Only recently have advanced methods of production allowed so many to enjoy more education, more leisure, and higher standards of living.

Production: Inputs into Outputs

Production transforms inputs, also called "factors of production," into outputs or products. Assembling a car, growing wheat, and cooking a meal are productive activities. **Outputs** or **products** are either tangible **goods** or intangible **services**. An automobile is a good; an auto tune-up is a service (combined with certain tangible replacement parts). Scissors and a comb are goods; a haircut is a service. Certain outputs of production, called intermediate goods, are inputs into the production of other goods. Steel and glass, for instance, are used to produce automobiles. Other products are for final consumer use.

Inputs to Production

Production inputs include land, unskilled labor, human skill (also called human capital), capital equipment, raw materials, and intermediate products (outputs from other production processes). Producing iron and steel, for example, involves all these inputs. Coal and iron ore are **raw materials**, while coke (partially burned coal) is an **intermediate product**.

- **Inputs to production:**
  1) land
  2) unskilled labor
  3) human capital
  4) capital equipment
  5) raw materials
  6) intermediate products
  7) organizing ability

Rail cars, ships, trucks for hauling, and furnaces and rolling mills for shaping metal are **capital equipment**. Unskilled workers provide **labor**, while managers, engineers, chemists, and skilled workers bring **human capital**. Owners of the firm add **organizing ability** (or hire it in senior management) and are willing to take risks. Finally, **land** is the site of production as well as the source of the minerals and other raw materials. All are inputs to the processes by which iron and steel are produced.

The Efficiency of Mass Production

Until the last two hundred years or so, production techniques were rather primitive, undergoing only gradual improvements. Now, however, due to **mass production** and the factory method of making goods, labor productivity is high and growing. The characteristics of mass production that have made this possible are dividing work into **specialized tasks**, using **standardizing parts** so they are interchangeable, and maintaining a **steady pace** to production. To accomplish this, managers and workers must thoroughly **organize** various processes before production begins, and then carefully **coordinate** operations and the flows of resources as it proceeds.

- **Characteristics of mass production:**
  1) specializing tasks
  2) standardizing parts for interchangeability
  3) keeping a steady pace
  4) organizing multiple processes
  5) coordinating ongoing work

Efficiencies of Continuous Production

To be most efficient, mass production must proceed steadily. For instance, you don't want to heat and cool a steel mill once a day; you want to run it continuously. Factories also must work steadily (though not necessarily day and night) so that they do not, for example, lose their skilled workers or connections to suppliers.

Steady economy-wide production promotes stable and high living standards. Recessions in economic activity or interruptions in resource supplies, however, interrupt the steady flow of production, causing factory managers to shut down plants and lay off workers for extended periods of time.

Efficiencies of Large Scale

Certain processes such as steel, petroleum refining, and auto production are especially suited to mass production on a large scale. These processes exhibit **economies of large scale**, so that average cost of production falls as the scale of the factory and the rate of output per period increase.

All production processes are not, however, created equal. Certain processes exhibit inefficiencies at large scale and are more efficient at medium or small scales. Businesses and factories, therefore, come in various sizes.

Flexibility of Mass Customization

The electronic revolution has dramatically changed the factory method, allowing for both the economies of scale and the flexibility of meeting custom orders. Computer scheduling of production, the arrival of parts, the shipping of finished goods, and computerized billing have freed factories from Henry Ford's decree that "Customers can have their cars in any color, as long as it's black." Instead, production of each item on certain assembly lines fits the customer's special order.

These flexible production methods developed under intense competition in private enterprise economies. A main force driving such relentless change in pursuit of efficient and flexible production is the profit-seeking entrepreneur.

Entrepreneurs and Production

- **Entrepreneurs:**
  1) organize the firm,
  2) assume risk, and
  3) monitor work

As initiators of production, **entrepreneurs** have driven progress in market economies over the last few centuries. An entrepreneur has three tasks: (1) organize production, bringing managerial skill and a brilliant idea or two; (2) assume risk; and (3) monitor ongoing work.

Entrepreneurs thrive in societies that promote personal freedom and allow above-average rewards for above-average individual effort. When the state manages or heavily regulates production, or when social envy limits economic rewards, entrepreneurial energy is squelched. Energetic risk-taking people will often leave a nation where commerce is restricted and emigrate to a nation where they can better exploit their own talents.

Organizing Inputs and Earning Revenues

Exhibit 12.1 shows that production involves transforming inputs into outputs. It also shows the entrepreneur's role as an organizer who contracts with resource suppliers. The entrepreneur also takes risks, paying input suppliers when they offer their services, or shortly after, but receiving sales revenues some time later. Product sales are never guaranteed, and the entrepreneur may never recover all costs, which is only one risk of the job.

Risk and Return in Production

By assuming risks of failure, entrepreneurs create opportunities to reap large returns above their costs. Risks can be substantial, however, restricting the field of willing entrepreneurs. **Lengthy delays** between initial investments and future receipt of sales revenues, and the uncertainty of future sales create risk.

To illustrate business risk, Expansion Point 12.1 explains a sad historical fact. Johannes Gutenberg, inventor of the first movable-metal-type printing press, went bankrupt because of delays in printing and selling his first mass-produced copies of the Bible.

Exhibit 12.1: Production Transforms Inputs into Outputs

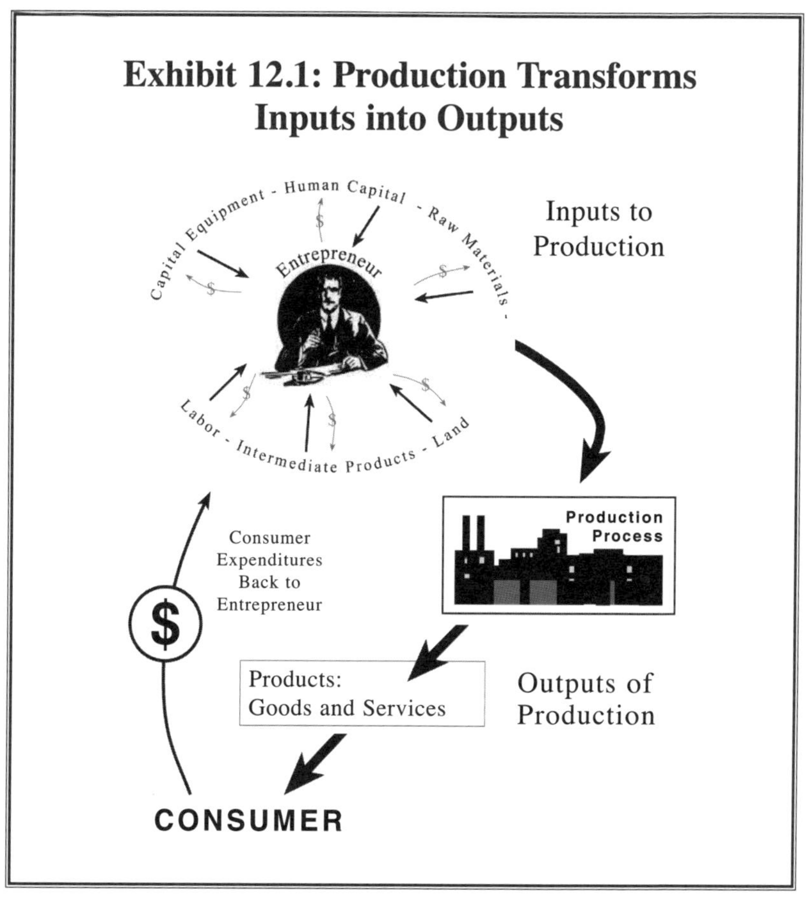

Businesses face other risks, such as potential **casualty losses** due to fire or other disasters. Theft of inventory or trade secrets, and liability for defective products also impose risk.

Profit, a Return for Risk. In return for risk, entrepreneurial owners deserve a reward. By law, business owners have a legal right to the residual income of the firm—the **profit** remaining after using revenues to pay costs. The law therefore calls the owners **residual claimants**. Of course, they also have a legal obligation to pay any unmet costs if revenues fall short.

• **Residual claimant:** the owner of a business has a legal claim to income in excess of costs

Profit, an Incentive to Monitor. The law gives an owner a clear incentive to run a firm efficiently and to assure that workers do not **shirk** their duties. As a result, what was called "superintendence" in the 1850s and what we now call "monitoring" is a third responsibility of the entrepreneur. As owner of the firm, the entrepreneur protects the investment by assuring that contractual obligations are met: workers must do their share of work, suppliers must deliver quality materials on time, and managers must act for the good of the business, not in their own narrow self-interests.

• **Shirking:** workers may not attend properly to their production duties

Limits to Entrepreneurial Ability

Very good entrepreneurs with more limited management skills can easily work themselves out of a job. As firms grow, owners

Expansion Point 12.1: Johannes Gutenberg's Bible—Winning and Losing at Printing

History teaches that Johannes Gutenberg (ca. 1398-1468) invented the movable-type printing press and used it to print the first mass-produced Bible. We are not taught, though, that Gutenberg went broke doing so. Gutenberg won in his secret technical quest to invent the press before others did, but he lost an entrepreneurial race to cover his costs with revenues from the sale of his Bibles.

Gutenberg solved two major technical obstacles to mass-producing books. He substituted metal type for imprecise wooden type and for more fragile wooden block carvings. He then developed a process to cast and grip the pieces of lead type in such a way that they could be held flat when inked and pressed on the paper page.

To apply his process, Gutenberg, who was not a rich man, had to borrow money in 1450 and 1452 from Johann Fust. A merchant in Mainz, Germany, Fust also became a partner in the venture in 1452 to further protect his investment.

Printing books in the 1450s was similar to making automobiles today: each requires a significant investment long before books or cars can be sold and costs recovered. While other craftsmen in other trades of Gutenberg's day had fewer expenses up front, Gutenberg needed printing equipment, metal, metal-working equipment, paper, and ink. For the 1200-page Bible, Gutenberg also had to hire extra laborers to operate his 10 presses, and to cast and arrange about 400,000 pieces of type for each of 10 runs of 130 pages each.

After five years, Gutenberg had not repaid the loans to Fust. In 1455, Fust sued and won in court to recover the loans. Gutenberg had to forfeit ownership of the machinery he had invented, the supplies, along with copies of—and even rights to revenue from—portions of the Bibles that he had already printed. Fust was able to hire Gutenberg's workers and to finish printing his copies of the Bible. He sold those copies and earned a profit on his investment and on Gutenberg's inventiveness.

The Gutenberg story illustrates that a long delay between beginning to pay costs of production and receiving sales revenue creates a significant risk for business organizers who must borrow money to get started. Entrepreneurs in business today face a similar threat to their success. Undercapitalization of the business (inadequate financial reserves to keep a business afloat until it returns adequate revenues) is one common reason why most new businesses fail.

Source: "Guild Hall: The Printer's Guild," and connected sites related to Peter Shoeffer's association with Gutenberg and Fust. Found at http://www.twingroves.district96.k12.il.us/Renaissance/guildhall/printer/printingguild.html#anchor1001704.

who were great initiators and risk takers may be bad bureaucrats and managers. Where once the owner could control all operations, growth requires delegating authority to others in a management team, a skill that not all entrepreneurs possess.

Time to Sell. When the firm grows rapidly, the entrepreneur may choose to sell the firm to others that have the organizational ability to cope with growing managerial responsibilities. Large corporations are always looking to buy profitable **start-up** firms from their owners, because they are often better at maintaining than at starting new firms. A dedicated entrepreneur will then return to a search for the next opportunity to start a new business.

Bad Endings. Very bad entrepreneurs are apparently more common than very good ones. The great majority of new businesses in the United States fail within the first three years. In 1997, over 166,700 U.S. businesses began, while over 83,300 failed.

In *The E-Myth Revisited,* author Michael E. Gerber (1995) offers one reason why so many entrepreneurs fail. Most people who start a business are unable to organize it or assess what the market wants or needs. They are simply good "technicians" and want to employ themselves to do what they enjoy.

Good plumbers, builders, and hairstylists often make lousy managers and entrepreneurs. Poorly organized, unable to keep accounts, unable to market themselves or their products well, they build a small business based on technical skill and sheer will to succeed with a small client base. When the business thrives, however, they are in big trouble, because a thriving business needs organization and direction. For a list of seven easy ways to let *your* business fail, see Expansion Point 12.2.

Expansion Point 12.2: How to Bankrupt Your Business

In 1997 in California, about 22,500 entrepreneurs launched new businesses, but about 20,100 failed. Not all those that failed had just started up, but most small businesses do fail in the first three years. According to business consultants, here is how to do it (fail) yourself:

1. Start out too big right away, or rapidly increase the size of the business later, without planning for adequate funds to keep it going through the inevitable lean times. The next downturn in business will catch you with inadequate capital to keep your business afloat.

2. Take on a partner that you don't know very well. Give him full authority to put you in debt and full access to the bank account too.

3. Attend to the technical parts of the job, all the things that you like to do and began a business to do, but don't take time to make a business plan or organize. Be sure not to sweat the details.

4. Stuff all your receipts in a shoe box and promise to attend to the bookkeeping next April. Until then, do ignore cash flows, net worth, and accounts payable or receivable.

5. Overwork your skilled help, and by all means, refuse to teach your unskilled help how to do the job well.

6. Focus on how *you* like to do the job, rather than on what your *customer* wants.

7. Have a bad attitude with customers and employees.

Sources: Coleman Management Services, "How to Fail in Business Without Really Trying," 1999. Found at http://www.stargate.ca/roncole/html/rcol2000.htm.

Michael Gerber, *The E-Myth Revisited: Why Most Small Businesses Don't Work and What to Do About It* (New York: Harper Business, 1995).

Producing Blue Jeans at Montana Jeans

You can learn about the economics and business of production by following the decisions and opening the books of a theoretical firm called Montana Jeans. Its books refer to the accounts that the firm keeps. Understanding two important accounting reports, the income statement and the balance sheet, will help us in our economic analysis of the firm. In our analysis, we will assume that the managers of Montana will behave rationally as they plan how many jeans to produce and at what price to offer them for sale. Let's look first at their goals.

Goals of the Firm

The owners at Montana have the normal range of human feelings and they are as benevolent as anyone else. In business, though, we assume that they seek either to **maximize profit** or to **maximize the value** of their firm. That may seem harsh, so let's qualify the goal by saying they intend to abide by the law, treat their workers with respect, and also give some of their profits to relieve the suffering of the poor around the world. Nevertheless, they watch the performance of their firm and hope to consistently generate more revenues than costs.

A firm's **profit** equals total revenues from product sales less total costs, including normal returns for organizing, risk taking, and providing any capital. The **value of the firm** is the wealth the owners would have if they sold the firm today. Unless a firm has just been sold, its value must be estimated as the value that someone might pay for owning all the assets and being able to claim the flow of profit from future sales.

Critics claim that firms have other goals than profits and value maximization, but the bottom lines of the two most important summary accounting statements of any firm—the income statement and the balance sheet—show the firm's profit and value. While accountants use them to audit the books, entrepreneurs and potential investors use them to assess potential future performance.

Montana's Income Statement

The **income statement** calculates the short-term accounting profit or loss of the firm. Accounting profit is calculated as total revenue less explicit costs of the business. The income statement is a detailed expression of the following simple equation for net income of the firm:

Net Income = Revenues - Accounting Costs

When net income is positive, it is an accounting profit. When net income is negative, it is an accounting loss.

Exhibit 12.2 shows the most recent income statement for Montana Jeans. Explicit costs are those involving actual payments of the firm's money, such as wages paid or resources purchased. Opportunity costs of an owner's time or the rents that the firm is foregoing by using its own equipment rather than renting it to others are ignored.

Exhibit 12.2: Montana Jeans Income Statement

Montana Jeans, Inc.
Income Statement, Jan. 1 to Dec. 31

Revenue:		
Gross Sales	$4,952,391	
Less Sales Returns	345,110	
Net Sales		**$4,607,281**
Cost of Goods Sold:		
Materials	780,000	
Labor	2,570,400	
Other Direct Costs	434,840	
Indirect Expenses	169,000	
Total Cost of Goods Sold		**$3,854,240**
Gross Profit (Loss)		**$753,041**
Expenses:		
Advertising	0	
Bad Debts	4,700	
Depreciation	10,750	
Insurance	9,900	
Interest	8,500	
Office Expenses	50,400	
Utilities	15,200	
Wages and Benefits	184,000	
Total Expenses		**$293,450**
Net Operating Income		**$459,591**

Gross revenues of the firm are the total value of sales less the value of returned merchandise. Costs of goods sold include the direct costs of actually producing the product, such as the costs of raw materials and labor. Indirect costs, such as managerial salaries and building rents, are expenses of the business that are not directly linked to making a specific unit of product, but which are still costs of producing the goods. Subtracting costs from revenues leaves the gross income of the firm.

In addition to direct and indirect costs of producing goods, the income statement considers other expenses, such as costs of advertising and selling the goods, depreciation (allowance for worn-out equipment), and interest costs of debt. Deducting these

- **Profit:** total revenues less total costs
- **Value of a firm:** market value of a firm, based on expected stream of future profits
- **Income statement:** accounting statement recording a firm's revenues, explicit costs, and net income

other expenses from gross income leaves net operating income, which is the profit or loss of the firm. That is why an income statement is also called a profit and loss statement.

Montana's Balance Sheet

The **balance sheet** of a firm calculates the net worth of the business as total assets (the value of what it owns) minus total liabilities (the value of what it owes) at a point in time:

Net Worth = Assets - Liabilities

Net worth is also called the firm's capital. Assets are the value of what the firm owns. Liabilities are the value of what it owes.

Exhibit 12.3 shows the most recent balance sheet for Montana Jeans. Assets of the firm include cash on hand, accounts receivable (the debts buyers owe to Montana), a deduction allowing for bad debts among the accounts receivables, the value of inventory of outputs, the value of inventory of inputs, the value of equipment and buildings owned by the firm less depreciation (allowance for worn-out equipment and buildings), and the value of land owned by the firm. Liabilities are what Montana owes its suppliers for previous materials and services, governments for taxes, workers for wages, short-term notes (loans), and long-term notes and mortgages (loans). Montana's net worth is one estimate of its value as a collection of separate parts.

Exhibit 12.3: Montana Jeans Balance Sheet

Montana Jeans, Inc.
Balance Sheet, December 31

Assets			**Liabilities**		
Current Assets:			**Current Liabilities**		
Cash		$224,300	Accounts Payable	$40,000	
Accounts Receivable	$40,510		Sales Taxes Payable	2,800	
Less Bad-Debt Reserves	2,800	37,710	Payroll Taxes Payable	32,600	
Merchandise Inventory		55,760	Accrued Wages Payable	95,000	
Materials Inventory		24,000	Short-Term Notes Payable	15,000	
Total Current Assets		**$341,770**	**Total Current Liabilities**	**$185,400**	
Fixed Assets:			**Long-Term Liabilities:**		
Equipment	120,000		Long-Term Notes Payable	50,000	
Less Depreciation	60,000	60,000	Mortgages Payable	30,000	
Buildings	95,000		**Total Long-Term Liabilities**	**$80,000**	
Less Depreciation	47,500	47,500			
Land		88,000	**Total Liabilities**		**$265,400**
Total Fixed Assets		**$195,500**			
			Capital (Net Worth):		**$271,870**
Total Assets		**$537,270**			
			Total Capital and Liabilities		**$537,270**

Public Accounting and Economic Efficiency

In the United States and other free-enterprise nations, publicly owned corporations must open their books to the public. They must regularly publish their income statements and balance sheets, with important economic effects. Publicly reported financial statements influence the firm's own stockholders and the investment decisions of other entrepreneurs. Corporations showing high profits will encourage other entrepreneurs to invest in a similar business. Corporate losses will discourage more investment.

• **Balance sheet:** accounting statement recording a firm's assets, liabilities, and net worth

As explained in chapter 2, allocative efficiency involves putting resources to their most valuable uses. Publicly reporting profits, by directing flows of capital in a market economy, increases the responsiveness of business to changing market conditions. This therefore increases allocative efficiency of a market economy by encouraging production of those goods and services most valued by its people.

The firm uses its books for internal monitoring and decision making as well. Auditors use the books for determining where money comes from and where it goes, and for detecting fraud. The books also reflect changing economic conditions and will signal when the firm needs new strategies. Higher resource costs or lower efficiency will reduce profits and prompt cost cutting. Increased demand will be reflected in higher revenues and, if costs are controlled, higher profits.

Accounting vs. Economic Valuations

Exhibit 12.2 shows that Montana is making an accounting profit of over $459,000. Accounting profits and losses, however, are different from economic profits and losses. This is because accountants consider only explicit costs where suppliers were paid in money or goods. Economists, on the other hand, include implicit costs when calculating opportunity costs. A firm that uses equipment, buildings, or land that it owns will have no current payments for such items, but it will have **opportunity costs** of using these resources (see chapter 2). By using equipment it owns, the firm loses potential income from renting them to another firm. Therefore, economic costs that include such implicit costs exceed accounting costs, and economic profits are less than accounting profits.

If full opportunity costs are important to economic decisions, why do accountants ignore implicit costs? The reason is that they are paid to set up a system to record actual expenses of the firm, not to estimate implicit costs. Such a system helps avoid and detect fraud in the business. Even so, economists recommend that managers estimate costs of doing business using implicit costs estimated from current market values of machines, buildings, and land that the firm owns and for which the firm makes no money payments. A few public corporations do report a statistic measuring economic value added (EVA).

Book Value vs. Market Value of the Firm

The net worth of a firm is also called its book value. Is the book value of the firm shown on its balance sheet, so that you would know what you would have to pay if you were to purchase it? Not necessarily; a selling price is always negotiable. Furthermore, at least two other factors may make the selling price higher or lower. One, the historical or book value of equipment differs from its current market value. Two, abnormal profits or losses may change a firm's market value more than its book value. Let's see why.

First, book value of equipment is recorded at historical purchase price less depreciation (declining value due to age and wear). Book values of equipment are historical costs, not current market values of the equipment. Historical costs are **sunk costs**, and they are irrelevant to economic decision making. Why do accountants record historical costs on a balance sheet and elsewhere on the books? It is because they are not paid to provide hypothetical estimates of what a machine *might* be worth *if* sold today. Even so, economists suggest that managers also estimate current market values in making economic decisions.

•**Sunk costs:** accounting costs or historical costs, as compared to economic opportunity costs

Second, book value of a firm may be less than the sale price because the firm is making a huge profit each year. No matter what a business costs initially, on the books, an unprofitable firm is not worth much. If, for example, you were to buy a well-kept, rather new, but unprofitable soft-ice-cream store at a great bargain, the market value of the firm would be quite low compared to its book value. If in the next year, however, soft ice cream suddenly came back into fashion in your area, you would be sitting on a gold mine. Each month, you would earn a high income on a relatively small investment. If you sold the store after it became profitable, sale price would then be greater than the firm's book value.

Economic Activity and Market Value of Firms

When economic activity fluctuates, profits of firms will fluctuate and so will their market values. When an economy is booming and sales are rising rapidly for many businesses, a firm's profits will tend to be above average and its market value will tend to be greater than its book value. When an economy is contracting and sales are stagnant or falling, profits will be lower or negative and a firm's market value will be less than book value.

How Profitable Is Montana Jeans?

Profitability is an important concept in economic analysis of market economies. Profits spur production and technological advancement. From its income statement and balance sheet, we can assess Montana Jeans' profitability. We will use two standard measures: **sales margin**, the profit as a proportion of total revenue (net sales); and **return on investment** (ROI), or profit as a proportion of net worth (capital or equity) of the firm.

Sales Margin = Net Income After Taxes / Net Sales

ROI = Net Income After Taxes / Net Worth

These rates of profit are calculated by finding the relevant figures on the books of the firm and making adjustments to income for taxes. Montana's income statement shows that what economists call total revenues and what accountants call net sales (total sales less returns) were $4,607,281. Net income or profit before taxes, also taken from the income statement, was $459,591. In percentage terms, the rate of profit was about 10 percent of total sales, but this fails to consider that government takes a portion as corporate income taxes.

The After-Tax Sales Margin

We must estimate the after-tax rate of return by estimating the tax on Montana's net income from average figures in the nation. The after-tax rate of profit is important to investors, because profits that are paid as business taxes are not really profits at all. Government taxes in the United States in 1996, for example, took about 35.5 percent of the net income of manufacturers. Montana's estimated after-tax net income would be ($459,591 * 0.645) = $296,436.

Now we can calculate the after-tax rate of profit out of total revenues, or sales margin, as ($296,436 / $4,607,281) = 0.064. In percentage terms, profit was 6.4 percent of sales.

The After-Tax Return on Investment

Montana's balance sheet shows that net worth or capital was $271,870. We use the income of the firm after taxes are removed to calculate an accounting rate of return on investment and divide that by net worth. The rate of profit on capital invested was ($296,436 / $271,870) = 1.090. In percentage terms, the after-tax profit was 109 percent of capital.

Evaluating Montana's Profitability

Are these rates of profit high? The rate of profit out of revenue is within the normal range for U.S. businesses. The rate of profit on capital invested is quite high, indicating that the book values of Montana's equipment or other fixed assets are significantly less than their market values.

Perhaps the market price of jeans is well above cost of production. An accountant values the firm with the historical value of equipment. If the current price of jeans is well above cost, some of the excess profitability might mean that the plant and equipment could be sold at higher market values than their historical costs. If so, economic profit would be less because of a higher charge for implicit cost (opportunity cost) of capital.

• **Two measures of a firm's profitability:**

1) **sales margin**, the ratio of net income after taxes to net sales

2) **return on investment**, the ratio of net income to net worth

Organizing Production

A producer must attend to important details about the best legal and managerial structure of the firm. The short story is that organization affects the profitability and risk of a business. The role of entrepreneurs in production, discussed earlier in the chapter, covers a few of the legal and organizational aspects of production. Here are additional details.

Legal Aspects of Production

In the first section of this chapter, you learn that entrepreneurs as owners are legally entitled to any residual income of the firm. Other laws influence what types of business organizations are legal, how businesses may contract with one another, and who is liable for damages that one business causes another. Economic factors, in turn, affect which organizational forms, which types of contracts, and which systems of legal liability are most efficient under various circumstances. What follows is a brief introduction to these few topics (among the many that could be chosen from the field of business law).

Legal Structure of Businesses

The U.S. legal system generally allows for three forms of business organization. The first, having a single owner, is called a **sole proprietorship**. The second, having two or more partners, is a **partnership**. The third, having shareholders, is a **corporation** that is legally distinct from any of its shareholding owners. Each form of ownership has advantages compared to the other, though the most advantages seem to be with single-owner firms or shareholder-owned corporations.

- **Sole proprietorship:** business with one owner who is personally liable for its debts
- **Partnership:** business with two or more owners who are personally liable for its debts
- **Corporation:** business entity with legal standing apart from its shareholders, who have limited liability for its debts; shares are transferable, and firm has continuity and access to more capital

Exhibit 12.4 shows the numbers and total business income for each type of business. About 73 percent of the firms in the United States are quite small, owned by sole proprietors. Fewer firms, about 7 percent, are organized as partnerships among several owners. Corporations, accounting for the remaining 20 percent, are more numerous than partnerships because of legal advantages mentioned below. Sole proprietorships, being generally small in size, account for only 5.1 percent of total business revenue, while partnerships, being a bit larger in average size but smaller in number, account for 5.5 percent. The remaining 89.4 percent of business revenues are earned by corporations.

Sole proprietorships and partnerships are personally owned businesses that cannot legally be distinguished from their owners. If you take the business to court, you are taking the owner or partners to court. Both are intact only if their proprietors or partners are alive. On the death of a partner, for example, the law requires the partnership to dissolve and reform, with heirs of the dead partner being paid for their share or otherwise compensated.

Exhibit 12.4: Sole Proprietors, Partnerships, and Corporations in the United States

	Sole Proprietors	Partnerships	Corporations
Number in 1995	16.4 million	1.6 million	4.5 million
Sales in 1995	$807 billion	$854 billion	$13,969 billion

Source: U.S. Bureau of the Census, 1999, *Statistical Abstract of the United States,* 1998, Table 856 (Lanham, MD: Bernan Associates), 540.

Large firms and some smaller firms are organized as **corporations** and are owned by their "shareholders," each owning one or more shares of a firm. A corporation has four distinct advantages over partnerships and proprietorships. It has **legal standing** to make contracts as a "body" or *corpus* that is independent of the humans who own shares of the company. The owners are also insulated from the debts of the firm and cannot lose more than their initial investment. This legal situation is called **limited liability**, because an individual owner's private property cannot be seized to pay for corporate debts (that is why English firms are called "limiteds" rather than corporations). Shares of a public corporation are traded on public stock exchange where almost anyone can become a part owner. This **transferability of shares** adds to the efficiency of the firm as minority shareholders come and go without disturbing the operation of the firm. The sale of shares enables a corporation to gather more capital than a proprietor or several partners could raise. Transferability also means that the corporation will have **continuity**, and will be able to exist longer than the lives of its owners if it is well managed.

As to control of the business, the personally owned firms do have advantages. Sole proprietorships give more control to the one owner, but partnerships give greater access to financial capital with some measure of control as a few partners pool wealth to invest in the firm. The corporation gives the least control to an individual owner, but the greatest protection from financial losses and the greatest access to financial capital through sales of shares of stock to more owners.

Legal Contracts

One of the most significant costs of running a business is writing and enforcing contracts with workers, other suppliers of resources, and buyers of product. With all of the effort that businesses and their lawyers put into writing contracts, you might think that all business contracts are written so as to cover most every contingency. Some contracts are in fact very detailed, especially those that banks use when lending money (see Mishkin 1998).

Many other contracts, however, are not very complete because specifying each and every contingency would be impossible. Especially when two businesses intend to carry out frequent transactions long into the future, specifying all future conditions under which they will trade could not be done. Instead, the firms will rely on **relational contracts** that involve mutual trust and an understanding that the agreement will be adapted to changing conditions in fair and mutually agreeable ways, according to norms of the contracting community (Williamson 1987, 71-72, 79).

- **Relational contracts** do not specify every contingency, but rely on trust.

More important than specifying every possible contingency is writing **incentive-compatible contracts**. Owners will find that their interests are not the same as their hired managers and workers unless they write contracts that reconcile their different goals. Managers and workers, for example, will want to increase the owner's profit if they too share in profits. Another approach is to pay managers bonuses that rise and fall with higher or lower profitability.

- **Incentive-compatible contracts:** reconcile the different interests of parties to the contract

Legal Liability of a Business

A business can be destroyed by a single mistake that causes great damages to others and for which it is found liable in the courts. Along with the potential for profit goes the responsibility for a harm or "tort" caused to others. Tort law specifies the conditions under which a firm or individual is liable for damages. Economists have shown that these conditions have economic significance. Judge Richard Posner (1972) is widely known among scholars in law and economics for his view that the laws of torts (and contracts as well) have developed in the common law to maximize economic efficiency, in the sense of maximizing wealth.

An example will show how different standards of liability for damages affect efficiency. Assume that Jim rammed his car into Joan's illegally double-parked car. Damaged cars are costly to individuals and society, because the repairs use scarce resources. Avoiding such auto accidents at relatively low cost is economically efficient. In tort law, a **negligence standard** puts responsibility on the party that caused the crash. Without going into all the details, Jim will have to pay Joan for damages if he could have prevented the accident at low cost. Since his windshield was muddy, the judge would rule that Jim was negligent in not cleaning it. This ruling will make Jim more careful to clean the windshield in the future, thus protecting economic wealth from damage. A **contributory-negligence** standard, however, would also consider that, at very low cost, Joan could have avoided the accident by parking legally out of the driving lane. Therefore, Joan could not collect damages if she could more easily have prevented the accident than Jim, making Joan more careful where she parks (Landsburg 1989, 395-96).

Management Methods

Business organizations vary in their styles of management. One corporate chief executive officer (CEO) might decree that the firm will be organized hierarchically, with power residing at the top, a strict chain of command, and discipline of workers strictly enforced. Another corporate CEO might allow for a more participatory form of management, with a flatter organizational structure in which power is shared and passed freely and workers are given freedom to offer and act on new ideas.

Which management style is better—a hierarchical form with command and control, or a participatory form with more freedom? That depends. The first corporate form may be most suitable to an industry under attack, where quick decisions must be made, or in a firm where mistaken decisions would be costly. The second corporate form would be more suitable to a business that requires workers to experiment and innovate, or to one whose workers are more independent-minded professionals. The U.S. Army, for example, is organized mainly on the hierarchical, command-and-control model, with chains of command clearly specified and enforced. Yet, the Army has a Special Forces unit in which soldiers are trained to operate in smaller groups, with soldiers acting much more independently than normal. Each form is suited to specific goals.

The quest for quality production in America has caused firms to rethink traditional management styles and organizational forms. Firms using assembly line production, where command and control was normal, have recently begun to empower their workers to make their own decisions. To ensure quality, many assembly line workers can now shut down the line if they spot a quality problem. And, where managers formerly gave direction to line workers and took no advice, now managers regularly seek new ideas from the workers, who may more thoroughly understand a production process and how to improve it.

Assessing Organizational Performance

How do businesses know whether a particular organizational form or another economic decision is beneficial to the firm? They use the efficiency measures introduced in chapter 2. Specifically, the firm can estimate average cost of producing each unit. Or the firm can estimate the average productivity of workers.

These measures are not, however, an adequate measure of efficiency when the firm is attempting to improve the quality of its product. As quality improves, normal measures of average cost may not decrease, but the average cost of *nondefective* products or

the costs of customer service may decline, and customer satisfaction may increase. Such complexities are why firms rely on measures of profitability to assess performance. Profitability can be compared among divisions of a firm or among firms in a similar business to determine how well management teams are doing.

Do Actual Firms Optimize?

An important question is whether firms really follow the techniques of economic analysis. For example, do firms really use the marginal method, choosing the output level at which marginal revenue equals marginal cost? Realism requires us to admit that many do not. Market competition, however, tests the methods by which firms do decide, rewarding those who act as if they do know economic theory and weeding out those making less-than-the best decisions. This is a long-run, not a moment-by-moment process, though.

Chapter Summary

1. Production transforms inputs such as raw materials, intermediate products, and the services of land, labor, equipment, and management into outputs of goods and services.

2. In a market economy, risk-taking private entrepreneurs and their hired managers are the main organizers of production.

3. Entrepreneurs as owners of a firm have a legal right to the residual income of the firm, called profit. They also have responsibility for debts of the firm and for monitoring productivity of workers. Entrepreneurs take significant risks, meaning that profit is not guaranteed in any venture.

4. The goals of a firm are assumed to be maximizing profit or the overall value of the firm. These goals correspond to the two major reports of the accounting books of any firm—the income statement and the balance sheet. The income statement shows profit or loss during each period, while the balance sheet shows the net worth (capital or equity) of the firm.

5. Two commonly calculated measures of profitability are the sales margin (net income / sales revenue) and the rate on investment (net income / equity invested).

6. Changes in market prices of inputs and outputs, and in other economic factors, will affect the firm's profitability and will, therefore, affect the firm's willingness to supply more or less product.

7. Three legal forms of business organization are sole proprietorship, partnership, and limited-liability corporation. Each form has advantages and disadvantages. Other legal rules affect contracts that a firm makes and liabilities for damages that it causes.

8. Business organizations vary in management style and in size based on their goals, transactions costs, and economic environment.

PROBLEMS FOR PRACTICE

12.1 What exactly is production?

12.2 List two examples of production of one good and one service not discussed in the text for which very special inputs are needed in their production.

12.3* Its books show that Acme Products has a net income of $113,482 on net sales of $2,383,410 and net worth of $1,400,952. What are the rates of profit out of net sales and net worth? Assume that the rate of taxation on Acme's income is about 30 percent.

12.4 a. What are a few of the risks that entrepreneurs face in organizing production? Add to the list in the text, if you can.

b. What exactly was the business risk that bankrupted entrepreneur Johannes Gutenberg in his quest to print the first mass-produced Bible? See Expansion Point 12.1.

12.5 Which of the following would increase or decrease the profitability of the firm? Explain how the books of the firm would be affected. Explain whether you mean economic or accounting profit. Explain how this is likely to affect the willingness of the firm to continue in business as it is.

a. Wages of workers rise.
b. The market value of the machinery the firm owns rises due to other valuable uses.
c. Product price rises due to higher demand.
d. The cost of an important raw material falls.
e. Accountants find an error in the books. The historical value of the equipment the firm owns is actually double the listed value.
f. Advertising costs will double next year. They comprise 20 percent of the firm's costs.

12.6* What are the various legal structures for organizing an advertising agency? How important is size of the agency and how important is creativity versus always being correct? What about a doctor's office? Which form would you favor for each and why?

12.7 What is a "tort" and why is it important to the owner of a business in the United States today?

12.8* If you were the CEO of a corporation in the electronics industry, what style of management would you tend to use and why?

For class discussion:

12.9 Do you think that greed is the main motive of most entrepreneurs? Some critics of capitalism do and this troubles them. Does it bother you that some entrepreneurs may be greedy? Explain your answer in terms of the functions of entrepreneurs and the alternative methods that society could use to organize production.

12.10 Institutional economists think that one of the most significant costs of production is the cost of negotiating and enforcing contracts. Think about firms that you know and consider any business training you have had. Do you agree with this assessment?

12.11 General Motors created a new organization to manufacture and sell its Saturn automobile. Briefly research what it tried to accomplish and why, and how successful the Saturn experiment has been. Be prepared to discuss the importance of organizational structure in light of General Motors' experience with its Saturn organization.

12.12 How could you apply the principles of Expansion Point 12.2 to the life of a college student? Can you bankrupt your efforts as a student? How might they apply to life in general, including relationships or spiritual life? Develop a list of applications for various contexts. Include relevant examples.

See Answer Key for hints/answers to starred (*) questions.

Chapter 13

PRICE THEORY

Determinants, Elasticity, and Market Structure

What this chapter will help you think about:

1. What factors cause shifts in demand and supply?
2. How can we analyze a shock to demand or supply?
3. What is price elasticity of demand?
4. How does elasticity of demand affect sellers' revenue?
5. What factors influence price elasticity of demand?
6. When evaluating elasticity of supply, what are the three planning periods?
7. What are the benefits of market exchange?
8. How do monopoly power and other market imperfections affect the benefits of market exchange?

- **Price theory:** explains why market prices (and output) change as they do
- **Determinants of demand & supply:** the lists of factors that cause demand and supply to shift, leading to changes in market price and quantity exchanged
- **Elasticity of demand & supply:** measures of the responsiveness of buyers and sellers to changes in price
- **Market structure:** presence of competitive or monopolistic characteristics, such as numbers of buyers and sellers, and freedom of exit and entry of firms

Price is what you pay in exchange for another product or resource. Because prices are so important in rationing scarce resources, a task of microeconomics has been to construct a theory of what determines market prices, based on the behavior of individual buyers and sellers. For this reason, microeconomics has also been called **price theory**. Price theory is methodological individualism in action.

Economists explain price determination using the model of demand and supply, the workhorse of economic analysis. As an economics student, you need a thorough understanding of a few more details about price theory. First, for what reasons do market prices change? These are called the **determinants of demand and supply**. Second, what determines how responsive buyers and sellers are to changes in prices? The technical terms for measuring responsiveness are **elasticity of demand** and **elasticity of supply**. Finally, how do variations in the structure of markets affect price determination? **Market structure** refers to the existence of competition or monopoly power in a market. In this chapter, we assess the effects of monopoly power on price and output.

Why Do Demand and Supply Shift?

According to demand-and-supply analysis, a market price changes because either demand increases or decreases, or supply increases or decreases. Price and quantity exchanged vary then only if one of the determinants of demand or supply changes. Exhibit 13.1 lists the determinants of demand and the determinants of supply. A change in any one of these factors will shift demand or supply and will cause a change in market price and quantity exchanged. Let's see how.

Exhibit 13.1: Determinants of Demand and Supply

Determinants of Demand	Determinants of Supply
1. consumer preferences	1. costs of production
2. consumer income	2. technology
3. prices of substitutes and complements	3. prices of goods related in production
4. expected future price	4. expected future price
5. government regulations, taxes, and subsidies	5. government regulations, taxes, and subsidies
6. interest rates	6. number of sellers in the market
7. number of potential buyers in the market	

Determinants of Demand

Price is the first determinant of demand. If the costs of construction increase and cause the prices of houses to increase, according to the law of demand, the quantity of houses that people demand will decrease. The nonprice determinants of demand, however, are all those other factors that cause a shift in demand. A changing price causes a change in quantity demanded. A shift in the nonprice determinants causes a shift in demand.

Exhibit 13.2 explains how each determinant of demand (listed in Exhibit 13.1) can cause higher demand for a good or service. Exhibit 13.3 then explains how the determinants of demand can cause *lower* demand for a good or service. Both exhibits contain an example for each determinant and a graph of the effects of the demand shift on price and quantity exchanged. Read carefully, and imagine your own examples.

Income, for example, is one of the nonprice determinants of demand. If the income of families who hope to be homeowners rose 20 percent (with building costs constant), we would expect an increase in the demand for houses at every price. This is a shift in demand, as shown in Exhibit 13.2. We are assuming that housing is a **normal good** and that more income causes higher demand.

• **Normal good:** if income increases, demand for such a good increases

The relationship of income changes to demand changes is not always this simple. For certain goods called economically **inferior goods**, as income rises, people buy less of a product. Low-income families, for example, are more likely to rent or buy a small, older house or apartment in many parts of the United States. As income rises, people tend to buy or rent newer and

• **Inferior good:** if income increases, demand for such a good decreases

Exhibit 13.2: What Changes in the Determinants of Demand Cause an *Increase* in Demand?

1. People like a good or service more.
A singer becomes popular, and sales of her CDs soar.

2. For a normal good, income rises.
With more income after graduation, a family eats more steaks.

For an inferior good, income falls.
A recession means the family has less income and buys more potatoes.

3. The price of a substitute in consumption rises.
If letter postage costs more, workers send more E-mails.

The price of a complement falls.
Airfare cuts mean that people will travel more and demand the use of more out-of-town hotel rooms.

4. Expected future price rises.
Expecting the state to sign a lucrative new production contract with their firm, insiders illegally buy more of their own stock.

5. A government regulation requires the product.
Seatbelt laws force car buyers to pay for them.

A tax on a good is lowered.
A tax on gasoline is cut and people drive more.

A government subsidy to buyers increases.
Loan subsidies encourage college attendance.

6. Interest rates fall.
Bank interest-rate cuts encourage more borrowing to buy cars.

7. The number of potential buyers increases.
A growing town population means more demand for products in its stores.

Graph of an Increase in Demand:
Price and quantity exchanged both increase.

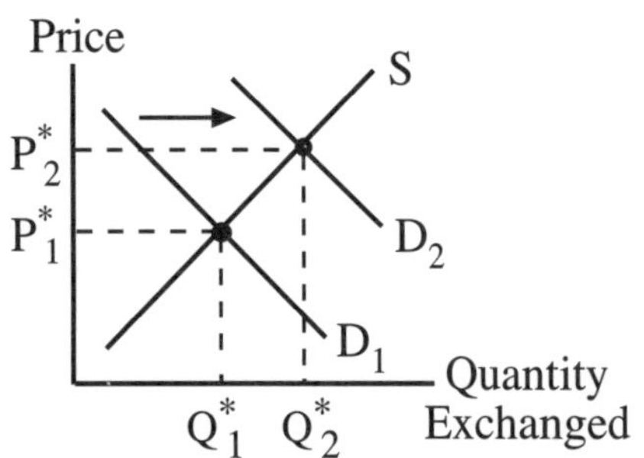

Exhibit 13.3: How Can the Determinants of Demand Cause a *Decrease* in Demand?

1. Buyers like a good or service less.
   Fear causes travelers to fly less often.

2. For a normal good, income decreases.
   Plant layoffs cause local car sales to flounder.

   For an inferior good, income increases.
   A pay raise means less shopping in bargain stores.

3. The price of a substitute in consumption falls.
   If the price of ABC soap falls, demand for XYZ soap falls.

   The price of a complement rises.
   Higher bus fare means lower sales for bus-stop vendors.

4. Expected future price falls.
   Expecting a bear market, investors buy fewer shares of stock now.

5. Government regulations restrict use of a good.
   A report that asbestos can cause cancer lowers the demand for existing houses with asbestos siding.

   A tax on a good increases.
   Due to a 10-percent U.S. tax on jewelry, Americans buy fewer diamond rings.

   A subsidy to buyers decreases.
   Energy-conservation subsidies end, and demand for house insulation falls.

6. Interest rates rise.
   Higher rates cause a drop in housing demand.

7. The number of potential buyers decreases.
   The end of a baby boom means lower demand for diapers and baby bottles.

Graph of a Decrease in Demand:
Price and quantity exchanged both decrease.

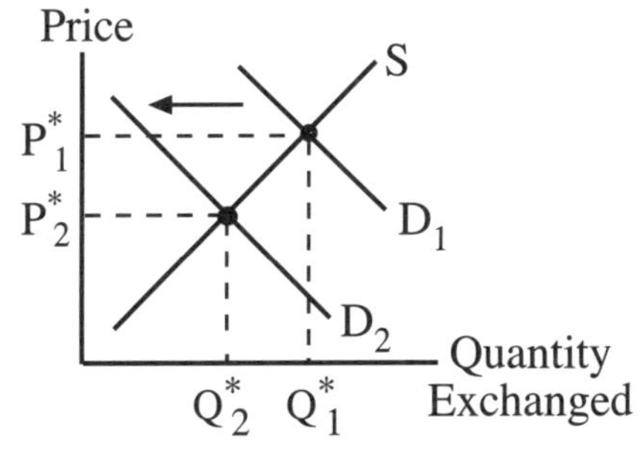

larger houses. Therefore, smaller, older houses and apartments are economically inferior goods. As people's incomes increase, they tend to buy or rent fewer of these properties.

A key to understanding Exhibits 13.2 and 13.3 is to recognize the importance of certain characteristics of goods and services. You already read about normal versus inferior goods in relation to changes in buyer income. What people like matters, and due to fads and fashions, likes and dislikes change over time. Another important characteristic is whether two goods related in consumption are **substitutes** or **complements**. Substitutes are used instead of one another, while complements are used together. Another characteristic of the market for many goods is that we have information about their future prices, which affect the good differently from current price. A higher current price causes quantity demanded to fall now. A higher *future* price, however, causes demand to increase at every price *now*.

- **Substitutes in consumption:** products that fulfill the same purposes
- **Complements in consumption:** products that are used together

Also recognize that many goods are subject to government regulation, taxes, and subsidies. Furthermore, the market for any good is subject to changing numbers of buyers and sellers, or demographic effects. Markets are also subject to the entry and exit of firms, due to profits and losses in competition.

Determinants of Supply

Price is also the first determinant of supply. If the price that people will pay for running shoes increases (as has happened over the past few decades), the quantity of running shoes that manufacturers supply will increase. A changing price due to a demand shift causes a change in quantity supplied. In the graphs of Exhibit 13.2 and 13.3, you will notice that when demand increases or decreases, the quantity supplied increases or decreases.

The nonprice determinants of supply are all those other factors that cause a shift in supply. For example, when the cost of materials used in running shoes rises, manufacturers and retailers pass along cost increases to buyers. Economists call this a decrease in supply. Alternatively, if manufacturers are able to use lower cost labor in foreign countries, they also pass these cost savings along as an increase in the willingness to sell the product or an increase in supply. The nonprice determinants of supply include cost of resources, technology, prices of substitutes or complements in production, expected future price, government regulations, taxes or subsidies, and the numbers of firms in the market.

Exhibit 13.4 explains how the determinants of supply (listed in Exhibit 13.1) can cause higher supply of a good or service. Exhibit 13.5 then explains how the determinants of supply can cause *lower* supply for a good or service. Here again, the exhibits contain examples and graphs of the effects of the supply shift on price and quantity exchanged. As with demand, try to imagine your own examples for each case.

→ MAIN DETERMINANT IS PRICE

Exhibit 13.4: What Changes in the Determinants of Supply Cause an *Increase* in Supply?

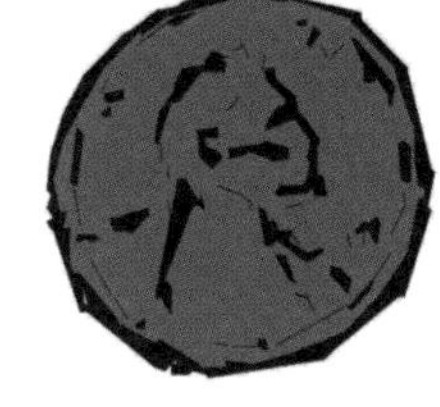

1. One or more of the costs of production decrease.
The cost of cooking oil falls, and bakeries increase supplies of cookies.

2. Technological change improves efficiency and lowers cost per unit.
Computer chips improve, and manufacturers offer them for less.

3. The price of a good that can be substituted in production falls.
Compact-car prices fall, and companies make more sport utility vehicles.

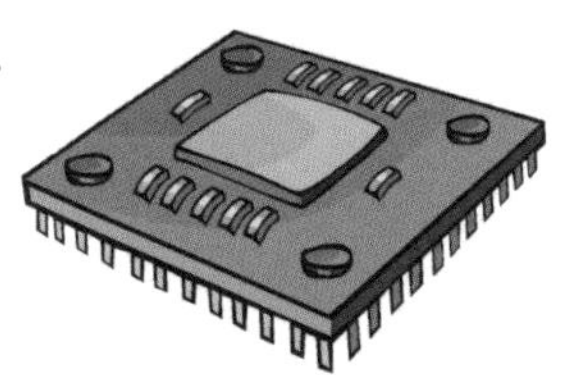

The price of a complement in production rises.
In winter, the price that people will pay for kerosene heating fuel rises, and refineries produce more gasoline, a by-product of kerosene.

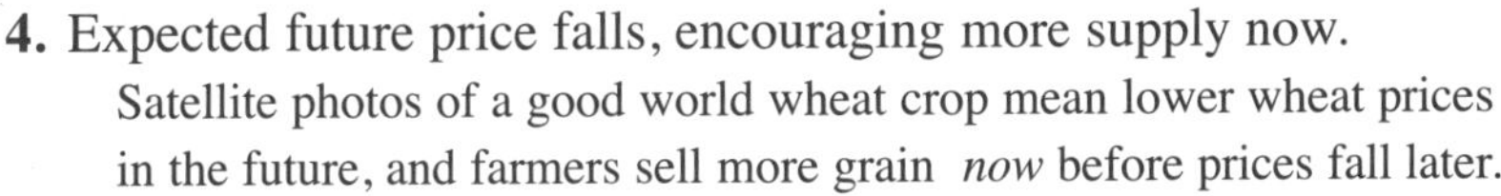

4. Expected future price falls, encouraging more supply now.
Satellite photos of a good world wheat crop mean lower wheat prices in the future, and farmers sell more grain *now* before prices fall later.

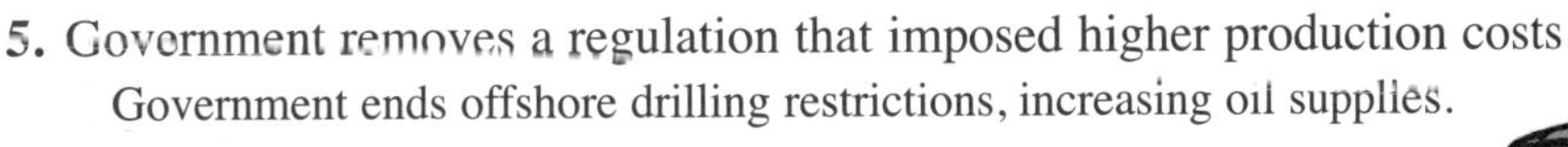

5. Government removes a regulation that imposed higher production costs.
Government ends offshore drilling restrictions, increasing oil supplies.

A tax on a resource used in production is lowered.
A tax on gasoline is cut, and companies with lower costs increase supply.

A government subsidy to producers increases.
The U.S. Congress renews farm subsidies, encouraging greater milk supply.

6. The number of sellers increases.
Increasing profitability of housing construction draws more builders into the market, and the supply of new houses increases.

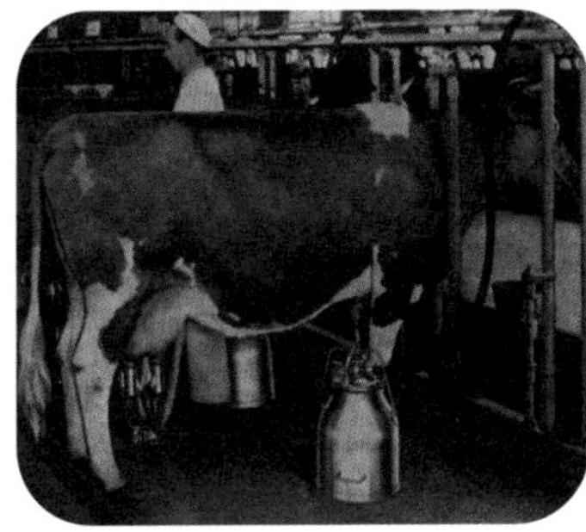

Graph of an Increase in Supply:

Price decreases and quantity exchanged increases.

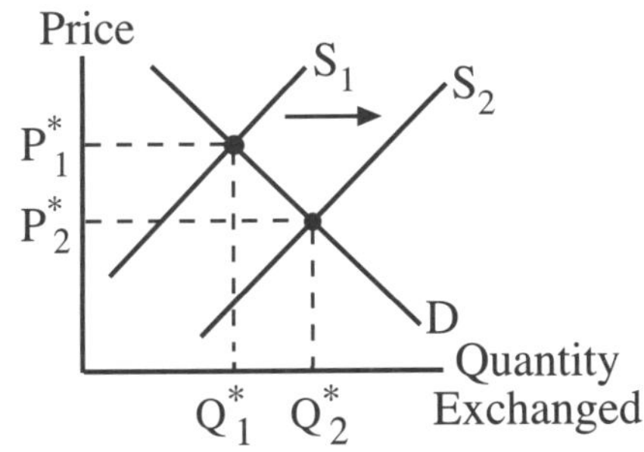

Exhibit 13.5: How Can the Determinants of Supply Cause a *Decrease* in Supply?

1. One or more of the costs of production increase.
   Workers demand higher wages, and the construction firm must charge more.

2. After a crisis, using older technology reduces efficiency.
   A war destroys farm equipment, and supplies of food decrease.

3. A higher price for a substitute in production makes the good more profitable.
   When action figures are profitable, toy companies cut production of other toys.

   The market price of a complement in production decreases.
   When the price of beef falls, butchers slaughter fewer cattle, and supplies of rawhide and bones (for making bonemeal) are lower.

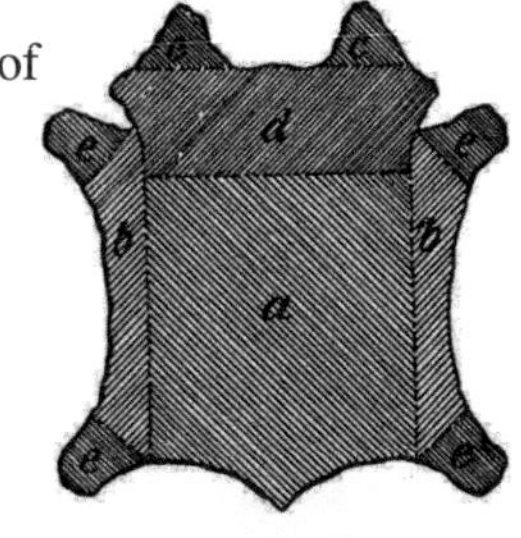

4. Expected future price rises.
   Expecting a drought in Asia to raise grain prices, farmers withhold grain supplies *now* in hopes of earning a higher profit later.

5. A government regulation raises production costs.
   OSHA requires mine ventilation equipment, reducing the supply of coal.

   A tax on a raw material increases, raising production costs.
   A higher tax on burning fossil fuels raises costs of electricity production at coal-fired generating plants, and companies cut electricity supplies.

   A subsidy to sellers decreases.
   A city stops giving tax breaks to local manufacturers, and they pass along costs to buyers (which is another way to say supply decreases).

6. The number of potential sellers decreases.
   Losses among computer manufacturers causes 25 percent of the firms to exit the industry, reducing the market supply of computers.

Graph of a Decrease in Supply:

Price increases and quantity exchanged decreases.

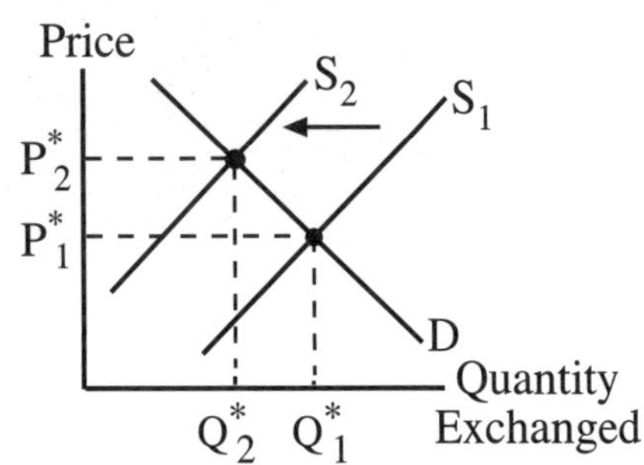

Disequilibrium and Adjustment: Five Steps to Analyzing Shifts in Demand or Supply

How do markets adjust when a determinant of demand or supply changes? In actual markets, more than one determinant will be changing at the same time. To keep introductory theory simple, however, principles-level explanations generally allow only one determinant to change at a time, holding other determinants constant.

For instructional purposes, practical questions about shifts in demand and supply take the following **general form**: what is the effect of a change in a single determinant of supply or demand on market price and output? For example, how will a drought in a coffee-producing region affect the worldwide price of coffee? A related question would be, what effect would a higher price of coffee have on the price of tea?

- **General form of demand and supply questions:** What is the effect of a change in one of the determinants of demand or supply on market price and output?

In economic theory, a change in a determinant of the demand for or the supply of some product shocks the market for that product. The shock creates a disequilibrium to which buyers and sellers react. Their adjustments will then restore equilibrium at a higher or lower price and higher or lower quantity sold. You should be able to carefully explain this process involving a shock, disequilibrium, and adjustment with the following **five-step method**. To illustrate, let's consider the question about how a drought in a coffee-growing region would affect the global market for coffee.

- **Market shock:** a change in a determinant of demand or supply that changes equilibrium price and output

- **Five steps to explaining market adjustments to demand and supply shocks:**
  1) assume initial equilibrium
  2) identify whether shock affects demand or supply
  3) explain the disequilibrium created
  4) explain price and output adjustments
  5) discuss real-world complications

First, Assume an Initial Equilibrium

Changing economic conditions constantly disturb markets. Realistically, market prices and outputs adjust constantly to numerous shocks. For instructional purposes, however, we will assume that one shock at a time affects a market in equilibrium. Therefore, assume an initial equilibrium of price and output in the market you are examining. Sketch an equilibrium of demand and supply in the market, labeling demand and supply curves, and equilibrium price and output.

Panel A of Exhibit 13.6 shows you such an initial equilibrium for the coffee market. The equilibrium price of $2.00 refers to the average retail price for a pound of coffee in the United States. The equilibrium quantity of coffee sold per year is 1.2 million tons.

Second, Identify the Type of Shock

Any shock to a product or resource market affects either demand or supply. You must identify whether the shock is a change in a determinant of demand or supply. You also must identify whether the shock increases or decreases demand or supply.

Exhibit 13.6: Effects of a Drought on the Coffee Market

Panel A

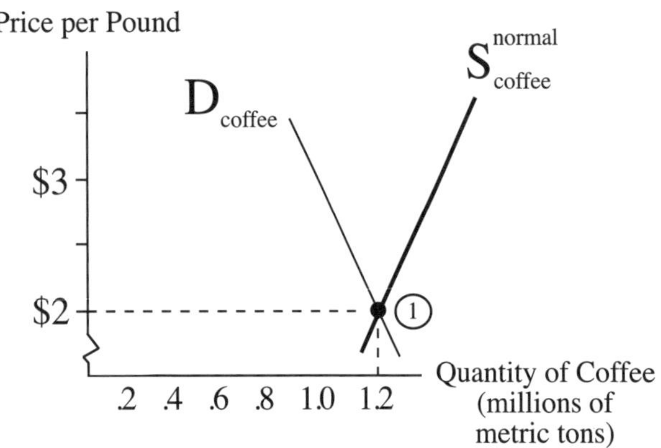

Panel B

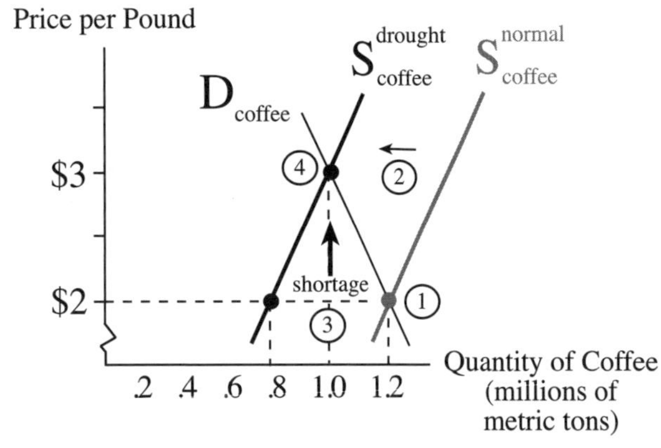

KEY

1) Initial Equilibrium	3) Disequilibrium
2) Shock to Supply	4) New Equilibrium

A drought in an agricultural market such as the coffee market, for example, causes a decrease in the willingness and ability to supply coffee. This decrease in supply is illustrated in Exhibit 13.6, Panel B, as the shift from S_{normal} to $S_{drought}$. Although supply appears to be moving up, this is a decrease in supply, with lower quantities supplied at every price.

Third, Identify the Disequilibrium Created in the Market

A shift in demand or supply creates disequilibrium at the old price of the product or resource. An increase in demand or decrease in supply creates a **shortage** at the old price. A decrease in demand or increase in supply creates a **surplus** at the old price.

A drought that reduces the supply of coffee creates a shortage of coffee at the initial equilibrium. The shortage is illustrated in Panel B of Exhibit 13.6. The amount of the shortage at a price of $2.00 per ton is 400 thousand tons.

Fourth, Explain Adjustments

Shortages and surpluses cause price changes. In a shortage, buyers try to outbid each other for limited goods or services as sellers take advantage of the opportunity to increase profit. In a surplus, sellers offer excess product at lower prices.

• **Shortage:** quantity demanded is greater than quantity supplied

In Panel B of Exhibit 13.6, the shortage causes the price of coffee to increase. The new equilibrium price is $3.00 per pound. The equilibrium quantity sold falls by 200 thousand to 1 million tons of coffee. As price rises, quantity demanded decreases, eliminating the shortage of coffee.

Fifth, Recognize Complications

The last step in analysis is to recognize that demand-and-supply analysis is a simplification of reality, an **abstract** model of actual market exchange that ignores irrelevant detail. What is irrelevant for economic instruction, however, is not irrelevant for understanding markets as a whole. So finish your analysis with comments about the details ignored in your analysis, especially important qualifications, secondary effects, and long-run effects.

Two important considerations are the secondary effects on other markets and the long-run effects of a protracted drought on supply. First, secondary effects could moderate a drought's impact on the coffee market. If significant numbers of coffee drinkers are also tea drinkers, for example, rising coffee prices will be moderated if many people switch to tea. Exhibit 13.7 illustrates that the demand for tea increases when the price of coffee increases. Furthermore, if the drought persists over several years, higher coffee prices worldwide would cause producers to plant more trees, increasing coffee supplies in the long run.

Exhibit 13.7: Demand for Tea Increases When the Price of Coffee Increases

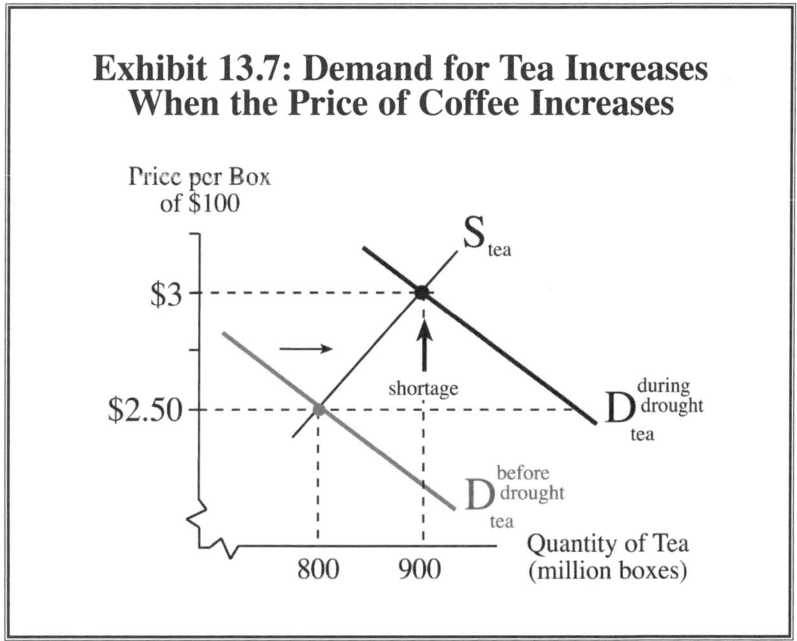

Coffee drinkers, however, may not quit drinking coffee until after rather dramatic increases in coffee prices. As coffee lovers say, "I need my fix in the morning." These are empirical questions: how substitutable is tea for coffee and how responsive is the demand for tea to a change in the price of coffee? We answer empirical questions, not with logical analysis of pure theory, but with statistical tests of the facts of the case. For example, we could gather historical data on coffee prices and the demand for tea, and try to isolate a statistical relationship between the two, holding other factors constant.

- **Surplus:** quantity demanded is less than quantity supplied

- **Abstract model:** a simplified representation of reality that ignores irrelevant detail, focusing instead on important instructional details

Finally, the market for coffee has no single price because coffee growers produce many varieties. Each variety of coffee would have its own equilibrium price. Moreover, to influence coffee prices, a drought must be widespread in a dominant coffee-producing region. A localized drought would reduce the revenues of local growers without affecting coffee prices significantly. Furthermore, drought is not the only cause of a shock to coffee supplies. As Expansion Point 13.1 explains, the coffee market is susceptible to other shocks as well, to both demand and supply.

Expansion Point 13.1: Coffee Prices Jump in 1997

In 1997, green (unroasted) coffee prices reached their highest levels in two decades due to market disturbances. A year earlier, in June of 1996, coffee purchased in a 60-kilogram bag had cost about $270. By mid-1997, coffee had risen to $460 per bag.

Shocks to both the demand for coffee and the supply of coffee caused the higher prices. As with other agricultural products, the supply of coffee can be volatile. In 1997, coffee supplies were not hurt by weather itself, but by labor unrest and by rumors of bad weather. Early in the year, South America, where a significant portion of the world's coffee is grown, experienced labor disturbances that interrupted coffee shipments. By March 1997, coffee prices were up about 75 percent, a three-year high.

Consumer demand for coffee is fairly steady, but the wholesale demand for coffee is more volatile. Shifts in wholesale demand due to weather reports and speculation can cause coffee prices to fluctuate. By June 1997, speculative demand for coffee pushed prices even higher on the worry that cold weather might frost the coffee crop.

Markets are complex, but the principles of demand and supply still apply. Both a decrease in supply and an increase in speculative demand create shortages that will cause coffee prices to increase.

Sources: Rhonda Shaffler, "Coffee Is a Costly Wake-Up," CNNFN, Monday, March 6, 1997. Found at http://cnnfn.com/hotstories/economy/9703/06/coffee_prices_pkg/index.htm.

Michael Rose, "Soaring Coffee Prices Jolt Roasters, Retailers," *Business Journal*, Portland, June 9, 1997. Found at http://www.amcity.com/portland/stories/060997/story3.html.

Elasticity of Demand and Shifting Supply

We know that when supply decreases and price rises quantity demanded for coffee falls, but by how much? That depends on how responsive buyers are to a price change. Economists use a **price elasticity of demand** to measure buyer responsiveness. Price elasticity of demand (E_d) equals the percentage change in quantity demanded divided by the percentage change in price. In math, the symbol delta (Δ) is read "change," so the definitional formula for elasticity of demand can be written:

$$E_d = \%\Delta Q_d / \%\Delta P$$

Illustrating Elasticity of Demand

We can illustrate variations in the responsiveness of buyer demand and in the price elasticity of demand by varying the slope of the demand curve. Elasticity and slope of the demand curve are not the same. The slope of the demand curve is the change in price divided by change in quantity demanded, while elasticity of demand is the ratio of *percentage* changes (with percentage change of quantity demanded in the numerator).

Exhibit 13.8 invites you to compare four different elasticities of demand. The graphs are of no particular product. Panel A illustrates totally responsive consumers, who change quantity

• **Price elasticity of demand** measures the responsiveness of buyers to a change in price; we calculate it as the percentage change in quantity demanded divided by percentage change in price.

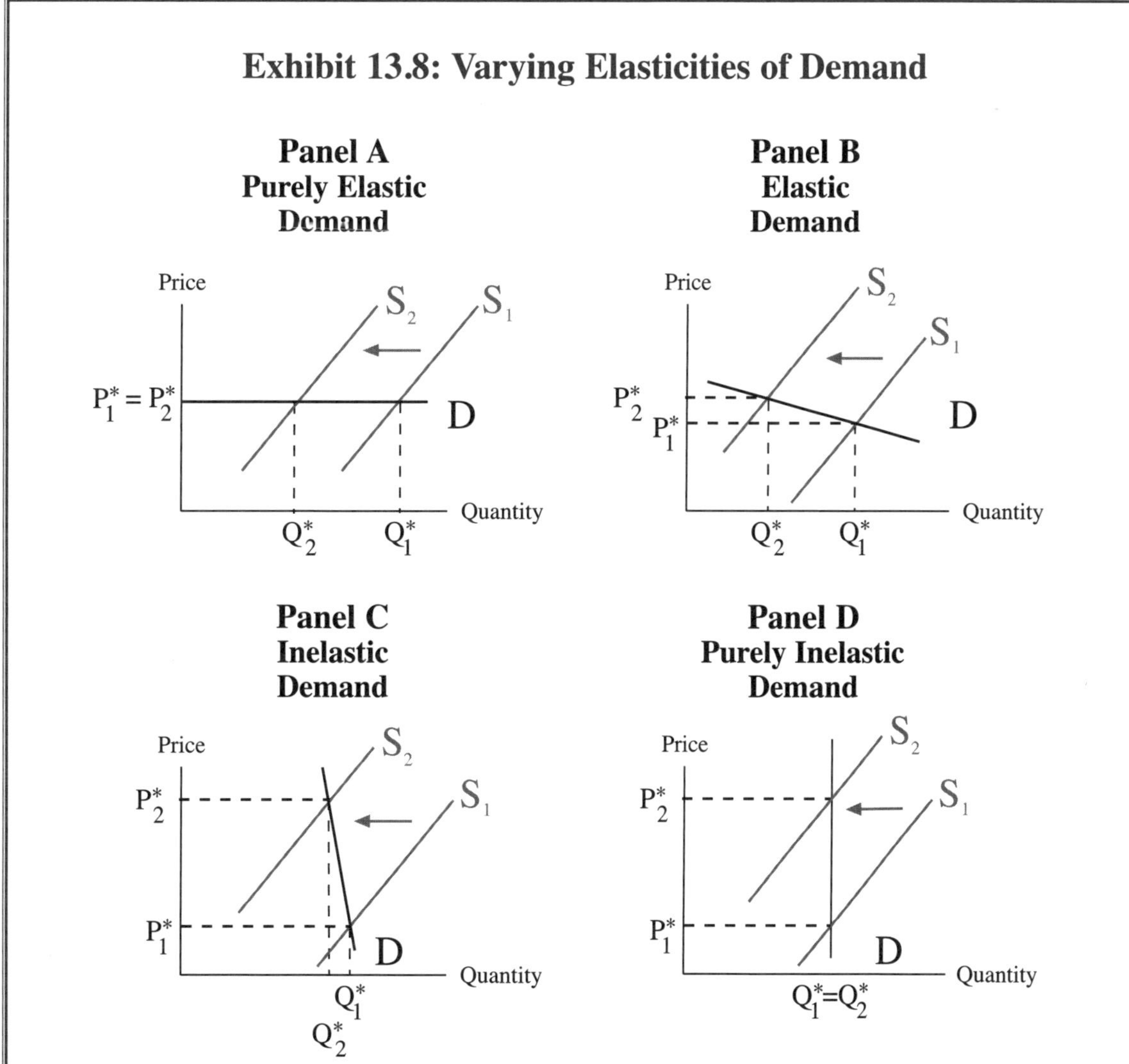

demanded at the mere hint of a price change. Therefore, no price change is needed to encourage them to find a substitute or to simply stop buying the product. We can use this case of purely elastic demand to illustrate the demand for agricultural products from an individual farmer (as opposed to market demand). If the farmer reduces his willingness to supply in half with a leftward shift in supply, as illustrated, product price does not change. Buyers would simply buy their corn, wheat, or beef from other farmers at the market price. One farmer's supply decisions do not affect product price because one farmer supplies so little of the market output.

Panel D on the other extreme illustrates totally unresponsive consumer demand. Even a sharp decrease in supply and a resulting higher price will not cause buyers to lower quantity demanded. This graph might illustrate the demand for heroin or some other very addictive drug. The graph shows why a drug dealer would be willing to give the first bit of heroin away for free. When the buyer is hooked, the dealer can then reduce supply, raising price to a very high level without losing the addicted customer.

Panels B and C of Exhibit 13.8 illustrate intermediate cases of **elastic** and **inelastic demand**. In both panels, shifting supply causes a change in product price and quantity demanded. In Panel B, the change in price is relatively less than the change in quantity demanded. This would illustrate demand for a product that is not a necessity or for which other substitutes exist. In Panel C, the change in price is relatively greater than the change in quantity demanded. This illustrates the demand for a good that is more of a necessity and for which few close substitutes exist. This graph could be used to illustrate increasing brand loyalty of a buyer.

For those who want to try the calculations, Expansion Point 13.2 shows how. It estimates the elasticity of demand for coffee (from Exhibit 13.6), using a formula for **percentage changes**.

Elasticity and Total Revenue

When the price of a product increases, will total revenue increase? Not necessarily. It depends on elasticity, on how responsive buyers are to the price increase. Let's see what happens to a coffee-seller's revenues when demand is inelastic and price increases. Total revenue (TR) equals price times quantity:

$$\mathbf{TR = P * Q}$$

When price of coffee increased, revenue to sellers of coffee increased by $1.2 billion. The old total revenue at retail was $4.8 billion while the new total revenue is $6.0 billion, as indicated in the following calculations:

$$\mathbf{TR_{old}} = [(1{,}200{,}000 \text{ tons}) * (2000 \text{ lbs. per ton}) * (\$2.00 \text{ per lb.})]$$
$$= \$4.8 \text{ billion}$$

- **Elastic demand:** elasticity of demand is greater than one (in absolute value) because $\%\Delta Q_d > \%\Delta P$

- **Inelastic demand:** elasticity of demand is less than one (in absolute value) because $\%\Delta Q_d < \%\Delta P$

- **Percentage change in any variable X** $= (\Delta X / \text{Avg. } X) * 100$ $= \{(X_{new} - X_{old}) / [(X_{new} + X_{old})/2]\} * 100$

Expansion Point 13.2: Calculating Price Elasticity of Demand

Whenever price and quantity change because of a known supply shift, we can estimate a price elasticity of demand. We first calculate the percentage changes in price and quantity demanded. Then we calculate the elasticity of demand.

The **percentage change in any variable** is the change in the variable divided by the average value of the variable, with everything multiplied by 100 to convert a ratio into a percent. Assume, as in the earlier example, that the coffee price increases from $2 to $3 per pound and quantity sold falls from 1.2 to 1.0 million tons. We calculate percentage changes as follows:

$$\begin{aligned}\%\Delta Q_d &= \{(Q_{new} - Q_{old})/[(Q_{new} + Q_{old})/2]\}*100\\ &= \{(1.0 - 1.2) / [(1.0 + 1.2)/2]\}*100\\ &= (-0.2 / 1.1)*100\\ &= -18\%\end{aligned}$$

$$\begin{aligned}\%\Delta P &= \{(P_{new} - P_{old})/[(P_{new} + P_{old})/2]\}*100\\ &= \{(\$3 - \$2)/[(\$3 + \$2)/2]\}*100\\ &= (\$1 / \$2.50)*100\\ &= 40\%\end{aligned}$$

The price elasticity of demand for coffee is the ratio of the two percentage changes:

$$\begin{aligned}E_d &= \%\Delta Q_d / \%\Delta P\\ &= -18\% / 40\%\\ &= -0.45\end{aligned}$$

The price elasticity of coffee demand is less than 1 in absolute value (removing the negative sign) because consumers were relatively unresponsive to the change in price. A 40-percent change in price caused only an 18-percent drop in quantity of coffee demanded. Demand, therefore, is **inelastic**. If the price elasticity of demand were greater than one, demand would be **elastic**, meaning that consumers were relatively responsive to a price change. While these numbers are hypothetical, they are realistic in that coffee lovers tend to drink it even at high prices.

A **simplified working formula** for price elasticity of demand results by canceling the two twos and the two 100s on top and bottom of the elasticity formula:

$$E_d = \frac{[(Q_{new} - Q_{old}) / (Q_{new} + Q_{old})]}{[(P_{new} - P_{old}) / (P_{new} + P_{old})]}$$

$$\begin{aligned}\mathbf{TR_{new}} &= [(1{,}000{,}000 \text{ tons}) * (2000 \text{ lbs. per ton}) * (\$3.00 \text{ per lb.})]\\ &= \$6.0 \text{ billion}\end{aligned}$$

This result is true because of a mathematical relation that the percentage change in total revenue equals the percentage change in price plus the percentage change in quantity demanded. The formula is

$$\%\Delta TR = \%\Delta P * \%\Delta Q$$

When consumers are relatively unresponsive to a price increase, total revenue to the seller will rise. When consumers are very responsive to a price increase, total revenue will fall. These relations among price elasticity of demand, price changes, and total revenue changes are summarized in the table of Exhibit 13.9.

If, in the example of a drought that reduces coffee supplies, the demand for coffee had been elastic, then a 40 percent increase in

• **Determinants of price elasticity of demand:**
1) share of budget
2) availability of substitutes
3) time to adjust

price would have caused a greater percentage decrease in quantity demanded. In that case, total revenue for coffee sellers would have decreased.

Exhibit 13.9 also summarizes the relation between price elasticity of demand and total revenue graphically. In the graph in Panel A, supply decreases and demand is very inelastic. As you can see, a large gain from a higher price more than offsets a small loss of revenue from reduced sales. In the graph of Panel B, supply decreases and demand is very *elastic*. Here, lost revenue from reduced sales offsets a small gain from a higher price.

Why Elasticity of Demand Varies

Whether consumer demand for a particular product is elastic or inelastic depends on at least **three factors**: (1) the proportion of the budget spent on the product, (2) the availability of substitutes for it, and (3) the time available to adjust buying patterns.

Exhibit 13.9: Price Elasticity of Demand, Price Changes, and Total Revenue Changes

Panel A
Inelastic Demand

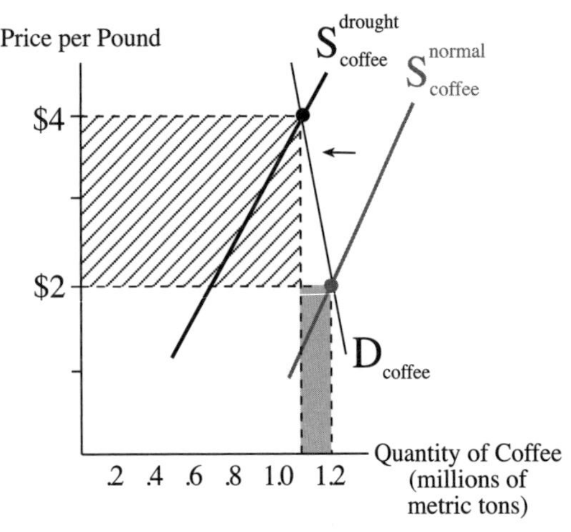

Panel B
Elastic Demand

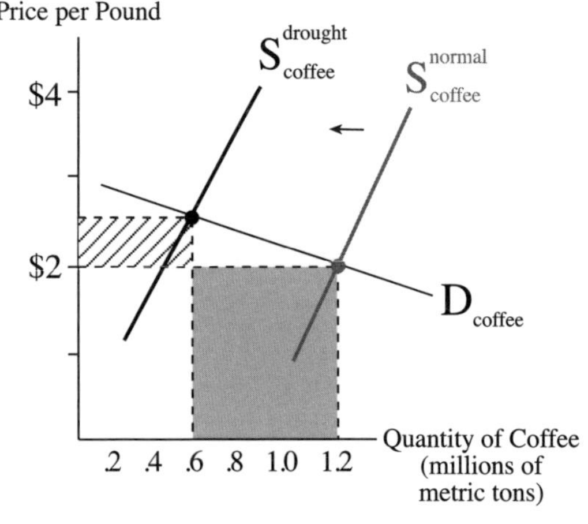

Price Elasticity of Demand*	Elasticity Designation	Price Change	Total Revenue Change
$E_d > 1$	elastic demand	increase decrease	decrease increase
$E_d = 1$	elastic demand	either	constant
$E_d < 1$	inelastic demand	increase decrease	increase decrease

*In absolute value

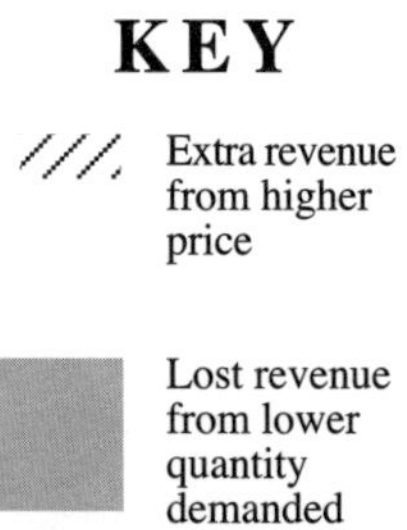

Share of the Budget. The more a family spends of its household **budget** on an item, the more responsive it will be to a change in its price. Households normally spend very little of their budget on salt, and when they need it, they buy it. Since food shoppers don't fret the price of salt, its demand is price inelastic.

The same is not true about other products like housing. If the price of a rental apartment doubles, a family most likely will look for another apartment. The demand for housing would tend to be more elastic than the demand for salt. The family budget can tolerate a doubling of the price of salt, but not of housing. Back in Exhibit 13.8, Panel B would illustrate housing demand while Panel C, or perhaps D, would illustrate demand for table salt.

Availability of Substitutes. The more **substitutable** other products are, the more responsive buyers will be to a price change. Salt has few substitutes, giving another reason for inelastic demand for salt. The demand for necessary prescription medicine would also be inelastic if no other substitutes exist.

Substitutability of products varies with how specific we are about type or brand name. The demand for a specific brand of a product will be more elastic than the demand for the entire product category, because specific brands are substitutable for one another, but the product overall may not have close substitutes. The demand for one brand of athletic shoes is more elastic (more responsive to a price change) than the overall demand for athletic shoes. The more specific the product, the more elastic is demand.

This principle is also true with demand for food and specific food products. In our diets, we can substitute one grain for another or one fruit for another. Therefore, if the price of apples goes up, we buy more pears or oranges. Our demand for food overall, however, is less responsive to a price change, because we need a certain amount in our diet and little else substitutes for food. Because agricultural supply is highly variable, the inelasticity of food demand poses special problems for farmers, as explained in Expansion Point 13.3 on the "Paradox of Agriculture."

Time to Respond. The third influence on elasticity of demand, **time for response**, is also related to substitutability. The more time consumers have to adjust their buying habits, the more elastic is their demand for any product. Exhibit 13.10 shows this effect on the demand for gasoline. If the price of gasoline rises today, buyers can't find immediate substitutes for gas. So the short-run demand for gasoline tends to be inelastic. Over time, however, gasoline users can buy smaller cars that use less gas, move or change jobs so that their homes are closer to their work, take fewer long trips by car, and so on. These are, in fact, the long-run responses of U.S. consumers in the years following the oil and gasoline crises of 1974 and 1979. The demand for gasoline is more elastic in the long run, as consumers have time to adjust.

Expansion Point 13.3: The Paradox of Agriculture

The paradox of agriculture, a traditional topic of microeconomics, made the news in the summers of 1997 to 1999. Farmers were complaining that a bumper crop, a crop spilling over the back bumper of the grain wagons, meant lower revenues, not higher revenues. Two factors cause the paradox: the extreme inelasticity of demand for raw agricultural products, and the variability of agricultural supply.

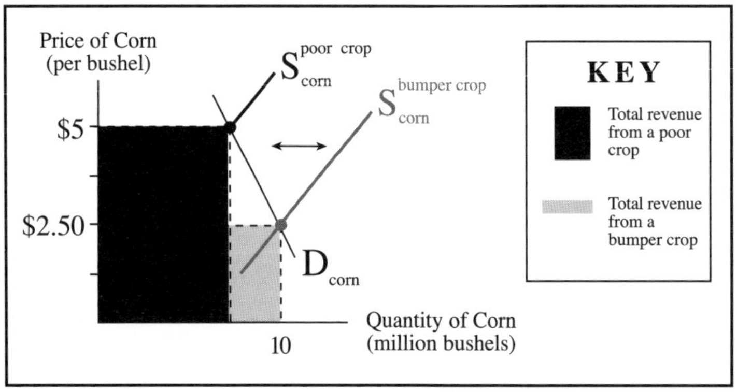

Economists have estimated a price elasticity of demand for agricultural products in the United States as low as about 0.2 (in absolute value). On the one hand, food is a necessity, but, on the other hand, people need only so much food. As a result, a 10 percent drop in prices only increases consumption of raw agricultural products like milk, wheat, and corn by 2 percent. The vagaries of nature create the weather variations that cause agricultural supplies to fluctuate from year to year.

As a result of inelastic demand and variable supply, farm incomes tend to fluctuate widely, as illustrated in the graph of the demand and supply for corn. When supply is high, the price of corn plummets to $2.50 and farm revenue declines to $25 million dollars. When supply is low, the price of corn increases to $5.00 and farm revenue rises to $40 million.

The crisis in 1999 actually began in 1997, a strange twist of circumstance as it turned out. The crisis of the late 1990s was rooted in two factors: bumper crops since 1997 and falling U.S. farm exports since 1997. Even during the drought of the summer of 1999, farmers outside the Eastern and Southern United States and farmers with clay-based soils were still reporting exceptional yields. The Asian financial crisis of 1997, meanwhile, had caused economic recession and reduced family incomes. Asians had less money to buy food, causing reduced grain exports from the United States and further downward pressure on prices.

A similar crisis had afflicted American farmers during the Great Depression of the 1930s. The Depression reduced incomes and demand for food in the cities, causing lower commodity prices and severely lower farm incomes. Potato farmers, for example, could not make enough revenue to pay even the cost of shipping potatoes to markets. The U.S. government had responded with commodity price supports that paid farmers a "fair price" during years when crop prices would otherwise be low. Over the years, the program grew into an agricultural welfare program, especially for large corporate farms.

The program of price supports, subsidies, and other farm aid continued in various forms until a Republican-led Congress passed the "Freedom to Farm" bill in 1996. Dwindling worldwide grain supplies and high U.S. farm prices in 1995 and 1996 suggested that farm supports were no longer needed. A wave of free-market sentiment also fueled the fire for reform. When Democratic President Bill Clinton signed it into law in December 1996, the bill began to phase out most farm subsidies through the year 2002.

Within two years of Freedom to Farm's passage, however, American farmers were in trouble from the Asian crisis and plummeting agricultural prices. Soybean prices fell from an average of $7.35 a bushel in 1996 to $5.46 in October 1998. Corn fell from an average of $3.25 a bushel in 1995 to $2.19 in October 1998.

Sources: U.S. Bureau of the Census, 1999, *Statistical Abstract of the United States: 1998,* Table 1128 (Lanham, MD: Bernam Associates), 681.

"Final Soybean CRC Harvest Price," November 18, 1998. Found at http://www.americanag.com/html/mforum/soyb1118.htm.

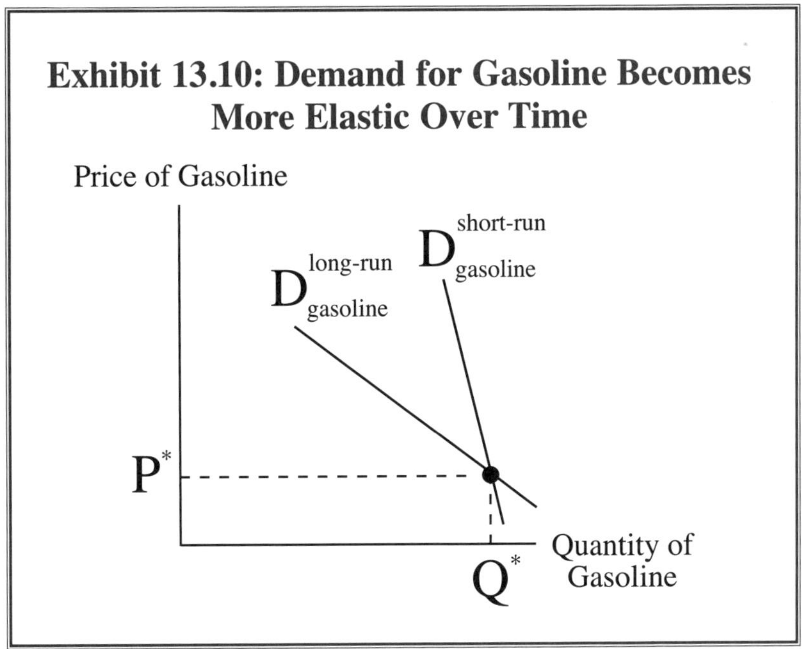

Elasticity of Supply

The responsiveness of sellers to a price change, called the **price elasticity of supply**, affects market price and quantity when demand is shifting. Elasticity of supply with respect to price equals the percentage change in quantity supplied over the percentage change in price:

$$E_S = \% \Delta Q_S / \% \Delta P$$

Let's consider why elasticity of supply varies and why that is important. The chief determinant of elasticity of supply is time. Except for the supply of land, the more time suppliers have to adjust, the more responsive supply will be.

A convenient way to summarize a supplier's adjustment time is to divide the supplier's planning horizon into three periods: the market period, short run, and long run. In the market period, quantity supplied is fixed, and we say that elasticity of supply is zero. In the short run, a manager can increase or decrease quantity supplied by varying the use of labor and other variable resources. In the short-run period, however, equipment is fixed in supply, limiting a seller's adjustment to changing demand conditions.

In the long run, all suppliers can vary their equipment and labor force, and supply is most responsive over time. Therefore, supply is more elastic in the long run than in the short-run period. Exhibit 13.11 shows the different elasticities of supply in the different planning periods.

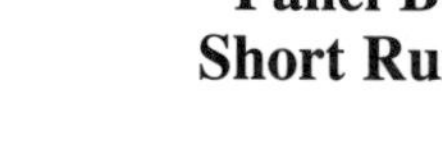

Exhibit 13.11: Elasticity of Supply and Bread Pricing in the Market Period, Short Run, and Long Run

Panel A
Market Period

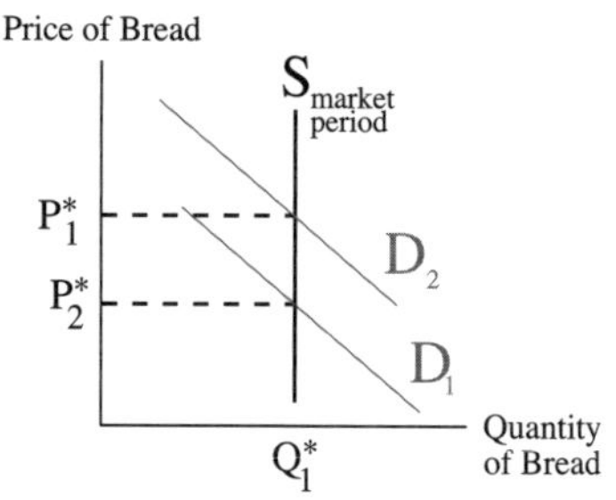

Panel B
Short Run

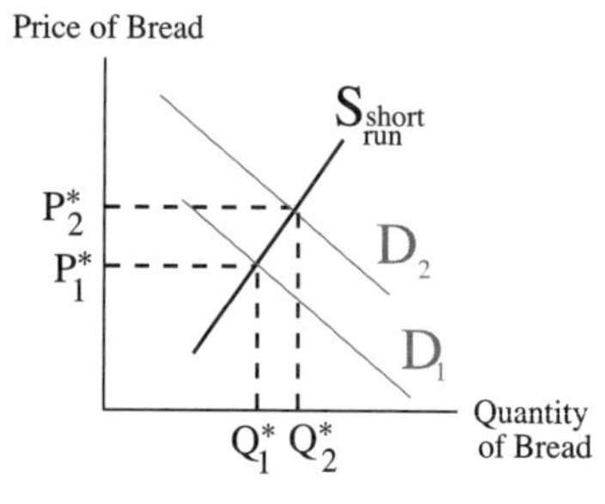

Panel C
Long Run

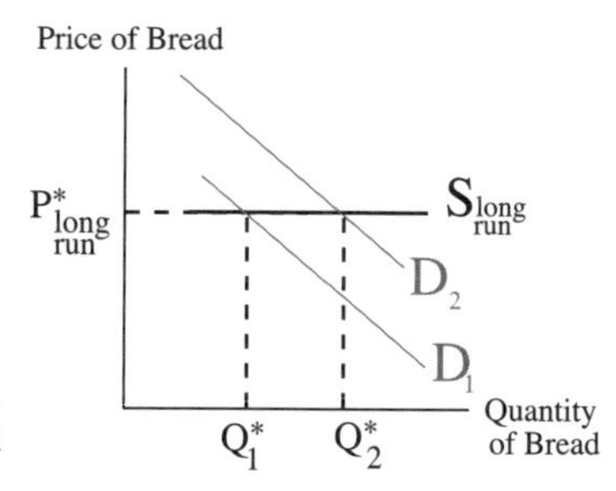

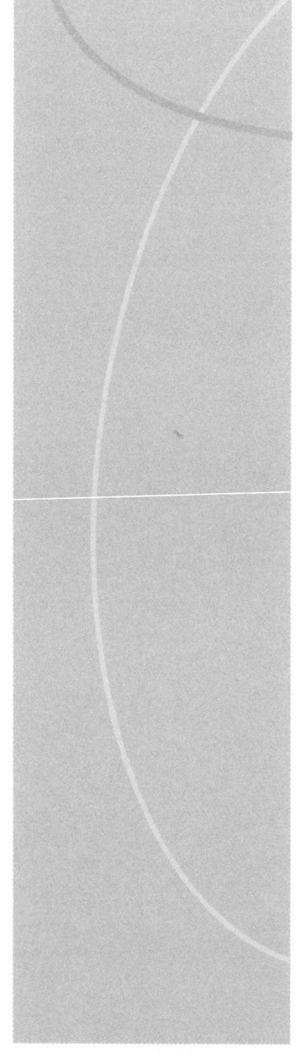

Supply in the Market Period

Panel A illustrates market-period supply of bread on a given day at a local farmer's market with shifting demand. The quantity of bread for the day cannot be increased or decreased, as shown by the vertical supply curve. Supply in the market period is purely inelastic. Whether or not the price of bread is negotiated up and down, the equilibrium price of bread—the price needed to clear the shelves, with no buyers unable to buy—is completely determined by the level of the demand for bread.

Bread prices in the United States don't appear to fluctuate, because the bakery prints prices on bread bags or on plastic tabs. At fixed prices, fluctuating bread demand leaves too little bread or too much bread each day. Yet, bread-truck drivers do assess how well bread is selling, using discount stickers on day-old bread to eliminate surpluses. So average bread prices do vary with demand.

Supply in the Short Run

Panel B of Exhibit 13.11 shows short-run supply of bread with shifting demand. In the short run, bread makers can adjust bread output by adjusting employment of workers. If demand is high, bakery managers can hire more laborers to work with existing baking equipment. The ability to supply more depends on the technical conditions of production. Therefore, in the short run, the price of bread depends on the interaction of supply and demand. If bakeries continually find they have too much day-old bread to sell at a discount, they will cut production by working their bakeries for fewer hours or operating fewer ovens.

Supply in the Long Run

Panel C of Exhibit 13.11 shows the long-run supply of bread

with shifting demand. It assumes that bread production is characterized by constant returns to scale (constant average costs), as explained in chapter 6. If that is true, then the equilibrium price of bread will be determined in the long run, not by shifting demand, but by the average costs of production when bakery equipment is being used efficiently. We assume constant average costs only for instructional purposes, not because the bread industry necessarily will exhibit constant costs.

• **Market structure:** presence of competitive or monopolistic characteristics, such as numbers of buyers and sellers, and freedom of exit and entry of firms

Market Structure and Price Theory

Market structure refers to the competitiveness or lack of it in a market. In a **purely competitive** market, **large numbers** of buyers and sellers compete in a market for a **homogeneous product**. Homogeneous means that every producer makes products with the exact same characteristics and all are perfect substitutes for one another. All sellers are **price takers**, meaning that a change in only one producer's supply will not influence market price. The purely competitive market is also subject to **free entry and exit** of firms.

• **Characteristics of pure competition:**
1) large numbers
2) homogeneous product
3) price-taking sellers
4) free entry and exit

In the United States, farming illustrates competitive conditions of large numbers, very similar or homogeneous products, price-taking farmers (as illustrated in the discussion earlier of Exhibit 13.8, Panel A), and free entry and exit. In Russia, where many workers are paid with products from the factory and where many gardeners grow the same crops, roadside sales of enameled pots and cucumbers approach competitive conditions.

In a market characterized by **monopoly**, only **one seller** offers a product that has no **close substitutes**. The monopolist is a **price searcher**, meaning that the firm searches for the price that maximizes profits. Complete **barriers to entry** by other firms protect the monopolist's position. No other firms can enter the market due to the monopolist's government license, a crucial patent or trade secret, or economies of large scale that make other smaller firms hopelessly inefficient.

• **Characteristics of monopoly:**
1) one seller
2) product with no close substitutes
3) price-searching seller
4) barriers to entry

Utilities illustrate monopoly power in practice. The local electric company has a government license as the only seller of a product with no close substitutes for lighting houses. Local telephone companies have similar monopoly franchises in the United States. Until the Internet, telephones were the only source of immediate communication over long distances.

The long-run supply of a product illustrated in Panel C of Exhibit 13.11 approximates conditions in certain competitive markets: constant average costs. If firms can enter and exit an industry without influencing resource costs, constant costs will prevail in the long run. We can use such a description of competitive markets to compare the effects of competitive and monopolistic conditions on social welfare.

Long-Run Competitive Pricing

To compare competition and monopoly, let's first consider certain key principles from microeconomic theory about long-run competitive-market pricing and profits. We are, in effect, starting with our conclusions (rather than deriving them). In the long run in a competitive market, the price of a product will tend toward average cost of production. In other words, profits will tend to zero in the long run. What is required for zero economic profits? Entry and exit must be relatively easy for firms. Free entry and exit adjusts the supplies of resources and product so that firms will only break even, covering all economic costs.

The Sock Market

Let's assume that a large number of domestic and foreign hosiery manufacturers produce standard types of socks for the U.S. clothing market and that the industry has constant average costs. Entry and exit into the industry are free. Exhibit 13.12 illustrates competitive pricing of socks in the long run. When sock producers have made all adjustments to capacity, the long-run price exactly covers all economic costs. On the price axis of the graph, $\mathbf{P_{lr} = AC}$ is read, "Price in the long run equals average cost of each unit produced."

Competition in the sock market benefits society by providing socks at a minimum cost without excess returns to anyone who produces and distributes them. We say that competition is productively and allocatively efficient. Productive efficiency describes how competition assures that sock producers will use the

Exhibit 13.12: Long-Run Competitive Pricing of Socks Made at Constant Average Costs

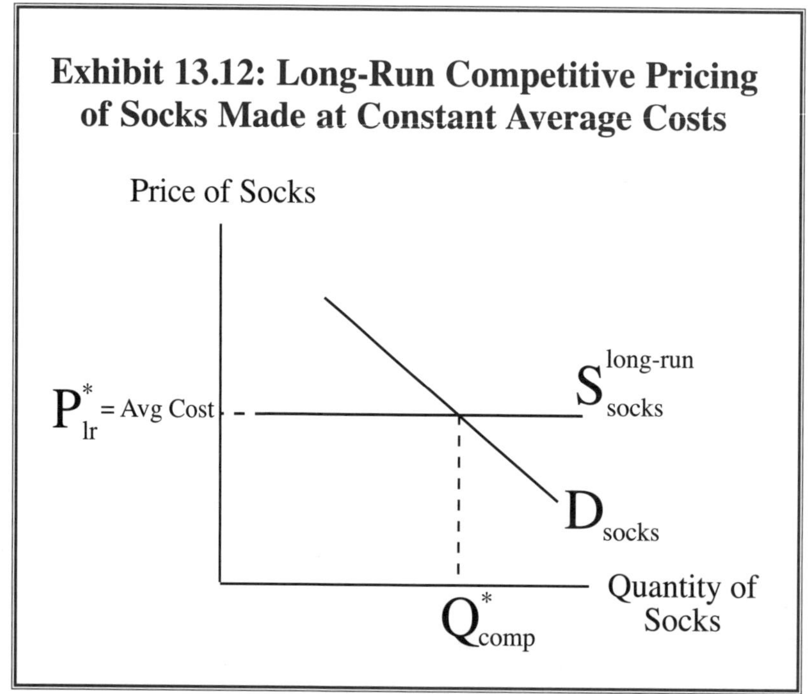

most efficient mixes of capital, labor, energy, and other inputs to production. Allocative efficiency describes how competition brings the right total quantity of capital, labor, and other inputs into each industry. This is assured by free entry and exit of firms in response to economic profits and losses.

A Qualification and Conclusion

One qualification about competitive efficiency has to do with whether prices reflect full information of economic conditions. Productive and allocative efficiency in competition both require that prices of goods and services reflect the actual benefits of the good to society and that the prices of productive inputs reflect actual scarcities or availabilities of the inputs.

The conclusion is that competition among firms reconciles the interests of a firm to make a profit with society's interests in using resources efficiently. This is true in pure theory, but arguable as a description of all industries in actual market economies. Where monopoly power exists, it interferes with the social benefits of competition. While some economists (especially those of the Chicago school) apply this principle to all markets, whether they seem competitive or not, critics of this approach emphasize the costs of monopoly power and the need for government regulation.

Monopoly Pricing

A monopolist is the only seller of a product with no close substitutes. A patent or some other barrier blocks entry into the industry. Economists and antitrust law in the United States both assume that firms that have monopoly power will use it to earn an economic profit. A monopolist has no guarantee that demand will allow for an economic profit, but if conditions allow, theory assumes that the monopolist will earn it through maximizing behavior.

Cornering the Sock Market

Let's assume that a powerful conglomerate of sock manufacturers develops, gaining control of the domestic sock industry and limiting entry by winning government protection against imports and other domestic competitors. What effect would such a change in market structure cause? The simplest way to illustrate monopoly power is to assume (without the proof of more advanced microeconomic analysis) that an unregulated monopoly will restrict output and charge a higher price, when compared to competitive price and output.

By restricting output below the competitive level and charging a higher price, monopoly reduces social welfare compared to purely competitive markets. Consumers must pay a price that is above average cost of production, implying that their limited income will meet fewer needs. As a whole, society is paying more for socks than it would pay under competitive conditions. The value of the last pair of socks produced under monopoly is also

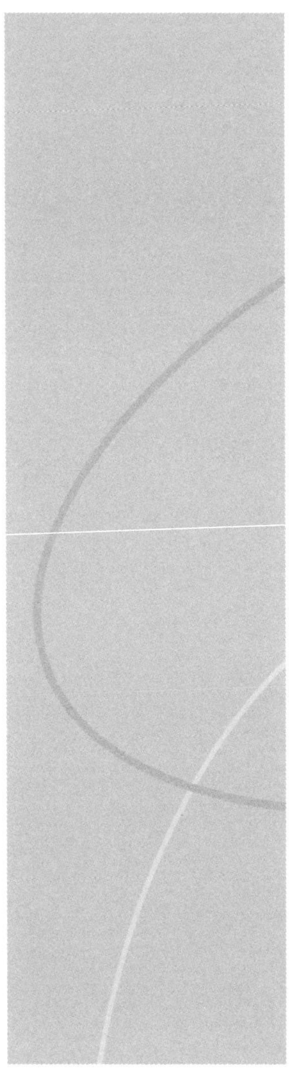

greater than the marginal cost, indicating that society is under-supplied with socks. Monopoly, therefore, violates the equi-marginal rule of optimality and allocative efficiency.

Figure 13.13 illustrates the effects on price when monopoly restricts output and charges "what the market will bear." P_{mon} and Q_{mon} are monopoly price and output. P_{comp} and Q_{comp} are purely competitive price and output. Notice that competitive supply exhibits a constant average cost and constant economies of larger scale in the industry being represented. The shaded area is a geometric representation of the value of monopoly profits [monopoly profit = (P_{mon} - Avg Cost) * Q_{mon}]. Under competitive conditions, remember, economic profits are zero due to the exit and entry of firms into the industry. Monopoly profits (excess or economic profits) here will not be eliminated because free entry or exit is impossible in such a market.

Qualifications

The conclusion that monopoly is socially inefficient is strictly true only when the production process exhibits no economies of large scale. Economies of scale means that as output increases by expanding the size of the production facility, average costs fall. In the case of economies of large scale, one or several very large firms might be socially more efficient than an industry with many smaller, competitive firms.

The view that monopoly restricts output and raises price to reap an economic profit is the basis for antitrust laws and regulation of business. Free-market economists, however, contend that all businesses must compete with one another and that no one has absolute monopoly power. Even the threat of entry by another firm, for example, might encourage a monopolist to price competitively (this is called a contestable market). Other questions surround the relative size of monopoly profits. In Exhibit 13.13, the shaded area makes monopoly profit appear to be about 1/3 of total revenue for the monopoly. This is an exaggeration compared to

Exhibit 13.13: Monopoly Restricts Output and Charges a Higher Price

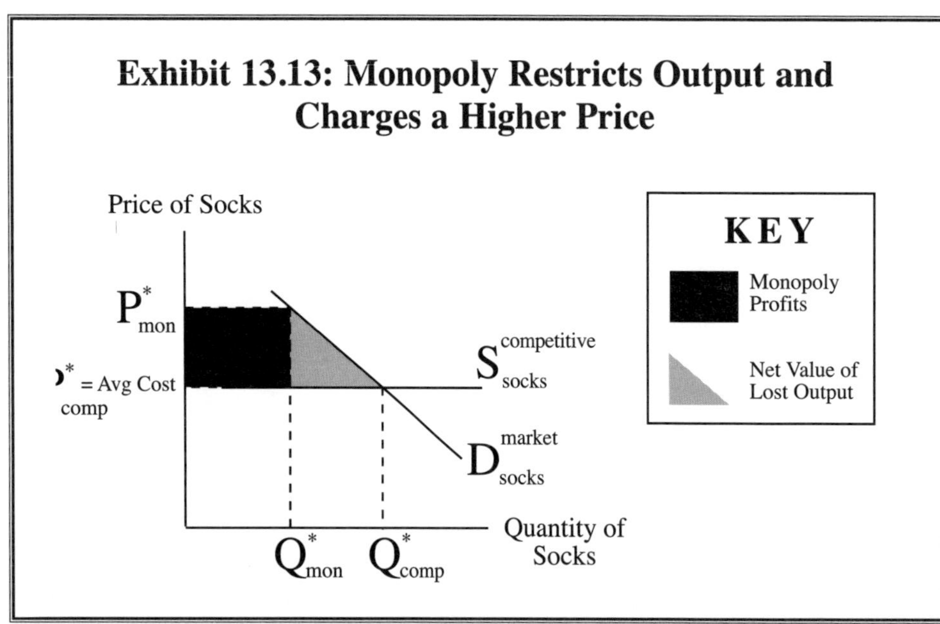

estimates for the United States that monopoly profits range from 0.1 percent to 10 percent of the total value of economic output.

Other Market Imperfections

Pure monopoly is not the only threat to the benefits of competitive market production and exchange. The theory of imperfect competition includes a range of possible defects. Economists, for example, have developed several other models of market structure to fill the gap between monopoly and pure competition. The two most commonly considered are monopolistic competition and oligopoly. Economists also consider imperfections due to asymmetric information between buyer and seller about the quality of the good or service being sold.

Monopolistic Competition

Monopolistic competition is a theory of an industry filled with many firms that can enter and exit easily, yet each one produces a different product. If firms develop and advertise differences in their products in an otherwise competitive market, the cost of advertising could be considered as an unwarranted cost. When a fast-food restaurant spends millions of dollars to tell us how different its food is from other similar restaurants, the firm can create limited monopoly power over people who identify with its products. If all restaurants do the same, advertising differences can enable them to raise prices above the competitive levels, reducing output to inefficient levels. The resulting "excess capacity" among firms in the industry is allocatively and productively inefficient. Monopolistically competitive markets, therefore, are less beneficial to society than the ideal of competition, primarily because of higher costs due to advertising differences and inefficiencies of restricted output.

• **Characteristics of monopolistic competition:**
1) large numbers
2) differentiated product
3) limited pricing power
4) free entry and exit
5) as a result of the first four, firms experience excess capacity and inefficiency

Oligopoly

Oligopoly is a theory of an industry dominated by a few large firms, although other fringe firms may also compete. When large firms can produce a product more efficiently than small firms can, as is true in auto production, a few large firms will dominate the industry. The potential for a few dominant firms to act as a **joint monopoly** makes oligopoly a potentially inefficient form of industrial organization in a market economy. Such collusion of firms in raising prices and dividing market shares systematically raises profits of the firm at the cost of general social welfare.

• **Characteristics of oligopoly:**
1) a few sellers
2) products may be differentiated or homogeneous
3) pricing may be competitive or monopolistic
4) significant barriers to entry

• **Joint monopoly:** oligopolistic firms collude and price as a pure monopolist would

Asymmetric Information

Another market imperfection, asymmetric information, occurs when one party to a trade knows more about conditions surrounding the trade. The seller often knows more about the quality of the product or about the seller's own willingness to meet contractual obligations. Unequal information among traders reduces the social benefits of exchange because it makes people

more fearful about some trades that could be potentially beneficial to them. Traders must pay more to gather information, to write effective contracts, and to monitor and enforce their provisions. This particular market information is given great attention in the "new microeconomics of the firm."

CHAPTER SUMMARY

1. A change in one of the determinants of demand for or supply of a product will cause a shift in demand or a shift in supply. Since these determinants change over time, equilibrium market price and output for most goods and services are constantly changing. Economic analysis of market adjustments begins with one change at a time, holding other factors constant.

2. Here is a five-step approach to analyzing a shift in demand or supply. First, assume an initial equilibrium. Second, identify whether the shock causes a shift in demand or supply. Third, determine whether the shift causes a shortage or surplus at the old price. Fourth, analyze the adjustment of price and output to a new equilibrium. Fifth, explain any limits or qualifications to the analysis, recognize real-world complications and secondary effects, and discuss any related issues that affect actual markets.

3. When supply shifts, quantity demanded and price will change. The price elasticity of demand determines by how much each changes for a given supply shift. Elasticity of demand measures the relative responsiveness of consumers to a change in price.

4. Price elasticity of demand equals the percentage change in quantity demanded divided by the percentage change in price. Price elasticity of demand is generally negative. If it is greater in absolute value than one, demand is said to be elastic. If it is less than one, demand is inelastic.

5. A price increase will increase total revenue of the seller if product demand is inelastic (consumers are relatively unresponsive to the price increase). A price increase will decrease total revenue if demand is elastic (consumers are relatively responsive to the price increase). The opposite results for changes in total revenue hold for a price decrease.

6. Demand for a product is more price elastic in three cases: when a higher proportion of the buyer's budget is used to buy the product, when close substitutes for the good are available, and when more time is available to the buyer for making economic adjustments and substitutions.

7. Price elasticity of supply of a product equals the percentage change in quantity supplied divided by the percentage change in price.

8. The elasticity of market supply varies with the planning horizon. In the market period, supply is purely inelastic because sellers cannot vary the quantity they have brought to market. In the short run, supply is more elastic. In the long run, supply depends on technical conditions of production and the effects of varying industry capacity on average costs of production. In a constant-cost industry, the long-run supply is purely elastic.

9. The long-run equilibrium of supply and demand in a competitive market is socially beneficial in theory. Competition assures productive and allocative efficiency.

10. In the absence of economies of large scale, a monopolist restricts output and charges a higher price, compared to a competitive market. Monopoly is neither productively nor allocatively efficient.

PROBLEMS FOR PRACTICE

13.1 Give your own examples for shifts in demand or supply caused by each of the various determinants of demand and supply. Draw the four different graphs that illustrate each of the cases. Also explain the effect of each of the four cases on price and quantity.

13.2* Give a five-step answer to these questions about demand and supply. Illustrate with a graph.

a. All Guatemalan producers of dresses for U.S. retail distribution are forced by concern about sweatshop labor conditions to double the wage paid to the people who sew dresses, from 30¢ to 60¢ an hour.
b. The same Guatemalan producers of dresses for U.S. retail distribution are able to find new suppliers of cotton cloth. The new price of cloth will be 40¢ a yard, 25 percent cheaper than the old price.
c. One producer of home appliances raises all prices by 10 percent, while other appliance makers hold the line. What will happen in the market for those appliances made by other producers?

13.3 Give examples of two products, each for which demand is (a) elastic, and (b) inelastic.

13.4* Please answer the following questions about price elasticity of demand. Be ready to explain each answer. These don't need detailed calculations.

a. If price increases by 10 percent and quantity demanded decreases by 20 percent, is demand elastic or inelastic?
b. If price increases and total revenue falls, is demand elastic or inelastic?
c. If the price of steak dinners changes from $10 to $11 and quantity demanded changes from 300 to 120 a week, is demand elastic or inelastic?
d. To John, going to the movies is a luxury, but buying news magazines is almost a necessity for his work. For which product will John's demand be less elastic?
e. For which will demand tend to be more elastic: the demand for food or the demand for lightbulbs?
f. You like hamburgers, let's say. Consider the following two market structures.
Case A: Fred's hamburger stand competes with Jim's drive-in and Mary's restaurant. All make good burgers.
Case B: Fred's hamburger stand is the only stand in town.
In which case would your demand for a hamburger at Fred's be more elastic?

13.5* Please answer the following questions about price elasticity of demand. Be ready to explain each answer. These questions require you to do calculations.

a. If the price of music CDs goes from $10 to $8 and quantity demanded goes from 200 to 240 units, what exactly is the elasticity of demand? Use the working formula and show your work.
b. Assume that the absolute value of the elasticity of demand for wheat on commodity markets is 0.35. If the price of wheat rose 10 percent, how much will the quantity demanded of wheat decrease? How much would total revenue increase or decrease?

13.6 What are the theoretical effects of monopoly power on market efficiency? Compare monopoly to a market structure with pure competition.

For class discussion:

13.7* Various economists have studied the competitiveness of the U.S. economy. Based on your casual observations, what do you think they found about U.S. markets? Are they highly competitive (in the sense of pure competition) or highly monopolized by one or a few dominant firms in each important industry? Give support for your answers, citing particular industries or examples. If you have time, research articles about the competitiveness of the U.S. economy.

See Answer Key for hints/answers to starred (*) questions.

Section III

Introduction to Macroeconomics

This final section is a brief introduction to macroeconomics, the study of what determines aggregate output, employment, and the general level of prices. Chapter 14 reviews the most commonly used measures and indicators of macroeconomic activity. It also reviews the aggregate demand and aggregate supply model, using it to explain the history of macroeconomic theory. Finally, the chapter explains the theory of monetarism and evidence in support of it. Chapter 15 discusses the circular flow model in detail, applying its insights to historical macroeconomic episodes.

Chapter 14

MACROECONOMICS

Concepts, Theory, and History

What this chapter will help you think about:

1. What is macroeconomics?
2. Under what historical conditions did macroeconomic analysis begin?
3. What are the major macroeconomic problems?
4. What are the important indicators of macroeconomic activity?
5. What is the circular flow model of the economy and what macroeconomic conclusions does it illustrate?
6. What is the aggregate demand and aggregate supply model?
7. How do classical and Keynesian macroeconomic views compare with the new macroeconomic consensus?
8. What are the conclusions, historical applications, and controversies of the quantity theory?

Macroeconomics explains changes in economic aggregates. To aggregate means to add together or to take as a whole. The macroeconomy refers to the total value of output, the general level of prices, and the levels of overall employment and unemployment. One protracted economic crisis, the Great Depression, forced economists to pursue macroeconomic analysis in earnest. Before investigating the historical beginnings of macroeconomics, we will examine basic macroeconomic concepts and models.

•**Macroeconomics:** the study of changes in aggregate economic activity and the general price level

Macroeconomic Concepts

To understand the history and theories of macroeconomics requires an introduction to a few important concepts of macroeconomics. In this section, we will concentrate on macroeconomic problems, macroeconomic statistics, and a simple model.

Macroeconomic Problems

Three related problems plague market economies: the business cycle, a changing price level, and excessive unemployment. Because these problems affect economic efficiency, they provide society with three economic goals: stable growth of economic output, stable prices, and full employment. These three problems and their corresponding goals are related, as the discussions of concepts, history, and theory will show.

Business Cycle

Industrial machines are most efficient when running steadily. The same is true for companies that use them. Starting and stopping industrial enterprises causes wasteful errors in planning and resource use. For example, each time a steel furnace is started, energy is used simply to heat it to operating capacity. Similarly, economic activity overall is most efficient when it proceeds steadily, using productive capacity efficiently.

With the growth of industrial economies, however, came recurrent fluctuations in economic activity. These recurring fluctuations of output, incomes, and employment are called the business cycle. Exhibit 14.1 reproduces from the chapter on government a graph of the **business cycle**. The business cycle's key feature is that the value of economic output rises and falls over time.

As illustrated, the business cycle has two distinct stages: an **expansion** and a **contraction**. An expansion is a period of rising economic activity. The expansion immediately after a contraction is a **recovery**. A very rapid expansion after a recovery is an economic **boom**. Expansions are never as smooth as in Exhibit 14.1. Market economies also experience periods of slow growth or no growth. A period of slow growth in the middle of an expansion is called a **slowdown** or **pause**.

A contraction is a period of falling value of real output. If a contraction in the United States lasts two quarters (six months) or more, the National Bureau of Economic Research calls it a **recession**. The United States experienced the onset of recessions in 1980, 1982, and 1990. A severe contraction that lasts for several years is called a **depression**. Russia experienced a

Exhibit 14.1: Stages of the Business Cycle

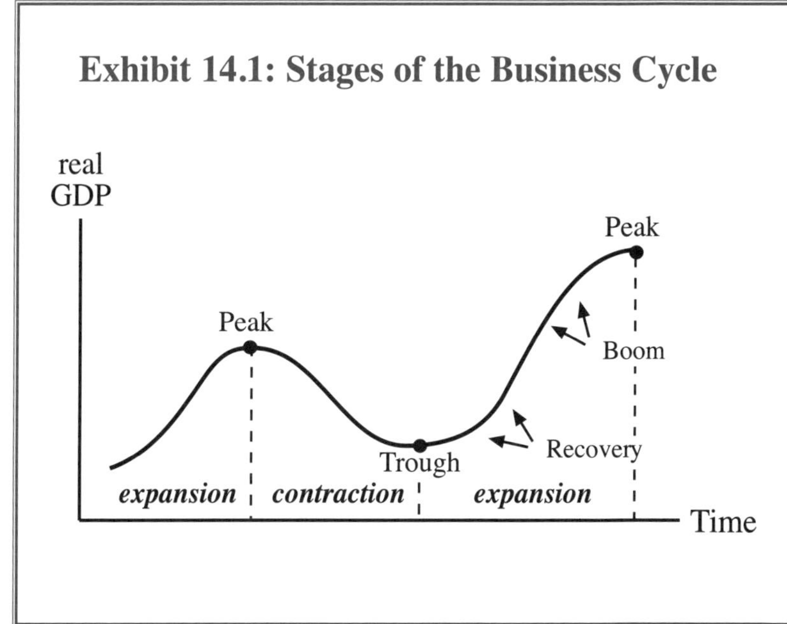

•**Expansion:** a period of rising economic activity

•**Contraction:** a period of falling economic activity

•**Recovery:** a period of expansion immediately after a contraction ends

•**Boom:** a rapid economic expansion

•**Slowdown or pause:** a period of slow growth during an expansion

•**Recession:** an economic contraction lasting at least two quarters

•**Depression:** an extended and severe contraction

depression in the early and mid-1990s after it abandoned communism and tried to convert to a market economy. Japan also experienced a depression in the 1990s. The United States and many of its trading partners, such as Britain, Canada, and France, experienced the Great Depression in the 1930s.

•**Turning points:** peaks and troughs in the business cycle

Peaks and troughs in economic activity are called **turning points**. A slowdown becomes a contraction at the peak of a business cycle. A contraction becomes a recovery at the trough of the business cycle.

Price Level Changes

•**Relative price:** the ratio of the price of one good to the price of another good

When the price of beef rises, with the prices of chicken, pork, and other foods constant, we say that the **relative price** of beef has increased. Relative price changes carry important information on which the efficiency of a market economy relies. They signal buyers and sellers about scarcities of resources and values to consumers of various products.

•**General price level:** an index of changes in all prices in an economy, or in one sector of it

When the prices of beef, chicken, pork, other foods, and other goods and services increase together, we say that the **general price level** has increased. Such fluctuations in the general level of prices can be harmful because they interfere with market signals and financial planning. They also can influence the distribution of wealth among lenders and borrowers.

•**Deflation:** ongoing decreases in the general price level

•**Inflation:** ongoing increases in the general price level

Two patterns of changes in the general level of prices, deflation and inflation, are particularly harmful. **Deflation** is a continual decline in the general level of prices. **Inflation** is a continual increase in the general level of prices. Because prices and wages do not easily adjust downward, many economists favor a moderate rate of inflation from 1-3 percent. Maintaining a stable rate of inflation also encourages efficiency in private planning.

Let's assume that inflation has been 1 percent over the last few years. An unexpected increase in the rate of inflation to 5 percent in the next year will transfer wealth from lenders to borrowers. That is because loan contracts had been based on an expected rate of inflation of 1 percent. If a lender demanded 6 percent nominal interest rate, the higher inflation would mean that the lender gets only a 1 percent real rate of return, not the expected 5 percent real rate. The borrower repays the loan with dollars that are less valuable than the loan contract anticipated.

•**Disinflation:** a falling rate of inflation

Unexpected deflation, on the other hand, transfers wealth from borrower to lender. The borrower repays the loan with dollars that are more valuable than the loan contract anticipated. **Disinflation**, a decrease in the rate of inflation, causes similar effects. In addition, deflation and disinflation both tend to cause temporary declines in economic activity. Federal Reserve policies of disinflation from 1979 to 1982 and from 1989 and 1990 contributed to recessions in the United States.

Unemployment

Workers are unemployed if they are willing and able to work, and age eligible, but could not find work during the survey week. To those who emphasize macroeconomic efficiency, full employment is the goal, because less-than-full employment means potential output is lost forever. Unemployment of labor and equipment imposes personal losses of income for households and businesses and, therefore, an overall loss to society.

Economists distinguish **four types of unemployment**: cyclical, structural, seasonal, and frictional. **Cyclical unemployment** rises and falls with the business cycle. It rises during a recession and falls during a boom. Cyclical unemployment has been one of the main concerns of traditional macroeconomic analysis of the business cycle.

- **Four types of unemployment:**
  1) cyclical
  2) structural
  3) seasonal
  4) frictional

Inefficiencies in the labor market cause **structural unemployment**. The indicator of structural unemployment is that job vacancies and unemployment are both high, even in a booming economy. High vacancies and high unemployment may mean that workers are not trained properly for the jobs that are open. Or perhaps people are uninformed about job openings, or they may not be mobile enough to get to vacant positions. Employment discrimination also contributes to structural unemployment.

Fluctuations of economic activity during the calendar year cause **seasonal unemployment**. For example, every winter brings seasonal declines in home building and in the employment of carpenters and others who construct the homes. Springtime brings layoffs in winter-sport industries. Various holidays and shopping seasons create other seasonal employment patterns. Job opportunities in retail sales increase at Christmas time and before school starts, and then diminish afterward.

The turnover of people quitting jobs and looking for new work creates **frictional unemployment**. Such turnover is normal in a healthy economy, as workers move out of jobs that are less valuable to jobs that are more valuable. They also move from work for which they are not suited to work for which they are suited. Previous estimates have suggested that turnover unemployment in the United States might be about 3 percent.

Measuring Macroeconomic Activity

Businesses want to estimate demand for their products and pressures on resource prices using economic indicators. Governments seek estimates of tax revenues and expenditures mandated by law from estimates of economic activity. Government and private agencies provide measures and indicators of economic activity for these purposes. The two main types of macroeconomic indicators are those that measure the level of economic activity and those that measure the general level of prices. As you will see, the two measures are related.

Nominal Gross Domestic Product

To measure economic activity, the U.S. Commerce Department calculates nominal gross domestic product (GDP). **Nominal GDP** equals the dollar value of all goods and services produced for final consumption during the year within a given political boundary such as the United States. Statisticians measure the values of goods and services using current-year market prices.

• **Nominal GDP:** market value, at current market prices, of final goods and services produced in a given year within a given political boundary

When equations contain measurements that are repeated, the Σ symbol is very helpful. It means, "sum together all values of the following." So the equation for nominal GDP in 2004 would be:

$$\textbf{Nominal GDP}^{2004} = \Sigma\,(Q_i^{2004} * P_i^{2004})$$

[where i is a sequential numbering of all goods from 1 to n]

This is simpler than it may look. Multiply the average price of apples in the year 2004 times quantity of apples produced for final consumption in the United States during the year 2004. This is the market value of apples produced during the year 2004. Do the same for all other fruits and food. Then do the same for clothes, housing, cars, and so on. Sum all those products to get nominal GDP.

In practice, the Commerce Department can estimate GDP by using either of two methods: an expenditure approach as outlined above, or an income approach. The **expenditure approach** calculates nominal GDP as the sum of what consumers, businesses, governments, and exporters spend each year. Since consumers and businesses also buy imports, the value of imports would have to be subtracted. The expenditure approach can be written as an equation using C for consumption, I for business investment, GS for government spending, and X – M for exports minus imports (net exports):

$$\textbf{Nominal GDP} = C + I + GS + (X - M)$$

Using the **income** approach, the Commerce Department could use income tax records to estimate GDP as the total value that people and organizations earn in producing and selling goods and services counted in GDP. Since self-employed individuals and businesses must file U.S. federal income taxes every quarter, the Commerce Department has good reason to estimate GDP each quarter. The income approach to estimating GDP is to add up the reported values of wages and salaries, profits, rents, and interest:

Nominal GDP = Wages & Salaries + Profits + Rents + Interest

Why use two approaches to estimate GDP? The task of estimating the value of output for a nation with trillions of dollars of goods and services each year is tremendous and also imprecise. As a result, estimators can use two methods to double-check their work. When income and expenditure estimates do not match, government statisticians calculate a "statistical discrepancy."

Real Gross Domestic Product

The problem with nominal GDP as an indicator of economic activity is that both quantity changes and price changes influence it. Therefore, economists calculate **real GDP** with the same approach except that they eliminate the effect of price changes.

•**Real GDP:** market value of goods and services using base-year prices to eliminate the effects of a changing general price level on nominal GDP

Calculating Real GDP the Old Way. We will show an older method in which economists used a fixed set of base-year prices (changing the base about every five or ten years). Economists chose a **base year** that had average economic conditions, hoping that it also had average price levels, undistorted by boom or recession. They then used base-year prices to calculate economic values that are free from year-to-year changes in the general price level. Officials changed the base year to reflect changing economic conditions such as falling prices of computers and introductions of new products such as VCRs and DVDs.

•**Base year:** a year of normal economic activity whose prices are used to calculate economic values that are free of the influence of yearly price changes

If the most recent base year was, say, 2000, then real GDP for 2004 is calculated with 2000 prices. The formula for real GDP for 2004 would be the same as the formula for nominal GDP, except that it would use the base year prices to calculate the market value of all goods and services.

$$\textbf{Real GDP}^{2004} = \Sigma\,(Q_i^{\;2004} * P_i^{2000})$$

When calculating real GDP for the year 2004, multiply the quantity of apples produced in 2004 by the average price of apples in the base year, 2000. Repeat this for all other final goods and services.

Exhibit 14.2 illustrates the calculation of nominal and real GDP for a simple economy that only produces three goods: bread, automobiles, and blue jeans. All three prices have risen between the base year 2000 and the current year of 2004. This causes nominal GDP to be larger than real GDP.

A problem with calculating the real GDP is that individual prices can change dramatically between the base year and the current year. These relative price changes can distort real GDP calculations. If computer prices have fallen between 2000 and 2004, then using 2000 prices to value the millions of computers sold will overstate real GDP in 2004.

A New Approach. In actual practice, the method that the Commerce Department has used since 1996 to calculate real GDP is more complex. It now uses a chain-weighted index that takes account of price changes each year. In effect, a new base year is

Exhibit 14.2: Calculating Real and Nominal GDP: A Simple Example

Consumer Goods	Output in 2004	Price in 2004	$P^{04}*Q^{04}$	Price in 2000	$P^{00}*Q^{04}$
Bread Loaves	120,000	$1.80	$216,000	$1.50	$180,000
Automobiles	30	$16,500.00	$495,000	$8,000.00	$240,000
Blue Jeans	54,000	$26.00	$1,404,000	$17.00	$918,000
		$\Sigma P^{04}Q^{04}$ =	$2,115,000	$\Sigma P^{00}Q^{04}$ =	$1,338,000

Nominal GDP for 2004 = $2,115,000

Real GDP for 2004 = $1,338,000

Implicit Deflator for GDP 2004 = $2,115,000 / $1,338,000
= 1.58

used every year. To calculate real GDP for 1999, 1998 prices were used. To calculate real GDP for 1998, 1997 prices were used.

Real GDP is the most complete measure of the overall level of economic activity. To chart the business cycle, you would most likely use time-series data on real GDP. Time-series data refers to the fact that GDP is measured as a series of observations over time. Statisticians calculate nominal and real GDP after each quarter. The ends of the four quarters of the year are on March 31, June 30, September 30, and December 31.

Economic Indicators

Nominal and real GDP are costly to calculate. In the United States, the Commerce Department must survey many businesses and gather huge amounts of tax data to estimate prices and outputs for all industries, and incomes for all businesses and families. Businesses, investors, and government planners, however, want up-to-date information about economic activity. If it is July 2004, the Commerce Department cannot release the next report on GDP until after the third quarter finishes, which means in October 2004.

To fill the information gap, the government and other agencies calculate three indices of indicators of economic activity: leading indicators, coincident indicators, and lagging indicators. The indices are calculated each week from sample data on the economy. Each index is a composite or average of the behavior of various economic indicators. Changes in the indicators are supposed to correspond to changes in real GDP, but the indicators sometimes turn when real GDP does not.

As the names imply, the economic indicators have different relations in time to real GDP. The index of **leading indicators** theoretically reaches a turning point six months before real GDP does. In the United States, changes in the money supply, the spread between the federal-funds rate and ten-year Treasury bonds (a measure of real interest rates for investors), boxcar loadings of freight, and housing permits are important leading indicators. The index of **coincident indicators** is supposed to move in time with real GDP. Two important coincident indicators are the index of industrial production and personal income (less government transfers). Changes in **lagging indicators** trail changes in GDP by up to six months. The unemployment rate is a lagging indicator of market activity at the end of a recession. The prime rate of interest, the rate that banks charge their best customers, also lags.

- **Index of leading indicators:** monthly measure of future economic activity that often anticipates turning points in real GDP by up to six months
- **Index of coincident indicators:** measure of current economic activity that can be measured more easily than GDP
- **Index of lagging indicators:** measure of economic activity that trails changes in GDP

The Unemployment Rate

While changes in the unemployment rate tend to lag changes in real GDP, unemployment is one of the more popular economic indicators. The press reports the rate of unemployment each month, highlighting it when it is changing or remaining high.

The U.S. Bureau of Labor Statistics (BLS) calculates the **unemployment** rate as the number of persons unemployed in a given week divided by the total labor force. The total labor force consists of all those people in the age-eligible population who are willing and able to work. The age-eligible population includes people 16 years or older who are not institutionalized (not prisoners or hospital patients). To be unemployed in a given survey week means that someone does no work but actively seeks employment. Actively seeking means submitting a job application or making calls to prospective employers. Exhibit 14.3 summarizes these relationships.

- **Unemployment rate:** number of people without a job who are willing to work, able to work, and looking for work, divided by the total labor force

Exhibit 14.3: The Labor Force and the Unemployed

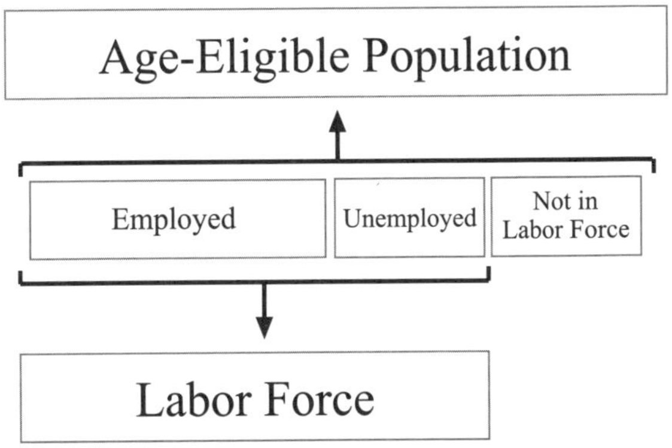

Age-Eligible Population

Employed | Unemployed | Not in Labor Force

Labor Force

The BLS conducts its employment surveys each week. From those surveys, the BLS estimates unemployment for individual cities, each of the states, and the entire nation. While the data are subject to revision, as soon as the BLS releases monthly data, they influence the opinions of economic policy makers and market analysts, who wait eagerly for the data.

Manufacturing Capacity Utilization

The Federal Reserve Board of Governors in Washington, D.C. publishes rates of manufacturing capacity utilization for specific industries and a rate for all industries combined. The rate compares current output to some measure of full capacity in the industry. According to recent historical data, a rate of 85 for overall manufacturing would be moderate, a rate of 92 would be high, and 78 would be low. These are only approximations to give you a rough idea of how to use the data.

Manufacturing capacity utilization is less important than it was in the 1960s and before. Manufacturing now contributes a smaller share of the U.S. economy, because the service sector is more influential in the economy than it was before.

Measuring the Price Level

Economists calculate a general level of all prices in the economy using data for real and nominal GDP. They also calculate indices of various groups of prices. For example, they calculate a separate index for consumer prices and another for producer prices. With a price index, economic analysts can compare prices from one year to the next and estimate the rate of inflation or deflation over time. Let's review calculations and uses of two measures of price changes: the implicit price deflator for GDP and the Consumer Price Index.

Price Deflator for GDP

• **GDP deflator:** a measure of the overall price level

Estimates of nominal GDP and real GDP for a particular year imply a price level for that year. It is called the implicit price deflator for GDP or, more simply, the **GDP deflator**. The price level can be used to remove the effects of rising prices. The GDP deflator equals the ratio of nominal GDP divided by real GDP:

GDP deflator = Nominal GDP / Real GDP

The GDP deflator for the base year is one because, in the base year, nominal and real GDP are equal. The reason they are equal is that, in the base year, current prices are the same as base-year prices.

Exhibit 14.2 includes a calculation of the GDP deflator for the year 2004. The price level is 1.58. The calculations of real and nominal GDP imply that prices have risen 58 percent between the hypothetical base year 2000 and the year 2004. Considering compounding each year, inflation equals roughly 9.5 percent per year [calculated as $(1.58^{1/5} - 1) * 100$].

Consumer Price Index

The Consumer Price Index (**CPI**) is a narrower measure of prices. The Bureau of Labor Statistics estimates a CPI for the nation and for each urban area in the United States. The CPI measures changes in a worker's cost of living each month, and is useful for negotiating appropriate wage changes each year. If an employer offers a 3 percent wage increase, but consumer prices are also rising by 3 percent, the wage offer provides for no increase in the real wage. The estimated increase in a worker's real wage equals the increase in nominal wage minus the increase in the CPI:

•**CPI:** a monthly measure of the price level for a market basket of urban consumer goods; consumer price index

$$\%\,\Delta\,\text{real wage} = \%\,\Delta\,\text{nominal wage} - \%\,\Delta\,\text{CPI}$$

Workers and their unions use the CPI in wage negotiations. Wage contracts sometimes include automatic **cost-of-living-adjustment (COLA) clauses** specifying that wages will increase by, say, 2 percent per year plus the growth in the CPI. Social Security payments and U.S. military and civil service wages are tied to changes in the CPI.

•**COLA:** provision of a wage contract specifying that wage increases will keep pace with changes in the CPI, cost-of-living adjustment

The CPI is calculated by first defining an average monthly market basket of goods and services for an urban worker's family of four. Perhaps it contains 10 pounds of beef, 8 pounds of chicken, 6.5 pounds of sugar, one three-bedroom apartment, so many shirts, shoes, and other clothes, and so on. The current-year CPI equals the cost of the market basket of goods at current prices as a percentage of the cost of those goods at *base-year* prices.

$$\text{CPI} = \frac{\text{cost of market basket at current prices}}{\text{cost of market basket at base-year prices}} * 100$$

If the cost of a monthly market basket of goods for the urban family grows from $1,675 in a hypothetical base year of 1994 to $2,040 in 2000, the CPI for 2000 is equal to 1.22 [calculated as ($2,040 / $1675) * 100]. Consumer prices have risen by 22 percent over six years, or about 4.1 percent per year.

With CPI values for two years, we can calculate a percentage change in the price level using either of the following formulas:

$$\%\,\Delta P^{04} = [(P^{04} - P^{03}) / P^{03}] * 100$$

$$\%\,\Delta P^{04} = [\ln(P^{04}) - \ln(P^{03})] * 100$$

If the CPI in 2004 were 134.7 and the CPI in 2003 were 132.5, then the yearly percent change in the CPI would equal 1.65 percent, using the logarithmic formula. The percentage change is

1.74 using the first formula. (The logarithmic formula gives the same percentage change no matter which price is considered the first. The other formula is more common, but it is not more accurate. It gives different answers, depending on whether the old or new price is in the denominator. For precise work, use the average price level in the denominator or the logarithm formula.)

Aggregate Demand and Aggregate Supply

A macroeconomic model should explain what causes changes in important macroeconomic variables such as real GDP, the general price level, and the levels of employment and unemployment. The model of aggregate demand and supply does just that. It explains changes in the level of economic activity, the general price level and, by implication, unemployment.

Exhibit 14.4 illustrates an initial equilibrium of aggregate demand and aggregate supply at P^*_1 and Q^*_1. A shift in either aggregate demand or aggregate supply will cause the price level or real GDP to change. An increase in aggregate demand raises price and output in the short run. A decrease in aggregate demand lowers price and output in the short run. An increase in aggregate supply lowers price but raises output. A decrease in aggregate supply increases price but lowers output. (Exhibit 14.4 shows a decrease in aggregate supply; more on that after a few basics.)

Aggregate Demand

Aggregate demand is the willingness of people and organizations in the economy to spend their money on goods and services. In terms of the expenditure approach to measuring GDP,

Exhibit 14.4: Equilibrium of Aggregate Demand and Aggregate Supply and the Effects of an Oil-Price Shock

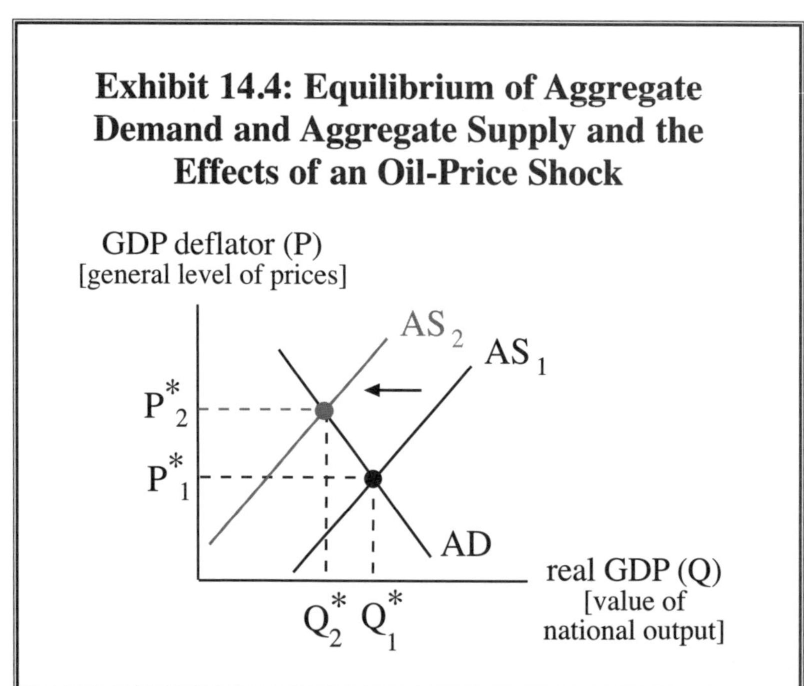

aggregate demand shows how values of aggregate expenditure vary with a changing price level. Using symbols introduced above, aggregate expenditure (AE) is defined as:

$$AE = C + I + GS + (X - M)$$

When prices rise, C, I, GS, and (X - M) tend to fall. For example, higher domestic prices cause families to buy less (C decreases). They also substitute imports for domestic products (M increases). Higher U.S. prices also cause foreigners to buy fewer exports (X decreases). Therefore, AE decreases at a higher price level. When prices fall, the reverse happens, and AE increases.

Aggregate Supply

Aggregate supply is the willingness of businesses in the economy to supply goods and services. Their willingness to sell varies with price levels. Higher prices encourage firms to supply more products, at least in the short run.

Shifting Aggregate Demand and Supply

Aggregate demand varies with changes in any factor that causes consumption, investment, government spending, or net exports to change. These include changes in the money supply, interest rates, exchange rates, foreign prices, and spending that is independent of other factors (called "autonomous" or self-induced changes in spending). A sudden swing in the mood of consumers or investors, for example, could lead to autonomous increases or decreases in spending, independent of current economic conditions. A recession overseas could lower export demand independent of what is happening in the domestic economy.

Aggregate supply varies due to improvements in technology, changing resource prices such as crude oil prices, and changes in contract, menu, and catalog prices. Price and inflation expectations also influence aggregate supply. If producers expect the general level of prices to be higher next year than last year, they will reduce their willingness to supply their products. Through this channel of price expectations, the money supply can affect aggregate supply by altering price expectations.

Higher Oil Prices: An Aggregate Supply Shock

Exhibit 14.4 illustrates the effects of an aggregate supply shock due to rising crude oil prices. In 1974 and 1979, OPEC, a cartel of oil-producing nations, shocked the global economy with two dramatic increases in the price of crude oil. Each of these oil price increases contributed to global recession and to higher general levels of prices in many nations.

How did higher prices affect the macroeconomies of Western nations? Oil was an important resource in industrial production. Higher oil prices meant higher resource costs for most industries. Producers passed higher costs on to consumers. The oil price increase also was a tax on consumer purchasing power, with much of the tax going overseas to oil-producing nations. Therefore, the graph shows an increase in the general price level from P^*_1 to P^*_2 and a recessionary decrease in real GDP from Q^*_1 to Q^*_2. As the graph implies, unemployment rose after both oil price shocks.

Historical Beginnings of Macroeconomics

- **Classical macroeconomics:**
  1) increases in the general level of prices are caused by a growing money supply;
  2) the market economy tends to full employment due to price flexibility; and
  3) price, not output, will adjust to a drop in aggregate demand

Up until the 1930s, systematic study of the aggregate economy was very limited, except for two ideas of what has come to be called **classical macroeconomics**. First, using the Quantity Theory (quantity-of-money theory of price), the majority of economists explained that more money caused the general level of prices to rise. Second, the majority believed that the overall level of employment would take care of itself, tending toward full employment where everyone who wanted a job could find one with a reasonably short search. Therefore, economic analysis until 1930 focused on what we now call microeconomics, especially theories of price and market activity.

Exhibit 14.5 uses the concepts of aggregate demand and aggregate supply to illustrate the simple classical view of macroeconomics. Classical aggregate supply, indicating the willingness of businesses to supply products, is purely inelastic. The vertical supply curve illustrates the classical belief that, if aggregate demand fell, the surplus of goods on the market would only be temporary. As illustrated in the graph, a decrease in aggregate demand causes prices to fall from P^*_1 to P^*_2 and real GDP to fall to $Q_{D\ temporary}$. In the long run, after price adjustments are complete, full employment is restored automatically without government intervention. Real GDP rises from $Q_{D\ temporary}$ to $Q_{full\ employment}$.

- **Say's Law:** supply of products creates its own demand by creating the income needed to buy them

Exhibit 14.5 illustrates what classical economists referred to as **Say's Law**: supply creates its own demand. The real question is how long such automatic adjustments take. During the Great Depression, automatic adjustments were long in coming.

The Roosevelt Era and Keynesian Economics

Lasting through the 1930s, the Great Depression challenged accepted economic wisdom about a self-correcting economy. Never mind that market-oriented economists would later indict the central bank and legislature on charges of policy mismanagement. Twenty-five percent unemployment in 1932 convinced policy makers that a cure required governmental activism. Economic activists labored on three fronts: theory, measurement, and policy.

Writing a Theory of Depression

John Maynard Keynes' *General Theory of Employment, Interest, and Money* (1936) explained what was wrong with the

Exhibit 14.5: Classical Full-Employment Economy

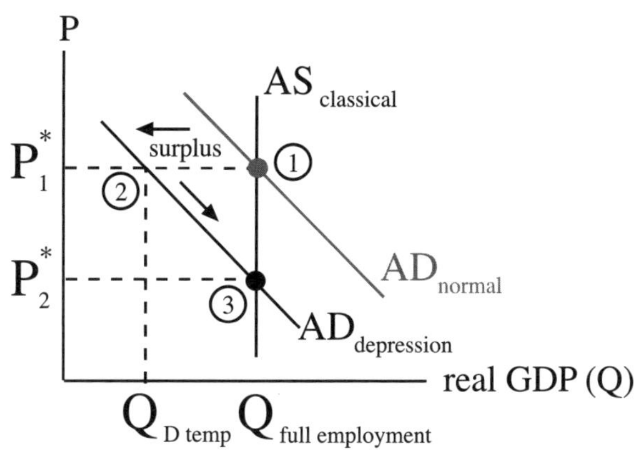

KEY

1. Initial equilibrium at full employment.
2. Decreasing demand leads to a temporary surplus of goods.
3. Prices decrease to return the economy quickly to full employment

private market economy and how government intervention could help. **Keynesian macroeconomics** focused on how private investment spending had plummeted in the 1930s because the 1929 stock market crash had left industry with excess capacity and investors with few if any projects that were likely to earn a future profit. Initially, prices were not flexible enough to allow for rapid automatic adjustments. Moreover, by the time prices did start to fall due to excess inventories of goods, consumers could not buy more because their incomes were also falling due to layoffs and lower wages. Households had no extra purchasing power to get the economy started and, because of excess capacity, businesses had no reason to invest. The economy needed government deficit spending, Keynes said, to stimulate aggregate spending and restore full employment.

Exhibit 14.6 illustrates Keynes' theory of depression. At prices above the current price, the aggregate supply is vertical, indicating that increases in aggregate demand will increase price, not output. This is identical to the classical view.

To represent inflexible prices, the aggregate supply curve has a purely elastic section at the current price level. This represents price rigidities due, for example, to contract, catalog, and menu prices. In the Keynesian view, a decrease in aggregate demand will cause a recession or depression because prices do not immediately adjust. This is represented by the shift in aggregate demand from AD_{normal} to $AD_{depression}$ and the new equilibrium output of $Q_{depression}$ at the initial price level (the change from 1 to 2). When prices do finally begin to fall (represented by the rotating aggregate supply), aggregate demand is also dropping because of falling incomes due to layoffs and falling wages (2 to 3). As a result, prices fall but the economy remains stuck in a depression.

- **Keynesian macroeconomics:**
  1) prices are initially inflexible downward;
  2) quantity, not price, adjusts to falling aggregate demand;
  3) when prices do finally fall, wages are falling too; and
  4) a market economy can become stuck at less than full employment

Exhibit 14.6: Keynesian Depression Economics

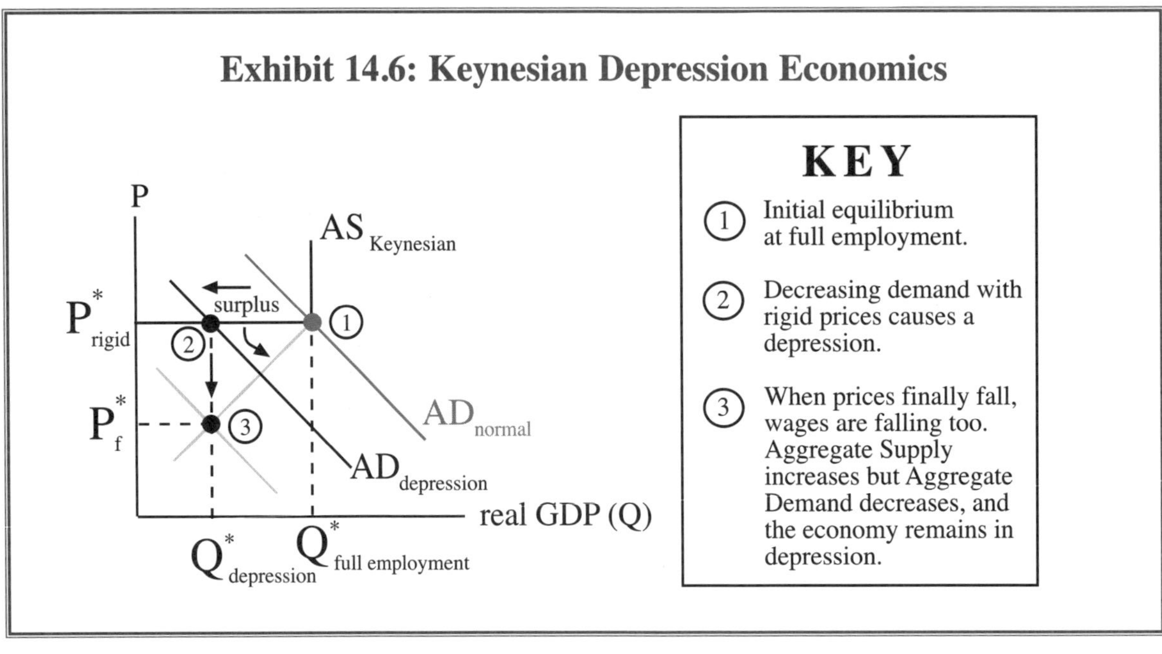
P
AS Keynesian
P^*_{rigid}
surplus
1
2
P^*_f
3
AD normal
AD depression
real GDP (Q)
$Q^*_{depression}$
$Q^*_{full\ employment}$
KEY
1 Initial equilibrium at full employment.
2 Decreasing demand with rigid prices causes a depression.
3 When prices finally fall, wages are falling too. Aggregate Supply increases but Aggregate Demand decreases, and the economy remains in depression.

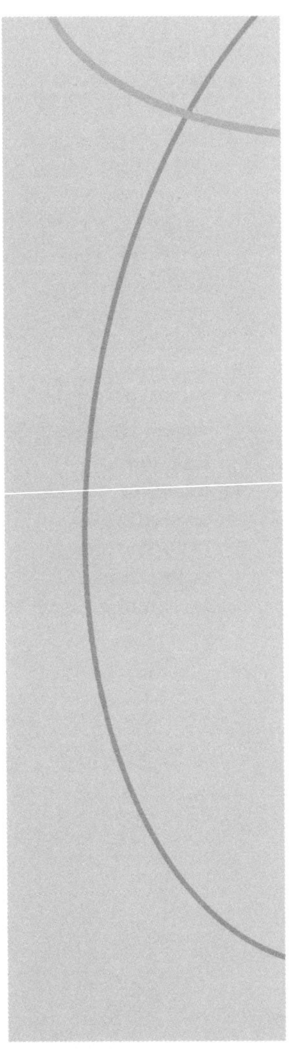

Did wages really fall in the Great Depression? I once asked my great aunt Sara, a Philadelphia schoolteacher until the 1960s, if it was so. She said, "Oh yes, the principal would come to our rooms and tell us, 'I'm sorry, but you are going to have to take a cut in pay.'" Historical data show that wages plummeted by 60 percent on average. Yet several other people I questioned about the Depression said that their families were unaffected. "Living in the hills of Kentucky," one woman said, "we were poor before the Depression, and we were poor during it." Two of Kentucky's important industries, coal and farming, were indeed in depression in the United States during the 1920s and 1930s.

Estimating Aggregate Economic Activity

In the 1940s, Simon Kuznets (1941) began to collect data in order to estimate measures of aggregate economic activity. Eventually the federal government would collect and publish the National Income Accounts. These included Gross National Product (GNP) as a measure of the dollar value of aggregate economic activity. Now we use a variant of GNP called Gross Domestic Product. The government has also published separate estimates of aggregate consumption expenditures, business investment, government spending, and net exports (exports minus imports).

Implementing Economic Policy

As the U.S. economy headed into the deepest part of the Depression from 1930 to 1932, President Herbert Hoover began programs to offset the economic decline. In January 1932, for example, in the face of inadequate Federal Reserve action, Hoover created the Reconstruction Finance Corporation to rescue a failing banking system. Hoover's programs, however, did not prevent Franklin D. Roosevelt from winning the presidency in 1932.

Roosevelt took office in 1933 with a one-hundred-day whirlwind legislative program called the New Deal. It created the Civilian Conservation Corp that employed three million, the Farm Credit Administration to regulate lending to farmers, the Federal Deposit Insurance Corporation to insure bank deposits and restore confidence in the banking system, the National Recovery Administration to set fair trade rules, minimum wages, and prices (ruled unconstitutional in 1935), and the Public Works Administration to construct courthouses, hospitals, tunnels, and other structures. In 1933, Roosevelt worked mainly through businesses under the view that government should be the spender of last resort. By 1935, he advocated a Second New Deal in which government was a guarantor of economic security and regulator of private enterprise. This initiative created the Social Security Administration to fund a public pension program, and the National Labor Relations Board to promote labor union organization.

The United States suffered through a Roosevelt depression in 1936 and 1937, caused by strict Federal Reserve monetary policies. By 1936, Germany had recovered fully from depression and was preparing for military aggression and domination. The United States did not recover until it began to supply exports to Europe at war and to prepare itself for war in the 1940s.

A Keynesian/Neoclassical Synthesis in the 1960s

After World War II, American economists integrated Keynesian macroeconomic activism and neoclassical microeconomic restraint. Government should actively use monetary and especially fiscal policy to stabilize the macroeconomy at full employment and free markets, and the price system should allocate capital and other resources to their most valued uses.

Macroeconomic **activism** meant not waiting for a full-scale depression to implement counter-cyclical stabilization policies. Government economists should watch every turn in the economic indicators and offset them with opposite changes in fiscal and monetary policy. A booming economy needed fiscal and monetary restraint: a budget surplus and slower growth in the money supply. An economy beginning a contraction needed fiscal and monetary stimulus: more deficit spending and more money in circulation. Economists called this **fine-tuning**.

• **Macroeconomic activism and fine-tuning:** the government should actively monitor economic indicators and offset fluctuations in real GDP

The Keynesian activist consensus peaked in the United States in the 1960s when President John F. Kennedy proposed a tax cut to stimulate a sluggish economy. His successor Lyndon Johnson pushed it through Congress in 1964. Keynesians were jubilant when the economy grew more rapidly for several years. Critics of activism contended that monetary policy was stimulating the economy. The Federal Reserve was creating new money to buy the Treasury debt that funded the tax cut, the Vietnam War, and a Great Society.

Keynesian Activism Falters

By 1970, clear evidence showed that fiscal policy could not control the economy as well as Keynesians believed. Through the 1970s, belief in Keynesian activism weakened as governments of industrialized economies seemed helpless against the twin macroeconomic problems of inflation and unemployment. In the Keynesian view of the macroeconomy, policy makers could trade off more inflation for less unemployment, or more unemployment for less inflation. In 1970, 1974, and 1980, however, both inflation and unemployment were growing or already high.

In the 1980s, Margaret Thatcher in Britain and Ronald Reagan in the United States rode waves of economic conservatism to power. They replaced Keynesian activism with a commitment to free markets and less government. Yet, because monetary conservatism experienced its own policy problems in the 1980s, academic macroeconomics was in turmoil. By the mid-1980s, academic economists were even reluctant to publish a macroeconomics text until a new consensus emerged.

The Current Consensus

A new consensus has developed that incorporates Keynesian concerns about market instability, but discards the idea that private market economies can become stuck in a permanent crisis of stagnation and unemployment. The consensus recognizes the validity of the classical view that markets do adjust over time.

- **The current macroeconomic consensus:**
  1) prices adjust sluggishly to a demand shock;
  2) sluggish price adjustment causes recessions and booms; and
  3) prices do adjust fully in the long run, returning the economy to full employment

The **current macroeconomic consensus** (if one exists) combines three ideas. First, market economies are subject to periodic shocks to aggregate demand and supply, including oil price changes, monetary surprises, changing expectations of investors and consumers, and changing government fiscal policies. Second, when such a macroeconomic shock occurs, prices and wages do not adjust instantaneously. They adjust sluggishly. Delayed price and wage adjustments cause a period of macroeconomic disequilibrium. Since prices and wages don't adjust, production quantities do, leading to fluctuations in employment. Third, prices and wages eventually adjust completely to macroeconomic shocks, leaving workers and productive equipment fully employed.

Exhibit 14.7 summarizes the current consensus using an aggregate demand and supply analysis that combines classical and Keynesian ideas. Panel A shows an initial macroeconomic equilibrium at a given price level (P^*_1) and full-employment real GDP ($Q_{full\ employment}$). The purely inelastic classical aggregate supply curve, indicated by $AS^{long\ run}$, represents a long-run tendency of the economy toward full employment. Full employment in this model is not an engineering concept of absolute maximum production. Instead, it is an economic concept of the most efficient level of output, the **natural level**. In the short run, firms may operate plants and equipment at higher rates than would be efficient in the long run. A more elastic short-run aggregate supply (AS_1) represents sluggish price adjustment to demand shocks.

Panel B shows the effects of an increase in aggregate demand when, say, the central bank increases the money supply. In the short run, output increases above full employment to Q^*_{temp}. The GDP deflator rises to P^*_{temp} because some prices are flexible. Yet, full adjustment of prices does not occur in the short run because other prices adjust sluggishly.

Panel B also illustrates that firms will adjust their willingness to supply product in the long run. Higher contract, catalog, and menu prices, and higher wage contracts reflect a reduced willingness to supply, shown as a drop in short-run aggregate supply to AS_2. In the long run, the economy is operating at a higher price level P^*_2 but at the economic full-employment level of output, the natural level.

•natural level of output: the level of real GDP to which the economy tends in the long run; corresponds to the classical idea of full employment with economic efficiency

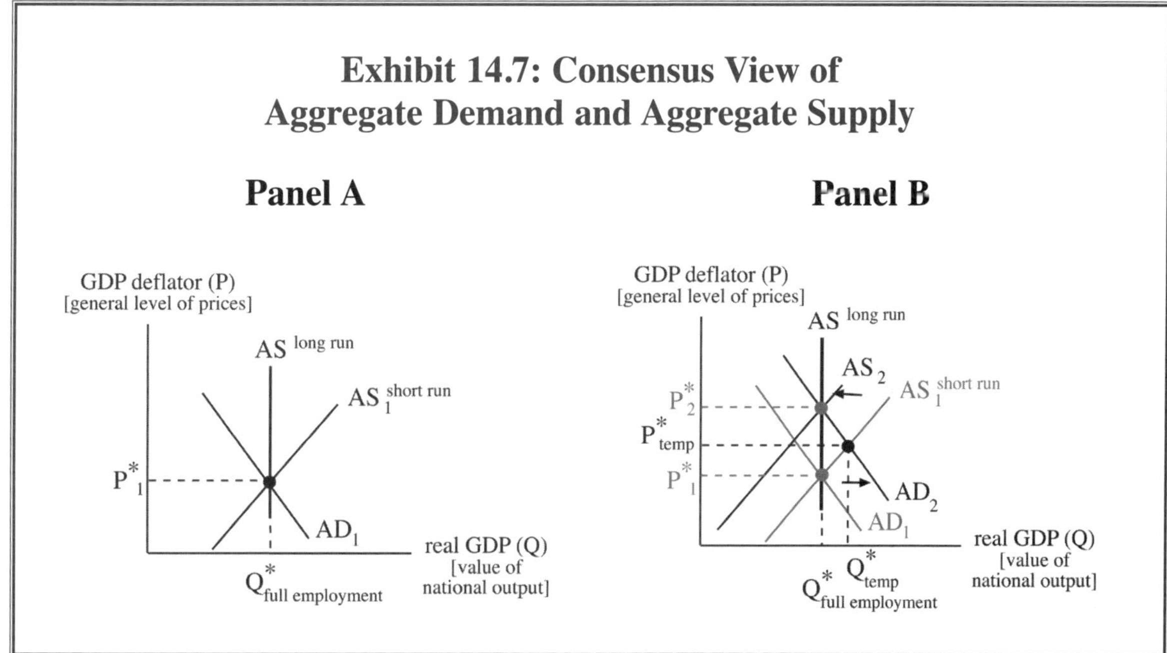

Theory and Evidence on Money and Economic Activity

Monetarists such as Milton Friedman have said that changes in the money supply impact economic activity and prices. Fiscalists and nonmonetarists believed that money had little impact on economic activity, especially compared to changes in government taxes and expenditures. Here is a brief survey of the view that money matters, the historical evidence, and criticisms of that view.

The Equation of Exchange

To represent monetarist views, we will use the algebra of what is called the equation of exchange. It expresses the relation of the money supply to economic activity as follows:

$$M * V = P * Q$$

Economic activity, represented on the right side of the equation, is measured by the value of transactions that consumers, investors, importers, and government make in the economy. The value of economic activity is measured as nominal gross domestic product (GDP). Nominal GDP is the product of real GDP (called Q for quantity of output per year) and the general level of prices or GDP deflator (called P for the average level of prices during the year). The percentage change in P is the rate of price inflation.

The left side of the equation measures the value of economic activity in the economy. M is the money supply and V is the velocity of money. M measures the average quantity of money in the economy at any point in time during the year. V measures the number of times each unit of money is used by consumers in a transaction for goods and services for final consumption.

In practice, U.S. statisticians estimate M from Federal Reserve Bank data, and P and Q from Commerce Department data. V is then calculated as (P * Q) / M. As a simple example, if estimates show that Q = 800, P = 1, and M = 200, then V = (800*1)/200 = 4 by definition.

The equation of exchange illustrates a simple principle. Changes in the stock of money can only affect these three factors: velocity of money, real output, or the general level of prices. For example, if prices double and velocity drops in half, then money has no effect on economic activity. That, in short, is an extreme **nonmonetarist view**: changes in the money supply affect only velocity of money—they have no dependable effect on real output or the price level.

- **Nonmonetarist view:** changes in the money supply are not the main causes of changes in economic activity or the price level

The Quantity Theory: A Monetarist View

The monetarist view is expressed in the Quantity Theory. It has several assumptions, the first of which is a rather stable velocity of money. A change in the money supply may instantly reduce velocity, but velocity will soon return to its average level. The second assumption is that money is **neutral** in the long run. Real output does not change in the long run with changes in the money supply. Real output depends on nonmonetary factors such as the amount and skill of laborers, the capital stock, and the level of technology it contains. Growth in real output depends on the rates of saving, investment, education, and research and development.

What are the main **conclusions** of the **Quantity Theory**? First, a change in the money supply will have short-run impacts on the level of economic activity that will not persist in the long run. Second, a change in the money supply will cause a proportional change in the price level. If the money supply doubles, prices will approximately double. As a result, you should think of the Quantity Theory as a **quantity-of-money theory of price**. As Milton Friedman puts it, inflation of prices is "everywhere a monetary phenomenon" (1963, 17).

- **Conclusions of the Quantity Theory:** a rise in the supply of money will, after a time, cause an approximately proportional rise in the general level of prices; it is a quantity-of-money theory of price

Inflation is defined as ongoing increases in the general level of prices, not one-time increases in prices due to, say, an oil shock. Inflation is measured as the percentage change of the general level of prices from year to year. U.S. inflation between 1996 and 1997 was just under 2 percent. According to monetarism, persistently low inflation indicates monetary restraint by the central bank.

- **Inflation:** ongoing increases in the general level of prices (not merely a one-time increase in prices)

What would happen if a central bank were not restrained? The quantity theory states that a money growth rate higher than what is needed to accommodate expanding trade will cause higher rates of inflation. Since a nation's level of economic activity rarely if ever grows faster than from 5 to 10 percent per year, an annual monetary growth rate of 20 percent can be expected to cause price inflation of roughly 10 to 15 percent or more. Correspondingly, an annual monetary growth rate of 200 percent can be expected to cause nearly 200 percent inflation per year.

Picturing Monetarism

Exhibit 14.8 illustrates the monetarist view of a one-time instantaneous doubling of the money supply. Such an instantaneous event is difficult to imagine in practice, but its theoretical effects are easier to explain. In each graph, the vertical axis measures changes in one variable of the equation of exchange, and the horizontal axis measures time. At time t_0, the central bank instantly doubles the money supply from 200 to 400. The money supply stays at this higher level permanently.

When the money supply doubles, how do velocity, real output, and the price level respond? The second panel shows that velocity immediately falls by half and then recovers quickly to its old level. The third panel shows that real output increases temporarily as the new money creates higher demand for goods and services. Since prices adjust sluggishly, output adjusts in the short run. In the long run, though, output falls back to its **natural level** to which it tends. While output is rising and then falling, unemployment would first fall below its natural level and then return to it. The long-run effect of the money-supply increase on price is featured in the fourth panel. It illustrates (but in no way proves) the belief that a doubling of the money supply will gradually double the price level from one to two.

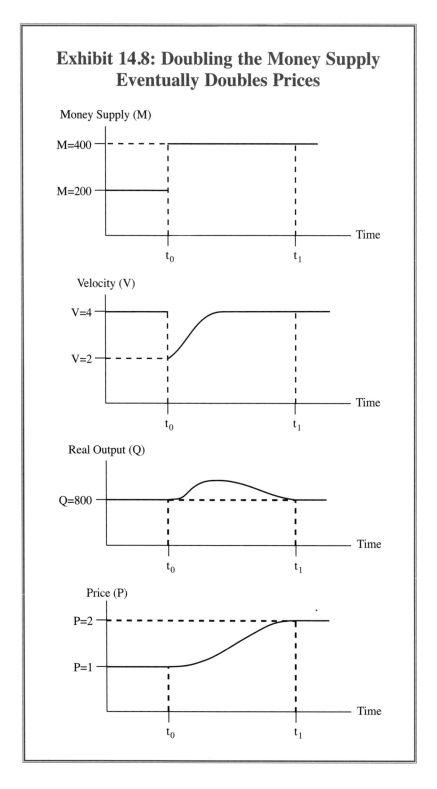

Exhibit 14.8: Doubling the Money Supply Eventually Doubles Prices

Money Supply (M)
M=400
M=200
Time
t_0 t_1

Velocity (V)
V=4
V=2
Time
t_0 t_1

Real Output (Q)
Q=800
Time
t_0 t_1

Price (P)
P=2
P=1
Time
t_0 t_1

How long is the long run? Evidence suggests that the time between an initial monetary shock (time t_0) and full adjustment of price (time t_1) could be five or more years. Such a long lag makes controlling economic activity more difficult. The lag may well be responsible for oscillating economic activity from 1997 to 2003.

Empirical Evidence and Criticisms

Actual economies are never as precise as such simple algebraic theories. Twentieth-century evidence in the United States tends at times to support and at other times to disconfirm the quantity theory. One assumption of the theory, that velocity is constant or at least stable and predictable, does not seem to have been true. Velocity generally fell in the Great Depression, rose through 1980, and then has fluctuated ever since. On the other hand, the prediction that a sharp fall in the growth rate of the money supply will cause a sharp fall in price inflation does seem to have been true in the early 1980s. As stated above, in October 1979, the Federal Reserve began lowering money growth dramatically. Within three years, U.S. inflation had dropped sharply.

• **Long-run neutrality of money:** an unexpected increase in the money supply may increase real GDP temporarily, but more money has no effect on real GDP in the long run

International evidence suggests that, over ten-year periods of time, high rates of money growth are indeed associated with high rates of price inflation. Exhibit 14.9 shows a statistical association between the rates of money-supply growth and inflation for six countries. Notice that, with a few minor exceptions, higher rates of money growth are linked with higher rates of inflation. While not proving causation, the statistical association of money growth with inflation lends support to the idea.

Exhibit 14.9 Statistical Association between Money Growth and Price Inflation

Country	Money-Supply Growth per Year 1980-90	Price Inflation per Year 1980-90
United States	8.4	3.7
Japan	9.0	1.5
Denmark	12.0	5.6
Guatemala	15.7	14.6
Botswana	25.9	12.1
Ghana	44.8	42.7
Uganda	88.0	107.0
Israel	101.8	101.4
Brazil	178.3	284.4
Argentina	368.5	395.1

Source: James Gwartney and Richard Stroup, *Introduction to Economics: The Wealth and Poverty of Nations* (New York: Dryden Press, 1994), 623-24.

The power of monetary policy is limited in the short run, however, because empirical measures of money are not always precisely related to the level of economic activity. Nonmonetarists

also argue that economic activity depends on money plus what are called **near monies**, highly liquid financial assets such as certain savings accounts. Liquid means easily converted into money. Thus, the amount of credit in the economy may be just as important as the quantity of money. Monetarism does, however, clearly define the effects of profligate monetary policy in the long run: excessive money growth generates more near monies, more debt, and higher inflation.

Chapter Summary

1. Macroeconomics deals with aggregate economic activity: the total value of output, the general level of prices, and the overall levels of employment and unemployment.

2. The major macroeconomic problems of capitalist economies have been the business cycle, unemployment, and a fluctuating general level of prices. Inflation is the problem of ongoing increases in the price level.

3. GDP is the market value of goods and services produced for final consumption in an economy during the year. Nominal GDP uses current prices to value output. Real GDP uses base-year prices.

4. The important measures of aggregate economic activity are real GDP, leading, lagging, and coincident indicators, the rate of unemployment, and the rate of manufacturing capacity utilization. The important measures of the general level of prices are the implicit price deflator for GDP and the Consumer Price Index.

5. Economists estimate the rate of price inflation each year by comparing values of the consumer price index (CPI) or the values of the price deflator for GDP between years.

6. The Aggregate Demand and Aggregate Supply Model of the macroeconomy explains changes in real GDP and the general level of prices. Shifts in the willingness to spend and the willingness to produce and supply goods cause changes in economic activity and prices.

7. Classical economists (through the 1920s) believed that price adjustments would eliminate any surplus of goods created by inadequate aggregate demand. John Maynard Keynes believed that price rigidities would prevent automatic adjustment. That was part of Keynes' explanation of the Great Depression. Another part was the expenditure multiplier effects that turned an initial drop in investment spending into a greater drop in national income.

8. Classical macroeconomics is represented by an inelastic (vertical) aggregate supply curve. Keynesian depression economics is represented with an aggregate supply curve that is purely elastic (horizontal) at the current price level.

9. The Quantity Theory asserts that the money supply and the price level are "proportional." A 10 percent increase in the money supply leads to approximately a 10 percent increase in price in the long run (over five to ten years).

10. Using the equation of exchange, the Quantity Theory, and empirical evidence, Milton Friedman and other monetarists claim that increasing the growth rate of money is the primary long-run cause for increases in the rate of inflation.

Problems for Practice

14.1* List the measures of economic activity. Which is most likely to be used in the following situations by the stated speakers?

a. Stock-market analysts assess the current state of the macroeconomy each month.

b. An economic researcher wants the best historical data for the 1990s on the overall dollar value of output in the United States each quarter.

c. A union official needs a measure of the overall health of labor markets for a speech.

d. An expert on U.S. industry wants to estimate changes in the level of manufacturing activity for the past thirty years.

14.2 What is the theoretical difference between what the CPI and the implicit deflator for GDP measure? Are the two calculated in the same ways?

14.3* A market basket of goods for the average urban family in the United States cost $2,149 in the current year and $1,895 in the base year.

a. What is the CPI for the current year?
b. If five years have passed between the base and current years, what was the approximate yearly rate of increase in consumer prices?

14.4* Use the following data for prices and output in a simple economy (and the old BEA method) to calculate nominal and real GDP and the GDP deflator. The base year is 1994 and the current year is 2000.

Consumer Goods	Output in 2000	Price in 2000	$P^{00}Q^{00}$	Price in 1994	$P^{94}Q^{00}$
Bread Loaves	39,000	$1.00		$0.80	
Automobiles	12	$21,500.00		$18,000.00	
Blue Jeans	17,000	$30.00	______	$24.00	______
		$\Sigma P^{00}Q^{00} =$		$\Sigma P^{94}Q^{00} =$	

Nominal GDP for 2000 =

Real GDP for 2000 =

Implicit Deflator for GDP 2000 =

14.5* Answer the following questions about macroeconomic measures.

a. What is the value of the GDP deflator in the base year?
b. What is the value of the CPI in the base year?
c. If prices fall for five years after the base year, nominal GDP will be (less than, equal to, greater than) real GDP.

14.6 Do classical and Keynesian views of the economy (as represented in the AD/AS models) agree or disagree on the effects of aggregate demand increases? Do they agree on the effects of aggregate demand decreases? Explain.

14.7 What is the monetarist view of the effects of a change in the money supply on the macroeconomy? What evidence can monetarists cite for this view? What are the objections to the monetarist view?

14.8* Exhibit 14.4 illustrated the effects on aggregate supply of an increase in crude oil prices. Using the AD/AS model, explain what you think the macroeconomic effects were of *declining* crude oil prices in 1982 and 1983.

For your portfolio:

14.9 Find quarterly U.S. data for the years 1967 through 1973 for the percentage growth rates of the M1 money supply, real GDP, the federal budget deficit, and federal spending. Try to determine whether the data support a monetarist or nonmonetarist hypothesis about the macroeconomy.

14.10 Examine quarterly U.S. data from 1978 to 1984 for the growth rates of M1 and M2 money supplies, real GDP, and the GDP deflator or CPI. Does the evidence suggest a relationship between the growth rate of the money supply, economic activity, and the price level? Explain. Graph the data over time.

For class discussion:

14.11 Evaluate the following summary of an economist's view of the importance of national income accounting. Then compare it to the response that follows. Be prepared to discuss your own views.

Comment on the National Income Accounts: The government must measure the level of economic activity. If it did not, it would not have any idea whether the private sector was producing enough of the appropriate kinds of products. In order to know whether the nation has the capacity to produce the military hardware, public schools, and public transportation system, doesn't the government need to measure actual production and potential productive capacity? Finally, don't we need to know what the levels of inflation and unemployment are so that the government can enact appropriate stabilization measures?

A response: This is a troubling justification for national income accounting unless one is prepared to accept intervention of the government into the microeconomy as well as the macroeconomy. The last sentence is traditional justification based on the assumed need to stabilize the macroeconomy with government policy. Everything that goes before, however, hints at a government-planned economy. Furthermore, I don't think the writer is correct at all here. If national income accounts are so necessary to building schools, national defense, and rail systems, how did Britain, America, Japan, Germany, and other industrialized nations carry out such projects before the 1930s when income accounting began in earnest? The writer overstates the need for aggregate information and understates the role of private capital markets, which financed the investments of risk-taking entrepreneurs. He also misunderstands the function of government officials: to ignore short-term economic fluctuations and private spending, and to spend public funds for the long run, building needed public capital.

See Answer Key for hints/answers to starred (*) questions.

Chapter 15

THE CIRCULAR FLOW

Income, Expenditure, Injections, and Leakages

What this chapter will help you think about:

1. What does the simple circular flow model illustrate?
2. What are the sources and uses of household income?
3. What factors cause changes in consumption spending?
4. How do we measure household standards of living, changes in the level of consumer prices, and consumer sentiments?
5. What are the sources and uses of business income?
6. Why are business-fixed investment and inventory investment important in the circular flow?
7. What are a few indicators of the overall level of production activity?
8. How do changes in injections of spending into and leakages out of the domestic circular flow affect economic activity?
9. What macroeconomic conclusions does the complete circular flow illustrate?
10. What are the theoretical limitations of the circular flow?

- **Macroeconomics:** the study of changes in aggregate economic activity and the general price level

In **macroeconomics**, we study causes of changing aggregate (overall) economic activity. In this chapter, we construct a **circular flow model** of linkages between important economic aggregates, especially aggregate income, expenditure on goods and services, and leakages from and injections into the spending stream.

- **Circular flow model:** shows how aggregate money expenditure and income move through sectors of the economy

We start with a simple circular flow of income and expenditure that includes only households and businesses. After explaining the macroeconomics of consumption and production, we will illustrate a rather complete circular flow. This more realistic representation of the macroeconomy assembles all of the partial money-flow diagrams that we will use to describe consumption, production, finance, government, and international trade.

The complete circular flow provides a framework for interpreting macroeconomic news of the day. You will see how the effects of a change in interest rates move from financial markets into different sectors of the economy. You will understand why shifts in business expectations about future profits or shifts in householder optimism about future incomes affect the level of economic activity. And you will see how a central bank influences domestic and international money conditions.

A Simple Circular Flow

In a market economy, people trade goods and services. In an *advanced* market economy with money, businesses hire labor and other resources from households and produce goods and services that households then buy with their income. Businesses and households therefore meet in product markets and resource markets. As Exhibit 15.1 illustrates, this creates a circular flow of household income and expenditure.

The model illustrates **two important features** of a market-oriented macroeconomy: product and resource markets are interdependent, and market economies are subject to feedback effects. Activity in the product market affects, and is affected by, activity in the resource market. If households suddenly get more fearful about future income and cut their spending on goods and services, businesses will suffer and will lay off workers. Household incomes will therefore drop, causing a further drop in consumption. Thus, the circular flow shows that changes in consumer spending will "feed back" into further changes in consumer spending. Fears of lower incomes may *cause* lower incomes.

Let's examine aggregate consumer and producer behavior in more detail. We will expand the model and discuss popular indicators of consumer and producer activity.

- **Simple circular flow:** the flow of income from businesses to households becomes the flow of expenditure from households to businesses, and back again.

- **Two features of a market-oriented macroeconomy**:
  1) product and resource markets are interrelated
  2) the economy is subject to feedback effects

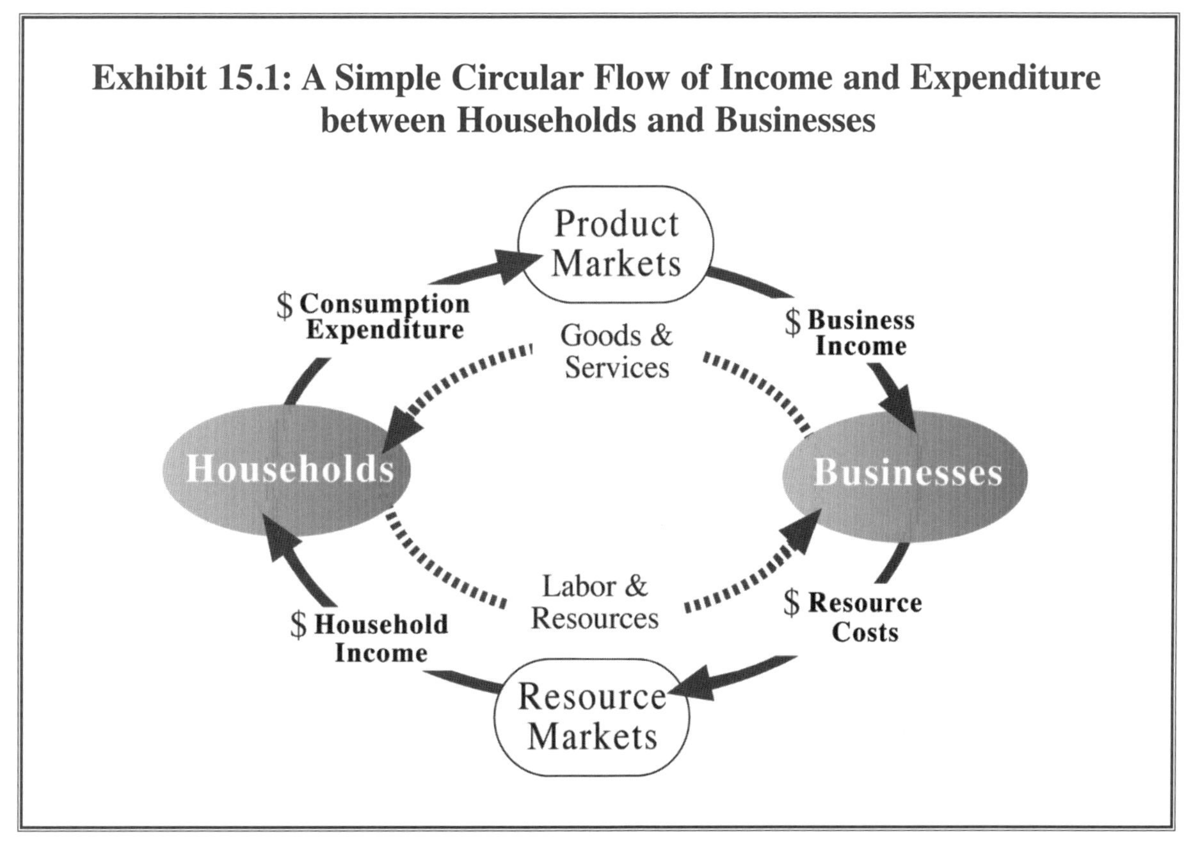

Households in the Circular Flow

Actual market economies are more complex than the simple circular flow. The aggregate economic activity of households, for example, includes more than one source and one use of income. Households not only earn income in resource markets, but they also borrow and withdraw savings from financial markets, and they receive government subsidies. Households have more uses of their incomes than spending on consumer products. They save, repay debt, and pay taxes. Let's view a picture of this increased complexity.

Illustrating Sources and Uses of Household Income

Exhibit 15.2 shows the flows of money into and out of the household budget. As in the simple circular flow, we are treating all households as one, and lumping their sources and uses of income into aggregate categories represented in the model.

Exhibit 15.2: Sources and Uses of Household Income

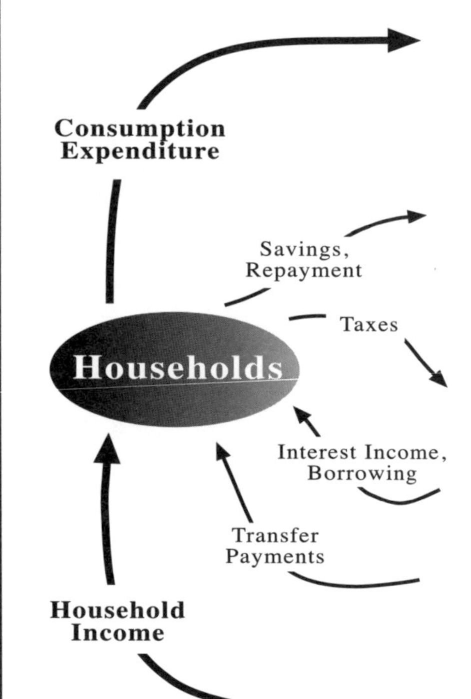

Sources of Household Income

Household income, called personal income in the national product accounts, comes primarily from wages and salaries for human labor and skill. Exhibit 15.3 shows data on total U.S. household (personal) income and its sources for 2001. For comparison, it also lists nominal GDP. At 64.8 percent of personal income, wages, salaries, and other labor income dominate. Transfer payments to persons equal about 13.2 percent of personal income.

Household income from the resource market also includes nonlabor income, such as **rental income** from leasing land to businesses and **profits** from organizing or owning a business. Household income can also come from **interest** received from lending money to financial markets. A household can supplement income by borrowing or drawing money out of savings—we will call this dissaving. Note that savings is your accumulated wealth, while saving (without the last "s") is the flow of income into stock of savings. Retirement income is largely drawn from savings.

Another income source is government **transfer payments** such as social security, poor relief, or unemployment compensation. Your family, friends, and nongovernmental organizations may also be a source of private transfers that we would simply call gifts. A bequest from a dead relative is a form of personal gift that also influences consumption.

Uses of Household Income

Households use their income first to pay **taxes** and then to make choices between **consumption expenditure** and **saving**, including **repaying loans**. A family's income tax liability is the amount it owes to various levels of government. On average, the higher a family's income, the higher the tax it owes. Governments also collect other taxes besides the income tax, but studies have shown that all U.S. taxes are roughly proportional to income.

Exhibit 15.3 shows the uses of personal income in the U.S. for 2001, including taxes, saving, and personal consumption expenditures for durable goods, nondurable goods, and services. Notice the very low personal saving rate of 1.4 percent of personal income. Personal taxes and payments are 15.0 percent of income.

Why Does Consumption Vary?

Exhibit 15.3 shows that total personal consumption expenditures were 70.0 percent of GDP in 2001. As a result, to understand what the level of economic activity will be in the next six months, economists watch consumer behavior and its determinants closely. Exhibit 15.2 suggests **which factors determine current levels of consumer expenditure**. Changes in personal income, interest rates, and government tax and transfer policies influence consumption. Less obvious but also important is the influence of changes in personal wealth.

- **Factors causing consumer spending to vary:**
  1) income
  2) interest rates
  3) taxes and transfers
  4) consumer sentiments
  5) personal wealth

The Relationship Between Income and Consumption

The dominant effect in Exhibit 15.2 is that consumer spending depends on the level of income. Furthermore, as shown in Exhibit 15.1, consumer spending will also influence the level of income. The more people buy, the more goods and services businesses produce, and the more those businesses pay to households as income. This is the feedback relationship between income and

Exhibit 15.3: Sources and Uses of U.S. Personal Income in 2001

Sources of Personal Income

Nominal GDP	Personal Income	Wages & Salaries	Other Labor Income	Proprietor's Income	Non-Labor Income	Government Transfers
$10,107.7	$8,724.7	$5,098.8	$553.9	$743.2	$1,553.1	$1,149.0

Uses of Personal Income

Nominal GDP	Personal Income	Personal Consumption Expenditures . . . on Durable Goods	on Nondurable Goods	on Services	Personal Saving	Personal Taxes & Pymnts
$10,107.7	$8,724.7	$858.0	$2,052.9	$4,150.3	$121.1	$1,306.3

Note: Amounts are in billions of current U.S. dollars; "advance estimates."
Source: "National Data," *Survey of Current Business*, February 2002, D-2, D-7. Found at www.bea.gov.

consumption. Expansion Point 15.1 illustrates the effect of income on consumption with algebra and with evidence suggesting that when U.S. income fell in 1990, U.S. consumption also fell.

Save or Borrow? Interest Rates, Culture, and Taxes

Household consumption spending depends on the willingness to save or borrow. At least three factors affect choices between saving and borrowing: interest rates, taxes, and culture. The rate of interest is a cost of borrowing money and a reward for saving. As a result, higher interest rates will tend to decrease borrowing and increase saving. Lower interest rates will tend to increase borrowing and decrease saving.

A family's willingness to save also depends on cultural attitudes about thrift and debt. Financial counselors exhort households: "Get out of debt and stay out of debt," and "prepare now for retirement." The easy availability of consumer credit and

Expansion Point 15.1: The Algebra and Evidence of a Relationship Between Income and Consumption

Mathematical economists say that consumption is a function of income. They express the relation with algebra such as this linear equation.

Consumer Spending = 0.95 * Household Income

This equation, called a consumption function, could be much more complex, but let's keep it simple. In it, we are assuming that households spend a constant fraction of their income. For every $10 of income, an average family spends $9.50 and saves or repays debt with the extra $0.50. If we recognize the effects of taxes, then we ought to rewrite the equation as follows:

Consumer Spending = 0.95 * [Income - Taxes]

Disposable income is the value of household income less taxes, so we can rewrite the equation as follows.

Consumer Spending = 0.95* Disposable Income

What evidence do we have of a direct relationship between income and consumption expenditure? Very good evidence comes from the recession of 1990 and 1991. A recession is a minimum of six consecutive months of a decline of economic output. From mid-1990 to early 1991, the U.S. economy was in such a recession. As a result, household incomes were falling between 1990 and 1991. The following table shows what happened to U.S. per capita disposable income and consumption expenditure between 1988 and 1993 ("per capita" means per person; we divide income and expenditure by total U.S. population).

Year	Per Capita Disposable Income	Per Capita Consumption Expenditure
1988	$17,621	$16,211
1989	$17,801	$16,430
1990	$17,941	$16,532
1991	$17,756	$16,249
1992	$18,062	$16,520
1993	$18,075	$16,810

Notice how income and consumption both rise rather smoothly in the first several years. In 1991, however, income falls due to the recession, and so does consumption. When income rebounds in 1992 and 1993, consumption again starts to rise. These historical data do not prove that consumption depends on the level of income, but they are consistent with the idea.

Source: U.S. Bureau of the Census, *Statistical Abstract of the United States: 1996,* 116th edition, Washington, DC, 1996.

such exhortations as, "Why wait?" influence others. Expansion Point 15.2 shows that, by 2002, households worldwide had waded deep into debt. Such borrowing shifts household consumption from the future to the present.

The tax code also influences consumption. Saving in an individual retirement account (IRA) reduces your tax liability this year and in the coming years, because income put into an IRA and yearly interest payments from it are not taxable until you retire. IRAs therefore encourage saving and discourage current consumption.

Tax Effects on Consumption

Income taxes have other effects on consumer spending through their impacts on disposable income and on decisions to work or not to work. Higher income-tax rates lower the proportion of their wages and salaries that people can spend, and therefore tend to discourage work effort and encourage leisure (or underground economic activity). Thus higher income taxes reduce consumption because of direct effects on disposable income and indirect effects on before-tax income. A lower tax has opposite effects.

Wealth Effects on Consumption

A family's level of **wealth** affects its consumption spending. A sudden increase in wealth can trigger more consumption. In the 1990s, many American families owned shares of stock directly or through their mutual funds. As stock prices rose, they felt wealthier and consumed more while saving less of their current income. By 1999, the saving rate was down to 0.5 percent, having hovered around 5 percent at the end of the 1980s.

Expansion Point 15.2: Households Were Deep in Debt in 2002

As U.S. householders burrowed deeper into debt in 2002, households elsewhere joined them.

An indicator of indebtedness is the ratio of household debt to household income. In the United States, the wealthiest 20 percent increased their debt from 80 to 120 percent of income from 1995 to 2002. In Australia, between 1990 and 2002, debt rose from 54 percent to a record 125 percent of household income (with a paltry 0.5 percent saving rate). In Singapore, the government sounded a warning over similarly rising debt levels.

Increasingly available credit cards are probably most to blame. In 1980, less than half of U.S. families had widely accepted credit cards, such as Visa and MasterCard. Families then were more likely to save than to borrow for larger consumer expenditures. Twenty years later, the vast majority of families had credit cards and received several offers a month for additional cards. No wonder debt increased 60 percent in the 1990s.

Why worry? High debt poses risks to families. Much household debt has a variable interest rate, and rising rates cause higher repayments. Worsened economic conditions or employment difficulties could reduce family income, also making debt repayment more difficult.

Sources: Josh Gordon, "Household Debt Hits Record Levels," *The Age* (28 September 2002). Found at http://www.theage.com.au/articles/2002/09/27/1032734326495.html.

Jon Hilsenrath, et al., "Debt Problems Hit Even the Wealthy," *Wall Street Journal* (9 October 2002): D1.

Denise Yeo, "Crushing Debt," *The Electric New Paper* (17 December 2002). Found at http://newpaper.asia1.com.sg/top/story/0,4136,10534,00.html.

Indicators of Household Conditions and Attitudes

Business analysts, labor union representatives, government policy makers, and economic researchers all want accurate measures of householders' well-being and their attitudes toward the economy. In this section, we will focus on measures of standards of living, consumer prices, and consumer sentiments.

Measuring Living Standards

- **Standard of living:** average level of consumption at a given time and place

Standard of living refers to average levels of human consumption at a given time or place. Consumption levels have increased so dramatically in the past two hundred years that a vast majority of "poor" families in the United States today have available to them luxuries such as telephones, televisions, and automobiles that would have astonished royalty two hundred years ago. Americans today take wheat bread for granted as a staple of life. In Poland in the late 1700s, however, peasants were "reduced to eating bread made from barley and oats . . . wheaten bread being only for the great lords." Most French and German peasants up to the late 1700s wore a "coarse cloth" made of wool or linen, and diseases of the skin such as scabies and ringworm were common among them due to lack of cleanliness (Braudel [1817] 1981, 125-26, 315).

How do economists and statisticians measure standards of living? The procedures are complex, requiring extensive historical investigation or statistical data collection, but the ideas are simple. When comparing standards of living in earlier centuries, they estimate the quantities of food, drink, and cloth available to the average peasant or to the nobility. As Fernand Braudel has done, they also compare housing size and construction, and the quality of amenities such as doors, windows, and floors.

- **Nominal Income:** household income in current money terms, before adjusting for changes in prices

- **Real Income:** nominal income divided by an indicator of the general price level; allows comparison of purchasing power of incomes when prices are different

Now, through extensive measurement and recording of data, the task is more mathematically precise, comparing how much a family can buy of various products with the average income for that year. The method is to first calculate average household income for each year. Before any adjustments for price changes, it is called **nominal income**. Then the statistician calculates an index of the price level. Dividing nominal household income by the price level for that year gives an estimate of **real income**, or income adjusted for price changes.

Real Income = Nominal Income / Price Level

With price level data, we can assess how much our standard of living has risen over the years. Let's say that, in 1992 (the base year of our example), the price level is arbitrarily set at 1.00 and that Mary's salary that year was $20,000. The real value and nominal value of Mary's income are the same. Let's say that by 1998 her salary is $30,000, but the price level is up to 1.50.

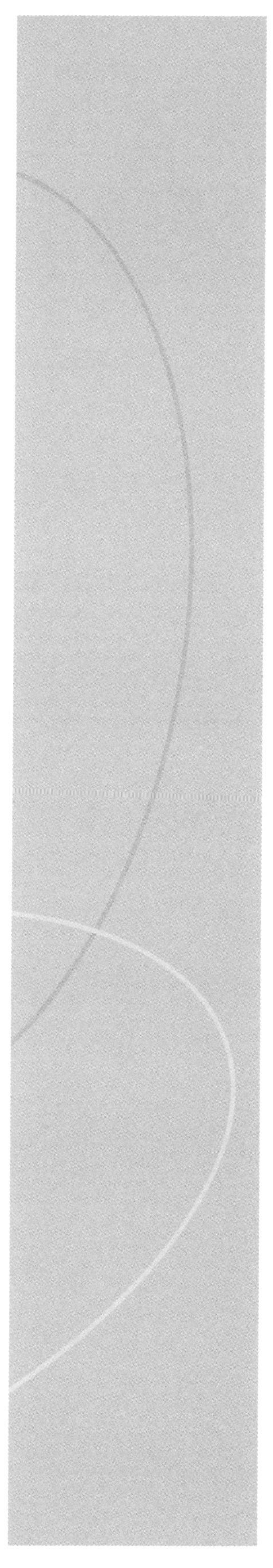

Mary's nominal income is about 50 percent higher, but is her real income higher? No, because ($30,000 / 1.5) = $20,000. Mary's purchasing power has not changed between 1992 and 1998.

The definition of real income implies that the percentage change (% Δ) in real income is as follows:

% Δ Real Income = % Δ Nominal Income - % Δ in Price

In Mary's case, the percentage change in nominal income and the percentage change in price are equal, so real income has not changed. Her standard of living is the same. If her nominal income had risen 50 percent but prices had only risen 30 percent, then her real income would be 20 percent higher.

Calculating changes in workers' standards of living, therefore, requires not only a measure of their nominal or money income, but a measure of price changes as well. This is why labor union representatives seek accurate estimates of changes in consumer prices. Bargaining for an increasing real wage depends on knowing the rate of inflation of consumer prices.

Measuring Changes in Consumer Prices

The U.S. Bureau of Labor Statistics (BLS) calculates a national Consumer Price Index (CPI) along with indexes for major urban areas of the country. The CPI measures changes in the general level of urban consumer prices, also called the rate of consumer price inflation. Values of the CPI over time can be used to convert nominal wages into real wages to assess what is happening to general standards of living.

Every month, the BLS sends shoppers out to buy an average market basket of consumer goods that urban consumers buy. They do so in every major urban area of the country. A market consists of fixed quantities of goods, such as five pounds of ground beef, one standard business suit, shirt, or blouse, the use of a three bedroom apartment, and so on. BLS statisticians then calculate how much the market basket costs each month. This gives them estimates of month-to-month changes in the urban cost of living. For year-to-year changes, the BLS can average monthly prices for each year.

Junk Food Cost of Living Index. You will understand BLS methods better by working through a simple hypothetical example in which we will calculate a junk food cost of living index. Exhibit 15.4 constructs a cost of living index with a market basket of junk food using items from the four basic food groups—chocolate, cola, potato chips, and pizza. Knowing prices in 2003 and 2004, and using a market basket in which quantities of food items are constant, we can see how much weekly spending for junk food changes between years. That allows us to construct a

Exhibit 15.4: Calculating a Junk Food Cost of Living Index

Weekly Market-Basket Goods	2003 Prices	2003 Weekly Spending	2004 Prices	2004 Weekly Spending
3 large chocolate bars	$0.89	$2.67	$0.99	$2.97
4 two-liter cola bottles	$1.09	$4.36	$0.99	$3.96
2 14 oz. bag of chips	$2.49	$4.98	$2.89	$5.78
1 16" pepperoni pizza	$10.99	$10.99	$11.49	$11.49
Total Spending		**$23.00**		**$24.20**

Cost of Living Index = (Weekly Spending Current Year) / (Weekly Spending Base Year)

Assume that 2003 is the base year. Then weekly spending in the base year is $23.000 and the costs of living index numbers for 2003 and 2004 are as follows:

Cost of Living Index 2003 = ($23.00) / ($23.00) = 1.000*

Cost of Living Index 2004 = ($24.20) / (($23.00) = 1.052

The conclusion is that the average prices of junk food were about 5.2 percent higher in 2004 compared to the base year of 2003.

* BLS publications report the CPI with a base year value of 100, not 1. This example converts the base value to 1 for ease of calculations. No accuracy is lost by such a change.

cost of living index showing that on average junk food prices rose a little more than 5 percent.

Comparing Salary Offers between Cities. BLS consumer price indexes are only for use in comparing price level changes between different time periods. The U.S. Chamber of Commerce, however, publishes city-by-city general price levels that can be used for cost of living comparisons of different regions of the country. Such index numbers can be helpful in comparing salary offers from different regions of the country.

Let's say that you have an offer of $48,000 to work in New York City where the price level is measured to be 1.58. You also have an offer to work in Knoxville, Tennessee, for only $32,000, but the price level is estimated as 0.95. This means that New York City prices are much higher than the U.S. average, but Knoxville prices are a bit below average. If you don't mind either city, which one would give you relatively more purchasing power? Divide each salary offer by its respective price index to compare offers.

Exhibit 15.5 shows that the dramatically higher salary in New York City will actually give you about 10 percent less purchasing power than the more modest Knoxville wage. Why? A house that costs $125,000 in Knoxville could cost $450,000 or more around New York City. Since real estate is more expensive in New York

Exhibit 15.5: Comparing Salaries in Different Cities

General Method	New York City	Knoxville
nominal salary offer	$48,000	$32,000
(divided by) estimated price index	1.58	0.95
(equals) comparable real salary	$30,380	$33,684

City, businesses there must also charge more for all other things they sell, including food, clothing, and appliances.

Substitution Bias in the CPI. A difficulty with the BLS CPI is that it has apparently overstated the rate of inflation during the past thirty years. Because the CPI assumes that consumers never change their market basket, it does not take into account consumers' willingness to substitute one good for another. When the price of ground beef goes up, some families will substitute ground turkey or another meat. The BLS did not allow for such substitutions, and CPI calculations make the family appear to be worse off, as if it is still buying beef.

One effect of this substitution bias is that official estimates of real wages were lower than they would have been without such a bias. Here is a hypothetical story with nice round numbers to illustrate the importance of this error. Assume that the average American low-skilled worker's wage was $3.00 an hour in 1970 and $10.00 an hour in 1995. The increase in nominal wage over the twenty five years equaled a yearly rate of about 5 percent. Assume that the CPI grew at a 5.5 percent rate from 1970 to 1995 without adjusting for substitution bias, but that it would have grown by only 4.5 percent if the bias had been eliminated.

What would be the effect on estimated real wages? Exhibit 15.6 shows that the real wage would seem to have fallen from $3 per hour to $2.62, measured in terms of 1970 purchasing power. When the bias is eliminated in these hypothetical calculations, the conclusion is reversed. Real wages have not fallen over the twenty-five-year period—they have risen.

Exhibit 15.6: Illustrating Effects of an Upward Bias in the CPI

Year	1970	1995 biased	1995 actual
Nominal Wage	$3.00	$10.00	$10.00
CPI*	1.00	3.81	3.00
Real Wage**	$3.00	$2.62	$3.33

BLS publications report the CPI with a base year value of 100, not 1. This chart converts the base value to 1 for ease of calculations. No accuracy is lost by such a change.

** Real Wage = Nominal Wage / CPI

This is approximately what occurred in the 1990s. Reports using the biased CPI criticized the American economic system for failing to deliver rising wages to low-skilled workers. Such criticisms were accompanied by various calls for government interventions to correct the problem. Instead, government statisticians corrected for the bias in the CPI and found that it had been overestimating the rate of consumer price inflation by 1 or 2 percent. At lower rates of inflation, new estimates suggested that workers' real wages had been rising, though rather slowly.

Consumer Sentiments

Data on uses of personal income for the United States in 2001 (Exhibit 15.3) show that household spending exerts a powerful influence on the economy. Personal consumer spending comprised 69.9 percent of GDP. As a result, a shift in the willingness of U.S. consumers to spend out of their personal incomes can cause fluctuations in aggregate economic activity and employment.

For this reason, economists track consumer attitudes toward the economy each month as early indicators of changes in their willingness to spend. Two commonly cited indices are the Conference Board's index of consumer confidence (www.conference-board.org) and the University of Michigan's consumer sentiment index (http://www.sca.isr.umich.edu). The consumer confidence index measures householders' attitudes about income and jobs in the next six months. A typical survey would ask whether the respondent thinks that jobs will be (a) more available, (b) neither more nor less available, or (c) less available in the next six months. (Answer (a) is clearly optimistic, and (c) is pessimistic.)

While income can influence consumption, economists watch these survey results as indicators of how consumer spending may lead to changes in national income, through the circular flow. Upturns in consumer sentiments and spending plans indicate a stronger economy in the near future. A downturn in sentiments and spending plans would be one early indicator of a coming economic contraction.

Consumerism and Materialism

Social critics direct our attention away from the question of whether consumer expenditures and standards of living are rising, and toward the question of whether more makes us better or even happier. While an economist is not trained to answer such questions, the student of economics who wishes to see life in its totality must wrestle with them.

The range of attitudes toward consumption is illustrated in the meanings of the term consumerism. On the one hand, consumerism is a movement to protect households from their own ignorance of market opportunities and risks, and from exploitation by unscrupulous businesses. Consumerism also refers to an excessive desire to shop for and buy consumer goods. This second meaning perverts the common sense idea that consuming goods and services is desirable, elevating it to the greatest thing.

Materialism (at least in one sense of the word) is the principle that "material well-being and the furtherance of material progress" are the highest human values (*Webster's Ninth Collegiate Dictionary*). Not all consumers are materialists, but many are. While most of us are not philosophers by training, we hold our personal philosophies dearly and act on them in spite of our words. A materialistic philosophy promotes consumption.

An important question is whether the standard analysis of the macroeconomics of consumption (as I have attempted to give in this chapter) *promotes* a materialistic philosophy. To the extent that it does, it ceases to be morally neutral, inviting criticism of its claim to scientific neutrality. Expansion Point 15.3 addresses the moral question, "How much consumption is enough?"

Expansion Point 15.3: How Much Consumption Is Enough?

Economics is materialistic, assuming that more goods and services are better. In the 1930s, U.S. economics courses taught high school students about the "point of satiety" (the point of complete satisfaction or of satisfaction to excess), but you don't hear that phrase much now. By assuming unlimited wants, economists ignore the question, "How much consumption is enough?" U.S. political leaders also rarely address the issue. They tend mainly to material rather than spiritual matters. Besides, steadily rising consumption promotes politically popular periods of prosperity.

Materialism seems inconsistent as the dominant philosophy of people who overwhelmingly believe in spiritual aspects of life (90 percent of Americans claim belief in God). Many are familiar with Jesus' quote of the Old Testament, "Man does not live on bread alone" (Luke 4:4 NIV). The passage is from Deuteronomy 8:3, which adds "but on every word that comes from the mouth of the Lord." Moses was reminding the Israelites of their inability to feed themselves while wandering in the desert, and of their reliance on God for food and other necessities of life.

Americans tend to allow the individual and private social groups, not government, to strike a balance between material and spiritual aspects of life. To America's social commentators and religious leaders falls the task of keeping the issue before the people, as Moses did with Israel.

How much consumption, then, is enough? What are the indicators of excess? Inordinate unhappiness compared to those with less material prosperity would suggest trouble. It is notable that Robert Lane (2000) reports that rates of psychological depression have been rising in the very market economies where a consumer mentality rules. Inadequate saving and imprudent borrowing, or working to excess to augment income, would also suggest a consumer fever. Perhaps the best indicator of too much consumption is when it simultaneously becomes a fever and yet fails to satisfy.

Another approach to detecting excess in consumption is to ignore self and focus on how it affects others, especially the most vulnerable. Lane also reports that, with standards of living and time at work on the rise, U.S. parents' time with children has been falling.

Source: Robert Lane, *The Loss of Happiness in Market Democracies* (Yale University, 2000).

Producers in the Circular Flow

As with consumer uses and sources of funds, business activity in the macroeconomy is more complex than the simple circular flow would indicate. Once again, we can illustrate this increased complexity with a picture of the flows of funds into and out of the business sector.

Illustrating Flows of Business Income and Expenditure

Businesses spend and borrow money to make money. They also pay taxes, supply goods and services to government, and deal with foreign traders, as shown in Exhibit 15.7. This figure describes money flows for one business or for all businesses of an economy.

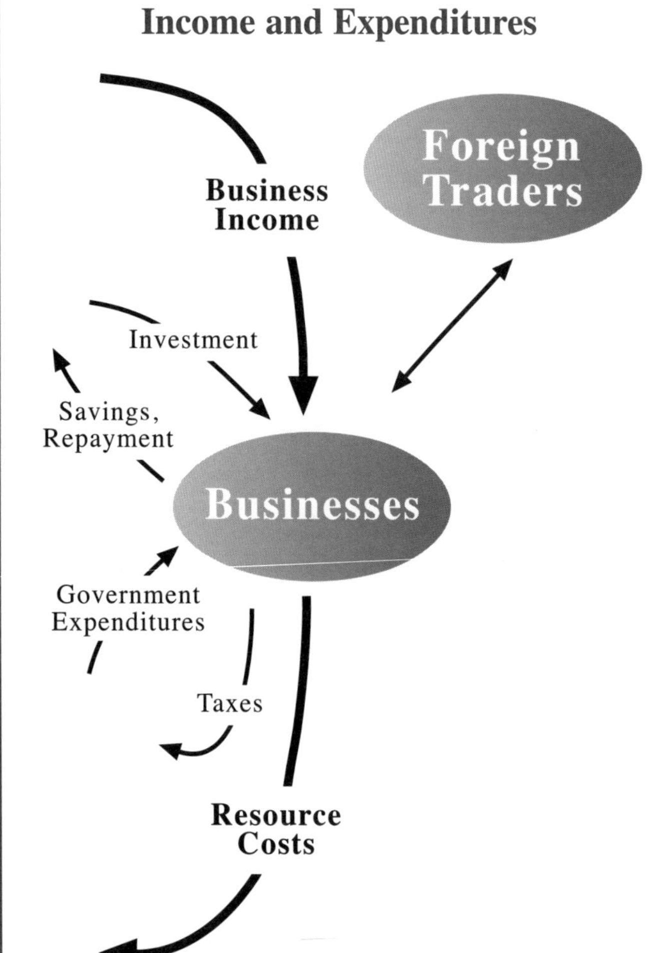

Business Income

Businesses earn income by selling goods and services to consumers. The major flow of business income in Exhibit 15.7 is consumer expenditure. Firms also earn income by selling to government and to foreign traders, as illustrated. Sales to foreign traders are called exports of goods and services.

Businesses with substantial bank accounts may also earn some interest income. Some businesses earn money by investing in other businesses and will earn investment income. These flows are not shown separately in the exhibit, but can be considered as an addition to the investment funds flowing into the firm from the financial sector.

Business Expenditures

A firm must pay costs of resources used in production, often before it earns any income from product sold. Resources include unskilled and skilled labor, capital equipment, land, raw materials, intermediate goods, and managerial or entrepreneurial ability. This flow is called resource costs in Exhibit 15.7. These costs of resources then become household income.

Firms also pay taxes to government, as illustrated. They pay income taxes and make payments for the sales taxes that governments charge consumers at the checkout counter. In the United States, these sales taxes are generally levied by states. In Canada and Europe, federal governments also levy sales taxes.

A firm often buys intermediate products and invests in new capital that it uses in production. This flow is not shown in the exhibit because it occurs within the business sector. The firm also buys both raw materials, intermediate product, and finished goods (for resale) from foreign traders. These purchases are called imports of goods and services. Most imported goods are bought by businesses acting as intermediaries for domestic consumers. Travel abroad, though, involves some direct purchases of imports by consumers, though this is not illustrated explicitly here.

Business Borrowing

When a firm wants to invest in an increase in equipment, buildings, or inventories of finished goods, raw materials, or intermediate product, it must either borrow from financial markets or use its own savings. Exhibit 15.7 shows the flow of investment funds into the firm. This is not the same as business income because it is not due to sales of goods or services, nor is the flow of investment funds from the bank the same as expenditure of those funds. Investment expenditure is a business-to-business exchange, and is not illustrated here.

Business Saving

A firm may have a positive cash flow, meaning that more money is flowing in than is flowing out. This is often true of established firms in mature industries. Such a firm will accumulate cash, at least temporarily, in its own checking account or some form of certificate of deposit. Some firms save for pending investments. Other firms accumulate cash in order to meet a future debt payment. At times, it is simply wise for a firm to have excess cash to guard against business uncertainties. In all of these cases, the firm is doing what many households do: saving its extra income.

Business Investment Is Crucial

In the circular flow of income and expenditure, business investment is as crucial as consumer spending. In the equation for aggregate expenditure, AE = C + I + GS + (X-M), I represents business investment. While business investment is not as large in money value as consumer spending (C) in total dollar value of GDP each year, it is crucial because of its volatility. We will study two types of business investment—fixed investment and inventory investment—examining the role of each in the circular flow.

• **Aggregate Expenditure (AE):** the sum of aggregate spending in the economy; AE = C + I + GS + (X-M) where:
- C = consumption
- I = investment
- GS = gov't spending
- X = exports
- M = imports

Fixed Investment

Fixed investment involves building new plants (factories, warehouses, and other buildings) and equipment. Once made,

• **Fixed investment:**
1) varies with the business cycle
2) contributes to the severity of the business cycle

such an investment is fixed because it is difficult to convert the buildings and machines to other uses. **Fixed investment** is related to the business cycle in two important ways: it varies with the business cycle while also contributing to the severity of the business cycle.

Fixed investment varies with the stage of the business cycle. During an expansion, businesses will be operating plant and equipment at higher capacities. If business managers expect good economic times to continue, they will invest in new plant and equipment because they expect it to be especially profitable. During a contraction, however, businesses will have significant excess capacity. They will not need more plant and equipment. They might need to replace worn-out capital, but during a contraction, a company can buy used equipment from other companies. A healthy company may even be able to buy whole companies as the prices of shares of stock fall during a contraction.

Fixed investment in plant and equipment also *contributes* to the business cycle in a market economy. During an economic boom, new investment exaggerates the boom by stimulating even more production of capital goods, more construction of buildings, and more income for the workers who build them. When the boom reaches a peak and a contraction begins, however, businesses cut back sharply on new investment and even replacement investment. While households try to protect their levels of past consumption during a contraction, businesses do not insist on maintaining steady patterns of investment. This cyclicality of fixed investment works through aggregate expenditure and the circular flow to make the cycle worse.

Inventory Investment

Businesses invest in inventories of finished goods when they produce products during the current period for measuring GDP, but don't sell them. Inventory investment can be of two kinds: intended or unintended. Each has a different role in the business cycle.

• **Inventory investment:** product produced but not sold during the current period of measuring GDP

Intended Inventory Investment. Businesses hold inventories for several reasons. They keep buffer stocks of finished goods to protect against sudden unexpected increases in the pace of sales. Losing a customer to a competitor because product is out of stock is costly to a business that depends on good customer relations for its income. Firms also run larger intended inventories just before a big selling season. Producers of rock salt for winter road treatment, for example, build inventories as winter approaches because weekly production during winter might not keep up with weekly demand. Toy manufacturers and retailers hold larger inventories going into the Christmas selling season.

Firms monitor actual inventories and adjust them toward target levels during the year and over the business cycle. They rebuild actual inventories that are less than target levels and cease production to trim inventories that are excessive. Excess inventories impose interest costs on firms, either because the firm had to borrow to pay for its production and storage or because the firm is losing interest income on money tied up in inventories.

Inventory cycles follow and contribute to the business cycle. As Expansion Point 15.4 explains, during the recession of 2001, U.S. firms cut production to trim inventories that had ballooned due to slowing sales. This is the general pattern. At the peak of economic activity, inventory adjustments contribute to an economic contraction. Near the trough at the end of a contraction, firms begin to rebuild inventories that have grown too lean to meet demand, contributing to the expansion that follows.

Unintended Inventory Investment. Not all changes in inventories are intentional. Unexpected decreases in sales lead to unintended investment in inventories. While such investments in additional goods are counted in GDP, they signal falling, not

Expansion Point 15.4: The Role of Investment in the Recession of 2001

Business investment played an important role in the U.S. recession of 2001. The onset of the contraction occurred in the first quarter of the year. The data below on percentage changes in business inventories signal both the onset of a problem and the response of businesses. Inventories were growing rapidly during the months of December 2000 to March 2001, the month the NBER later declared as the beginning of the recession. From April until June, inventories then fell rather quickly.

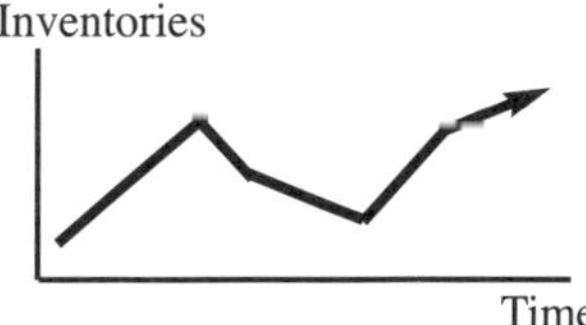

Changes in U.S. Business Inventories 12/00 to 12/01

12/00	1/01	2/01	3/01	4/01	5/01	6/01
0.5%	0.4%	0.0%	0.2%	-0.3%	-0.4%	-0.2%

We can interpret the inventory data as follows. Until March, the data show unintended inventory accumulation, as customers slowed their rate of purchases. After March, businesses responded with production cutbacks to reestablish inventory balance.

Business-fixed investment also played a major role in the downturn. The following chart reports fixed investment in the United States from the fourth quarter of 2000 to the fourth quarter of 2001. Fixed investment fell 3.3 percent from the first quarter to the second, but between the first and the fourth quarter, it fell 14.6 percent. This dramatic decline worsened the recession.

Trillions of Dollars of U.S. Fixed Investment 12/00 to 12/01

IV/00	I/01	II/01	III/01	IV/01
$1.63	$1.78	$1.72	$1.67	$1.52

The recession was reaching a trough near the end of 2001. Economists contended that continued low fixed investment would put a drag on the coming recovery. Declining inventories, however, could not persist in the face of rising demand at the beginning of a recovery in late 2001. Declining inventories in December 2001 suggested that production would recover further in early 2002 to catch up with consumer demand.

Sources: "Month-to-month Change in Business Inventories," *Econoday*. Found at http://www.econoday.com/client-demos/demoweekly/2001/November/15/busi_inv.html.

GPDI, National Income and Product Accounts, Bureau of Economic Analysis. Found at www.bea.gov/briefrm/tables/ebrm.htm.

"Consumer Prices Slip; Industrial Production, Inventories Fall, Pointing to Future Recovery," *CNNMoney* (16 January 2002). Found at http://money.cnn.com/2002/01/16/economy/.

rising, economic activity. Because sales were less than expected, firms will cut production and lay off workers. Economic activity will therefore decline.

In the other direction, unexpected increases in sales lead to unintended decreases in inventories. These inventory reductions will temporarily offset the measured increase in sales of final goods, but they signal that firms need to increase production with the resulting positive effects on income and GDP.

What Causes Changes in Investment?

If fixed investment and inventory investment are volatile, what causes their fluctuations? Expected profitability of investment, which depends on a manager's assessments of future economic activity, directly affects fixed and planned-inventory investments. Interest rates are inversely related, with higher rates choking off investment.

Other Indicators of Production Activity

Fixed and inventory investment are two crucial indicators of business activity, but by no means are they the only ones. What analysts want are indicators of current and forthcoming production activity and of current producer prices.

Indicators of production include the Federal Reserve's rate of manufacturing capacity utilization and its index of industrial production. Building permits and housing starts are useful indicators of residential construction activity. The Bureau of the Census' estimate of monthly retail sales gauges final sales to consumers. For detailed reviews of these and several other production indicators, see Gary Clayton and Gerhard Giesbrecht's *Everyday Economic Statistics* (1995).

The Bureau of Labor Statistics' producer price index (PPI) measures prices for the first rather than final sale of a manufacturer's product. The PPI is more volatile than the CPI each month and over the last 15 years has grown more slowly than the CPI due to global competition and other factors (Clayton and Giesbrecht 1995, 95).

The Complete Circular Flow

You have seen diagrams of the flows of money into and out of households and businesses. We can combine them with the financial, government, and international sectors into the complete circular flow of income and expenditure. The circular flow illustrates important macroeconomic relations, allowing us to trace the effects of factors that influence income and output through the various sectors. More than other models, the circular flow can show the many indirect effects of economic change.

Picturing Macroeconomic Activity

Exhibit 15.8 shows the circular flow as one main flow with a number of secondary flows. The main circular flow, shown as the thickest lines, represents flows of expenditure and income between households and businesses. Other important flows involve financing commerce, government, and international commerce. The picture also illustrates money flows reflecting central-bank interventions in domestic and foreign financial markets.

Leakages and Injections

Following a useful tradition of Keynesian economics, economists call these other flows **leakages** out of and **injections** into the circular flow. A leakage drains spending for real GDP from the domestic economy. An injection adds spending for real GDP to the domestic economy.

- **Leakages from the circular flow:**
  1) saving
  2) taxes
  3) imports

Leakages and injections come in pairs. Saving is a leakage from the circular flow, while investment is an injection into the circular flow. Taxes are a leakage, and government spending and transfer payments are injections into the circular flow. Imports are a leakage, while exports are an injection.

- **Injections into the circular flow:**
  1) investment
  2) gov't spending
  3) exports

Economic activity responds to the **balance of leakages and injections**. Keynesian thinking holds that when injections into the circular flow are greater than leakages, income and output will increase. When leakages exceed injections, aggregate income and output will decrease. Most interesting to economists are unpredicted changes in leakages or injections.

- **If injections exceed leakages:** income and output will increase

- **If leakages exceed injections:** income and output will decrease

Unexpected injections of more spending into the economy, therefore, will give at least a temporary boost to economic activity. For example, when European economies rebound from a recession, their people increase purchases of U.S. exports. This injects additional spending into the domestic U.S. circular flow. In export-producing industries, more workers have more income to spend on domestic products.

The same is true for a sudden burst of investment spending. When firms invest in new technology such as computer hardware and software, the additional spending means higher incomes for firms and workers producing computers and software. This eventually filters through retail and other businesses in the domestic economy. Swings in consumer sentiments can cause similar bursts of spending, independent of the level of income.

Real vs. Money Flows

In Exhibit 15.8, only money flows are recorded. Real flows of goods and services, and changing ownership of assets in the opposite direction are implied. For example, consumer expenditure includes the dollars you pay to the food store in return for real bags of groceries. When a business pays money for heavy equipment, the payment is a money flow and the machinery is the real flow of goods. When a foreign investor buys a U.S. Treasury bond, the money flows in while ownership of the bond flows out.

Exhibit 15.8: The Complete Circular Flow of Income and Expenditure

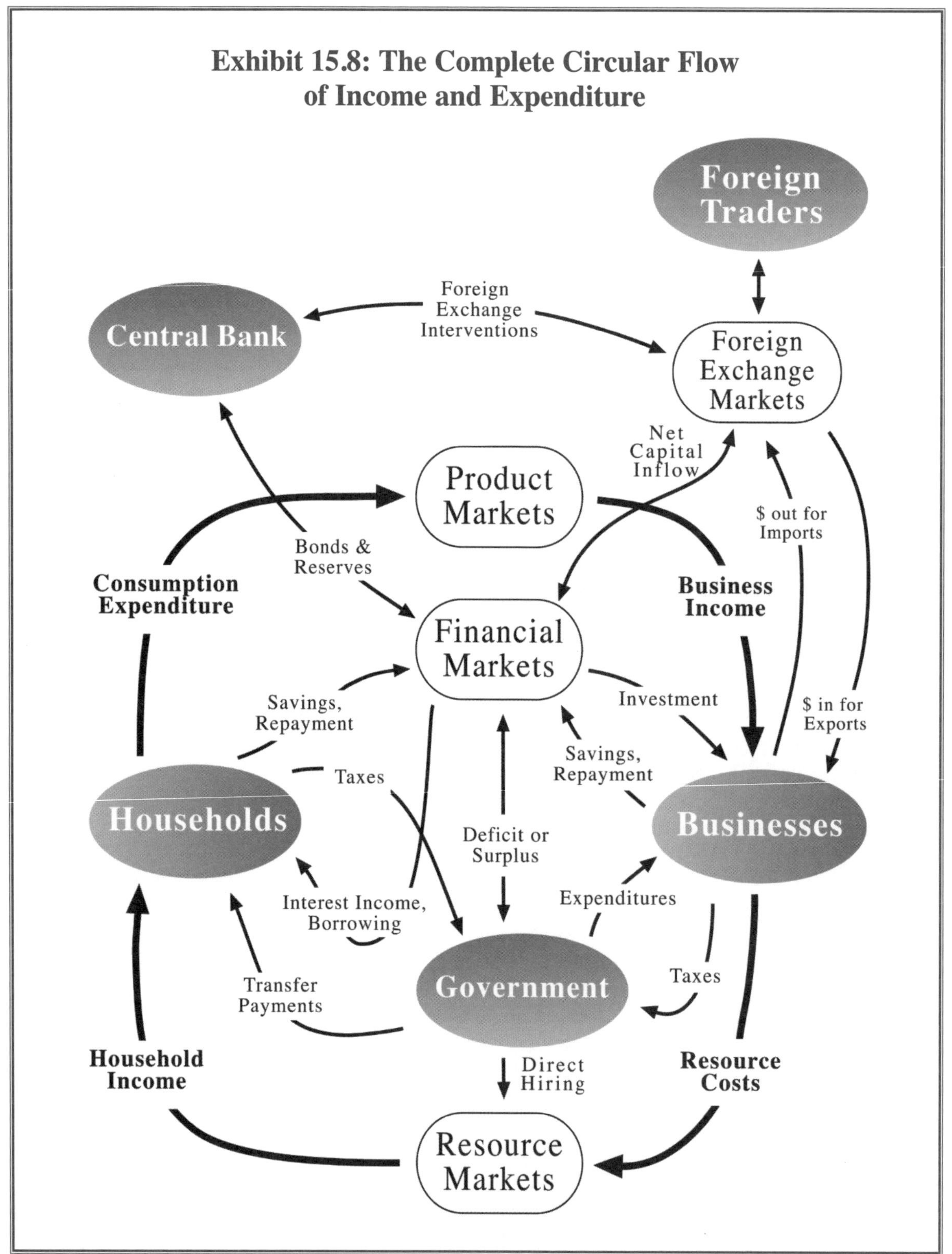

The Sum of the Parts: Interdependence and Complexity of Effects

What conclusions can we draw about the sum of the parts of the circular flow? Clearly the sectors are interdependent, not isolated. Furthermore, a shock to the economy will have complex effects as it works through various channels.

As shown in Exhibit 15.8, a mixed economy is composed of interdependent sectors and markets. Representatives of government, households, and businesses meet in financial, resource, and product markets. Consumers buy goods and services in product markets. Businesses and government buy labor services, land use, and capital-equipment services in resource markets. Ownership of financial assets changes hands in financial markets. Traders swap international currencies in the foreign-exchange market, which is an extension of domestic financial markets. Moreover, decisions in one sector affect opportunities and decisions in other sectors.

Because of the varied channels of influence in a macroeconomy, policy changes and other economic shocks will have complex effects. The relation between income and consumption is just one of five complexities.

Consumption and Income

What effects do your consumption decisions have on your own employment? They are negligible when we consider only your own spending and your own employment. When we consider the whole economy, however, the effects of many people's decisions to spend more or less can be dramatic. More spending can mean more jobs in the short run, though it will also mean less investment and output for the future. Less spending means fewer jobs, but over time a higher saving rate would mean more investment.

In Exhibit 15.8, the circulation of money between households and businesses is the dominant circular flow, creating an important macroeconomic interdependence. The level of consumption depends on the level of income, which depends on the level of consumption. This "feedback" between income and consumption is important to Keynesian analysis of the Great Depression. Perhaps you can imagine how higher consumer spending leads to more demand for household-supplied resources and higher household income, allowing for even more consumer spending. In a depression, John Maynard Keynes said, less income leads to less consumption, which leads to less income, and so on.

Government Borrowing and Private Saving and Investment

What are the effects of government borrowing on the interest rates for your next car loan or real estate mortgage? You probably don't give that much thought, but financial analysts do. They bid the interest rates on Treasury bonds up and down on news of

increases and decreases in government borrowing. Passage of the Deficit Reduction Act of 1993, for example, immediately preceded and apparently caused about a 2 percent fall in long-term bond interest rates. This led to lower interest rates for personal home and auto loans as well. Economists attributed the economic boom of the 1990s partly to this drop in interest rates and to its effects on business investment in new technology.

Another important interdependent relationship exists among financial market flows. If the government borrows huge sums of money to finance a deficit, that may crowd investors out of the market for loanable funds. Of course, more private saving or a net capital inflow could also fund the extra borrowing, but the point is clear. One flow affects another in financial markets.

Government Stimulus Policy: Domestic Channels with International Effects

A government that wishes to stimulate the domestic economy during a recession in economic activity can use various channels. It can cut income taxes and stimulate consumption spending among working families, or it can increase transfer payments to specifically poor families, increasing their consumption spending. Government can target investment tax credits to stimulate fixed investment by businesses. Or it can increase its own spending for projects that increase sales of private goods and services and that stimulate private or public hiring of workers.

Yet, since all of these channels for economic stimulus encourage consumer spending, the stimulus effect will leak abroad to other countries. When U.S. consumers increase spending, a fraction goes for imported goods and services. Thus, Canada, Europe, Japan, and the rest of the world will feel the effects of a policy designed to stimulate the U.S. economy.

Central Banking

A central bank adds money to or takes money away from the circular flow. The central bank, however, does not directly control the speed of the flow of money as it is spent in the economy. Even so, central bank policies indirectly influence the rate of spending by consumers and businesses through their influences on interest rates and the quantity of money. Lower interest rates encourage spending and discourage saving. Higher rates do the opposite. More money encourages spending, and less constrains spending.

Here again, however, international effects can moderate the effects of government policy. Lower interest rates will decrease the flow of investment into a country and increase the flow of investment funds out of the country (through the net-capital-inflow channel). This is because many investors search internationally for the highest rates of return on financial assets such as government and private debt. Alternatively, higher interest rates will attract foreign investment and keep domestic investment funds at home. Therefore, international financial flows will tend to moderate the ability of a central bank to influence interest rates.

The ability of a central bank to control monetary policy depends on its independence from the political influences in government. Therefore, it is significant that the central bank sits apart from the government in Exhibit 15.8. By law, the Federal Reserve (the Fed, which is the U.S. central bank) is independent of political influence in its week-to-week operation. While the U.S. Congress regularly reviews the Fed's policies, studies have shown that a more independent central bank is associated with lower rates of price inflation, a prime goal of most central bankers.

International Financial Crises and Domestic Markets

With the circular flow, we can also illustrate how international financial crises can affect different sectors of the domestic economy. A financial crisis in Asia in 1997 and 1998 lowered demand for U.S. agricultural exports, but also caused a capital flight (a rapid and speculative exit of foreign investment funds) that became a net capital inflow into U.S. financial markets. As a result, while farmers suffered from slow exports, interest rates fell because of the additional loanable funds. Stock market prices also rose due to additional foreign demand for the safety of the United States market.

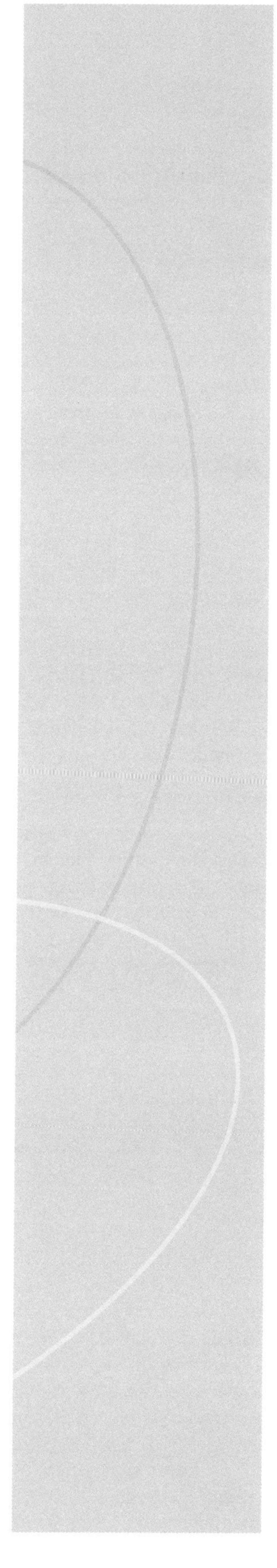

Shortcomings of the Circular Flow

The circular flow is not a complete model. The price level, for example, appears nowhere in the model. The economists who designed it assumed that prices were constant. Economists who believe that price changes and inflation are important to macroeconomic policy, however, expect to see a model that incorporates them. Another macro model is needed to explain periods of rising or falling prices.

The circular flow also does not explain other important economic issues such as economic growth or short-term or long-term shifts in the patterns of production in various industries, such as the rise of the service economy in the United States during the last half of the twentieth century.

The circular flow model is not a poor model. It is an excellent teaching device, especially concerning macroeconomic interrelationships and the feedback between income and consumption. Yet, the circular flow simply cannot explain *every* important macroeconomic issue. That is why the student of macroeconomics must learn a variety of models, each of which contributes to a more complete understanding of macroeconomic activity. Aggregate demand and supply, for example, highlights the influences on the general price level and real GDP, while the Phillips Curve (a historic relationship between rates of inflation and unemployment) highlights inflation and unemployment dynamics over time.

Chapter Summary

1. The simple circular flow of income and expenditure illustrates that households and businesses interact in product and resource markets, and that household income and consumption expenditure are directly related.

2. A chart of the uses and sources of personal income illustrates different choices that consumers make about augmenting and spending income. Sources of income include wages, salaries, transfers, borrowing, and withdrawals from savings. Uses of income include taxes first, and then spending, saving, and paying off loans out of disposable income.

3. Changes in the level of household income, interest rates, government taxes and transfers, and wealth will cause changes in household consumption spending, borrowing, and saving.

4. Standards of living before the 1900s have been estimated by historians who compare quantities of food, drink, and cloth available, and type and size of housing. The U.S. Bureau of Labor Statistics estimates standards of living, dividing nominal wages by an index of consumer prices to estimate real wages.

5. The consumer price index (CPI) has in the past had a substitution bias because it did not allow for the fact that consumers change the mix in their market basket of goods and services when prices change.

6. Indexes of consumer sentiments give important information into household plans for spending in the near future.

7. Flows of business income and expenditure illustrate the overall picture of business activity, from borrowing for investment and earning revenue from sales to paying taxes to government and the costs of resources to households.

8. Business-fixed investment and investment in inventories signal changes in economic activity and also cause changes in economic activity, adding to business cycle fluctuations. Inventory investment may be either intended or unintended. Levels of fixed investment and intended inventory investment depend on managers' expectations of future profitability of the investments and on interest rates.

9. Economic analysts use other indicators of production activity and the producer price index to monitor current business activity and costs.

10. The circular flow of income and expenditure illustrates interdependencies in the macroeconomy. The most important is the feedback between aggregate income and aggregate consumption.

11. The circular flow model also can illustrate the indirect effects of various policies and economic events. Government borrowing, for instance, also affects household consumption and saving, as well as business investment through its effects on interest rates in financial markets. The Asian financial crisis caused capital inflows into the United States, but also decreased the demand for U.S. agricultural products.

12. The circular flow is not able to explain all macroeconomic events. It ignores prices and, therefore, cannot explain changes in the rate of inflation. It also cannot explain economic growth.

Problems for Practice

15.1 Briefly compare and contrast the conclusions that we can derive about the macroeconomy from the simple circular flow and the more complete circular flow. For example, do both include leakages and injections into the circular flow? Do both illustrate the interdependence of product and resource markets?

15.2 Through the recession of 2001, consumer spending remained relatively strong, while fixed investment fell dramatically. What are the possible reasons that consumer spending did not drop, according to the theoretical determinants of changes in consumption explained in this chapter?

15.3* Expansion Point 15.1 gives evidence on per capita U.S. consumption expenditure and disposable income from 1988 to 1993. What was the average rate of saving out of disposable income? Is it close to 0.05, as implied by a hypothetical consumption function where income is 0.95 times disposable income?

15.4* Assume that, in the year just past, nominal income per capita in the United States was $18,700 and the price level was 1.30. (a) What was real income per capita? (b) If income eight years earlier, in the base year, was $14,000, were Americans better off or worse off in the current year?

15.5 Why is the consumer price index biased and how does this bias affect estimates of the increase in real wages in the United States since 1970?

15.6 Business investment is only a small fraction of consumer spending, which is about 70% of GDP in any year. Why is business investment an important factor in determining the level of economic activity?

15.7 Which is important in causing a recession—changes in inventory investment or changes in fixed investment? What does theory say and what does evidence from the 2001 U.S. recession suggest?

15.8* If leakages from the circular flow are greater than injections into it, what will happen to the level of economic activity? Explain. Is the opposite true if injections are greater than leakages?

15.9 Draw and label the complete circular flow from memory. Tell stories about economic theory, current economic conditions, or events from macroeconomic history, making reference to your chart. For example, if interest rates are falling now, refer to the chart to illustrate the effects of interest-rate changes.

For your portfolio:

15.10* In a group of three or four students, establish your own market basket of goods for a hypothetical consumer. Follow the example in Exhibit 15.4. That means figuring how much of a good you use each week. You have to allow for how fast equipment such as a computer will wear out. If, for instance, your computer would last about three years (52 * 3 years) then each week you use up (wear out) about 1/(52*3) of the computer's life and value per week. Each person should then check the prices of three goods this year and last year in the same week. When you come together with your prices, use your group's market basket to calculate a price index.

15.11 Search business literature for two current articles on aggregate consumption and two current articles on production and investment in the domestic economy. Also search Web sites containing economic statistics and find recent values of indicators of consumer and producer activity. Write a one-page report on the current state of the economy from your articles and include statistics on these two sectors.

For class discussion:

15.12 Consider Expansion Point 15.3 and the discussion of materialism and consumerism in the text. Do you think the relative prosperity of the United States is an indication of excessive consumerism and an abandonment of spiritual interests? Do you find any other compelling evidence in the United States today of an excessively materialistic philosophy?

See Answer Key for hints/answers to starred (*) questions.

Chapter 16

The Financial System

Saving and Investment in the Circular Flow

What this chapter will help you think about:

1. What are the six functions of financial activity?
2. What are the major flows into and out of financial markets?
3. How do financial flows affect economic activity?
4. How do financial markets encourage foreign commerce?
5. How does the central bank influence financial markets?
6. How do financial flows affect macroeconomic activity?
7. How do interest rate changes affect financial markets?
8. What are the types of financial risk and their effects on financial market activity?

A healthy financial system encourages economic growth, and improves the efficiency of distribution of goods and services. This chapter focuses mainly on the functions and history of a private financial system with government regulation. You will also find a few comments in the overview about centrally controlled finance, as practiced in Soviet-Russian central planning.

- **Finance:** to pay for something; to lend, borrow, or otherwise provide money to make a payment

To **finance** something means to pay for it or, more narrowly, to arrange for a loan. We talk about financing an investment with a commercial loan or financing an automobile with a consumer loan. In a market economy, however, finance is broader than just lending, involving the monetary system and insurance industry, for example. As you will see in the picture of financial flows, financial activities and institutions weave together the private and public, foreign and domestic, and monetary and real (goods and services) sectors of a market economy.

- **Financial markets:**
  1) in bond markets, governments and corporations sell debt
  2) in stock markets, individuals and organizations buy and sell shares of corporate ownership
  3) in foreign-exchange markets, people trade national currencies

Financial Markets

Financial activity occurs when buyers and sellers of financial assets meet directly in **stock markets, bond markets**, and **foreign-exchange markets**. A market is a system by which buyers and sellers exchange things. In financial markets, people exchange financial assets, not goods or resources. Corporations sell bonds, which are claims to a future flow of funds in repayment of the debt. Individuals and organizations trade stock certificates, which are shares of ownership in a corporation. People trade currencies of various nations.

Financial activity also occurs indirectly as intermediaries such as commercial banks, investment banks, insurance companies, pension funds, and mutual funds provide financial services to government, businesses, and individuals. Financial services include holding deposits and returning them on demand, underwriting the issues of new bonds and stocks, insuring people against various calamities, and managing assets in a pension fund or mutual fund.

Six Functions of a Financial System

A financial system has at least **six functions:** making payments, changing currencies, extending credit, taking deposits, raising capital, and insuring against risks. These six functions involve purchases at home and abroad, the banking system, the stock and bond market, and the insurance business.

- **Six functions of finance:**
  1) making payments
  2) changing currencies
  3) extending credit
  4) taking deposits
  5) raising capital
  6) insuring against risk

Moving Money in Payment

A financial system must first provide a means of **making payments** for goods, services, and resources in normal commerce. This includes providing money as a means of exchange and providing for methods of changing ownership and perhaps location of the money.

Changing Currencies

Second, and closely related, a financial system provides for paying across national borders by facilitating **currency exchanges**. Money that is accepted in one country often is not accepted in another. For large transactions, the dollar is an exception because it is a world reserve currency. Normally, though, you could not use a dollar to buy goods and services in another country. The same is true to a greater extent for other currencies.

While money changing is distinct from lending and other functions of commercial banks, the same banks that take deposits and make loans often will also change currencies. Those with branches in different countries are most likely to do so. Banks have economies of scope in handling money, in that it is more efficient to conduct all these operations involving money within the same organization.

Extending Credit

As noted above, the common meaning of "finance" is **extending credit** for consumption and productive investment. Shoppers write their own loans for many retail purchases through credit card transactions. Borrowers secure funds for cars, houses, and commercial loans by signing a contract at the bank.

Taking Deposits

As part of the same process of moving money from savers to investors and spenders, commercial and savings banks **take deposits**. A deposit provides the depositor with convenience,

safety, and a modest return. People traditionally have deposited money in banks, but have more recently found that other institutions such as money-market mutual funds are willing and legally able to take a kind of deposit. As a result, the share of commercial banks in financial activity declined in the last two decades of the twentieth century.

Direct finance in bond markets allows corporations and governments to go directly to savers. Only those with well-established reputations for repayment and a favorable current credit rating need offer their bonds.

Raising Capital

Fifth, a financial system allows for the sharing of investment risks by assisting corporations in **raising capital**. Capital as used here refers to ownership in a business venture. While a deposit in a bank is a claim on money today or in the future, a share of ownership in capital is a claim on future income from a going concern that produces a product. Shareholders are paid dividends when the company makes a profit (income after expenses). Selling stock spreads the risks of investment because, unlike bondholders, shareholders suffer losses if the company's costs exceed revenues.

A financial system provides avenues for investors to buy and sell shares of businesses. Investment banks underwrite a firm's issue of new shares of stock by buying them and then reselling them. The New York Stock Exchange and other exchanges also facilitate the buying and selling of existing shares of stock of corporations.

Insuring Against Casualty Risks

In the final function, financial markets allow traders and others to **insure against casualty risks** of enterprise and investment through a system of insurance. The industry has blossomed from insuring sailing vessels and their contents against disaster several hundred years ago into a vast system of insuring houses, lives, and quarterbacks' throwing arms today. Companies now specialize in life insurance, disability insurance, auto insurance, homeowner's insurance, physician's malpractice insurance, and so on. The industry depends on carefully measuring future probabilities of accidents based on past occurrences, and then setting rates for the future that will cover those risks.

Consumers in Financial Markets

Finance is not reserved for the corporate elite. Consumers participate in all aspects of finance. They use money and the payments system every time they use their credit card. They borrow funds, and make investments in deposits, government bonds, and the stock market. Most have forms of insurance, especially since banks demand home mortgage insurance and states generally demand auto insurance. When traveling abroad, consumers also buy foreign currencies.

By the 1990s, U.S. consumers could consider numerous investments and electronic tools for buying and managing them. They also faced a wider variety of risks, as collapsing "dot.com" stock prices and the Enron scandal of 2001 illustrated. As an introduction to financial markets, see the practical hints for managing your own finances in Expansion Point 16.1. They illustrate institutional details and economic principles affecting financial decisions.

Expansion Point 16.1: Practical Tips for Personal Finance

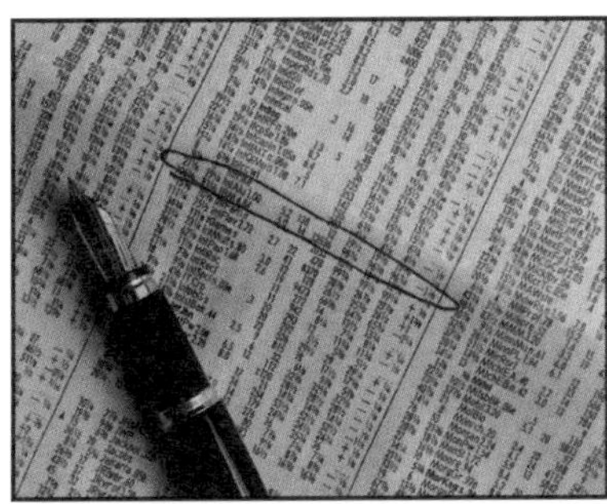

Here are nine common recommendations about personal finance. They are offered for illustrative purposes only and are not intended as a comprehensive plan for personal finance or as advice on specific investments that you might be considering.

1. Paying off debt is usually the best investment you can make, especially when the interest rates are higher than you can expect to make in other investments. Taking available cash and paying off a loan that charges 15 percent gives you an unusually high and sure return.

2. Accumulate three to six times your monthly salary in a liquid savings account, especially if your job is not secure. Liquid means easily converted to money at low cost. Money-market accounts are very liquid but still pay a modest rate of interest. Mutual funds that invest in short-term U.S. government bills are relatively risk free.

3. Diversify your holdings of different financial instruments. If one investment suffers, perhaps another will thrive. Don't invest heavily in one type of asset such as real estate, stocks of a particular company or industry, or corporate bonds. Mutual funds provide low-cost diversification.

4. But don't overdiversify when buying stock-market mutual funds. Studies show that purchasing shares in three or so funds yields a diversified portfolio. Any more funds leads to extra headaches of keeping accounts straight.

5. Adjust your mix of assets as you age. A 30-year-old investor, for example, will on average put more money into riskier "growth" stocks and less in more secure U.S. Treasury bills than a 50-year-old investor will. When very near retirement, the investor would generally want more retirement wealth in less risky assets, even though they tend to pay lower rates of return.

6. Take advantage of government tax exemptions in an Individual Retirement Account (IRA) and in company-sponsored investment plans such as a 401-K plan.

7. Choose the largest deductibles to get the best rates when buying insurance. If the deductible is $1,000, you pay for any damages up to that amount and the company pays anything more. And consider carefully how often you apply for small claims against the company. Instead, keep a savings account for emergencies to cover deductibles. Yet, don't cut corners on coverage.

8. Shop among local lenders for loans and compare the interest costs, other expenses, and particular terms of each loan. Loans do differ, so force lenders to compete for your business. The same is true when opening a deposit account or buying a certificate of deposit.

9. Avoid certain traps of saving for a child's education. Prepaying college tuition may sound great, until your child decides to attend another school. Putting savings in your child's name for education is a mistake too, because college aid formulas reduce financial aid when money is in a child's savings than when in a family's savings.

Source: Stephanie Gallagher, *Money Secrets the Pros Don't Want You to Know* (New York: Amacon, 1995).

Money Flows through Financial Markets

As a further overview of the financial system, let's examine the relationship of financial flows. Exhibit 16.1 illustrates the flows into and out of financial markets. It illustrates one of their main functions: channeling funds from savers to investors. These flows shift purchasing power among households, businesses, and governments from those who want to save for the future to those who want to spend and invest now. Such financial flows increase economic efficiency because savers are not always the best at choosing and organizing new investment projects.

Implied Flows of Assets and Obligations

In Exhibit 16.1, for every flow of money in one direction through financial markets, a written obligation to provide a service or a title to an asset flows in the other. All of this is specified in the financial contracts that people sign.

Quid pro quo is required for a legal contract: something for something. Borrowers sign loan contracts with lenders, promising to repay the loan in the future according to specified terms in return for money today. Insurance contracts shift risk for individual or business calamities to the insurer, and the insurer takes on an obligation to repay losses under specified conditions in return for insurance premiums today. Pension contracts specify the rate at which and conditions under which the firm is obligated to repay the pensioner in return for pension payments now.

Specific Money Flows

Exhibit 16.1 illustrates that at least five groups of people and organizations meet in financial markets: households, the government's treasury, the central bank, foreign investors, and businesses. Let's consider how each interacts with the markets.

Household Finance

Households **save** and **borrow** money mainly through financial markets and their institutions. Flows of funds from households into financial markets include saving every month and repayment of loans as well. Flows from financial markets to households also include borrowing and interest income. These flows are quite sensitive to changes in interest rates and in perceptions about the future health of the economy, which affects future income.

- **Budget deficit:** expenditures exceed revenues
- **Balanced budget:** revenues equal expenditures
- **Budget surplus:** revenues exceed expenditures

Government Finance

The government borrows from financial markets when it has a **budget deficit** and saves or repays existing debt when it has a **budget surplus**. A deficit means expenditures exceed revenues. A surplus means revenues exceed expenditures. In a **balanced budget**, revenues equal expenditures.

Government borrowing in the United States has been extensive, especially between 1980 and 1995. Such borrowing raises interest rates in financial markets, **crowding out** private borrowers from the market. High interest rates, however, also can draw private saving into the market.

• **Crowding out:** government deficit borrowing causes higher interest rates and lower private consumption and investment

Businesses and families require flows of private saving to replace worn-out houses, cars, factories, productive equipment, and other used-up resources. Adequate flows of saving also allow for new investments. The higher the rates of saving and investing are today, the higher future national income will be.

Therefore, governments must be careful not to take too much saving away from private uses. When the U.S. government committed to less borrowing in its 1993 deficit-reduction plan, financial markets responded with a two-percent drop in long-term interest rates. Lower rates then increased private investment and consumption, contributing to an economic boom through the 1990s.

Exhibit 16.1: Financial-Market Money Flows

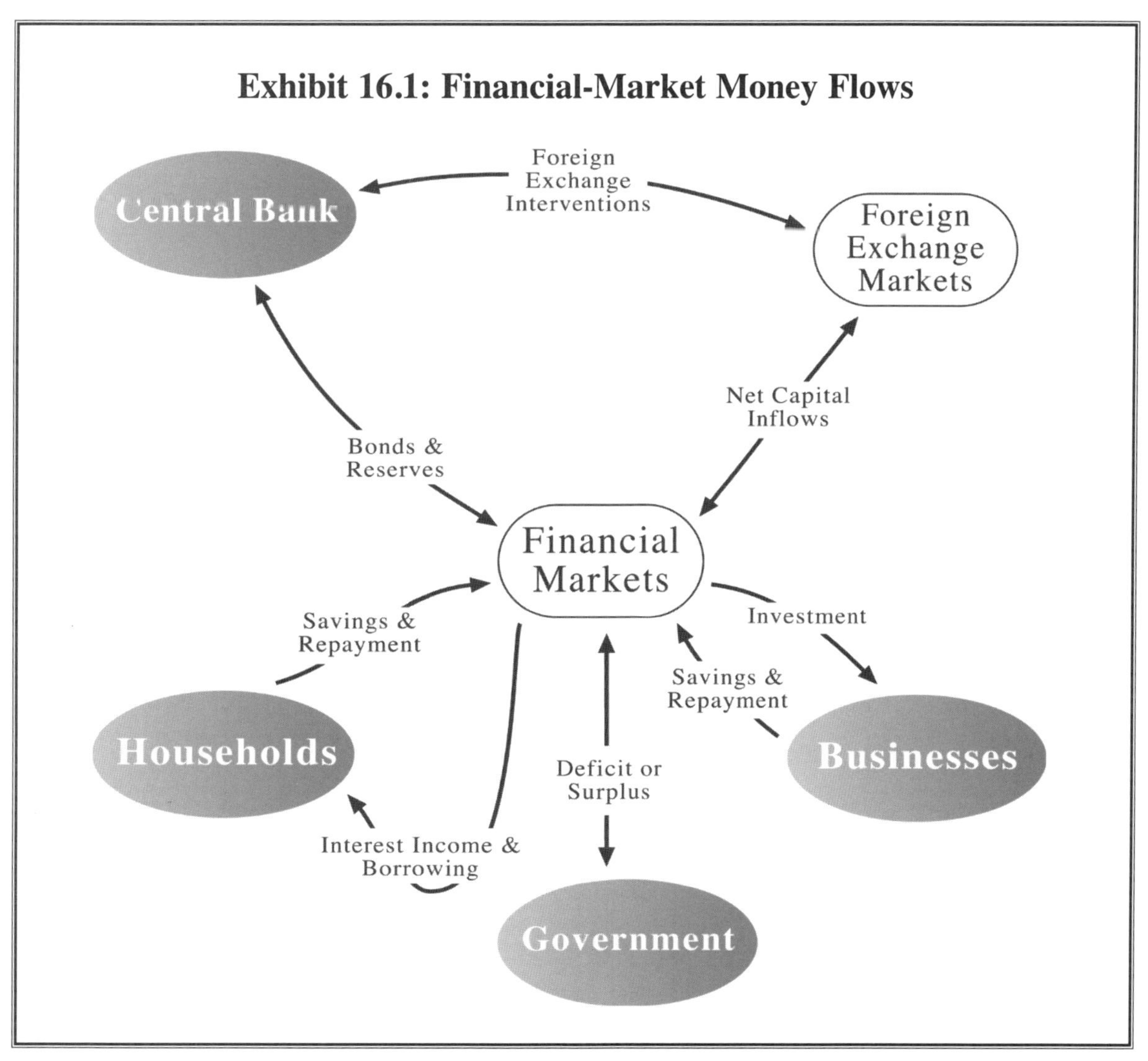

Business Finance

Businesses finance new investment either by **borrowing** money or by **issuing new shares** of stock. Commercial banks provide business loans. Financial intermediaries help with both. Investment banks assist in selling stock, a process called underwriting because the bank agrees to buy shares and then resell them. Businesses then must repay loans or pay dividends to shareholders out of the additional income that the investment is supposed to provide. Businesses with more cash flow than they need also may choose to save temporarily in their own bank accounts, certificates of deposit, or other short-term securities.

Foreign Exchange Markets

Businesses conduct many financial transactions across national boundaries. International transactions involve flows of funds through foreign exchange markets. Importers, for example, must swap their national currency for the currency of the nation from which they are buying goods.

The Role of Commercial Banks

Importers, exporters, and foreign investors use commercial banks to fund their transactions and change currencies. Exhibit 16.1 can give a distorted idea of banks as separate from foreign exchange markets. International and domestic banking are not separate. To serve their customers, most large commercial banks have branches or correspondent (partner) banks in other nations. Therefore, in Exhibit 16.1, domestic financial markets are directly connected to foreign exchange markets.

Net Capital Inflows

The flow of funds from foreign markets into domestic financial markets is called a capital inflow. The flow from domestic markets to foreign markets is a capital outflow. The inflow minus the outflow for any period is called a **net capital inflow**, a net flow of wealth into domestic financial markets.

- **Net capital inflow:** investment funds flowing into a nation less funds flowing out

If the net inflow into the United States is positive, then investors (they could be foreign or American) with foreign assets are buying dollars and using them to buy investments in U.S. financial markets. If the net capital inflow is negative, then investors are selling dollars on average to buy other currencies in order to buy foreign assets.

Net capital inflows respond to changing perceptions of global risk. After 1997, the Asian financial crisis increased perceptions of risk and caused a rise in the net flow of capital into the United States. Capital flows also react to changing domestic and foreign interest rates. High U.S. interest rates in the 1980s attracted foreign funds into the bond market. Government Treasury bonds were especially popular, and in the 1980s the United States became a net debtor nation for the first time in the twentieth century.

Central Bank Activities

A central bank operating like the U.S. Federal Reserve (Fed) is able to influence financial markets very directly by buying and selling government debt. Because the Fed participates in a public auction, its bond-market activities are called **open-market operations.** The Fed **buys** U.S. Treasury obligations to increase bank reserves and the supply of money. The Fed **sells** treasuries to decrease bank reserves and the money supply.

The central bank undertakes **defensive operations** in the bond market to offset changes in the money market, such as changes in consumer desires to have paper money. If consumers want more currency, as they did in South Florida after Hurricane Andrew wrecked Homestead in August 1992, the Fed must supply currency and offset the drain of deposits with more reserves. The central bank also undertakes **dynamic operations** to influence overall economic activity and the price level. Buying bonds will tend, in normal circumstances, to decrease interest rates and stimulate borrowing, spending, and output in the economy. To reduce upward pressure on prices, the Fed would have to reduce bond purchases and slow the growth of the money supply.

Discount Lending

The central bank also can lend reserves to member banks that have temporary needs. The Fed calls these discount loans because the bank must sell the Fed eligible securities at a discount price as collateral for the loan. The Fed can influence the willingness of banks to borrow and can signal changes in its policy by changing the **discount rate**, the rate at which member banks borrow reserves. A quarter-percent change in the discount rate is a moderate policy change. A 1 percent change is a more severe change. Banks do have an alternative to borrowing at the Fed's "discount window"; to meet reserve requirements, banks can borrow from each other in the **federal funds market**. The average interest rate on federal funds, however, responds quickly to changes in the Fed's discount rate and in its open-market bond sales and purchases. These loans are also reported to the Fed as changes in banks' reserves.

Foreign Exchange Interventions

The central bank will from time to time intervene in foreign exchange markets, and this is illustrated as a direct connection of the two. The Fed, for instance, carries out the international currency operations of the U.S. Treasury. Together, the two agencies decide on purchases and sales of foreign currencies, mainly British pounds, German marks, and Japanese yen.

With these purchases, the Fed adjusts the value of the dollar when it is too high or too low against other currencies. If the dollar were too strong against the yen, for example, the Fed would buy yen and sell dollars. More dollars in circulation would weaken the

- **Central-bank open-market operations:** buy bonds to increase bank reserves and the money supply; sell bonds to decrease bank reserves and the money supply
- **Defensive open-market operations** offset changes in money market conditions and consumers' demand for paper money.
- **Dynamic open-market operations** are intended to influence overall economic activity and the price level.
- **Discount rate:** the rate that the Fed charges to member banks that borrow to meet reserve requirements
- **Federal funds market:** a market in which banks lend excess reserves to other banks with inadequate reserves; borrowers pay the "federal funds rate"

• **Sterilize:** the Fed offsets a foreign-exchange intervention with an opposite open-market operation

dollar's value. The Fed would sell yen to strengthen the dollar. Most often, when the Fed buys dollars internationally, it **sterilizes** the operation by simultaneously selling dollars domestically.

Effects of Financial Flows on the Macroeconomy

How do these financial flows affect the level of economic activity? We will examine the direct effects of the flows and the factors that cause variations in the flows. The most important factors are interest rates, inflation, and perceived levels of risk.

Investment Is an Injection

Business investment injects spending into the circular flow of household income and expenditure on goods and services. A burst of new investment stimulates economic activity in the short run. A decline in investment puts a drag on economic activity.

Saving as a Leakage

Saving is a leakage from the spending stream. If households choose to save more of a given level of income, consumption must drop (unless borrowing simultaneously increases). This decline in consumption will slow down the economy. A decrease in saving, however, will reduce the amount of money leaking out of the spending stream. Less saving generally means more consumption.

Increased repayment of loans has an effect similar to a higher rate of saving, putting a drag on economic activity. Household borrowing for additional consumption above the level of household income has an effect similar to a lower rate of saving. It stimulates the economy, causing more output and income.

When saving rises and borrowing falls, the short-run impact on the economy may be negative, but the long-run impact should be positive. Higher savings and less borrowing will force interest rates down and make loans for investment cheaper. Businesses have lists of projects waiting for investment funds and, at high interest rates, only the most profitable are undertaken. As interest rates fall, more investments are expected to be profitable and more will be undertaken. This increased investment increases the capital stock of the economy and increases productivity of labor. Higher productivity allows for higher wages and higher standards of living.

The Role of Interest Rates

Financial market analysts watch interest rates very carefully because changes in rates have powerful economic effects. Changing interest rates have at least three kinds of effects. They affect interest income on savings and interest payments on loans. They also affect financial incentives for savers and investors. In addition, they alter the prices and desirability of other asset prices.

Interest Income and Loan Payments. Changing interest rates tend to affect middle-aged householders and retirees differently. The reason is that middle-aged people tend to have more debt than savings, while retirees tend to have more savings than debt. Higher interest rates, for example, increase interest income from money-market investments like Treasury bills and short-term certificates of deposit (CDs). At the same time, higher rates increase payments on variable-rate loans.

When interest rates rise, homeowners with variable-rate mortgages mourn. However, retirees rejoice because they tend to invest more heavily in CDs and other money-market accounts. A 1 percent increase in interest rates means $1,000 more income on every $100,000 invested in CDs, but it also causes interest payments on a variable rate loan to increase by the same amount for a $100,000 loan.

Changing Incentives. Interest-rate changes alter incentives with respect to levels of saving and investment. A higher interest rate will encourage more saving and less consumption, while tending to cause less borrowing and investment. Higher interest rates create a drag on economic activity, reducing spending for consumption and investment, leading businesses to reduce levels of production. Lower rates encourage increasing economic activity with the opposite effects on spending and output.

Expansion Point 16.2 explains how changes in the U.S. rate of consumer saving and borrowing during the last two decades of the twentieth century appear to have responded to changing interest rates. The economic effects of such fluctuations can be significant in the short run and the long run. In the short run, fluctuations in saving and borrowing affect the level of economic activity by influencing the business cycle. In the long run, fluctuating rates of saving and borrowing affect the accumulation of capital and the productivity of labor.

Higher domestic interest rates also will attract more foreign investment in domestic bonds and other debt. This effect works through a rising net capital inflow when domestic rates are relatively high compared to foreign rates.

Changing Financial Asset Prices. Stock market prices react to interest rate changes, as do bond market prices. Higher interest rates, for example, change the desirability of stocks versus bonds and other money-market opportunities. Higher interest rates tend to cause investors to favor bonds that pay market rates of interest.

Another effect of interest rates on stock-share prices works through borrowing for stock market investments, or what is called buying on margin. In the U.S., stock market investors may borrow up to half of the money for stock purchases. A higher interest rate

Expansion Point 16.2: Why the Lower Saving Rates and More Borrowing in the United States?

In the 1980s and the 1990s, Americans gradually decreased their rate of saving and increased their willingness to take on new debt to finance current consumption. The following table, for example, lists the rate of household saving out of personal disposable income from 1968 to 1998.

U.S. Rate of Family Saving Out of Personal Disposable Income

Year	1968	1978	1988	1998*
Rate of Saving	7.7%	7.5%	5.4%	0.5%

*estimated

Source: National Bureau of Economic Research, *Economic Report of the President* (February 1999): 362. Found at www.nber.org

What would cause such shifts in saving and borrowing activity? Economists identify at least four reasons.

First, falling interest rates could encourage borrowing and discourage saving. In fact, U.S. interest rates fell from a historic high in 1982 to rather low levels in the late 1990s.

Second, if families felt more confident about rising future incomes, they would tend to borrow more and save less now. Family incomes did rise in the United States from 1982 to 1999 in an economic boom that was interrupted only briefly in 1990 and 1991.

Third, consumers might have an increase in wealth that makes them more willing to borrow and less willing to save. This also happened during the two stock market booms of the 1980s and 1990s.

Fourth, lower costs of additional borrowing would encourage more consumer debt. This too happened for two reasons. Bankruptcy laws became more lenient. Bankruptcy is a legal action to get relief from people you owe when your debts are greater than your assets (negative net worth). Personal credit cards also were more easily available. Widespread issuing of credit cards after the 1960s depended on the ability of banks and retail stores to use telephone lines and high-speed computers to track which individuals were good and bad credit risks.

Another reason for less saving and more borrowing that is harder for economists to explain is that Americans may simply have become less thrifty during the two decades. We can see evidence, however, that economic factors do seem to matter, in data from the recession of 1980 to 1982. In those years, when U.S. interest rates were at historic highs, the saving rate rose to an average for the three years of 9.0 percent. When interest rates fell in 1983, the saving rate fell to 6.7 percent.

would increase the cost of stock market investing on margin. This would decrease the demand for stocks and their prices as well.

Interest rates affect bond prices inversely. When interest rates increase, the value of a bond issued earlier at lower interest rates decreases. If a 30-year bond that sells for $1,000 today pays $50 for every $1,000 of face value to be repaid at maturity, it pays a five percent yield to maturity. If market rates rise to 10 percent, investors would want interest payments of $100 per $1,000 of face value. Therefore, they will be willing to buy this bond only at a lower price (or what is called at a discount off the face value).

The Effects of Financial Risk

Investors respond to changes in the perceived risks of different investments. Perceptions of greater financial risk interfere with the smooth financing of business operations. In bond markets, an increase in the risk that corporations could not repay their obligations would decrease the willingness of investors to buy bonds. Higher risk of bonds would therefore decrease the bond prices and increase interest rates.

We are referring here to a particular kind of risk, the risk that a business will default on its obligation to repay debt. Default risk is only one type of financial risk. Expansion Point 16.3 compares a variety of risks that investors face.

In stock markets, an increase in the risks of a business failure also affects stock prices. The failure of Enron Corporation, for example, caused investors to fear that other firms might also be hiding their desperate financial situations with accounting tricks. When such fears are widespread, perceived risk of investing in stocks will be higher. This will lower the demand for and prices of shares of affected stocks.

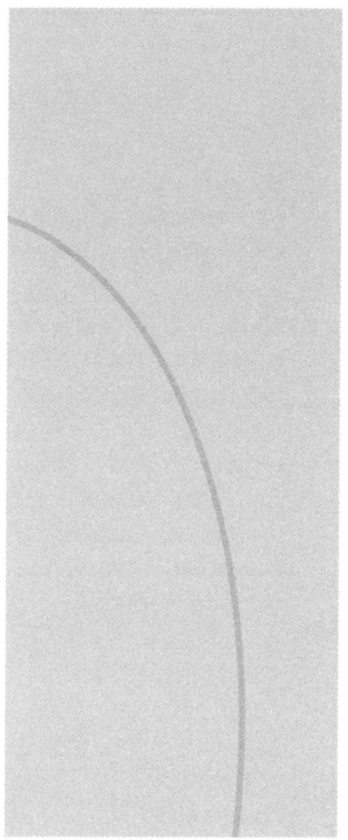

Chapter Summary

1. Financial markets provide six functions: making payments for commerce, changing currencies, lending money, taking deposits, directing scarce capital to its most productive uses, and pooling risk. An economy's financial system develops to meet people's demands for such services. An *efficient* financial system reduces the cost and risk of making transactions.

2. The financial system includes stock markets, bond markets, and foreign exchange markets. Because financial intermediaries such as banks, pension funds, and insurance companies provide valuable services, they also have been important in making payments, making loans, taking deposits, rationing capital, sharing risk, and changing currencies.

3. Households save and borrow through financial markets and their intermediaries. Governments borrow and repay debts through financial markets. The central bank influences the money supply by buying and selling bonds in bond markets. Foreign investment flows into and out of a nation's financial system, depending on domestic and foreign interest rates. Businesses borrow from financial markets for investment and save their own excess funds there, and use investment banks to issue new bonds and shares of stock.

4. The flows of income into and out of financial markets have important economic effects. More saving and less investment put a drag on economic activity. More borrowing and more investment stimulate economic activity.

5. Foreign exchange markets encourage commerce across national boundaries. Foreign exchange markets are integrated with domestic banks and financial markets.

6. A nation's central bank has important effects on financial markets and macroeconomic flows. The central bank controls the money supply and influences interest rates. A central bank can influence both the money supply and interest rates by buying and selling treasury bonds. It also influences financial market stability by lending to member banks.

7. Changes in interest rates and perceptions of financial market risk have important effects on financial market flows and on financial asset prices.

Expansion Point 16.3: Types of Financial Risk

FORTY-NINE YEARS WITHOUT LOSS OF PRINCIPAL OR INTEREST TO ANY INVESTOR
Our Last Offering at 8%
Lower interest rates, talked about for months, are now a reality. ¶ We are making our last 8% offering of National Capital First Mortgage Investments, secured by business property in Washington, D. C. ¶ As our next offering will be at 7%, we suggest that you act promptly. ¶ Our Ten-Month Investment Savings Plan pays 8%.
$100, $500, $1000; Maturities: 2 to 10 years
THE F. H. SMITH COMPANY
Founded 1873
815 FIFTEENTH STREET N.W.
WASHINGTON, D. C.
Address
Dept. 8

Financial activity involves identifiable risks. Once you understand the varieties of risk, you will soon see that few if any investments are risk free. Here are seven different risks. The first three concern the risks of lending, the fourth concerns international investments, and the rest are more general.

1. **Default risk** is what people mean when they say, "I want an investment with no risk." To default means to fail to pay a debt. In the 1930s, many families lost their life savings when banks defaulted on their obligations. Default risk of a U.S. Treasury bond is considered to be zero. Default risk of "junk bonds" is considered to be much higher, especially if economic activity collapses; thus, the term junk bond.

2. **Interest-rate risk** results from rising interest rates. Although people consider thirty year U.S. Treasury bonds to be risk free, the potential for rising interest rates makes them risky. The risk is that you will put, say, $10,000 into a bond at 6 percent interest, and then the market rate on bonds next year will rise, say, to 8 percent. You are stuck for twenty nine years with a bond that will pay 2 percent less than what you could have earned had you waited a year to invest. If you must sell the bond early (which you can do in the bond market), you will lose principal on your investment because, after interest rates fall, investors won't pay as much for your bond as you did initially.

3. **Reinvestment risk**, the reverse of interest-rate risk, results from falling interest rates. Following on the last example, perhaps you decide not to buy a thirty year bond this year at 6 percent, and buy a 1 year bond at 4 percent instead. You plan to buy another bond, perhaps a 30-year bond, next year. The problem is that next year interest rates may have fallen. When you reinvest in a new 1 year bond, rates may be down to 3 percent.

4. **Exchange-rate risk** is created by flexible currency-exchange rates that can foil your international investment plans. Any time you invest in foreign markets, whether in stocks, bonds, factories, or whatever, and hope to convert your future earnings back into your domestic currency, you risk a fall in the value of the foreign currency. [See Problem 16.10 at the end of the chapter.]

5. **Casualty risk** is due to the possibility of a disaster befalling your investment. Your ship doesn't come in with its treasure because it fell victim to pirates or rocky shoals. Your investment is lost when the building housing your business is lost in a flood. Your business depends on a key person who suddenly dies. Disasters like these are why we buy insurance.

6. A different business trouble is the **risk of fraud** or **theft**. You enter into an investment scheme that promises to make you rich, only to find that the scheme is a scam. For instance, your partner in a business runs up $200,000 of debt and then runs out on you. Traders avoid fraud and theft by wise and careful researching of investment opportunities and potential partners. Corporations also limit risk of fraud by limiting a shareholder's liability.

7. A group of additional risks can be classified as **general business risk**. Businesses fail because of bad planning, unexpected cycles in economic activity, unforeseen shifts in costs of resources or product demand, and inadequate financial resources. Most investors in a business understand that they are risking their capital due to these problems.

PROBLEMS FOR PRACTICE

16.1 What are the six functions of a financial system? List specific ways in which the functions are related.

16.2 Illustrate with a chart the flows of funds into and out of financial markets.

16.3 How do savings, consumer borrowing, repaying loans, and business investment affect the circular flow of income and expenditure in a market economy? Which flows increase economic activity?

16.4 How do changing interest rates affect financial flows and the economy? How do interest-rate changes affect stock and bond prices? How does greater financial risk affect financial investments?

16.5* Consider these interest-rate and present-value problems.

a. On a loan of $40,000 at 8.3 percent annual interest, payable monthly, what interest will you pay in the first month?

b. How much extra income would you have to earn each month to equal the earning power of $4,500,000 in the bank? Assume that the annual interest rate on such deposits is 7.5 percent.

c. What is the risk-free equivalent wealth value of having yearly income of $45,000? Assume that risk-free interest rates are 0.045 per year (4.5 percent annual interest).

d. You are in an automobile accident and a jury awards you a lump sum settlement of $100,000 for your injuries. The insurance company asks you to take a structured settlement instead. They offer to pay $20,000 a year for seven years starting today. If your rate of discount is 8 percent, should you take the lump sum or the structured settlement?

e. If the nominal interest rate on a one-year bond is 6.4 percent and the expected inflation rate is 2 percent, what is the expected real rate of return? Why can a lender or borrower not be sure of the real rate of return when making a loan contract?

16.6 In a market economy, what function do changing interest rates serve? Do investors pay attention to nominal interest rates or to real interest rates?

16.7* What causes interest rates to change? List the factors, first, according to causes in the market and, second, according to the three parts of any nominal interest rate. Use graphs and charts as needed to illustrate.

16.8* What would the following tell you about the current state of financial markets? What is happening in the economy currently, or what would you expect to happen in the economy in the near future?

a. The FOMC has announced that it has increased its target rate for federal funds from 3.5 percent to 3.75 percent.

b. The federal funds rate is drifting lower every day during the past few weeks, even though the FOMC's target remains steady at 5.25 percent.

c. The spread between ten-year Treasury notes and an average of five important ten-year corporate bond rates has decreased from 1.30 to 0.85 percent during the past six months.

d. The Fed has been increasing the money supply rapidly during the past three months. Instead of falling, interest rates on thirty-year mortgages and thirty-year bonds have been rising. Explain why with regard to inflation.

16.9* Consider this problem after reading Expansion Point 16.2 on risk. As an illustration of the problem of exchange-rate risk, assume that in 1992, you lent $10,000 to a business in Thailand, to be repaid with interest in 1999. Initially, you converted the $10,000 to 250,000 Thai bahts because $1 = 25 bahts was the exchange rate. According to your deal, in 1999, you were to get back 400,000 bahts (just under 10 percent per year interest). Because the government promised to keep the exchange rate fixed at $1 = 25 bahts to eliminate exchange-rate risk, you were planning on exchanging your baht for $16,000 (we are ignoring costs of changing currencies). Instead, the Asian crisis forces the Thai government to allow the baht to fall to $1 = 42 bahts in 1997. How much of a return on your money will you have when you convert back to dollars?

16.10 Summarize the differences between the roles of the U.S. Treasury and the Federal Reserve in U.S. financial markets. Who has more independence and power to influence interest rates: the Secretary of the U.S. Treasury or the Chairman and Board of Governors of the Federal Reserve?

Economics in film and literature:

16.11 For a story of financial intrigue, investments gone bad, sudden fortune, and life in London, England's Marshalsea debtors' prison, read the book *Little Dorritt* by Charles Dickens or review the video, starring Sir Alec Guinness.

See Answer Key for hints/answers to starred (*) questions.

For your portfolio:

16.12 What is the current state of financial markets? What are the causes of its current state? What do you expect to happen over the next six months? Search government and private Web site sources of economic data. Search recent articles for information.

16.13 Research on the Internet or in a newspaper's financial page to find the interest rates at which consumers can save (lend money to the bank). Find the rates at which consumers can borrow from the bank. Savings rates include rates on certificates of deposit, checkable deposits, money-market deposit accounts, or regular passbook savings accounts. Borrowing rates include interest rates for home mortgages, auto loans, or credit card debt. Observe which rates are higher or lower. What do you think explains the differences in rates for savings and borrowing? Why might each of these rates vary over time?

For class discussion:

16.14 Debtors' prisons were banned in the United States some time ago. How do you think banning debtors' prison affects the willingness of individuals to borrow money? The U.S. Congress recently considered making bankruptcy laws more strict, so that consumers could no longer automatically cancel credit card debts. How would lenient laws and strict laws affect borrowing behavior? Which type of laws would bankers prefer?

Answer Key
And Hints to Problems

Introduction: Faith and Learning

I.3 You might ask your philosophy teacher to weigh in on this. Or look up the topic of positive vs. normative thinking in a dictionary of philosophy.

I.7 Most college libraries contain Bible commentaries. The reference section will usually contain complete volumes. The stacks will hold individual studies on each book of the Bible. These go verse by verse through the text. Certain commentaries focus on critical issues (with frequent use of Greek or Hebrew), while others are more homiletical, focusing on the lessons that the verses contain.

I.8 See the comment for I.7 above. You would use similar commentaries for these topics.

Chapter 1: Scarcity

1.1 This complaint against economics, that scarcity is a thing of the past, is contradicted by the added statement about available radio-frequency bands. If the electromagnetic spectrum is "filling up," then this is nothing other than a description of scarcity on the radio spectrum. A call to have a meeting of users is a call to discuss how to ration a scarce good. Is scarcity really dead? The statement betrays itself.

1.2 Perhaps such a system would seem fair, but it would be quite inefficient. Some people don't like milk and they would have to sell it to others. Other people like milk very much and would rather buy milk than soda or other foods. They would have more trouble finding a supplier. All this extra exchange would waste scarce time and resources.

1.3 Use either standard history books, economic history books, or a scholarly encyclopedia.

1.4 Your answer should address how free-market exchange of food and how government rationing work. Have you ever seen beef cattle or hogs being auctioned? Have you participated in a government program to distribute surplus cheese or lived on a farm that benefited from government subsidies?

Consider when first-come, first-served is at work or when equal shares prevail. Is food distribution ever arbitrary? How does your family deal with food? Do parents sell food to children or make them work for it? What about food in the school cafeteria or at a local fast-food restaurant? What about food-stamp programs?

1.8 Local newspapers abound with articles on government policies addressing scarcity. Politicians constantly make economic choices about how to allocate public funds for roads, education, national defense, or social welfare. Other articles discuss market exchange and private enterprise. You can also search *Business Week*, *USA Today*, *The Wall Street Journal*, and other business and financial publications.

You may also see articles about shortages of certain goods, especially in countries where prices are held artificially low or where economic conditions are changing and prices are adjusting. A drought or a frost, for example, will cause a temporary shortage of agricultural goods until market prices adjust. A sudden increase in demand for new computers or a toy whose price is fixed will also cause shortages.

1.10 This statement is generally true, but students might take issue with it on certain theological grounds. For example, miracles in the Old Testament and Jesus' miracles and those of His disciples in the New Testament suggest a temporary divine breaking of scarcity's bonds. Or a person could argue that "love of a child" is not an economic issue. Yet those with more than one child quickly find that time to show that love is very scarce! So the general point can be debated but never fully dismissed.

1.12 The text disagrees. Tools and other inventions, as well as human skill do enhance productivity.

1.18 First your group must decide about property rights. Who owns the cookies? If the person who received them owns the cookies, the group's choices are limited to revolt and theft or a constitutional amendment.

If the entire group owns the cookies, then a variety of distribution methods are possible. Here are only a few ideas. (1) Give equal numbers to each person. (2) Give cookies to each person directly or inversely proportional to her weight. (3) Allow the holder of the cookies to give them out according to his whim. (4) Have each student write a letter of appeal to the cookie holder, telling how many she should get and why (this is called "rent-seeking" behavior). (4) Allow people to bid for the cookies and then dispense the funds collected equally to group members. (5) You could combine any of the other methods, especially (1) to (3), with a subsequent cookie exchange in which individuals can buy cookies from and sell them to each other.

Either method 4 or 5 should result in a somewhat efficient distribution of cookies, in which those who want them most can get the amounts they want. Notice how either method 4 or combining methods 1 and 5 would blend fairness and efficiency.

Chapter 2: Scarcity and Economics

2.1 See the explanations at the beginning of each major section of the chapter.

2.2 If demand and supply are normal, market price will: a. fall, b. rise, c. fall, d. rise, e. fall if minimum was above equilibrium wage, f. fall, g. rise.

2.3 Graph the following: a. supply decrease, b. demand decrease, c. demand increase, d. supply increase.

2.4 a. Higher demand tends to increase both price and quantity exchanged, but higher supply tends to decrease price and increase quantity. Therefore, quantity exchanged will be higher, but the effect on price is uncertain, depending on which factor has more influence.

b. Lower demand will cause decreased price and quantity, but higher supply will further decrease price and increase quantity. Therefore, quantity exchanged is uncertain, but price should surely fall.

2.5 Calculate average cost of producing each unit (total cost / quantity produced):

Process	**A**	**B**	**C**
Quantity Produced	100	110	90
Total Cost	$1550	$1600	$1500
Average Cost	$15.50	$14.55	$16.67

Method B, the machine-intensive method, is the most efficient process. Of the three production processes, method B's total cost is highest, but its quantity is highest too. The result is that its average cost is lowest.

A government commitment to labor-intensive methods does not change the definition of efficiency.

In the example, if labor-intensive methods such as Methods A or C were more efficient, they would have lower total labor costs. The test of efficiency is that, for producing a given output, labor-intensive methods should yield the lowest average cost. A test of efficiency in the market place is to look at the methods actually practiced by the most profitable companies in the market. If labor-intensive methods were efficient, then you would observe them being used. For instance, you would more likely see household workers washing clothes by hand than using washing machines. In fact, you can see hand washing of clothes in countries where labor's wages are very low.

2.6 Different prices for the same good imply either different costs of delivery or exchange inefficiency. Perhaps the costs of retail carpet-store space are higher in Atlanta. Perhaps installation and delivery costs are higher because wages in Atlanta might generally be higher than in Bristol.

Where cost differences cannot account for the $10 price difference, you would conclude that exchange is not fully efficient. An enterprising trader could buy carpet in Bristol and ship it to Atlanta to sell, so long as the cost to ship and sell was not greater than $10. A trader might buy carpet at the factory if the cost was less than $20 (and shipping costs were not excessive). Factories, however, are not always willing to sell to all comers, preferring to sell only to licensed dealers of their products. Such restrictive practices of factories could also be the cause of the different prices.

2.7 According to the completed chart below, the United States has the most productive workers among the three nations. In 1990, an average U.S. worker produced $53,533 worth of goods and services per year. An average Japanese worker produced $43,617 per year. A Chinese worker averaged $3,632. Although China's total economy was larger than Japan's, Japan's workers were more productive due to their more industrialized economy. A larger stock of equipment makes workers more productive.

Productivity of U.S. and Chinese workers increased more than productivity of Japanese workers did. This is in large part because of three different factors: the United States emerged from a recession between 1990 and 1995, Japan entered an extended recession, and China continued to allow increasing free enterprise in its Southeastern provinces.

1995 Data

Nation	Productivity of Labor
China	$5,666
Japan	$43,719
United States	$88,956

1990 Data

Nation	Productivity of Labor
China	$3,632
Japan	$42,617
United States	$53,552

Source: "Selected OECD Countries: Economic Profile." Profile of Organization for Economic Cooperation and Development accessed from CIA Web site: http://www.odci.gov/cia/publications/khies97/c/tab7.htm (*and* tab16.htm).

2.8 a. Set up the equation where the time and ticket costs of both flights are equal as follows:

(3 hours * Wage) + $3000 = (6 hours * Wage) + $600

Solve the equation for the wage as follows:

(3 hours * Wage) + (6 hours * W) = $3000 + $600

9 hours * Wage = $3600

Wage = $3600 / 9 hours

Wage = $400 per hour

Only those business travelers with very high hourly wages will choose the Concorde!

b. Consider the effects of fears and the effects of low wages.

Note: this problem and the solution are based on a similar discussion in James Gwartney and Richard Stroup's *Economics: Public and Private Choice*, Ch. 1.

2.9 a. Voluntary exchange will usually benefit both parties, no matter what they think. They are trading something they don't want to someone who wants it much more. Thus the different perspectives and also the gains from trade arise from different psychological evaluations of economic value.

b. The seller is probably using "profit" to describe the total revenue. If opportunity costs of time and the value of the goods sold are subtracted from revenues, the profit might actually be a loss.

2.10 Keep the survey short. You might ask the following questions, or something like them:

(1) Which is more efficient?
- a. Post Office
- b. (list the name of a private package service)
- c. both are equally efficient

(2) Which of these is more efficient in using new technology? Serving the American people?
- a. government
- b. (list a private automobile producer)
- c. both are equally efficient

(3) Which of the following is more likely to create new technology?
- a. government planning agency
- b. private business
- c. neither is more likely

Randomly select people to survey. Pick every fifth name from a local list or ask every fifth person who walks by. Think how your methods could have biased your results.

When interpreting the statistical results, remember that you are surveying what people think, not estimating what actual economic measures of efficiency would indicate. Be able to explain whether you think people's perceptions of efficiency are realistic.

Chapter 3: What Is Economics?

3.8 & 9 For both questions, do note that a text on the history of economic thought is different from a text on economic history. Search your library catalog under both of these topics.

Chapter 4: Economic Behavior

4.3 a. Consider college fraternities, sororities, and service organizations.

b. Students sometimes copy each other's homework because the teacher insists that they hand it in. Drivers use radar detectors to avoid speeding tickets. Policemen wait until cars go past to turn on radar guns, thus foiling radar detectors.

c. As the story goes, a woman always cut the end off her ham when cooking it because her mother had always done it and because she thought it must make it taste better. When she called her mother to ask why, her mother said grandmother always did it. She called her grandmother, who said that she did it because the pan was too small for the whole ham.

d. Twenty-four cans of soft drink in a refrigerator that four people share communally (with no clear property rights) will be consumed faster than six cans of soda in a private refrigerator of one person. If you don't believe it, try an experiment.

e. Merchants who sell complex services (auto, appliance, and electronic repairs) have been shown in televised sting operations to have cheated their ignorant customers.

f. Certain ethically minded people who receive too much change from a merchant or a customer point out the error and give the extra money back.

g. Negotiators often don't give their best offer in the first round. They hope to get more than they would settle for. Thus, negotiation includes various strategies for hiding one's true intents. [See also the answers to (b)].

4.5 Think of testing as a strategic game. Do teachers and students have the same goals? Also think in terms of benefits and costs. How does the policy affect a student's costs or benefits of not studying for the first round of an exam?

4.8 Less competitive people do prefer cooperative

games, but others turn most everything into a competitive game. Throwing a plastic saucer in the yard was originally a noncompetitive pastime. College-aged players soon made it a competitive game somewhat like football. Wouldn't those forced to play noncompetitive basketball begin comparing the total scores of their games with scores of other games?

Chapter 5: Economic Method

5.4 Think about editing a paper you have written. The extra benefits of editing diminish as you spend more time editing. On the other hand, the extra costs of more editing rise because time used becomes more scarce. The costs of the time can be measured in the lower grades you may get in other courses. By the way, computer word processors and spell checkers lower the costs of editing your paper! Consequently, college papers seem to be better edited now than they were when students used typewriters.

5.5 The lost value is the sum of the differences between what the last two consumers would be willing to spend and what they actually spend per can. For the sixth person, this is $0 because the two are the same. For the fifth person, the lost value is ($0.80 - $0.70) = $0.10. That is also the net loss per hour of the restriction.

5.6 The last few thousand dollars are taxed at the marginal rate of 40 percent, not the average tax rate of 25 percent. If the Jones family income were reduced by $1000, it would pay $400 less in taxes and would only lose $600 of net income. Therefore, the marginal tax rate is relevant to good economic decision making. As explained in the text, economic thinking is marginal thinking.

5.8 The equilibrium condition allows you to set the expression for Q_s equal to the expression for Q_d:

$$\mathbf{1 + 4P = 15 - 3P}$$

Rearranging terms by subtracting 1 from both sides and adding 3P to both sides yields:

$$7P = 14$$

$$P^* = \mathbf{\$2}$$

When P* = $2, Q* = (1 + 4*2) = (15 - 3*2) = **9**.

5.11 One other factor might be whether any other machines or sources of soft drinks have become available to buyers.

Chapter 6: What Is an Economy?

6.2 Review Expansion Points 6.1 and 6.2 for examples of personal and governmental policy mistakes. Make your explanation no longer than each of these expansion points. If you can't think of an example, survey teachers.

6.4 Compare, for example, giving food stamps to poor families in the United States and the Japanese government's cooperation with business in directing the economy (industrial policies). Food stamps enable poor families to buy certain types of healthy foods with government funds. This shows high concern for individual economic security, but not for state security. Put this policy in the lower right. As a nation, Japan has a moderate system of poor relief, but a high concern for state economic security and economic self-sufficiency, expressed in its industrial policies. Put Japan more towards the upper left-hand corner.

Chapter 7: Economic Endowments

7.1 Within 50 miles of my town, we have salt mines, dairy cattle and grazing lands, several world-class industries that make products for export, a brisk logging industry, and four colleges and universities with their accumulations of human capital, buildings, books, and equipment. In the 1820s, a working canal connected my town to other regions, but now we use railroads a bit and highways a lot.

7.2 See Exhibit 7.4 and the related discussion.

7.3 The firm that is most efficient at cleaning pollution will sell its rights to the firm that is least efficient at eliminating pollution. For a given level of pollution, the economic value of output from the affected firms will be greater than with across-the-board identical pollution restrictions for all firms.

7.4 You might want to take a quick look at the history of coal mining in Wales before watching the movie. Take note of when the pace of mining there began to slow.

7.5 For example, consider how the end of the Cold War between Russia and the United States affected the following: commerce in areas around closed military bases, the electronics industry and Silicon Valley, the weapons industry, and the aircraft industry.

7.6 For an example of a religious institution that becomes an economic institution, see Expansion Point 7.4 on the Sabbath and U.S. blue laws.

7.8 If you are confident, is it based on anything more than faith in progress in the future? If you are not confident, what are your thoughts on the steady technological progress that has occurred in the last three centuries?

Chapter 8: Wealth and Poverty

8.1 Varying the definition of "poor" is crucial here.

8.10 See Expansion Point 8.1 on perspectives on

wealth before you answer.

Chapter 9: Economic Growth

9.5 Consider that a cost of running a business is monitoring whether or not workers are being productive, and a cost of exchange is assuring that agreements will be kept. Consider why it would be inefficient for you to invest in a food-importing business that ended up being a fraud. Consider how increased shoplifting and employee theft might be inefficient.

9.6 All three are consistent.

9.9 If you do not find one of these two texts, you will want to find an *economic history* book.

Chapter 10: Government

10.2 Be sure to read about the various perspectives on the nature of government at the end of the chapter. This is helpful for answering the third question.

Chapter 11: Consumption

11.1 Of consumption, production, and distribution, consumption is primary. See the discussion at the beginning of the chapter.

11.2 The demand for durables would drop more. We need a steady flow of many nondurable goods. Durable goods can be repaired rather than replaced when incomes are low. Durable-goods purchases are therefore generally more postponable. Even so, some nondurable goods are luxuries, not necessities, and the demand for luxuries will drop more than the demand for necessities.

11.3 a. The stapler is a durable good since it provides services over many years. When the stapler gets old and begins to misfire occasionally, you can postpone buying a new one if the business is not going well and money is tight.

b. Though a stapler may last many years, the staples would probably be considered a nondurable good, since they are used up and have to be repurchased much more regularly than the stapler. When a box is empty, you generally would not postpone buying a new one, even if money were tight.

c. Modest as it is, the stapler is a good investment because it is used in a business to produce income.

11.5 For definitions, start with a regular dictionary. Then consult a dictionary, an encyclopedia of religion, or a Bible dictionary. For the Zakat, you might try the Web site <http://www3.geocities.com/Athens/ Academy /7368/ essay_zakat.htm>.

11.6 The student who got more than expected would, other things being equal, be happier. This depends on whether you consider just the wealth at hand in assessing rationality. If so, having different attitudes for the same gifts makes no sense. The human mind, though, evaluates disappointments and surprises along with the wealth at hand. The psychological issue of how we evaluate and the moral matter of thankfulness might therefore be more important than questions about narrow economic rationality.

11.7 For example, how many of the tips are strategies for pre-committing to a long-run plan, as described in Expansion Point 11.4? Do any tips incorporate ideas about opportunity costs?

11.8 The key is to identify your conflicting wants and the strategies by which you assure that, in each case, one of those wants is sure to win out.

11.11 Consider how each choice will affect all members of the family. Explain how you would balance various interests and evaluate competing needs and wants. Also be sure to have clear family goals in mind as you decide. What are you maximizing, and what is not so important?

Chapter 12: Production

12.3 The rates of profit are as follows:
Sales Margin
(rate of profit on total revenues) =
($113,482 * 0.70) / $2,383,410 = 0.033 or 3.3%.
Return on Investment
(rate of profit on capital invested) =
($113,482 * 0.70) / $1,400,952 = 0.057 or 12.7%.

12.6 How important is it for the agency to be large? How important is creativity? How important is independence? A large agency is more likely to be a partnership or perhaps a corporation. When creativity is important, a partnership with shared responsibilities or sole proprietorship is often preferred to a corporate hierarchy. Doctors often share offices, but don't form large partnerships. Sharing offices saves money on clerical and building costs, while being sole proprietors or small partnerships allows doctors to be independent.

12.8 Electronics is a varied business. Making components requires precision and an emphasis on zero mistakes since they are difficult to find in a complex circuit board. Research and development on the other hand requires freedom and creativity. For this reason, electronics manufacturers might have to run the research division much like a college campus, with individual freedom for its employees. On the other hand, management might seek to have components produced in a highly regimented factory environment where quality is strictly monitored, even if by the workers themselves.

Chapter 13: Price Theory

13.2 a. (1) Dresses are selling at an initial equilibrium, say $2.50 each. (2) The wage increase reduces producer's willingness to supply. (3) A shortage of Guatemalan dresses develops at the old price. (4) Dress prices rise and fewer dresses are sold to U.S. buyers. (5) Guatemalan producers may try to cut costs by making sewers work faster for their higher wage. Guatemalan producers may move their factories to another nation where wages are lower than 60¢ per hour. U.S. retailers may seek out other suppliers.

13.4 a. Elastic: elasticity equals -2.0 = (-20/10).

b. Elastic because a big consumer response lowers revenues.

c. Without doing the math, the percentage change in quantity demanded looks so much bigger than the percentage change of price in the opposite direction. Consumers are responsive and demand for steaks is said to be elastic.

d. John's demand for news magazines would be less elastic.

e. The demand for lightbulbs is more elastic.

f. Case A, in which substitutes are available.

13.5 a. Price elasticity of demand equals -0.82 (0.82 in absolute value). Demand is somewhat inelastic.

b. Quantity demanded would decrease 3.5 percent. Total revenue would increase 6.5 percent.

13.7 Particular examples make for excellent discussion. Understand, however, that the issue rests on a thorough empirical study of the U.S. economy. One approach used by researchers is to compare average industry prices with estimates of average costs of production for each industry. If price is equal or close to average cost, the industry is deemed competitive. As mentioned in the text, one important study is by Arnold C. Harberger. Some microeconomics texts cite and explain his study and responses to it. You might ask your instructor for an intermediate text that might have a copy of such a citation.

Chapter 14: Macroeconomics

14.1 a. Use the indices of leading and coincident economic indicators.

b. Use historical data on real GDP.

c. Use the national rate of unemployment and changes in the number of jobs.

d. Use the rate of manufacturing capacity utilization.

14.3 a. CPI for the current year = ($2149 / $1895) * 100 = 113.4

b. 2.5 to 2.6 percent per year.

14.4 Here are the calculations.

Consumer Goods	Output in 2000	Price in 2000	$P^{00}Q^{00}$	Price in 1994	$P^{94}Q^{00}$
Bread Loaves	39,000	$1.00	$39,000	$0.80	$31,200
Automobiles	12	$21,500.00	$258,000	$18,000.00	$216,000
Blue Jeans	17,000	$30.00	$510,000	$24.00	$408,000
			$\Sigma P^{00}Q^{00}$ = $807,000		$\Sigma P^{94}Q^{00}$ = $655,200

Nominal GDP for 2000 = $807,000

Real GDP for 2000 = $655,200

Implicit Deflator for GDP 2000 = 1.23

14.5 a. 1.0 b. 100 c. Nominal GDP is less than real GDP.

14.8 Your graph should show an increase in real GDP and a decrease in the general level of prices. In actual practice, the oil-price decrease contributed to falling inflation (rather than falling prices) during 1982 to 1984.

Chapter 15: The Circular Flow

15.3 In 1988, the saving rate was 0.08 = ($17,621 - $16,211) / $17,621. By 1993, the saving rate was down to 0.07.

Exhibit 15.3 gives data for 2001. The saving rate out of disposable personal income is 0.1388 = $121.1 / ($8724.7 - $1306.3), or approximately 1.6 percent, not even close to 5 percent.

15.4 a. Real income is $14,385 = $18,700 / 1.30.

b. Last year, each person had approximately $385 more purchasing power, measured at base-year prices. Since real income last year was greater than income in the base year, Americans are estimated to have been better off last year. At base-year prices, they had $385 more to spend. [Remember that nominal income and real income are the same in the base year.]

15.8 Economic activity should decline. Yes, the reverse would tend to be true.

15.10 Shop local stores for prices. Ask managers about prices last year. Read through newspaper ads from this year and last to find old and new prices. You can also use last year's and this year's catalogs for things you buy. The library will have magazines and newspapers with prices in advertisements. You may have a good memory. If so, use it, but do attempt to document the accuracy of your prices.

Chapter 16: The Financial System

16.5 a. $3320 = $40,000 * 0.083. Dividing that by 12 months, the monthly interest due is $276.67.

b. $337,500 per year = $4,500,000 / 0.075, so you would need approximately $337,500 / 12 or $28,125. [This answer ignores compounding of interest during the 12 months.]

c. $1 million = $45,000 / 0.045. That is, $1 million in the bank would pay an interest income of $45,000 per year.

d. The net present value of the seven payments is only $92,457.54. [Discount each year's payment of $20,000 by dividing by a discount factor of (1.08) to the power of zero through six for each successive year.] This is less than $100,000. Reject the structured settlement.

e. 4.4 percent = 6.4 - 2.0. We can't be sure what the actual inflation rate will be over the period of the loan contract.

16.7 The reasons are given in several places. Read about the effects of the central bank's policies. Also read about the effects of changing saving and investment flows.

16.8 a. The Federal Reserve thinks that interest rates are too low. They are restricting the supply of bank reserves and, therefore, restricting the supply of money. This may ease inflation and slow economic growth.

b. Demand for loans must be low, leaving banks with excess reserves and less need to borrow reserves from other banks. Lower demand for reserves pushes the federal funds rate down. This could mean that economic activity is weakening, causing less loan demand.

c. The spread measures the risk of corporate bonds (compared to relatively default-risk-free Treasury bonds). This probably means that economic activity is improving, creating expectations of higher corporate income in the next few months or years. This would mean corporations are more able to repay interest and principal on their bonds.

d. Mortgage markets must be expecting that the Fed's actions will cause higher future inflation. This would lead to higher inflation premiums on mortgage interest rates.

16.9 Multiply your 400,000 bahts by $1 / 42 bahts to get your return in dollars. We are ignoring costs of making the exchange of currencies. How many dollars do you get back? How did you do?

Reference List

Introduction

Allen, Diogenes. 1993. The end of the modern world. *Christian Scholar's Review* (June): 339-47.

Benson, Bruce L. 1997. The spontaneous evolution of commercial law. In *Reputation: Studies in the voluntary elicitation of good behavior.* Daniel B. Klein, ed. Ann Arbor, MI: University of Michigan Press.

Berkouwer, G. C. 1976. *The church.* Grand Rapids, MI: Eerdmans.

Black, Robert. 1998. Without a *strategic plan* the people perish? *Journal of Biblical Integration in Business* (Fall): 124-37.

Blaug, Mark. 1985. *Economic theory in retrospect.* 4th ed. Cambridge: Cambridge University Press.

Edersheim, Alfred. 1898. *Life and times of Jesus the Messiah.* Grand Rapids, MI: Christian Classics Ethereal Library.

Farley, John E. 1994. *Sociology.* 3rd ed. Englewood Cliffs, NJ: Prentice Hall.

Fee, Gordon and Douglas Stuart. 1982. *How to read the Bible for all its worth.* Grand Rapids, MI: Zondervan.

Fowler, Michael. 1996. Counting in Babylon. Found at: http://www.phys.virginia.edu/classes/109N/lectures/babylon.html.

Griffiths, Brian. 1984. *The creation of wealth.* Downers Grove, IL: InterVarsity Press.

Hocksbergen, Roland. 1994. Is there a Christian economics? *Christian Scholar's Review* 24, no. 2 (December): 126-42.

Holmes, Arthur. 1975. *The idea of a Christian college.* Grand Rapids, MI: Eerdmans.

Iannaccone, Laurence. 2002. Religious extremism: The good, the bad, and the deadly. From a presentation at the meetings of the European Public Choice Society. Belgirate, Italy. Article may be found at http://faculty.washington.edu.

Klein, Daniel B., ed. 1997. *Reputation: Studies in the voluntary elicitation of good behavior.* Ann Arbor, MI: University of Michigan Press.

Lange, John Peter. [1865-1879] 1946. *Commentary on the Holy Scriptures.* Translated from the German and edited with additions by Philip Schaff. Grand Rapids, MI: Zondervan, 1960.

Lunn, John and Robin Klay. 1994. The Neoclassical economics model in a postmodern world. *Christian Scholar's Review* 24, no. 2 (December): 143-63.

Mason, John. 1993. Biblical teaching and the objectives of welfare policy. *ACE Bulletin* 22 (Fall): 7-30.

Newcomb, Simon. 1886. The basis and method of economic science. In *Principles of political economy.* New York: Harper & Brothers.

North, Douglass. 1990. *Institutions, institutional change, and economic growth.* Cambridge: Cambridge University Press.

Osterhaven, M.E. 1984. Covenant. In *Evangelical dictionary of theology.* Ed. Walter Elwell. Grand Rapids, MI: Baker Book House.

Smith, Adam. [1776] 1981. *An inquiry into the nature and causes of the wealth of nations.* Glasgow Ed. Edited by R.H. Campbell and A.S. Skinner. Indianapolis, IN: Liberty Fund.

Solomon, Robert C. 1993. Business ethics. In *A companion to ethics.* Ed. Peter Singer. Oxford, England: Blackwell.

Stott, John. 1982. *Between two worlds.* Grand Rapids, MI: Eerdmans.

Surdyk, Lisa K. 2002. God's economy: Teaching students key biblical principles. *Journal of Biblical Integration and Business* (Fall): 69-98.

Tiemstra, John. 1993. Christianity and economics: A review of recent literature. *Christian Scholar's Review* (March): 227-247.

U. S. Bureau of the Census. 1999. *Statistical abstract of the United States: 1998.* Lanham, MD: Bernan Associates.

CHAPTER 1

Encyclopedia Britannica. 1999. Steam engine. In *Encyclopedia Britannica.* CD-ROM.

Cash, James. 1999. *Nightly business report.* Public Broadcasting System, 10 February.

Covey, Stephen R., A. Roger Merrill, and Rebecca Merrill. 1996. *First things first: To live, to love, to learn, to leave a legacy.* New York: Fireside/Simon and Schuster, 1994.

Dickens, Charles. *A Christmas carol.* An Online Library of Literature, 1999: http://www.literature.org/Works/CharlesDickens/christmas-carol/.

Federal Bureau of Investigation. *Crime statistics in the United States*. 1997. FBI Uniform Crime Report. Found at: http://www.winner-intl.com/statistics.html.

Goldberg, Michael. 1972. A philosophy of Christmas. In *Carlyle and Dickens*. Athens, GA: University of Georgia Press.

Hammer, Michael and James Champy. 1993. *Reengineering the corporation: A manifesto for business revolution*. New York: HarperBusiness.

Henderson, Hazel. 1997. Interview by Kevin Kelley. *Wired* (February). Found at http://www.wired.com.

Marx, Karl and Friedrich Engels. 1848. *Communist manifesto*.

Smith, Adam. [1776] 1981. *An inquiry into the nature and causes of the wealth of nations*. Glasgow Ed. Edited by R.H. Campbell and A.S. Skinner. Indianapolis, IN: Liberty Fund.

Winston, Stephanie. 1994. *The organized executive: New ways to manage time, paper, people, and the electronic office*. Rev. ed. New York: W.W. Norton.

CHAPTER 2

Grant, Eugene W. and W. Grant Ireson. 1987. The comparison of alternatives. In *Managerial economics and operations research: Techniques, applications, and cases*. 5th ed. Edited by Edwin Mansfield. New York: W.W. Norton.

Marshall, Alfred. 1890. *Principles of economics*.

Selected OECD Countries: Economic profile. Organization for Economic Cooperation and Development. Found at http://www.odci.gov/cia/publications/khies97/c/tab7.htm *and* http://www.odci.gov/cia/publications/khies97/c/tab16.htm.

Smith, Adam. [1776] 1981. *An inquiry into the nature and causes of the wealth of nations*. Glasgow Ed. Edited by R.H. Campbell and A.S. Skinner. Indianapolis, IN: Liberty Fund.

Wogaman, Philip. 1986. *Economics and ethics: A Christian inquiry*. Philadelphia: Fortress Press.

CHAPTER 3

BEA News Release. 26 February 1999. *Gross domestic product: Fourth quarter 1998*. Found at http://www.bea.doc.gov/bea/newsrel/gdp498.htm.

Bentham, Jeremy. 1780. *An introduction to the principles of morals and legislation*.

Blackstone, William. 1765. *Commentaries on the laws of England*.

Brock, Gerald. 1994. The Christian economist as dream interpreter. *ACE Bulletin* (Fall): 5-8.

Chamberlain, Edward. [1933] 1950. *Theory of monopolistic competition*, 6th ed. Cambridge, MA: Harvard University Press.

Friedman, Milton and Anna Schwartz. 1963. *A monetary history of the United States, 1867-1960*. Princeton, NJ: Princeton University Press.

Friedman, Milton and Rose Friedman. 1980. *Free to choose*. Philadelphia: Harcourt, Brace, Jovanovich.

Grinnols, Earl. 1994. Panel discussion: What should ACE do? *ACE Bulletin* (Fall): 34-36.

Halteman, James. 1988. *Market capitalism and Christianity*. Grand Rapids: Baker Books.

Halteman, James. 1990. An Anabaptist approach to economic systems. *ACE Bulletin* (Fall): 6-13.

Hayek, Friedrich. 1944. *The road to serfdom*. Chicago: University of Chicago Press.

Heilbroner, Robert. 1967. *The worldly philosophers*. 3d ed. New York: Clarion.

Heyne, Paul. 1994. Passing judgments. *ACE Bulletin* (Spring): 9-10.

Hocksbergen, Roland. 1994. Is there a Christian economics? *Christian Scholar's Review* 24, no. 2 (December): 126-42.

Keynes, John Maynard. 1936. *The general theory of employment, interest, and money*. New York: Harcourt, Brace, Jovanovich.

Lunn, John and Robin Klay. 1994. The neoclassical economics model in a postmodern world. *Christian Scholar's Review* 24, no. 2 (December): 143-63.

Marshall, Alfred. 1890. *Principles of economics*.

Marx, Karl. 1865. Profit is made by selling a commodity at its value. In *Value, price, and profit*. Ed. Eleanor Marx Aveling. Found at http://csf.Colorado.EDU/psn/marx/Archive/1864-IWMA/1865-VPP/.

Marx, Karl. 1867. *Das Kapital*.

Mason, John. 1993. Biblical teaching and the objectives of welfare policy. *ACE Bulletin* (Fall): 7-30.

Mason, John. 1994. Panel discussion: What should ACE do? *ACE Bulletin* (Fall): 36-39.

Mun, Thomas. 1664. *England's treasure by foreign trade*.

Oser, Jacob and Stanley Brue. 1988. *Evolution of economic thought*. 4th ed. Philadelphia: Harcourt, Brace, Jovanovich.

Plato. *Republic*.

Richardson, J. David. 1988. Frontiers in economics and Christian scholarship. *Christian Scholar's Review* (June): 381-400.

Richardson, J. David. 1994. What should (Christian) economists Do? . . . Economics! *ACE Bulletin* (Spring): 12-15.

Robinson, Joan. 1933. *Imperfect competition*. London: Macmillan and Co.

Rosser, J. Barkley and Marina W. Rosser. 1995. *Comparative economics in a transforming world Economy*. Chicago: Irwin.

Ruskin, John. 1862. *Unto this last*.

Smith, Adam. [1776] 1981. *An inquiry into the nature*

and causes of the wealth of nations. Glasgow Ed. Edited by R.H. Campbell and A.S. Skinner. Indianapolis, IN: Liberty Fund.

Spiegel, Henry William. 1991. *History of economic thought*. 3rd ed. Durham, NC: Duke University Press.

Tiemstra, John et al. 1990. *Reforming economics*. Lewiston, NY: Edwin Mellen Press.

Tiemstra, John. 1993. Christianity and economics: A review of recent literature. *Christian Scholar's Review* (March): 227-247.

Tiemstra, John. 1994. What should Christian economists do? Doing economics, but differently. *ACE Bulletin* (Spring): 3-11.

CHAPTER 4

Ainsworth, Diane. 2000. Prof wins for work to model irrational behavior. UC Berkeley *Campus News* (14 June). Found at http://www.berkeley.edu/news/features/2000/06/16_macarthur.html.

Cameron, Rondo. 1993. *A concise economic history of the world*. 2d ed. Cambridge: Oxford University Press.

Commons, John. 1924. *Legal foundations of capitalism*. New York: Macmillan.

Coughlin, Ellen K. 1995. Rational fascists? Sociologist probes people's motives for supporting the Nazi party. *The Chronicle of Higher Education* (23 June): A10.

Etzioni, Amitai. 1988. *The moral dimension: Toward a new economics*. New York: The Free Press.

Feldstein, Martin. 1995. The economics of health care: What have we learned? What have I learned? *American Economic Review* 85, no. 2 (May): 28-31.

Frank, Robert H. et al. 1993. Does studying economics inhibit cooperation? *Journal of Economic Perspectives* 7: 159-171.

Hirshleifer, David and Tyler Shumway. 2001. Good day sunshine: Stock returns and the weather. From http://www-personal.umich.edu/~shumway/papers.dir/weather.pdf.

Krueger, Anne. 1996. The political economy of controls: American sugar. In *Empirical studies in institutional change*. Eds. Lee Alston, Thrainn Eggertsson, and Douglass North. Cambridge: Oxford University Press.

Marwell, G. and R. E. Ames. 1981. Economists free ride, does anyone else? *Journal of Public Economics* 15: 295-310.

Nicholson, Walter. 1993. *Intermediate microeconomics*. 5th ed. New York: Dryden.

Putnam, Robert. 1995. Bowling alone: America's declining social capital. *Journal of Democracy* 6, no. 1 (January): 75-78.

Schmit, Julie. 1995. Study shows jets running on fumes. *Rochester Democrat and Chronicle* (4 April): 1A.

U. S. Bureau of the Census. *Statistical abstract of the United States: 1998*, Table 638, Percent of adult population doing volunteer work: 1995. Lanham, MD: Bernan Associates: p. 396.

CHAPTER 5

Friedman, Milton and Rose Friedman. 1980. *Free to choose*. Philadelphia: Harcourt, Brace, Jovanovich.

Samuelson, Paul. 1958. *Economics*, 4th ed. New York: McGraw-Hill.

CHAPTER 6

Dorner, Dietrich. 1996. *The Logic of failure,* 1st American ed. New York: Metropolitan Books.

Hayek, Friedrich. 1944. *The road to serfdom*. Chicago: University of Chicago Press.

Keynes, John Maynard. 1936. *The general theory of employment, interest, and money*. New York: Harcourt, Brace, Jovanovich.

Landes, David. 1999. *The wealth and poverty of nations*. New York: W.W. Norton.

Morse, Jennifer Roback. 1995. The modern state as an occasion of sin. *Bulletin of ACE* (Fall).

Novak, Michael. 1982. *The spirit of democratic capitalism*. New York: Touchstone.

Nove, Alec. 1969. *An economic history of the U.S.S.R*. New York: Penguin Press.

Quinn, Jane Bryant. 1999. Investors buying stocks on margin online are best positioned to hear "crack of doom." *Buffalo News* (4 April): C-13.

Smith, Adam. [1776] 1981. *An inquiry into the nature and causes of the wealth of nations*. Glasgow Ed. Edited by R.H. Campbell and A.S. Skinner. Indianapolis, IN: Liberty Fund.

Smith, Stephen L. S. 1994. Integration and differentiation: Economics at Christian colleges, *Bulletin of the Association of Christian Economists* (Fall): 9-23.

CHAPTER 7

Cameron, Rondo. 1993. *A concise economic history of the world*. 2d ed. Cambridge: Oxford University Press.

Crumm, David. 1998. In a restless world, families strive to heed their religion's call to remember the Sabbath. *Buffalo News* (5 September): A-11.

Gay, Craig M. 1994. On learning to live with the market economy. *Christian Scholar's Review* (December): 180-195.

Oxford companion to the Supreme Court. 1992. Sunday closing laws. Cambridge: Oxford University Press: 847-848.

Sowell, Thomas. 1994. *Race and culture*. New York: Basic Books.

World almanac and book of facts: 1995. Mahway, NJ: World Almanac.

CHAPTER 8

Adie, D. K. 1984. Wealth, Christian view of. In *Evangelical dictionary of theology*. Ed. Walter Elwell. Grand Rapids, MI: Baker Book House.

Belshaw, Deryke, Robert Calderisi, Christ Sugden, eds. 2001. *Faith in development: Partnership between the world bank and the churches of Africa*. Washington, D.C.: World Bank.

Camp, Jean and Brian Anderson. 1999. Grameen phone . . . *Information Impacts* (December). Found at http://www.cisp.org/imp/december_99/12_99camp.htm.

Cox, W. Michael and Richard Alm. 1999. *Myths of rich and poor*. New York: Basic Books.

Economic report of the president. 1999. National Bureau of Economic Research. Accessed at http://www.nber.com

Emerson, Ralph Waldo. 1996. Quoted in *Columbia world of quotations*. http://www.bartleby.com.

Friedman, Milton and Rose Friedman. 1980. *Free to choose*. Philadelphia: Harcourt, Brace, Jovanovich.

Human development report 1998. United Nations Development Programme. Found at http://www.hdr.undp.org/reports/global.

Human development report 2001: Making new technologies work for human development. New York: Oxford University Press.

Merriam-Webster, Inc. 1987. *Merriam-Webster's collegiate dictionary*, 9th ed. Springfield: MA.

Mishkin, Frederic S. 1998. *Money, banking, and financial markets*. 5th ed. Boston: Addison-Wesley.

Murray, John. 1995. Human capital in religious communes: Literacy and selection of nineteenth century Shakers. In *Explorations in economic history* 32, issue 2 (April): 217.

Pope John Paul II. October 5, 1979. Remarks about the [Catholic] campaign for human development. Accessed at http://www.usccb.org/cchd/pope1979.htm.

Shao, John. 2001. Alleviating poverty in Africa. In *Faith in development: Partnership between the world bank and the churches of Africa*. Eds. Deryke Belshaw, Robert Calderisi, and Chris Sugden. Washington, D.C.: World Bank.

Smith, Adam. [1776] 1981. *An inquiry into the nature and causes of the wealth of nations*. Glasgow Ed. Edited by R.H. Campbell and A.S. Skinner. Indianapolis, IN: Liberty Fund.

Sowell, Thomas. 1994. *Race and culture*. New York: Basic Books.

Subsistence theory of wages. *The encyclopedic dictionary of economics*. 1991. 4th ed. Guilford, CT: Dushkin Publishing Group: 237.

U. S. Bureau of the Census. 1999. *Statistical abstract of the United States: 1998*. Tables 747 and 767. Lanham, MD: Bernan Associates: 473,482.

U. S. Bureau of the Census. 2001. *The marginal effects of taxes and transfers on poverty estimates: 2000*. http://www.census.gov/hhes/poverty/poverty00/tablef.html.

U. S. Bureau of the Census. 2002. *Statistical abstract of the United States: 2001*. Section 13: Income, expenditure, and wealth. Table No. 689: Household and nonprofit organization sector balance sheet, 1980 to 2002. Found at http://www.census.gov/prod/2002pubs/01statab/stat-ab01.html.

U. S. Bureau of the Census. 2000. Found at: http://www.census.gov/hhes/income/income00/inctab7.html.

U. S. Bureau of the Census. *Statistical abstract of the United States: 2000*. Tables 673, 679.

U. S. Bureau of the Census. *Statistical abstract of the United States: 2001*. Table 685.

World development report 2000-2001: Attacking poverty. Oxford: Oxford University Press.

World Bank. 2001. *Empowering the poor through decentralization: Brazil Rural Poverty Alleviation Program*. Found at http://poverty.worldbank.org/library/view/10057.

World development report 2000-2001. The World Bank Group. Found at: http://www worldbank.org/poverty/wdrpoverty.

World Hope International. August 2003. *Microenterprise: Ministry overview*. Found at http://www.worldhope.net/microenterprise/micro.htm.

CHAPTER 9

Black, R.A. 1994. John Commons on customer goodwill and the economic value of business ethics . . . *Business Ethics Quarterly* 4, no. 3: 359-365.

Byrne, John A. et al. 2002. How to fix corporate governance. *Business Week* (6 May): 68-78.

Cameron, Rondo. 1993. *A concise economic history of the world*. 2nd ed. Cambridge: Oxford University Press.

Commons, John. 1924. *Legal foundations of capitalism*. New York: Macmillan.

Creswell, Julie. 2002. Banks on the hot seat. *Fortune* (2 September): 79-82.

Dos Santos, Theotonio. 1991. Reprint. The structure of dependence. In *The theoretical evolution of international political economy*. Eds. George Crane and Abla Amawi. New York: Oxford University Press. Original edition, *American Economic Review* 16 (1970).

France, Mike and Wendy Zeller. 2002. Enron's fish

story. *Business Week* (25 February): 39-40.

Gill, Richard T. 1963. *Economic development: Past and present*. Englewood Cliffs, NJ: Prentice Hall.

Gimein, Mark. 2002. You bought. They sold. *Fortune* (2 September): 64-74.

Harrison, Lawrence E. 1985. *Underdevelopment is a state of mind: The Latin American case*. Cambridge: Harvard University Press.

Kaufman, R.R., Daniel S. Giller, and Harry I. Chernotsky. 1975. Preliminary test of the theory of dependency. *Comparative Politics* (April). Cited in Lawrence E. Harrison, *Underdevelopment is a state of mind: The Latin American case* (Cambridge: Harvard University Press, 1985).

Klein, Daniel B., ed. 1997. *Reputation: Studies in the voluntary elicitation of good behavior.* Ann Arbor, MI: University of Michigan Press.

Landes, David. 1999. *The wealth and poverty of nations*. New York: W.W. Norton.

Lenin, Vladimir. 1939. *Imperialism: The highest state of capitalism*. New York: International Publishers. Reprinted in *The evolution of international political economy*, George T. Crane and Abla Amawi, eds. New York: Oxford University Press, 1991.

McGuffey, William H. [1836] 1982. *Eclectic readers*. Reprint, Fenton, MI: Mott Media.

North, Douglass and Barry Weingast. 1989. Constitutions and commitment: The evolution of institutions governing public choice in seventeenth-century England. *Journal of Economic History* 49 (No. 4, December). Reprinted in *Empirical studies in institutional change*. 1996. Eds. Lee Alston, Thrainn Eggertsson, and Douglass North. Cambridge: Oxford University Press, 134-165.

North, Douglass. 1990. *Institutions, institutional change, and economic growth*. Cambridge: Cambridge University Press.

Shrock-Shenk, David. 1998. Why I won't thank God for all my things this Thanksgiving. *Mennonite Brethren Herald* 37, nos. 11 and 12 (12 June).

Smith, Adam. [1776] 1981. *An inquiry into the nature and causes of the wealth of nations*. Glasgow Ed. Edited by R.H. Campbell and A.S. Skinner. Indianapolis, IN: Liberty Fund.

Smith, Adam. 1759. *The theory of moral sentiments*.

Smith, Adam. 1766. Lectures on the influence of commerce on manners. In *Lectures on jurisprudence*. Reprinted in *Reputation: Studies in the voluntary elicitation of good behavior*. 1997. Ed. Daniel B. Klein. Ann Arbor, MI: University of Michigan Press.

Tullock, Gordon. 1985. Adam Smith and the prisoner's dilemma. *Quarterly Journal of Economics*: 1073-1081. Reprinted in Klein, 1997.

U. S. Bureau of the Census. 1999. *Statistical abstract of the United States: 1998*. Lanham, MD: Bernan Associates.

U. S. Bureau of the Census. 2002. *Statistical abstract of the United States: 2001*. Found at http://www.census.gov.

Wallis, John and Douglass North. 1986. Measuring transaction sector in the American economy, 1870-1970. In *Long-term factors in American economic growth*. Eds. S.L. Engerman and R.E. Gallman. Chicago: University of Chicago Press.

CHAPTER 10

Boutrous, Theodore J., Jr. 1994. Rule of law: The Supreme Court remembers property rights. *Wall Street Journal* (29 June): A17.

Franzen, Robin. 1994. Oregon's takings tangle. *Planning* 60 (No. 6, June): 13.

Gwartney, James and Richard Stroup. 1994. Economic report of the president. In *Introduction to economics: The wealth and poverty of nations*. New York: Dryden Press.

Hamilton, Alexander. 1793. *Report on manufactures*.

Hayek, Friedrich. 1944. *The road to serfdom*. Chicago: University of Chicago Press.

Krueger, Anne. 1996. The political economy of controls: American sugar. In *Empirical studies in institutional change*. Eds. Lee Alston, Thrainn Eggertsson, and Douglass North. Cambridge: Oxford University Press.

Oxford companion to the Supreme Court. 1992. Laissez-faire constitutionalism. Cambridge: Oxford University Press: 492-493.

Rhoads, Stephen E. 1985. Kind hearts and opportunity costs. Reprinted in *Annual editions microeconomics*. 2d ed. (Guilford, CT: Dushkin, 1993).

Rutherford, Samuel. 1644. *Lex rex*.

Smith, Adam. [1776] 1981. *An inquiry into the nature and causes of the wealth of nations*. Glasgow Ed. Edited by R.H. Campbell and A.S. Skinner. Indianapolis, IN: Liberty Fund.

Stone, Andrew, Brian Levy, and Ricardo Paredes. 1996. Public institutions and private transactions. In *Empirical studies in institutional change*. Eds. Lee Alston, Thrainn Eggertsson, and Douglass North. Cambridge: Oxford University Press.

CHAPTER 11

Black, R.A. 1991. Endogenous demand for alcohol and self-command: A model of the temperance solution. *Handbook of behavioral economics* 2B: 453-472.

Dappen, Andy. 1997. *Shattering the two-income myth*. Brier. WA: Brier Books.

Elster, Jon. 1985. *Ulysses and the sirens: Studies in rationality and irrationality.* Cambridge: Cambridge University Press.

Etzioni, Amitai. 1988. *The moral dimension: Toward*

a new economics. New York: The Free Press.

Friedman, Milton and Rose Friedman. 1980. *Free to choose*. Philadelphia: Harcourt, Brace, Jovanovich.

Galbraith, John Kenneth. 1958. Consumer behavior and the dependence effect. In *The affluent society*. New York: Houghton Mifflin. Reprinted in Edwin Mansfield, *Microeconomics: Selected readings*. 1979. New York: Norton.

Hayek, Freidrich A. 1961. The non sequitur or the "dependence effect." In *Southern Economic Journal* (April); reprinted in Mansfield, 1979.

Homer. 1952. *The Odyssey*. Translated by Samuel Butler. Encyclopedia Britannica Great Books series.

Lebenstein, Harvey. 1950. Bandwagon, snob, and Veblen effects. In *Quarterly Journal of Economics* (May); reprinted in Mansfield, 1979.

Nader, Ralph. 1965. *Unsafe at any speed*. New York: Grossman.

Schelling, Thomas. 1984. Self-command in practice, in policy, and in a theory of traditional choice. *American Economic Review* 74 (May): 1-11.

Sidgwick, Henry. 1883. *Principles of political economy*.

CHAPTER 12

Coleman Management Services. 1999. *How to fail in business without really trying*. Found at http://www.stargate.ca/roncole/html/rcol2000.htm.

Gerber, Michael. 1995. The e-myth revisited: Why most small businesses don't work and what to do about it. New York: HarperBusiness.

Guild Hall: The printer's guild and connected sites: http://www.twingroves.district96.k12.il.us/Renaissance/guildhall/printer/printingguild.html#anchor1001704.

Landsburg, Stephen. 1989. *Price theory and applications*. New York: Dryden.

Mishkin, Frederic S. 1998. *Money, banking, and financial markets*. 5th ed. Boston: Addison-Wesley.

Posner, Richard. 1972. *Economic analysis of the law*. New York: Little Brown.

U. S. Bureau of the Census. 1999. Statistical abstract of the United States: 1998. Table No. 856. Lanham, MD: Bernan Associates.

Williamson, Oliver. 1987. *The economic institutions of capitalism*. New York: Free Press.

CHAPTER 13

Final soybean CRC harvest price. 1998 (18 November). Found at http://www.american-ag.com/html/mforum/soyb1118.htm.

Rose, Michael. 1997. Soaring coffee prices jolt roaster, retailers. (Portland) *Business Journal* (9 June). Found at http://www.amcity.com/portland/stories/060997/story3.html.

Shaffler, Rhonda. 1997. Coffee is a costly wake-up. *CNNFN* (6 March). Found at http://cnnfn.com/hotstories/economy/9703/06/coffee_prices_pkg/index.htm.

U.S. Bureau of the Census. 1999. *Statistical abstract of the United States: 1998*. Table No. 1128. Lanham, MD: Bernan Associates.

CHAPTER 14

Friedman, Milton and Anna Schwartz. 1963. *A monetary history of the United States, 1867-1960*. Princeton: Princeton University Press.

Gwartney, James and Richard Stroup. 1994. *Introduction to economics: The wealth and poverty of nations*. New York: Dryden Press.

Keynes, John Maynard. 1936. *The general theory of employment, interest, and money*. New York: Macmillan.

Kuznets, Simon, with Lillian Epstein and Elizabeth Jenks. 1941. *National income and its composition, 1919-1938*. New York: National Bureau of Economic Research.

CHAPTER 15

Braudel, Fernand. [1817] 1981. *The structures of everyday life*. Trans. Miriam Kochan. Rev. Sian Reynolds. Reprint: New York: Harper and Row.

Clayton, Gary and Gerhard Giesbrecht. 1995. *Everyday economic statistics*. New York: McGraw-Hill.

Consumer prices slip; industrial production, inventories fall, pointing to future recovery. 2002. *CNNMoney* (16 January). Found at http://money.cnn.com/2002/01/16/economy/.

Gordon, Josh. 2002. Household debt hits record levels. *The Age* (28 September). Found at http://www.theage.com.au/articles/2002/09/27/1032734326495.html.

Hilsenrath, Jon et al. 2002. Debt problems hit even the wealthy. *Wall Street Journal* (9 October): D1.

Lane, Robert. 2000. *The loss of happiness in market democracies*. New Haven, CT: Yale University.

Month-to-month change in business inventories. 2001. *Econoday* (15 November). Found at http://www.econoday.com/client-demos/demoweekly/2001/November/15/busi_inv.html.

National Data. 2002. *Survey of current business*. Found at http://www.bea.gov

U .S. Bureau of Economic Analysis. *GPDI, National income and product accounts*. Found at http://www.bea.gov/briefrm/tables/ebrm.htm.

U. S. Bureau of the Census. 1996. *Statistical sbstract of the United States: 1996*. 116th ed. Washington, D.C.

Yeo, Denise. 2002. Crushing debt. *The Electric New Paper* (17 December). Found at http://www.newpaper.asia1.com.sg/top/story/0,4136,10534,00.html.

CHAPTER 16

National Bureau of Economic Research. *Economic report of the president*. February 1999. Found at www.nber.org.

Gallagher, Stephanie. 1995. *Money secrets the pros don't want you to know*. New York: Amacom.

ANSWER KEY

Gwartney, James and Richard Stroup. 1990. *Economics: public and private choice*. 5th ed. San Diego, et al.: Harcourt, Brace, Jovanovich.

Selected OECD countries: Economic profile. Found at: http://www.odci.gov/cia/publications/khies97/c/tab7.htm and http://www.odci.gov/cia/publications/khies97/c/tab16.htm.

Index